Tennessee History

A BIBLIOGRAPHY

Tennessee History

A BIBLIOGRAPHY

Sam B. Smith

EDITOR AND COMPILER

Luke H. Banker

ASSISTANT EDITOR

THE UNIVERSITY OF TENNESSEE PRESS

KNOXVILLE

THE SUPPORT OF THE

Tennessee Historical Commission

IN MAKING THIS PUBLICATION POSSIBLE

IS GRATEFULLY ACKNOWLEDGED.

Library of Congress Cataloging in Publication Data

Smith, Sam B.   1929–
    Tennessee history, a bibliography.

    1. Tennessee—History—Bibliography. I. Title.
Z1337.S55   016.91768   74-8504
ISBN 0-87049-158-X

For Sue

Foreword

J. Franklin Jameson, sometime editor of the *American Historical Review,* and Chief of the Division of Manuscripts at the Library of Congress, often mused that fate had confined him to the simple role of a powder monkey, passing forward ammunition for others to fire off. Even though Jameson was unduly modest and had actually written a substantial amount of history, the role of the powder monkey does not seem an unworthy one. It is in fact with such a spirit that this volume is presented in the hope that it will provide ammunition for others to fire off for many years to come, by revealing needed areas of research and providing direction for new interpretations of Tennessee history.

Some years ago, Misses Laura E. Luttrell and Pollyanna Creekmore published a bibliography of the ninety-five counties of the state. A few years later, William T. Alderson and Robert H. White brought forth an initial bibliography of Tennessee history. It was instructive to discover, however, that nothing of the scope of this work had ever before been attempted. Thus an obvious need for a larger, more comprehensive, and current bibliography of Tennessee history provided the stimulus for this effort.

In the preparation of this volume the compiler was ever torn between a desire for comprehensiveness and a need to be somewhat selective. The result seems to be weighted on the side of comprehensiveness, although quite obviously, everything written on Tennessee history could not be, and should not have been included. An effort was made, however, to achieve a balance, for this volume could easily have been three times as long or one-third its size. The compiler always viewed this work as primarily a research tool and his effort has been to indicate the diversity and wealth of information about Tennessee.

It is hoped that the overall result of this work, which carries through the calendar year 1972, will help to fill an existing need; in time, it should be updated and improved upon.

Acknowledgments

John Donne's famous statement "No man is an island, entire of itself" is in no way brought home to one so vividly as when he attempts a work of this magnitude. I am indebted to a multitude of persons and institutions across the state and country for help which in many cases went far beyond the call of ordinary duty. In the order of their aid, I would like to thank LeRoy P. Graf, head of the Department of History at the University of Tennessee at Knoxville, who first suggested this work and was generous with released time while I was a member of the faculty there; the University of Tennessee Faculty Research Fund for a summer grant freeing me to work without interruption; the fine reference staff of the University of Tennessee Library, headed by Eleanor Goehring, with the special assistance of Jane Marks; the Special Collections Unit of the University of Tennessee Library, whose director, John Dobson, was unfailingly helpful and suggestive; the McClung Collection of the Knoxville-Knox County Public Library, whose able head, William MacArthur, gave generously the use of his facilities; the Tennessee State Library and Archives, whose fine reference staff, including Doris Glasser, Max Mendelsohn, Peggy Wildman, and Lucia Drier always rendered prompt and courteous service; and my student assistant, Don Thompson, whose tireless effort in checking entries helped reduce substantially the margin of error.

To achieve maximum accuracy as well as authority, most of the longer sections have been read by persons knowledgeable in their special fields. Their suggestions, which were extremely helpful, have been incorporated into the manuscript. For the time from their busy lives and schedules I would like to express my gratitude to Kendall Cram, associate state librarian of Tennessee; Dewey Grantham of Vanderbilt University; Hugh Lefler of the University of North Carolina; Harriet C. Owsley, former director of the Manuscript Division of the Tennessee State Library and Archives; Robert Remini of the University of Illinois, Chicago; Mary U. Rothrock, emeritus member of the Tennessee Historical Commission; Henry Lee Swint of Vanderbilt University; Jacques Voegeli, chairman of the Department of History at Vanderbilt University;

Herbert Weaver of Vanderbilt University; and Richard Weesner, former president of the Tennessee Historical Society.

A special word of appreciation is due David J. Harkness, director of Library Services for the Division of Continuing Education of the University of Tennessee, who generously shared his knowledge of Tennessee literature in helping to compile and annotate the section on literature relating to Tennessee history.

Another special note of gratitude is due Isabel Howell, former director of the State Library Division of the Tennessee State Library and Archives, who shared her intelligence and experience in aiding organization of the manuscript and in suggesting additional titles.

I am particularly indebted to Stanley J. Folmsbee, professor emeritus of history, the University of Tennessee, whose bibliographical essay appears as part of this work. Because of his sponsorship of innumerable masters' theses and several doctoral dissertations during his tenure of four decades at the University, Professor Folmsbee has been responsible for more scholarly writing about Tennessee than any other person. In addition, he was editor of the East Tennessee Historical Society's *Publications* and author of a considerable body of distinguished scholarly works.

Roy Nicks, chancellor of the University of Tennessee at Nashville, has given so much help in so many ways that my indebtedness to him is a large one. Also, I would like to thank his competent staff, including Charles Zuzak, dean of the College of Arts and Science. Evelyn Walton and Jackie Golden, also of the University at Nashville, demonstrated a spirit of helpfulness in giving typing assistance at a particularly important time.

My own staff, including my secretary, Linda Keeton, gave unstintingly of itself in a time of substantial stress. Carese Parker was helpful in a number of ways. I am ever grateful to my assistant editor, Luke H. Banker, whose energy and initiative greatly aided the completion of this work.

Finally, my deep appreciation is reserved for my mother-in-law, Mrs. R. L. Fitzsimmons, who cared for our three sons during the final days of manuscript preparation, and for my wife, Sue, who typed the manuscript and whose intelligence, understanding, and good spirit in the face of heavy additional responsibilities helped make possible the compilation of this bibliography.

Statement of Method

In an effort to be as thorough as possible in searching for Tennessee material, a personal exploration was made at the Tennessee State Library and Archives, the Joint Universities Library at Vanderbilt University, the McClung Room of the Knoxville-Knox County Public Library, and the Special Collections unit and main library of the University of Tennessee at Knoxville. In addition, an extensive search was made in America and Canada for as many relevant masters' theses and doctoral dissertations as could be discovered. Some one thousand of these are included in this volume, most of which should be available for use through interlibrary loan.

The primary scholarly periodicals were thoroughly examined for pertinent Tennessee material, and important articles were chosen for inclusion in this work. The decision was also made to include appropriate articles from popular periodicals, the rationale being that, despite their popular nature, they often elucidate, and are suggestive of, topics, areas, and sources not covered in scholarly periodicals. This is particularly true for the last four decades. Also, a relative dearth of monographic treatment of twentieth-century Tennessee pointed to the advisability of including these articles.

It has been nearly thirty years since a bibliography of Tennessee county history was published; therefore, the latter portion of this work deals extensively with that subject. It is obvious that there has been included peripheral, and even marginal, material for many of our counties. Such inclusion seems to be justified on the basis that very little has been written about many of our counties and that any information is better than none at all. In an effort to obtain as much material as possible on the counties, an attempt was made to contact some seventy-five county historians who have been appointed by county courts under permissive legislation passed by the General Assembly several years ago. The names and addresses of the county historians, several of whom responded to my request for information, are given at the beginning of the entries for each county. This list was generously supplied by Robert M. McBride, editor of the *Tennessee Historical Quarterly*. The county historians are usually at the center of all activity relating to historical interests in their counties. They should be helpful in locating material which, because of its nature, is difficult to find, e.g., typescripts, newspaper articles, scrapbooks, and family biographies and histories. Many of these source materials are to be found, however, in the local county library or at the State Library and Archives.

In an effort to indicate the diversity and wealth of information about Tennessee, the compiler has included documents and papers (largely published in historical periodicals) where such materials are not already a part of larger published collections, such as presidential papers. Selected works of folklore and good literary volumes which focus upon biography and our social and cultural background have also been included. Finally, the fields of natural science such as geology, botany, and zoology have some small representation here.

For the most part, there has been no attempt to treat the field of genealogy. It is a huge field of its own and deserves separate treatment.

As far as possible, entries have been collated with the *National Union Catalog.* In addition, all places of publication in Tennessee have been entered without the state's abbreviation; this has also been done in cases of very well-known cities, and those where a state university is publishing. If an important city outside Tennessee has the same name as a city or town in the state, even though the latter is very small, the former is entered with its state abbreviation, the latter without: Cleveland; Cleveland, O.—Philadelphia; Philadelphia, Pa. After the first citation of a book, subsequent references use a shortened form of title, if possible, and omit the facts of publication. However, in the case of articles in periodicals, the full citation is repeated at each entry for the convenience of the reader. Unless otherwise indicated, each entry designated as "Thesis" is a Master's thesis, and each entry designated as "Diss." is a Ph.D. dissertation. It will be noted that some duplication of entries has been permitted for what seemed to me valid reasons, but this has been kept to a minimum.

It would have been helpful if every important entry could have been annotated. Time and space have not allowed this, however, and only a few representative works have been so described.

In undertaking this work, I am acutely aware of the pitfalls inherent in such an effort, for inevitably there will be material which should have been included and perhaps much which might well have been omitted. Nonetheless, it is hoped that this volume will prove useful in helping to understand our past, illuminate our present, and give us hope, confidence and renewed purpose for our future at this the 200th anniversary of self-government in Tennessee.

Abbreviations for
Periodicals Frequently Cited

AH	*American Heritage*
AHM	*American Historical Magazine*
AHR	*American Historical Review*
Annals	*Annals of the American Academy of Political and Social Science*
ETHS*P*	East Tennessee Historical Society's *Publications*
FCHQ	*Filson Club History Quarterly*
JAH	*Journal of American History*
JSH	*Journal of Southern History*
JTAS	*Journal of the Tennessee Academy of Science*
MVHR	*Mississippi Valley Historical Review*
NCHR	*North Carolina Historical Review*
PSQ	*Political Science Quarterly*
TFSB	*Tennessee Folklore Society Bulletin*
THM	*Tennessee Historical Magazine*
THQ	*Tennessee Historical Quarterly*
TLR	*Tennessee Law Review*
VLR	*Vanderbilt Law Review*
WTHS*P*	West Tennessee Historical Society *Papers*

Contents

A Bibliographical Essay
on the History of Tennessee

Stanley J. Folmsbee

From the time when it was the abode of prehistoric Indians, Tennessee has received the attention of writers of history. Archaeologists have looked upon the state as a fertile field for investigation of its prehistoric remains. Accounts left by early white explorers and hunters in the region have also received considerable attention, and the Tennessee country has been viewed as an important frontier in the advancement of civilization in the New World. Especially significant in the minds of historians was the creation by persons within the boundary of that area of a homespun government. The Watauga Association, as it was called, was formed before constitutional government became available and the state of Tennessee was organized. Historians have also recognized Tennessee as the source of Jacksonian Democracy, and of the origins of the anti-Jackson movement which led to creation of the Whig party.

Few states, historians agree, have been as seriously cursed with the evil of sectionalism as has Tennessee, especially during the Civil War and Reconstruction. Even so, it was the last state to join the Confederacy and the first to return to the Union.

In later years, Tennessee has been in the national spotlight and has drawn the attention of historians by such events as the "War of the Roses," the "Coal Miners' War," the Scopes trial, the establishment of the Tennessee Valley Authority, and the making of the atomic bomb. Tennessee has indeed a notable history. In this essay reviewing the treatment of that history, we shall assess outstanding books on the various topics considered.

The most recent comprehensive, one-volume history of Tennessee is *Tennessee, A Short History* (Knoxville, 1969; rpt. 1972), by Stanley J. Folmsbee, Robert E. Corlew, and the late Enoch L. Mitchell. This book is a condensation and revision of their earlier two-volume work entitled *History of Tennessee* (New York, 1960). The single other effort by a trained historian, Thomas P. Abernethy, *From Frontier to Plantation in Tennessee; A Study in Frontier*

Democracy (Chapel Hill, 1932), treats only the period to the beginning of the Civil War. The Great Depression of the 1930s led to the compiling of *Tennessee: A Guide to the State* (New York, 1939; rpt. 1972), by the Federal Writers' Project of the WPA. Other one-volume works, exclusive of strictly school histories, include Z. Cartter Patten, *A Tennessee Chronicle* (Chattanooga, 1953); W. R. Garrett and A. V. Goodpasture, *History of Tennessee, Its People and Its Institutions* (Nashville, 1900; rpt. 1905); James Phelan, *History of Tennessee: the Making of a State* (Boston, 1888); and Goodspeed, *History of Tennessee* (Nashville, 1887; rpt. 1972), which in its several editions includes histories of various counties and cities.

Most of the multivolume histories of Tennessee, as well as of many other states, have been the work of the Lewis Historical Publishing Company of New York, which for many years has been employing historians to write two-volume histories of their respective states, accompanied by two other volumes containing biographies and family histories. The books for Tennessee were published in 1960, with Stanley J. Folmsbee, Robert E. Corlew, and Enoch L. Mitchell as authors. In 1933 the same company, using the imprint "American Historical Society," published *Tennessee: A History, 1673-1932*, 4 vols., with two well-researched volumes of narrative history being contributed mainly by Philip M. Hamer. Still useful is *Tennessee: The Volunteer State, 1769-1923*, by John Trotwood Moore and Austin P. Foster, 4 vols. (Chicago and Nashville, 1923), comprising one volume of history and three volumes of biography. Ten years earlier the Lewis company published the eight-volume work, *A History of Tennessee and Tennesseans*, by Will T. Hale and Dixon L. Merritt, containing three volumes of history and five of biographical sketches.

There are several excellent works of collective biography of Tennesseans. Prior to publication of William T. Alderson's compilation of biographies of notable living personages, *Tennessee Lives* (Hopkinsville, Ky., 1971), Senator Kenneth D. McKellar compiled interesting sketches of *Tennessee Senators As Seen by One of Their Successors* (Kingsport, 1942; rpt. 1944). Many years earlier, Mary B. Temple, daughter of a notable East Tennessean, Oliver P. Temple of Knoxville, published over his name *Notable Men of Tennessee from 1833 to 1875, Their Times and Their Contemporaries* (New York, 1912), which he had prepared to honor the Unionists of the state (largely of East Tennessee) during the Civil War period. John Allison's *Notable Men of Tennessee: Personal and Genealogical, with Notes* (Atlanta, 1905) is more general in its treatment, both topically and geographically. While women were still struggling for the right of suffrage, Mrs. Annie Somers Gilchrist wrote a biographical work entitled *Some Representative Women of Tennessee* (Nashville, 1902). Two very important books, *Sketches of the Bench and Bar of Tennessee* (Knoxville, 1898), and *Sketches of Prominent Tennesseans* (Nashville, 1888), were compiled by Joshua W. Caldwell and William S. Speer, respectively. In 1893 the A. D. Smith Company of Chattanooga published *East Tennessee—Historical and Biographical,* which, in addition to essays descriptive of topography, geology, and natural resources, includes sketches of "none but honourable men," notable in such fields as law, medicine, and journalism. Not to be overlooked, of course, are the sketches of Tennesseans in the *Dictionary of American Biography,* 20 vols. and index (New York, 1928-36), plus later supplements. The names of Tennesseans included are listed in ETHSP 4 (1932), 171-73; 7 (1935), 172-74; and 9 (1937), 165-67.

A new era in archaeological investigation in the state, especially in East Tennessee, began with the establishment of the Tennessee Valley Authority, whose lakes were about to engulf many sites of former Indian habitation. Cooperation of TVA with the University of Tennessee led to scientific investigation of Indian mounds, first in the Norris Basin by William S. Webb, and later by Thomas M. N. Lewis and Madeline Kneberg on Hiwassee Island, in Chickamauga Basin, and in many other places across the state. After making their reports, published by the University of Tennessee Press, Lewis and Kneberg made an outstanding contribution to the general public by translating those reports into layman's language in an attractive, well-illustrated volume, *Tribes that Slumber: Indian Times in the Tennessee Region* (Knoxville, 1958; rpt. 1960, 1966, 1970). After their departure, their work was carried on by the University's Department of Anthropology which they had created. Although excavational activity of earlier archaeologists was not so scientific or thorough as twentieth-century work, the annual reports of the Smithsonian Institution and the work of Gates P. Thruston, *The Antiquities of Tennessee . . .* (Cincinnati, 1890, 1897; rpt. Knoxville, 1964, 1972) contain significant contributions to our knowledge of Tennessee archaeology. Many years earlier, Tennessee's first archaeologist as well as its first historian, John Haywood, published *The Christian Advocate* (Nashville, 1819), which included historical archaeology with religious topics. Some of this work was incorporated in his *Natural and Aboriginal History of Tennessee* (Nashville, 1823). Mary U. Rothrock edited a reprint of the latter work (Jackson, 1959) and contributed a short biography of Haywood.

The dean of Tennessee historians, Judge Samuel Cole Williams, sometime after having acquired an outstanding reputation with his *History of the Lost State of Franklin* (Johnson City, 1924; rpt.

1933, 1970), treated the preceding periods of Tennessee history in equal detail. One book, published in Johnson City while the TVA was in its state of rapid development, was *Dawn of Tennessee Valley and Tennessee History, 1541-1776* (Johnson City, 1937). Although, like his other works, excessively eulogistic of the pioneers, it still remains the best one-volume work on the period. In 1930 Williams had published *Beginnings of West Tennessee in the Land of the Chickasaws, 1541-1841* (Johnson City, 1930; rpt. Nashville, 1971) the first and still the best work on the early history of that part of the state. The only significant work dealing with the beginning of Middle Tennessee, A. W. Putnam, *History of Middle Tennessee; or, Life and Times of Gen. James Robertson* (Nashville, 1859), was reprinted in 1971 as one of the Tennesseana Editions of the University of Tennessee Press, with an introduction by Stanley F. Horn and a new index by Hugh and Cornelia Walker. The "Bible" of early Tennessee history by James G. M. Ramsey, *The Annals of Tennessee to the End of the Eighteenth Century* (Charleston, S.C., 1853), was reprinted in 1967 by the East Tennessee Historical Society, with the addition of a biographical sketch of Dr. Ramsey by William H. Masterson, "Annotations Relating Ramsey's *Annals of Tennessee* to Present-Day Knowledge" by Stanley J. Folmsbee, and a new index. More recently, it was reprinted in New York by Arno in 1971.

Another invaluable early work, of social history, *The Tennessee Gazetteer, or Topographical Dictionary . . .* by Eastin Morris (Nashville, 1834), has been recently reprinted along with Matthew Rhea's *Map of the State of Tennessee, 1832,* edited by Robert M. McBride with an introduction by Mary U. Rothrock (Nashville, 1971). In 1823 John Haywood brought forth as a companion volume to his *Natural and Aboriginal History* what may be considered the first general history of the state: *The Civil and Political History of the State of Tennessee* (Knoxville, 1823; rpt. Knoxville, 1969; New York, 1971). It should be mentioned at this point that good accounts of the early history of Tennessee may be found in histories of the Old Southwest and of the West, such as John A. Caruso, *The Appalachian Frontier* (Indianapolis, 1959); Archibald Henderson, *The Conquest of the Old Southwest* (New York, 1920); Constance Skinner, *Pioneers of the Old Southwest* (New Haven, 1919); Theodore Roosevelt, *The Winning of the West,* 6 vols. (New York, 1889-96); and pertinent volumes of a recent and significant mammoth work: Lawrence H. Gipson, *The British Empire before the American Revolution,* 15 vols. (New York, 1936-70). The gathering and preservation of materials for writing the history of Tennessee and the Old Southwest are described by William B. Hesseltine in *Pioneer Mission: The Story of Lyman Copeland Draper* (Madison,

Wis., 1954), and in his edited work *Dr. J. G. M. Ramsey: Autobiography and Letters* (Nashville, 1954).

An invaluable collection of accounts written by some thirty early travelers into the boundaries of Tennessee and edited by Samuel C. Williams was published under the title *Early Travels in the Tennessee Country* (Johnson City, 1928; rpt. Nashville, 1970). His editing of *Lieutenant Henry Timberlake's Memoirs, 1756-1765* (Johnson City, 1927; rpt. Marietta, Ga., 1948), first published in London, 1765, made more readily available and usable the best description of the life of Cherokee Indians in the East Tennessee region for that period. Francis Harper has produced the best edition of *The Travels of William Bartram* (New Haven, 1958), a work significant for its description of the area including the Overhill Cherokee country. Accounts of earlier exploration are to be found in Charles W. Alvord and Lee Bidgood, *The First Explorations of the Trans-Allegheny Region by the Virginians, 1650-1674* (Cleveland, O., 1912), which made available for the first time reports recovered from the British Archives of the Needham and Arthur expedition into the East Tennessee region in 1673. The voyage of Marquette and Jolliet down the Mississippi in 1673 has been restudied in Raphael N. Hamilton, *Marquette's Explorations: The Narratives Reexamined* (Madison, Wis., 1970). La Salle's voyages of 1682 are well described in Paul Chesnel, *History of Cavalier de la Salle, 1643-1687* (New York and London, 1932). Thomas Walker, *Journal of an Exploration . . . 1750* (Boston, 1888), describing Sullivan County, and *The Journal of Daniel Smith* [1779-80] (Nashville, 1915) are also important. Volume 3 of Reuben Gold Thwaites' monumental thirty-two-volume work, *Early Western Travels 1748-1846* (Cleveland, O., 1904), includes both the travel accounts of André Michaux, 1793-1796, and the narrative by his son, François André Michaux, who traveled through Tennessee in 1802. These Frenchmen made significant observations about what they saw on their journeys from Middle to East Tennessee. Bibliographic references to many early travel accounts may be found in Thomas D. Clark, ed., *Travels in the Old South, a Bibliography,* 3 vols. (Norman, Okla., 1956-69).

The first effort to establish an English settlement in Tennessee is best described in Philip M. Hamer, *Fort Loudoun on the Little Tennessee* (Raleigh, N.C., 1925), which is a reprint of two articles in the *North Carolina Historical Review* of that year. A briefer booklet, published by the Fort Loudoun Association and written by Paul Kelly, *Historic Fort Loudoun* (Vonore, 1958, 1961), is a good later work which includes on opposite pages a modern map of the region and one drawn by Timberlake in the 1760s. David H. Corkran, *The Cherokee Frontier; Conflict and Survival, 1740-62*

(Norman, 1962, 1966), has an excellent account of the colorful
and tragic history of Fort Loudoun, as do most general works on
early Tennessee published since 1925. Works on this topic prior to
this date are not so reliable; for example, see corrections of Ramsey
in the annotations of the 1967 edition of *Annals of Tennessee.*

Other than in general works mentioned above, the beginnings of
permanent settlement in the Tennessee country are well covered in
biographies of Tennessee pioneers: Carl Driver, *John Sevier* (Chapel
Hill, 1932); Thomas E. Matthews, *General James Robertson* (Nashville, 1934); Samuel C. Williams, *William Tatham: Wataugan* (Johnson City, 1947); and John Bakeless, *Master of the Wilderness:
Daniel Boone* (New York, 1939).

The only one-volume treatment of the state in the American
Revolution is *Tennessee during the Revolutionary War* (Nashville,
1944), by Samuel C. Williams. This title is being reprinted (1974)
by the University of Tennessee Press. Although in general quite
reliable, it is marred by the author's refusal to accept a viewpoint
which has gained consensus that British agents, instead of inciting
the Cherokee Indians to ravage the frontier in 1776, actually tried
to restrain them from making their initial attacks. Other works on
the Revolutionary War include Thomas P. Abernethy, *Western
Lands and the American Revolution* (New York, 1937, 1959),
which has inaccuracies but remains important; John R. Alden, *The
South in the Revolution 1763-1789* (Baton Rouge, 1957, 1962);
and the eulogistic but still valuable work, Lyman C. Draper, *King's
Mountain and Its Heroes* (Cincinnati, 1881; rpt. Spartanburg, S.C.,
1967; Baltimore, 1971), the basic work on this subject.

For the period from the American Revolution to statehood, the
pioneering work *History of the Lost State of Franklin,* by Samuel
C. Williams (Johnson City, 1924; rpt. Nashville, 1972), remains the
best one-volume treatment of the "Lost State." The territorial
period of Tennessee is best covered in the biography of the governor of the Southwest Territory: *William Blount,* by William H.
Masterson (Baton Rouge, 1954; rpt. Westport, Conn., 1970). Many
of the basic documents of this period are printed in Clarence E.
Carter, ed., *The Territorial Papers of the United States,* vol. 4: *The
Territory South of the River Ohio, 1790-1796* (Washington, D.C.,
1936; rpt. New York, 1972), and much private correspondence is
available in *The John Gray Blount Papers,* vols. 1 and 2, ed. Alice
Keith; vol. 3, ed. William H. Masterson (Raleigh, N.C., 1952, 1965).
Intrigues by Tennesseans with the Spanish are clarified in Arthur
P. Whitaker, *The Spanish-American Frontier, 1783-1795* (Boston,
1927; rpt. Gloucester, Mass., 1962; Lincoln, Neb., 1969), and in
Driver, *John Sevier,* mentioned earlier.

The attainment of statehood is best described in Samuel C.

Williams, *The Admission of Tennessee into the Union* (Nashville, 1945), and in John D. Barnhart's analysis of early western constitutions: *Valley of Democracy* (Bloomington, Ind., 1953). A Supreme Court judge from Tennessee, Edward T. Sanford, wrote *The Constitutional Convention of Tennessee of 1796* (Nashville, 1896); and a noted attorney, Joshua W. Caldwell, produced *Studies in the Constitutional History of Tennessee* (Cincinnati, 1895, 1907), covering not only that convention but earlier and later constitutional developments.

The best general work on the middle period—statehood to Secession—is Abernethy's *From Frontier to Plantation in Tennessee,* although an older, eulogistic work, S. G. Heiskell, *Andrew Jackson and Early Tennessee History* (Nashville, 1920), is still useful. Eric R. Lacy makes an important contribution to understanding political issues of this era in *Vanquished Volunteers: East Tennessee Sectionalism from Statehood to Secession* (Johnson City, 1965), a work in which he analyzes legislative and congressional voting records of East Tennessee. Robert H. White in the first four volumes of his editorial work, *Messages of the Governors of Tennessee* (Nashville, 1952-72), illuminates much more than the texts of the messages. Much of his coverage deals with outstanding personalities such as Andrew Jackson and their impact upon the matters at public issue in their time. The most recent, objective biography of Jackson is by Robert V. Remini, *Andrew Jackson* (New York, 1966). Remini, who also wrote *The Election of Andrew Jackson* (Philadelphia, 1963) and *Andrew Jackson and the Bank War* (New York, 1967), is consultant editor for the forthcoming volumes of the Andrew Jackson papers, edited by Sam B. Smith and Harriet C. Owsley. This work is a greatly needed supplement to John Spencer Bassett's edition of *Correspondence of Andrew Jackson,* 7 vols. (Washington, D.C., 1926-35), which includes less than one-tenth of existing Jackson material. Bassett was also the author of the best single biographical treatment of Jackson, *Life of Andrew Jackson,* 2 vols. (Garden City, N.Y., 1911, 1916, 1925, 1928, 1931; rpt., 2 vols. in 1, Hamden, Conn., 1967). Marquis James, *Andrew Jackson: The Border Captain* (New York, 1933) and *Andrew Jackson: Portrait of a President* (New York, 1937, 1961), later published as *Life of Andrew Jackson,* 2 vols. (New York, 1938), is a highly competent later work. Briefer and more recent Jackson titles include Arthur M. Schlesinger, Jr., *The Age of Jackson* (Boston, 1945); Harold S. Syrett, *Andrew Jackson: His Contribution to American Tradition* (Indianapolis, 1953); John W. Ward, *Andrew Jackson: Symbol for an Age* (New York, 1953, 1955, 1962); Marvin Meyers, *The Jacksonian Persuasion* (Stanford, 1957; rpt. New York, 1960); Glyndon G. Van Deusen, *The Jacksonian Era, 1828-1848* (New

York, 1959); and Charles G. Sellers, ed., *Andrew Jackson: A Profile* (New York, 1971). The century-old work of James Parton, *Life of Andrew Jackson,* 3 vols. (New York, 1859, 1860, 1861; rpt. Boston, 1863, 1887-88; rpt. New York, 1972), is still of great value, especially for the early period, as are two authorized works by Jackson's associates: John H. Eaton and John Reid, *The Life of Andrew Jackson* (Philadelphia, Pa., 1817, 1824, 1828, 1878; rpt. New York, 1971) and Samuel Putnam Waldo, *Memoirs of Andrew Jackson* (Hartford, Conn., 1819, 1820; rpt. New York, 1825; Chambersburg, Md., 1828).

Coverage of Tennessee's other President of the period, James K. Polk, is much less voluminous. Only two volumes of the projected definitive biography by Charles G. Sellers have appeared: *James K. Polk: Jacksonian 1795-1843* (Princeton, 1957); and *James K. Polk: Continentalist, 1843-1846* (Princeton, 1966). The best one-volume biography probably is Eugene I. McCormac, *James K. Polk: A Political Biography* (Berkeley, 1922; rpt. New York, 1965). The President's own meticulous journal, edited by Milo M. Quaife, *The Diary of James K. Polk during His Presidency, 1845 to 1849,* 4 vols. (Chicago, 1910), has been condensed into one volume by Allan Nevins, ed., *Polk: The Diary of a President, 1845-1849* (New York, 1929, 1952, 1968). Two welcome volumes of *The Correspondence of James K. Polk: I, 1817-1832; II, 1833-1834,* edited by Herbert Weaver and Paul H. Bergeron (Nashville, 1969-), have recently appeared. Although biographies of the third President from Tennessee, Andrew Johnson, will be described later in this essay, the three volumes in print of *The Papers of Andrew Johnson: I, 1822-1851; II, 1852-1857; III, 1858-1860,* eds. LeRoy P. Graf and Ralph W. Haskins (Knoxville, 1967-) deserve mention here as especially valuable for the period.

There is an excellent biography of Polk's Whig opponent, *John Bell of Tennessee,* by Joseph H. Parks (Baton Rouge, 1950). Parks also wrote *Felix Grundy: Champion of Democracy* (Baton Rouge, 1949). Sam Houston is the subject of several significant works: Marquis James, *The Raven* (New York, 1929, 1935; rpt. Garden City, 1946; rpt. New York, 1956, 1962; rpt. Dunwoody, Ga., 1968); Llerena Friend, *Sam Houston, the Great Designer* (Austin, 1954, 1969); Marion K. Wisehart, *Sam Houston, American Giant* (Washington, D.C., 1962); and Amerlia W. Williams and Eugene C. Barker, eds., *The Writings of Sam Houston,* 8 vols. (Austin, 1938-43).

Although much has been written about David Crockett, most studies have been about the mythical rather than the historical Crockett. No biography in book form based on authentic sources appeared until 1956, when the University of North Carolina Press published *David Crockett: The Man and the Legend,* written by the late James A. Shackford and edited by his brother, John B. Shackford. Crockett's "Autobiography," written with the aid of a ghost writer, was published as *A Narrative of The Life of David Crockett of the State of Tennessee* (Philadelphia, Pa., and Baltimore, 1834). Many reprint editions of the "Autobiography" unfortunately have been distorted by the inclusion of the spurious *Col. Crockett's Exploits and Adventures in Texas* (Philadelphia, Pa., 1836). Although this latter work is of doubtful validity, it has usually been accepted as genuine and thus, until recently, has been published in the same volume with Crockett's *Narrative.* In 1973, however, a facsimile of the first edition of the *Narrative,* supplemented by an introduction and annotations by the late James A. Shackford and Stanley J. Folmsbee, was published by the University of Tennessee Press.

Books on the period from the granting of statehood to the eve of Secession include works on various topics. There are several dealing with the Creek War and the War of 1812. Specialized works include James W. Holland, *Andrew Jackson and the Creek War* (Tuscaloosa, Ala., 1969); Mrs. Dunbar Rowland, *Andrew Jackson's Campaign against the British, or, The Mississippi Territory in the War of 1812* (New York, 1926); Robert B. McAfee, *History of the Late War in the Western Country* (Lexington, Ky., 1816; Bowling Green, O., 1919); and H. S. Halbert and T. H. Ball, *The Creek War of 1813 and 1814* (Chicago and Montgomery, 1895; ed. Frank L. Owsley, Jr., University, Ala., 1969). More general works are Reginald Horsman, *The Causes of the War of 1812* (Philadelphia, Pa., 1962; rpt. New York, 1971), and Julius W. Pratt, *Expansionists of 1812* (New York, 1925; rpt. Gloucester, Mass., 1949, 1957).

The Cherokee and their removal are described in such monographs as Henry T. Malone, *Cherokees of the Old South: A People in Transition* (Athens, Ga., 1956, 1966); Marion Lena Starkey, *The Cherokee Nation* (New York, 1946); Grace S. Woodward, *The Cherokees* (Norman, 1963, 1965, 1969); John P. Brown, *Old Frontiers: The Story of the Cherokee Indians from Earliest Times to the Date of Their Removal to the West, 1838* (Kingsport, 1938; rpt. New York, 1971); and Charles C. Royce, comp., "Indian Land Cessions in the United States," *Eighteenth Annual Report, Bureau of American Ethnology* (Washington, D.C., 1899). Royce's invaluable account, "The Cherokee Nation of Indians" is a part of the *Fifth Annual Report of the Bureau of American Ethnology* (Washington, D.C., 1887).

General works about the Southern Indians and about federal Indian policy are also useful: Robert S. Cotterill, *The Southern Indians: The Story of the Civilized Tribes before Removal* (Norman,

1954, 1966); O. B. Peake, *A History of the United States Indian Factory System, 1795-1822* (Denver, 1954); Francis P. Prucha, *American Indian Policy in the Formative Years* (Cambridge, Mass., 1962); Reginald Horsman, *Expansion and American Indian Policy, 1789-1812* (East Lansing, Mich., 1967); and Grant Foreman, *Indian Removal: The Emigration of the Five Civilized Tribes of Indians* (Norman, 1932, 1953, 1972). Foreman's excellent biography *Sequoyah* (Norman, 1938, 1959) is the best on the subject.

The outstanding work on missionary activity among the Cherokee is Robert S. Walker, *Torchlights to the Cherokees: The Brainerd Mission* (New York, 1931). Also significant are Ralph H. Gabriel, *Elias Boudinot, Cherokee, and His America* (Norman, 1941); Althea Bass, *Cherokee Messenger* (Norman, 1936, 1968), a biography of Samuel Austin Worcester; John M. Wooten, *Red Clay Council Ground, 1832-1838; Last Capital of the Cherokee Nation East of the Mississippi River* (Cleveland, 1938); and George W. Wood, *Report of Mr. Wood's Visit to the Choctaw and Cherokee Missions, 1855* (Boston, 1855).

The only general work on the Chickasaw Indians in book form is Arrell M. Gibson, *The Chickasaws* (Norman, 1971).

Early post-statehood travel accounts, in addition to the work of F. A. Michaux mentioned earlier, also available in Williams, *Early Travels,* include Francis Baily, *Journal of a Tour in 1796/97 in the Unsettled Parts of North America* (London, 1856; rpt. Louisville, 1959; rpt. Carbondale, 1969). Among the later accounts and guides cited in Clark, *Travels in the Old South,* previously mentioned, are *The Journal of the Rev. Francis Asbury,* 3 vols. (New York, 1827; rpt. Nashville, 1958; rpt. London, 1958); Mrs. Anne Royall, *Sketches of History, Life, and Manners of the United States* (New Haven, 1826); James Hall, *Statistics of the West* (Cincinnati, 1836); and Mrs. Frances Trollope, *Domestic Manners of the Americans,* 2 vols. (London, 1832).

Aspects of economic and social history in the early years have been summarized by Albert C. Holt, *The Economy and Social Beginnings of Tennessee* (Nashville, 1923) and for the entire period in such works as Thomas H. Freeman IV, *An Economic History of Tennessee* (Nashville, 1965) and Paul Barnett, *Industrial Development in Tennessee* (Knoxville, 1941). Two general works with the title *Development of Banking in Tennessee* have appeared, one by Claude A. Campbell (Nashville, 1932) and the other by Warren P. Gray (New Brunswick, N.J., 1948), both of which represent sound scholarship. Works on transportation include Stanley J. Folmsbee, *Sectionalism and Internal Improvements in Tennessee, 1796-1845* (Knoxville, 1939); T. J. Campbell, *The Upper Tennessee* (Chattanooga, 1932); Byrd Douglas, *Steamboatin' on the Cumber-*

land (Nashville, 1961); Jonathan Daniels, *Devil's Backbone: The Story of the Natchez Trace* (New York, 1961); Donald Davidson, *The Tennessee,* 2 vols. (New York, 1946, 1948); Ulrich B. Phillips, *A History of Transportation in the Eastern Cotton Belt to 1860* (New York, 1908, 1968); Thomas D. Clark, *The Beginning of the L & N* (Louisville, 1933), and *A Pioneer Southern Railroad from New Orleans to Cairo* (Chapel Hill, 1936). The compendious *History of Transportation in the United States before 1860,* B. H. Meyer, et al., sponsored by the Carnegie Foundation (Washington, D.C., 1917), is a storehouse of information, as is a companion work, vol. 1 of Victor S. Clark, comp., *History of Manufacturers in the United States, 1607-1914* (Washington, D.C., 1916-28).

In regard to agriculture and Negro slavery in the state, new viewpoints have resulted from the use of statistics based upon original returns of the 1850 and 1860 United States census, e.g., Chase Mooney, *Slavery in Tennessee* (Bloomington, Ind., 1957; rpt. Westport, Conn., 1971); Blanche Henry Clark, *The Tennessee Yeomen, 1840-1860* (Nashville, 1942); and Frank L. Owsley, *Plain Folk of the Old South* (Baton Rouge, 1949). These works established the facts that slavery was not so widespread in Tennessee and the South as had previously been thought and that the nonslaveholding yeoman farmer was the backbone of the population. Older works, such as Caleb Patterson, *The Negro in Tennessee, 1790-1865* (Austin, 1922; rpt. New York, 1968), and Ulrich B. Phillips, *American Negro Slavery* (New York, 1918; rpt. Baton Rouge, 1966), and *Life and Labor in the Old South* (Boston, 1929; rpt. New York, 1958), are still useful, although they should be read along with such modern works as Kenneth M. Stampp, *The Peculiar Institution* (New York, 1956). In view of Tennessee's geographic location, Frederick Bancroft, *Slave-Trading in the Old South* (Baltimore, 1931), and Wendell H. Stephenson, *Isaac Franklin, Slave Trader and Planter of the Old South* (University, La., 1938), are of special interest. The availability of some early nineteenth-century contemporary writings should perhaps be noted also: C. R. Barteau, *Brief Review: What Has Been Done in Tennessee . . . Tennessee and the Institution of Slavery* (Hartsville, 1861); Elihu Embree, *The Emancipator* (Jonesborough, 1820; rpt., with a biographical sketch of Embree by Robert H. White, Nashville, 1932); and the Federal Writers' Project, *Tennessee Narrative,* vol. 15 of *Slave Narratives* (Washington, D.C., 1941).

Social life of the middle period of Tennessee history has been described by F. Garvin Davenport in his *Cultural Life in Nashville on the Eve of the Civil War* (Chapel Hill, 1941). Earlier works, with a contemporary flavor, are John Allison, *Dropped Stitches in*

Tennessee History (Nashville, 1897, 1971); J. C. Guild, *Old Times in Tennessee* (Nashville, 1878; rpt. Knoxville, 1971); J. W. M. Breazeale, *Life As It Is; or, Matters and Things in General* (Knoxville, 1842, 1969); and John C. Gunn, *Gunn's Domestic Medicine* (Knoxville, 1830; rpt. Madisonville, 1834; rpt. Cincinnati, 1859).

Perception of the Civil War and Reconstruction period may be gained by studying biographies of Andrew Johnson and William Gannaway Brownlow. The best works on Johnson are Robert W. Winston, *Andrew Johnson, Plebeian and Patriot* (New York, 1928, 1969, 1970) and George F. Milton, Jr., *The Age of Hate: Andrew Johnson and the Radicals* (New York, 1930; rpt. Hamden, Conn., 1965), the latter work being more biographical than the title indicates. Also valuable are Eric L. McKitrick, *Andrew Johnson and Reconstruction* (Chicago, 1960); Milton Lomask, *Andrew Johnson: President on Trial* (New York, 1960) and *Andy Johnson: Tailor Who Became President* (New York, 1962); Joseph G. De Roulhac Hamilton, *Life of Andrew Johnson, 17th President of the United States* (Greeneville, 1928, 1930); the earlier work, James S. Jones, *Life of Andrew Johnson, 17th President of the United States* (Greeneville, 1901); and Lillian Foster, comp., *Andrew Johnson, President of the United States: His Life and Speeches* (New York, 1866). Clifton R. Hall, *Andrew Johnson: Military Governor of Tennessee* (Princeton, 1916), is a specialized study.

The only book-length biography of William Gannaway Brownlow is E. Merton Coulter, *William G. Brownlow, Fighting Parson of the Southern Highlands* (Chapel Hill, 1937; rpt. with an introduction by James W. Patton, Knoxville, 1971). One of his own works, *Sketches of the Rise, Progress, and Decline of Secession; with a Narrative of Personal Adventures among the Rebels* [known as *Parson Brownlow's Book*] (Philadelphia, Pa., 1862; rpt. with introduction by Thomas B. Alexander, New York, 1968), is a fascinating and invaluable introduction to Brownlow's thought pattern. There is one excellent nonbiographical summary of this period: James W. Patton, *Unionism and Reconstruction in Tennessee, 1860-1869* (Chapel Hill, 1934; rpt. Gloucester, Mass., 1966).

The background of Tennessee's secession is described in an outstanding work: Mary E. R. Campbell, *The Attitude of Tennesseans toward the Union, 1847-1861* (New York, 1961), although the biographies of Johnson, Brownlow, John Bell, as well as Temple's *Notable Men,* mentioned previously, and also William B. Hesseltine, ed., *Dr. J. G. M. Ramsey: Autobiography and Letters* (Nashville, 1954), are significant on this topic for both the prewar and the war periods. An important general work, E. Merton Coulter, *The Confederate States of America,* A History of the South, vol. 7 (Baton Rouge, 1950), includes a treatment of Tennessee.

For the military campaigns, the best account is a two-volume study of the Army of Tennessee: Thomas L. Connelly, *Army of the Heartland: The Army of Tennessee, 1861-1862* and *Autumn of Glory: The Army of Tennessee, 1862-1865* (Baton Rouge, 1967 and 1971, respectively). The older work, Stanley F. Horn, *The Army of Tennessee: A Military History* (Indianapolis, 1941; rpt. Norman, 1953, 1968), remains a vital account and interpretation. Individual campaigns and battles are well described in Fairfax Downey, *Storming the Gateway: Chattanooga, 1863* (New York, 1960, 1969); James J. Hamilton, *The Battle of Fort Donelson* (South Brunswick, N.J., 1968); Capt. John D. Shellenbarger, *The Battle of Spring Hill* (Cleveland, O., 1913) and *The Battle of Franklin, Tennessee* (Cleveland, O., 1916); Orlando M. Poe, *Personal Recollections of the Occupation of East Tennessee and the Defense of Knoxville* (Detroit, 1889; rpt. Knoxville, 1963); Digby G. Seymour, *Divided Loyalties: Fort Sanders and the Civil War in East Tennessee* (Knoxville, 1963); Stanley F. Horn, *The Decisive Battle of Nashville* (Baton Rouge, 1956; rpt. Knoxville, 1968); Grady McWhiney, *Braxton Bragg and Confederate Defeat* (New York, 1969) deals with Shiloh; and Alexander F. Stevenson, *The Battle of Stone's River* (Boston, 1884).

Biographies of commanders are numerous and valuable, especially those of Nathan Bedford Forrest, the best of which is Robert S. Henry, *"First with the Most" Forrest* (Indianapolis, 1944). The same author edited *As They Saw Forrest* (Jackson, 1956). Andrew N. Lytle, *Bedford Forrest and His Critter Company* (New York, 1931, 1947, 1960), and the near-contemporary work, Thomas Jordan and J. P. Pryor, *The Campaigns of Lieut.-Gen. N. B. Forrest* (New Orleans, 1868), are also significant. Other biographies of Confederate generals are *The Gallant Hood,* by John P. Dyer (Indianapolis, 1950); *General Edmund Kirby Smith, C.S.A.* (Baton Rouge, 1954) and *General Leonidas Polk, C.S.A., The Fighting Bishop,* by Joseph H. Parks (Baton Rouge, 1962); *Life of Albert Sidney Johnston,* by William P. Johnston (New York, 1878); and *Lee's Lieutenants,* by Douglas S. Freeman, 3 vols. (New York, 1942-44). *Morgan and His Raiders: A Biography of the Confederate General,* by Cecil F. Holland (New York, 1942), and *Champ Ferguson: Confederate Guerilla,* by Thurman Sensing (Nashville, 1942), are probably the best works on these guerilla leaders. The most recent works on the famous Coleman Scout Sam Davis are *Sam Davis: Confederate Hero* (Smyrna, 1947) and *Sam Davis, Hero of the Confederacy and of the Coleman Scouts* (Nashville, 1971) by Edythe J. R. Whitley. Of the biographies of Union generals involved in Tennessee campaigns, Freeman Cleaves, *Rock of Chickamauga: The Life of General George H. Thomas* (Norman, 1948); Samuel C. Williams, *General John T. Wilder: Commander of the Lightning Brigade* (Bloomington, Ind.,

1936); Lloyd Lewis, *Sherman, Fighting Prophet* (New York, 1932); and the contemporary work, S. M. Bowman and R. B. Irwin, *Sherman and His Campaigns: A Military Biography* (Cincinnati, 1865), probably are the most significant. Of the host of memoirs and "regimental" histories by participants, in addition to Sherman's *Memoirs* (Bloomington, Ind., 1957), the most useful are William R. Carter, *History of the First Regiment of Tennessee Volunteer Cavalry* (Knoxville, 1902); Alexander Eckel, *History of the Fourth Tennessee Cavalry, U.S.A.* (Knoxville, 1929), and his *Andersonville: Seven Months' Experience of Two Tennessee Boys in Andersonville and Five Other Rebel Prisons* (Knoxville, n.d.); and John W. Rowell, *Yankee Cavalrymen: Through the Civil War with the Ninth Pennsylvania Cavalry* (Knoxville, 1971). Significant works of Confederates are *The Reminiscences of Newton Cannon, First Sergeant, 11th Tennessee Cavalry, C.S.A.*, ed. Campbell H. Brown (Franklin, 1963); *Civil War Diary of Capt. J. J. Womack, Company E, 16th Regiment of Tennessee Volunteers* (McMinnville, 1961); and [Richard R.] *Hancock's Diary: or, A History of the Second Tennessee Confederate Cavalry* (Nashville, 1887); *Dr. Quintard, C.S.A., Chaplain and Second Bishop of Tennessee*, ed. A. H. Noll (Sewanee, 1905); and *"Co. Aytch" . . . Side Show of the Big Show*, by Samuel R. Watkins, ed. Bell I. Wiley (Jackson, 1952). Instructive personal accounts of the War are found in *Tennessee's War, 1861-1865, Described by Participants*, ed. Stanley F. Horn (Nashville, 1965), and two works by Bell I. Wiley: *The Life of Johnny Reb* and *The Life of Billy Yank* (Indianapolis, 1943 and 1952).

There are two excellent summaries of Reconstruction in the state: Thomas B. Alexander, *Political Reconstruction in Tennessee* (Nashville, 1950; rpt. New York, 1968), and James W. Patton, *Unionism and Reconstruction in Tennessee, 1860-1869*, previously mentioned. Older works such as John R. Neal, *Disunion and Restoration in Tennessee* (New York, 1899) and James W. Fertig, *The Secession and Reconstruction of Tennessee* (Chicago, 1898) are still useful, although the latter has some inaccuracies, such as his treatment of the Reconstruction Convention. For the entire period of 1857 to 1869, vols. 5 and 6 of White, *Messages of the Governors*, mentioned earlier, contain important information. Topical and general works important to Tennessee are George R. Bentley, *A History of the Freedmen's Bureau* (Philadelphia, Pa., 1955; rpt. New York, 1970); E. Merton Coulter, *The South during Reconstruction*, A History of the South, vol. 8 (Baton Rouge, 1947); Richard O. Curry, ed., *Radicalism, Racism, and Party Realignment: The Border States during Reconstruction* (Baltimore, 1970); Jonathan T. Dorris, *Pardon and Amnesty under Lincoln and Johnson* (Chapel Hill, 1953); Robert S. Henry, *The Story of*

Reconstruction (Indianapolis, 1938; rpt. Gloucester, Mass., 1963);
Stanley F. Horn, *Invisible Empire: The Story of the Ku Klux Klan,
1866-1871* (Boston, 1939; rpt. New York, 1969; rpt. Cos Cob,
Conn., 1969; 2nd enl. ed., Montclair, N.J., 1969) which is still the
definitive work on the subject; and J. C. Lester and D. L. Wilson,
Ku Klux Klan. Its Origin, Growth and Disbandment (Nashville,
1884; rpt. New York, 1905, 1971). There are several good works
about the Negro during the period; especially useful are Alrutheus
A. Taylor, *The Negro in Tennessee, 1865-1880* (Washington, D.C.,
1941) and Bell I. Wiley, *Southern Negroes, 1861-1865* (New Haven,
1965).

Fine political and military histories for the period from 1870 to
1972 are available. For the early part of the period, while Robert
L. Taylor was the dominant figure, Dan M. Robison, *Bob Taylor
and the Agrarian Revolt in Tennessee* (Chapel Hill, 1935) is the
outstanding work. Vols. 6 and 7 of White's *Messages of the Governors* cover the period from 1869 to 1899; vol. 8, ed. Dan M.
Robison and Robert M. McBride (Nashville, 1972), the final
volume of this series, covers the period from 1899 to 1907. There
is nothing in book form about Tennessee and the Spanish-American
War except a few accounts by participants, such as that contained
in *Memoirs of Cordell Hull,* 2 vols. (New York, 1948), which also
covers his relationship to World Wars I and II. For World War I,
Tom Skeyhill, ed., *Sergeant York: His Own Story and War Diary*
(New York, 1928) is good biography; for World War II, Gene
H. Sloan, *With the Second Army, Somewhere in Tennessee* (Kansas
City, 1956) and George H. Butler, *The Military March of Time in
Tennessee, 1939-1944* (Nashville, 1945) are important.

There are several biographies and autobiographies of twentieth-
century Tennessee leaders. Mention has been made of Hull's
Memoirs; the only biography of Hull is Harold B. Hinton, *Cordell
Hull* (New York, 1942), although Julius W. Pratt in vols. 12 and 13
of the *American Secretaries of State and Their Diplomacy* series
describes Hull's diplomatic career thoroughly and quite favorably.
Joseph B. Gorman, *Kefauver: A Political Biography* (New York,
1971) is the best single biography of this distinguished U.S. senator.
Albert Gore, another outstanding former U.S. senator, has written
The Eye of the Storm: A People's Politics for the Seventies (New
York, 1970). Other twentieth-century Tennessee political figures
who have received biographical treatment are Newell Sanders, Ben
W. Hooper, Edward H. Crump, and Austin Peay.

Party history and organization are treated in Austin P. Foster
and Albert H. Roberts, *Tennessee Democracy: A History of the
Party and Its Representative Members—Past and Present,* 4 vols.
(Nashville, 1940); John W. Kilgo, *Campaigning in Dixie with Some*

Reflections on Two-Party Government (New York, 1945); and William Goodman, *Inherited Domain: Political Parties in Tennessee* (Knoxville, 1954).

Four vital issues are treated in *Prohibition and Politics: Turbulent Decades in Tennessee, 1885-1920,* by Paul E. Isaac (Knoxville, 1965); in *The Woman's Suffrage Movement in Tennessee,* by A. Elizabeth Taylor (New York, 1957); in Jennings Perry, *Democracy Begins at Home: The Tennessee Fight on the Poll Tax* (New York, 1944); and in Richard C. Cortner, *The Apportionment Cases* (Knoxville, 1971), which describes the landmark Tennessee case of *Baker* v. *Carr* and other reapportionment cases heard by federal courts.

In addition to treatment in the general works by Freeman, Barnett, Campbell, and Gray mentioned previously in discussion of the pre-Civil War period, economic developments since 1865 are dealt with more specifically in Hermann Bokum, *The Tennessee Hand-Book and Immigrants Guide* (Philadelphia, Pa., 1868)—a part of the Brownlow administration's campaign for immigrants; Joshua W. Caldwell, *East Tennessee: Its Agricultural and Mineral Resources* (New York, 1867); Morrow Chamberlain, *A Brief History of the Pig Iron Industry of East Tennessee* (Chattanooga, 1942). Significant recent studies are Leonard P. Curry, *Rail Routes South: Louisville's Fight for the Southern Market, 1865-1872* (Lexington, Ky., 1969); Kincaid A. Herr, *The Louisville & Nashville Railroad* (Louisville, 1943, 1959, 1964); Richard E. Prince, *The Nashville, Chattanooga and St. Louis Railway* (Green River, Wyo., 1967); John F. Stover, *The Railroad of the South, 1865-1900* (Chapel Hill, 1955); Earl C. Case, *The Valley of East Tennessee: The Adjustment of Industry to Natural Environment* (Nashville, 1925); John B. McFerrin, *Caldwell and Company: A Southern Financial Empire* (Chapel Hill, 1939; rpt. Nashville, 1969); James E. Thorogood, *A Financial History of Tennessee since 1870* (Sewanee, 1949); and J. Fred Holly, *Protective Labor Legislation and Its Administration in Tennessee* (Knoxville, 1956).

The problems of race and the contribution of the Negro in Tennessee are described in Alrutheus A. Taylor, *The Negro in Tennessee, 1865-1880,* previously mentioned; C. Vann Woodward, *The Strange Career of Jim Crow* (New York, 1955, 1957); Margaret Anderson, *The Children of the South* (New York, 1966), which describes desegregation in Clinton; Benjamin Muse, *Ten Years of Prelude* (New York, 1964), which contains a chapter on the Clinton difficulties; Charles W. Cansler, *Three Generations: The Story of a Colored Family of Eastern Tennessee* (Kingsport, 1939); L. H. Schuster, E. A. Epps, and V. W. Henderson, *Business Enterprises of Negroes in Tennessee* (Nashville, 1961); Wilma Dykeman and James Stokely, *Neither Black nor White* (New York, 1957) and *Seeds of*

Southern Change: The Life of Will Alexander [founder of the Southern Regional Council] (Chicago, 1962); Nikki Giovanni, *Gemini* [an autobiography including life in Knoxville and Nashville] (New York, 1971); Hugh Davis Graham, *Crisis in Print: Desegregation and the Press in Tennessee* (Nashville, 1967); Herman H. Long and Vivian W. Henderson, *Negro Employment in Tennessee State Government* (Nashville, 1962); Mingo Scott, *The Negro in Tennessee Politics and Governmental Affairs, 1865-1965* (Nashville, 1965); Tennessee State Planning Commission, *Human Relations in Tennessee* (Nashville, 1970); and Charles E. Wynes, ed., *The Negro in the South since 1865* (Tuscaloosa, Ala., 1965).

The experience of the Great Depression and the New Deal in the state led to such works as *National Youth Administration . . . 1935, 1936 . . . in Tennessee* (Nashville, 1936), and W. L. Simpson, *Review of Civil Works Administration Activities in Tennessee* (Nashville, 1935). Literature on the basic New Deal contribution in Tennessee, the TVA, is, however, much more extensive and includes two guides: Harry C. Bauer, comp., *An Indexed Bibliography of the Tennessee Valley Authority* (Knoxville, 1933-40, various editions), and Bernard L. Foy, comp., *The TVA Program— A Bibliography* (Knoxville, 1943-48, several editions). Among the most significant books on TVA are the following: J. Haden Alldredge, et al., *A History of Navigation on the Tennessee River System, House Doc.* 254, 75th Cong., 1st sess. (Washington, D.C., 1937); Carlton R. Ball, *A Study of the Work of the Land-Grant Colleges in the Tennessee Valley Area in Cooperation with the Tennessee Valley Authority* (Knoxville, 1939); Wilmon H. Droze, *High Dams and Slack Waters: TVA Rebuilds a River* (Baton Rouge, 1965), which supplements Thomas J. Campbell's pre-TVA work, *The Upper Tennessee: Comprehending Desultory Records of River Operations in the Tennessee River Valley* (Chattanooga, 1932); Clarence L. Hodge, *The Tennessee Valley Authority: A National Experiment in Regionalism* (Washington, D.C., 1938; rpt. New York, 1968); Victor C. Hobday, *Sparks at the Grassroots: Municipal Distribution of TVA Electricity in Tennessee* (Knoxville, 1969); T. L. Howard, *The TVA and Economic Security in the South* (Chapel Hill, 1936); Preston J. Hubbard, *Origins of the TVA, the Muscles Shoals Controversy, 1920-1932* (Nashville, 1961; rpt. New York, 1968); David E. Lilienthal, *The Journals of David E. Lilienthal,* vol. 1, *The TVA Years* (New York, 1964) and *TVA: Democracy on the March* (New York, 1944, 1953); John R. Moore, ed., *The Economic Impact of TVA* (Knoxville, 1967); Charles H. Pritchett, *The Tennessee Valley Authority: A Study in Public Administration* (Chapel Hill, 1943); Wilson Whitman, *God's Valley: People and Power along the Tennessee River* (New York, 1939);

Joseph S. Ransmeier, *The Tennessee Valley Authority: A Case Study in the Economics of Multiple Purpose Stream Planning* (Nashville, 1942); *Recreational Development of the Southern Highlands Region* (Knoxville, 1938); Gordon R. Clapp, *The TVA: An Approach to the Development of a Region* (Chicago, 1955); Roscoe C. Martin, ed., *TVA: The First Twenty Years* (Knoxville, Tenn., and University, Ala., 1956); Norman I. Wengert, *Valley of Tomorrow: The TVA and Agriculture* (Knoxville, 1952); and James E. Williams, *The Industrial Development Policy of the Tennessee Valley Authority . . . 1935-1950* (Knoxville, 1950).

Two significant works on Oak Ridge should be mentioned: Leslie R. Groves, *Now It Can Be Told: The Story of the Manhattan Project* (New York, 1962) and George O. Robinson, *The Oak Ridge Story: The Saga of a People Who Share in History* (Kingsport, 1950).

The best general survey of education in the South and in Tennessee is the work by Charles W. Dabney, *Universal Education in the South,* 2 vols. (Chapel Hill, 1936). Henry A. Bullock, *A History of Negro Education in the South: From 1619 to the Present* (Cambridge, Mass., 1967) is an excellent survey of the education of the Negro. An invaluable survey of educational literature for the pre-Civil War period is Edgar W. Knight, ed., *A Documentary History of Education in the South before 1860,* 5 vols. (Chapel Hill, 1949-53). Two outstanding general works concerning Tennessee are Robert H. White, *Development of the Tennessee State Education Organization, 1776-1929* (Nashville, 1929), and Andrew D. Holt, *The Struggle for a State System of Public Schools in Tennessee, 1903-1936* (New York, 1938, 1972). The contributions of two outstanding educators are surveyed in Charles Lee Lewis, *Philander Priestly Claxton: Crusader for Public Education* (Knoxville, 1948) and Laurence McMillin, *The Schoolmaker: Sawney Webb and the Bell Buckle Story* (Chapel Hill, 1971).

In the field of higher education the only general survey, Lucius S. Merriam, ed., *Higher Education in Tennessee* (Washington, D.C., 1893), is out of date, but there is a good work on private institutions: John S. Diekhoff, et al., *A Study of Private Higher Education in Tennessee* (Nashville, 1970). There are, also, numerous works on individual colleges and universities. For the state university there are three older works of significance: Moses White, *Early History of the University of Tennessee* (Knoxville, 1879); Thomas C. Karns, *The University of Tennessee,* rpt. from Merriam, *Higher Education* (Washington, D.C., 1893); and Edward T. Sanford, *Blount College and The University of Tennessee* (Knoxville, 1894). The University of Tennessee has published in the University of Tennessee *Record* several booklets on various periods, all being results of modern research. Three are by Stanley J. Folmsbee: *Blount College and*

East Tennessee College, 1794-1840 (1946); *East Tennessee University, 1840-1879* (1959); and *Tennessee Establishes a State University: First Years of the University of Tennessee, 1879-1887* (1961). Two more are by James R. Montgomery: *The Volunteer State Forges Its University: The University of Tennessee, 1887-1919* (1966) and *Threshold of a New Day: The University of Tennessee, 1919-1946* (1971). In progress by these two authors is a one-volume work on the University of Tennessee, 1794-1970. There is also a good study of a former private institution which is now a part of the University of Tennessee system: Gilbert E. Govan and James W. Livingood, *The University of Chattanooga: Sixty Years* (Chattanooga, 1947). Two excellent works by Edwin Mims treat Vanderbilt: *History of Vanderbilt University* (Nashville, 1946) and *Chancellor Kirkland of Vanderbilt* (Nashville, 1940). There is also a biography of the founder: *Bishop Holland Nimmons McTyeire,* by John J. Tigert (Nashville, 1955). Henry N. Snyder's, *Vanderbilt University in Some of Its Relations to Higher Education in the South* (Nashville, 1898), is also significant.

Alfred L. Crabb, *The Genealogy of George Peabody College for Teachers Covering a Period of One Hundred and Fifty Years* (Nashville, 1935) is probably the best general history of Peabody College, although John E. Windrow, *John Berrien Lindsley: Educator, Physician, Social Philosopher* (Chapel Hill, 1938) is an excellent biography of a noted president of its predecessor, the University of Nashville. There are several good descriptions of the smaller schools of the state.

Religious developments in Tennessee are well described in several general works: William W. Sweet, *Religion on the American Frontier, 1783-1840,* 4 vols. (New York, 1931-46); Walter B. Posey, *Religious Strife on the Southern Frontier* (Baton Rouge, 1965) and *Frontier Mission: A History of Religion West of the Southern Appalachians to 1861* (Lexington, Ky., 1966); Catherine C. Cleveland, *The Great Revival in the West, 1797-1805* (Chicago, 1916); and Kenneth K. Bailey, *Southern White Protestantism in the Twentieth Century* (New York, 1964; rpt. Gloucester, Mass., 1968).

There are also several good works on the evolution controversy and the Scopes trial: Willard B. Gatewood, Jr., ed., *Controversy in the Twenties: Fundamentalism, Modernism, and Evolution* (Nashville, 1969); Leslie Henri Allen, ed., *Bryan and Darrow at Dayton: The Record and Documents of the "Bible-Evolution Trial"* (New York, 1967); L. Sprague DeCamp, *The Great Monkey Trial* (Garden City, N.Y., 1968); Ray Ginger, *Six Days or Forever? Tennessee v. John Thomas Scopes* (Boston, 1958; rpt. New York, 1969); John T. Scopes and James Presley, *Center of the Storm: Memoirs of John T. Scopes* (New York, 1967); and Jerry R. Tompkins, ed.,

D-Days at Dayton: Reflections on the Scopes Trial (Baton Rouge, 1965).

In the church demoninational field, the most authoritative works on Tennessee and Southern Baptists are Walter B. Posey, *The Baptist Church in the Lower Mississippi Valley, 1776-1845* (Lexington, Ky., 1957); Rufus B. Spain, *At Ease in Zion: A Social History of the Southern Baptists, 1865-1900* (Nashville, 1967); O. W. Taylor, *Early Tennessee Baptists, 1769-1832* (Nashville, 1957). Davis C. Wooley and N. W. Cox, *Encyclopedia of Southern Baptists,* 3 vols. (Nashville, 1958-71) includes a monograph on Tennessee Baptists.

The most authoritive works on the various branches of the Christian church are David Edwin Harrell, Jr., *Quest for a Christian America: The Disciples of Christ and American Society to 1866* (Nashville, 1966); Herman A. Norton, *Tennessee Christians: A History of the Christian Church in America* (Nashville, 1971); and Winfred E. Garrison and Alfred T. De Groot, *The Disciples of Christ: A History* (St. Louis, 1948, 1958).

Studies in Cumberland Presbyterian History, by Thomas H. Campbell (Nashville, 1944), is the most recent work on that denomination, but B. W. McDonnold, *History of the Cumberland Presbyterian Church* (Nashville, 1892); R. V. Foster, *A Sketch of the History of the Cumberland Presbyterian Church* (New York, 1895); and Thaddeus C. Blake, *The Old Log House: A History and Defense of the Cumberland Presbyterian Church* (Nashville, 1878) are still useful.

For the Episcopalians, Arthur H. Noll, *History of the Church in the Diocese of Tennessee* (New York, 1900) is still standard, except for West Tennessee, where Ellen Davies Rodgers, *The Romance of the Episcopal Church in West Tennessee, 1832-1964* (Brunswick, 1964) makes a substantial supplement to the church's history in this area.

The only works on the Lutherans in Tennessee are by C. W. Cassell, W. J. Finck, and E. O. Henkel, eds., *History of the Lutheran Church in Virginia and East Tennessee* (Strasburg, Va., 1930) and by Socrates Henkel, *History of the Evangelical Lutheran Tennessee Synod* (New Market, Va., 1890).

Although literature about the Methodists is extensive, there is no one work of general coverage. The nearest approach to a broad treatment is in conference histories such as Richard N. Price, *Holston Methodism. From Its Origin to the Present Time,* 5 vols. (Nashville, 1903-13) and Cullen T. Carter, *History of the Tennessee Conference and a Brief Summary of the General Conference of the Methodist Church from the Frontier in Middle Tennessee to the Present Time* (Nashville, 1948). Carter also wrote several other works on Methodism in the area. For the early period, *The Journal of the Rev. Francis Asbury,* 3 vols. (New York, 1821; rpt. Nashville, 1958) and the *Autobiography of Peter Cartwright* (Cincinnati, 1859; rpt. Nashville, 1946) are basic works, but they should be supplemented by John B. McFerrin, *History of Methodism in Tennessee,* 3 vols. (Nashville, 1869-73, 1874, 1875); Walter B. Posey, *The Development of Methodism in the Old Southwest, 1783-1824* (Tuscaloosa, Ala., 1933); and William W. Sweet, ed., *The Rise of Methodism in the West: Being the Journal of the Western Conference, 1800-1811* (Nashville, 1920). Three works by Isaac P. Martin: *Elijah Embree Hoss* (Nashville, 1942, 1944); *Methodism in Holson* (Knoxville, 1945); and *A Minister in the Tennessee Valley: Sixty-seven Years* (Nashville, 1954), are descriptive of the Methodists in East Tennessee. For the Southern Methodist church, after the division, Albert H. Redford, *History of the Organization of the Methodist Episcopal Church, South* (Nashville, 1871); *Biographical Sketches of Eminent Itinerant Ministers . . . Methodist Episcopal Church, South* (Nashville, 1859); and *Autobiography of Rev. A. B. Wright, of the Holston Conference, Methodist Episcopal Church, South* (Cincinnati, 1896) are important.

Leading works on the Presbyterians are J. E. Alexander, *A Brief History of the Synod of Tennessee from 1817-1887* (Knoxville, 1890); Walter B. Posey, *The Presbyterian Church in the Old Southwest, 1778-1838* (Richmond, Va., 1952); and Ernest T. Thompson, *Presbyterians in the South: 1607-1861,* vol. 1 (Richmond, Va., 1963-).

Literature relating to the Roman Catholic church is represented by V. F. Daniel, *The Life, Times, and Character of the Right Reverend Richard P. Miles* [founder of the church in Tennessee] (Washington, D.C., c. 1925); George J. Flanigen, *History of Catholic Faith in Tennessee* (Memphis, c. 1960) and his edited work, *Catholicity in Tennessee: A Sketch of Catholic Activities in the State, 1541-1937* (Nashville, 1937).

This historiographical essay, being merely suggestive, is naturally incomplete. It is simply one person's effort to list what he considers the outstanding works in the field, knowing as he does so that this is a subject about which there is ample room for disagreement.

Tennessee History

A BIBLIOGRAPHY

General Reference Materials

BIBLIOGRAPHIES AND CHECKLISTS

Alderson, William T., and Robert H. White. *A Guide to the Study and Reading of Tennessee History.* Nashville: Tennessee Hist. Comm., 1959. 87 pp.

Allen, Ronald R. *Tennessee Books: A Preliminary Guide.* Knoxville: The Author, 1969. 63 pp.

Beasley, Gladys Mays, and Mary Friel Brown, comps. *Tennessee through the Printed Page; a Classified List of Materials Relating to Tennessee for School Libraries.* Nashville: Nashville Pub. Schools, 1940; rev. ed., 1942. 32 pp.

Conner, Martha. "A Contribution toward a Bibliography of Tennessee History." Thesis, Pennsylvania State Univ., 1920.

Cram, Kendall J. *Guide to the Use of Genealogical Material in the Tennessee State Library and Archives.* Nashville: State Library and Archives, 1964. 24 pp.

Historical Records Survey, Tennessee. *List of Tennessee Imprints, 1793-1840,* vol. 16. Nashville: Hist. Records Survey, WPA, 1941. 97 leaves.

——. *Check List of Tennessee Imprints, 1841-1850,* vol. 20. Nashville: Hist. Records Survey, WPA, 1941. 138 leaves.

Horn, Stanley F. "Twenty Tennessee Books." *THQ* 17 (1958), 3-18.

——. "Twenty More Tennessee Books." *THQ* 30 (1971), 26-49.

List of Tennessee State Publications. Nashville: State Library and Archives, 1954- . This list is published annually.

Luttrell, Laura E., and Pollyanna Creekmore, comps. *Writings on Tennessee Counties.* Nashville: Tennessee Hist. Comm., 1944. 50 pp. Rpt. from *THQ*, Sept., Dec. 1943; March 1944. References are found for all 95 counties.

Luttrell, Laura E., Martha L. Ellison, and Pollyanna Creekmore, eds. "Writings on Tennessee History." ETHSP 2-40 (1930-68).

Millirons, Martha Woolbright. "A Bibliographical Checklist of Tennessee Imprints in Small Towns, 1867-1876, with an Introductory Essay on an Inquiry into Reconstruction Publications of Village Tennessee, 1867-1876." Thesis, Univ. of Tennessee, 1963.

Mitchell, Eleanor Drake. "A Bibliographical Checklist of Tennessee Imprints, 1861-1866, with an Introductory Essay on the Civil War Press in Tennessee." Thesis, Univ. of Tennessee, 1949.

———. *A Preliminary Checklist of Tennessee Imprints, 1861-1866.* Charlottesville: Bibliog. Soc. of the Univ. of Virginia, 1953. 98 leaves.

Preliminary Check-List of Tennessee Legislative Documents. Nashville: State Library and Archives, 1954. Unpaged. These legislative documents consist of session laws, legislative journals, collected public documents and statutes. Issued one volume to which the statutes were added later.

Springer, Patricia. "Bibliography of Historical Material of Tennessee in Nashville Libraries." Thesis, George Peabody College, 1930.

Tennessee Newspaper Directory. Nashville: Tennessee Press Assoc., 1973- . 40 pp. This is an annual list.

Tennessee Newspapers. A Cumulative List of Microfilmed Tennessee Newspapers in the Tennessee State Library and Archives, July 1969. Progress Report. Nashville: State Library and Archives, 1969- . 127 pp. In 1955 the library began to film all available Tennessee newspapers. This is a continuing program and the list is periodically updated.

Major Manuscript Guides and Resources

Corbitt, D. C., and Roberta C., trans. and eds. "Papers from the Spanish Archives Relating to Tennessee and the Old Southwest, 1783-1800." ETHSP 9-44 (1937-72).

Cram, Kendall J., ed. *Guide to the Use of Genealogical Material in the Tennessee State Library and Archives.*

Hamer, Philip M., ed. *A Guide to Archives and Manuscripts in the United States.* New Haven: Yale Univ. Press, 1961. 775 pp. This is the first attempt in recent times to document manuscript collections in American institutions. It has been largely superseded by the *National Union Catalog of Manuscript Collections.*

Historical Records Survey, Tennessee. *Guide to Collections of Manuscripts in Tennessee.* Nashville: Hist. Records Survey, WPA, 1941. 38 leaves.

——. "The Historical Records Survey in Tennessee: A Review of Five Years." ETHS*P* 13 (1941), 91-101.

Lawson McGhee Library. *Calvin M. McClung Historical Collection.* Knoxville: The Library, 1971. 16 pp.

Library of Congress. *The National Union Catalog of Manuscript Collections: Based on Reports from American Repositories of Manuscripts.* Ann Arbor, Mich.: Edwards, 1959-61- . An outstanding description of important manuscript resources located in American institutions. Periodic additions are made to the catalog.

Luttrell, Laura E., and Mary U. Rothrock, comps. *Calvin Morgan McClung Historical Collection of Books, Pamphlets, Manuscripts, Pictures and Maps Relating to Early Western Travel and the History and Genealogy of Tennessee and Other Southern States, Presented to Lawson McGhee Library by Mrs. Calvin M. McClung.* Knoxville: Knoxville Litho., 1921. 191 pp.

Mississippi Valley Collection Bulletin. Memphis: Memphis State Univ., 1968- .

Moore, John Trotwood. *The Draper Manuscripts As Relating to Tennessee.* Nashville: Brandon, 1919. 30 pp.

Owsley, Harriet C., ed. *Guide to the Processed Manuscripts of the Tennessee Historical Society.* Nashville: Tennessee Hist. Comm., 1969. 70 pp. A superb aid to finding manuscript collections located in the State Library and Archives.

——. *Registers of the Manuscript Section, Tennessee State Library and Archives.* Nashville: State Library and Archives, 1959-70.

——. "The Tennessee Historical Society: Its Origin, Progress, and Present Condition." *THQ* 29 (1970), 227-42.

Rose, Kenneth. "The Story of a Music Collection." *THQ* 15 (1956), 356-63.

Sioussat, St. George L. *A Preliminary Report upon the Archives of Tennessee.* Washington, D.C.: Government Printing Office [hereafter cited as GPO], 1908, 41 pp.; rpt. from *American Historical Association Annual Report, 1906,* II, 197-238.

GENERAL HISTORIES AND REFERENCE WORKS

Alderson, William T., and Robert M. McBride. *Landmarks of Tennessee History.* Nashville: Tennessee Hist. Soc., 1965. 321 pp. A compendium of cover articles appearing in the *THQ* in the 1960s, describing in detail 15 of the state's most important historic sites.

Davidson, Donald. *The Tennessee: The Old River, Frontier to Secession,* Rivers of America Series, vol. 1. New York: Rinehart, 1946. 342 pp.

——. *The Tennessee: The New River, Civil War to TVA,* Rivers of America Series, vol. 2. New York: Rinehart, 1948. 377 pp.

Federal Writers' Project. *Tennessee: A Guide to the State,* American Guide Series. New York: Viking, 1939; rpt. New York: Hastings House, 1949; rpt. New York: Somerset, 1972. 558 pp. A product of the WPA program in Tennessee, this volume contains a general narrative of the state's history plus a tourist's guide to major highways and cities of the state.

Folmsbee, Stanley J., Robert E. Corlew, and Enoch L. Mitchell. *History of Tennessee.* 4 vols. New York: Lewis, 1960. This set contains 2 vols. of narrative history and 2 vols. of biography. It is the most recent and useful edition of the individual state histories and contains a high degree of accuracy and readability.

——. *Tennessee, A Short History.* Knoxville: Univ. of Tennessee Press, 1969. 640 pp. Rpt. 1972, 656 pp. A revised and condensed edition of their 4-vol. *History of Tennessee,* especially useful as a college textbook.

Foster, Austin P., and Albert H. Roberts. *Tennessee Democracy, a History of the Party and Its Representative Members—Past and Present.* 4 vols. Nashville: Democratic Hist. Assoc., 1940.

Hale, Will T., and Dixon L. Merritt. *A History of Tennessee and Tennesseans: The Leaders and Representative Men in Commerce, Industry and Modern Activities.* 8 vols. Chicago: Lewis, 1913.

Hamer, Philip M., ed. *Tennessee: A History, 1673-1932.* 4 vols. New York: American Hist. Soc., 1933.

Killebrew, Joseph B., et al. *Introduction to the Resources of Tennessee.* Nashville: Tavel, Eastman & Howell, 1874. 1193 pp. This is a survey study of the resources of Tennessee, together with a county-by-county study of geography, archaeology, rivers and creeks, timber, crop statistics, products, roads, railroads, institutions, etc. A major work.

McBride, Robert M., ed. *More Landmarks of Tennessee History.* Nashville: Tennessee Hist. Comm., 1969. 393 pp. A continuation of the work initiated by the editor in cooperation with William T. Alderson, this is a compendium of more recent cover articles from the *THQ,* describing 19 additional historic sites.

Moore, John Trotwood, and Austin P. Foster. *Tennessee: The Volunteer State, 1769-1923.* 4 vols. Nashville: Clarke, 1923.

Vol. 1 surveys Tennessee history to 1923. Moore suggests in his foreword that Tennessee well illustrates Frederick J. Turner's thesis that the frontier experience was the largest element in shaping American life and institutions. This work fails to develop that view, however, and tends to be a collection of documents connected by narrative, with few exceptions covering only political history.

Tennessee Old and New. Sesquicentennial Edition 1796-1946. 2 vols. Nashville: Tennessee Hist. Comm. and Tennessee Hist. Soc., 1946. This is a compendium of outstanding articles, most of which were extracted from previous publications of the Tennessee Historical Society.

White, Robert H., ed. *Messages of the Governors of Tennessee.* 8 vols. Nashville: Tennessee Hist. Comm., 1952-72. Vol. 8 published posthumously, completed by Dan M. Robison and Robert M. McBride. Not only are the basic messages of the governors through 1907 recorded here, but there is also a highly entertaining narrative which illuminates the fundamental issues of the day.

BRIEF SUMMARIES OF STATE HISTORY

Alderson, William T. *Tennessee History in Brief.* Nashville: Tennessee Hist. Comm., 1964. 16 pp.

——. "Tennessee, a Historical Introduction." *Antiques,* Sept. 1971, pp. 378-81.

Moore, Mary Daniel. "Tennessee." *History of Homes and Gardens in Tennessee,* ed. Roberta Sewell Brandau, 24-28. Nashville: Garden Study Club, 1936.

Tennessee State Department of Education. *Tennessee, Current and Historic Facts, June 1948.* Nashville: State of Tennessee, 1948. 90 pp.

ONE-VOLUME GENERAL HISTORIES AND SCHOOL TEXTS

Abernethy, Thomas P. *From Frontier to Plantation in Tennessee; A Study in Frontier Democracy.* Chapel Hill: Univ. of North Carolina Press, 1932. 392 pp. Rpt. Memphis: Memphis State College Press, 1955. Rpt., Southern Historical Publications, no. 12. Tuscaloosa: Univ. of Alabama Press, 1967. The author treats Tennessee's social, economic, and political history from the white man's earliest settlement in the area until the Civil War.

Barrett, Albert T. *Tennessee.* New York: Macmillan, 1904. 61 pp. Supplementary volume to Ralph S. Tarr and Frank M. McMurry. *Home Geography, and the Earth as a Whole.* (New York, 1900).

Caldwell, Mary French. *Tennessee, the Volunteer State,* Commemorative State Books Series. Chicago: Rich Text Press, 1968. 214 pp. Elementary school text.

Carpenter, William H. *History of Tennessee, from Its Earliest Settlement to the Present Time,* Lippincott's Cabinet Histories of the States. Philadelphia, Pa.: Lippincott, 1854, 1856, 1858. 284 pp.

Creekmore, Betsey Beeler. *Arrows to Atoms; the Story of East Tennessee.* Knoxville: Univ. of Tennessee Press, 1959. 142 pp. Chaps. on East Tennessee reprinted from *Knoxville* (Knoxville: Univ. of Tennessee Press, 1958).

Dyer, Gustavus Walker. *A School History of Tennessee,* National History Series. Chicago: National Bk., 1919. 279 pp. Elementary school text.

Dyer, John Pope. *Tennessee History for All.* Chattanooga: n.p., 1949. 52 pp.

Dykeman, Wilma, and James Stokely. *The Border States: Kentucky, North Carolina, Tennessee, Virginia, West Virginia,* Time-Life Library of America. New York: Time-Life, 1968. 192 pp.

Folmsbee, Stanley J., Robert S. Corlew, and Enoch L. Mitchell. *Tennessee, A Short History.*

Foster, Austin P. *The Volunteer State, a School History.* Dallas: Southern, 1936. 341 leaves. Elementary school text.

Free, George D. *History of Tennessee from Its Earliest Discoveries and Settlements to the End of the Year 1894.* Church Hill, Ky.: The Author, 1895; rev. ed. Nashville: The Author, 1896. 224 pp. Elementary school text.

Garrett, William R., and Albert V. Goodpasture. *History of Tennessee, Its People and Its Institutions.* Nashville: Brandon, 1900, 1905. 351 pp. Elementary school text.

Goodspeed Publishing Company. *A History of Tennessee from the Earliest Times to the Present.* 6 vols. Nashville: Goodspeed, 1886, 1887; rpt. Columbia: Woodward & Stinson, 1971, 1972. Rpt. Nashville: Elder, 1972. This work is one of a series of state histories produced during the late 1800s. It is divided by volume into histories of a number of Tennessee counties; each volume includes a narrative history of the state up to the Civil War.

Karns, Thomas Conner. *Tennessee History Stories.* Richmond, Va.: B. F. Johnson, 1904. 274 pp. Elementary school text.

Larew, Charles Lynnval. *Historic Tennessee: A Brief Historical and Biographical Sketch of Tennessee and Tennesseans Prepared Especially for the Busy Reader.* Knoxville: Historic Tennessee, 1937, 1938. 56 pp.

McGee, Gentry R. *A History of Tennessee from 1663 to 1900 for Use in Schools.* New York: American Bk., 1900, 1911; rev. ed., 1919; rev. & enl., ed. C. B. Ijams, 1924; rev. & enl., ed. C. B. Ijams, 1930; rpt. Nashville: Elder, 1971. 352 pp. Elementary school text.

McMurry, Charles A. *The Tennessee Reader.* Richmond, Va.: Johnson, 1925. 355 pp. Elementary school text.

Parks, Joseph H., and Stanley J. Folmsbee. *The Story of Tennessee.* Oklahoma City: Harlow, 1952, 1954, 1958, 1963, 1968. 424 pp. Elementary school text.

Paschall, Edwin. *Old Times; or, Tennessee History, for Tennessee Boys and Girls.* Nashville: The Author, 1869. 294 pp. Elementary school text.

Patten, Cartter. *A Tennessee Chronicle.* Chattanooga: privately printed, 1953. 286 pp.

Phelan, James. *History of Tennessee; the Making of a State.* Boston: Houghton, 1888. 478 pp.

———. *School History of Tennessee.* Philadelphia, Pa.: E. H. Butler, 1889. 233 pp. Elementary school text.

Rothrock, Mary U. *This is Tennessee; a School History.* Knoxville: The Author, 1963, 1968. 491 pp. Elementary school text.

Scates, Silas E. *A School History of Tennessee.* Yonkers-on-Hudson, N.Y.: World Bk., 1925. 395 pp. Rev. ed., 1931. 404 pp. 2nd rev. ed., 1936. 418 pp. Elementary school text.

White, Robert H. *Tennessee, Its Growth and Progress.* Nashville: The Author, 1936, 1943; rev. ed., 1947. 709 pp. Elementary school text.

COLLECTIVE BIOGRAPHY

Alderson, William T., ed. *Tennessee Lives.* Hopkinsville, Ky.: Historical Record Assoc., 1971. 448 pp.

Allison, John, ed. *Notable Men of Tennessee. Personal and Genealogical, with Notes.* 2 vols. Atlanta: Southern Hist. Assoc., 1905. A more recent but considerably less important work, with shorter sketches than those of Speer's *Sketches,* cited below.

Bass, Frank E., ed. *Who's Who in Tennessee; a Reference Edition Recording the Biographies of Contemporary Leaders in Tennessee with Special Emphasis on Their Achievements in Making the Volunteer State One of America's Greatest.* Hopkinsville, Ky.: Historical Record Assoc., 1961. 774 pp.

Biographical Directory: Tennessee General Assembly, 1796- , eds. Dan M. Robison (1967-69) and Robert M. McBride (1970-). Nashville: State Library and Archives, 1967- . A series of biographical sketches by counties of persons who have served in the Tennessee State General Assembly from 1796 to the present.

Caldwell, Joshua W. *Sketches of the Bench and Bar of Tennessee.* Knoxville: Ogden, 1898. 402 pp. A very good collective biography focusing upon lives of outstanding legal figures in East Tennessee.

Chavannes, Cecile. *East Tennessee Sketches.* Knoxville: Albert Chavannes, 1900. 112 pp.

Dyer, Gustavus Walker, ed. *Library of American Lives, Tennessee Edition, a Source Edition Recording the Contemporary History of the Nation through the Medium of the Life History of Its Most Constructive Contributors. Chronicling the Genealogical and Memorial Records of Its Prominent Families and Personages.* 2 vols. Nashville: Historical Record Assoc., 1949.

East Tennessee, Historical and Biographical. Chattanooga: A. D. Smith, 1893. 545 pp.

Gaines, George Towns. *Fighting Tennesseans.* Kingsport: Privately printed, 1931. 127 pp. Biographical sketches of early settlers.

Gilchrist, Annie Somers. *Some Representative Women of Tennessee.* Nashville: McQuiddy, 1902. 173 pp.

Gillum, James L. *Prominent Tennesseans, 1796-1938.* Lewisburg: *Who's Who,* 1940. 286 pp.

Goodpasture, Albert B. "A Dictionary of Distinguished Tennesseans." *AHM* 8 (1903), 105-23.

Green, John W. *Lives of the Judges of the Supreme Court of Tennessee, 1796-1947.* Knoxville: Archer and Smith, 1947. 337 pp.

Haile, Mrs. Herbert, ed. *Catholic Women of Tennessee, 1937-1956.* Nashville: Marshall & Bruce, 1956. 421 pp.

Johnson, Allen, and Dumas Malone. *Dictionary of American Biography.* 20 vols. New York: Scribners, 1928-36. Supplements:

Harris E. Starr, ed., 1944; Robert L. Schuyler, 1958. The names of Tennesseans included in the first twenty volumes are listed in the East Tennessee Historical Society *Publications* 4 (1932), 171-73; 7 (1935), 172-74; and 9 (1937), 165-67.

Jones, J. S., comp. *Biographical Album of Tennessee Governors from 1790 through 1903.* Knoxville: The Author, 1903. 30 cards.

Laughlin, Samuel H. "Sketches of Notable Men." *THM* 4 (1918), 73-78.

McKellar, Kenneth D. *Tennessee Senators As Seen by One of Their Successors.* Kingsport: Southern, 1942, 1944. 625 pp.

Memorial and Biographical Record; an Illustrated Compendium of Biography, Containing a Compendium of Local Biography, Including Biographical Sketches of Prominent Old Settlers and Representative Citizens of Part of the Cumberland Region of Tennessee with a Review of Their Life Work. . . . Also a Compendium of National Biography. Chicago: Ogle, 1898. 514 pp.

Men of Tennessee. Chattanooga: n.p., 1930. 180 pp.

Moore, W. A. G. *Historical Album of East Tennessee.* Knoxville: Newman, 1898. 22 pp.

Oldham, Bethenia McLemore. *Tennessee and Tennesseans.* Clarksville: W. P. Titus, 1903. 198 pp.

Robison, Dan M. "Biographical Directory of the Tennessee General Assembly," *THQ* 25 (1966), 351-59.

Speer, William S., comp. and ed. *Sketches of Prominent Tennesseans. Containing Biographies and Records of Many of the Families Who Have Attained Prominence in Tennessee.* Nashville: A. B. Tavel, 1888. 579 pp. The finest, most authentic work of its time in the field of collective biography.

Temple, Oliver P. *Notable Men of Tennessee from 1833 to 1875, Their Times and Their Contemporaries,* comp. and arr. Mary B. Temple. New York: Cosmopolitan, 1912. 467 pp. An important and substantial work focusing primarily upon East Tennessee. Published posthumously.

Wallace, Louis D., ed. *Makers of Millions, Not for Themselves but for You; Stories of Tennesseans Whose Accomplishments for Agriculture Brought Renown to Their State and Caused an Appreciating and Benefited Public to Propose Their Admission to the Tennessee Agricultural Hall of Fame.* Nashville: Tennessee Dept. of Agriculture, 1951. 354 pp.

Who's Who in Tennessee: A Biographical Reference Book of Notable Tennesseans of To-Day. Memphis: Paul and Douglass, 1911. 670 pp.

Early Period

GENERAL HISTORIES

Albright, Edward. *Early History of Middle Tennessee*. Nashville: Brandon, 1909. 207 pp.

Breazeale, J. W. M. *Life As It Is; or, Matters and Things in General: Containing, amongst Other Things, Historical Sketches of the Exploration and First Settlement of the State of Tennessee; Manners and Customs of the Inhabitants; Their Wars with the Indians; Battle of King's Mountain; History of the Harps (Two Noted Murderers); a Satirical Burlesque on the Practice of Electioneering; Legislative, Judicial and Ecclesiastical Incidents; Descriptions of Natural Curiosities; a Collection of Anecdotes, &c.* Knoxville: James Williams, 1842; rpt. Nashville: Charles Elder, 1969. 256 pp. A good history of early Tennessee, this work is primarily known for its vivid description of two notorious outlaws, Micajah and Wiley Harp, who terrorized the Natchez Trace and other trails.

Goodpasture, Albert V. "Moses Fisk's Historical Sketch of Tennessee." *AHM* 2 (1897), 17-26.

Haywood, John. *The Christian Advocate. By a Tennessean*. Nashville: Thomas G. Bradford, 1819. 357 pp. The first historical work of Tennessee by Tennessee's first historian. It deals especially with religious topics and aboriginal history; the author was to incorporate much of this work into his *Natural and Aboriginal History*.

——. *The Civil and Political History of the State of Tennessee, from Its Earliest Settlement up to the Year 1796; Including the Boundaries of the State*. Knoxville: Heiskell & Brown, 1823; rpt. Nashville: Methodist Pub. House, 1891, 1915; rpt. Knoxville: Tenase, 1969. Rpt., First American Frontier Series. New York: Arno, 1971. 504 pp. An effort "to record the memorable achievements of the eminent men of Tennessee" by Tennessee's first historian. Armstrong, Zella. *Index to John Haywood's Civil and Political History of the State of Tennessee*. Chattanooga: Lookout, 1939. 26 pp.

——. *The Natural and Aboriginal History of Tennessee, up to the First Settlements Therein by the White People, in the Year 1768.* Nashville: G. Wilson, 1823. 390 pp. Rev. ed., introd., biog. of Haywood, and annots. Mary U. Rothrock. Jackson: McCowat-Mercer, 1959. 438 pp. This is the first published history of Tennessee, concentrating primarily upon aboriginal history and based primarily upon observations and personal interviews.

Morris, Eastin. *The Tennessee Gazetteer, or Topographical Dictionary; Containing a Description of the Several Counties, Towns, Villages, Post Offices, Rivers, Creeks, Mountains, Valleys, &c. in the State of Tennessee, Alphabetically Arranged to Which Is Prefixed a General Description of the State: Its Civil Divisions, Resources, Population, &c. and a Condensed History from the Earliest Settlements Down to the Rise of the Convention in the Year 1834. With an Appendix Containing a List of Practicing Attorneys at Law in Each County; Principal Officers of the General and State Governments; Times of Holding Courts; and Other Valuable Tables.* Nashville: W. H. Hunt, 1834. 178 pp. Rpt. with Matthew Rhea's *Map of the State of Tennessee, 1832,* introd. Mary U. Rothrock. Nashville: Gazetteer Press, 1971. 325 pp. This volume contains a brief history of the state to 1796, together with a summary of proceedings of the General Assembly from 1796 to 1834. It also gives much useful information on towns and communities, similar in content to that which is now found in city directories.

Morse, Jedidiah, comp. *The American Gazetteer.* 3rd ed., rev. and corr. Boston: Thomas & Andrews, 1810. Rpt., First American Frontier Series. New York: Arno, 1971. 600 pp. This work includes an early Tennessee map and description of the state. First published in 1797.

Ramsey, James G. M. *Annals of Tennessee to the End of the Eighteenth Century: Comprising Its Settlement, as The Watauga Association, from 1769 to 1777; a Part of North-Carolina, from 1777 to 1784; the State of Franklin, from 1784 to 1788; a Part of North-Carolina, from 1788 to 1790; the Territory of the U. States, South of the Ohio, from 1790 to 1796; the State of Tennessee, from 1796 to 1800.* Charleston, S. C.: Walker & James, 1853. 744 pp. Rpt. Philadelphia, Pa.: Lippincott, 1853, 1860; rpt. Kingsport: Kingsport Press, 1926; rpt. Knoxville: East Tennessee Hist. Soc., 1967, 1972. Rpt., First American Frontier Series. New York: Arno, 1971. 744 pp. The 1972 edition is an enlarged, augmented work with a biographical sketch of Ramsey by William H. Masterson and "Annotations Relating Ramsey's *Annals of Tennessee* to Present Day Knowledge" by

Stanley J. Folmsbee. Index, biographies, and annotations. Ramsey's work was the first major effort after that of John Haywood to compile the history of Tennessee. Based upon source materials of some of the earlier public figures of the state, this work is rich in its description of pioneer life. Fain, J. Tyree. *Fain's Critical and Analytical Index and Genealogical Guide to Ramsey's Annals of Tennessee, Embracing All Proper Names as well as Important Topical Subjects.* Nashville: P. Hunter, 1920. 86 pp.

Walker, William A., Jr. "Tennessee, 1796-1821." Diss., Univ. of Texas, 1959.

Williams, Samuel Cole. *Beginnings of West Tennessee in the Land of the Chickasaws, 1541-1841.* Johnson City: Watauga, 1930. 331 pp. Rpt. Nashville: Blue & Gray, 1971. The first history of this portion of the state ever written, it tells the story of the land between the Tennessee and Mississippi rivers.

——. *Dawn of Tennessee Valley and Tennessee History, 1541-1776.* Johnson City: Watauga, 1937. 495 pp. The author considers this his best book. It is an outstanding history of the region which became Tennessee.

PREHISTORY AND ARCHAEOLOGY

East Tennessee

Bachman, Ernest A., Jr. "The Nickajack Dam Sites." *Tennessee Archaeologist* 22 (1966), 6-12.

Fischer, F. William. "A Woodland Site in Campbell County." *Tennessee Archaeologist* 7 (1951), 39-42.

Gillingham, G. O. "Tennessee Valley Authority Aids American Archaeology; Cherokee Village Sites Discovered near Caryville, Tennessee." *Scientific American,* Nov. 1934, p. 248.

Gough, H. F. "First Tennessee Valley Authorities; Indian Mounds and Village Sites Soon to Be Submerged by Reservoirs." *Scientific American,* Feb. 1935, pp. 80-82.

Haile, Joshua. "Antiquities of Jackson County, Tennessee." *Smithsonian Institution Annual Report 1874,* pp. 384-86. Washington, D.C.: GPO, 1875.

Harrington, Mark Raymond. *Cherokee and Earlier Remains on Upper Tennessee River.* New York: Heye Foundation, 1922. 321 pp.

Jordan, Douglas F. "A Clovis Point from Sullivan County." *Tennessee Archaeologist* 12 (1956), 15-16.

Kneberg, Madeline. "Chipped Stone Artifacts of the Tennessee Valley Area." *Tennessee Archaeologist* 13 (1957), 55-56.

Law, Annie E. "Antiquities of Blount County, Tennessee." *Smithsonian Institution Annual Report 1874*, p. 375. Washington, D.C.: GPO, 1875.

Lewis, Thomas M. N., and Madeline Kneberg. *The Prehistory of the Chickamauga Basin in Tennessee, a Preview.* Knoxville: Dept. of Anthropology, Univ. of Tennessee, 1941. Various pagings.

———. *Hiwassee Island, an Archaeological Account of Four Tennessee Indian Peoples.* Knoxville: Univ. of Tennessee, 1946; rpt. 1970. 204 pp. Partially based on field reports by Charles H. Nash. The 1970 reprint has the addition of a foreword by James B. Griffin.

———. "The Camp Creek Site." *Tennessee Archaeologist* 13 (1957), 1-48. Relates to Greene County.

McCormick, J. C. "Mound in Jefferson County, Tennessee." *Smithsonian Institution Annual Report 1887*, pp. 571-74. Washington, D.C.: GPO, 1889.

Moore, Clarence Bloomfield. *Aboriginal Sites on Tennessee River.* Philadelphia, Pa.: The Author, 1915. 428 pp.

Polhemus, Richard R., and James H. "The McCullough Bend Site." *Tennessee Archaeologist* 22 (1966), 13-24. Relates to Claiborne and Grainger counties.

Seever, William. "James Christian, Archaeologist." *THM* 4 (1918), 248-51. Relates to Roane and adjacent counties.

Webb, William S. "The Prehistory of East Tennessee." *ETHSP* 8 (1936), 3-8.

———. *An Archaeological Survey of the Norris Basin in Eastern Tennessee,* Smithsonian Institution, Bureau of American Ethnology Bulletin 118. Washington, D.C.: GPO, 1938. 398 pp.

Middle Tennessee

Broster, John B. "The Ganier Site: A Late Mississippian Village on the Cumberland River." *Middle Cumberland Culture* 3 (1972), 51-78. Relates to Davidson County.

Butler, Brian M. *Hoover-Beason Rock Shelter 40-Cn4. Cannon County, Tennessee.* Nashville: Tennessee Archaeological Soc., 1971. 71 pp.

Cambron, James W. "Harpeth River Point." *Tennessee Archaeologist* 26 (1970), 15-18.

Clark, W. M. "Antiquities of Tennessee." *Smithsonian Institution Annual Report 1877*, pp. 269-76. Washington, D.C.: GPO, 1878. Relates to Williamson County.

Dowd, John T. "Excavation of a Tennessee Overhang: Mill Creek Overhang." *Tennessee Archaeologist* 25 (1969), 1-19. Relates to Davidson County.

——. "A Woodland Burial in Middle Tennessee." *Tennessee Archaeologist* 26 (1970), 1-14.

——. *The West Site: A Stone Box Cemetery in Middle Tennessee.* Nashville: Tennessee Archaeological Soc., 1972. 73 pp.

Dowd, John T. and John B. Broster. "Cockrills Bend Site." *Journal of Southeastern Indian Antiquities Survey* 1 (1972), 8-19. Relates to Davidson County.

Dragoo, Don W. "Investigations at a Paleo-Indian Site in Stewart County, Tennessee." *Eastern States Archaeological Federation Bulletin* 24 (1965), 12-13.

Faulkner, Charles H., ed. *Archaeological Investigations in the Tims Ford Reservoir Tennessee, 1966.* Knoxville: Dept. of Anthropology, Univ. of Tennessee, 1968. 276 pp.

——. *The Old Stone Fort: Exploring an Archaeological Mystery.* Knoxville: Univ. of Tennessee Press, 1968. 70 pp. Rpt. 1971. 80 pp. An investigation of a partially-walled enclosure located on 50 acres in Coffee County.

Ferguson, Robert B. "The Arnold Village Sites Excavations of 1965-1966." *Middle Cumberland Culture* 3 (1972), 1-50. Relates to Williamson County.

Glenn, Leonidas Chalmers. *The Thruston Collection, Vanderbilt University.* Nashville: n.p., 1910. 31 pp. Rpt. from *Vanderbilt Quarterly* (1910), 243-74.

Haile, Joshua. "Mounds on Flynn's Creek, Jackson County, Tennessee." *Smithsonian Institution Annual Report 1881*, pp. 611-12. Washington, D.C.: GPO, 1883.

Halley, R. A. "Tennessee Archaeology at St. Louis." *AHM* 9 (1904), 257-73. Relates to the Thruston collection.

Lyons, Sidney E., and Glenn Koons. "Preliminary Report on Sherd-lined Stone-Box Graves in the Clarksville Area." *Tennessee Archaeologist* 20 (1964), 1-5.

McGaw, Robert A., and Richard W. Weesner. "Tennessee Antiquities

Re-exumed: The New Exhibit of the Thruston Collection at Vanderbilt." *THQ* 24 (1965), 121-35; 136-42.

McMahan, Basil B. *The Mystery of Old Stone Fort.* Nashville: Tennessee Bk., 1965. 95 pp. Relates to Coffee County.

Morse, Dan F., et al. "Fluted Points from Smith County, Tennessee." *Tennessee Archaeologist* 20 (1964), 16-34.

Myer, William Edward. "Two Prehistoric Villages in Middle Tennessee." *Forty-first Annual Report of the Bureau of American Ethnology to the Secretary of the Smithsonian Institution, 1919-1924,* pp. 485-614. Washington, D.C.: GPO, 1928.

Peacock, Charles K. "Mound Bottom Pictoglyph." *Tennessee Archaeologist* 5 (1949), 8-9. Relates to Cheatham County.

——. *Duck River Cache; Tennessee's Greatest Archaeological Find.* Chattanooga: J. B. Graham, 1954. 33 pp.

Robertson, Robert Stoddart. "Antiquities of Nashville, Tennessee." *Smithsonian Institution Annual Report 1877,* pp. 276-78. Washington, D.C.: GPO, 1878.

Smith, Arthur G. "Paleo-Indian Tools from Ringgold Creek, Montgomery County, Tennessee." *Tennessee Archaeologist* 12 (1956), 11-15.

Stack, Guy. "A Late Mississippi Site in Davidson County (ca. 1500)." *Tennessee Archaeologist* 5 (1949), 22-23.

Thruston, Gates P. *The Antiquities of Tennessee and the Adjacent States, and the State of Aboriginal Society in the Scale of Civilization Represented by Them; a Series of Historical and Ethnological Studies.* Cincinnati: R. Clarke, 1890, 1897; rpt. Knoxville: Tenase, 1964, 1972. 369 pp. A fine, descriptive work important to Tennessee for the results of archaeological investigations of Stone-Grave Peoples of Tennessee, featuring various sites in Middle Tennessee counties.

——. "The Old Stone Fort near Manchester, Tennessee." *AHM* 1 (1896), 253-56.

——. *Tennessee Archeology at St. Louis—the Thruston Exhibit.* Milwaukee: n.p., 1904. Rpt. from *The Wisconsin Archaeologist* 3 (1904), 132-48.

Wardle, H. N. "Ancients of the Bow of the Tennessee." *Harper's Monthly Magazine,* Sept. 1916, pp. 580-99.

Webb, William S., and David L. DeJarnette. *An Archaeological Survey of Pickwick Basin in the Adjacent Portions of the States of Alabama, Mississippi and Tennessee,* Smithsonian Institution,

Bureau of American Ethnology Bulletin 129. Washington, D.C.: GPO, 1942. 536 pp.

Wright, Daniel F. "Antiquities of Tennessee." *Smithsonian Institution Annual Report 1874*, pp. 371-74. Washington, D.C.: GPO, 1875. Relates to Montgomery County.

Yeatman, Harry C. "Surface Material from Maury County, Tennessee." *Tennessee Archaeologist* 20 (1964), 59-79.

Young, T. Hugh. "A Study of Stone Graves of Middle Tennessee." *Illinois State Archaeological Society Journal* 6 (1949), 7-12.

West Tennessee

Beaudoin, Kenneth L. *A Report of Excavation Made at the T. O. Fuller Site, Shelby County, Tennessee between March 8, 1952 and April 30, 1953. Conducted by Memphis Archaeological and Geological Society.* Memphis: Privately printed, 1953. 37 leaves.

——. "An Adventure into the Prehistory of the Memphis Area." *THQ* 13 (1954), 291-96.

Fischer, Fred W., and Charles H. McNutt. "Test Excavations at Pinson Mounds, 1961." *Tennessee Archaeologist* 18 (1962), 1-13.

Lewis, Thomas M. N., and Madeline Kneberg. *The Archaic Horizon in Western Tennessee.* Knoxville: Dept. of Anthropology, Univ. of Tennessee, 1947. 39 pp.

——. "The Nuckolls Site." *Tennessee Archaeologist* 14 (1958), 61-79. Relates to Benton County.

——. *Eva, An Archaic Site.* Knoxville: Univ. of Tennessee Press, 1961. 174 pp. Rpt., 1970. 188 pp. Relates to Benton County's 7,000-year-old site.

Myer, William Edward. "Recent Archaeological Discoveries in Tennessee." *Art and Archaeology* 14 (1922), 141-50. Relates to Madison County.

Nash, Charles H. "Choctaw Blowguns." *Tennessee Archaeologist* 16 (1960), 1-9.

——. "The Human Continuum of Shelby County, Tennessee." WTHSP 14 (1960), 5-31.

Nash, Charles H., and Rodney Gates, Jr. "Chucalissa Indian Town." *THQ* 21 (1962), 103-21.

Nuckolls, John B. "The Pinson Mounds." *Tennessee Archaeologist* 14 (1958), 1-8.

Null, James M. "Aboriginal Structures in Carroll County, Tennessee." *Smithsonian Institution Annual Report 1882,* pp. 768-69. Washington, D.C.: GPO, 1884.

Parmalee, Paul W. "Vertebrate Remains from the Chucalissa Site, Tennessee." *Tennessee Archaeologist* 16 (1960), 84-89. Comments by Charles H. Nash, pp. 90-91.

Printup, Dan. "Memphis State University Buffalo River Archaeological Survey." *Tennessee Archaeologist* 19 (1963), 29-42.

Stelle, J. Parish. "An Account of Aboriginal Ruins." *Smithsonian Institution Annual Report 1870,* pp. 408-20. Washington, D.C.: GPO, 1871. Relates to Hardin County.

Taylor, F. G. "Early Chipped Flint Objects from West Tennessee." *Tennessee Archaeologist* 13 (1957), 81-87.

Webb, William S., and David L. DeJarnette. *Archaeological Survey of Pickwick Basin.*

Statewide Area

"Antiquarian Riches of Tennessee." *Magazine of American History,* Oct. 1890, pp. 319-20.

Carr, Lucien. "Observations on the Crania from the Stone Graves in Tennessee." *11th Annual Report of the Trustees of the Peabody Museum of American Archaeology and Ethnology,* vol. 2, pp. 361-84. Cambridge: Salem Press, 1878.

——. *The Mounds of the Mississippi Valley, Historically Considered.* Frankfort, Ky.: Yeoman, 1883. 107 pp. Rpt. *Twelfth Annual Report of the Bureau of Ethnology to the Secretary of the Smithsonian Institution, 1890-1891,* pp. 503-99. Washington, D.C.: GPO, 1893.

DeWitt, John H. "William Edward Myer." *THM* 8 (1924), 225-30. Myer, an archaeologist with the Bureau of American Ethnology and a native of Carthage, Tenn., died in 1923.

Faulkner, Charles. "Tennessee Birdstones." *Tennessee Archaeologist* 21 (1965), 39-54.

——. "Tennessee Radiocarbon Dates." *Tennessee Archaeologist* 23 (1967), 12-30.

Holmes, William H. "Illustrated Catalogue of a Portion of the Collections Made during the Field Season of 1881." *Third Annual Report of the Bureau of Ethnology to the Secretary of the Smithsonian Institution, 1881-82,* pp. 433-507. Washington, D.C.: GPO, 1884. Includes findings in Cocke, Sevier, Roane, and Jefferson counties.

——. "Ancient Pottery of the Mississippi Valley." *Fourth Annual Report of the Bureau of Ethnology to the Secretary of the Smithsonian Institution, 1882-83,* pp. 367-436. Washington, D.C.: GPO, 1886. Includes findings in portions of Tennessee.

Jones, Joseph. *Explorations of the Aboriginal Remains of Tennessee,* Smithsonian Institution Publication 250. Washington, D.C.: Smithsonian Institution, 1876; rpt. Knoxville: Tenase, 1970. 171 pp.

Kneberg, Madeline. "The Tennessee Area." *Archaeology of Eastern United States,* ed. James B. Griffin, pp. 190-99. Chicago: Univ. of Chicago Press, 1952.

Lewis, Thomas M. N. "On Folsom Arrowpoints." *Tennessee Archaeologist* 1 (1945), 14-15.

Lewis, Thomas M. N., and Madeline Kneberg Lewis, eds. *Ten Years of the "Tennessee Archaeologist."* Chattanooga: Graham, 1954. 259 pp.

——. *Tribes That Slumber: Indian Times in the Tennessee Region.* Knoxville: Univ. of Tennessee Press, 1958, 1960, 1966, 1970. 208 pp. An outstanding description of the social and cultural traditions of the Cherokee Indians and their predecessors in Tennessee.

McElwee, W. E. "Aboriginal Remains in Tennessee." *THM* 6 (1920), 200-205.

Mallery, Garrick. "Picture-Writing of the American Indian." *Tenth Annual Report of the Bureau of Ethnology to the Secretary of the Smithsonian Institution, 1888-89,* pp. 3-807. Washington, D.C.: GPO, 1893. Material on pp. 114-15 relates to Tennessee petroglyphs.

Myer, William Edward. "Recent Archaeological Discoveries in Tennessee." *Art and Archaeology,* Sept. 1922, pp. 140-50.

Provine, William A. "Some Early Archaeological Finds in Tennessee." *THM* 5 (1919), 216-28.

Stack, Guy. "The First Tennessee Farmers." *Tennessee Archaeologist* 5 (1949), 1-4.

Thomas, Cyrus. *Catalog of Prehistoric Works East of the Rocky Mountains,* Smithsonian Institution, Bureau of Ethnology Bulletin 12. Washington, D.C.: GPO, 1891. 246 pp.

"TV Archaeology; Indian Kitchen Middens in Tennessee Excavated, Flooded." *Scientific American,* May 1943, p. 209.

EARLY EXPLORATION

Alvord, Clarence W., and Lee Bidgood. *The First Explorations of the Trans-Allegheny Region by the Virginians, 1650-1674.* Cleveland, O.: Arthur H. Clark, 1912. 275 pp.

Armstrong, Zella. *Who Discovered America? The Amazing Story of Madoc.* Chattanooga: Lookout, 1950. 216 pp.

Bakeless, John Edwin. *Master of the Wilderness: Daniel Boone.* New York: Morrow, 1939. 480 pp.

——. *Fighting Frontiersman, the Life of Daniel Boone,* Morrow Junior Books. New York: Morrow, 1948. 260 pp.

Bourne, Edward G., ed. *Narratives of the Career of Hernando De Soto in the Conquest of Florida As Told by a Knight of Elvas, and in a Relation by Luys Hernandez de Biedma, Factor of the Expedition; . . . Together with an Account of de Soto's Expedition Based on the Diary of Rodrigo Ranjel, His Private Secretary, Translated from Oviedo's Historia General y Natural de las Indias,* Trail Makers Series. 2 vols. New York: Barnes, 1904; rpt. New York: Allerton, 1922; rpt. New York: AMS, 1972.

Burrus, Ernest J. "Father Jacques Marquette, S.J., His Priesthood in the Light of the Jesuit Roman Archives." *Catholic Historical Review* 41 (1955-56), 257-71.

Chesnel, Paul. *History of Cavelier de LaSalle, 1643-1687; Explorations in the Valleys of the Ohio, Illinois and Mississippi, taken from his Letters, Reports to King Louis XIV, also the Reports of Several of his Associates, Official Acts and Contemporaneous Documents.* New York: Putnam, 1932. 232 pp.

Crane, Verner W. "The Tennessee River as the Road to Carolina: The Beginnings of Exploration and Trade." *MVHR* 3 (1916-17), 3-18.

——. *The Southern Frontier, 1670-1732.* Durham: Duke Univ. Press, 1928. Rpt., American History: Viewpoints and Perspectives Series. Philadelphia: Porcupine, 1928; rpt. Ann Arbor: Univ. of Michigan Press, 1956. 391 pp.

Fishwick, Marshall W. "Daniel Boone and the Pattern of the Western Hero." *FCHQ* 27 (1953), 119-38.

Folmsbee, Stanley J., and Madeline Kneberg Lewis. "Journals of the Juan Pardo Expeditions, 1566-1567." *ETHSP* 37 (1965), 106-21.

Gipson, Lawrence H. *The British Empire before the American*

Revolution. 15 vols. Vols. 1-3, Caldwell, Id.: Caxton, 1936; vols. 4-15, New York: Knopf, 1939-70.

Hamilton, Raphael N. *Marquette's Explorations: The Narratives Reexamined.* Madison: Univ. of Wisc. Press, 1970. 275 pp.

Hansborough, Helen. "French Exploration of the Mississippi Valley in the 17th Century." Thesis, Univ. of Cincinnati, 1932.

Henderson, W. A. "The Adventures of De Soto." *THM* 6 (1920), 3-13.

Jacobs, Wilbur R., ed. *Indians of the Southern Colonial Frontier; The Edmond [Edmund] Atkin Report and Plan of 1755.* Columbia: Univ. of South Carolina Press, 1954; rpt. Lincoln: Univ. of Nebraska Press, 1967. 108 pp.

Kincaid, Robert L. *The Wilderness Road.* Indianapolis: Bobbs-Merrill, 1947; rpt. Harrogate: Lincoln Memorial Univ. Press, 1955; rpt. Middlesboro, Ky.: n.p., 1966. 392 pp.

——. "The Wilderness Road in Tennessee." *ETHSP* 20 (1948), 37-48.

Klutts, William A. "Fort Prudhomme: Its Location." *WTHSP* 4 (1950), 28-40.

Milton, George F. "East Tennessee in Colonial Days." *Sewanee Review* 3 (1894-95), 290-306, 410-20.

Putnam, Albigence W. *History of Middle Tennessee; or, Life and Times of Gen. James Robertson.* Nashville: The Author, 1859. 668 pp. Rpt., Tennesseana Editions, with an introduction by Stanley F. Horn and index by Hugh and Cornelia Walker. Knoxville: Univ. of Tennessee Press, 1971. 708 pp.

——. "Memoir of Daniel Boone." *AHM* 1 (1896), 128-33.

Ramsey, J. G. M. *Annals of Tennessee.*

Rowland, Dunbar, ed. *A Symposium on the Place of Discovery of the Mississippi River by Hernando De Soto.* Jackson: Mississippi Hist. Soc., 1927. 103 pp.

Steck, Francis B. "The Jolliet-Marquette Expedition, 1673." Diss., Catholic Univ., 1927.

Swanton, John R., ed. *Final Report of the United States De Soto Expedition Commission.* House Ex. Doc. 71, 76th Cong., 1st sess. Washington, D.C.: GPO, 1939. 400 pp.

Williams, Samuel Cole. *Early Travels in the Tennessee Country, 1540-1800.* Johnson City: Watauga, 1928; rpt. Nashville: Franklin Bk. Rpts., 1970. 540 pp. A series of extracts from the writings of more than thirty early visitors to the territory now the State of Tennessee.

Young, J. P. "Fort Prudhomme: Was It the First Settlement in Tennessee?" *THM* 2 (1916), 235-44; rpt. in *Tennessee Old and New,* I, 51-60.

EARLY TRAVEL ACCOUNTS

Anderson, T. A. *The Ocoee District, South East Tennessee in the United States of America, Especially the Hundred Thousand Acres, and the Gold Region, With A Sketch of the Character of the People Who Inhabit East Tennessee Generally.* London: J. Leath, 1842. 28 pp.

Baily, Francis. *Journal of a Tour in the Unsettled Parts of North America, in 1796 & 1797,* ed. A. De Morgan. London: Baily, 1856. 439 pp. Rpt. Louisville, Ky.: Lost Cause, 1959. Rpt., abridg. ed., Travels on the Western Waters Series, ed. Jack D. L. Holmes. Carbondale: Southern Illinois Univ. Press, 1969.

Bartram, William. *Travels Through North & South Carolina, Georgia, East & West Florida, the Cherokee Country, the Extensive Territories of the Muscogulges, or Creek Confederacy, and the Country of the Chactaws; Containing an Account of the Soil and Natural Productions of Those Regions, Together with Observations on the Manner of the Indians. Embellished with Copper Plates.* Philadelphia, Pa.: James & Johnson, 1791. 522 pp. Rpt. London: James & Johnson, 1792. 520 pp. Rpt., as *The Travels of William Bartram,* ed. Mark Van Doren. New York: Dover, 1928, 1947, 1955, 1963. 414 pp. Rpt., Naturalist's ed., ed. Francis Harper. New Haven: Yale Univ. Press, 1958. 727 pp. Of the many editions of this work, both English and French, perhaps the best is the one edited by Francis Harper. Bartram was a botanist who traveled through the Southeast in the mid-1770s.

Bass, John M. "Half an Hour with Some Early Visitors to Tennessee." *AHM* 5 (1900), 99-114; rpt. in *Tennessee Old and New,* I, 247-59.

Campbell, Patrick, ed. *Travels in the Interior Inhabited Parts of North America. In the Years 1791 and 1792, In Which Is Given an Account of the Manners and Customs of the Indians, and the Present War between Them and the Federal States, the Mode of Life and System of Farming among the New Settlers of Both Canadas, New York, New England, New Brunswick, and Nova Scotia; Interspersed with Anecdotes of People, Observations on the Soil, Natural Productions, and Political Situation of These Countries.* Edinburgh: J. Guthrie, 1793; rpt. Toronto: Champlain Soc., 1937. Rpt., H. H. Langton, ed. Westport, Conn.: Greenwood, 1968. 387 pp.

Clark, Thomas D. *Travels in the Old South: A Bibliography,* American Exploration and Travel Series, No. 19. 3 vols. Norman: Univ. of Oklahoma Press, 1956-69.

——. *Travels in the New South: A Bibliography,* American Exploration and Travel Series, Vol. 36. 2 vols. Norman: Univ. of Oklahoma Press, 1962.

Featherstonhaugh, George William. *A Canoe Voyage up the Minnay Sotor; with an Account of the Lead and Copper Deposits in Wisconsin; of the Gold Region in the Cherokee Country: and Sketches of Popular Manners; &c. &c. &c.* 2 vols. London: R. Bentley, 1847; rpt. St. Paul: Minnesota Hist. Soc., 1970.

Imlay, Gilbert. *A Topographical Description of the Western Territory of North America; Containing a Succinct Account of Its Soil, Climate, Natural History, Population, Agriculture, Manners, and Customs. With an Ample Description of the Several Divisions into Which the Country is Partitioned. . . .* 2nd ed., London: J. Debrett, 1793. 433 pp. Rpt., rev. ed., 1797. 598 pp. Rpt. New York: Dover, 1928; rpt. New York: Barnes and Noble, 1940. Copy, American Culture Series, 122: 7- . Ann Arbor: Univ. Microfilms, 1960. Rpt., American Scene Series. New York: Da Capo, 1968; rpt. Clifton, N.J.: Kelley, 1972. First appearing in London in 1792, this popular book was published in many editions with varying titles, in both London and New York in the 1790s; in 1793 it was published in both Dublin and Berlin.

Ingersoll, Ernest. *To the Shenandoah and Beyond: The Chronicle of a Leisurely Journey through the Uplands of Virginia and Tennessee, Sketching Their Scenery, Noting Their Legends, Portraying Social and Material Progress, and Explaining Routes of Travel.* New York: Leve & Alden, 1885. 125 pp.

Inman, E., ed. *Stories of Hatfield the Pioneer . . . His Experiences in the Wilderness of East Tennessee, Kentucky and South Indiana.* New Albany, Ind.: G. Fishback, 1889, 1890. 278 pp.

Michaux, François André. *Travels to the Westward of the Alleghany Mountains, in the States of the Ohio, Kentucky, and Tennessee, in the Year 1802 . . . ,* Collection of Modern and Contemporary Voyages and Travels, vol. 1. London: R. Phillips, 1805. 96 pp. Rpt. London: Crosby, 1805. 294 pp. Rpt. in *Early Western Travels, 1748-1846 . . . ,* vol. 3, ed. Reuben G. Thwaites (see below). A translation from the first French edition (Paris, 1804).

"Night on the Banks of the Tennessee River." *Blackwood's Magazine* 56 (1844), 278-89.

Owsley, Harriet C., ed. "Travel through the Indian Country in the Early 1800's; the Memoirs of Martha Philips Martin." *THQ* 21 (1962), 66-81.

Palmer, Frederick A. "Westerners at Home: Comments of French and British Travelers on Life in the West, 1800-1840." Diss., Univ. of Illinois, 1948.

Patton, James Welch. "The Tennessee Valley As Seen by a British Traveler in 1837." *THM* (ser. 2) 3 (1932-37), 45-58. The traveler was George William Featherstonhaugh.

——., ed. "Thomas Lenoir's Journey to Tennessee in 1806." *THQ* 17 (1958), 156-66.

Provine, William A., ed. "'A Tour in 1807 down the Cumberland, Ohio and Mississippi rivers from Nashville to New Orleans,' by Dr. John R. Bedford." *THM* 5 (1919), 40-68, 107-28.

Smith, Daniel. *A Short Description of the Tennassee Government, or The Territory of the United States South of the River Ohio, to Accompany and Explain a Map of That Country.* Philadelphia: Mathew Carey, 1793. 20 pp. Rpt. 1796. 44 pp. Rpt. New York: Mott, 1797. 47 pp. Rpt. in Imlay, *Topographical Description,* 3rd ed., 512-43. Rpt. Boston: Massachusetts Hist. Soc., 1936. 36 pp. Rpt., chronological notes by Mrs. Cartter Patten. Chattanooga: n.p., 1962. 26 leaves.

Stockton, Ernest Looney. *History Excursions into Tennessee—Its Early Heritage.* Kingsport: Kingsport Press, 1941. 51 pp.

Thwaites, Reuben Gold, ed. *Early Western Travels, 1748-1846; a Series of Annotated Reprints of Some of the Best and Rarest Contemporary Volumes of Travel, Descriptive of the Aborigines and Social and Economic Conditions in the Middle and Far West, during the Period of Early American Settlement.* 32 vols. Cleveland, O.: Clark, 1904-7; rpt. New York: AMS, 1966. Vol. 3 includes accounts of André Michaux's travels into Kentucky, 1793-96, François André Michaux's travels west of the Alleghenies, 1802, and Thaddeus Mason Harris's tour northwest of the Alleghenies, 1803.

Torrey, Bradford. *Spring Notes from Tennessee.* Boston: Houghton, 1896. 223 pp.

Walker, Thomas. *Journal of an Exploration in the Spring of the Year 1750.* Boston: Little, 1888. 69 pp. Rpt. in *First Explorations of Kentucky,* ed. Josiah Stoddard Johnson, Filson Club Publications no. 13. Louisville: John P. Morton, 1898. 84 pp. Rpt., titled *A Bit of Pioneer American History, As Told by Dr. Walker's Personal Journal and Map of His Journey,* ed. Marion Rust. [Ky.?]: n.p., 19-? 8 pp.

Warner, Charles Dudley. *On Horseback: A Tour in Virginia, North Carolina and Tennessee. With Notes of Travel in Mexico and California.* Boston: Houghton, 1888. 331 pp.

Williams, Samuel Cole, ed. *Early Travels in the Tennessee Country.*

EARLY SETTLEMENT

Alderman, Pat, and Lee B. Andrews. *The Overmountain Men; Early Tennessee History, 1760-1780. The Exploration, Settlement and Founding of the First Free Government in America; Its Struggles for Survival, Culminating in the Battle of King's Mountain.* Erwin: Wingreen, 1958. 61 pp. Rev. & enl., Johnson City: Overmountain Press, 1970. 286 pp.

Beasley, Paul W. "The Life and Times of Isaac Shelby." Diss., Univ. of Kentucky, 1968.

Caruso, John A. *The Appalachian Frontier; America's First Surge Westward.* Indianapolis: Bobbs-Merrill, 1959. 408 pp.

Cooke, John White. "Isaac Shelby, 1750-1796." Thesis, Vanderbilt Univ., 1959.

Fink, Paul M. "Jacob Brown of Nolichucky." *THQ* 21 (1962), 235-50.

———. "Russell Bean, Tennessee's First Native Son." ETHS*P* 37 (1965), 31-48.

Goodpasture, Albert V. "Why the First Settlers of Tennessee Were from Virginia." *THM* 5 (1919), 229-31.

Henderson, Archibald. *The Conquest of the Old Southwest; the Romantic Story of the Early Pioneers into Virginia, the Carolinas, Tennessee, and Kentucky, 1740-1790.* New York: Century, 1920. 395 pp.

———. "The Treaty of Long Island of Holston, July, 1777." *NCHR* 8 (1931), 55-116.

Patten, Cartter. *A Tennessee Chronicle.*

Pauley, James H. "Early North Carolina Migrations into the Tennessee Country, 1768-1782: A Study in Historical Demography." Thesis, Middle Tennessee State Univ., 1969.

Price, Prentiss. "Two Petitions to Virginia of the North of Holston Men, 1776, 1777." ETHSP 21 (1949), 95-110.

Skinner, Constance L. *Pioneers of the Old Southwest: A Chronicle of the Dark and Bloody Ground*, Chronicles of America Series, vol. 18. New Haven: Yale Univ. Press, 1919, 1920, 1921. 304 pp. This work is concerned with the type of people who took the first steps in westward settlement. The author sees them as freedom-loving persons who moved west to avoid the constraints of organized society. Daniel Boone is her prime example, but she devotes chapters to John Sevier and other early Tennesseans.

Williams, Samuel Cole. "Tidence Lane, Tennessee's First Pastor." *THM* (ser. 2) 1 (1930-31), 40-48; rpt. in *Tennessee Old and New*, I, 222-30.

———. "Hazard's Proposed Colony in the Tennessee Country—1755." *THM* (ser. 2) 2 (1931-1932), 50-61.

———. "Fort Robinson on the Holston." ETHSP 4 (1932), 22-31.

———. "Shelby's Fort." ETHSP 7 (1935), 28-37.

———. "Stephen Holston and Holston River." ETHSP 8 (1936), 26-34.

———., comp. "Western Representation in North Carolina Assemblies." ETHSP 14 (1942), 106-12.

FORT LOUDOUN

Cook, Thomas H. "Old Fort Loudoun, the First English Settlement in What Is Now the State of Tennessee and the Fort Loudoun Massacre." *THM* 7 (1921), 111-33.

DeWitt, John H. "Old Fort Loudoun." *THM* 3 (1917), 250-56; rpt. in *Tennessee Old and New*, I, 61-68.

Hamer, Philip M. *Fort Loudoun on the Little Tennessee*. Raleigh, N.C.: Edwards & Broughton, 1925. 39 pp.

———. "Anglo-French Rivalry in the Cherokee Country, 1754-1757." *NCHR* 2 (1925), 303-22.

———. "Fort Loudoun in the Cherokee War 1758-1761." *NCHR* 2 (1925), 442-558.

Kelly, Paul. *Historic Fort Loudoun*. Vonore: Fort Loudoun Assoc., 1958, 1961. 42 pp.

———. "Fort Loudoun: The After Years, 1760-1960." *THQ* 20 (1961), 303-22; rpt. in *Landmarks of Tennessee*, 219-38.

Morrison, A. J. "Fort Loudoun and Its Author." *Virginia Magazine of History* 32 (1924), 88-89.

Radford, P. M. "Old Fort Loudoun." *AHM* 2 (1897), 33-44.

Stone, Richard G., Jr. "Captain Paul Demere at Fort Loudoun, 1757, 1760." *ETHSP* 41 (1969), 17-32.

WATAUGA

Allen, Ben, and Dennis T. Lawson. "The Wataugans and the 'Dangerous Example.'" *THQ* 26 (1967), 137-47.

Caldwell, Joshua W. "The Watauga Association." *AHM* 3 (1898), 312-15.

Goodpasture, Albert V. "The Watauga Association." *AHM* 3 (1898), 103-20.

Hamer, Philip M., ed. "Correspondence of Henry Stuart and Alexander Cameron with the Wataugans." *MVHR* 17 (1930-31), 451-59.

——. "The Wataugans and the Cherokee Indians in 1776." *ETHSP* 3 (1931), 108-26.

Herndon, G. Melvin. *William Tatham and the Culture of Tobacco: Including a Facsimile Reprint of an Historical and Practical Essay on the Culture and Commerce of Tobacco by William Tatham.* Coral Gables: Univ. of Miami Press, 1969. 506 pp. Tatham was a Watauga settler.

Hyder, N. E. "Watauga Old Fields." *AHM* 8 (1903), 253-55.

McGill, J. T. "Andrew Greer." *THM* 2 (1916), 204-7. Greer was a Watauga settler and trader.

Williams, Samuel Cole. "William Tatham, Wataugan." *THM* 7 (1921), 154-79.

——. *William Tatham, Wataugan.* Nashville: n.p., 1923. 26 pp. Rev. & enl., Johnson City: Watauga, 1947. 109 pp.

CUMBERLAND SETTLEMENTS

Arnow, Harriette Simpson. *Seedtime on the Cumberland.* New York: Macmillan, 1960. 449 pp.

——. *Flowering of the Cumberland.* New York: Macmillan, 1963. 441 pp.

Bright, John Morgan. *Donelson and the Pioneers of Middle Tennessee.* Washington, D.C.: Globe, 1880. 35 pp. Centennial oration delivered at the Capitol in Nashville on Centennial Day, April 24, 1880.

Carr, John. *Early Times in Middle Tennessee.* Nashville: E. Stevenson & F. A. Owen, 1857. 248 pp. Rpt. Nashville: Parthenon Press, 1958. 112 pp. A description by one of the earliest pioneers in Middle Tennessee of conditions there during the period from 1780 to 1800. This book is composed of a series of sketches originally written for the *Christian Advocate* and the *Southwestern Monthly.*

Durham, Walter. "Kasper Mansker: Cumberland Frontiersman." *THQ* 30 (1971), 154-77.

——. "Thomas Sharp Spencer, Man or Legend." *THQ* 31 (1972), 240-55.

Goodpasture, Albert V. "Dr. James White—Pioneer, Politician, Lawyer," *THM* 1 (1915), 282-91; rpt. in *Tennessee Old and New,* I, 260-68.

Henderson, Archibald. "Richard Henderson: The Authorship of the Cumberland Compact and the Founding of Nashville." *THM* (ser. 3) 2 (1916), 155-74; rpt. in *Tennessee Old and New,* I, 93-111.

Horn, Stanley F. "The Cumberland Compact." *THQ* 3 (1944), 65-66.

Matlock, J. W. L. "John Cotten: Reluctant Pioneer." *THQ* 27 (1968), 277-86. *See also* Stanley J. Folmsbee, "The Journal of John Cotten, the 'Reluctant Pioneer'—Evidences of its Unreliability." *THQ* 28 (1969), 84-94.

Parks, Edd Winfield. *Long Hunter, the Story of Big-Foot Spencer,* illus. Edward Shenton. New York: Farrar, 1942. 270 pp.

Pope, Charles Monty. "John Donelson: Pioneer." Thesis, Univ. of Tennessee, 1969.

Quarles, Robert T., and Robert H. White, eds. *Three Pioneer Tennessee Documents: "Donelson's Journal," "Cumberland Compact," "Minutes of the Cumberland Court."* Nashville: Tennessee Hist. Comm., 1964. 40 pp.

Robison, Dan M. "Robert Hays, Unsung Pioneer of the Cumberland Country." *THQ* 26 (1967), 263-78.

Towles, S. S. "The Three Transylvania Towns: Boonesborough, Nashville and Henderson." *Register of the Kentucky Historical Society* 34 (1936), 77-80.

Williams, Samuel Cole. "Ann Robertson: An Unsung Tennessee Heroine." *THQ* 3 (1944), 150-55; rpt. in *Tennessee Old and New,* II, 15-20.

JAMES ROBERTSON

Baker, Blanche. "James Robertson: Frontiersman." Thesis, George Peabody College, 1926.

Garret, William R., ed. "The Correspondence of General James Robertson." *AHM* 1 (1896), 71-91, 189-94, 281-91, 390-96; 2 (1897), 59-86, 172-77, 278-79, 354-75; 3 (1898), 74-83, 267-98, 348-94; 4 (1899), 66-96, 163-92, 247-86, 336-81; 5 (1900), 67-96, 162-90, 252-86.

Lewis, Eugene C. "James Robertson, Nashville's Founder." *AHM* 8 (1902), 285-94; rpt. in *Tennessee Old and New,* I, 84-92.

Matthews, Thomas Edwin. *General James Robertson, Father of Tennessee.* Nashville: Parthenon Press, 1934. 588 pp.

Putnam, Albigence W. *History of Middle Tennessee.*

Ranson, James Morris. "The Life and Career of General James Robertson." Thesis, Univ. of Tennessee, 1966.

Sprague, L. T. "General James Robertson, the Father of Tennessee." *Outing,* Aug. 1907, pp. 606-13.

Tennessee in the American Revolution

Abernethy, Thomas P. *Western Lands and the American Revolution,* The Univ. of Virginia Institute for Research in the Social Sciences Monograph 25. New York: Appleton, 1937, 1959. Rpt. New York: Russell, 1959. 413 pp.

Adams, Randolph G. "Two Documents on the Battle of King's Mountain." *NCHR* 8 (1931), 348-52.

Alden, John Richard. *The South in the Revolution, 1763-1789,* a History of the South, vol. 3. Baton Rouge: Louisiana State Univ. Press, 1957, 1962. 442 pp.

Alderman, Pat. *One Heroic Hour at King's Mountain, October 7, 1780.* Erwin: n.p., 1968. 64 pp. Rpt. in Alderman and Andrews, *Overmountain Men,* 61-144.

Allen, Penelope J., comp. *Tennessee Soldiers in the Revolution: A Roster of Soldiers Living during the Revolutionary War in the Counties of Washington and Sullivan. Taken from the Revolutionary Army Accounts of North Carolina.* Bristol: King, 1935. 71 pp.

Armstrong, Zella. *Some Tennessee Heroes of the Revolution; Compiled from Pension Statements.* Chattanooga: Lookout, 1933. Unpaged.

Bailey, James D. *Commanders at King's Mountain.* Gaffney, S.C.: E. H. De Camp, 1926. 431 pp.

Burnett, Swan M. *The Over Mountain Men: Some Passages from a Page of Neglected History.* Washington, D.C.: American Hist. Reg., 1895. 23 pp.

Calendar of the Tennessee and King's Mountain Papers of the Draper Collection of Manuscripts. Madison: Wisconsin Hist. Soc., 1929. 138 pp.

Carpenter, Hugh. *King's Mountain, an Epic of Revolution: With Historical and Biographical Sketches, and Illustrations.* Knoxville: The Author, 1936. 137 pp.

Chandler, Helen Deane. *A Brief Description of the Battle of King's Mountain, 'The Turning Point of the American Revolution,'*

Fought in York County, S.C., October 7, 1780. Together with Brief Accounts of Previous Celebrations, Illustrations Showing the Battlefield and Monuments and Interesting Data concerning 150th Anniversary Celebration to be Held on the Battleground October 7, 1930. Gastonia, N.C.: Publicity Comm. of the Sesquicentennial Celebration Comm., 1930. 47 pp.

Claiborne, Nathaniel H. *Notes on the War in the South; with Biographical Sketches of the Lives of Montgomery, Jackson, Sevier, the Late Gov. Claiborne, and Others.* Richmond, Va.: William Ramsay, 1819. Rpt., First American Frontier Series. New York: Arno, 1971. 112 pp.

Draper, Lyman C. *King's Mountain and Its Heroes: History of the Battle of King's Mountain, October 7th, 1780, and the Events Which Led to It.* Cincinnati: P. G. Thomson, 1881; rpt. New York: Dauber & Pine, 1929; rpt. Marietta, Ga.: Continental, 1954. Rpt., North Carolina Heritage Series, vol. 5. Spartanburg, S.C.: Reprint Co., 1967; rpt. Baltimore: Genealogical Pub., 1971. 612 pp. The definitive account of this Revolutionary War battle in which a substantial number of Tennesseans participated.

Foster, Stephen. "The Battle of King's Mountain." *AHM* 1 (1896), 22-45.

Garrett, William R., ed. "Revolutionary and Military Pensioners—List for Tennessee, June 1, 1840." *AHM* 3 (1898), 120-32.

Gilmore, James R. [pseud. Edmund Kirke]. *The Rear-Guard of the Revolution.* New York: Appleton, 1886. 317 pp.

Goodrich, William. "Invincible Tennesseans." *AHM* 3 (1898), 223-29.

Henri, Florette. *King's Mountain.* Garden City, N.Y.: Doubleday, 1950. 340 pp. Fiction.

Kirke, Edmund. *See* Gilmore, James R.

McCown, Mary Hardin, ed. "A King's Mountain Diary." *ETHSP* 14 (1942), 102-5.

Putnam, Albigence W., ed. " 'Another Account of the Battle of King's Mountain,' by Robert Campbell and 'A Letter Relative to the Battle of King's Mountain.'" *AHM* 1 (1896), 40-47.

Ramsey, James G. M. [?] *Tales of the Revolution, by a Young Gentleman of Tennessee.* Nashville: Hunt, Tardiff, 1833. 179 pp.

Stone, Maggie H. "Joseph Greer, 'King's Mountain Messenger': A Tradition of the Greer Family." *THM* 2 (1916), 40-42.

Tyson, Lawrence Davis. *Tennessee's Part in the Revolution: Address at Valley Forge, at the Presentation of the Tennessee State Flag and Inauguration of Tennessee Sunday, April 24, 1927.* Valley Forge, Pa.: Tennessee Soc. of Colonial Dames, 1927. 14 pp.

White, Katherine Keogh. *The King's Mountain Men: The Story of the Battle, with Sketches of the American Soldiers Who Took Part.* Dayton, Va.: Joseph K. Ruebush, 1924; rpt. Baltimore: Genealogical Pub., 1966, 1970. 271 pp.

Williams, Samuel Cole. "The Battle of King's Mountain: As Seen by the British Officers." *THM* 7 (1921), 51-66, 104-10.

——. "The First Volunteers from the 'Volunteer State.'" *THM* 8 (1924), 132-39; rpt. in *Tennessee Old and New,* I, 213-21.

——. "The First Territorial Division Named for Washington." *THM* (ser. 2) 2 (1931-32), 153-64; rpt. in *Tennessee Old and New,* I, 201-12.

——. *Tennessee During the Revolutionary War.* Nashville: Tennessee Hist. Comm., 1944. 294 pp. Rpt. Knoxville: Univ. of Tennessee Press, 1974. This work treats civil as well as military affairs during the Revolutionary War. It reveals that these overmountain people took part in several Revolutionary War battles besides the one at King's Mountain.

Wilson, Samuel C. "Colonel Elijah Clarke in the Tennessee Country." *Georgia Historical Quarterly* 25 (1941), 151-58. Clarke was in this area during the Revolutionary War.

Young, Carol Furlong. "A Study of Some Developing Interpretations of the History of Revolutionary Tennessee." *ETHSP* 25 (1953), 24-36.

State of Franklin

Alden, George H. "The State of Franklin." *AHR* 8 (1902-3), 271-89.

Black, Henry C. "Some Forgotten Constitutions: Franklin." *Constitutional Review* 10 (1926), 115-19.

Cannon, Walter Faw. "Four Interpretations of the History of the State of Franklin." ETHS*P* 22 (1950), 3-18.

Clemens, Will M. "Lost State of Franklin." *New England Magazine*, Feb. 1903, pp. 772-74.

Davis, Charles Elton. "Theodore Roosevelt, Franklin Historian." Thesis, Kansas State Univ., 1961.

A Declaration of Rights, Also, the Constitution, or Form of Government, Agreed to, and Resolved upon, by the Representatives of the Freemen of the State of Frankland, Elected and Chosen for that Particular Purpose, in Convention Assembled, at Greeneville, the 14th of November, 1785. Philadelphia, Pa.: Francis Bailey, 1786. 23 pp. Rpt., *AHM* 1 (1896), 50-63.

DeWitt, John H. "History of the Lost State of Franklin." *THM* 8 (1924), 167-70.

Driver, Carl S. *John Sevier: Pioneer of the Old Southwest.* Diss., Vanderbilt Univ., 1929. Nashville: n.p., 1929. 11 leaves. Chapel Hill: Univ. of North Carolina Press, 1932. 240 pp.

Fink, Paul M. "Some Phases of the History of the State of Franklin." *THQ* 16 (1957), 195-213.

Fitch, William Edward. *The Origin, Rise and Downfall of the State of Franklin under Her First and Only Governor, John Sevier,* Publications of the New York Society of the Order of the Founders and Patriots of America, vol. 25. New York: The Society, 1910. 24 pp.

Garrett, William R., ed. "The Provisional Constitution of Frankland." *AHM* 1 (1896), 48-63.

Goodpasture, Albert V., ed. "Constitution of the State of Franklin" *AHM* 9 (1904), 399-408; rpt. in *Tennessee Old and New,* I, 13-26.

Hagy, James W., and Stanley J. Folmsbee. "Arthur Campbell and the Separate State Movements in Virginia and North Carolina." *ETHSP* 42 (1970), 20-46. Relates to the State of Franklin.

Lacy, Eric Russell. "The Persistent State of Franklin." *THQ* 23 (1964), 321-32.

McGill, J. T. "Franklin and Frankland: Names and Boundaries." *THM* 8 (1924), 248-57.

Miller, Helen Topping. *The Sound of Chariots: A Novel of John Sevier and the State of Franklin.* Indianapolis: Bobbs-Merrill, 1947. 288 pp. Fiction, but fair history.

Williams, Samuel Cole. *History of the Lost State of Franklin.* Johnson City: Watauga, 1924. 371 pp. Rev. ed., New York: Press of the Pioneers, 1933. 378 pp.; rpt. Nashville: Franklin Bk. Rpts., 1970; rpt. Knoxville: Tenase, 1970; rpt. Clifton, N.J.: Kelley, 1971. The first of a long series of works on Tennessee history written by Judge Williams of Johnson City. He illustrates that a movement toward separate statehood existed on all frontiers in the 1780s, but a de facto government was achieved only by Franklin.

The Southwest Territory
and William Blount

The Acts and Ordinances of the Governors and Judges of the Territory of the United States of America South of the River Ohio. Knoxville: George Roulstone, 1793. c. 4 pp.

Acts Passed at First Session of General Assembly . . . Territory of the United States South of the River Ohio. Knoxville: George Roulstone, 1794. 101 pp.

Bentley, George F. "Printers and Printing in the Southwest Territory, 1790-1796." *THQ* 8 (1949), 332-44.

Blount, William. *The Blount Journal, 1790-1796: The Proceedings of Government over the Territory of the United States of America, South of the River Ohio, William Blount, Esquire, in His Executive Department as Governor.* Nashville: Tennessee Hist. Comm., 1955. 166 pp. A reprint of "Governor Blount's Journal," William R. Garrett, ed., cited below.

———. *Proceedings on the Impeachment of William Blount, a Senator from the State of Tennessee, for High Crimes and Misdemeanors.* Philadelphia, Pa.: J. Gales, 1799. 102 pp.

Carter, Clarence Edwin, ed. *The Territory South of the River Ohio, 1790-1796.* The Territorial Papers of the United States, vol. 4, United States Department of State Publication no. 855. Washington, D.C.: GPO, 1936. Rpt. New York: AMS, 1973. This volume contains numerous items of correspondence from the Southwest Territorial Governor William Blount to national government officials, especially to the secretary of war.

Cobb, P. L. "William Cobb—Host of Governor William Blount." *THM* 9 (1925), 241-63.

Corbitt, D. C. "Exploring the Southwest Territory in the Spanish Records." *ETHSP* 38 (1966), 109-18.

Davidson, Elizabeth Huey. "The Life of William Blount." Thesis, Univ. of Tennessee, 1928.

Garrett, William R., ed. "Governor Blount's Journal." *AHM* 2 (1897), 213-77; rpt., titled *The Blount Journal, 1790-1796,* cited above.

Gilmore, James R. [pseud. Edmund Kirke]. *The Advance-Guard of Western Civilization.* New York: Appleton, 1888. 343 pp. Includes history of Tennessee and the Old Southwest.

Goodpasture, Albert V. "William Blount and the Old Southwest Territory." *AHM* 8 (1903), 1-13.

Hamer, Philip M., ed. "Letters of Governor William Blount." ETHS*P* 4 (1932), 122-37.

Keith, Alice B., and William H. Masterson, eds. *The John Gray Blount Papers.* 3 vols. Raleigh: North Carolina Dept. of Archives and Hist., 1952, 1965. Vol. 1 (1952), 1764-89; vol. 2 (1952), 1790-95; vol. 3 (1965), 1796-1802, ed. William H. Masterson.

Keith, Alice B. "Three North Carolina Blount Brothers in Business and Politics, 1783-1812." Thesis, Univ. of North Carolina, 1940.

Kirke, Edmund. *See* Gilmore, James R.

Masterson, William H. "William Blount and the Establishment of the Southwest Territory, 1790-1791." ETHS*P* 23 (1951), 3-31.

——. *William Blount,* Southern Biography Series. Baton Rouge: Louisiana State Univ. Press, 1954. Rpt. Westport, Conn.: Greenwood, 1970. 378 pp.

——. "The Land Speculator and the West—the Role of William Blount." ETHS*P* 27 (1955), 3-8.

Prucha, Francis P. *The Sword of the Republic: The United States Army on the Frontier, 1783-1846,* Wars of the United States Series, Louis Morton, ed. New York: Macmillan, 1969. 442 pp.

Runnion, Helen. "The Political Career of William Blount." Thesis, George Peabody College, 1927.

Smith, Delle Dulaney. "The Public Career of William Blount, 1790-1800." Thesis, Univ. of Virginia, c. 1927.

Storm, Colton, ed. "Up the Tennessee in 1790: The Report of Major John Doughty to the Secretary of War." ETHS*P* 17 (1945), 119-32.

Thompson, Isabel. "The Blount Conspiracy." ETHS*P* 2 (1930), 3-21.

United States Congress. House of Representatives. Committee on Impeachment of William Blount. *Report of Committee Appointed to Prepare Articles of Impeachment against William Blount.* Philadelphia, Pa.: Fenno, 1797. 16 pp.

White, Kate. "John Chisholm, a Soldier of Fortune." ETHS*P* 1 (1929), 60-66. Chisholm was an aide to Blount.

Williams, Samuel Cole. *Phases of Southwest Territory History (a Contribution to the Celebration of the Sesqui-centennial of the Territory, October 13, 1940).* Johnson City: Watauga, 1940. 26 pp.

——. "The Southwest Territory to the Aid of the Northwest Territory, 1791." *Indiana Magazine of History* 37 (1941), 152-57.

——. *History of the Southwest Territory, 1790-1796,* ed. Robert L. Kincaid. Nashville: Tennessee Hist. Comm., 1960. 223 leaves.

Wright, Marcus Joseph. *Some Account of the Life and Services of William Blount, an Officer of the Revolutionary Army, Member of the Continental Congress, and of the Convention Which Framed the Constitution of the United States, Also Governor of the Territory South of the Ohio River, and Senator in Congress U.S. 1783-1797. Together with a Full Account of His Impeachment and Trial in Congress, and His Expulsion from the U.S. Senate.* Washington, D.C.: E. J. Gray, 1884. 142 pp.

Spanish and Other Intrigues

Abernethy, Thomas Perkins. *The Burr Conspiracy.* New York: Oxford Univ. Press, 1954; rpt. Gloucester, Mass.: P. Smith, 1968. 301 pp.

Alvord, Clarence W. *The Mississippi Valley in British Politics; a Study of the Trade, Land Speculation, and Experiments in Imperialism Culminating in the American Revolution.* 2 vols. Cleveland, O.: Arthur H. Clark, 1916-17; rpt. New York: Russell, 1959.

Allison, John. "The 'Mero District.'" *AHM* 1 (1896), 115-27; rpt. in *Tennessee Old and New,* I, 145-54.

Beard, William E. "Colonel Burr's First Brush with the Law." *THM* 1 (1915), 3-20.

Bounds, T. Gordon. "James Wilkinson and the Spanish Intrigue." Thesis, Univ. of Tennessee, 1938.

Corbitt, D. C., and Roberta C., trans. and eds. "Papers from the Spanish Archives Relating to Tennessee and the Old Southwest, 1783-1800." ETHSP 9-44 (1937-72).

Cox, Zachariah. *An Estimate of Commercial Advantages by Way of the Mississippi and Mobile Ribers to the Western Country. Principles of a Commercial System; and the Commencement and Progress of a Settlement on the Ohio River to Facilitate the Same;*

with a Statement of Facts. Knoxville: The Author, 1797; rpt. Nashville: J. M'Laughlin, 1799. c. 54 pp. Rpt. in *Historical and Philosophical Society of Ohio Quarterly Publication* 8 (1913), 37-91.

Garrett, William R., ed. "The Capture of Aaron Burr." *AHM* 1 (1896), 140-53.

Henderson, Archibald. "The Spanish Conspiracy in Tennessee." *THM* 3 (1917), 229-49.

Holmes, Jack D. L. "Fort Ferdinand of the Bluffs: Life on the Spanish-American Frontier, 1795-1797." WTHSP 13 (1959), 38-54.

——. "Spanish-American Rivalry over the Chickasaw Bluffs, 1780-1795." ETHSP 34 (1962), 26-57.

——. "The Ebb-Tide of Spanish Military Power on the Mississippi: Fort San Fernando De Las Barrancas, 1795-1798." ETHSP 36 (1964), 23-44.

Johnson, Georgia B. K. "Spain and the Cherokee Indians, 1783-1798." Thesis, Univ. of Tennessee, 1929.

McKernan, Frank M. "The Intrigues of James Wilkinson in the Old Southwest, 1783-1803." Thesis, Univ. of Cincinnati, 1939.

Matthews, Thomas E. "The Spanish 'Conspiracy' in Tennessee." *THM* 4 (1918), 69-72.

Whitaker, Arthur P. "The Old Southwest, 1783-1791." Diss., Harvard Univ., 1924.

——. "Spanish Intrigue in the Old Southwest: An Episode, 1788-89." *MVHR* 12 (1925), 155-76.

——. "The Muscle Shoals Speculation, 1783-1789." *MVHR* 13 (1926), 365-86.

——. *The Spanish-American Frontier: 1783-1795; the Westward Movement and the Spanish Retreat in the Mississippi Valley,* introd. Samuel Eliot Morison. Boston: Houghton, 1927; rpt. Gloucester, Mass.: P. Smith, 1962. Rpt., Bison Bks. Lincoln: Univ. of Nebraska Press, 1969. 255 pp.

——. *The Mississippi Question, 1795-1803: A Study in Trade, Politics, and Diplomacy.* New York: Appleton, 1934; rpt. Gloucester, Mass.: P. Smith, 1962. 342 pp.

Williams, Samuel Cole. "The Conquest of the Old Southwest." *THM* 5 (1919), 212-15.

——. "French and Other Intrigues in the Southwest Territory, 1790-1796." ETHSP 13 (1941), 21-35.

Statehood for Tennessee

Abernethy, Thomas P. *The South in the New Nation, 1789-1819,* A History of the South, vol. 4. Baton Rouge: Louisiana State Univ. Press, 1961. 529 pp.

Andrews, I. W. "Admission of Tennessee." *Magazine of American History* 18 (1887), 306.

Barnhart, John D. *Valley of Democracy: The Frontier versus the Plantation in the Ohio Valley, 1775-1818.* Bloomington: Indiana Univ. Press, 1953. 338 pp.

Cross, Nathaniel. "The Admission of Tennessee into the Union." *AHM* 1 (1896), 230-37; 5 (1900), 241-47.

Preyer, Norris Watson. "The Congressional Fight over the Admission of Kentucky, Tennessee, Louisiana, and Alabama into the Union." Thesis, Univ. of Virginia, 1950.

Roosevelt, Theodore. *The Winning of the West,* The Sagamore Series, vols. 8-13. 6 vols. New York: Putnam, 1900; rpt. Philadelphia: Gebbie, 1903; rpt. New York: *Review of Reviews,* 1904; rpt. New York: Current Literature, 1905; rpt. Putnam, 1920; 1 vol. abridg., introd. Christopher Lasch, New York: Hastings House, 1963. Rpt., ed. Harvey Wish. Gloucester, Mass.: P. Smith, 1971. 320 pp. Rpt., 6 vols. New York: Somerset, 1972. In these volumes, Roosevelt views the settlement of the trans-Appalachian West as part of the great forward movement of English-speaking peoples. Particularly significant in the American migration was the settlement of the Old Southwest. Working largely from primary sources, he devotes several chapters to the Tennessee country, from its earliest settlement until statehood.

White, R. L. C. "The Great Seal of the State of Tennessee." *AHM* 6 (1901), 193-212; rpt. in *Tennessee Old and New,* I, 231-46.

Williams, Charlotte. "Legislative History of the Admission of Tennessee into the Federal Union." Thesis, Vanderbilt Univ., 1939.

——. "Congressional Action on the Admission of Tennessee into the Union." *THQ* 2 (1943), 291-315; rpt. in *Tennessee Old and New,* I, 27-50.

Williams, Samuel Cole. "The Admission of Tennessee into the Union." *THQ* 4 (1945), 291-319.

——. *The Admission of Tennessee into the Union.* Nashville: Tennessee Hist. Comm., 1945. 31 pp.

JOHN SEVIER

Carter, Clyde Cass. "Administrations of John Sevier." Thesis, Vanderbilt Univ., 1928.

Commission Book of Governor John Sevier, 1796-1801. Nashville: Tennessee Hist. Comm., 1957. 68 pp.

DeWitt, John H., ed. "Journal of John Sevier." *THM* 5 (1919), 156-94, 232-66; 6 (1920), 18-68.

Driver, Carl S. *John Sevier.* The author interprets Sevier in light of 20th-century scholarship, separating him from romantic legend. He expresses concern that our perspective of Tennessee's first governor has been distorted by the dominant position of Andrew Jackson in the state's history. He concludes that Sevier, when considered in terms of his own time, had remarkable abilities and should occupy a "position of some dignity and importance above others of his time and section."

Flournoy, Fitzgerald. "John Sevier, Huguenot Frontiersman and Commonwealth Builder." *The Huguenot* 7 (1935), 129-39.

Gilmore, James R. [pseud. Edmund Kirke]. *John Sevier as a Commonwealth Builder. A Sequel to "The Rear-Guard of the Revolution."* New York: Appleton, 1887. 321 pp.

Henderson, William A. *"Nolachucky Jack." Lecture of William A. Henderson to the Board of Trade of the City of Knoxville, January 7th, 1873.* Knoxville: *Press and Herald,* 1873. 22 pp.

Hildreth, Howard P. "John Sevier and Isaac Shelby." *Virginia Cavalcade* 14 (1964), 10-15.

Kirke, Edmund. *See* Gilmore, James R.

Perry, Catherine. "Life of John Sevier." Thesis, Vanderbilt Univ., 1923.

Sevier, Cora Bales, and Nancy S. Madden. *Sevier Family History, with the Collected Letters of General John Sevier, First Governor of Tennessee, and 28 Collateral Family Lineages.* Washington, D.C.: Kaufman, 1961. 558 pp.

Sevier, George W. "General John Sevier, a Sketch By His Son." *THM* (ser. 2) 1 (1930-31), 207-14.

Temple, Oliver P. *John Sevier, Citizen, Soldier, Legislator, Governor, Statesman, 1744-1815,* foreword Mary Boyce Temple. Knoxville: Zi-po Press, 1910. 28 pp.; rpt. in *Tennessee Old and New,* I, 155-66.

Turner, Francis Marion. *Life of General John Sevier.* New York: Neale, 1910. 226 pp.

Wilkie, Katherine E. *John Sevier, Son of Tennessee; Born: September 25, 1745, Died: September 24, 1815.* New York: Messner, 1958. 192 pp.

Williams, Samuel Cole. "Tennessee's First Military Expedition, 1803." *THM* 8 (1924), 171-90.

———., ed. "Executive Journal of Gov. John Sevier." ETHS*P* 1-7 (1929-35).

Land Speculation and Disposition

Alexander, Maude. "Public Lands of Tennessee." Thesis, George Peabody College, 1927.

Barnhart, John. *Valley of Democracy: The Frontier versus the Plantation in the Ohio Valley, 1775-1818.*

Bramlett, A. L. "North Carolina's Western Lands." Diss., Univ. of North Carolina, 1928.

Cartwright, Betty Goff Cook, and Lillian Johnson Gardiner, comps. *North Carolina Land Grants in Tennessee, 1778-1791,* foreword by Robert T. Quarles, Jr. Memphis: n.p., 1958. 199 pp.

Chappell, Gordon T. "Land Speculation and Taxation in Tennessee, 1790-1834." Thesis, Vanderbilt Univ., 1936.

Cumming, William P. *The Southeast in Early Maps, with an Annotated Check-List of Printed and Manuscript Regional and Local Maps of Southeastern North America during the Colonial Period.* Princeton: Princeton Univ. Press, 1958. 275 pp. Rev. ed., 1962. 284 pp.

Garrett, William R., and John Bass, eds. "Memorials Relative to Public Lands Claimed by the University of North Carolina." *AHM* 6 (1901), 268-82.

———. "Some Early North Carolina Legislation (1776)." *AHM* 6 (1901), 260-67. This legislation affected the area which is now Tennessee.

Goodpasture, Albert V. "Education and the Public Lands in Tennessee." *AHM* 4 (1899), 210-28.

Henry, Robert Selph. "Tennesseans and Territory." *THQ* 12 (1953), 195-203.

Hughes, Cleo A. "Speculation and Settlement in West Tennessee." Thesis, George Peabody College, 1968.

Jones, Thomas B. "The Public Lands of Tennessee." *THQ* 27 (1968), 13-36.

Keith, Alice B., and William H. Masterson, eds. *The John Gray Blount Papers.*

Leftwich, Nina. *Two Hundred Years at Muscle Shoals, Being an Authentic History of Colbert County, 1700-1900, with Special Emphasis on the Stirring Events of the Early Times.* Tuscumbia, Ala.: Privately printed, 1935; rpt. Northport, Ala.: Am. Southern, 1965. 279 pp.

"Legislature of Tennessee." *Niles' Weekly Register* 21 (1822), 299-300. This article refers to legislative action relating to the disposition of public land.

Rippy, Jird H. "A History of the School Lands of Tennessee." Thesis, George Peabody College, 1929.

Waite, Mariella D. "The North Carolina Land Cession of 1784." Thesis, Univ. of Florida, 1956.

Warden, Kenneth Wilson. "The History of the Administration of the Tennessee School Fund." Thesis, George Peabody College, 1920. This fund was derived from the sale of public land.

Whitaker, Arthur P. "The Muscle Shoals Speculation, 1783-1789." *MVHR* 13 (1926-27), 365-86.

Whitney, Henry D. *The Land Laws of Tennessee, Being a Compilation of the Various Statutes of North Carolina, the United States, and Tennessee, Relative to Titles to Lands within the State of Tennessee, from the Second Royal Charter to the Present Time; the Constitutional and Statutory Provisions concerning the Establishment and Change of the Boundary of the State, and of Each County; Tables Showing the Date of Each Hiatus, Editorial Notes, etc. to Which Is Added a Digest of Decisions on the Land Laws.* Chattanooga: J. M. Deardorff, 1891; rpt. Cincinnati: W. H. Anderson, 1893. 1136 pp.

Williams, Samuel Cole. "Henderson and Company's Purchase within the Limits of Tennessee." *THM* 5 (1919), 5-27.

Williams, Sarah V. "History of the Tennessee Public School Lands." Thesis, Vanderbilt Univ., 1944.

———. "Tennessee Public School Lands." *THQ* 3 (1944), 335-48.

BOUNDARY DISPUTES

Coulter, E. Merton. "The Georgia-Tennessee Boundary Line." *Georgia Historical Quarterly* 35 (1951), 269-306.

Davis, Ben T. "The Kentucky-Tennessee Line." *Kentucky State Bar Association Proceedings* (1925), 175-91.

De Vorsey, Louis, Jr. "The Virginia-Cherokee Boundary of 1771." ETHSP 33 (1961), 17-31.

———. *The Indian Boundary in the Southern Colonies, 1763-1775.* Chapel Hill: Univ. of North Carolina Press, 1966. 267 pp. The author describes this boundary as extending from the Ohio River south to the Florida Peninsula and west to the Mississippi River; the inclusive area was the focal point for Anglo-Indian relations in the Southeast.

Garrett, William R. *History of the South Carolina Cession, and the Northern Boundary of Tennessee,* Tennessee Historical Society Papers, 1884. Nashville: Southern Methodist Pub., 1884. 32 pp.

———., ed. "Southern Boundary Line of Tennessee, Report of Select Committee." *AHM* 5 (1900), 27-40.

———. "Northern Boundary of Tennessee." *AHM* 6 (1901), 18-39; rpt. in *Tennessee Old and New,* I, 404-24.

Hardesty, Charles Hugh. "The Kentucky-Tennessee Boundary Line." Thesis, Univ. of Louisville, 1928.

Henry, Robert S. "The Extension of the Northern Line of Tennessee to the West of the Cumberland Gap-Matthews Line." *THM* 6 (1920), 177-84.

Johnston, J. Stoddard. "Kentucky-Tennessee Boundary Line: History of the Line 36:30, the Boundary Line between Virginia and North Carolina and between Kentucky and Tennessee." *Register of the Kentucky Historical Society* 6 (1908), 23-35.

Luckett, William Wallace. "Important Boundary Disputes of Tennessee." Thesis, George Peabody College, 1926.

McCullar, Albert L. "The Kentucky-Tennessee Boundary Dispute." Thesis, Univ. of Kentucky, 1933.

Rouse, William H. "The Romance of a Boundary Line." *Virginia State Bar Association Proceedings,* 42nd annual meeting (c. 1931), 258-73.

Smith, Daniel. "The Journal of General Daniel Smith, August, 1779 to July, 1780 . . .", ed. St. George L. Sioussat. *THM* 1 (1915), 40-65. Rpt. Chattanooga: Cartter Patten, 1962. Smith was a member of the Boundary Commission to extend the line between Virginia and North Carolina.

Williams, Samuel Cole. "The North Carolina-Tennessee Boundary Line Survey, 1799." *THM* 6 (1920), 46-57.

NATCHEZ TRACE

Breazeale, J. W. M. *Life As It Is.*

Coates, Robert M. *The Outlaw Years: The History of the Land Pirates of the Natchez Trace.* New York: Macaulay, 1930. 308 pp.

Cotter, John L. "Prehistoric People along the Natchez Trace." *Journal of Mississippi History* 12 (1950), 231-37.

Cotterill, Robert S. "The Natchez Trace." *THM* 7 (1921), 27-35.

Daniels, Jonathan. *The Devil's Backbone: The Story of the Natchez Trace,* American Trail Series. New York: McGraw, 1962. 278 pp. This is the story of the Natchez Trace from De Soto's expedition in the 16th century until the creation of the Natchez Trace Parkway in the 20th century. The work's contents include brief sketches of many personalities and events playing significant roles in Tennessee history.

Dillon, Richard. *Meriwether Lewis: A Biography.* New York: Coward-McCann, 1965; rpt. New York: Putnam, 1968. 364 pp. Lewis died on the Natchez Trace.

Hudson, Susan. "The Natchez Trace." *DAR Magazine,* Oct. 1960, p. 576.

Jamison, Lena Mitchell. "The Natchez Trace: A Federal Highway of the Old Southwest." *Journal of Mississippi History* 1 (1939), 82-99.

Keating, Bern. "Today along the Natchez Trace, Pathway through History." *National Geographic Magazine,* Nov. 1968, pp. 641-67.

Marshall, Park. "The True Route of the Natchez Trace. The Rectification of a Topographical Error." *THM* 1 (1915), 173-82.

Moore, J. H. "The Death of Meriwether Lewis." *AHM* 9 (1904),

218-30; rpt. in *Tennessee Old and New,* I, 288-98.

Ogden, Florence S. "The Natchez Trace." *DAR Magazine,* Feb. 1964, pp. 108- .

Phelps, Dawson A. "Stands and Travel Accomodations on the Natchez Trace." *Journal of Mississippi History* 11 (1949), 1-54.

———. "Travel on the Natchez Trace: A Study of Its Economic Aspects." *Journal of Mississippi History* 15 (1953), 155-64.

———. "The Natchez Trace in Tennessee History." *THQ* 13 (1954), 195-203.

———. "The Tragic Death of Meriwether Lewis." *William and Mary Quarterly* 13 (1956), 305-18.

———. "The Natchez Trace, Indian Trail to Parkway." *THQ* 21 (1962), 203-18; rpt. in *Landmarks of Tennessee,* 241-56.

———. "Genesis of the Natchez Trace Parkway." WTHSP 19 (1965), 58-68.

Phelps, Dawson A., and Edward H. Ross. "Names Please: Place Names along the Natchez Trace." *Journal of Mississippi History* 14 (1952), 217-56.

Sioussat, St. George L., ed. "Roll of Tennessee Cavalrymen in the Natchez Expedition." *THM* 2 (1916), 295-98.

Swain, J. "Natchez Trace: A Journey to the Grave of Meriwether Lewis." *Everybody's Magazine,* Sept. 1905, pp. 329-36.

U.S. National Park Service. *Natchez Trace Parkway Survey. Letter to the Secretary of Interior Transmitting in Response to Senate Resolution no. 222, a Report of a Survey of the Old Indian Trail, Known as the Natchez Trace, Made by the Department of the Interior, through the National Park Service, Pursuant to an Act Approved May 21, 1934, with a View to Constructing a National Road on this Route to Be Known As the Natchez Trace Parkway.* Sen. Doc. 148, 76th Cong., 3rd sess., Washington, D.C.: GPO, 1941. 167 pp.

Wellman, Paul I. *Spawn of Evil; the Invisible Empire of Soulless Men Which for a Generation Held the Nation in a Spell of Terror.* Garden City, N.Y.: Doubleday, 1964; rpt. New York: Curtis, 1971. 350 pp. Describes outlaws along the early Tennessee routes of travel, including John A. Murrell, the Harp brothers, et al.

Cherokee and Other Indians
of Tennessee

EARLY INHABITANTS

Adair, James. *The History of the American Indians; Particularly
Those Nations Adjoining to the Mississippi, East and West Florida,
Georgia, South and North Carolina, and Virginia; Containing an
Account of Their Origin, Language, Manners , Religious and
Civil Customs, Laws, Form of Government, Punishments, Con-
duct in War and Domestic Life, Their Habits, Diet, Agriculture,
Manufactures, Diseases and Method of Cure . . . . With Observa-
tions on Former Historians, the Conduct of Our Colony Gov-
ernors, Superintendents, Missionaries &c. Also an Appendix
Containing a Description of the Floridas, and the Mississippi
Lands, with Their Productions—the Benefits of Colonizing
Georgiana, and Civilizing the Indians—and the Way to Make All
the Colonies More Valuable to the Mother Country. . . .* London:
E. & C. Dilly, 1775. 464 pp. Rev. ed., *Adair's History of the
American Indians*, ed. and annot. Samuel Cole Williams. Johnson
City: Watauga, 1930; rpt. Nashville: Nat. Soc. of Colonial Dames
of Am., 1953. Rpt. 1775 ed., American Studies Series, introd.
Robert F. Berkhofer, Jr. New York: Johnson Rpt., 1968. 508 pp.
Rpt. 1930 ed., New York: Arno, 1971. Adair was a trader among
the Cherokees and Chickasaws from 1735 to 1768. His account,
objective and balanced, is of the greatest importance.

Bailey, Carolyn S. *Stories from an Indian Cave; the Cherokee Cave
Builders*, Just Right Books. Chicago: Whitman, 1924. 217 pp.

Blanton, John O. *Pre-historic Man in Tennessee. The Problem
Solved. A Centennial Booklet.* Tracy City: Tracy City *News*,
1896. 20 pp. This is a period piece and is unreliable at best.

Brown, Anna B. A. "The Early Inhabitants of Tennessee." *AHM* 2
(1897), 147-52.

Corkran, David H. "Cherokee Pre-History." *NCHR* 34 (1957),
455-66.

Fischer, Fred W. "Before the Cherokee." *JTAS* 27 (1953), 265-68.

Guthe, Alfred K. "Tennessee's Paleo-Indian." *Tennessee Archaeologist* 22 (1966), 67-77.

Lewis, Thomas M. N. "The Lure of Prehistoric Tennessee." *JTAS* 10 (1935), 153-59.

——. *Annotations Pertaining to Prehistoric Research in Tennessee.* Knoxville: Dept. of Anthropology, Univ. of Tennessee, 1937. 28 pp.

——. "The Paleo-Indian Problem in Tennessee." *Tennessee Archaeologist* 9 (1953), 38-40.

Lewis, Thomas M. N., and Madeline Kneberg. *The First Tennesseans; an Interpretation of Tennessee Prehistory.* Knoxville: Dept. of Anthropology, Univ. of Tennessee, 1955. 111 leaves. This publication was revised and enlarged and issued as *Tribes That Slumber.*

——. *Tribes That Slumber.*

Lowrie, Walter, and Matthew St. Clair Clarke, eds. *American State Papers. Indian Affairs.* 2 vols. Washington, D.C.: Gales & Seaton, 1832-34. These volumes contain much primary material relating to the national government's relations with various Indian tribal groups between 1789 and 1814. A large part of this information concerns Indian affairs of the Southwest Territory and of the State of Tennessee.

Mooney, James. *The Aboriginal Population of America North of Mexico,* Smithsonian Miscellaneous Collections, vol. 80, no. 7. Washington, D.C.: Smithsonian Institution, 1928. 40 pp.

Myer, William E. "Indian Trails of the Southeast." *Forty-Second Annual Report of the Bureau of American Ethnology to the Secretary of the Smithsonian Institution, 1924-1925,* pp. 727-857. Washington, D.C.: GPO, 1928. Rpt. Nashville: Blue and Gray Press, 1971.

Shetrone, Henry Clyde. *The Mound-Builders; a Reconstruction of the Life of a Prehistoric American Race, through Exploration and Interpretation of Their Earth Mounds, Their Burials, and Their Cultural Remains.* New York: Appleton, 1930; rpt. Port Washington, N.Y.: Kennikat, 1964. 508 pp.

Silverberg, Robert. "And the Moundbuilders Vanished from the Earth." *American Heritage* 20 (1969), 60- .

Swanton, John R. "Aboriginal Culture in the Southeast." *Forty-Second Annual Report of the Bureau of American Ethnology to the Secretary of the Smithsonian Institution, 1924-1925,* pp. 677-726. Washington, D.C.: GPO, 1928.

Thomas, Cyrus. "The Cherokees Probably Mound Builders." *Fifth Annual Report of the Bureau of Ethnology to the Secretary of the Smithsonian Institution, 1833-84*, pp. 87-107. Washington, D.C.: GPO, 1887.

———. *The Cherokees as Mound Builders*, Smithsonian Institution Bureau of Ethnology Bulletin 8, pp. 31-37. Washington, D.C.: GPO, 1889.

———. *The Cherokees in Pre-Columbian Times*, Fact and Theory Papers no. 4. New York: N. D. C. Hodges, 1890. 97 pp.

Webb, William S. "The Prehistory of East Tennessee." ETHS*P* 8 (1936), 3-8.

Yarrow, H. C. "A Further Contribution to the Study of the Mortuary Customs of the North American Indians." *First Annual Report of the Bureau of Ethnology to the Secretary of the Smithsonian Institution, 1879-1880*, pp. 89-203. Washington, D.C.: GPO, 1881.

EARLY TRADE RELATIONS

Alden, John Richard. *John Stuart and the Southern Colonial Frontier: A Study of Indian Relations, War, Trade, and Land Problems in the Southern Wilderness, 1754-1775*, Univ. of Michigan Publications, History and Political Science, vol. 15. Ann Arbor: Univ. of Michigan Press, 1944; rpt. London: Oxford Univ. Press, 1944; rpt. Staten Island, N.Y.: Gardian, 1966. 384 pp.

Buchanan, D. P. "The Relations of the Cherokee Indians with the English in America prior to 1763." Thesis, Univ. of Tennessee, 1923.

Corkran, David H. *The Cherokee Frontier: Conflict and Survival, 1740-1762*. Norman: Univ. of Oklahoma Press, 1962, 1966. 302 pp.

De Filipis, M., ed. "An Italian Account of Cherokee Uprisings at Fort Loudoun and Fort Prince George, 1760-1761." *NCHR* 20 (1943), 247-58.

Franklin, W. Neil. "Virginia and the Cherokee Indian Trade, 1673-1752." ETHS*P* 4 (1932), 3-21.

———. "Virginia and the Cherokee Indian Trade, 1753-1775." ETHS*P* 5 (1933), 22-38.

Goodpasture, Albert V. "Portrait of Judge [Judd's] Friend."

THM 4 (1918), 155-56. Cherokee chief in London with Timberlake in the 1760s.

Hamer, Philip M. "Anglo-French Rivalry in the Cherokee Country, 1754-1757." *NCHR* 2 (1925), 303-22.

———. "Fort Loudoun in the Cherokee War, 1758-1761." *NCHR* 2 (1925), 442-58.

Henderson, Archibald. *The Conquest of the Old Southwest.*

Hunter, George. *George Hunter's Map of the Cherokee Country and the Path Thereto in 1730, with Comments, by A. S. Salley, Jr.,* South Carolina Hist. Comm. Bulletin 4. Columbia, S.C.: State Co., 1917. 5 pp.

McDermott, John F., ed. *The Western Journals of Dr. George Hunter, 1796-1805.* Philadelphia, Pa.: American Philosophical Soc., 1963. 133 pp.

Peake, O. B. *A History of the United States Indian Factory System, 1795-1822.* Denver, Colo.: Sage Books, 1954. 340 pp.

Philopatrios [pseud.]. *Some Observations on the Two Campaigns against the Cherokee Indians, in 1760 and 1761.* Charleston, S.C.: Timothy, 1762. 88 pp.

Rothrock, Mary U. "Carolina Traders among the Overhill Cherokees, 1690-1760." ETHSP 1 (1929), 3-18; rpt. in *Tennessee Old and New,* I, 69-83.

Thomas, Cyrus. *The Problem of the Ohio Mounds,* Smithsonian Institution Bureau of Ethnology Bulletin 8. Washington, D.C.: GPO, 1889. 54 pp. Contains a chapter on the Cherokees.

Timberlake, Henry. *The Memoirs of Lieut. Henry Timberlake (Who Accompanied the Three Cherokee Indians to England in the Year 1762), Containing Whatever He Observed Remarkable, or Worthy of Public Notice, during His Travels to and from That Nation; Wherein the Country, Government, Genius, and Customs of the Inhabitants, Are Authentically Described. Also the Principal Occurrences during Their Residence in London. Illustrated with an Accurate Map of Their Overhill Settlement, and a Curious Secret Journal, Taken by the Indians out of the Pocket of a Frenchman They Had Killed.* London: The Author, 1765. 160 pp. Rpt., titled *Lieut. Henry Timberlake's Memoirs, 1756-1765,* ed. Samuel Cole Williams. Johnson City: Watauga, 1927; rpt. Marietta, Ga.: Continental, 1948; rpt. First American Frontier Series. New York: Arno, 1971. 197 pp.

Williams, Samuel Cole, ed. *Dawn of Tennessee Valley and Tennessee History, 1541-1776.*

COLONIAL AND NATIONAL RELATIONSHIPS: 1763-1800

Adair, James. *History of the American Indians.*

Alden, John R. "Imperial Management of Indian Affairs in the South 1756-1775." Diss., Univ. of Michigan, 1939.

———. *John Stuart and the Southern Colonial Frontier.*

Baynton, Benjamin. *Authentic Memoirs of William Augustus Bowles, Esquire, Ambassador from the United Nations of Creeks and Cherokees, to the Court of London.* London: R. Fauldner, 1791. 79 pp. Rpt. Tarrytown, N.Y.: W. Abbatt, 1916. 25 pp. Rpt., 1791 ed., First American Frontier Series. New York: Arno, 1971.

Connelly, Thomas Lawrence. "Indian Warfare on the Tennessee Frontier, 1776-1794: Strategy and Tactics." ETHSP 36 (1964), 3-22.

Cotterill, Robert S. "Federal Indian Management in the South, 1789-1825." *MVHR* 20 (1933-34), 333-52.

———. "The Virginia-Chickasaw Treaty of 1783." *JSH* 8 (1942), 483-96. It was negotiated at Nashborough.

———. *The Southern Indians; the Story of the Civilized Tribes before Removal,* The Civilization of the American Indian Series, vol. 38. Norman: Univ. of Oklahoma Press, 1954, 1966. 255 pp. This work treats the major tribes of the South from the colonial period to the Removal, with emphasis upon the last quarter of the 18th century.

De Vorsey, Louis. "The Virginia-Cherokee Boundary of 1771." ETHSP 32 (1961), 17-31.

———. *The Indian Boundary in the Southern Colonies, 1763-1775.*

Downes, Randolph C. "Indian Affairs in the Southwest Territory, 1790-1796." *THM* (ser. 2) 3 (1932-37), 240-68.

———. "Cherokee-American Relations in the Upper Tennessee Valley, 1776-1791." ETHSP 8 (1936), 35-53.

———. "Cherokee-American Relations 1790-1795." *JSH* 8 (1942), 350-73.

Eaton, Miriam Boyd. "A History of the Cherokee Indians 1763-1776." Thesis, Univ. of Tennessee, 1928.

Foreman, Grant. "Captain John Stuart's Sketch of the Indians." *Chronicles of Oklahoma* 11 (1933), 667-72.

Frost, Ralph Walter. "A History of the Cherokee Indians of the Tennessee Region from 1783-1794." Thesis, Univ. of Tennessee, 1925.

Ganyard, Robert L. "Threat from the West: North Carolina and the Cherokee, 1776-1778." *NCHR* 45 (1968), 47-66.

Garrett, William R., ed. "Joseph Brown's Narrative." *AHM* 5 (1900), 200-203. Reminiscences of Middle Tennessee campaigns c. 1780.

Givan, Francis P. "Indian Affairs in the Southern Department, 1763-1785." Thesis, Univ. of Louisville, 1956.

Hamer, Philip M. "The British in Canada and the Southern Indians, 1790-1794." ETHS*P* 2 (1930), 107-34.

——., ed. "Correspondence of Henry Stuart and Alexander Cameron with the Wataugans." *MVHR* 17 (1930), 451-59.

——. "John Stuart's Indian Policy during the Early Months of the American Revolution." *MVHR* 17 (1930-31), 351-66.

——. "The Wataugans and the Cherokee Indians in 1776." ETHS*P* 3 (1931), 108-26.

Hemperley, Marion R., ed. "Benjamin Hawkins' Trip across Western and Northern Georgia, 1798." *Georgia Historical Quarterly* 41 (1972), 415-31. The trip to Tellico for the Treaty of 1798.

Herron, Richard W. "The Southern Indians as a Factor in the Relations of Spain and the U.S., 1783-1795." Thesis, Univ. of Cincinnati, 1938.

Horsman, Reginald. *Expansion and American Indian Policy, 1783-1812.* East Lansing: Michigan State Univ. Press, 1967. 209 pp. Horsman describes the tension between the nation's desire to expand because of population pressure, strategic reasons, and growing nationalism, and a genuine desire to treat the Indian fairly according to the developing national tradition.

Jackson, George B. "John Stuart: Superintendent of Indian Affairs for the Southern District." *THM* 3 (1917), 165-91.

Kimery, Greer Jackson. "Return Jonathan Meigs; Cherokee Indian Agent, 1801-1823." Thesis, Univ. of Tennessee, 1948.

McMurry, Donald L. "The Indian Policy of the Federal Government and the Economic Development of the Southwest, 1789-1801." *THM* 1 (1915), 21-39, 106-19.

Marshall, Peter D. "Imperial Regulation of American Indian Affairs 1763-1774." Diss., Yale Univ., 1959.

O'Donnell, James H., III. *The Southern Indians in the American Revolution.* Diss., Duke Univ., 1963. Knoxville: Univ. of Tennessee Press, 1973.

——. "The Virginia Expedition against the Overhill Cherokee, 1776." ETHS*P* 39 (1967), 13-25.

Peake, O. B. *A History of the United States Indian Factory System, 1795-1822.*

Pound, Merritt B. *Benjamin Hawkins, Indian Agent.* Athens: Univ. of Georgia Press, 1951. 270 pp. A biography of the best of the Indian agents sent to the South by the federal government. The author views Hawkins as being responsible for our Indian policy from 1783 to 1812. He suggests that, had Hawkins lived longer, our treatment of the Indians might have reflected greater credit upon the nation.

Shaw, Helen L. *The British Administration of the Southern Indians, 1756-1783.* Diss., Bryn Mawr, 1929. Lancaster, Pa.: Lancaster Press, 1931. 205 pp.

Stuart, John. *A Sketch of the Cherokee and Choctaw Indians.* Little Rock: Woodruff & Pew, 1837. 42 pp.

White, Kate. "John Adair, the Entry Taker." *THM* 8 (1924), 112-18.

Williams, Samuel Cole. "Colonel Joseph Williams' Battalion in Christian's Campaign." *THM* 9 (1925), 102-14. The 1776 movement against the Overhill Cherokees.

General History of the Cherokees

Allen, Ivan Ernest. *The Cherokee Nation: Fort Mountain, Vann House, Chester Inns, New Echota.* Atlanta: Allen, 1958. 59 pp.

Bleeker, Sonia. *The Cherokee; Indians of the Mountains.* New York: Morrow, 1952. 159 pp. Juvenile.

Brown, John P. *Old Frontiers: The Story of the Cherokee Indians from Earliest Times to the Date of Their Removal to the West, 1838.* Kingsport: Southern, 1938. Rpt., First American Frontier Series. New York: Arno, 1971. 570 pp.

Corn, James Franklin. *Red Clay and Rattlesnake Springs: A History of the Cherokee Indians of Bradley County, Tennessee.* Cleveland: n.p., 1959. 108 pp.

Cotterill, Robert S. *The Southern Indians.*

Dale, Edward Everett, and Gaston Litton. *Cherokee Cavaliers; Forty Years of Cherokee History As Told in the Correspondence of the Ridge-Watie-Boudinot Family,* The Civilization of the American Indian Series. Norman: Univ. of Oklahoma Press, 1939. 319 pp.

Derthick, Lawrence G. "The Indian Boundary Line in the Southern District of British North America, 1763-1779." Thesis, Univ. of Tennessee, 1930.

Donaldson, Thomas, ed. *Eastern Band of Cherokees in North Carolina.* Washington, D.C.: U.S. Census Office, 1892.

Driver, Leota S. "Colonel Richard Sparks—The White Indian." *THM* (ser. 2) 2 (1931-32), 96-110.

Farrand, Max. "The Indian Boundary Line." *AHR* 10 (1904-5), 782-91.

Fitzgerald, Mary N. *The Cherokees.* Knoxville: Coleman, 1937, 1939. 42 pp.

Foreman, Carolyn T. *Indians Abroad, 1493-1938,* The Civilization of the American Indian Series. Norman: Univ. of Oklahoma Press, 1943. 247 pp. The story of Indians taken to Europe and other parts of the world by the white man from the time of Columbus, including the 18th-century trips to England by Overhill Cherokee leaders.

Foreman, Grant. *The Five Civilized Tribes,* The Civilization of the American Indian Series, introd. John R. Swanton. Univ. of Oklahoma Press, 1934, 1971. 455 pp.

Gilbert, William H., Jr. *The Eastern Cherokees.* Diss., Univ. of Chicago, 1934. Smithsonian Institution, Bureau of American Ethnology Anthropological Papers no. 23, pp. 169-413. Washington, D.C.: GPO, 1943.

Goodpasture, Albert V. "Indian Wars and Warriors of the Old Southwest, 1730-1807." *THM* 4 (1918), 3-49, 106-45, 161-210, 252-89.

Gregg, Polly. "Change in Attitude toward the Indian As the Frontier Line Advanced." Thesis, East Tennessee State Univ., 1954.

Gulick, John. *Cherokees at the Crossroads,* University of North Carolina Institute for Research in Social Science Monographs. Chapel Hill: The Institute, 1960. 202 pp.

Hagy, James William, and Stanley J. Folmsbee. "The Lost Archives of the Cherokee Nation (1763-1772)." *ETHSP* 43 (1971), 112-22; (1772-1775) 44 (1972), 114-25.

Hale, William T. *The Backward Trail; Stories of the Indians and Tennessee Pioneers.* Nashville: Cumberland, 1899. 183 pp.

Kephart, Horace. *The Cherokees of the Smoky Mountains; a Little Band that has Stood against the White Tide for Three Hundred Years; Rewritten from the Papers of Horace Kephart.* Ithaca, N.Y.: Atkinson, 1936. 36 pp.

Knapp, David, Jr. "The Chickamaugas." *Georgia Historical Review*

51 (1967), 194-96. The Chickamaugas were offspring of the Cherokees.

McCall, William A. *Cherokees and Pioneers.* Asheville, N.C.: Stephens, 1952. 106 pp.

Malone, Henry Thompson. *Cherokees of the Old South: A People in Transition.* Athens, Ga.: Univ. of Georgia Press, 1956, 1966. 238 pp.

Parker, Thomas V. "Relations of the United States Government with the Cherokee Tribe." Diss., New York Univ., 1906.

——. *The Cherokee Indians, with Special Reference to Their Relations with the United States Government,* The Grafton Historical Series. New York: Grafton, 1907. 116 pp.

Pate, James Paul. "The Chickamauga: A Forgotten Segment of Indian Resistance on the Southern Frontier." Diss., Mississippi State Univ., 1969.

Prucha, Francis P. *American Indian Policy in the Formative Years: The Indian Trade and Intercourse Acts, 1780-1834.* Cambridge, Mass.: Harvard Univ. Press, 1962; rpt., Bison Bks. Lincoln: Univ. of Nebraska Press, 1970. 303 pp.

Reed, Gerard Alexander. "The Ross-Watie Conflict: Factionalism in the Cherokee Nation, 1839-1865." Diss., Univ. of Oklahoma, 1967.

Royce, Charles C. "The Cherokee Nation of Indians." *Fifth Annual Report of the Bureau of Ethnology to the Secretary of the Smithsonian Institution, 1883-84,* pp. 129-378. Washington, D.C.: GPO, 1887.

Smith, William R. L. *The Story of the Cherokees.* Cleveland: Church of God Pub., 1928. 229 pp.

Stambaugh, Samuel C., Amos Kendall, George W. Paschal, M. St. Clair Clarke. *A Faithful History of the Cherokee Tribe of Indians, from the Period of Our First Intercourse with Them, Down to the Present Time. The Reasons and Considerations Which Produced a Separation of the Tribe at an Early Period; Organizing a Nation East and a Nation West of the Mississippi River. With a Full Exposition of the Causes Which Led to Their Subsequent Division into Three Parties, and Involved Them in Their Present Deplorable Condition, and of the Nature and Extent of Their Present Claims.* Washington, D.C.: J. E. Dow, 1846. 40 pp.

Starkey, Marion L. *The Cherokee Nation.* New York: Knopf, 1946. 355 pp. A survey history of the Cherokees, this easily read work represents sound scholarship.

Swanton, John R. *The Indians of the Southeastern United States,* Smithsonian Institution Bureau of American Ethnology Bulletin 137. Washington, D.C.: GPO, 1946. 943 pp.

——. *The Indian Tribes of North America,* Smithsonian Institution Bureau of American Ethnology Bulletin 145. Washington, D.C.: GPO, 1952. 726 pp. Bibliography, 643-82.

Wales, G., and M. Roberts. *Indian Battles, Murders, Sieges and Forays in the South-west.* Nashville: n.p., 1853.

Wardell, Morris L. *A Political History of the Cherokee Nation, 1838-1907,* The Civilization of the American Indian Series, vol. 17. Norman: Univ. of Oklahoma Press, 1938. 383 pp.

Whitaker, Arthur P. "Spain and the Cherokee Indians, 1783-1796." *NCHR* 4 (1927), 252-69.

Wilkins, Thurman. *Cherokee Tragedy: The Story of the Ridge Family and the Decimation of a People.* New York: Macmillan, 1970. 398 pp. An eminent Cherokee family, the Ridges were in ascendant tribal leadership until toppled by their stand on western migration.

Woodward, Grace S. *The Cherokees,* The Civilization of the American Indian Series, vol. 65. Norman: Univ. of Oklahoma Press, 1963, 1965, 1969. 359 pp. This is a history of the Cherokees from the colonial period to the early 20th century, when Oklahoma was granted statehood.

Cultural History

Adair, John, comp. *Compiled Laws of the Cherokee Nation, Published by Authority of the General Council.* Talequah, I. T.: *National Advocate,* 1881. 370 pp. Rpt., Cherokee characters. Talequah: *National Advocate,* 1881. 335 pp.

Anderson, Thomas A. *Description of Hiwassee Old Town.* London: n.p. 1842. 8 pp.

Ballenger, Thomas L. "The Development of Law and Legal Institutions among the Cherokees." Diss., Univ. of Oklahoma, 1938.

Bartram, William. *Travels.* Bartram's description of the Cherokees and other southeastern Indians of that period is wholly important for the quality of his observation of folkways and mores.

Bass, Althea. *Cherokee Messenger,* The Civilization of the American Indian Series, vol. 12. Norman: Univ. of Oklahoma Press, 1936, 1968. 348 pp. The lives and work of Samuel Worcester and his wife, missionaries to the Cherokees from 1825 to 1859. Worcester translated the Christian Bible and a hymnbook into the Cherokee tongue.

Bloom, Leonard. "The Acculturation of the Eastern Cherokee: Historical Aspects." *NCHR* 19 (1942), 323-58.

Bushnell, David I., Jr. *Native Cemeteries and Forms of Burial East of the Mississippi,* Smithsonian Institution Bureau of American Ethnology Bulletin 71. Washington, D.C.: GPO, 1920. 160 pp. Cherokee burial customs are described pp. 90-93.

Dickson, John. "The Judicial History of the Cherokee Nation from 1721 to 1835." Diss., Univ. of Oklahoma, 1964.

Dugger, Shepherd M. *The War Trails of the Blue Ridge, Containing an Authentic Description of the Battle of Kings Mountain, the Incidents Leading up to and the Echoes of the Aftermath of This Epochal Engagement, and Other Stories Whose Scenes Are Laid in the Blue Ridge.* Banner Elk, N.C.: The Author, 1932. 324 pp.

Eggan, Frederick R., ed. *Social Anthropology of North American Tribes.* Chicago: Univ. of Chicago Press, 1937. 456 pp. Rpt. Chicago: Univ. of Chicago Press, 1955. 574 pp. Includes section on the Eastern Cherokee social organization.

Fitzgerald, Mary Newman. *The Cherokee and His Smoky Mountain Legends.* 3rd ed. Asheville, N.C.: Stephens, 1946. 44 pp.

Foster, George Everett. *Literature of the Cherokees: Also, Bibliography and the Story of Their Genesis, Social Organization, Law and Religion, Presented to Professor A. R. Radcliffe-Brown upon the Occasion of His Accepting the Chair of Social Anthropology at Oxford University.* Ithaca, N.Y.: *Democrat* Press, 1889; rpt. Muscogee, I.T.: *Phoenix,* 1889. 12 pp.

——. *Reminiscences of Travel in Cherokee Lands. An Address Delivered before the Ladies' Missionary Society of the Ithaca, New York, Congregational Church, 1898.* Ithaca, N.Y.: *Democrat* Press, 1899. 76 pp. Bound with Foster's *Story of the Cherokee Bible.*

Gearing, Fred. "The Structural Poses of 18th Century Cherokee Villages." *American Anthropologist* 60 (1958), 1148-57.

Gaston, Litton. "Enrollment Records of the Eastern Band of Cherokee Indians." *NCHR* 17 (1940), 199-231.

Hill, J. J., comp. *Old Cherokee Families: "Old Families and Their Genealogy"... with a Comprehensive Index.* Norman: Univ. of Oklahoma Press, 1968. 476 pp.

Holland, Cullen J. "The Cherokee Indian Newspapers, 1828-1906:

The Tribal Voice of a People in Transition." Diss., Univ. of Minnesota, 1956; copy, Ann Arbor, Mich.: Univ. Microfilms, no. 22, 491, 1956. 606 pp.

Laws of the Cherokee Nation: Adopted by the Council at Various Periods 1808-1835. Printed for the Benefit of the Nation. Tahlequah, C.N.: *Cherokee Advocate,* 1852. 179 pp.

Lewis, Thomas M. N., and Madeline Kneberg. "The Cherokee 'Hothouse.'" *Tennessee Archaeologist* 9 (1953), 2-5.

Mahoney, James W. *The Cherokee Physician . . . As Given by Richard 'Foreman.* Chattanooga: J. M. Edney, 1846. 416 pp.

Malone, Henry T. "A Social History of the Eastern Cherokee Indians from the Revolution to Removal." Diss., Emory Univ., 1952.

Mooney, James. "The Sacred Formulas of the Cherokees." *Seventh Annual Report of the Bureau of Ethnology to the Secretary of the Smithsonian Institution, 1885-86,* pp. 301-97. Washington, D.C.: GPO, 1891.

———. "Myths of the Cherokee." *Nineteenth Annual Report of the Bureau of American Ethnology to the Secretary of the Smithsonian Institution, 1897-98,* pp. xxxviii-ix, 3-568. Washington, D.C.: GPO, 1900. Rpt., American Indian History Series. St. Clair Shores, Mich.: Scholarly Press, 1970. Rpt., Landmarks in Anthropology Series. New York: Johnson Rpt., 1970. Rpt. Nashville: Elder, 1972. 576 pp.

———. *The Swimmer Manuscript: Cherokee Sacred Formulas and Medicinal Prescriptions,* rev., completed, and ed. Frans M. Olbrechts, Smithsonian Institution Bureau of American Ethnology Bulletin 99. Washington, D.C.: GPO, 1932. 319 pp. Rpt. Nashville: Elder, 1972.

Myer, William E. "Indian Trails of the Southeast." *Forty-Second Annual Report of the Bureau of American Ethnology to the Secretary of the Smithsonian Institution, 1924-1925,* pp. 727-857. Washington, D.C.: GPO, 1928. Rpt. Nashville: Blue & Gray, 1971. 132 pp.

Reid, John P. *A Law of Blood: The Primitive Law of the Cherokee Nation.* New York: New York Univ. Press, 1970. 340 pp.

Speck, Frank G., Leonard Broom, and Will West Long. *Cherokee Dance and Drama.* Berkeley: Univ. of California Press, 1951. 106 pp.

Starr, Emmet. *Early History of the Cherokees: Embracing Aboriginal*

Customs, Religion, Laws, Folklore and Civilization. Claremore, Okla.: n.p., 1917. 254 pp.

——. *History of the Cherokee Indians and Their Legends and Folklore.* Oklahoma City: Warden, 1921. 680 pp. Rpt., 1921 ed., Millwood, N.Y.: Kraus, 1969. Rev. ed., ed. Jack Gregory and Rennard Strickland. Fayetteville, Ark.: n.p., 1967.

CHEROKEE LEADERS

John Ross

Eaton, Rachael C. *John Ross and the Cherokee Indians.* Diss., Univ. of Chicago, 1919. Menasha, Wis.: Banta, 1914. 212 pp. Rpt. Muskogee, Okla.: *Star,* 1921. 153 pp.

Meserve, John Bartlett. "Chief John Ross." *Chronicles of Oklahoma* 13 (1935), 421-37.

Ruskin, Gertrude McDaris. *John Ross, Chief of an Eagle Race.* Chattanooga: John Ross House Assoc., 1963.

Sequoyah

Bird, Traveller. *Tell Them They Lie. The Sequoyah Myth.* Los Angeles: Western Lore, 1971. 148 pp. This work develops the dubious thesis that Sequoyah was a mythical figure.

Buttrick, Daniel S., and David Brown. *TSVLVKI SQCLVLV: A Cherokee Spelling Book.* Knoxville: Heiskell & Brown, 1819. 62 pp.

Coblentz, Catherine C. *Sequoya.* New York: Longmans, Green, 1946, 1948; rpt. New York: McKay, 1962. 199 pp.

Foreman, Grant. *Sequoyah,* The Civilization of the American Indian Series, vol. 16. Norman: Univ. of Oklahoma Press, 1938, 1959. 90 pp. The best biography of this noble Cherokee who gave his people their first syllabary, that they might have a written language.

Foster, George Everett. *Se-quo-yah; the American Cadmus and Modern Moses. A Complete Biography of the Greatest of Redmen, around Whose Wonderful Life Has Been Woven the Manners, Customs and Beliefs of the Early Cherokees, Together with a Recital of Their Wrongs and Wonderful Progress toward Civilization,* illus. Miss C. S. Robbins. Philadelphia, Pa.: Off. of the Indian Rights Assoc., 1885; rpt. Tahlequah,

C.N.: Stone, 1885. Rpt. New York: B. Franklin, 1971.

Marriott, Alice L. *Sequoyah: Leader of the Cherokees,* Landmark Series. New York: Random, 1956. 180 pp. A popular brief account of Sequoyah for juveniles.

Williams, Samuel Cole. "Nathaniel Gist, Father of Sequoyah." ETHS*P* 5 (1933), 39-54.

Nancy Ward

Burns, Annie Walker, comp. *Military and Genealogical Records of the Famous Indian Woman; Nancy Ward. . . .* Washington, D.C.: n.p., 1957. 286 leaves.

Foreman, Carolyn Thomas. *Indian Women Chiefs.* Muskogee [?], Okla.: n.p., 1954. 86 pp. A good account of Nancy Ward is included.

King, Elisha Sterling. *The Wild Rose of Cherokee; or, Nancy Ward, "The Pocahontas of the West." A Story of the Early Exploration, Occupancy and Settlement of the State of Tennessee. A Romance, Founded on and Interwoven with History.* Nashville: Univ. Press, 1895. 119 pp. Rpt. Etowah: Myrtle K. Tatum, 1938. 130 pp. Romantic fiction.

McClary, Ben Harris. "Nancy Ward: The Last Beloved Woman of the Cherokees." *THQ* 21 (1962), 352-64.

Tucker, Norma. "Nancy Ward, Ghighau of the Cherokees." *Georgia Historical Quarterly* 53 (1969), 192-200.

CHRISTIAN MISSIONS

Anderson, Rufus. *Memoir of Catharine Brown, a Christian Indian of the Cherokee Nation.* Boston: Armstrong, and Crocker & Brewster, 1825; New York: Haven, 1825. 180 pp. 2nd ed., Boston: Crocker & Brewster; New York: Haven, 1825. 144 pp. Rev. ed., Philadelphia Pa.: Am. Sunday School Union, 1832. 138 pp.

Bass, Althea. *Cherokee Messenger.* Biography of Samuel A. Worcester, missionary to the Cherokees.

Berkhofer, Robert F. "Protestant Missionaries to the American Indians, 1789 to 1862." Diss., Cornell Univ., 1960.

Crouch, William Ward. "Missionary Activities among the Cherokee Indians, 1757-1838." Thesis, Univ. of Tennessee, 1932.

Edwards, Martha L. "Government Patronage of Indian Missions." Diss., Univ. of Wisconsin, 1916.

Fleming, Robert. *Sketch of the Life of Elder Humphrey, First Baptist Missionary to the Cherokee Indians.* Philadelphia, Pa.: King & Baird, 1852.

Foster, George E. *Story of the Cherokee Bible. An Address, with Additional and Explanatory Notes, Delivered before the Meeting of the Ladies' Missionary Society of the First Congregational Church, Ithaca, N.Y., Feb. 5, 1897,* Cherokee History Series. Enl. 2nd ed., Ithaca, N.Y.: *Democrat* Press, 1899. 89 pp. With this is bound Foster's *Reminiscences of Travel in Cherokee Lands.*

Gabriel, Ralph H. *Elias Boudinot, Cherokee, and His America.* Norman: Univ. of Oklahoma Press, 1941. 190 pp. A biography of a Cherokee leader who, with his New England-born wife, exemplified American Protestantism confronting not only a race problem, but also one of adjustment between two radically different cultures.

Malone, Henry Thompson. "The Early Nineteenth Century Missionaries in the Cherokee Country." *THQ* 10 (1951), 127-39.

Moffitt, James W. "Early Baptist Missionary Work among the Cherokees." ETHSP 12 (1940), 16-27.

——. "A History of Early Baptist Missions among the Five Civilized Tribes." Diss., Univ. of Oklahoma, 1946.

Queener, Verton M. "Gideon Blackburn." ETHSP 6 (1934), 12-28. Blackburn was a Presbyterian missionary to the Cherokees in the early 1800s.

Walker, Robert S. *Torchlights to the Cherokees: The Brainerd Mission.* New York: Macmillan, 1931. 339 pp. Brainerd was an outstanding center of Christian mission to the Cherokees and was located near Chattanooga from 1817 to 1838.

Williams, Samuel Cole. "An Account of the Presbyterian Mission to the Cherokees, 1757-1759." *THM* (ser. 2) 1 (1930-31), 125-38.

——. "Christian Missions to the Overhill Cherokees." *Chronicles of Oklahoma* 12 (1934), 66-73.

Wood, George W. *Report of Mr. Wood's Visit to the Choctaw and Cherokee Missions, 1855.* Boston: T. R. Marvin, 1855. 24 pp.

Treaties: 1800-1839

Coe, Robert H. "Benjamin Hawkins, Indian Agent from 1796-1817." Thesis, Univ. of Tennessee, 1926.

Goodpasture, Albert V., ed. "McMinn Correspondence on the

Subject of Indian Treaties in the Years 1815, 1816, and 1817."
AHM 8 (1903), 377-94.

Kimery, Greer Jackson. "Return Jonathan Meigs, Cherokee Indian Agent, 1801-1823." Thesis, Univ. of Tennessee, 1948.

Lea, John M. "Indian Treaties of Tennessee." *AHM* 6 (1901), 367-80.

Malone, Henry T. "Return Jonathan Meigs: Indian Agent Extraordinary." ETHS*P* 28 (1956), 3-22.

——. "Cherokee-White Relations on the Southern Frontier in the Early Nineteenth Century." *NCHR* 34 (1957), 1-14.

Peake, Ora Brooks. *A History of the United States Indian Factory System, 1795-1822.* Denver: Sage Bks., 1954. 340 pp.

Pound, Merritt B. *Benjamin Hawkins.*

Royce, Charles C. "The Cherokee Nation of Indians." *Fifth Annual Report of the Bureau of Ethnology to the Secretary of the Smithsonian Institution, 1883-84,* pp. xlii-iv, 129-378. Excellent treatment of treaties.

Starr, Emmet. *Cherokees "West," 1794-1839.* Oklahoma City: Warden, 1921. 164 pp.

Treaties between the United States and the Cherokee Nation from 1785. Tahlequah, C.N.: n.p., 1870.

Wooten, John Morgan. *Red Clay in History.* Cleveland: n.p., 1935. 11 pp.

——. *Red Clay Council Ground, 1832-1838; Last Capital of the Cherokee Nation East of the Mississippi River.* Cleveland: n.p., 1935. 15 pp.

REMOVAL

Abel, Annie H. "The History of the Events Resulting in Indian Consolidations West of the Mississippi." *American Historical Association Annual Report, 1906,* II, 233-450. Washington, D.C.: GPO, 1908.

Brown, John P. "Cherokee Removal, an Unnecessary Tragedy." ETHS*P* 11 (1939), 11-19.

Corn, James F. "Removal of the Cherokee from the East." *FCHQ* 27 (1953), 37-51.

Foreman, Grant, ed. "Journey of a Party of Cherokee Emigrants."

MVHR 18 (1931-32), 232-45. Early evacuation of a group from Ross's Landing.

———. *Indian Removal: The Emigration of the Five Civilized Tribes of Indians*, The Civilization of the American Indian Series, vol. 2. Norman: Univ. of Oklahoma Press, 1932; new ed., 1953; rpt. 1932 ed., 1972. 415 pp. An account of the removal of the southern Indians by the federal government following the election of Andrew Jackson. Foreman stresses the government's failure to comprehend its task, resulting in much unnecessary suffering by the emigrants. He does, however, commend the regular army for its work, which he considers to have been far superior to that of most militia troops and civilians connected with removal.

———. *Advancing the Frontier, 1830-1860*, The Civilization of the American Indian Series, vol. 4. Norman: Univ. of Oklahoma Press, 1933, 1968. 363 pp. Foreman describes the advancing frontier in Oklahoma in terms of the arrival of the immigrant Indians from the East and the steadily advancing chain of military forts near the Territory.

Gabriel, Ralph H. *Elias Boudinot.*

Hoffman, William S. "Andrew Jackson, State Rightist: The Case of the Georgia Indians." *THQ* 11 (1952), 329-45.

McGhee, Lucy Kate, comp. "Cherokee and Creek Indians. Returns of Property Left in Tennessee and Georgia, 1838." Washington, D.C.: Unpublished typescript, 1957. 32 leaves.

Memorial of the Cherokee Representatives Submitting the Protest of the Treaty of New Echota. Washington, D.C.: n.p., 1836.

Myers, Minnie Hazel. "Tennessee's Policy in the Removal of the Cherokee." Thesis, Univ. of Tennessee, 1937.

Prucha, Francis P. "Andrew Jackson's Indian Policy: A Reassessment." *JAH* 56 (1969-70), 527-39.

———. "Indian Removal and the Great American Desert." *Indiana Magazine of History* 59 (1963), 299-322.

Radford, P. M. "The Cherokee Indians: Their Expatriation from Georgia." *AHM* 2 (1897), 139-46.

Royce, Charles C., comp. "Indian Land Cessions in the United States." *Eighteenth Annual Report of the Bureau of American Ethnology to the Secretary of the Smithsonian Institution, 1896-97*, pp. 521-964. Washington, D.C.: GPO, 1899. Rpt., First American Frontier Series. New York: Arno, 1971. 477 pp.

Sioussat, St. George L. "Tennessee and the Removal of the Chero-kees." *Sewanee Review* 16 (1908), 337-44.

Underwood, Thomas Bryan, and Moselle S. Sandlin, adapts. *Legends of the Ancient Cherokees,* adapted from *Nineteenth Annual Report of the Bureau of American Ethnology to the Secretary of the Smithsonian Institution, 1897-98.* Asheville, N.C.: Stephens, 1956; rpt. as *Cherokee Legends and the Trail of Tears.* Knoxville: Newman, 1956. 32 pp. Includes the John Burnett version of the Cherokee Removal, courtesy of the Museum of the Cherokee Indian, Cherokee, N.C.

——. *The Story of the Cherokee People.* Knoxville: Newman, 1961. 48 pp.

Wilkins, Thurman. *Cherokee Tragedy.*

Wills, Jesse E. *Meditations on the American Indian.* Nashville: The Author, 1971. 86 pp.

Young, Mary E. "Indian Removal and Land Allotment: The Civilized Tribes and Jacksonian Justice." *AHR* 64 (1958-59), 31-45.

THE CHICKASAWS

Braden, Guy B. "The Colberts and the Chickasaw Nation." *THQ* 17 (1958), 222-49, 318-35.

Caldwell, Norman W. "The Chickasaw Threat to French Control of the Mississippi." *Chronicles of Oklahoma* 16 (1938), 465-92.

Gibson, Arrell M. *The Chickasaws,* The Civilization of the American Indian Series, vol. 109. Norman: Univ. of Oklahoma Press, 1971. 312 pp.

Higgins, Joseph. "The Chickasaw Nation." *THM* 8 (1924), 140-41.

Malone, James H. *The Chickasaw Nation; a Short Sketch of a Noble People, Souvenir of Memphis Centenary Celebration, May 19-24, 1919.* Kansas City: E. L. Mendenhall, 1919. 175 pp.; enl. ed., Louisville, Ky.: Morton, 1922. 537 pp.

Marshall, Park. "Cushman's History of the Indians—Choctaws, Chickasaws and Natchez." *THM* 9 (1925), 59-65.

Phelps, Dawson A. "The Chickasaw, the English and the French, 1699-1744." *THQ* 16 (1957), 117-33.

Porter, James D. "The Chickasaw Treaty of 1818."*AHM* 9 (1904), 252-56.

Swanton, John R. "Social and Religious Beliefs and Usages of the Chickasaw Indians." *Forty-Fourth Annual Report of the Bureau of American Ethnology to the Secretary of the Smithsonian Institution, 1924-1925,* 169-273. Washington, D.C.: GPO, 1928.

Underhill, Ruth M. *Red Man's Religion: Beliefs and Practices of the Indians North of Mexico.* Chicago: Univ. of Chicago Press, 1965, 1972. 301 pp.

THE CREEKS

Caughey, John W. *McGillivray of the Creeks,* The Civilization of the American Indian Series, vol. 18. Norman: Univ. of Oklahoma Press, 1938, 1959. 385 pp. An outstanding biography and collection of papers of this, the greatest of the Creek leaders, a half-breed whose diplomacy and wile enabled the Creeks of the late 18th century to contend with the white man for a generation longer than they might otherwise have done.

Claiborne, W. C. C. *Official Letter Books of W. C. C. Claiborne, 1801-1816,* ed. Dunbar Roland. 6 vols. Jackson: Mississippi Dept. of Archives and Hist., 1917; rpt. New York: AMS, 1972.

Curry, J. L. M. "Creek Indians: Historical Facts and Personal Reminiscences." *AHM* 2 (1897), 103-12.

Downes, Randolph C. "Creek-American Relations, 1790-1795." *JSH* 8 (1942), 350-73.

Garrett, William R. and John M. Bass. "Proceedings of Courts-Martial in the Creek War." *AHM* 6 (1901), 251-59.

——., eds. "Documents Relating to the Creek War." *AHM* 7 (1902), 209-18.

Halbert, Henry S., and T. H. Ball. *The Creek War of 1813 and 1814.* Chicago: Donohue & Henneberry, 1895; Montgomery, Ala.: White, Woodruff & Fowler, 1895. Rpt., Southern History Publications 15, ed. Frank L. Owsley, Jr. Tuscaloosa: Univ. of Alabama Press, 1969. 331 pp. This work is considered the most detailed and accurate of older works treating the Creek War. Owsley considers the authors' most valuable contribution to be their use of manuscripts and reminiscences of contemporaries.

Owsley, Frank L., Jr. "Benjamin Hawkins, Political Leader and Indian Agent." Thesis, Univ. of Alabama, 1951.

——. "Benjamin Hawkins, the First Modern Indian Agent." *Alabama Historical Quarterly* 30 (1968), 7-13.

———. "The Fort Mims Massacre." *Alabama Review* 24 (1971), 192-203.

Putnam, Albigence W., ed. "Alexander McGillivray, The Creek Chief." *AHM* 4 (1899), 304-15. Letters with no annotations.

Swanton, John R. *Early History of the Creek Indians and Their Neighbors,* Smithsonian Institution Bureau of American Ethnology Bulletin 73. Washington, D.C.: GPO, 1922. Rpt., Landmarks in Anthropology Series. New York: Johnson Rpts., 1971. 492 pp.

———. "Social Organization and Social Usages of the Indians of the Creek Confederacy." *Forty-Second Annual Report of the Bureau of American Ethnology to the Secretary of the Smithsonian Institution, 1924-1925,* pp. 31-672. Washington, D.C.: GPO, 1928. Rpt., Landmarks in Anthropology Series. New York: Johnson Rpts., 1970. 472 pp.

Whitaker, Arthur P. "Alexander McGillivray, 1783-1789." *NCHR* 5 (1928), 181-203, 289-309.

Woodward, Thomas S. *Woodward's Reminiscences of the Creek, or Muscogee Indians, Contained in Letters to Friends in Georgia and Alabama.* Montgomery, Ala.: Berrett & Wimbish, 1859; rpt. Tuscaloosa: Alabama Bk. Store; rpt. Birmingham: Birmingham Bk. Exchange, 1939. 168 pp. Rev. ed., Birmingham: Southern Univ. Press, 1970. 149 pp.

Andrew Jackson

Bibliographies

Shaw, Ronald E. *Andrew Jackson, 1767-1845: Chronology, Documents, Bibliographical Aids.* Dobbs Ferry, N.Y.: Oceana, 1969. 123 pp. For grades 9-12.

Wise, W. Harvey, Jr., and John W. Cronin, comps. *A Bibliography of Andrew Jackson and Martin Van Buren,* Presidential Bibliographical Series, vol. 5. Washington, D.C.: Riverford, 1935. 72 pp. Rpt., New York: B. Franklin, 1970. 66 pp.

General Histories and Biographies

Abernethy, Thomas P. "Andrew Jackson and the Rise of Southwestern Democracy." *AHR* 33 (1927-28), 64-77.

———. "The Political Geography of Southern Jacksonianism." *ETHSP* 3 (1931), 35-41.

———. *From Frontier to Plantation in Tennessee.* One of the earliest modern critiques of Jackson and Jacksonian Democracy.

Allison, John. *Dropped Stitches in Tennessee History.* Nashville: Marshall & Bruce, 1897; rpt. Nashville: Charles Elder, 1971. 152 pp.

"Andrew Jackson." *DAR Magazine,* Mar. 1966, p. 204.

"Andrew Jackson." *Harper's New Monthly Magazine* 10 (1855), 145-72.

Andrist, Ralph K. *Andrew Jackson: Soldier and Statesman,* American Heritage Junior Library, consultant Arthur M. Schlesinger, Jr. New York: *American Heritage,* 1963. 153 pp.

Bassett, John Spencer. *The Life of Andrew Jackson.* 2 vols. Garden City, N.Y.: Doubleday, 1911. Rpt. New York: Macmillan, 1916, 1925, 1928, 1931. Rpt., 2 vols. in 1, Hamden, Conn.: Shoe String, 1967. 766 pp. Probably the best single biography of Jackson available.

——., ed. *Correspondence of Andrew Jackson,* Carnegie Institution of Washington Dept. of Historical Research Publication 371. 7 vols. Washington, D.C.: Carnegie Institution, 1926-35; rpt. Millwood, N.Y.: Kraus, 1969. The 7th volume is an index comp. by D. M. Matteson.

Beard, William E. "Democracy's Two-Thirds Rule Rounds Out a Century." *THM* (ser. 2) 2 (1931-32), 87-95.

Benson, Lee. *The Concept of Jacksonian Democracy: New York as a Test Case.* Princeton: Princeton Univ. Press, 1961; rpt. New York: Atheneum, 1964. 351 pp.

Blau, Joseph L., ed. *Social Theories of Jacksonian Democracy: Representative Writings of the Period 1825-1850.* New York: Hafner, 1947. Rpt., The American Heritage Series, vol. I. New York: Bobbs-Merrill, 1954. 383 pp.

Bowers, Claude G. *The Party Battles of the Jackson Period.* Boston: Houghton, 1922, 1924, 1928; rpt. New York: Octagon, 1965. 506 pp.

——. *Making Democracy a Reality: Jefferson, Jackson, Polk.* Memphis: Memphis State College Press, 1954. 170 pp.

Brady, Cyrus Townsend. *The True Andrew Jackson,* The "True" Series. Philadelphia, Pa.: Lippincott, 1906. 504 pp.

Briggs, Carolyn V. "Andrew Jackson: Frontier Statesman." Thesis, Tennessee State A & I Univ., 1961.

Brown, John F., and William White. *Messages of Gen. Andrew Jackson: With a Short Sketch of His Life.* Concord, N.H.: n.p., 1837. 429 pp.

Brown, William G. *Andrew Jackson,* The Riverside Biographical Series, vol. 1. Boston: Houghton, 1900. 156 pp.

Buell, Augustus C. *History of Andrew Jackson, Pioneer, Patriot, Soldier, Politician, President.* 2 vols. New York: Scribners, 1904.

Burke, John Emmett. "Andrew Jackson As Seen by Foreigners." *THQ* 10 (1951), 25-45.

By an American Officer. Civil and Military History of Andrew Jackson, Late Major General in the Army of the United States, and Commander in Chief of the Southern Division. New York: P. M. Davis, 1825. 359 pp.

By a Free Man. *A Brief and Impartial History of the Life and Actions of Andrew Jackson.* Boston: Stimpson & Clapp, 1831.

Campbell, Tom W. *Two Fighters and Two Fines: Sketches of the*

Lives of Matthew Lyon and Andrew Jackson. Little Rock: Pioneer, 1941. 557 pp.

Catterall, Ralph Charles Henry. *The Second Bank of the United States,* The Decennial Publications of the University of Chicago, 2nd Series, vol. 1. Chicago: Univ. of Chicago Press, 1903; rpt., Chicago Reprint Series. Chicago: Univ. of Chicago Press, 1960. 538 pp.

Cave, Alfred A. "The Jacksonian Movement in American Historiography." Diss., Univ. of Florida, 1961; copy, Ann Arbor: Univ. Microfilms, 1962.

——. *Jacksonian Democracy and the Historians,* University of Florida Monographs, Social Sciences, no. 22. Gainesville: Univ. of Florida, 1964. 86 pp. A useful guide to the bibliography of the Jackson era prior to 1964.

Clark, John B., Jr. "Andrew Jackson: Fire Fighter." *THQ* 19 (1960), 162-65.

Cobbett, William. *Life of Andrew Jackson, President of the United States of America.* Baltimore: J. Robinson, 1834. 81 pp. Rev. ed. London: Mills, Jarnett, & Mills, 1834. 142 pp. Rpt. New York: Richards, 1834. 16 pp.

Colyar, Arthur St. Clair. *Life and Times of Andrew Jackson: Soldier—Statesman—President.* 2 vols. Nashville: Marshall & Bruce, 1904. Rpt. in Thomas Wesley Martin, *Horseshoe Bend Military Park,* pp. 202-93. Birmingham: Horseshoe Bend Battle Park Assoc., 1957. 293 pp.

Cooper, James Fenimore. *The American Democrat; or, Hints on the Social and Civic Relations of the United States of America.* Cooperstown, N.Y.: H. & E. Phinney, 1838. 192 pp. Rpt., ed. H. L. Mencken. New York: Knopf, 1931. 134 pp. Rpt., introd. H. L. Mencken and introd. note Robert E. Spiller. New York: Vintage, 1956. 190 pp. Rpt. New York: Funk, 1969. 184 pp. Rpt., Classic Series. Ed. George Dekker and Larry Johnston. Baltimore: Penguin, 1970; rpt. Gloucester, Mass.: P. Smith, 1972. 236 pp.

Dangerfield, George. *The Era of Good Feelings.* New York: Harcourt, 1952. Rpt., Harbinger Bks. New York: Harcourt, 1963. 525 pp.

De Tocqueville, Alexis. *Democracy in America,* trans. Henry Reeve. 4 vols. London: Sanders & Atley, 1835-40. Abridg. eds., The World's Classics Series, trans. Henry Reeve, ed. Henry Steele Commager. New York, London: Oxford Univ. Press, 1947. 513 pp. 1952. 599 pp. New ed., trans. George Lawrence, ed.

J. P. Mayer. New York: Doubleday, 1969. 778 pp. From the original edition, in French (Brussels, 1835), through the many recent ones, only 3 of which are cited here, this justly famous work has gone through many editions both in Europe and in the United States.

Doherty, Herbert J., Jr., ed. "Andrew Jackson on Manhood Suffrage: 1822." *THQ* 15 (1956), 57-60.

Eaton, John H., ed. *The Life of Andrew Jackson, Major General in the Service of the United States: Comprising a History of the War in the South, from the Commencement of the Creek Campaign, to the Termination of Hostilities before New Orleans.* Philadelphia, Pa.: M. Carey and Son, 1817 (425 pp.); rpt. S. F. Bradford, 1824 (468 pp.); rev. ed., McCarty & Davis, 1828 (338 pp.); rpt. Claxton, Ramsen & Haffelfinger, 1878 (362 pp.). Rpt. 1824 ed., First American Frontier Series. New York: Arno, 1971. 468 pp. Chs. 1-4 were written by Major John Reid, an eyewitness; the rest were edited by Eaton.

Floyd, Viola Caston. "Andrew Jackson, the Boy." *DAR Magazine,* Feb. 1967, pp. 141- .

Foster, Austin P. "The Purposes of the Andrew Jackson Memorial Association." *THM* 1 (1915), 206-8.

Foster, Genevieve. *Andrew Jackson: An Initial Biography.* New York: Scribners, 1951. 112 pp. Fiction.

Francis, Mary C. *A Son of Destiny; the Story of Andrew Jackson.* New York: Federal, 1902. 459 pp.

Goldman, Perry M. "Political Rhetoric in the Age of Jackson." *THQ* 29 (1970), 360-71.

Goodpasture, Albert V. *Andrew Jackson, Tennessee and the Union; a Paper by Albert V. Goodpasture, Read before the Tennessee Historical Society, Tuesday, June 11, 1895,* Tennessee Hist. Soc. Papers. Nashville: Brandon, 1895. 23 pp. Rpt. in *AHM* 1 (1896), 209-23; rpt. in *Tennessee Old and New,* I, 188-200.

———. "Genesis of the Jackson-Sevier Feud." *AHM* 5 (1900), 115-23; rpt. in *Tennessee Old and New,* I, 167-75.

Goodwin, Philo A. *Biography of Andrew Jackson, President of the United States, Formerly Major General in the Army of the United States.* Hartford, Conn.: Clapp & Benton, 1832; rpt. New York: R. H. Towner, 1833. 456 pp.

Green, Fletcher M. "On Tour with President Andrew Jackson." *New England Quarterly Review* 36 (1963), 208-28.

Hailperin, Herman. "Pro-Jackson Sentiment in Pennsylvania." *Pennsylvania Magazine of History and Biography*, July 1926, 193-238.

Hammond, Bray. *Banks and Politics in America, from the Revolution to the Civil War.* Princeton: Princeton Univ. Press, 1957. 771 pp. A study of the entrepreneurial ambitions of the men around Jackson which deemphasizes the President's role in the Bank War.

Heiskell, Samuel Gordon. *Andrew Jackson and Early Tennessee History.* 3 vols. Nashville: Ambrose, 1918, 1920-21. A narrative and documentary history of the state from the early period to the presidency of Polk. The whole work, however, leads to and focuses upon Jackson.

Henig, Gerald S. "The Jacksonian Attitude toward Abolitionism in the 1830's." *THQ* 28 (1969), 42-56.

Hoffman, William S. *Andrew Jackson and North Carolina Politics.* Chapel Hill: Univ. of North Carolina Press, 1958. 134 pp.

Hofstadter, Richard. "William Leggett, Spokesman of Jacksonian Democracy." *PSQ* 58 (1943), 581-94.

——. "Andrew Jackson and the Rise of Liberal Capitalism." *The American Political Tradition and the Men Who Made It,* ed. Richard Hofstadter, 45-67. New York: Knopf, 1948. The best brief statement of the entrepreneurial thesis.

Horn, Stanley F., ed. "Some Jackson-Overton Correspondence." *THQ* 6 (1947), 161-75.

Hugins, Walter E. "Ely Moore: The Case History of a Jacksonian Labor Leader." *PSQ* 65 (1950), 105-25.

——. *Jacksonian Democracy and the Working Class, a Study of the New York Workingmen's Movement, 1829-1837,* Stanford Studies in History, Economics, and Political Science, no. 19. Stanford: Stanford Univ. Press, 1960. 286 pp. Hugins views Jackson as the product rather than the originator of Jacksonian Democracy. He views the urban workingman as a part of the Jacksonian coalition and seeks to clarify his aspirations.

James, Marquis. *Andrew Jackson: The Border Captain.* Indianapolis: Bobbs-Merrill, 1933. 461 pp. Rpt., The Universal Library, no. 47. New York: Grosset, 1969.

——. *Andrew Jackson: Portrait of a President.* Indianapolis: Bobbs-Merrill, 1937. 627 pp. Rpt., The Universal Library, no. 94. New York: Grosset, 1961.

——. *The Life of Andrew Jackson.* 2 vols. in 1. Indianapolis: Bobbs-Merrill, 1938. 972 pp. A combination of the 2 volumes above, this is a popular, generally accurate, but intensely partisan appraisal of Jackson's life. It is the most readable biography of Jackson and is recommended particularly to laymen.

Jenkins, John Stilwell, ed. *Life and Public Services of Gen. Andrew Jackson, Seventh President of the United States; Including the Most Important of His State Papers.* Buffalo: G. H. Derby, 1850, 1852; rpt. New York: Saxton, Barker, 1860. 397 pp.

Johnson, Gerald W. *Andrew Jackson, an Epic in Homespun.* New York: Minton, Balch, 1927. 306 pp.

Judson, Clara I. *Andrew Jackson, Frontier Statesman.* Chicago: Follett, 1954. 224 pp.

Karsner, David. *Andrew Jackson, the Gentle Savage.* New York: Brentano's, 1929. 399 pp.

Kendall, Amos. *Life of Andrew Jackson, Private, Military and Civil. With Illustrations,* no. 1-7. New York: Harper, 1843-44. Only 7 numbers were published in pamphlet form.

Ketchum, Richard N. "Faces from the Past: Andrew Jackson." *AH* 13 (1961), 16 ff.

Lee, Major Henry, Jr. *A Vindication of the Character and Public Services of Andrew Jackson; in Reply to the Richmond Address, Signed by Chapman Johnson, and to Other Electioneering Calumnies.* Boston: True & Greene, 1828. 51 pp.

Lewis, Alfred Henry. *When Men Grew Tall; or, The Story of Andrew Jackson.* New York: Appleton, 1907. 330 pp.

Lossing, B. J. "Andrew Jackson." *Harper's New Monthly Magazine,* Jan. 1855, pp. 145-72.

McCormick, Richard P. "New Perspectives in Jacksonian Politics." *AHR* 65 (1960), 288-301.

MacDonald, William. *Jacksonian Democracy, 1829-1837,* The American Nation Series, vol. 15. New York: Harper, 1906. Rpt., ed. Albert B. Hart. New York: Harper, 1968, 1971; rpt. New York: AMS, 1971. 345 pp.

McLemore, Richard A. "The French Spoliation Claims, 1816-1836; A Study in Jacksonian Diplomacy." Diss., Vanderbilt Univ., 1933; *THM* (ser. 2) 2 (1931-32), 234-54. Rpt. Nashville: The Author, 1932. 21 pp.

——. *Franco-American Diplomatic Relations, 1816-1836.* University:

Louisiana State Univ. Press, 1941; rpt. Port Washington, N.Y.: Kennikat, 1971. 227 pp.

Madeleine, Sister M. Grace. *Monetary and Banking Theories of Jacksonian Democracy.* Thesis, Univ. of Pennsylvania. Philadelphia: Privately printed, 1943; rpt. Port Washington, N.Y.: Kennikat, 1970. 186 pp.

Meadowcroft, Enid L. *The Story of Andrew Jackson,* Signature Series. New York: Grosset, 1953. 182 pp.

Meyers, Marvin. "The Jacksonian Persuasion." *American Quarterly* 5 (1953), 3-15.

———. *The Jacksonian Persuasion: Politics and Belief.* Diss., Columbia Univ., 1957; copy, Ann Arbor: Univ. Microfilms, 1957. Stanford: Stanford Univ. Press, 1957. 231 pp. Rpt. New York: Vintage, 1960. 292 pp. The author considers Jacksonian Democracy a broad political, social, and intellectual movement. Pondering why this current evoked powerful political emotions, he concludes that the Jacksonian struggles to regain agrarian republican values collided with revolutionary undercurrents of materialism in an increasingly acquisitive age.

Miles, Edwin A. *Jacksonian Democracy in Mississippi,* The James Sprunt Studies in History and Political Science, vol. 42. Chapel Hill: Univ. of North Carolina Press, 1960. 192 pp. The author traces the evolution of the Mississippi Democratic party in the Jackson era and the development of political democracy within the state during the same period.

Nicolay, Helen. *Andrew Jackson, the Fighting President.* New York: Century, 1929. 335 pp.

Ogg, Frederic A. *The Reign of Andrew Jackson; a Chronicle of the Frontier in Politics,* The Chronicles of America Series, vol. 20. New Haven: Yale Univ. Press, 1919, 1920, 1921. 249 pp.

Ostrogorskii, Moisei. *Democracy and the Organization of Political Parties,* trans. Frederick Clarke; preface James Boyce. 2 vols. New York: Macmillan, 1902, 1908. Rev. ed., abridg. and ed. Seymour Martin Lipset. 2 vols. Chicago: Quadrangle, 1964. This work outlines the development of the political structure during the Jacksonian period, the evolution from the party caucus to the convention system for nominating presidential candidates, and the growth of political organization at all levels of government.

Parks, Joseph H., ed. "Letter Describes Andrew Jackson's Last Hours." *THQ* 6 (1947), 176-78.

Parton, James. *Life of Andrew Jackson.* 3 vols. New York: Mason, 1860, 1861; rpt., 1 vol., 1863; rpt., 1 vol., Boston: Mason & Hamlin, 1863. 479 pp. Rpt., 3 vols., Boston: Houghton, 1887-88. Vol. 3 rpt., titled *The Presidency of Andrew Jackson,* Harper Torchbooks, ed. Robert V. Remini. New York: Harper, 1967. 468 pp. Rpt., 3 vols., New York: Johnson Rpts., 1972. Written by the finest of 19th-century American biographers, this was the first substantial biography of Jackson. Parton's work is particularly good for the early period. It is less objective and more sharply critical of his later life.

Peck, Charles Henry. *The Jacksonian Epoch.* New York: Harper, 1899. 472 pp.

Pessen, Edward. "The Workingmen's Movement in the Jackson Era." *MVHR* 43 (1958), 428-43.

———. *Most Uncommon Jacksonians: The Radical Leaders of the Early Labor Movement.* Albany: State Univ. of New York Press, 1967. 208 pp.

———. *Jacksonian America: Society, Personality, and Politics.* Homewood, Ill.: Dorsey, 1969. 408 pp. The most recent, most adversely critical study of Jackson.

———. *New Perspectives on Jacksonian Parties and Politics.* Boston: Allyn, 1969. 291 pp.

"President Andrew Jackson." *Blackwood's Magazine* 91 (1862), 643-62.

Provine, William A., ed. "Jackson Correspondence." *THM* 7 (1921), 137-39.

Ranck, James B. "Andrew Jackson and the Burr Conspiracy." *THM* (ser. 2) 1 (1930-31), 17-28; rpt. in *Tennessee Old and New,* I, 176-87.

Remini, Robert. *Andrew Jackson,* Rulers and Statesmen of the World Series, vol. 2. New York: Twayne, 1966. 212 pp. The best and most recent short account of Jackson's life.

Richardson, James D., comp. and ed. *A Compilation of the Messages and Papers of the Presidents,* House Miscellaneous Doc. 210, 53rd Cong., 2nd Sess., vols. 2, 3. Washington, D.C.: GPO, 1896-99. Rpt. New York: Bur. of Nat. Art and Literature, 1903, 1911, 1912, 1917. Rpt. New York: Johnson Rpts., 1969.

Schlesinger, Arthur M., Jr. *The Age of Jackson.* Boston: Little, 1945. 577 pp. The author attempts to explain the politics of the Jackson era in terms of the movement of ideas. He believes that Jacksonian Democracy was not so much a product of random forces as it was of reasoned, systematic ideas about society emanating from the East and South rather than from the West. This study rekindled scholarly controversy over the Jacksonian period.

Schultzman, Lucy. "Jacksonian Historiography, 1948-1969." Thesis, Murray State Univ., 1970.

Sellers, Charles G., Jr. "Andrew Jackson versus the Historians." *MVHR* 44 (1958), 615-34.

———. *Jacksonian Democracy,* Service Center for Teachers of History, Publication no. 9. Washington, D.C.: The Center, 1958. 18 pp.

———., ed. *Andrew Jackson; A Profile.* New York: Hill and Wang, 1971. 231 pp.

Sharp, James R. *The Jacksonians versus the Bank; Politics in the States after the Panic of 1837.* New York: Columbia Univ. Press, 1970. 392 pp.

Sioussat, St. George L. "Some Phases of Tennessee Politics in the Jackson Period." *AHR* 14 (1908), 51-69.

Smith, Culver H. "The Washington Press in the Jackson Period." Diss., Duke Univ., 1933.

———. "Andrew Jackson, *Post Obitum.*" *THQ* 4 (1945), 195-221.

Smith, Walter Buckingham. *Economic Aspects of the Second Bank of the United States,* Studies in Economic History. Cambridge, Mass.: Harvard Univ. Press, 1953; rpt. Westport, Conn.: Greenwood, 1953. 314 pp.

Smyth, Clifford. *Andrew Jackson, the Man Who Preserved Union and Democracy,* Builders of America Series, vol. 17. New York: Funk, 1931. 174 pp.

Somit, Albert. "Andrew Jackson: Legend and Reality." *THQ* 7 (1948), 291-313.

Sullivan, William A. "Did Labor Support Andrew Jackson?" *PSQ* 62 (1947), 569-80.

Sumner, William Graham. *Andrew Jackson as a Public Man. What He Was, What Chances He Had, and What He Did with Them,* American Statesmen Series, vol. 17. Boston: Houghton, 1882, 1883, 1885, 1888, 1890, 1899, 1909 [?], 1910, 1917; rpt., Great Presidents Series, 1924; rpt., American Biography Series, vol. 32, 1969. Rpt. 1882 ed., New York: Haskell, 1969; Westport, Conn.: Greenwood, 1969. 402 pp.

Syrett, Harold C. *Andrew Jackson; His Contribution to the*

American Tradition, Makers of the American Tradition Series. Indianapolis: Bobbs-Merrill, 1953; rpt. Westport, Conn.: Greenwood, 1971. 298 pp. Syrett identifies as the basic contribution of Jackson his recognition that the first principle of a democracy was that the majority would govern.

Taylor, Joe Gray. "Andrew Jackson and the Aaron Burr Conspiracy." WTHSP 1 (1947), 81-90.

Thorpe, Francis N., ed. *The Statesmanship of Andrew Jackson As Told in His Writings and Speeches.* New York: Tandy-Thomas, 1909. 538 pp.

Turner, Frederick Jackson. *The Rise of the New West, 1819-1829,* The American Nation Series, vol. 14. New York: Harper, 1906; rpt. Gloucester, Mass.: P. Smith, 1959, 1961. 363 pp. Rpt., foreword and biblio. Ray A. Billington. New York: Collier, 1962. 252 pp. Rpt., 1906 ed., New York: Harper, 1968.

——. *The Frontier in American History.* New York: Holt, 1920, 1921, 1923, 1926, 1947, 1950, 1962, 1969.

——. *The United States, 1830-1850; the Nation and Its Sections,* eds. M. H. Crissey, Max Farrand, and Avery Craven. New York: Holt, 1935; rpt. Gloucester, Mass.: P. Smith, 1958; rpt. New York: Norton, 1965. 602 pp. Incomplete; published posthumously.

Van Deusen, Glyndon G. *The Jacksonian Era, 1828-1848,* The New American Nation Series. New York: Harper, 1959; rpt. 1963. 290 pp. Van Deusen projects a revisionist view of Jackson in stating his thesis that Jackson had little constructive legislation to his credit, since the destruction of the Bank had questionable results. He views as Jackson's most permanent influences his conception of the presidency and his enlargement of executive authority.

Waldo, Samuel Putnam. *Memoirs of Andrew Jackson, Major-General in the Army of the United States; and Commander in Chief of the Division of the South.* Hartford, Conn.: S. Andrus, 1819. 316 pp. 3rd ed., Hartford: Andrus, 1819. 312 pp. 5th ed., Hartford: Russell, 1819, 1820. 336 pp. Rpt. New York: Davis, 1825. 359 pp. Rpt. Chambersburg, Md.: Pritts, 1828. 306 pp.

Walker, Alexander. *The Life of Andrew Jackson, to Which Is Added an Authentic Narrative of the Memorable Achievements of the American Army at New Orleans, in the Winter of 1814, '15.* Philadelphia, Pa.: G. G. Evans, 1860. 414 pp.

Ward, John William. *Andrew Jackson: Symbol for an Age.* Diss., Univ. of Minnesota, 1953; copy, Ann Arbor: Univ. Microfilms, Publication 6163. 1953. New York: Oxford Univ. Press, 1955;

rpt. Galaxy Bk. no. 73, 1962. 274 pp. The author depicts Jackson as a product of his region, symbolizing in his person forces from the West at work upon the nation.

Watson, Thomas E. *The Life and Times of Andrew Jackson.* Thomson, Ga.: Jeffersonian Pub., 1912. 408 pp.

White, Leonard Dupee. *The Jacksonians; a Study in Administrative History, 1829-1861.* New York: Macmillan, 1954, 1956; rpt. New York: Free Press, 1965. 593 pp. This work is important for pointing up the fact that Jackson removed slightly more than 10 percent of all officeholders in the 8 years of his presidency.

Wright, Frances F. *Andrew Jackson, Fighting Frontiersman,* Makers of America Series. New York: Abingdon, 1958. 127 pp. Juvenile.

FAMILY AND PERSONAL LIFE, AND MISCELLANY

Brown, Rosalie B. "Andrew Jackson and the Greasy Cove Race Track." *THM* (ser. 2) 2 (1931-32), 62-66.

Caldwell, Mary French. *General Jackson's Lady: A Story of the Life and Times of Rachel Donelson Jackson, Beloved Wife of General Andrew Jackson, Seventh President of the United States.* Nashville: The Author, in cooperation with the Ladies' Hermitage Assoc., 1936. 555 pp.

DeWitt, John H. "Andrew Jackson and His Ward, Andrew Jackson Hutchings." *THM* (ser. 2) 1 (1930-31), 83-106.

Doss, Richard B. "Andrew Jackson; Road Builder." *Journal of Mississippi History* 16 (1954), 1-21.

Erwin, Andrew. *Gen. Jackson's Negro Speculations, and His Traffic in Human Flesh, Examined and Established by Positive Proof.* Nashville: n.p., 1828. 16 pp.

Floyd, Viola Caston. "Andrew Jackson Equestrian Statue." *DAR Magazine,* Dec. 1961, pp. 676- .

Frost, John. *Pictorial Life of Andrew Jackson; Embracing Anecdotes, Illustrative of his Character. For Young People.* Philadelphia, Pa.: Lindsay & Blakiston, 1845. 183 pp. Rpt. Hartford: Belknap & Hamersley, 1847. 512 pp.

Galloway, Linda Bennett. "Andrew Jackson, Jr." Thesis, Vanderbilt Univ., 1949.

——. "Andrew Jackson, Junior." *THQ* 9 (1950), 195-216, 306-43.

——. *Andrew Jackson, Jr., Son of a President; a Biographical Study,*

Exposition-Lochinvar Series. New York: Exposition Press, 1966. 85 pp.

Gardiner, Francis T. "The Gentleman from Tennessee." *Surgery, Gynecology and Obstetrics with International Abstracts of Surgery* 88 (1949), 404-11. A clinical description of Jackson's physical ills.

Goff, Reda C. "A Physical Profile of Andrew Jackson." *THQ* 28 (1969), 297-309.

Govan, Christine N. *Rachel Jackson, Tennessee Girl,* The Childhood of Famous Americans Series. Indianapolis: Bobbs-Merrill, 1955, 1962. 192 pp. Juvenile historical fiction by a Tennessee writer.

Harris, Max F. *The Andrew Jackson Birthplace Problem; a Report Prepared for the Historic Sites Division of the State Dept. of Archives and History.* Raleigh, N.C.: North Carolina Dept. of Archives and Hist., 1963. 56 pp.

Herd, Elmer D. *Andrew Jackson, South Carolinian; a Study of the Enigma of His Birth.* Lancaster, S.C.: Lancaster Co. Hist. Comm., 1963. 64 pp.

Kegley, Tracy M. "James White Stephenson: Teacher of Andrew Jackson." *THQ* 7 (1948), 38-51.

Kupfer, Barbara Stern. "A Presidential Patron of the Sport of Kings: Andrew Jackson." *THQ* 29 (1970), 243-55.

Reardon, Virginia. "Family and Home Life of Andrew Jackson." Thesis, Vanderbilt Univ., 1934.

Satterfield, R. B. "The Early Public Career of Andrew Jackson Donelson, 1799-1846." Thesis, Vanderbilt Univ., 1948.

Symonds, Susan Clover. "Portraits of Andrew Jackson: 1815-1845." Thesis, Univ. of Delaware, 1968.

Vance, Marguerite. *The Jacksons of Tennessee.* New York: Dutton, 1953, 1955. 181 pp.

Walker, Arda S. "The Social and Economic Views of Andrew Jackson." Thesis, Univ. of Tennessee, 1941.

——. "Andrew Jackson: Planter." ETHSP 15 (1943), 19-34.

——. "The Educational Training and Views of Andrew Jackson." ETHSP 16 (1944), 22-29.

——. "The Religious Views of Andrew Jackson." ETHSP 17 (1945), 61-70.

——. "Andrew Jackson: Frontier Democrat." ETHSP 18 (1946), 19-34.

White, Robert H. "Elizabeth Hutchinson Jackson, the Mother of President Andrew Jackson." *THM* (ser. 2) 3 (1932-37), 179-84.

THE CREEK WAR AND THE WAR OF 1812

Adair, John, and Andrew Jackson. *Letters of . . . Relative to the Charge of Cowardice Made by the Latter against the Kentucky Troops at New Orleans.* Lexington, Ky.: T. Smith, 1824. 63 pp.

Allen, Penelope, comp. *Tennessee Soldiers in the War of 1812, Regiments of Col. Allcorn and Col. Allison.* Chattanooga: Tennessee Soc., USD of 1812, 1847. 65 pp.

Aristides. *See* Van Ness, William Peter.

Armstrong, Zella, comp. *Twenty-four Hundred Tennessee Pensioners: Revolution—War of 1812.* Chattanooga: Lookout, 1937. 121 pp.

Boom, Aaron. "John Coffee, Citizen Soldier." *THQ* 22 (1963), 223-37.

Brooks, Charles B. *The Siege of New Orleans.* Seattle: Univ. of Washington Press, 1961. 334 pp.

Brown, Roger H. "The War Hawks of 1812: An Historical Myth." *Indiana Magazine of History* 60 (1964), 137-51.

Brown, Wilburt S. *The Amphibious Campaign for West Florida and Louisiana, 1814-1815; a Critical Review of Strategy and Tactics at New Orleans.* University: Univ. of Alabama Press, 1969. 233 pp.

Carter, Samuel. *Blaze of Glory; the Fight for New Orleans, 1814-1815.* New York: St. Martin, 1971. 351 pp.

Chappell, Gordon T. "The Life and Activities of John Coffee." Diss., Vanderbilt Univ., 1941.

——. "The Life and Activities of General John Coffee." *THQ* 1 (1942), 125-46.

——. "John Coffee: Land Speculator and Planter." *Alabama Review* 22 (1969), 24-43.

De Conde, Alexander. "The War Hawks of 1812: A Critique." *Indiana Magazine of History* 60 (1964), 152-54.

Ewing, Robert. "Portrait of General Robert Armstrong." *THM* 5 (1919), 75-80. Staff officer of Andrew Jackson at New Orleans.

Folk, Reau E. *Battle of New Orleans, Its Real Meaning; Exposure of Untruth Being Taught Young America concerning the Second Most Important Military Event in the Life of the Republic.* Nashville: Ladies' Hermitage Assoc., 1935. 48 pp.

Garrett, William R., ed. "Report of Gen. Andrew Jackson to Gov. Willie Blount. 'Battle of Tehopiska or the Horseshoe.'"*AHM* 4 (1899), 291-96.

Garrett, William R., and John M. Bass, eds. "Letters from John Coffee." *AHM* 6 (1901), 174-90.

Goodpasture, Ernest W. "General Nathaniel Taylor and Some Papers Relating to His Service in the War of 1812." *AHM* 9 (1904), 193-200.

Halbert, Henry S., and Timothy H. Ball. *The Creek War of 1813 and 1814.*

Hamer, Philip M., ed. "A Muster Roll of Captain Jacob Tipton's Company in St. Clair's Campaign." ETHS*P* 3 (1931), 150-53.

Holland, James W. *Andrew Jackson and the Creek War; Victory at the Horseshoe.* Tuscaloosa: Univ. of Alabama Press, 1969. 47 pp.

Horsman, Reginald. *The Causes of the War of 1812.* Diss., Univ. of Indiana, 1958; film reprod., Bloomington: Univ. of Indiana, 1958. Philadelphia, Pa.: Univ. of Pennsylvania Press, 1962. Rpt., Perpetua Bks. New York: A. S. Barnes, 1962; rpt. New York: Octogan, 1971. 345 pp.

——. "Who Were the War Hawks?" *Indiana Magazine of History* 60 (1964), 121-36. Relates to the War of 1812.

Latour, Arsène Lacarrière. *Historical Memoir of the War in West Florida and Louisiana, in 1814-15. With an Atlas,* trans. H. B. Nugent. Philadelphia, Pa.: John Conrad, 1816. 441 pp. Rpt., Quadricentennial Edition of the Floridiana Fascimile & Reprint Series, ed. Jane Lucas de Grummond. Gainesville: Univ. of Florida Press, 1964. 264 pp. This is one of the more important contemporary accounts of the Battle of New Orleans.

McAfee, Robert B. *History of the Late War in the Western Country, Comprising a Full Account of all the Transactions in that Quarter, from the Commencement of Hostilities at Tippecanoe, to the termination of the Contest at New Orleans on the Return of Peace.* Lexington, Ky.: Worsley & Smith, 1816. 534 pp. Rpt. Great American Historical Classics Series. Bowling Green, O.: Hist. Pub. Co., 1919. 591 pp.

McCown, Mary Hardin. "The 'J. Hartsell Memora': The Journal of a Tennessee Captain in the War of 1812." ETHS*P* 11 (1939), 93-115; 12 (1940), 118-46.

McCown, Mary Hardin, and Inez E. Burns, eds. *Soldiers of the War of 1812 Buried in Tennessee: A Short History.* Johnson City: Tennessee Soc., USD of 1812, 1959. 156 pp.

McGovern, James R., ed. *Andrew Jackson and Pensacola: A Sesqui-centennial Commemoration.* Pensacola: Jackson Day Sesquicenten-nial Comm., 1971. 80 pp.

McGowin, N. Floyd. "Some Aspects of Waning British Influence in the Middle Gulf Region." *THQ* 17 (1958), 131-40.

Maiden, Leota Driver. "Colonel John Williams." ETHS*P* 30 (1958), 7-47.

Moore, Mrs. John Trotwood. "Commissioned Officers of the Tennes-see Militia for the Year 1815, and Justices of the Peace, 1815." *THM* (ser. 2) 1 (1930-31), 222-28.

——., ed. "Record of Commissions of Officers in the Tennessee Militia, 1796-1815." *THQ* 1-9 (1942-50), 15 (1956).

Nagy, James Emerick. "A Biographical Sketch of Brigadier General Joseph Martin." Thesis, George Peabody College, 1932.

Official Record from the War Department of the Court Martial Which Tried, and the Orders of General Jackson for Shooting the Six Militia Men together with Official Letters from the War Depart-ment, Ordered to Be Printed by Congress, Showing That These American Citizens Were Inhumanely Massacred. Concord, N.H.: J. B. Moore, 1828. 52 pp. The first edition was reprinted in 1921, in the Publications of the Mississippi Historical Society, under the title *Mississippi Territory in the War of 1812.* The present edition is revised and amplified.

Owsley, Frank L., Jr. "The Role of the South in the British Grand Strategy in the War of 1812." *THQ* 31 (1972), 22-38.

Pelham, Samuel Clay. "Jackson's Creek Campaign as a Factor in the War of 1812." Thesis, George Peabody College, 1926.

Phelps, Dawson A., ed. "The Diary of a Chaplain in Andrew Jackson's Army." *THQ* 12 (1953), 264-81. This relates to the Creek wars and War of 1812.

Pratt, Julius W. *Expansionists of 1812.* New York: Macmillan, 1925; rpt. Gloucester, Mass.: P. Smith, 1949, 1957. 309 pp.

Provine, William A., ed. "Extracts from 'The Military Instructor.'" *THM* 8 (1924), 215-19. The Tennessee militia c. 1810.

Remini, Robert V. "Andrew Jackson's Account of the Battle of New Orleans." *THQ* 26 (1967), 23-42.

Risjord, Norman. "The War Hawks and the War of 1812." *Indiana Magazine of History* 60 (1964), 155-58.

Roland, Eron O. Moore. *Andrew Jackson; Campaign against the British, or, The Mississippi Territory in the War of 1812.* New York: Macmillan, 1926. 424 pp.

Silver, James W. "Edmund Pendleton Gaines: Exponent of the Frontier." Diss., Vanderbilt Univ., 1935.

——. *Edmund Pendleton Gaines: Frontier General.* Baton Rouge: Louisiana State Univ. Press, 1949. 291 pp. Gaines was a professional soldier whose career spanned the period from the War of 1812 to the Mexican War. He was commander of the regular forces in the West for most of the time from 1821 to 1842. Gaines believed that the solution to the Indian problem was not removal, but detribalization and education in agriculture.

Sioussat, St. George L., ed. "Letters of General John Coffee to His Wife, 1813-1815, with Introduction and Notes by John H. DeWitt." *THM* 2 (1916), 264-95.

Swint, Henry Lee. "Andrew Jackson and the War in the South." Thesis, Vanderbilt Univ., 1930.

Van Ness, William P. [pseud. Aristides]. *A Concise Narrative of General Jackson's First Invasion of Florida, and of His Immortal Defence of New Orleans: With Remarks.* New York: E. M. Murden & A. Ming, Jr., 1827. 40 pp.

Walker, Alexander. *Jackson and New Orleans. An Authentic Narrative of the Memorable Achievements of the American Army, under Andrew Jackson, before New Orleans, in the Winter of 1814, '15.* New York: J. C. Derby, 1856. 411 pp. Rpt. in his *Life of Andrew Jackson.* An early and still valuable account of the famous battle.

Walker, William A., Jr. "Martial Sons: Tennessee Enthusiasm for the War of 1812." *THQ* 20 (1961), 20-37.

Watson, Elbert L. *Tennessee at the Battle of New Orleans,* Battle of New Orleans Sesquicentennial Historical Booklet no. 5. New Orleans: Battle of New Orleans 150th Anniversary Comm. of Louisiana, 1965. 48 pp.

White, Robert H. "The Volunteer State." *THQ* 15 (1956), 53-56.

Williams, Samuel Cole. "A Forgotten Campaign." *THM* 8 (1924), 266-76. The Florida campaign of Col. John Williams in 1812.

——. "Brigadier-General Nathaniel Taylor." *ETHSP* 12 (1940), 28-44.

Young, Mary E. "The Creek Frauds: A Study in Conscience and Corruption." *MVHR* 47 (1955), 411-37.

Young, Rogers W. "Andrew Jackson's Movements on the Lower Natchez Trace during and after the War of 1812." *Journal of Mississippi History* 10 (1948), 87-103.

THE SEMINOLE WAR AND FLORIDA

A Concise Narrative of the Seminole Campaign. By an Officer, Attached to the Expedition. Nashville: M'Lean & Tunstall, 1819. 41 pp.

Doherty, Herbert J., Jr. "The Governorship of Andrew Jackson." *Florida Historical Quarterly* 33 (1954), 3-31.

——. "Andrew Jackson's Cronies in Florida Territorial Politics. With Three Unpublished Letters to His Cronies." *Florida Historical Quarterly* 34 (1955), 3-29.

Horn, Stanley F., ed. "Tennessee Volunteers in the Seminole Campaign of 1836: The Diary of Henry Hollingsworth." *THQ* 1 (1942), 269-74, 344-66; 2 (1943), 61-73, 163-78, 236-56.

McGovern, James R., ed. *Andrew Jackson in Tennessee.* Pensacola: Jackson Day Sesquicentennial Comm. of Pensacola, 1971.

McQueen, Ray A. "The Role of Andrew Jackson in the Acquisitions of the Floridas." Diss., Univ. of Pittsburgh, 1942.

Mahon, John K. *History of the Second Seminole War 1835-1842.* Gainesville: Univ. of Florida Press, 1967. 387 pp.

Perkins, Samuel. *General Jackson's Conduct in the Seminole War Delineated in a History of That Period, Affording Conclusive Reasons Why He Should Not Be the Next President.* Brooklyn: Advertiser Press, 1828. 39 pp.

Thomas, David Y. "Jackson's Attitude in the Seminole War." *AHM* 9 (1904), 145-52.

Thompson, Arthur W. *Jacksonian Democracy on the Florida Frontier,* University of Florida Monographs, Social Sciences, no. 9. Gainesville: Univ. of Florida Press, 1961. 88 pp.

THE 1820s AND PRESIDENTIAL POLITICS

Bergeron, Paul H. "A Test for Jacksonians: Sam Houston on Trial." *ETHSP* 38 (1966), 16-29.

Brown, Everett S. "The Presidential Election of 1824-1825." *PSQ* 40 (1925), 384-403.

Haller, Mark H. "The Rise of the Jackson Party in Maryland, 1820-1829." *JSH* 28 (1962), 307-26.

Harlan, Louis R. "Public Career of William Berkeley Lewis." *THQ* 7 (1948), 3-37. Lewis was Jackson's political intimate and trusted friend.

Hay, Robert P. "The Case for Andrew Jackson in 1824: Eaton's 'Wyoming Letters.'" *THQ* 29 (1970), 139-51.

——. "The Presidential Question: Letters to Southern Editors, 1823-24." *THQ* 31 (1972), 170-86.

Kelsay, Isabel Thompson. "The Presidential Campaign of 1828." ETHS*P* 5 (1933), 69-80.

Morgan, William G. "John Quincy Adams versus Andrew Jackson: Their Biographers and the 'Corrupt Bargain' Charge." *THQ* 26 (1967), 43-58.

Nagel, Paul C. "The Election of 1824: A Reconsideration Based on Newspaper Opinion." *JSH* 24 (1960), 315-29.

Remini, Robert V. *The Election of Andrew Jackson,* Critical Periods of History Series. Philadelphia, Pa.: Lippincott, 1963. 224 pp. Remini contends that the election of Jackson was not an accident, but an event instigated by politicians who hoped their efforts would inaugurate a political revolution.

Sellers, Charles G., Jr. "Banking and Politics in Jackson's Tennessee, 1817-1827." *MVHR* 41 (1954-55), 61-84.

——. "Jackson Men with Feet of Clay." *AHR* 62 (1957), 537-51.

Smith, Culver H. "Propaganda Technique in the Jackson Campaign of 1828." ETHS*P* 6 (1934), 44-66.

Stenberg, Richard R. "Jackson, Buchanan, and the Corrupt Bargain Calumny." *Pennsylvania Magazine of History and Biography* 58 (1934), 61-85.

Weston, Florence. *The Presidential Election of 1828.* Diss., Catholic Univ. of America 1938 [?]; Washington: Ruddick, 1938. 217 pp.

The President: 1829-37

Ahl, Frances Norene. *Andrew Jackson and the Constitution.* Boston: Christopher, 1939. 168 pp.

Albjerg, Victor L. "Jackson's Influence on Internal Improvement." *THM* (ser. 2) 2 (1931-32), 259-69.

Anderson, Hattie M. "The Jackson Men in Missouri in 1828." *Missouri Historical Review* 34 (1940), 301-34.

Aronson, Sidney H. *Status and Kinship in the Higher Civil Service: Standards of Selection in the Administration of John Adams, Thomas Jefferson, and Andrew Jackson.* Diss., Columbia Univ., 1961. Publication of the Center for the Study of the History of

Liberty in America. Cambridge: Harvard Univ. Press, 1964. 274 pp. This work illustrates the close similarity with which these three presidents dealt with federal appointments.

Baily, Myrtice Maud. "Tennessee's Attitude toward the Jackson-South Carolina Nullification Controversy, 1832-1833." Thesis, George Peabody College, 1932.

Barbee, David Rankin. "Andrew Jackson and Peggy O'Neale." *THQ* 15 (1956), 37-52.

Barker, Eugene C. "President Jackson and the Texas Revolution." *AHR* 12 (1906-7), 788-809.

Bassett, John Spencer. "Notes on Jackson's Visit to New England, June, 1833." *THM* 8 (1924), 119-31.

Bergeron, Paul H. "Politics and Patronage in Tennessee during the Adams and Jackson Years." *Prologue* 2 (1970), 19-24.

Bower, Robert T. "Note on 'Did Labor Support Jackson?: The Boston Story.'" *PSQ* 65 (1950), 441-44.

Brown, Richard H. "The Missouri Crisis, Slavery, and the Politics of Jacksonianism." *South Atlantic Quarterly* 65 (1966), 55-72.

Bugg, James L., ed. *Jacksonian Democracy: Myth or Reality?,* American Problem Studies. New York: Holt, 1962; rpt. Dryden Editions, 1965. Rpt. Gloucester, Mass.: P. Smith, 1971. 122 pp.

Cain, Marvin R. "William Wirt against Andrew Jackson: Reflections on an Era." *Mid-America* 47 (1965), 113-38.

Chase, James Staton. "Jacksonian Democracy and the Rise of the Nominating Convention." *Mid-America* 45 (1963), 229-49.

Cherokee Removal. *See* Cherokee and Other Indians of Tennessee: Removal.

Chroust, Anton-Herman. "Did President Jackson Actually Threaten the Supreme Court of the US with Nonenforcement of Its Injunction against the State of Georgia?" *American Journal of Legal History* 4 (1960), 76-78.

Clifton, Frances. "John Overton as Andrew Jackson's Friend." *THQ* 11 (1952), 23-40.

Cobun, Frank E. "The Educational Level of the Jacksonians." *History of Education Quarterly* 7 (1967), 515-20.

Cole, Donald B. "The Presidential Election of 1832 in New Hampshire." *Historical New Hampshire* 21 (1966), 32-50.

———. *Jacksonian Democracy in New Hampshire, 1800-1851.* Cambridge, Mass.: Harvard Univ. Press, 1970. 283 pp.

Curtis, James C. "Andrew Jackson and His Cabinet—Some New Evidence." *THQ* 27 (1968), 157-64.

Dangerfield, George. *The Awakening of American Nationalism, 1815-1828,* New American Nation Series. New York: Harper, 1965; rpt. 1966. 331 pp.

Darling, Arthur B. "Jacksonian Democracy in Massachusetts 1824-1848." *AHR* 29 (1924), 271-87.

Davis, Alfred McFarland. "A Tempest in a Teapot." *THM* 8 (1924), 191-210. Harvard's conferring of the LL.D. degree upon President Jackson.

Dorfman, Joseph. "The Jackson Wage Earner Thesis." *AHR* 54 (1947), 296-306.

Eriksson, Erik M. "Official Newspaper Organs and Their Activities, 1825-1837: A Study in Jacksonian Politics." Diss., Univ. of Iowa, 1922.

——. "The Federal Civil Service under President Jackson." *MVHR* 13 (1927), 517-40.

Ershkowitz, Herbert, and William G. Shade. "Consensus or Conflict? Political Behavior in the State Legislatures during the Jacksonian Era." *JAH* 58 (1971), 591-621.

Esarey, Logan. "The Organization of the Jacksonian Party in Indiana." *Proceedings of the Mississippi Valley Historical Association* 7 (1913-14), 220-44.

Fish, Carl R. *The Civil Service and the Patronage,* Harvard Historical Studies, vol. II. New York: Longmans, Green, 1905. Rpt. New York: Russell, 1963. 280 pp.

——. *The Rise of the Common Man 1830-1850,* A History of American Life, vol. 6. New York: Macmillan, 1937. Rpt. New York: Quadrangle, 1971. 391 pp.

Freehling, William W. *Prelude to Civil War: The Nullification Controversy in South Carolina, 1816-1836.* New York: Harper, 1966; rpt., Torchbook Series, 1968. 395 pp. The best study of this controversy.

Gammon, Samuel R., Jr. *The Presidential Campaign of 1832.* Diss., Johns Hopkins Univ., 1922. Johns Hopkins University Studies in Historical and Political Science, Ser. 40, no. 1. Baltimore: Johns Hopkins Univ. Press, 1922; rpt. New York: Da Capo, 1972. 180 pp.

Gatell, Frank Otto. "Spoils of the Bank War: Political Bias in the Selection Pet Banks." *AHR* 70 (1964), 35-58.

——. *The Jacksonians and the Money Power, 1829-1840,* Berkeley Readings in American History Series, vol. 7. Chicago: Rand McNally, 1963, 1967. 59 pp.

——. "Money and Party in Jacksonian America: A Quantitative Look at New York City's Men of Quality." *PSQ* 82 (1967), 235-52.

Goldman, Perry M. "Political Virtue in the Age of Jackson." *PSQ* 87 (1972), 46-62.

Govan, Thomas P. "John M. Berrien and the Administration of Andrew Jackson." *JSH* 5 (1939), 447-67.

Hammond, Bray. "Jackson, Biddle, and the Bank of the United States." *Journal of Economic History* 7 (1947), 1-23.

——. "Jackson's Fight with 'Money Power.'" *AH* 7, No. 4 (1956), 8- .

——. *Banks and Politics in America, from the Revolution to the Civil War.*

Hugins, Walter Edward. *Jacksonian Democracy.*

Jackson, Carlton. "The Internal Improvement Vetoes of Andrew Jackson." *THQ* 25 (1966), 261-79.

——. "Another Time, Another Place—The Attempted Assassination of President Andrew Jackson." *THQ* 26 (1967), 184-90.

Longaker, Richard P. "Andrew Jackson and the Judiciary." *PSQ* 71 (1956), 341-64.

——. "Was Jackson's Kitchen Cabinet a Cabinet?" *MVHR* 44 (1957-58), 94-108.

Lowe, Gabriel L., Jr. "John H. Eaton, Jackson's Campaign Manager." *THQ* 11 (1952), 99-147.

McBride, Robert M., ed. "Andrew Jackson and the Bank of the United States." *THQ* 21 (1962), 377-78.

McCormick, Richard P. "New Perspectives on Jacksonian Politics." *AHR* 65 (1960), 288-301.

——. *The Second American Party System: Party Formation in the Jacksonian Era.* Chapel Hill: Univ. of North Carolina Press, for American Assoc. for State & Local History, Nashville, 1966; rpt., Chapel Hill Books, 1968. 389 pp. A section on Tennessee is included.

McDaniel, Glen. "The Politics of Andrew Jackson." Thesis, Southern Methodist Univ., 1933.

MacDonald, William. *Jacksonian Democracy.*

McFaul, John M., and Frank Otto Gatell. "The Outcast Insider: Reuben M. Whitney and the Bank War." *Pennsylvania Magazine of History and Biography* 91 (1967), 114-15.

McGrane, Reginald C. *The Panic of 1837; Some Financial Problems of the Jacksonian Era.* Chicago: Univ. of Chicago, 1924; rpt. New York: Russell, 1965. 260 pp.

McKenney, Thomas L. *Essays on the Spirit of Jacksonianism, As Exemplified in Its Deadly Hostility to the Bank of the United States.* Philadelphia, Pa.: J. Harding, 1835. 151 pp.

McNiell, Sarah Brown. "Andrew Jackson and Texas Affairs, 1819-1836." ETHSP 28 (1956), 86-101.

Marshall, Lynn L. "The Authorship of Jackson's Bank Veto Message." *MVHR* 50 (1963-64), 466-77.

Miller, Douglas T. *Jacksonian Aristocracy; Class and Democracy in New York, 1830-1860.* New York: Oxford Univ. Press, 1967. 228 pp.

Moore, Powell. "The Revolt against Jackson in Tennessee, 1835-1836." *JSH* 2 (1936), 335-59.

Morris, Richard B. "Andrew Jackson, Strikebreaker." *AHR* 55 (1949-50), 54-68.

Pessen, Edward. "The Workingman's Movement of the Jacksonian Era." *MVHR* 43 (1956), 428-43.

——. "The Workingman's Party Revisited." *Labor History* 4 (1963), 203-26.

——. *New Perspectives.*

Prucha, Francis P. *The American Indian Policy in the Formative Years: The Indian Trade and Intercourse Acts, 1780-1834.*

——. "Andrew Jackson's Indian Policy: A Reassessment." *JAH* 56 (1969), 527-39.

Remini, Robert V. *Andrew Jackson and the Bank War; a Study in the Growth of Presidential Power,* Norton Essays in American History Series. New York: Norton, 1968, 1969. 192 pp. The author studies this struggle as a political phenomenon. He argues that the destruction of the Bank of the United States occurred because it was caught in a clash between two willful, proud, and stubborn men.

Richards, Leonard L. *Gentlemen of Property and Standing: Anti-Abolition Mobs in Jacksonian America.* New York: Oxford Univ. Press, 1970; rpt., Galaxy Books, 1971. 196 pp.

Royall, William L. *Andrew Jackson and the Bank of the United States. Including a History of Paper Money in the United States, and a Discussion of the Currency Question in Some of Its Phases,* Economic Monographs, no. 19. New York: Putnam, 1880. 65 pp.

Scheiber, Harry N. "The Pet Banks in Jacksonian Politics and Finance, 1833-1841." *Journal of Economic History* 23 (1963), 196-214.

Sellers, Charles G., Jr. "Andrew Jackson versus the Historians." *MVHR* 44 (1957-58), 615-34.

Smith, Wayne W. "Jacksonian Democracy on the Chesapeake. The Political Institutions." *Maryland Historical Magazine* 62 (1967), 381-93.

Smoot, Joseph G., ed. "A Presbyterian Minister Calls on Presidential Candidate Andrew Jackson." *THQ* 21 (1962), 287-90.

Somit, Albert. "Andrew Jackson as Political Theorist." *THQ* 8 (1949), 99-126.

———. "Andrew Jackson as Administrative Reformer." *THQ* 13 (1954), 204-23.

Stenberg, Richard R. "Jackson, Anthony Butler and Texas." *Southwestern Social Science Quarterly* 13 (1932), 264-86.

———. "The Texas Schemes of Jackson and Houston 1829-1836." *Southwestern Social Science Quarterly* 15 (1934), 229-50.

———. "Jackson's 'Rhea Letter' Hoax." *JSH* 2 (1936), 480-96.

———. "The Jefferson Birthday Dinner, 1830." *JSH* 4 (1938), 334-45.

Strasser, Donald H. "Andrew Jackson and His Political Lieutenants." Thesis, Univ. of Maryland, 1962.

Sullivan, John. "Jackson Caricatured: Two Historical Errors." *THQ* 31 (1972), 39-44.

Sullivan, William A. "Did Labor Support Andrew Jackson?" *PSQ* 62 (1947), 569-80.

Temin, Peter. *The Jacksonian Economy,* Norton Essays in American History Series. New York: Norton, 1969. 208 pp.

Timberlake, Richard H., Jr. "The Specie Circular and the Distribution of the Surplus." *Journal of Political Economy* 68 (1960), 109-17.

Walker, Arda S. "Andrew Jackson: Frontier Democrat." ETHSP 18 (1946), 59-86.

Wallace, Sarah Agnes, ed. "Opening Days of Jackson's Presidency As Seen in Private Letters." *THQ* 9 (1950), 367-71.

White, Leonard D. *The Jacksonians.*

Wilburn, Jean A. *Biddle's Bank: The Crucial Years.* New York: Columbia Univ. Press, 1967. 149 pp.

Wilson, Major L. "Andrew Jackson: The Great Compromiser." *THQ* 26 (1967), 64-78.

———. "The Concept of Time and the Political Dialogue in the United States, 1828-1848." *American Quarterly* 19 (1967), 619-644.

———. "Liberty and Union: An Analysis of Three Concepts Involved in the Nullification Controversy." *JSH* 33 (1967), 331-55.

Young, Mary E. "Indian Removal and Land Allotment: The Civilized Tribes and Jacksonian Justice." *AHR* 64 (1958), 31-45.

DEVELOPING OPPOSITION

Bergeron, Paul H. "The Jacksonian Party on Trial: Presidential Politics in Tennessee, 1836-1856." Diss., Vanderbilt Univ., 1965.

Dewey, Donald O. "Madison's Response to Jackson's Foes." *THQ* 20 (1961), 167-76.

Hooper, Ernest Walter. "The Presidential Election of 1836 in Tennessee." Thesis, Univ. of North Carolina, 1949.

Moore, Powell. "The Political Background of the Revolt against Jackson in Tennessee." *ETHSP* 4 (1932), 45-66.

Murphy, James Edward. "Jackson and the Tennessee Opposition." *THQ* 30 (1971), 50-69.

Satterfield, R. Beeler. "The Uncertain Trumpet of the Tennessee Jacksonians." *THQ* 26 (1967), 79-96.

Van Deusen, Glyndon. "Some Aspects of Whig Thought and Theory in the Jacksonian Period." *AHR* 63 (1958), 305-22.

David Crockett

Abbott, John S. C. *David Crockett: His Life and Adventures,* American Pioneers and Patriots Series. New York: Dodd, 1874. 350 pp.

Allen, Charles Fletcher. *David Crockett, Scout, Small Boy, Pilgrim, Mountaineer, Soldier, Bear-Hunter, and Congressman, Defender of the Alamo.* Philadelphia, Pa.: Lippincott, 1911. 308 pp.

Blair, Walter. *Davy Crockett, Frontier Hero; the Truth As He Told It, The Legend as Friends Built It.* New York: Coward-McCann, 1955. 215 pp.

Catron, Anna Grace. "The Public Career of David Crockett." Thesis, Univ. of Tennessee, 1955.

Clarke, Matthew St. Clair. *Life and Adventures of Colonel David Crockett of West Tennessee.* Cincinnati: Privately printed, 1833.

Cooper, Texas Jim. "A Study of Some David Crockett Firearms." ETHSP 38 (1966), 62-69.

Crockett, David. *A Narrative of The Life of David Crockett of the State of Tennessee.* Philadelphia, Pa.: E. L. Carey & A. Hart, 1834. Rpt., Tennesseana Editions, with an introduction and annotations by James A. Shackford and Stanley J. Folmsbee, Knoxville: Univ. of Tennessee Press, 1973. 224 pp. Many reprints of this "genuine" Autobiography were published in 1834-36; after 1836 the title was usually combined with other works supposedly written by Crockett. The text portion of the edition of 1973 is a facsimile; the Introduction and the notes, based on a dissertation by James Atkins Shackford, and edited by Stanley J. Folmsbee, separate the man from the myth, correct many factual errors, and explain obscure historical and political allusions.

——. *An Account of Col. Crockett's Tour to the North and Down East, in the Year of Our Lord One Thousand Eight Hundred and Thirty-four. His Object Being to Examine the Grand Manufacturing Establishments of the Country; and Also to Find Out the Condition of Its Literature and Morals, the Extent of Its Commerce, and the Practical Operation of "The Experiment." Written by Himself.* Philadelphia, Pa.: E. L. Carey & A. Hart, 1835; rpt. Boston: Ticknor, 1835. 234 pp. Rpt. New York: Graham, 1848. Rpt. in *Life of Col. David Crockett,* 171-238. Philadelphia, Pa.: Evans, 1860. Rpt. Philadelphia, Pa.: Patter, 1882. Rpt. in *Davy Crockett's Own Story As Written by Himself,*

———. *The Crockett Almanacks. Nashville Series, 1835-1838,* ed. Franklin J. Meine. Chicago: Caxton Club, 1955. 150 pp.

———. *The Autobiography of David Crockett,* The Modern Student's Library. New York: Scribners, 1923. 328 pp.

———. *The Adventures of Davy Crockett, Told Mostly by Himself.* New York: Scribners, 1934, 1955, 1958. 258 pp.

———. *Davy Crockett's Own Story As Written by Himself; the Autobiography of America's Great Folk Hero,* illus. Milton Glaser. New York: Citadel, 1955. 377 pp. A collection of Crockett's autobiographical works.

The Crockett Tavern and Pioneer Museum. Morristown: n.p., n.d. Unpaged pamphlet.

Dorson, Richard M., ed. *Davy Crockett: American Comic Legend.* New York: Spiral, 1939. 171 pp. Selections from *The Crockett Almanacks* (1835-56).

Ellis, Edward S. *Life of Colonel David Crockett: Comprising His Adventures as Backwoodsman and Hunter; His Services as Soldier and Scout in the Creek War; His Electioneering Canvasses; His Career as Congressman; His Tour through the Northern States; and His Services and Death in the Texan War of Independence. To Which Are Added, Sketches of General Sam Houston, General Santa Anna, Rezin P. and Colonel James Bowie.* Philadelphia, Pa.: Parter & Coates, 1884. 271 pp.

Evans, Mona. "David Crockett: An Interpretation." Thesis, Vanderbilt University, 1924.

Folmsbee, Stanley J. "David Crockett and His Autobiography." ETHSP 43 (1971), 3-17.

Folmsbee, Stanley J., and Anna Grace Catron. "The Early Career of David Crockett." ETHSP 28 (1956), 58-65.

———. "David Crockett: Congressman." ETHSP 29 (1957), 40-78.

———. "David Crockett in Texas." ETHSP 30 (1958), 48-74.

Foster, Austin P. "David Crockett." THM 9 (1925), 166-77; rpt. in *Tennessee Old and New,* I, 275-87.

French, Janie P. C., and Zella Armstrong. *Davy Crockett and the Crockett Family.* Chattanooga: Lookout, 1951. 29 pp.

Garrett, William R., ed. "Letters of Davy Crockett." *AHM* 5 (1900), 41-47.

Gates, Margaret Haynes. "Fact and Fiction in the Early Biographies of David Crockett." Thesis, Univ. of Illinois, 1929.

Hogue, Albert R. *Davy Crockett and Others in Fentress County Who Have Given the County a Prominent Place in History.* Crossville: *Chronicle,* 1955. 32 pp.

Kelly, C. C. *Tennessee's Hero of the Alamo, Col. David Crockett, and Business Men's Directory.* Lawrenceburg: n.p., 1922. 24 pp.

Lake, Mary Daggett. "The Family of David Crockett in Texas." *THM* (ser. 2) 3 (1932-37), 174-78.

McBride, Robert. "David Crockett and His Memorials in Tennessee." *THQ* 26 (1967), 219-39.

Meadowcroft, Enid L. *The Story of Davy Crockett,* Signature Series. New York: Grosset, 1952. 178 pp. Fiction.

Morrison, John, and Bob Hamsley. *The Real David Crockett: A Short, Authentic, Illustrated, History of Tennessee's Famous Hunter, Frontiersman, Soldier, Legislator, Statesman, Patriot, and Hero of the Alamo, Colonel David Crockett.* Lawrenceburg: n.p., 1955. 38 pp.

Morrow, Temple Houston. "Address of Temple Houston Morrow Delivered at the Unveiling of Monument to David Crockett at His Old Home near Trenton, Tennessee, October 13, 1950." WTHSP 5 (1951), 5-13.

Null, Marion Michael. *The Forgotten Pioneer: The Life of Davy Crockett.* New York: Vantage, 1954. 183 pp.

Pearson, Josephine A. "The Tennessee Woman Trecker—Elizabeth—Widow of David Crockett." *THM* (ser. 2) 3 (1932-37), 169-73.

Rourke, Constance M. *Davy Crockett.* New York: Harcourt, 1934. 276 pp. Rpt., illust. James MacDonald; introd. and study guides Geraldine Murphy, 1955. 262 pp. Rpt., illust. Walter Seaton. Garden City, N.Y.: Jr. Deluxe Eds., 1956. 256 pp.

Shackford, James Atkins. "The Autobiography of David Crockett: An Annotated Edition." 2 vols., Diss., Vanderbilt Univ., 1948. Shackford's Introduction and voluminous notes in this dissertation later became the foundation for the Shackford-Folmsbee edition (1973) of *A Narrative of the Life of David Crockett* (see s. v. David Crockett; Shackford and Folmsbee, eds.).

———. "The Authorship of David Crockett's Autobiography." *Boston Public Library Quarterly* 3 (1951), 294-304.

——. *David Crockett: The Man and the Legend,* ed. John B. Shackford. Chapel Hill: Univ. of North Carolina Press, 1956. 338 pp. An effort to achieve an authentic biography of Crockett and to separate the man from legend.

——. "David Crockett and North Carolina." *NCHR* 28 (1957), 298-315.

Shackford, James Atkins, and Stanley J. Folmsbee, eds. *A Narrative of the Life of David Crockett.* A facsimile edition of the 1834 autobiographical work, with an introduction and annotations by the editors.

Sprague, William C. *Davy Crockett,* True Stories of Great American Series. New York: Macmillan, 1915. 189 pp.

Stiffler, Stuart A. "Davy Crockett: The Genesis of Heroic Myth." *THQ* 16 (1957), 134-40.

Stout, S. H. "David Crockett." *AHM* 7 (1902), 3-21.

Torrence, Robert M., and Robert L. Whittenburg. *Colonel "Davey" Crockett.* Washington, D.C.: N. Fagan, 1956. 23 pp.

Turner, H. S. "Andrew Jackson and David Crockett." *Magazine of American History* 27 (1892), 385-87.

James Knox Polk

Armistead, George H., Jr. "The Void Provision of a President's Will." *THQ* 15 (1956), 136-40.

Bonner, James C., ed. "Andrew Jackson Comments on Polk's Cabinet." *THQ* 27 (1968), 287-88.

Burt, Jesse C., ed. "Editor Eastman Writes James K. Polk." ETHS*P* 39 (1967), 103-17.

Chandler, Walter. "Centenary of James K. Polk and His Administration." WTHS*P* 3 (1949), 27-38.

Chase, Lucien B. *History of the Polk Administration.* New York: Putnam, 1850. 512 pp.

Everett, Robert B. "James K. Polk and the Election of 1844 in Tennessee." WTHS*P* 16 (1962), 5-28.

Goodpasture, Albert V. "The Boyhood of President Polk." *THM* 7 (1921), 36-50; rpt. in *Tennessee Old and New,* I, 333-48.

Graebner, Norman A. "James K. Polk's Wartime Expansionist Policy." ETHS*P* 23 (1951), 32-45.

———. "Polk, Politics and Oregon." ETHS*P* 24 (1952), 11-25.

———. "James K. Polk: A Study in Federal Patronage." *MVHR* 38 (1953), 613-32.

Hay, Thomas Robson. "Who Is James K. Polk?" *THM* 7 (1921), 235-42.

Hickman, George H. *The Life and Public Services of the Hon. James K. Polk, with a Compendium of His Speeches on Various Public Measures. Also, a Sketch of the Life of the Hon. George Mifflin Dallas.* Baltimore: Hickman, 1844. 40 pp.

Horn, James J. "Trends in Historical Interpretation: James K. Polk." *NCHR* 42 (1965), 454-64.

Hoyt, Edwin Palmer. *James Knox Polk.* Chicago: Reilly & Lee, 1965. 155 pp. Juvenile.

Jenkins, John Stilwell. *James Knox Polk, and a History of His Administration; Embracing the Annexation of Texas, the*

Difficulties with Mexico, the Settlement of the Oregon Question, and Other Important Events. Buffalo, N.Y.: J. E. Beardsley, 1850; rpt. Auburn, N.Y.: J. M. Alden, 1851; rpt. New Orleans: Burnett & Bastwick, 1854. 395 pp.

Learned, H. Barrett. "The Sequence of Appointments to Polk's Original Cabinet: A Study in Chronology, 1844-1845." *AHR* 30 (1924-25), 76-83.

Ledford, Delmus. "James K. Polk and the Mexican War: A Survey of Changing Interpretations." Thesis, Univ. of Tennessee, 1962.

Lomask, Milton. *This Slender Reed; a Life of James K. Polk,* Ariel Series. New York: Farrar, 1966. 176 pp. Juvenile.

McCormac, Eugene I. *James K. Polk: A Political Biography.* Berkeley: Univ. of California Press, 1922; rpt. New York: Russell, 1965. 746 pp. An excellent work which focuses upon Polk's presidential years.

McCoy, Charles A. *Polk and the Presidency.* Austin: Univ. of Texas Press, 1960, 1962. 238 pp.

Moore, Powell. "James K. Polk and Tennessee Politics, 1839-1841." *ETHSP* 9 (1937), 31-52.

——. "James K. Polk and the 'Immortal Thirteen.'" *ETHSP* 11 (1939), 20-33.

——. "James K. Polk: Tennessee Politician." *JSH* 17 (1951), 493-516.

Morrell, Martha McBride. *"Young Hickory," the Life and Times of President James K. Polk.* New York: Dutton, 1949. 381 pp.

Parks, Joseph H., ed. "Letters from James K. Polk to Samuel II. Laughlin, 1835-1844." *ETHSP* 18 (1946), 147-67.

——., ed. "Letters from James K. Polk to Alfred O. P. Nicholson, 1835-1849." *THQ* 3 (1944), 67-80.

Polk, James Knox. *The Diary of James K. Polk during His Presidency, 1845 to 1849, Now First Printed from the Original Manuscript in the Collections of the Chicago Historical Society,* ed. Milo M. Quaife; introd. Andrew C. McLaughlin, Chicago Historical Society Collections, vols. 6-9. Chicago: McClurg, 1910; rpt. Millwood, N.Y. Kraus, 1969.

——. *Polk: The Diary of a President, 1845-1849, Covering the Mexican War, the Acquisition of Oregon, and the Conquest of California and the Southwest,* ed. Allan Nevins. New York: Longmans, Green, 1929, 1952, 1957, 1968; rpt. New York: Putnam, 1968. 412 pp. An abridgement of the 4 vol. Quaife edition listed above.

——. *Correspondence of James K. Polk,* eds. Herbert Weaver and Paul H. Bergeron, Polk Project Series. 2 vols. to date. Nashville: Vanderbilt Univ. Press, 1969, 1972- . Vol. 1 (1969) covers 1819-32; vol. 2 (1972), 1833-34.

Sellers, Charles G. "The Early Career of James K. Polk, 1795-1839." Diss., Univ. of North Carolina, 1950.

——. "Jim Polk Goes to Chapel Hill." *NCHR* 29 (1952), 189-203.

——. "Colonel Ezekiel Polk: Pioneer and Patriarch." *William and Mary Quarterly* 10 (1953), 80-93.

——. "James K. Polk's Political Apprenticeship." ETHS*P* 25 (1953), 37-53.

——. *James K. Polk, Jacksonian, 1795-1843.* Princeton: Princeton Univ. Press, 1957. 526 pp. Vol. 1 of the definitive work on Polk. In this broad-gauged description, Sellers presents him as the last national leader who had a chance of resolving the growing sectional conflict within a structure of Jeffersonian-Jacksonian convictions.

——. *James K. Polk, Continentalist, 1843-1846.* Princeton: Princeton Univ. Press, 1966. 513 pp. Vol. 2 of the definitive biography of Polk. Sellers considers his accomplishments in the presidency remarkable in view of prevailing sectional tension and general apprehension about his competence and stature.

Sioussat, St. George L., ed. "Letters of James K. Polk to Cave Johnson, 1833-1848." *THM* 1 (1915), 209-56.

——. "Letters of James K. Polk to Andrew Jackson Donelson, 1843-1848." *THM* 3 (1917), 51-73.

Wallace, Sarah Agnes, ed. "Letters of Mrs. James K. Polk to Her Husband." *THQ* 11 (1952), 180-91, 282-88.

Walton, Brian G. J. "James K. Polk and the Democratic Party in the Aftermath of the Wilmot Proviso." Diss., Vanderbilt Univ., 1968.

West, Earl Irvin. "Religion in the Life of James K. Polk." *THQ* 26 (1967), 357-71.

Wiggins, J. Lexie. "Tennessee Whig Opposition to the Polk Administration, 1844-1848." Thesis, Middle Tennessee State Univ., 1972.

Williams, Emma Inman, ed. "Letters of Adam Huntsman to James K. Polk." *THQ* 6 (1947), 337-64.

Tennessee and Texas: 1820-50

Akins, Troy. "The Attitude of Tennessee toward the Annexation of Texas." Thesis, George Peabody College, 1928.

Binkley, William C. *The Texas Revolution.* Baton Rouge: Louisiana State Univ. Press, 1952. 131 pp. This work consists of four lectures delivered in 1950. The author views the immediate causes of the revolution as the substitution of centralism for federalism in Mexico and the decision to use force to effect the change upon the Americans in Texas.

Furber, George C. *The Twelve Months Volunteer; or, Journal of a Private, in the Tennessee Regiment of Cavalry, in the Campaign, in Mexico, 1846-47; Comprising Four General Subjects: I. A Soldier's Life in Camp; Amusements; Duties; Hardships; II. A Description of Texas and Mexico, As Seen on the March; III. Manners; Customs; Religious Ceremonies of the Mexicans; IV. The Operations of All the Twelve Months Volunteers Including a Complete History of the War with Mexico Embellished with Correct Engravings, from Drawings by the Author.* Cincinnati: J. A. & U. P. James, 1848. 624 pp. Rpt. 1848, 1849. 640 pp.

Gilley, Billy Hawkins. "Tennessee Opinion of the Mexican War As Reflected in the State Press." Thesis, Univ. of Tennessee, 1953.

———. "Tennessee Opinion of the Mexican War As Reflected in the State Press." ETHSP 26 (1954), 7-26.

Graf, Le Roy P., and Ralph W. Haskins, eds. "Blackston McDannel to Andrew Johnson: An East Tennessean in the Mexican War." ETHSP 32 (1960), 106-16.

Heiman, Adolphus. "Concise Description of the Services of the First Regiment of Tennessee Volunteers Commanded by Col. W. B. Campbell in the War with Mexico in 1846 and 1847." *AHM* 2 (1897), 324-35.

Karsch, Robert F. "Tennessee's Interest in the Texan Revolution, 1835-1836." Thesis, Vanderbilt Univ., 1934.

———. "Tennessee's Interest in the Texan Revolution, 1835-1836." *THM* (ser. 2) 3 (1932-37), 206-39.

Pierce, Gerald S. "The Great Wolf Hunt: Tennessee Volunteers in Texas, 1842." WTHSP 19 (1965), 5-20.

Rutland, Robert. "Captain William B. Walton, Mexican War Volunteer." *THQ* 11 (1952), 171-79.

Sioussat, St. George L., ed. "Mexican War Letters of Col. William Bowen Campbell, of Tennessee, Written to Governor David Campbell, of Virginia, 1846-1847." *THM* (ser. 1) 1 (1915), 129-67.

Smothers, Marion B. "Tennesseans Participating in the Annexation of Texas, 1821-1845." Thesis, East Tennessee State Univ., 1967.

Stephenson, Nathaniel W. *Texas and the Mexican War; a Chronicle of the Winning of the Southwest,* Chronicles of America Series, vol. 24. New Haven: Yale Univ. Press, 1921. 273 pp.

SAM HOUSTON

Barbee, David Rankin. "Sam Houston—The Last Phase." *THQ* 13 (1954), 12-64.

Bergeron, Paul H. "A Test for Jacksonians: Sam Houston on Trial." ETHSP 38 (1965), 16–29.

Bruce, Henry. *Life of General Houston, 1793-1863,* Makers of America Series. New York: Dodd, 1891. 232 pp.

Bryan, George Sands. *Sam Houston,* True Stories of Great Americans Series. New York: Macmillan, 1917. 183 pp.

Busfield, Roger M., Jr. "The Hermitage Walking Stick: First Challenge to Congressional Immunity." *THQ* 21 (1962), 122-30. Relates to Sam Houston.

Crane, William C. *Life and Select Literary Remains of Sam Houston of Texas.* Philadelphia, Pa.: Lippincott, 1884. 672 pp.

Creel, George. *Sam Houston, Colossus in Buckskin.* New York: Cosmopolitan, 1928, 340 pp.

Elliott, Sarah Barnwell. *Sam Houston,* Beacon Biographies of Eminent Americans Series. Boston: Small, Maynard, 1900, 1917. 149 pp.

Friend, Llerena. *Sam Houston, the Great Designer.* Austin: Univ. of Texas Press, 1954, 1969. 394 pp.

Garrett, William R., ed. "Letters of Gen. Sam Houston." *AHM* 4 (1899), 297-303.

Gregory, Jack, and Rennard Strickland. *Sam Houston with the Cherokees, 1829-1833.* Austin: Univ. of Texas Press, 1967. 206 pp.

Hefley, Estella G. "Sam Houston and Secession." Thesis, Vanderbilt Univ., 1930.

Houston, Samuel. *The Autobiography of Sam Houston,* ed. Donald Day and Harry H. Ullom. Norman: Univ. of Oklahoma Press, 1954. 298 pp. The editors present their subject not only as a great Texan but as a great American as well, a unique man who followed his star and fulfilled his destiny.

——. *The Writings of Sam Houston,* ed. Amerlia W. Williams and Eugene C. Barker. 8 vols. Austin: Univ. of Texas Press, 1938-43. Rpt. Austin: Jenkins, 1971.

James, Bessie R., and Marquis James. *Six Feet Six, the Heroic Story of Sam Houston.* Indianapolis: Bobbs-Merrill, 1931. 251 pp. Juvenile.

James, Marquis. *The Raven: A Biography of Sam Houston.* Indianapolis: Bobbs-Merrill, 1929; rpt. New York: Blue Ribbon, 1935, 1936; rpt. Garden City, N.Y.: Halcyon House, 1949. 489 pp. Rpt., Biographies of Distinction Series. New York: Grosset, 1956; rpt. New York: Paperback Libr., 1962; rpt. Dunwoody, Ga.: Berg, 1968. 384 pp. The most easily read biography of Sam Houston. Recommended particularly for laymen.

Lester, Charles Edwards. *Sam Houston and His Republic.* New York: Burgess, Stringer, 1846. 208 pp.

—— [alleged author]. *The Life of Sam Houston. (The Only Authentic Memoir of Him Ever Published).* New York: J. C. Derby, 1855; rpt. Philadelphia, Pa.: Davis, Porter & Coates, 1866; rpt. Philadelphia: J. E. Potter, 1867. Rpt. Austin: Jenkins, 1970. Rpt. Freeport, N.Y.: Books for Libraries Press, 1972. 402 pp.

McAlister, Hill. "Sam Houston." *THM* (ser. 2) 3 (1932-37), 197-205.

Mayfield, John S. *Sam Houston: Fugitive from Justice.* Nashville: Privately printed, c. 1927. 6 pp.

Mooney, Booth. *Sam Houston,* Library of American Heroes Series. Chicago: Follett, 1966. 144 pp. Juvenile.

Shearer, Ernest C. "Sam Houston and Religion." *THQ* 20 (1961), 38-50.

——. "The Mercurial Sam Houston." *ETHSP* 35 (1963), 3-20.

Smith, Beatrice Merle. "Sam Houston in Tennessee." Thesis, Univ. of Tennessee, 1932.

Turner, Martha Anne. *Sam Houston and His Twelve Women; the Ladies Who Influenced the Life of Texas' Greatest Statesman.* Austin: Pemberton, 1966. 96 pp.

Wiley, Evelyn. "Sam Houston's Career in Tennessee." Thesis, Vanderbilt Univ., 1939.

Wilson, Elizabeth. "Sam Houston, a Statebuilder." Thesis, George Peabody College, 1928.

Wisehart, Marion Karl. *Sam Houston, American Giant.* Washington, D.C.: Luce, 1962. 712 pp.

Wright, Frances F. *Sam Houston, Fighter and Leader,* Makers of America Series. Nashville: Abingdon, 1953. 128 pp.

William Walker: Filibusterer

Bass, John M. "William Walker."*AHM* 3 (1898), 207-22; rpt. in *Tennessee Old and New*, II, 112-23.

Crites, Walter W. "The Gray-Eyed Man of Destiny." *American West*, Nov. 1972, 4- .

Dufour, Charles L. *Gentle Tiger: The Gallant Life of Roberdeau Wheat.* Baton Rouge: Louisiana State Univ. Press, 1957. 232 pp. Wheat was a Tennessee filibuster with Walker in Central America.

Greene, Laurence. *The Filibuster; the Career of William Walker.* Indianapolis: Bobbs-Merrill, 1937; rpt. New York: B. Franklin, 196[?]. 350 pp.

Holman, Catherine Payne. "William Walker, Man of Controversy." Thesis, Austin Peay State Univ., 1968.

Hudson, Randall O. "The Filibuster Minister: The Career of John Hill Wheeler as United States Minister to Nicaragua, 1854-1856." *NCHR* 49 (1972), 280-97. Wheeler was an associate of William Walker.

Scroggs, William O. "William Walker and the Steamship Corporation in Nicaragua." *AHR* 10 (1904-5), 792-811.

——. "William Walker's Designs on Cuba." *MVIIR* 1 (1914-15), 198-211.

——. *Filibusters and Financiers: The Story of William Walker and His Associates.* New York: Macmillan, 1916; rpt. New York: Russell, 1969. 408 pp.

Sioussat, St. George L., ed. "Papers of Major John P. Heiss, of Nashville." *THM* 2 (1916), 137-47, 208-30. Heiss was a Nashville journalist and Walker aide.

——. "Walker-Heiss Papers. Some Diplomatic Correspondence of the Walker Regime in Nicaragua." *THM* 1 (1915), 331-45; 2 (1916), 147-49.

——. "With Walker in Nicaragua. The Reminiscences of Elleanore (Callaghan) Ratterman." *THM* 1 (1915), 315-30.

Wallace, Edward S. "The Gray-eyed Man of Destiny: William Walker and His Imperialist Filibusters in Nicaragua." *AH* 9 (1957), 26.

Slavery

[For the Negro and slavery at the county level, see individual county histories.]

Bancroft, Frederic. *Slave Trading in the Old South.* Baltimore: J. H. Furst, 1931. 415 pp.

Barteau, C. R. *Brief Review: What Has Been Done in Tennessee . . . Tennessee and the Institution of Slavery.* Hartsville: *Plaindealer,* 1861. 20 pp. Rpt., Confederate Imprints Collection Series. New York: Arno, 1972.

Bontemps, Arna. *American Missionary Association Archives in the Fisk University Library.* Nashville: n.p., 1947.

Bryan, Louise Miller. "Some Aspects of Slavery in Tennessee." Thesis, George Peabody College, 1924.

Catterall, Helen H. T. *Judicial Cases concerning American Slavery and the Negro,* Carnegie Institution of Washington Dept. of Historical Research Publication 374. 5 vols. Washington, D.C.: Carnegie Institution, 1926-37; rpt. New York: Octagon, 1968. An outstanding work summarizing important cases in various states; Tennessee, 1827-66, is covered in vol. 2.

Dillon, Merton L. "Three Southern Anti-slavery Editors: The Myth of the Southern Anti-slavery Movement." ETHSP 42 (1970), 47-56.

Embree, Elihu. *The Emancipator.* Jonesborough: n.p., 1820. Rpt., with biog. of Embree by Robert H. White, Nashville: B. H. Murphy, 1932. 112 pp.

England, James Merton. "The Free Negro in Ante-Bellum Tennessee." Diss., Vanderbilt Univ., 1941.

——. "The Free Negro in Ante-Bellum Tennessee." *JSH* 9 (1943), 37-58; Nashville: Joint Univ. Librs. 21 pp.

Federal Writers' Project. *Tennessee Narratives,* vol. 15 of *Slave Narratives, A Folk History of Slavery in the United States from Interviews with Former Slaves.* 17 vols. Washington, D.C.: LC, 1941; rpt. Detroit: Singing Tree, 1968.

Finnie, Gordon E. "The Antislavery Movement in the Upper South." *JSH* 35 (1969), 319-42.

Galpin, W. Freeman, ed. "Letters of an East Tennessee Abolitionist." ETHSP 3 (1931), 134-49. The abolitionist was Ezekiel Birdseye.

Hanson, Eliza Maud. "The Anti-Slavery Movement in Tennessee." Thesis, George Peabody College, 1930.

Henry, H. M. "The Slave Laws of Tennessee."*THM* 2 (1916), 175-203.

Hoss, E. E. "Elihu Embree, Abolitionist." *AHM* 2 (1897), 113-38.

Howell, Isabel. "John Armfield, Slave-Trader." *THQ* 2 (1943), 3-29.

Imes, William Lloyd. "The Negro in Tennessee before the Civil War, a Sociological Study." Thesis, Fisk Univ., 1912.

———. "The Legal Status of the Free Negroes and Slaves in Tennessee." *Journal of Negro History* 4 (1919), 254-72.

McMillan, Fay C. "Major Themes in Southern Negro Folklore." Thesis, East Tennessee State Univ., 1961.

McNeilly, James H. *Religion and Slavery, a Vindication of the Southern Churches.* Nashville: Methodist Episcopal Church, So., 1911. 88 pp.

Martin, Asa Earl. "The Anti-slavery Societies of Tennessee." *THM* 1 (1915), 261-81.

Mathews, Donald G. "Antislavery, Piety, and Institutionalism: The Slavery Controversies in the Methodist Episcopal Church, 1780-1844." Diss., Duke Univ., 1962.

———. *Slavery and Methodism, a Chapter in American Morality.* Princeton: Princeton Univ. Press, 1965. 329 pp. This study identifies the many ways in which the Methodist Church, second only to the Quakers in its early protest against slavery, sought to help the slaves through the American Colonization Society and missions. The author concludes that the issue so polarized the church that the split into northern and southern churches was inevitable.

Mooney, Chase C. "Slavery in Tennessee." Diss., Vanderbilt Univ., 1939. *Slavery in Tennessee,* Indiana Univ. Soc. Science Series, Publication 17. Bloomington: Indiana Univ. Press, 1957; rpt. Westport, Conn.: Greenwood, 1971. 250 pp.

———. "Some Institutional and Statistical Aspects of Slavery in Tennessee." *THQ* 1 (1942), 195-228.

———. "The Question of Slavery and the Free Negro in the Tennessee Constitutional Convention of 1834." *JSH* 12 (1946), 487-509.

Orr, Horace E. "The Tennessee Churches and Slavery (with Special Reference to East Tennessee)." Thesis, Univ. of Tennessee, 1924.

Parks, Edd Winfield. "Dreamer's Vision: Frances Wright at Nashoba, 1825-1830." *THM* (ser. 2) 2 (1932), 75-86.

Patterson, Caleb P. *The Negro in Tennessee, 1790-1865: A Study in Southern Politics.* Diss., Columbia Univ., 1923. Austin: Univ. of Texas Press, 1922; rpt. New York: Negro Univ. Press, 1922; rpt. New York: AMS, 1968. 213 pp. An early interpretation of the condition of the Negro in Tennessee, pointing up progress he had made under the system and emphasizing some sentiment for gradual emancipation.

Pease, William, and Jane H. Pease. "A New View of Nashoba." *THQ* 19 (1960), 99-109.

Phillips, Ulrich B. *American Negro Slavery: A Survey of the Supply, Employment and Control of Negro Labor As Determined by the Plantation Regime.* New York: Appleton, 1918. Rpt. Gloucester, Mass.: P. Smith, 1959; rpt. Baton Rouge: Louisiana State Univ. Press, 1966. 529 pp. An important work, but seriously marred by a fundamentally racist position.

——. *Life and Labor in the Old South.* Boston: Little, 1929, 1963; rpt. New York: Grosset, 1958. 375 pp.

Posey, Walter B. "Influence of Slavery upon the Methodist Church in the Early South and Southwest." *MVHR* 17 (1930-31), 530-42.

——. "The Slavery Question in the Presbyterian Church in the Old Southwest." *JSH* 15 (1949), 311-24.

Quarles, Benjamin. *The Negro in the American Revolution.* Chapel Hill: Univ. of North Carolina, 1961, 1967; rpt. New York: Norton, 1973. 231 pp. The author stresses that the Negro's contribution to the success of the Revolution was substantial. He states, however, that the Negro's primary loyalty was to principle rather than to group.

Roberts, Johnnie Mae Brigg. "A Survey of the Published Literature Relative to History of Anti-slavery Societies in Tennessee, 1815-1837: A Study in American History." Thesis, Tennessee State A&I Univ., 1953.

Roethler, Michael D. "Negro Slavery among the Cherokee Indians, 1540-1866." Diss., Fordham Univ., 1964.

Stephenson, Wendell H. *Isaac Franklin, Slave Trader and Planter of the Old South.* University: Louisiana State Univ. Press, 1938. 368 pp.

Swint, Henry Lee. "Ezekiel Birdseye and the Free State of Frankland." *THQ* 3 (1944), 226-36.

Trabue, Charles C. "The Voluntary Emancipation of Slaves in Tennessee As Reflected in the State's Legislation and Judicial Decisions." *THM* 4 (1918), 50-68; rpt. in *Tennessee Old and New*, II, 93-111.

Ward, Thomas L. "Anti-slavery Sentiment in the Upper South, 1820-1833." Thesis, Univ. of Tennessee, 1949.

Watson, Andrew Polk. "Primitive Religion among Negroes in Tennessee." Thesis, Fisk Univ., 1932.

Webb, Barsha Ruth. "The Attitude of Members of Congress from Tennessee on the Slavery Question, 1829-1858." Thesis, Univ. of Tennessee, 1931.

Wiley, Bell I. "Cotton and Slavery in the History of West Tennessee." Thesis, Univ. of Kentucky, 1929.

——. *Southern Negroes, 1861-65.* New Haven: Yale Univ. Press, 1965. 366 p.

Secession

Barbee, David Rankin. "The Line of Blood: Lincoln and the Coming of the War." *THQ* 16 (1957), 3-54.

Bratton, Madison. "The Unionist Junket of the Tennessee and Kentucky Legislatures in January, 1860." ETHS*P* 7 (1935), 64-80.

Campbell, Mary E. R. "Tennessee's Attitude toward Secession." Thesis, Vanderbilt Univ., 1929.

——. "Tennessee and the Union, 1847-1861." Diss., Vanderbilt Univ., 1937.

——. "Tennessee and the Union, 1847-1861." ETHS*P* 10 (1938), 71-90.

——. "The Significance of the Unionist Victory in the Election of February 9, 1861, in Tennessee." ETHS*P* 14 (1942), 11-30.

——. "Tennessee's Congressional Delegation in the Sectional Crisis of 1859-1860." *THQ* 19 (1960), 348-71.

——. *The Attitude of Tennesseans toward the Union, 1847-1861.* New York: Vantage, 1961; rpt. Deer Park, N.Y.: Brown Bk., 196[?]. 308 pp. The author concludes that the majority of Tennesseans, thinking war to be inevitable, prepared for it with all speed in the years immediately before 1861.

Clark, Herbert Leon. "Tennessee: A Reluctant Seceder, 1847-1861." Thesis, Tennessee State A&I Univ., 1966.

Craven, Avery O. *The Growth of Southern Nationalism, 1848-1861,* A History of the South, vol. 6. Baton Rouge: Louisiana State Univ. Press, 1953; Austin: Littlefield Fund for Southern History of the Univ. of Texas, 1953. 433 pp. The author attempts to explain how the American states drifted into the Civil War through the breakdown of the democratic processes in government.

——. *The Coming of the Civil War.* New York: Scribners, 1942; rpt. Chicago: Univ. of Chicago Press, 1957. 491 pp. Concentrating on the period between 1800 and 1861, Craven concludes that the conflict was inevitable.

Dumond, Dwight L. *The Secession Movement, 1860-1861.* Diss., Univ. of Michigan, 1929. New York: Macmillan, 1931; rpt. Westport, Conn.: Greenwood, 1931; rpt. New York: Octagon, 1963. 294 pp.

Fertig, James Walter. *The Secession and Reconstruction of Tennessee.* Diss., Univ. of Chicago, 1898. Chicago: Univ. of Chicago Press, 1898; rpt. New York: AMS, 1972. 108 pp.

Hamer, Marguerite B. "The Presidential Campaign of 1860 in Tennessee." ETHSP 3 (1931), 3-22.

Henry, J. Milton. "The Tennessee Conservatives and Secession, 1847-61." Diss., Univ. of Chicago, 1951.

——. "The Revolution in Tennessee, February, 1861, to June, 1861." *THQ* 18 (1959), 99-119.

Herndon, Dallas T. *The Nashville Convention of 1850.* Alabama Hist. Soc. *Transactions* 5 (1904), 203-37; rpt. Montgomery: Alabama Hist. Soc., 1905. 35 pp.

Jennings, Thelma. "A Reappraisal of the Nashville Convention." Diss., Univ. of Tennessee, 1968.

——. "Tennessee and the Nashville Conventions of 1850." *THQ* 30 (1971), 70-82.

Johnson, Andrew P. "The Nashville Convention of 1850." Thesis, Vanderbilt Univ., 1927.

McFerrin, Thomas Sumner. "Southern Sentiment and the Nashville Convention of 1850." Thesis, Florida State Univ., 1965.

Partin, Robert Love. "The Secession Movement in Tennessee." Diss., George Peabody College, 1935.

Porter, David L. "Attitude of the Tennessee Press toward the Presidential Election of 1860." *THQ* 29 (1970), 390-95.

Queener, Verton M. "East Tennessee Sentiment and the Secession Movement, November, 1860-June, 1861." ETHSP 20 (1948), 59-83.

Reynolds, Donald E. *Editors Make War: Southern Newspapers in the Secession Crisis.* Diss., Tulane Univ., 1965. Nashville: Vanderbilt Univ. Press, 1966, 1970. 304 pp.

Sheeler, J. Reuben. "The Development of Unionism in East Tennessee, 1860-1866." *Journal of Negro History* 29 (1944), 166-201.

Sioussat, St. George L. "Tennessee, the Compromise of 1850, and the Nashville Convention." *THM* (ser. 1) 4 (1918), 215-47.

Sydnor, Charles S. *The Development of Southern Sectionalism, 1819-1848,* A History of the South, vol. 5. Baton Rouge: Louisiana State Univ. Press, 1948, 1968. 400 pp. An attempt to trace the causes and development of disunity in the South. It treats both internal problems and federal relations with the South.

Civil War

[For historic sites of Civil War battles, see individual county histories.]

BIBLIOGRAPHIES

Nevins, Allan, James I. Robertson, Jr., and Bell I. Wiley, eds. *Civil War Books; a Critical Bibliography*. 2 vols. Baton Rouge: Louisiana State Univ. Press, 1967-69.

United States War Department Library. *Military Literature in the War Department Library Relating Chiefly to the Participation of the Individual States in the War for the Union*. Washington, D.C.: GPO, 1897, 1899; rpt., titled *Bibliography of State Participation in the Civil War, 1861-1866*, 1913. 1140 pp.

GENERAL ACCOUNTS

Catton, Bruce. *The American Heritage Short History of the Civil War*, Laurel-Leaf Library. New York: Dell, 1960, 1965. 286 pp. A 1-vol. edition of the narrative portion of the 2-vol. *The American Heritage Picture History of the Civil War* (New York, 1960).

——. *Grant Moves South*. Boston: Little, Brown, 1960. 564 pp.

——. *The Centennial History of the Civil War*. 3 vols. Garden City, N.Y.: Doubleday, 1961-65.

Coulter, E. Merton. *The Confederate States of America, 1861-1865*, A History of the South, vol. 7. Baton Rouge: Louisiana State Univ. Press, 1950. 644 pp. This is probably the best general work on the war's military, political, social, and economic impact upon the South that is available.

Eaton, Clement. *A History of the Southern Confederacy*. New York: Macmillan, 1954, 1961. 351 pp. Rpt. New York: Collier, 1961; rpt. New York: Free Press, 1965. 349 pp.

Freeman, Douglas S. *Lee's Lieutenants, a Study in Command*. 3 vols. New York: Scribner's, 1942-44.

Henry, Robert Selph. *The Story of the Confederacy*. Indianapolis: Bobbs-Merrill, 1931; rpt. Garden City, N.Y.: Garden City, 1933. Rev. ed., foreword Douglas S. Freeman, Indianapolis: Bobbs-

Merrill, 1936; rpt. New York: Grosset, 1937; rpt. New York: New Home Libr., 1943; rpt. New York: Bobbs-Merrill, 1957. 514 pp.

Roland, Charles P. *The Confederacy,* History of American Civilization Series. Chicago: Univ. of Chicago Press, 1960. 218 pp.

ARMY OF TENNESSEE

Connelly, Thomas Lawrence. "Metal, Fire and Forge: The Army of Tennessee, 1861-1862." Diss., Rice Univ., 1963.

——. *Army of the Heartland: The Army of Tennessee, 1861-1862.* Baton Rouge: Louisiana State Univ. Press, 1967. 305 pp.

——. *Autumn of Glory: The Army of Tennessee, 1862-1865.* Baton Rouge: Louisiana State Univ. Press, 1971. 558 pp.

Crisp, James Allen. "The Religious Awakening in the Army of Tennessee." Thesis, Duke Univ., 1964.

Drake, Edwin L., ed. *The Annals of the Army of Tennessee and Early Western History, Including a Chronological Summary of Battles and Engagements in the Western Armies of the Confederacy.* Nashville: A. D. Haynes, 1878. 432 pp.

Du Bose, John Witherspoon. *General Joseph Wheeler and the Army of Tennessee.* New York: Neale, 1912. 476 pp.

Dyer, John P. "Some Aspects of Cavalry Operations in the Army of Tennessee." *JSH* 8 (1942), 210-25.

——. *"Fightin' Joe" Wheeler,* Southern Biography Series. University: Louisiana State Univ. Press, 1941. 417 pp.

Gow, June Isobel. "Chiefs of Staff in the Army of Tennessee under Braxton Bragg." *THQ* 27 (1968), 341-60.

——. "Military Administration in the Confederacy: The Army of Tennessee, 1862-1864." Diss., Univ. of British Columbia, 1970.

Horn, Stanley F. *The Army of Tennessee: A Military History.* Indianapolis: Bobbs-Merrill, 1941; rpt. Norman: Univ. of Oklahoma Press, 1953, 1968. 503 pp. This work corrects what the author considers to have been neglect of the Army of Tennessee in Civil War literature. Horn believes that, despite the gallantry of this army which saw battle throughout the state, it could not succeed because of ever-changing and inexpert leadership.

McWhiney, Grady. *Braxton Bragg and Confederate Defeat: Field Command.* New York: Columbia Univ. Press, 1969- . 421 pp. Vol. 1 of a projected 2-vol. work.

Ridley, Bromfield L. *Battles and Sketches of the Army of Tennessee.* Mexico, Mo.: Missouri Printing, 1906. 662 pp.

BATTLES OF FORTS HENRY AND DONELSON, FEBRUARY 1862

Bearss, Edwin C. "Unconditional Surrender: The Fall of Fort Donelson." *THQ* 21 (1962), 47-65, 140-61.

——. "The Fall of Fort Henry, Tennessee." WTHS*P* 17 (1963), 85-107.

——. "The Construction of Fort Henry and Fort Donelson." WTHS*P* 21 (1967), 24-47.

"A Confederate Private at Fort Donelson, 1862." *AHR* 31 (1925-26), 477-84.

Confederate States of America, House of Representatives, Special Committee on the Recent Military Disasters. *Report of the Special Committee, on the Recent Military Disasters at Forts Henry and Donelson, and the Evacuation of Nashville.* Richmond, Va.: *Enquirer,* 1862. 178 pp. Rpt. in CSA, *Official Reports of Battles,* Confederate Imprints Collection Series. New York: Arno, 1972.

Cooling, Benjamin Franklin III. "The Battle of Dover, February 3, 1863." *THQ* 22 (1963), 143-51.

——., ed. "A Virginian at Fort Donelson: Excerpts from the Prison Diary of John Henry Guy." *THQ* 27 (1968), 176-90.

Cummings, Charles M. "Forgotten Man at Fort Donelson: Bushrod Rust Johnson." *THQ* 27 (1968), 380 97.

Hamilton, James J. *The Battle of Fort Donelson.* South Brunswick, N.J.: Yoseloff, 1968. 378 pp.

Provine, William A., ed. "General John B. Floyd's Report of the Battle of Fort Donelson." *THM* 5 (1919), 152-55.

Roland, Charles P. "Albert Sydney Johnston and the Loss of Forts Henry and Donelson." *JSH* 23 (1957), 45-69.

Stonesifer, Roy P., Jr. "The Forts Henry-Heiman and Fort Donelson Campaigns: A Study of Confederate Command." Diss., Pennsylvania State Univ., 1965.

——. "Gideon J. Pillow: A Study in Egotism." *THQ* 25 (1966), 340-50.

Treichel, James A. "Lew Wallace at Fort Donelson." *Indiana Magazine of History* 59 (1963), 3-18.

Walker, Peter Franklin. "Command Failure: The Fall of Forts Henry and Donelson." *THQ* 16 (1957), 335-60.

Battle of Shiloh, April 1862

Biel, John G., ed. "The Battle of Shiloh: From the Letters and Diary of Joseph Dimmit Thompson." *THQ* 17 (1958), 250-74.

Deaderick, John Barron. *Shiloh, Memphis, and Vicksburg.* Memphis: West Tennessee Hist. Soc., 1960. 32 pp.

Hurst, T. H. "Battle of Shiloh." *AHM* 7 (1902), 22-37.

——. "Battle of Shiloh." *THM* 5 (1919), 81-96.

McWhiney, Grady. "Braxton Bragg at Shiloh." *THQ* 21 (1962), 19-30.

——. *Braxton Bragg and Confederate Defeat.* New York: Columbia Univ. Press, 1969. 407 pp. Treats the battle of Shiloh.

Morrison, John Franklin. *The Battle of Shiloh. A Sketch of the Battle of Shiloh, in the War Between the States (Civil War) Fought April 6 and 7, 1862, at Pittsburg Landing, in Hardin County, Tennessee, and of Military Events Both prior to and after the Battle.* Lawrenceburg: Lawrence Co. Hist. Soc., 1962. 23 leaves.

Rice, De Long. *The Story of Shiloh.* Nashville: Brandon, 1919. 64 pp. Rpt. Jackson: McCowat-Mercer, 1924. 70 pp. Rpt. Memphis: Julia M. Rice, 1961. 47 pp.

Roland, Charles P. *Albert Sidney Johnston: Soldier of Three Republics.* Austin: Univ. of Texas Press, 1964. 384 pp.

Wallace, Harold Lew. "Lew Wallace's March to Shiloh Revisited." *Indiana Magazine of History* 59 (1963), 19-30.

Wiley, Bell I. "Johnny Reb and Billy Yank at Shiloh." WTHS*P* 26 (1972), 5-12.

Williams, T. Harry. "Beauregard at Shiloh." *Civil War History* 1 (1955), 17-34.

Worthington, Thomas. *Shiloh; or, The Tennessee Campaign of 1862: Written Especially for the Army of the Tennessee in 1862.* Washington, D.C.: M'Gill & Witherow, 1872. 164 pp.

Battles of Stones River and Murfreesboro, December 1862–January 1863

Bearss, Edwin C. "Cavalry Operations in the Battle of Stones River." *THQ* 19 (1960), 23-53, 110-44.

Rosecrans, William Starke. *Report on the Battle of Murfreesboro, Tennessee.* Washington, D.C.: GPO, 1863. 571 pp.

Stevenson, Alexander F. *The Battle of Stone's River near Murfreesboro', Tenn. December 30, 1862, to January 3, 1863.* Boston: James R. Osgood, 1884. 197 pp.

Thruston, Gates P. *Personal Recollections of the Battle in the Rear at Stones River, Tennessee.* Nashville: Brandon, 1906. 21 pp.

BATTLES OF CHICKAMAUGA, SEPTEMBER 1863, AND CHATTANOOGA, NOVEMBER 1863

"The Battles for Chattanooga." *Civil War Times Illustrated* (Special Supplement), Aug. 1971, pp. 4-50.

Catton, Bruce. "The Miracle on Missionary Ridge." *AH* 20 (1969), 60-72.

Cleaves, Freeman. *Rock of Chickamauga, the Life of General George H. Thomas.* Norman: Univ. of Oklahoma Press, 1948. 328 pp.

Downey, Fairfax D. *Storming of the Gateway; Chattanooga, 1863.* New York: McKay, 1960, 1969. 303 pp.

Funk, Arville L., ed. "A Hoosier Regiment at Chattanooga." *THQ* 22 (1963), 280-87.

Hay, Thomas R. "The Battle of Chattanooga." *Georgia Historical Quarterly* 8 (1924), 121-41.

Howard, O. O. "Campaign of Chattanooga." *Atlantic Monthly,* Aug. 1876, pp. 203-19.

Kimberley, R. L. "Raising the Seige at Chattanooga." *Lippincott's Magazine* 18 (1876), 211-15.

Lynde, Francis. *Chickamauga and Chattanooga National Military Park. With Narratives of the Battles of Chickamauga, Lookout Mountain and Missionary Ridge.* Chattanooga: Birchmore, 1895. 39 pp. Rpt. Chattanooga Community Assoc., 1930. 36 pp.

McWhiney, H. Grady. "The Ordeal of Command: Bragg before Chickamauga." Diss., Columbia Univ., 1960.

O'Connor, Richard. *Thomas, Rock of Chickamauga.* New York: Prentice-Hall, 1948. 385 pp.

Proudfoot, Merrill, and Stanley J. Folmsbee, eds. "Three Yankee Soldier-Brothers in the Battle of Chattanooga: Three Letters." *ETHSP* 35 (1963), 100-105.

Reed, Samuel R. *The Vicksburg Campaign, and the Battles about Chattanooga under the Command of General U. S. Grant in 1862-63; an Historical Review.* Cincinnati: R. Clarke, 1882. 201 pp.

Rogers, Jesse Littleton. *The Civil War Battles of Chickamauga and Chattanooga.* Chattanooga: Andrews, 1942. 31 pp.

Shanks, W. F. G. "Chattanooga and How We Held It." *Harper's New Monthly Magazine,* Jan. 1868, pp. 137-49.

Tucker, Glenn. *Chickamauga: Bloody Battle in the West.* Indianapolis: Bobbs-Merrill, 1961. 448 pp.

BATTLE OF KNOXVILLE, NOVEMBER 1863

Burrage, H. S. "Retreat from Lenoir and Siege of Knoxville." *Atlantic Monthly* 18 (1866), 21-30.

Davidson, James F. "Michigan and the Defense of Knoxville." ETHSP 35 (1963), 21-53.

Fink, Harold S. "The East Tennessee Campaign and the Battle of Knoxville in 1863." ETHSP 29 (1957), 79-117.

Poe, Orlando M. *Personal Recollections of the Occupation of East Tennessee and the Defense of Knoxville. A Paper Read before Michigan Commandery of the Military Order of the Loyal Legion of the United States, December 5, 1888.* Detroit: Ostler, 1889; rpt. Knoxville: East Tennessee Hist. Soc., 1963. 48 pp.

Seymour, Digby Gordon. *Divided Loyalties: Fort Sanders and the Civil War in East Tennessee.* Knoxville: Univ. of Tennessee Press, 1963. 244 pp. Writing to commemorate the Battle of Fort Sanders in its centennial year, Seymour covers developments throughout the war in East Tennessee. His contention is that control of the region was of great significance in determining the war's outcome.

Trent, Henry Gibson, Jr. "The Battle of Knoxville." Thesis, Southern Methodist Univ., 1950.

BATTLES OF FRANKLIN AND SPRING HILL, NOVEMBER 1864

Banks, Robert W. *The Battle of Franklin, November 30, 1864, The Bloodiest Engagement of the War Between the States.* New York: Neale, 1908. 88 pp.

Copley, John M. *A Sketch of the Battle of Franklin, Tenn.; with*

Reminiscences of Camp Douglas. Austin: Von Boeckmann, 1893. 206 pp.

Cox, Jacob D. *The March to the Sea: Franklin and Nashville,* Campaigning the Civil War, vol. 10. New York: Scribners, 1882. Rpt., The Army in the Civil War, vol. 10, 1885. Rpt., Campaigns of the Civil War, vol. 12. New York: J. Brussie, 1959. 265 pp.

——. *The Battle of Franklin, Tennessee, November 30, 1864. A Monograph.* New York: Scribners, 1897. 351 pp.

Crownover, Sims. "The Battle of Franklin." *THQ* 14 (1955), 291-322.

Gist, W. W. "The Battle of Franklin, the Key to the Last Campaign in the West." *THM* 6 (1920), 213-65.

Hay, Thomas Robson. "The Battle of Spring Hill." *THM* 7 (1921), 74-91.

——. "The Cavalry at Spring Hill." *THM* 8 (1924), 7-23.

Kinnard, Arthur H., Jr. "Events Leading to and Consequences of the Battle of Franklin, Tennessee." Thesis, Tennessee State A&I Univ., 1964.

McDonough, James L. "West Point Classmates—Eleven Years Later: Some Observations on the Spring Hill-Franklin Campaign." *THQ* 28 (1969), 182-96.

Robertson, James I., Jr. "The Human Battle of Franklin." *THQ* 24 (1965), 20-30.

Robison, Dan M. "The Carter House, Focus of the Battle of Franklin." *THQ* 22 (1963), 3-21.

Scofield, Levi T. *The Retreat from Pulaski to Nashville, Tenn.* Cincinnati: H. C. Sherick, 1886. 28 pp. Rev. ed. includes addition of *Battle of Franklin, Tennessee, November 30th, 1864; with Maps, Sketches, Portraits and Photographic Views.* Cleveland, O.: Caxton, 1909. 67 pp.

Shellenberger, John K. *The Battle of Spring Hill, Tennessee, November 29, 1864; a Refutation of the Erroneous Statements Made by Captain Scofield in His Paper Entitled "The Retreat from Pulaski to Nashville."* Cleveland, O.: Arthur H. Clark, 1913. 49 pp.

——. *The Battle of Franklin, Tennessee, November 30, 1864; a Statement of the Erroneous Claims Made by General Schofield [sic], and an Exposition of the Blunder Which Opened the Battle.* Cleveland, O.: Arthur H. Clark, 1916. 42 pp.

Wade, James Earl. "Hood's Campaign of 1864 from the Fall of Atlanta to the Battle of Franklin." Thesis, Auburn Univ., 1965.

Battle of Nashville, December 1864

Beard, William E. *The Battle of Nashville; Including an Outline of the Stirring Events Occurring in One of the Most Notable Movements of the Civil War—Hood's Invasion of Tennessee.* Nashville: Marshall & Bruce, 1913. 44 pp.

Boynton, Henry V. *Was General Thomas Slow at Nashville? With a Description of the Greatest Cavalry Movement of the War and General James H. Wilson's Cavalry Operations in Tennessee, Alabama, and Georgia.* New York: Harper, 1896. 95 pp.

Corn, John F., Jimmy Ellis, and Joe Rudis, photographers; text Bill Kovach. *The Battle of Nashville; a Pictorial Record of the Centennial Re-enactment, Warner Park, December 12, 1964.* Nashville: n.p., 1965.

Cox, Jacob D. *The March to the Sea: Franklin and Nashville.*

"Hood's Nashville Campaign." *Civil War Times Illustrated,* Dec. 1964, pp. 5 ff.

Horn, Stanley F. *The Decisive Battle of Nashville.* Baton Rouge: Louisiana State Univ. Press, 1956. 181 pp. Rpt. Knoxville: Univ. of Tennessee Press, 1968. 200 pp. The author considers this battle, a classic still studied in military schools, the "high-water mark of the Southern Confederacy's last aggressive action."

———. "Nashville—The Most Decisive Battle of the Civil War." *Civil War Times Illustrated,* Dec. 1964, pp. 5-11.

Kirby, James E. "The McKendree Chapel Affair." *THQ* 25 (1966), 360-70.

Otis, Ephraim A. *The Nashville Campaign.* Chicago: n.p., 1899.

Parman, Susan Katharine. "The Battle of Nashville." Thesis, George Peabody College, 1932.

Statewide Warfare

Aden, Mrs. R. F. "In Memoriam, Seventh Tennessee Cavalry, C.S.A." *WTHSP* 17 (1963), 108-17.

Alexander, Harbert L. Rice. "The Armstrong Raid Including the Battles of Bolivar, Medon Station and Britton Lane." *THQ* 21 (1962), 31-46.

Alexander, Thomas B. "Neither Peace nor War: Conditions in Tennessee in 1865." *ETHSP* 21 (1949), 33-51.

———. "Is Civil War History Polarized?—A Question Suggested by the Career of Thomas A. R. Nelson." *ETHSP* 29 (1957), 10-39.

Alvarez, Eugene, ed. "James C. Holt: Prisoner of War." *THQ* 25 (1966), 169-75.

Anderson, William M. "The Union Side of Thompson's Station." *THQ* 29 (1970), 396-406.

Black, Robert C. *The Railroads of the Confederacy.* Chapel Hill: Univ. of North Carolina Press, 1952. 360 pp.

Black, Roy W., Sr., ed. "William J. Rogers' Memorandum Book." WTHS*P* 9 (1955), 59-92.

Bogle, Robert V. "Defeat through Default: Confederate Naval Strategy for the Upper Mississippi River and Its Tributaries, 1861-1862." *THQ* 27 (1968), 62-71.

Born, Kathryn. "The Unionist Movement in Eastern Tennessee during the Civil War and Reconstruction Period." Thesis, Univ. of Wisconsin, 1933.

Bowman, S. M., and R. B. Irwin. *Sherman and His Campaigns: A Military Biography.* Cincinnati: C. F. Vent, 1865. 512 pp.

Bratcher, James T., ed. "An 1866 Letter on the War and Reconstruction." *THQ* 22 (1963), 83-86.

Brown, Campbell H. "Carter's East Tennessee Raid, the Sailor on Horseback Who Raided His Own Backyard." *THQ* 22 (1963), 66-82.

Buck, Irving A. *Cleburne and His Command.* New York: Neale, 1908. 382 pp. Rpt., foreword Bell I. Wiley, Jackson: McCowat-Mercer, 1959. 378 pp.

Burns, Amanda McDowell, and Lela M. Blankenship. *Fiddles in the Cumberlands.* New York: Smith, 1943. 310 pp. A pro-Confederate account of the Civil War in that region, it includes a diary of Amanda Burns.

Burt, Jesse C., Jr. "Sherman's Logistics and Andrew Johnson." *THQ* 15 (1956), 195-215.

——. "East Tennessee, Lincoln, and Sherman." ETHS*P* 34 (1962), 3-25; 35 (1963), 54-75.

Campbell, James B. "East Tennessee during the Federal Occupation, 1863-1865." ETHS*P* 19 (1947), 64-80.

Carter, William Randolph. *History of the First Regiment of Tennessee Volunteer Cavalry in the Great War of the Rebellion, with the Armies of the Ohio and Cumberland, under Generals Morgan, Rosecrans, Thomas, Stanley and Wilson. 1862-1865.* Knoxville: Gaut-Ogden, 1902. 335 pp.

Catton, Bruce. "The Army of the Cumberland: A Panoramic Show with W. D. T. Travis' Panorama." *AH* 19 (1967), 40-49.

Clark, Sam L., ed. "A Confederate Officer Visits Richmond." *THQ* 11 (1952), 86-91.

Clark, Sam L., and H. D. Riley, Jr., eds. "Outline and the Organization of the Medical Department of the Confederate Army and Department of Tennessee, by S. H. Stout." *THQ* 16 (1957), 55-82.

Cochran, Anna Delle. "Unionism in East Tennessee during the Civil War." Thesis, Univ. of Texas, 1931.

Cooper, William J., Jr. "A Reassessment of Jefferson Davis as War Leader: The Case from Atlanta to Nashville." *JSH* 36 (1970), 189-204.

Cosby, Helen Louise. "Union Sentiment in Tennessee during the Civil War Period." Thesis, George Peabody College, 1929.

Cotterill, Robert S. "The Louisville and Nashville Railroad, 1861-1865." *AHR* 29 (1923-24), 700-15.

Crego, Arthur Van Voorhis. "The Organization and Functions of the Staff of the Confederate Army of Tennessee." Thesis, Louisiana State Univ., 1965.

Criswell, Grover C., Jr., and Clarence L. Criswell. *Confederate and Southern State Currency; A Descriptive Listing, Including Rarity,* Criswell's Currency Series, vol. 1. Pass-a-Grille Beach, Fla.: Criswell, 1957. 277 pp. Rev. ed., Iola, Wis.: Krause, 1964. 291 pp.

Culp, Frederick M. "Captain George King's Home Guard Company, CSA." WTHSP 15 (1961), 55-78.

Cummings, Charles M. "Robert Hopkins Hatton: Reluctant Rebel." *THQ* 23 (1964), 169-81.

——. "Otho French Strahl: 'Choicest Spirit to Embrace the South.'" *THQ* 24 (1965), 341-55.

Cunningham, H. H. "Confederate General Hospitals: Establishment and Organization." *JSH* 20 (1954), 376-94.

Daniel, W. Harrison. "Protestant Clergy and Union Sentiment in the Confederacy." *THQ* 23 (1965), 284-90.

Deaderick, John Barron. "Civil War Campaigns in Tennessee." WTHSP 10 (1956), 53-77.

De Berry, John H. "Confederate Tennessee." Diss., Univ. of Kentucky, 1967.

Directory of Civil War Monuments and Memorials in Tennessee. Nashville: Civil War Centennial Comm., 1963. 93 pp.

Drake, James Vaulx. *Life of General Robert Hatton, Including His Most Important Public Speeches; Together with Much of His Washington and Army Correspondence.* Nashville: Marshall & Bruce, 1867. 458 pp.

Dwight, Allan. *See* Taylor, Allan, and Lois Dwight Cole.

Dyer, John P. *The Gallant Hood.* Indianapolis: Bobbs-Merrill, 1950. 383 pp. Concentrating on Gen. John B. Hood's Civil War years, Dyer believes that the key to understanding this failure-filled life lies in the General's impetuous personality.

Eaton, Clement. *A History of the Southern Confederacy.* This story of the Confederacy from Secession to Appomattox attempts to present a balanced social, political, and military history. Eaton largely counters the legends of glamorous life in the Old South and in the Confederacy, stressing the detrimental effects which they had upon subsequent generations of Southerners.

Eckel, Alexander. *History of the Fourth Tennessee Cavalry, U.S.A. War of the Rebellion, 1861-1865.* Knoxville: Stubley, 1929. 150 pp.

Fitch, John. *Annals of the Army of the Cumberland: Comprising Biographies, Descriptions of Departments, Accounts of Expeditions, Skirmishes, and Battles; Also Its Police Record of Spies, Smugglers, and Prominent Rebel Emmissaries. Together with Anecdotes, Incidents, Poetry, Reminiscences, etc., and Official Reports of the Battle of Stone River.* Philadelphia, Pa.: Lippincott, 1863. 671 pp. Rev. 5th ed., 1864. 716 pp.

Flynn, Ralph. "Rev. James Hugh McNeilly, Confederate Chaplain." Thesis, Vanderbilt Univ., 1964.

Garrett, Beatrice Lydia. "The Confederate Government and the Unionists of East Tennessee." Thesis, Univ. of Tennessee, 1932.

[The] Great Panic: Being Incidents Connected with Two Weeks of the War in Tennessee. By an Eye-Witness. Nashville: Johnson & Whiting, 1862. 36 pp.

Guild, George B. *A Brief Narrative of the Fourth Tennessee Cavalry Regiment, Wheeler's Corps, Army of Tennessee.* Nashville: n.p., 1913. 268 pp.

Hancock, Richard Ramsey. *Hancock's Diary: or, A History of the Second Tennessee Confederate Cavalry, with Sketches of First and Seventh Battalions; Also, Portraits and Biographical Sketches.* Nashville: Brandon, 1887. 644 pp.

Hartje, Robert G. "Van Dorn Conducts a Raid on Holly Springs and Enters Tennessee." *THQ* 18 (1959), 120-33.

——. "The Gray Dragoon Wins His Final Victory." *THQ* 23 (1964), 38-58.

——. *Van Dorn, the Life and Times of a Confederate General.* Nashville: Vanderbilt Univ. Press, 1967. 359 pp. This frank appraisal of Van Dorn's life (1820-1863) concentrates on his military activities. Hartje contends that, like many others North and South, he was a second-rate military leader motivated largely by his desire for personal glory.

Hay, Thomas Robson. *Hood's Tennessee Campaign.* New York: Neale, 1929. 272 pp.

Head, Thomas A. *Campaigns and Battles of the Sixteenth Tennessee Infantry Regiment, Tennessee Volunteers.* Nashville: Cumberland Presbyterian Pub., 1885; rpt., introd. Stanley F. Horn, McMinnville: Womack, 1961. 488 pp.

Hendricks, Allan. "Afloat in Dixie." *Lippincott's Magazine* 66 (1900), 581-88. On the Tennessee River during the Civil War.

Henry, Robert Selph. *The Story of the Confederacy.*

Hesseltine, William B. "The Underground Railroad from Confederate Prisons to East Tennessee." ETHSP 2 (1930), 55-69.

House, Boyce. "Confederate Navy Hero Put the Flag Back in Place!" *THQ* 19 (1960), 172-75.

Huddleston, Edwin Glenn. *The Civil War in Middle Tennessee.* Nashville: Nashville *Banner,* 1965. 159 pp.

Johnston, William P. *Life of Gen. Albert Sidney Johnston, Embracing His Services in the Armies of the United States, the Republic of Texas, and the Confederate States.* New York: Appleton, 1878. 755 pp.

Jones, Archer. "Tennessee and Mississippi, Joe Johnston's Strategic Problem." *THQ* 18 (1959), 134-47.

Jones, James P., ed. "The Yankees' Jeff Davis in Tennessee." *THQ* 19 (1960), 166-71. Davis was a Union soldier with a famous Confederate name.

Jordan, John L. "Was There a Massacre at Fort Pillow?" *THQ* 6 (1947), 99-133.

Lewis, Elizabeth Lumpkin. "The Organization of Tennessee's Forces, 1861." Thesis, Univ. of Texas, 1930.

Lewis, Lloyd. *Sherman, Fighting Prophet.* New York: Harcourt, 1932. 690 pp.

Lindsley, John Berrien, ed. *The Military Annals of Tennessee, Confederate. First Series: Embracing a Review of Military Operations, with Regimental Histories and Memorial Roles, Compiled from Original and Official Sources.* Nashville: J. M. Lindsley, 1886. 910 pp.

Livermore, Thomas L. *Numbers and Losses in the Civil War in America, 1861-1865.* Boston: Houghton, 1900, 1901; rpt., Civil War Centennial Series, Bloomington: Indiana Univ. Press, 1957; rpt. Millwood, N.Y.: Kraus, 1968. 150 pp.

Livingood, James W. "The Chattanooga *Rebel.*" ETHSP 39 (1967), 42-55.

McBride, Robert M. "The 'Confederate Sins' of Major Cheairs." *THQ* 23 (1964), 121-35.

McKee, James W., Jr. "Felix K. Zollicoffer: Confederate Defender of East Tennessee." ETHSP 43 (1971), 34-58; 44 (1972), 17-40.

MacLeod, Xavier Donald. *The Rebellion in Tennessee.* Washington, D.C.: McGill, Witheraw, 1862. 11 pp.

McMurray, William Josiah, D. J. Roberts, and R. J. Neal. *History of the Twentieth Tennessee Regiment Volunteer Infantry, C.S.A.* Nashville: The Authors, 1904. 520 pp.

McMurtry, R. Gerald. "Zollicoffer and the Battle of Mill Springs." *FCHQ* 29 (1955), 303-19.

Merrill, James M. "Capt. Andrew Hull Foote and the Civil War on Tennessee Waters." *THQ* 30 (1971), 83-93.

Mitchell, Enoch L., ed. "Letters of a Confederate Surgeon in the Army of Tennessee to His Wife." *THQ* 4 (1945), 341-53.

Moore, Albert B. *Conscription and Conflict in the Confederacy.* New York: Macmillan, 1924, 1963. 367 pp.

Muir, Andrew Forest. "William P. Johnson, Southern Proletarian and Unionist." *THQ* 15 (1956), 330-38.

Myers, Raymond E. *The Zollie Tree,* Filson Club Publication, 2nd Series. Louisville, Ky.: Filson Club Press, 1964. 200 pp. Biography of Felix Zollicoffer.

Nashville, Chattanooga and St. Louis Railway, Passenger Dept. *The Story of the "General," 1862.* Chicago: Poole Bros., 1917. 32 pp.

Nason, W. A. *With the Ninth Army Corps in East Tennessee.* Providence: Rhode Island Soldiers and Sailors Hist. Soc., 1891. 70 pp.

Nisbet, James C. *Four Years on the Firing Line.* Chattanooga: Imperial, 1914. 445 pp. Rev. ed., Bell I. Wiley, ed., Jackson: McCowat-Mercer, 1963. 267 pp.

Owsley, Frank L. *State Rights in the Confederacy.* Chicago: Univ.

of Chicago Press, 1925; rpt. Gloucester, Mass.: P. Smith, 1961. 289 pp.

Owsley, Harriet C. "Peace and the Presidential Election of 1864." *THQ* 18 (1959), 3-19.

Quintard, Charles. *Doctor Quintard, Chaplain, C.S.A. and Second Bishop of Tennessee; being his Story of the War (1861-1865) ed. and extended by the Rev. Arthur Howard Noll.* Sewanee: Univ. Press, 1905. 183 pp.

Parks, Joseph H. *General Edmund Kirby Smith, C.S.A.,* Southern Biography Series. Baton Rouge: Louisiana State Univ. Press, 1954. 537 pp.

——. *General Leonidas Polk, C.S.A., the Fighting Bishop,* Southern Biography Series. Baton Rouge: Louisiana State Univ. Press, 1962. 408 pp. Episcopal bishop and Confederate general, Polk sought reconciliation between North and South by helping to establish the University of the South. When reconciliation failed, he joined the Confederate army, where he died observing battle.

Partain, Robert. "The Civil War in East Tennessee As Reported by a Confederate Railroad Bridge Builder." *THQ* 22 (1963), 238-58.

Pennington, Edgar Legare. "The Battle at Sewanee." *THQ* 9 (1950), 217-43.

Pittenger, William. *The Great Locomotive Chase: a History of the Andrews Railroad Raid into Georgia in 1862, by William Pittenger, a Member of the Expedition.* Philadelphia: Lippincott, 1863, 1864; rpt. Philadelphia: Daughaday, 1864; rpt. Philadelphia, Pa.: Lippincott, 1882; rpt. Washington, D.C.: *National Tribune,* 1885; rpt. New York: War, 1887; rpt. New York: Alden, 1889; rpt. Philadelphia, Pa.: Penn, 1910, 1917. Rpt. San Marino, Calif.: Golden West Bks., 1965. 416 pp. Issued under at least 4 different titles, this work appeared in 1863, 1864, and 1887 as *Daring and Suffering;* in 1882 and 1885, as *Capturing a Locomotive. The Great Locomotive Chase . . .* was the title of the 1889 ed.; in 1965 it was called *In Pursuit of the General; a History of the Civil War Railroad Raid.*

Provine, William B. "The Legend of 'Long Tom' at Cumberland Gap." *THQ* 24 (1965), 255-64.

Ramsdell, Charles W. *Behind the Lines in the Southern Confederacy,* ed. Wendell H. Stephenson. Baton Rouge: Louisiana State Univ. Press, 1944; rpt. Westport, Conn.: Greenwood, 1944. 136 pp.

Randall, James G. *The Civil War and Reconstruction.* Boston: Heath,

1937, 1953. 971 pp. Rev. ed., with David Donald, 1961, 1969. 820 pp. This is one of the standard college textbooks concentrating on the years between 1850 and 1877. Randall prepared the work in order to synthesize the results of the enormous amount of scholarship devoted to this era. In so doing, he rejects the contention held by numerous scholars that the conflict was inevitable.

Ripley, C. Peter. "A Period of Discontent: The 31st Illinois in Tennessee."*THQ* 29 (1970), 49-61.

Ritt, Arnold. "The Escape of Federal Prisoners through East Tennessee, 1861-1865." Thesis, Univ. of Tennessee, 1965.

Robison, Dan M. "The Whigs in the Politics of the Confederacy." ETHS*P* 11 (1939), 3-10.

Rule, William. *The Loyalists of Tennessee in the Late War. A Paper Read before the Ohio Commandery of the Military Order of the Loyal Region of the United States, April 6, 1887.* Cincinnati: H. C. Sherick, 1887. 23 pp.

Rushing, Clarence A., Jr. "Isaac Burton Tigrett and the 'Rebel Route.'" Thesis, Tennessee Technological Univ., 1965.

Schroeder, Albert W., Jr. "Writings of a Tennessee Unionist." *THQ* 9 (1950), 244-72, 344-61.

Scott, Samuel W., and Samuel P. Angel. *History of the 13th Regiment, Tennessee Volunteer Cavalry, U.S.A., Including a Narrative of the Bridge Burning; the Carter County Rebellion, and the Loyalty, Heroism and Suffering of the Union Men and Women of Carter and Johnson Counties, Tennessee, during the Civil War.* Knoxville: n.p., 1903. 510 pp.

Scott, William Blair. "The Topographical Influences on the Campaigns in Middle and West Tennessee during the First Year of the Civil War." Thesis, Univ. of Tennessee, 1953.

Sherman, William T. *Memoirs of General William T. Sherman.* 2 vols. New York: Appleton, 1875.

Smith, Frank Prigmore. "The Military History of East Tennessee, 1861-1865." Thesis, Univ. of Tennessee, 1936.

Sneed, John L. T. *Tennessee and Her Bondage: A Vindication and a Warning.* Memphis: *Public Ledger,* 1881. 16 pp.

Strobridge, Truman R., ed. "The Letters of D. C. Donnohue, Special Agent for the Procuring of Cotton Seed." *THQ* 21 (1962), 379-86.

Stuart, Reginald C. "Cavalry Raids in the West: Case Studies of Civil War Cavalry Raids." *THQ* 30 (1971), 259-76.

Taylor, Allan, and Lois Dwight Cole [pseud. Allan Dwight]. *Linn Dickson, Confederate.* New York: Macmillan, 1934. 264 pp. Fiction.

Temple, Oliver Perry. *East Tennessee and the Civil War.* Cincinnati: R. Clarke, 1899. 588 pp. Rpt., Black Heritage Library Collection, Knoxville: Burmar Books, 1972. Written to vindicate the Unionists of East Tennessee in separating from the South and adhering to the national government, Temple's work is valuable especially because he was an eyewitness to many events he describes.

Tennessee Civil War Centennial Commission. *Guide to the Civil War in Tennessee.* Nashville: Tennessee Dept. of Conservation, 1960. 32 pp.

——. *Index to Tennessee Confederate Pension Applications.* Nashville: State Library and Archives, 1964. 323 pp.

——. *Tennesseans in the Civil War: A Military History of Confederate and Union Units with Available Rosters of Personnel.* 2 vols. Nashville: Civil War Centennial Commission, 1964-65. This is a history of all Tennessee military units, together with rosters of all Tennesseans, both Confederate and Union, with their ranks and the names of the companies and regiments in which they served.

Tennessee State Library and Archives, *Index to Questionnaires of Civil War Veterans.* Nashville: State Library and Archives, 1962. 33 pp.

Van Horne, Thomas B. *History of the Army of the Cumberlands; Its Organization, Campaigns, and Battles, Written at the Request of Major-General George H. Thomas Chiefly from His Private Military Journal and Official and Other Documents Furnished by Him.* 2 vols. Cincinnati: R. Clarke, 1875, 1876.

Vaughan, Alfred J. *Personal Record of the Thirteenth Regiment, Tennessee Infantry. By Its Old Commander.* Memphis: S. C. Toof, 1897. 95 pp.

Walker, Peter Franklin. "Defense of Tennessee, September, 1861-February, 1862." Thesis, Vanderbilt Univ., 1956.

West, James Durham. "The Thirteenth Tennessee Regiment—Confederate States of America." *THM* 7 (1921), 180-93.

White, Lonnie J. "Federal Operations at New Madrid and Island Number Ten." *WTHSP* 17 (1963), 47-67.

Williams, Kenneth P. "The Tennessee River Campaign and Anna Ella Carroll." *Indiana Magazine of History* 46 (1950), 221-48.

Williams, Samuel Cole. "General John T. Wilder." *Indiana Magazine of History* 31 (1935), 169-203.

———. *General John T. Wilder, Commander of the Lightning Brigade.* Bloomington: Indiana Univ. Press, 1936. 105 pp. Wilder, one of Sherman's most expert aides, came South after the Civil War to marry a Chattanooga girl and cast his fortune with this region. He became a wealthy ironmaster.

———. *The Lincolns and Tennessee.* Harrogate: Dept. of Lincolniana, Lincoln Memorial Univ., 1942; rpt. Johnson City: Watauga, 1842. 33 pp.

Williams, T. Harry. *P. G. T. Beauregard: Napoleon in Gray,* Southern Biography Series. Baton Rouge: Louisiana State Univ. Press, 1955. 345 pp. Rpt. New York: Collier, 1962. 416 pp.

Wingfield, Marshall. "Old Straight: A Sketch of the Life and Campaigns of Alexander P. Stewart, C.S.A." *THQ* 3 (1944), 99-130. Stewart was one of two Tennesseans who attained the rank of lieutenant general in the Civil War.

———. *General A. P. Stewart, His Life and Letters.* Memphis: West Tennessee Hist. Soc., 1954. 259 pp.

Womack, James J. *Civil War Diary of Capt. J. J. Womack, Company E, 16th Regiment, Tennessee Volunteers (Confederate).* McMinnville: Womack, 1961. 115 pp.

Worsham, William J. *Old Nineteenth Tennessee Regiment, C.S.A. June, 1861. April, 1865.* Knoxville: Paragon, 1902. 235 pp.

Wright, Marcus Joseph, comp. *Tennessee in the War, 1861-1865; Lists of Military Organizations and Officers from Tennessee in Both the Confederate and Union Armies; General and Staff Officers of the Provisional Army of Tennessee, Appointed by Governor Isham G. Harris.* New York: A. Lee, 1908. 228 pp.

Wynne, Robert Bruce. "Topographical Influences upon the 1863 Campaigns in East Tennessee and Northern Georgia." Thesis, Univ. of Tennessee, 1962.

Young, John Preston. *The Seventh Tennessee Cavalry. (Confederate.) A History.* Nashville: Methodist Pub. House, 1890. 227 pp.

Zornow, William Frank. "State Aid for Indigent Soldiers and Their Families in Tennessee, 1861-1865." *THQ* 13 (1954), 297-300.

GUERRILLA WARFARE, COLEMAN SCOUTS, AND OTHER CAVALRY RAIDERS

Bakeless, John. *Spies of the Confederacy.* Philadelphia, Pa.: Lippincott, 1970. 456 pp.

Bejach, Lois D. "The Journal of a Civil War 'Commando'—DeWitt Clinton Fort." WTHSP 2 (1948), 5-32.

Blankenship, Lela McDowell. *When Yesterday Was Today.* Nashville: Tennessee Bk., 1966. 194 pp. Novel of guerrilla warfare in the Tennessee highlands during the Civil War.

Braly, Mary Gramling. "If I Had a Thousand Lives." *THM* (ser. 2) 1 (1930-31), 261-69. The story of Sam Davis.

Brents, John A. *The Patriots and Guerrillas of East Tennessee and Kentucky. The Suffering of the Patriots. Also the Experience of the Author as an Officer in the Union Army. Including Sketches of Noted Guerrillas and Distinguished Patriots.* New York: The Author, 1863. 171 pp.

Brown, Dee Alexander. *The Bold Cavaliers. Morgan's 2nd Kentucky Cavalry Raiders.* Philadelphia, Pa.: Lippincott, 1959. 353 pp.

Cunningham, S. A. "Sam Davis." *AHM* 4 (1899), 195-209.

Daniel, John S., Jr. "Special Warfare in Middle Tennessee and Surrounding Areas, 1861-62." Thesis, Univ. of Tennessee, 1971.

Duke, Basil Wilson. *History of Morgan's Cavalry.* Cincinnati: Miami Printing, 1867. 578 pp. Rpt., Civil War Centennial Series, ed. Cecil F. Holland. Bloomington: Indiana Univ. Press, 1960; rpt. Millwood, N.Y.: Kraus, 1968. 595 pp.

Ellis, Daniel. *Thrilling Adventures of Daniel Ellis, the Great Union Guide of East Tennessee, for a Period of Nearly Four Years during the Great Southern Rebellion. Written by Himself. Containing a Short Biography of the Author.* New York: Harper, 1867. 430 pp; rpt., Black Heritage Library Collection, Freeport, N.Y.: Bks. for Libraries, 1972.

Epstein, Samuel, and Beryl Epstein. *The Andrews Raid; or, The Great Locomotive Chase, April 12, 1862.* New York: Coward-McCann, 1956. 253 pp. Juvenile.

Frantz, Mabel Goode. *Full Many a Name: The Story of Sam Davis, Scout and Spy, C. S. A.* Jackson: McCowat-Mercer, 1961. 143 pp.

Hale, Jonathan D. *Champ Ferguson: A Sketch of the War in East Tennessee Detailing Some of the Awful Murders on the Border and Describing One of the Leading Spirits of the Rebellion.* Cincinnati: n.p., 1862. 20 pp.

Holland, Cecil Fletcher. *Morgan and His Raiders: A Biography of the Confederate General.* New York: Macmillan, 1942. 373 pp. This favorable treatment confines itself to John Hunt Morgan's activities as leader of cavalry raiders during the Civil War. Holland, working largely from previously untouched materials, depicts his subject as one of the most popular figures of the Confederacy.

Knapp, David. *The Confederate Horsemen.* New York: Vantage, 1966. 302 pp.

O'Neill, Charles K. *Wild Train: The Story of the Andrews Raiders.* New York: Random House, 1956. 482 pp. This is the story of the capture of a Confederate train by a small group of Union soldiers in April, 1862, and of the ensuing chase which has become legend.

Pittard, Mabel Baxter. "The Coleman Scouts." Thesis, Middle Tennessee State Univ., 1953.

Roberson, B. L. "The Courthouse Burnin'est General." *THQ* 23 (1964), 372-78. Story of Hylan B. Lyon.

Romaine, William B. *Story of Sam Davis.* Pulaski: *Pulaski Citizen,* 1928. 15 pp.

Rowell, Adelaide. *On Jordan's Stormy Banks: A Novel of Sam Davis, the Confederate Scout.* Indianapolis: Bobbs-Merrill, 1948. 368 pp.

Rowell, John W. *Yankee Cavalrymen: Through the Civil War with the Ninth Pennsylvania Cavalry.* Knoxville: Univ. of Tennessee Press, 1971. 296 pp. Two enlisted men and their diaries describe the considerable cavalry activity of this unit in Tennessee.

Sensing, Thurman. *Champ Ferguson, Confederate Guerilla.* Nashville: Vanderbilt Univ. Press, 1942. 256 pp.

Swiggert, Howard. *The Rebel Raider: A Life of John Hunt Morgan.* Indianapolis: Bobbs-Merrill, 1934. 341 pp.

Whelan, Paul A. "Unconventional Warfare in East Tennessee, 1861-1865." Thesis, Univ. of Tennessee, 1963.

Van Noppen, Ina W. *Stoneman's Last Raid.* Boone [?], N.C.: North Carolina State College, 1961. 112 pp.

Whitley, Edythe J. R. *Sam Davis: Confederate Hero, 1842-1863.* Smyrna: n.p., 1947. 147 pp.

——. *Sam Davis, Hero of the Confederacy, 1842-1863, Coleman's Scouts.* Nashville: Blue & Gray Press, 1971. 251 pp.

Nathan Bedford Forrest: "Wizard of the Saddle"

Crawford, Charles W. "A Note on Forrest's Race for Home." *Georgia Historical Review* 50 (1966), 288-90.

Henry, Robert Selph. *"First with the Most" Forrest.* Indianapolis: Bobbs-Merrill, 1944. 558 pp.

——. ed. *As They Saw Forrest; Some Recollections and Comments of Contemporaries.* Jackson: McCowat-Mercer, 1956. 306 pp.

Howell, Elmo. "William Faulkner's General Forrest and the Uses of History." *THQ* 29 (1970), 287-94.

Hubbard, John Milton. *Notes of a Private.* Memphis: E. H. Clarke, 1909. 189 pp. Hubbard was from Company E, 7th Tennessee Regiment, Forrest's Cavalry Corps, C.S.A.

Johnston, John. "Forrest's March out of West Tennessee." WTHS*P* 12 (1958), 138-48.

Jordan, Thomas, and J. P. Pryor. *The Campaigns of Lieut. Gen. N. B. Forrest, and of Forrest's Cavalry.* New Orleans: Blelock, 1868; rpt. New York: B. Franklin, 1971. 704 pp.

Leftwich, William G., Jr. "The Battle of Brice's Cross Roads." WTHS*P* 20 (1966), 5-19.

Lowry, Audrey Blakeley. "A Study of the Battle of Johnsonville." Ed.S. diss., George Peabody College, 1956.

Luckett, William W. "Bedford Forrest in the Battle of Brice's Cross Roads." *THQ* 15 (1956), 99-110.

Lytle, Andrew N. *Bedford Forrest and His Critter Company.* New York: Minton, Balch, 1931; rpt. Putnam, 1947; rev. ed., McDowell, Obolensky, 1960. 402 pp.

McCain, William D. "Nathan Bedford Forrest: An Evaluation." *Journal of Mississippi History* 24 (1962), 203-25.

Mitchell, Enoch L., ed. "Nathan Bedford Forrest Accepts Counsel." *THQ* 22 (1963), 382-83.

Moore, Carey Moffett, comp. *Nathan Bedford Forrest and the Civil War in Memphis; a Subject Bibliography of Books and Other References.* Memphis: Memphis Pub. Libr., 1961. 42 pp.

Morton, John Watson. *The Artillery of Nathan Bedford Forrest's Cavalry, "The Wizard of the Saddle."* Nashville: Methodist Pub. House, 1909. 374 pp.

Sheppard, Eric William. *Bedford Forrest, The Confederacy's Greatest Cavalryman.* New York: Dial, 1930. 320 pp.

Stowe, John Joel, Jr. "The Military Career of Nathan Bedford Forrest." Thesis, George Peabody College, 1930.

Weller, Jac. "Nathan Bedford Forrest: An Analysis of Untutored Military Genius." *THQ* 18 (1959), 213-51.

Williams, Edward F., III. *Fustest with the Mostest: The Military Career of Tennessee's Greatest Confederate, Lt. Gen. Nathan*

Bedford Forrest. Memphis: Southern Bks., 1969. 32 pp.

——. "The Johnsonville Raid and Nathan Bedford Forrest State Park." *THQ* 28 (1969), 225-51.

Williams, Edward F., III, and H. K. Humphreys, eds. *Gunboats and Cavalry, The Story of Forrest's 1864 Johnsonville Campaign, As Told to J. P. Pryor and Thomas Jordan.* Memphis: Nathan Bedford Forrest Trail Comm., 1965. 24 pp.

Wyeth, John A. *Life of General Nathan Bedford Forrest.* New York: Harper, 1899, 1908. 655 pp. Rpt. as *That Devil Forrest; Life of General Nathan Bedford Forrest,* foreword Henry Steele Commager; maps, Jean Tremblay. New York: Harper, 1959. 614 pp. Rpt., original title, New York: B. Franklin, 1970. The author, a private under Forrest, concentrates on the general's Civil War career.

Naval Warfare

General Naval Warfare

Merrill, James M. *Battle Flags South: The Story of Civil War Navies on the Western Waters.* Rutherford, N.J.: Fairleigh Dickinson Univ. Press, 1970. 334 pp.

——. "Captain Andrew Hull Foote and the Civil War on Tennessee Waters." *THQ* 30 (1971), 83-93.

Milligan, J. D. *Gunboats down the Mississippi.* Annapolis: U.S. Naval Institute, 1965. 217 pp.

Newcomer, Lee N. "The Battle of Memphis, 1862." *WTHSP* 12 (1958), 41-57.

David G. Farragut: United States Admiral

Barnes, James. *David G. Farragut,* Beacon Biographies of Eminent Americans. Boston: Small, Maynard, 1899. 132 pp.

Chavanne, Rose N. *David Farragut, Midshipman.* New York: Coward-McCann, 1941. 152 pp.

Farragut, Loyall. *The Life of David Glasgow Farragut, First Admiral of the United States Navy, Embodying His Journal and Letters.* New York: Appleton, 1879, 1882, 1907. 586 pp. Written by Admiral Farragut's son.

Lewis, Charles L. *David Glasgow Farragut.* 2 vols. Annapolis: U.S.

Naval Institution, 1941-1943. This is the best biography of this outstanding Navy admiral from Tennessee.

Mahan, Alfred Thayer. *Admiral Farragut,* Great Commanders. New York: Appleton, 1892, 1895, 1901. 333 pp. Rpt., Makers of American History. New York: J. A. Hill, 1904. Rpt. 1895 ed., American Biography Series no. 32. New York: Haskell House, 1968. Rpt. 1895 ed., Westport, Conn.: Greenwood, 1969; rpt. 1892 ed., 1970.

Spears, John Randolph. *David G. Farragut,* American Crisis Biographies. Philadelphia, Pa.: G. W. Jacobs, 1905. 407 pp.

Stevens, William O. *David Glasgow Farragut, Our First Admiral.* New York: Dodd, 1942. 241 pp.

Williams, Samuel C. "The Farraguts and Tennessee." *THQ* 5 (1946), 320-27.

Matthew F. Maury: Confederate States Admiral

Beard, William E. "The Pathfinder of the Seas." *THQ* 5 (1946), 328-32.

Beaty, Janice. *Seeker of Seaways; a Life of Mathew Fontaine Maury, Pioneer Oceanographer.* New York: Pantheon, 1966. 165 pp. For grades 7 and up.

Caldwell, Andrew Jackson. "Matthew Fontaine Maury." *THM* (ser. 2) 1 (1930-31), 276-78.

Corbin, Diana Fontaine M., comp. *A Life of Matthew Fontaine Maury.* London: Low, Marston, Searle & Rivington, 1888. 326 pp. Compiled by his daughter.

Hawthorne, Hildegarde. *Matthew Fontaine Maury, The Trail Maker of the Seas.* New York: Longmans, Green, 1943. 226 pp.

Lewis, Charles L. *Matthew Fontaine Maury, the Pathfinder of the Seas.* Annapolis: U.S. Naval Institute, 1927. Rpt. New York: AMS, 1969. 264 pp. The best biography of this eminent Confederate naval leader from Tennessee.

"The Pathfinder of the Seas: Matthew Fontaine Maury." *Virginia Cavalcade* 2 (1952), 11-16.

Wayland, John Walter. *The Pathfinder of the Seas; the Life of Matthew Fontaine Maury,* introd. William J. Shawalter. Richmond, Va.: Garrett & Massie, 1930. 191 pp.

Williams, Frances Leigh. *Matthew Fontaine Maury, Scientist of the Sea.* New Brunswick: Rutgers Univ. Press, 1963. 720 pp.

Personal Wartime Accounts, Diaries, and Recollections

Abbott, Martin, ed. "The South As Seen by a Tennessee Unionist in 1865: Letters of H. M. Watterson." *THQ* 18 (1959), 148-61.

Alderson, William T., ed. "The Civil War Reminiscences of John Johnston, 1861-1865." *THQ* 13 (1954), 65-82, 156-78, 244-76, 329-54; 14 (1955), 43-81, 142-75.

——. "The Civil War Diary of Captain James Litton Cooper, September 30, 1861, to January, 1865." *THQ* 15 (1956), 141-73.

Bejach, Wilena Roberts. "Civil War Letters of a Mother and Son." *WTHSP* 4 (1950), 50-71.

Bokum, Hermann. *The Testimony of a Refugee from East Tennessee.* Philadelphia, Pa.: Privately printed, 1863. 24 pp.

Boldrick, Charles C. "Father Abram J. Ryan, the Poet-Priest of the Confederacy." *FCHQ* 46 (1972), 201-18.

Branch, Mary Polk. *Memoirs of a Southern Woman "Within the Lines," and a Genealogical Record.* Chicago: Joseph G. Branch, 1912. 107 pp.

Campbell, Andrew Jackson. *Civil War Diary,* ed. Jill K. Garrett. Columbia: n.p., 1965. 132 pp.

Cannon, Newton. *The Reminiscences of Newton Cannon,* ed. Campbell Brown; introd. Stanley F. Horn. Franklin: Carter House Assoc., 1963. 84 pp. From Holographic material provided by his grandson, Samuel M. Fleming, Jr.

Cleveland, Charlotte, and Robert Daniel, eds. "The Diary of a Confederate Quartermaster." *THQ* 11 (1952), 78-85.

Coffman, Edward M., ed. "Memoirs of Hylan B. Lyon, Brigadier General, C.S.A." *THQ* 18 (1959), 35-53.

Cunningham, Sumner A. *Reminiscences of the 41st Tennessee Regiment.* Shelbyville: Shelbyville *Commercial,* 1867. 57 pp.

Dana, Charles A. *Recollections of the Civil War; with the Leaders at Washington and in the Field in the Sixties.* New York: Appleton, 1898. 296 pp. Rpt., The Collier Books Civil War Classics Series, introd. Paul M. Angle. New York: Collier, 1963. 255 pp.

Duncan, Thomas D. *Recollections of Thomas D. Duncan, a Confederate Soldier.* Nashville: McQuiddy, 1922. 213 pp.

Eckel, Alexander. *Andersonville: Seven Months' Experience of Two Tennessee Boys in Andersonville and Five Other Rebel Prisons.* Knoxville: Stubley, n.d. 32 pp.

Fleming, Doris, ed. "Letters from a Canadian Recruit in the Union Army." *THQ* 16 (1957), 159-66.

Grant, Nicholas B. *The Life of a Common Soldier, 1862-1865.* La Follette: LaFollette Press, n.d. 36 pp.

Hancock, Richard Ramsey. *Hancock's Diary.*

Harrison, Lowell H. "The Diary of an 'Average' Confederate Soldier." *THQ* 29 (1970), 256-71.

Heartsill, William W. *Fourteen Hundred and 91 Days in the Confederate Army. A Journal Kept by W. W. Heartsill for Four Years, One Month, and One Day. Or, Camp Life, Day by Day, of the W. P. Lane Rangers from April 19, 1861, to May 20, 1865,* ed. Bell I. Wiley. Jackson: McCowat-Mercer Press, 1953. 332 pp.

Holden, John A. "Journey of a Confederate Mother." WTHS*P* 19 (1965), 36-57.

Holman, W. J., Jr., ed. "War Experience of a Confederate Officer." *THQ* 10 (1951), 149-60.

Horn, Stanley F., ed. "The Papers of Major Alonzo Wainwright." *THQ* 12 (1953), 182-84.

——., comp. and ed. *Tennessee's War, 1861-1865, Described by Participants.* Nashville: Tennessee Civil War Centennial Comm., 1965. 364 pp. This volume contains excerpts from more than 100 sources, arranged chronologically.

Jones, Katharine M. *Heroines of Dixie, Confederate Women Tell Their Story of the War.* Indianapolis: Bobbs-Merrill, 1955. 430 pp. Included is a profile of Mrs. William G. Harding of Nashville.

Martin, John M., ed. "A Methodist Cricuit Rider between the Lines: The Private Journal of Joseph J. Pitts, 1862-1864." *THQ* 19 (1960), 252-69.

Massey, Mary E. "Southern Refugee Life during the Civil War." *NCHR* 20 (1943), 1-21, 132-56.

——. *Refugee Life in the Confederacy.* Baton Rouge: Louisiana State Univ. Press, 1964. 327 pp.

——. *Bonnet Brigades,* Impact of the Civil War Series. New York: Knopf, 1966. 371 pp.

Meriwether, Elizabeth Avery. *Recollections of 92 Years, 1824-1916.* Nashville: Tennessee Historical Comm., 1958. 262 pp. This work concentrates on the Civil War memories of a Memphis suffragette, the first woman to cast a ballot in Tennessee.

Merrill, James M., ed. "'Nothing to Eat but Raw Bacon': Letters from a War Correspondent 1862." *THQ* 17 (1958), 141-55.

Moon, Anna Mary, ed. "Civil War Memoirs of Mrs. Adeline Deaderick." *THQ* 7 (1948), 52-71.

——. "A Southern Woman, in 1897, Remembers the Civil War." *ETHSP* 21 (1949), 111-15.

Morgan, Julia. *How It Was; Four Years among the Rebels.* Nashville: Privately printed, 1892. 204 pp.

Noyes, Edward, ed. "Excerpts from the Civil War Diary of E. T. Eggleston." *THQ* 17 (1958), 336-58.

Osborn, George C., ed. "A Tennessean at the Siege of Vicksburg: The Diary of Samuel Alexander Ramsey Swan, May-July, 1863." *THQ* 14 (1955), 353-72.

Partin, Robert. "A Confederate Sergeant's Report to His Wife during the Campaign from Tullahoma to Dalton." *THQ* 12 (1953), 291-308.

——. "A Confederate Sergeant's Report to His Wife during the Bombardment of Fort Pillow." *THQ* 15 (1956), 243-52.

——. "'The Momentous Events' of the Civil War As Reported by a Confederate Private-Sergeant." *THQ* 18 (1959), 69-86.

——. "The Wartime Experiences of Margaret McCalla: Confederate Refugee from East Tennessee." *THQ* 24 (1965), 39-53.

Quenzel, Carrol H. "A Billy Yank's Impressions of the South." *THQ* 12 (1953), 99-105.

Quintard, Charles Todd. *Dr. Quintard, Chaplain C.S.A. and Second Bishop of Tennessee; Being His Story of the War (1861-1865),* ed. Arthur Howard Noll. Sewanee: Univ. of the South Press, 1905. 183 pp.

Rowell, John W. *Yankee Cavalrymen.*

Simkins, Francis Butler, and James W. Patton. *The Women of the Confederacy.* Richmond, Va.: Garrett & Massie, 1936; rpt. 1971. 306 pp.

Skipper, Elvie Eagleton, and Ruth Gove, eds. "'Stray Thoughts': The Civil War Diary of Ethie M. Foute Eagleton." *ETHSP* 40 (1968), 128-37; 41 (1969), 116-28.

Smith, Ophia D. "The Incorrigible 'Miss Ginger.'" *WTHSP* 9 (1955), 93-118. An unusual Tennessee woman of the Civil War.

Smith, W. A., and Wallace Milam, eds. "The Death of John Hunt Morgan: A Memoir of James M. Fry." *THQ* 19 (1960), 54-63.

Trimble, Sarah Ridley, ed. "Behind the Lines in Middle Tennessee, 1863-1865: The Journal of Bettie Ridley Blackmore." *THQ* 12 (1953), 48-80.

Underwood, Betsy Swint. "War Seen Through a Teen-ager's Eyes." *THQ* 20 (1961), 177-87.

Vaughan, Alfred J. *Personal Record of the Thirteenth Regiment, Tennessee Infantry. By Its Old Commander.*

Watkins, Samuel R. *"Co. Aytch," Maury Grays, First Tennessee Regiment; or, A Side Show of the Big Show,* introd. Bell I. Wiley. Jackson: McCowat-Mercer, 1952; rpt. New York: Macmillan, 1962. 231 pp.

Wiley, Bell I. "Camp Newspapers of the Confederacy." *NCHR* 20 (1943), 327-35.

——. *The Life of Johnny Reb: The Common Soldier of the Confederacy.* Indianapolis: Bobbs-Merrill, 1943. 444 pp. Rpt. in *The Common Soldier in the Civil War.* 2 vols. in 1. New York: Grosset, 1958. This is a fine effort to depict the daily life of the Confederate soldier, based upon diaries and letters.

——. *The Plain People of the Confederacy.* Baton Rouge: Louisiana State Univ. Press, 1943; rpt. Gloucester, Mass.: P. Smith, 1971. 104 pp. A survey of life among the common folk, black and white alike, during the turbulent days of Civil War.

——. *The Life of Billy Yank, the Common Soldier of the Union.* Indianapolis: Bobbs-Merrill, 1952. 454 pp. Rpt. in *The Common Soldier in the Civil War.* 2 vols. in 1. New York: Grosset, 1958.

——. *The Life of Billy Yank* and *The Life of Johnny Reb.* 2 vols. Garden City, N.Y.: Doubleday, 1971.

Williamson, John C., ed. "The Civil War Diary of John Coffee Williamson." *THQ* 15 (1956), 61-74.

Womack, James J. *Civil War Diary of Capt. J. J. Womack, Company E, 16th Regiment, Tennessee Volunteers (Confederate).* McMinnville: Womack, 1961. 115 pp.

William G. Brownlow

Brownlow, William G. *Helps to the Study of Presbyterianism; or, an Unsophisticated Exposition of Calvinism, with Hopkinsian Modifications and Policy, with a View to a More Easy Inter-*

pretation of the Same. To Which Is Added a Brief Account of the Life and Travels of the Author; Interspersed with Anecdotes. Knoxville: T. F. S. Heiskell, 1834. 299 pp.

———. *A Political Register, Setting Forth the Principles of the Whig and Locofoco Parties in the United States, with the Life and Public Services of Henry Clay. Also an Appendix Personal to the Author; and a General Index.* Jonesborough: Jonesborough *Whig,* 1844. 249 pp.

———. *Americanism Contrasted with Foreignism, Romanism, and Bogus Democracy, in the Light of Reason, History, and Scripture; in Which Certain Demagogues in Tennessee, and Elsewhere, Are Shown up in Their True Colors.* Nashville: The Author, 1856. 208 pp.

———. *The Great Iron Wheel Examined; or, Its False Spokes Extracted, and an Exhibition of Elder Graves, Its Builder. In a Series of Chapters.* Nashville: The Author, 1856. 331 pp.

———. *A Sermon on Slavery: A Vindication of the Methodist Church, South: Her Position Stated. Delivered in Temperance Hall, in Knoxville, on Sabbath, August 9th, 1857, to the Delegates and Others in Attendance at the Southern Commercial Convention.* Knoxville: Kinsloe & Rice, 1857. 31 pp.

———. *Ought American Slavery to Be Perpetuated? A Debate between Rev. W. G. Brownlow and Rev. A. Pryne. Held at Philadelphia, September, 1858.* Philadelphia, Pa.: The Authors, 1858; rpt. Miami: Mnemosyne, 1969. 305 pp. Rpt., Black Heritage Library Collection. Freeport, N.Y.: Bks. for Librs., 1971.

———. *Brownlow, the Patriot and Martyr, Showing His Faith and Works, As Reported by Himself.* Philadelphia, Pa.: Weir, 1862. 144 pp.

———. *Portrait and Biography of Parson Brownlow, the Tennessee Patriot.* Indianapolis: Asher, 1862. 72 pp.

———. *Sketches of the Rise, Progress, and Decline of Secession; with a Narrative of Personal Adventures among the Rebels.* Philadelphia: G. W. Childs, 1862. Rpt., American Scene Series, introd. Thomas B. Alexander. New York: Da Capo, 1968. 458 pp. Brownlow, a vehemently pro-Union East Tennessean Methodist minister, newspaper editor, and radical Reconstructionist, expresses his views of the developments occurring in America, particularly in the South, during 1861 and 1862.

Conklin, Royal Forrest. "The Public Speaking Career of William Gannaway (Parson) Brownlow." Diss., Ohio Univ., 1967.

Coulter, E. Merton. "Parson Brownlow's Tour of the North during the Civil War." ETHS*P* 7 (1935), 3-27.

———. *William G. Brownlow, Fighting Parson of the Southern Highlands.* Chapel Hill: Univ. of North Carolina Press, 1937. 432 pp. Rpt., introd. James W. Patton. Knoxville: Univ. of Tennessee Press, 1971. 458 pp. The vacuity of Brownlow's life, which created great disturbances but produced nothing enduring, is depicted in this work. Although exaggeration and extremes in sentiment and conduct marred his whole life, he remains a figure of considerable interest and perplexity.

Fink, Paul M. "The Lighter Side of History." ETHS*P* 39 (1967), 26-41.

Garrett, William R., ed. "A Proclamation by William G. Brownlow, Governor of Tennessee." *AHM* 3 (1897), 151-54. Announcing a reward for the apprehension of Isham G. Harris.

Graf, LeRoy P., ed. "'Parson' Brownlow's Fears: A Letter about the Dangerous, Desperate Democrats." ETHS*P* 25 (1953), 111-14.

Haley, Nancy Marlene. "'Cry Aloud and Spare Not': The Formative Years of Brownlow's *Whig,* 1839-1841." Thesis, Univ. of Tennessee, 1966.

Humphrey, Stephen F. "The Man Brownlow from a Newspaper Man's Point of View." ETHS*P* 43 (1971), 59-70.

Lattimore, R. B. "A Survey of William G. Brownlow's Criticisms of the Mormons, 1841-1857." *THQ* 27 (1968), 249-56.

Lilton, Theodore. "Sketch of Parson Brownlow."*Independent,* May 22, 1862.

Parson Brownlow, and the Unionists of East Tennessee: With a Sketch of His Life . . . Together with an Interesting Account of Buell's Occupation of Tennessee, Beadle's Dime Biographical Library, no. 13. New York: Beadle, 1962. 96 pp.

Patton, James W. "The Brownlow Regime in Tennessee." Diss., Univ. of North Carolina, 1929.

———. "The Senatorial Career of William G. Brownlow." *THM* (ser. 2) 1 (1930-31), 153-64.

Queener, Verton M. "The Pre-Civil War Period of the Life of William G. Brownlow." Thesis, Univ. of Tennessee, 1930.

———. "William G. Brownlow as an Editor." ETHS*P* 4 (1932), 67-82.

Andrew Johnson

[*See also* Reconstruction.]

"Andrew Johnson." *DAR Magazine,* Nov. 1965, p. 884.

Bacon, George Washington. *Life and Speeches of President Andrew Johnson. Embracing His Early History, Political Career, Speeches, Proclamations, etc. With a Sketch of the Secession Movement, and His Course in Relation Thereto; Also His Policy as President of the United States.* London: Bacon, 1865. 106 pp. Rpt. 1866 [?]. 137 pp.

Bainder, Herman C. "Maryland's Reaction to Andrew Johnson, 1865-1868." Thesis, Univ. of Maryland, 1949.

Baumgardner, James Lewis. "Inconsistent Men of Principle: Future Liberal Republicans and the Johnson Administration." Thesis, Univ. of Tennessee, 1964.

——. "Andrew Johnson and the Patronage." Diss., Univ. of Tennessee, 1968.

Bentley, Hubert Blair. "Andrew Johnson, Governor of Tennessee, 1853-1857." Diss., Univ. of Tennessee, 1972.

Bible, Mary Ozelle. "The Post-presidential Career of Andrew Johnson." Thesis, Univ. of Tennessee, 1936.

Bowen, David W. "Andrew Johnson and the Negro." ETHSP 40 (1968), 28-49.

Caskey, Willie Malvin. "The Administration of Governor Andrew Johnson 1853-1857." Thesis, George Peabody College, 1928.

——. "First Administration of Governor Andrew Johnson." ETHSP 1 (1929), 43-59.

——. "The Second Administration of Governor Andrew Johnson." ETHSP 2 (1930), 34-54.

Conway, Moncure D. "The President's Defense." *Fortnightly Review* 5 (1866), 98-106.

Cox, John H., and La Wanda Cox. "Andrew Johnson and His Ghost Writers." *MVHR* 48 (1961-62), 460-79.

——. *Politics, Principle, and Prejudice, 1865-1866; Dilemma of Reconstruction America.* New York: Free Press of Glencoe,

1963. Rpt., Studies in American Negro Life. New York: Atheneum, 1969. 294 pp. This work discusses Johnson's alleged efforts to put together a coalition of conservative Republicans and Democrats during Reconstruction.

DeWitt, David M. *The Impeachment and Trial of Andrew Johnson, Seventeenth President of the United States; a History.* New York: Macmillan, 1903; Rpt., introd. Stanley I. Kutler. Madison: State Hist. Soc. of Wisconsin, 1967. 646 pp.

DeWitt, John H., Jr. "Andrew Johnson and the Hermit." *THQ* 27 (1968), 50-61.

Dobson, Wayne W. "Some Phases of the Congressional Career of Andrew Johnson." Thesis, East Tennessee State Univ., 1952.

Dunning, William A. *A Little More Light on Andrew Johnson,* rpt. from Massachusetts Hist. Soc. *Proceedings,* Nov. 1905. Cambridge, Mass.: J. Wilson, 1905. 13 pp.

Foster, G. Allen. *Impeached: The President Who Almost Lost His Job.* New York: Criterion, 1964. 175 pp.

Foster, Lillian, comp. *Andrew Johnson, President of the United States: His Life and Speeches.* New York: Richardson, 1866. 316 pp.

Gerson, Noel B. *The Yankee from Tennessee.* Garden City, N.Y.: Doubleday, 1960. 382 pp. Historical fiction.

Gipson, Lawrence H. "The Statesmanship of President Johnson." *MVHR* 2 (1915-16), 363-83.

Godkin, E. L. "Impeachment of Andrew Johnson." *The Nation* 3 (1866), 310; 4 (1867), 170-72, 214-15; 6 (1868), 184-85, 404-5.

Gossweiler, Richard C. "Communiques from the 'Firing Line': Andrew Johnson Learns about Louisiana, 1865-1869." Thesis, Univ. of Tennessee, 1965.

Graf, LeRoy P. "Andrew Johnson and the Coming of the War." *THQ* 19 (1960), 208-21.

——. "Andrew Johnson and Learning." *Phi Kappa Phi Journal* 42 (1962), 3-14.

Graf, LeRoy P., and Ralph W. Haskins, eds. *The Papers of Andrew Johnson.* 3 vols. to date. Knoxville: Univ. of Tennessee Press, 1967- . Vol. 1 (1967), 1822-51; vol. 2 (1970), 1852-57; vol. 3 (1972), 1858-60. The first 3 volumes of a projected 10-volume series bring Johnson from the obscurity of his tailor shop to the verge of national attention as a Southerner defending the Union.

Graf, LeRoy P., Ralph W. Haskins, and Patricia P. Clark. "The Pension Office to Congressman Andrew Johnson: A List, 1843-1853." ETHSP 38 (1966), 97-108.

The Great Impeachment and Trial of Andrew Johnson, President of the United States. With the Whole Preliminary Proceedings in the House of Representatives, and in the Senate of the United States. Together with the Eleven Articles of Impeachment, and the Whole of the Proceedings in the Court of Impeachment, with the Verbatim Evidence of All of the Witnesses, and Cross-Examinations of Them, with the Speeches of the Managers and the Counsel on Both Sides, with the Decision of Chief Justice Chase, and the Verdict of the Court. With Portraits of Andrew Johnson; Chief Justice Chase; General U. S. Grant; Hon. Edwin M. Stanton; Hon. Benjamin F. Wade; Hon. Benjamin F. Butler; Hon. Thaddeus Stevens; Major-Gen. Lorenzo Thomas. Philadelphia, Pa.: T. B. Peterson, 1868. 289 pp.

Green, Margaret. *Defender of the Constitution: Andrew Johnson.* New York: Messner, 1962. 192 pp. Juvenile.

Hall, Clifton R. *Andrew Johnson: Military Governor of Tennessee.* Diss., Princeton Univ., 1914. Princeton: Princeton Univ. Press, 1916. 234 pp. An attempt to depict the personality of Andrew Johnson from 1862 to 1865. Hall views Johnson's experience in reconstructing his own state as good training for his work at the national level.

Halperin, Bernard Seymour. "Andrew Johnson, the Radicals, and the Negro, 1865-1866." Diss., Univ. of California (Berkeley), 1966.

Hamilton, Joseph G. de Roulhac. *Life of Andrew Johnson, Seventeenth President of the United States.* Greeneville: Brown, 1928, 1930. 33 pp.

Haskins, Ralph W. "Andrew Johnson and the Preservation of the Union." ETHSP 33 (1961), 43-60.

——. "Internecine Strife in Tennessee: Andrew Johnson versus Parson Brownlow." THQ 24 (1965), 321-40.

Hays, Willard Murrell. "Andrew Johnson's Reputation: A Study of Changing Interpretations." Thesis, Univ. of Tennessee, 1958.

——. "Andrew Johnson's Reputation." ETHSP 31 (1959), 1-31; 32 (1960), 18-50.

Index to the Andrew Johnson Papers. Washington, D.C.: GPO, 1963. 154 pp.

Johnson, Andrew. *Speeches of Andrew Johnson, President of the*

United States, biogr. introd. Frank Moore. Boston: Little, Brown, 1865, 1866; rpt. New York: B. Franklin, 1968. 494 pp.

Jones, James Sawyer. *Life of Andrew Johnson, Seventeenth President of the United States.* Greeneville: East Tennessee Pub., 1901; rpt. New York: AMS, 1970. 400 pp.

——. "Alta Vela: Why Judge Black Withdrew from the Impeachment Trial of President Johnson." *AHM* 7 (1902), 244-48.

Lomask, Milton. *Andrew Johnson: President on Trial.* New York: Farrar, 1960. 376 pp.

——. *Andy Johnson: The Tailor Who Became President.* New York: Ariel, 1962. 181 pp.

Mackay, Charles. "President Johnson and the Reconstruction of the Union." *Fortnightly Review* 4 (1866), 477-90.

McKitrick, Eric L. *Andrew Johnson and Reconstruction.* Chicago: Univ. of Chicago Press, 1960. 533 pp. The author presents Johnson's political career in a more favorable light than some previous historians have done.

McSpadden, J. Walker. *Storm Center: A Novel about Andy Johnson.* New York: Dodd, 1947. 393 pp.

Milton, George F. *The Age of Hate: Andrew Johnson and the Radicals.* New York: Coward-McCann, 1930; rpt. Hamden, Conn.: Archon, 1965. 787 pp. This is an excellent work in the tradition of "life-and-times" histories. The fact that the author is a Tennessean sympathetic to Johnson makes this early revisionist work important to us.

——. "Andrew Johnson: Man of Courage." *ETHSP* 3 (1931), 23-34; rpt. in *Tennessee Old and New,* II, 76-86.

Nettels, Curtis. "Andrew Johnson and the South." *South Atlantic Quarterly* 25 (1926), 55-64.

Notaro, Carmen Anthony. "History of the Biographic Treatment of Andrew Johnson in the Twentieth Century." *THQ* 24 (1965), 143-55.

O'Donough, James L., and William T. Alderson, eds. "Republican Politics and the Impeachment of Andrew Johnson." *THQ* 26 (1967), 177-83.

Ortiz-Garcia, Angel Luis. "Andrew Johnson's Veto of the First Reconstruction Act." Diss., Carnegie-Mellon Univ., 1970.

Patton, James W. "Tennessee's Attitude toward the Impeachment and Trial of Andrew Johnson." *ETHSP* 9 (1937), 65-76.

Phifer, Gregg. "Andrew Johnson Takes a Trip." *THQ* 11 (1952), 3-22.

——. "Andrew Johnson Argues a Case." *THQ* 11 (1952), 148-70.

——. "Andrew Johnson Delivers His Argument." *THQ* 11 (1952), 212-34.

——. "Andrew Johnson Loses His Battle." *THQ* 11 (1952), 291-328.

——. "Andrew Johnson versus the Press in 1866." ETHS*P* 25 (1953), 3-23.

Poore, Benjamin P., ed. *Trial of Andrew Johnson, President of the United States, before the Senate of the United States, on Impeachment by the House of Representatives for High Crimes and Misdemeanors.* 3 vols. Washington, D.C.: GPO, 1868. Rpt., Law, Politics, and History Series. 3 vols. in 2. New York: Da Capo, 1970. This is the word-for-word official record of the impeachment proceedings against Andrew Johnson.

Ramage, Burr J. "Andrew Johnson's Administration." *South Atlantic Quarterly* 1 (1902), 171-81, 256-64.

Rayner, Kenneth. *Life and Times of Andrew Johnson, Seventeenth President of the United States.* Written from a National Standpoint. By a National Man. New York: Appleton, 1866. 363 pp.

Reece, Brazilla Carroll. *The Courageous Commoner; A Biography of Andrew Johnson.* Charleston, W. Va.: Education Foundation, 1962. 168 pp.

Robison, Dan M., ed. "Andrew Johnson on the Dignity of Labor." *THQ* 23 (1964), 80-85.

Roske, Ralph J. "Republican Newspaper Support for the Acquittal of President Johnson." *THQ* 11 (1952), 263-73.

Ross, Edmund G. *History of the Impeachment of Andrew Johnson, President of the United States, by the House of Representatives, and His Trial by the Senate, for High Crimes and Misdemeanors in Office, 1868.* Santa Fe: New Mexican, 1896. 180 pp.

Royall, Margaret Shaw. *Andrew Johnson—Presidential Scapegoat: A Biographical Re-evaluation.* New York: Exposition, 1958. 175 pp.

Russell, Robert G. "Prelude to the Presidency: The Election of Andrew Johnson to the Senate." *THQ* 26 (1967), 148-76.

Severn, William. *In Lincoln's Footsteps; the Life of Andrew Johnson.* New York: Washburn, 1966. 215 pp. Juvenile.

Sioussat, St. George L. "Andrew Johnson and the Early Phases of the Homestead Bill." *MVHR* 5 (1918-19), 253-87; *THM* 6 (1920), 14-45.

Steele, Robert V. P. [pseud. Lately Thomas]. *The First President Johnson: The Three Lives of the Seventeenth President of the United States of America.* New York: Morrow, 1968. 676 pp.

Stryker, Lloyd P. *Andrew Johnson; a Study in Courage.* New York: Macmillan, 1929, 1930, 1936; rpt. 1971. 881 pp. The author describes Johnson as being in the tradition of Lincoln and embracing his program of compassion and reconciliation for the South. Stryker's villains are the Radicals in Congress who blocked Johnson's efforts and ultimately attempted to impeach him.

Tappan, George L. *Andrew Johnson—Not Guilty.* New York: Comet, 1954. 139 pp.

Thomas, Lately. *See* Robert V. P. Steele.

Wagstaff, Thomas. "Andrew Johnson and the National Union Movement." Diss., University of Wisconsin, 1967.

Wells, Ruth Marguerite. "Andrew Johnson, Senator from Tennessee, 1857-1862." Thesis, Univ. of Pennsylvania, 1933.

Williams, Harry. "Andrew Johnson as a Member of the Committee on the Conduct of the War." ETHSP 12 (1940), 70-83.

Winston, Robert W. *Andrew Johnson, Plebian and Patriot.* New York: Holt, 1928; rpt. New York: Barnes & Noble, 1969; rpt. New York: AMS, 1970. 549 pp.

Reconstruction

[*See also* Andrew Johnson.]

Alexander, Thomas B. "Political Reconstruction in Tennessee."
Diss., Vanderbilt Univ., 1947. *Political Reconstruction in Tennessee.* Nashville: Vanderbilt Univ. Press, 1950; rpt. New York:
Russell, 1968. 292 pp. Primarily a study of the political aspects
of Reconstruction in Tennessee, it presents the state's experience
as unique for the South in that local Unionists reestablished civil
government, Radicalism was a home-grown commodity, and its
Radical regime was the first to be overthrown.

——. "Kukluxism in Tennessee, 1865-1869." *THQ* 8 (1949),
195-219.

——. "Neither Peace nor War: Conditions in Tennessee in 1865."
ETHS*P* 21 (1949), 35-51.

——. "Whiggery and Reconstruction in Tennessee." *JSH* 16 (1950),
291-305.

Allen, Ward. "A Note on the Origin of the Ku Klux Klan." *THQ* 23
(1964), 182.

Andrews, Rena Mazyck. "Johnson's Plan of Restoration in Relation
to That of Lincoln." *THM* (ser. 2) 1 (1930-31), 165-81.

Bascom, Major Dick. *The Carpet-bagger in Tennessee.* Clarksville:
J. Jay Buck, 1869.

Beale, Howard K. *The Critical Year: A Study of Andrew Johnson
and Reconstruction.* New York: Harcourt, 1930. Rpt., American
Classics Series. New York: Ungar, 1958. 454 pp.

Belissary, Constantine G. "Tennessee and Immigration, 1865-1880."
THQ 7 (1948), 229-48.

Bentley, George R. *A History of the Freedmen's Bureau.* Philadelphia,
Pa.: Univ. of Pennsylvania Press, 1955; rpt. New York: Octagon,
1970. 298 pp. Bentley treats the work of this federal agency,
which existed from 1865 to 1872, and the various wartime efforts
which preceded it. He concludes that, in the short run, the bureau
reaped benefits for the newly freed black, but in the long run
much of its work hurt the black, since whites reacted adversely to
the rapid changes it initiated, responding with increased racial
hostility.

Biggs, Riley O. "Development of Railroad Transportation in East Tennessee during the Reconstruction Period." Thesis, Univ. of Tennessee, 1934.

———. "The Cincinnati Southern Railway: A Municipal Enterprise." ETHSP 7 (1935), 81-102.

Burton, Ray Berry. "The Financing of Reconstruction in Tennessee." Thesis, Univ. of Pennsylvania, 1966.

Campbell, E. G. "Indebted Railroads—a Problem of Reconstruction." JSH 6 (1940), 167-88.

Campbell, James B. "Some Social and Economic Phases of Reconstruction in East Tennessee, 1864-1869." Thesis, Univ. of Tennessee, 1946.

———. "East Tennessee during the Radical Regime, 1865-1869." ETHSP 20 (1948), 84-102.

Chadsey, Charles E. "The Struggle between President Johnson and the Congress over Reconstruction." Diss., Columbia Univ., 1896.

Coulter, E. Merton. The South during Reconstruction, 1865-1877, a History of the South, vol. 8. Baton Rouge: Louisiana State Univ. Press, 1947. 426 pp. The author treats the events in the South of the period as symbolic of what he feels was happening in the nation—erosion of local and state rights as they were assimilated by the central government.

Curry, Richard O., ed. Radicalism, Racism, and Party Realignment: The Border States during Reconstruction. Baltimore: Johns Hopkins Univ. Press, 1970. 331 pp.

Darrah, Marsha. "Political Career of Col. William B. Stokes of Tennessee." Thesis, Tennessee Technological Univ., 1968.

Davis, Susan Lawrence. Authentic History, Ku Klux Klan, 1865-1877. New York: American Libr. Service, 1924. 316 pp.

Dorris, Jonathan T. Pardon and Amnesty under Lincoln and Johnson; the Restoration of the Confederates to Their Rights and Privileges, 1861-1898, introd. J. G. Randall. Chapel Hill: Univ. of North Carolina Press, 1953. 459 pp.

Durham, Gertrude. "Public Education in Tennessee during the Reconstruction Period." Thesis, Univ. of Tennessee, 1936.

Everett, Edward. Account of the Fund for the Relief of East Tennessee; with a Complete List of Contributors. Boston: Little, 1864. 99 pp.

Feistman, Eugene G. "Radical Disfranchisement and the Restoration of Tennessee, 1865-1866." THQ 12 (1953), 135-51.

Fertig, James Walter. *The Secession and Reconstruction of Tennessee.*

Folmsbee, Stanley J. "The Radicals and the Railroads." *Tennessee,* ed. Philip M. Hamer II, 659-73.

Franklin, John Hope. *Reconstruction: After the Civil War,* Chicago History of American Civilization. Chicago: Univ. of Chicago Press, 1961. 258 pp.

Fraser, Walter J., Jr. "John Eaton, Jr., Radical Republican: Champion of the Negro and Federal Aid to Southern Education, 1869-1882." *THQ* 25 (1966), 239-60.

Garrett, William R., and J. M. Bass, eds. "Ku Klux Mysteries." *AHM* 6 (1901), 46-47.

Golden, Dean Clyde. "The Operation of the Freedmen's Bureau in Tennessee, 1865-1870." Thesis, Memphis State Univ., 1963.

Graf, LeRoy P. "'Parson' Brownlow's Fears: A Letter about the Dangerous Desperate Democrats." *ETHSP* 25 (1953), 111-14.

Green, John W. "Judges of the Reconstruction Era, 1865-1870." *TLR* 17 (1942), 413-22.

Henry, Robert S. *The Story of Reconstruction.* Indianapolis: Bobbs-Merrill, 1938; rpt. Gloucester, Mass.: P. Smith, 1963. 633 pp.

Hesseltine, William B. "Methodism and Reconstruction in East Tennessee." *ETHSP* 3 (1931), 42-61.

——. "Tennessee's Invitation to Carpetbaggers." *ETHSP* 4 (1932), 102-15.

Hollingsworth, Harold M. "George Andrews—Carpetbagger." *THQ* 28 (1969), 312-23.

Horn, Stanley F. *Invisible Empire: The Story of the Ku Klux Klan, 1866-1871.* Boston: Houghton, 1939. 434 pp. Rpt., American Historical Series no. 47. New York: Haskell, 1969; enl. ed., Cos Cob, Conn.: Edwards, 1969; rpt. New York: Gordon, 1969; 2nd enl. ed., Criminology, Law Enforcement, and Social Problems Series no. 81. Montclair, N.J.: Patterson Smith, 1969. 452 pp. The author's premise is that the Klan, in its early stages, was designed to preserve some degree of law and order in the South after the War.

Howse, Nathaniel Roosevelt. "Political Activities of the Republican Party in the State of Tennessee, 1860-1870." Thesis, Tennessee State A&I Univ., 1951.

Hume, Richard. "The Black-and-Tan Constitutional Conventions of

1867-69 in the Former Confederate States." Diss., Univ. of Washington, 1969.

Jordan, Weymouth T. "The Freedmen's Bureau in Tennessee." ETHSP 11 (1939), 47-61.

Kent, Anne Poindexter. "The Ku Klux Klan in Tennessee." Thesis, Univ. of Tennessee, 1935.

Lester, John C., and Daniel L. Wilson. *Ku Klux Klan. Its Origin, Growth and Disbandment.* Nashville: Wheeler, Osborn & Duckworth, 1884. 117 pp. Rpt. New York: Neale, 1905; rpt. New York, AMS, 1970; rpt. St. Clair Shores, Mich.: Scholarly Press, 1972. 198 pp.

M'Donnold, R. L. "The Reconstruction Period in Tennessee." *AHM* 1 (1896), 307-28.

McFarlin, Brenda Mack. "The Ku Klux Klan in Middle Tennessee, 1866-1869." Thesis, Middle Tennessee State Univ., 1971.

McLone, Helen S. "Reconstruction Governors of Four Border States: Tennessee, Missouri, Kentucky, and Arkansas." Thesis, Univ. of Illinois, 1952.

Merry, Preston Robert. "The Freedmen's Bureau in Tennessee, 1865-1869." Thesis, Fisk Univ., 1938.

Mitchell, Enoch L. "The Role of General George Washington Gordon in the Ku Klux Klan." WTHSP 1 (1947), 73-80.

Neal, John Randolph. *Disunion and Restoration in Tennessee. . . .* Diss., Columbia Univ., 1899. New York: Knickerbocker, 1899. 80 pp.

Owens, Susie L. *The Union League of America: Political Activities in Tennessee, the Carolinas, and Virginia, 1865-1870.* New York: New York Univ., 1947. 23 pp.

Patton, James W. *Unionism and Reconstruction in Tennessee, 1860-1869.* Chapel Hill: Univ. of North Carolina Press, 1934; rpt. Gloucester, Mass.: P. Smith, 1966. 267 pp. Tennessee was the last state to secede from the Union and the first of the seceded states to be restored to its constitutional relations with the Union. It was the only southern state to escape military reconstruction; the author credits William G. Brownlow for saving it from this fate.

Phillips, Paul D. "A History of the Freedmen's Bureau in Tennessee." Diss., Vanderbilt Univ., 1964.

——. "White Reaction to the Freedmen's Bureau in Tennessee." *THQ* 25 (1966), 50-62.

*Revised and Amended Prescript of the Order of the * * * [Ku Klux Klan]*. Pulaski: Pulaski *Citizen,* 1868. 24 pp. Rpt., *AHM* 5 (1900), 3-26. Rpt. in Southern History Assoc. *Publications,* vol. 7, 1903, pp. 327-48. Rpt. in *Documents Relating to Reconstruction,* ed. Walter L. Fleming, vol. 2. Morgantown: Univ. of West Virginia Press, 1904. 32 pp. Rpt. Baton Rouge: n.p., 1908. 24 pp. The original *Prescript* was printed secretly in the office of the Pulaski *Citizen,* 1867.

Romine, William Bethel, and Mrs. William Bethel Romine. *Story of the Original Ku Klux Klan.* Pulaski: Pulaski *Citizen,* 1934. 29 pp.

Schruben, Francis W. "Edwin M. Stanton and Reconstruction." *THQ* 23 (1964), 145-68.

Sharp, Joseph A. "The Downfall of the Radicals in Tennessee." *ETHSP* 5 (1933), 105-24.

Sheeler, J. Reuben. "The Development of Unionism in East Tennessee, 1860-1866." *Journal of Negro History* 29 (1944), 166-203.

Sherrod, Isa Lee. "The Ku Klux Movement in Tennessee." Thesis, George Peabody College, 1935. This study comprehends the period from 1865 to the 1920s.

Smith, George Winston. "Some Northern Wartime Attitudes towards the Post-Civil War South." *JSH* 10 (1944), 253-74.

Smith, Rosalyn Atkinson. "Emerson Etheridge as a Candidate in the Tennessee Gubernatorial Election of 1867." Thesis, Univ. of Tennessee, 1969.

Snow, Marshall S. "A Yankee Schoolmaster's Reminiscences of Tennessee." *THM* 6 (1920), 279-83.

Stampp, Kenneth Milton. *The Era of Reconstruction, 1865-1877.* New York: Knopf, 1965; rpt. New York: Random, 1967. 228 pp. A readable synthesis of revisionist literature on Reconstruction.

Stonehouse, Merlin. "Lincoln's Carpetbagger, J. W. North." Diss., Univ. of California at Los Angeles, 1961.

——. *John Wesley North and the Reform Frontier.* Minneapolis: Univ. of Minnesota Press, 1965. 272 pp.

Swint, Henry Lee. *The Northern Teacher in the South, 1862-1870.* Nashville: Vanderbilt Univ. Press, 1941; rpt. New York: Octagon, 1967. 221 pp. Swint points up the difficulty which idealistic persons from the North found when they came South after the Civil War to aid the Negro and poor white.

——., ed. "Reports from Educational Agents of the Freedmen's Bureau in Tennessee, 1865-1870." *THQ* 1 (1942), 51-80, 152-70.

Tallant, James Glenn. "Political Readjustment in Tennessee, 1869-1870." Diss., George Peabody College, 1943.

Taylor, Alrutheus A. *The Negro in Tennessee, 1865-1880.* Washington, D.C.: Associated Pub., 1941. 306 pp. Taylor traces the adjustment of race relations in Tennessee from 1865 to 1880 and describes Negro participation in social and political life.

Taylor, Edward Morton. "Tennessee during Secession and Reconstruction." Thesis, Western Kentucky Univ., 1933.

Taylor, Jerome Gregg, Jr. "The Public Career of Joseph Alexander Mabry." Thesis, Univ. of Tennessee, 1970.

Thruston, Gates P. "A Relic of the Reconstruction Period in Tennessee." *AHM* 6 (1901), 243-50.

Trealease, Allen. *White Terror.* New York: Harper, 1971. 557 pp. The most recent account of the Ku Klux Klan.

Walker, Arda S. "John Henry Eaton, Apostate." ETHSP 24 (1952), 26-43.

Walker, Joseph E. "The Negro in Tennessee during the Reconstruction Period." Thesis, Univ. of Tennessee, 1933.

Wilkin, Mary, ed. "Some Papers of the American Cotton Planters' Association, 1865-1866." *THQ* 7 (1948), 335-61; 8 (1949), 49-62.

Williams, Frank B. "John Eaton, Jr., Editor, Politician, and School Administrator 1865-1870." *THQ* 10 (1951), 291-319.

Wilson, Theodore Brantner. *The Black Codes of the South,* Southern Historical Publications no. 6. University: Univ. of Alabama Press, 1965. 177 pp.

Military History from the Spanish-American War to 1972

Amis, Reese. *History of the 114th Field Artillery. First Tennessee Field Artillery.* Nashville: Benson, 1920. 133 pp.

Bryan, Charles F., Nelle Major, and Eleanor Keeble, comps. *Civilian Defense in Tennessee, 1940-1945,* Tennessee State Planning Commission Publication no. 157. Nashville: State Planning Comm., 1945. 15 pp.

Burt, Jesse C., Jr., ed. "Efforts for an Army Camp at Tullahoma, 1916-1917." *THQ* 10 (1951), 55-73.

Butler, George H., ed. *The Military March of Time in Tennessee, 1939-1944. Prentice Cooper, Governor. Six Year Consolidated Report, the Military Department and the Selective Service System.* Nashville: Tennessee Adjutant General's Off., 1945. 190 pp.

Cates, John H. *Company E, One Hundred and Seventeenth Infantry, 30th Division in World War I.* Johnson City: East Tennessee State Univ. Press, 1964. 113 pp.

"Completing the Battleship Tennessee." *Scientific American,* May 29, 1920, pp. 603- .

Cooling, B. Franklin. "The Tennessee Maneuvers, June, 1941." *THQ* 24 (1965), 265-80.

Cowan, Samuel K. *Sergeant York and His People.* New York: Funk, 1922; rpt. New York: Grosset, 1941. 292 pp. This is perhaps the best assessment to date of Sergeant York, his early life, religious conviction, and military experience.

Dorsett, Dona Carolyn. "The Opinion of Selected Tennessee Newspapers with Regard to American Entry into World War One and Rejection of the Versailles Treaty." Thesis, Univ. of Tennessee, 1963.

History of the American Legion, Department of Tennessee, 1919-1933. Knoxville: Knoxville Litho., 1933. 335 pp.

Howard, Philip Joseph. "The Tennessee Press and the Cuban Crisis of 1898." Thesis, Middle Tennessee State Univ., 1969.

Hoyer, Raymond A. "The Soldier Town." *Journal of Educational Sociology* 15 (1942), 487-97). Relates to Tullahoma, Coffee County.

Lea, Luke. "The Attempt to Capture the Kaiser," ed. William Alderson. *THQ* 20 (1961), 222-61.

McGaw, Robert A. "A Likeness of Sergeant York." *THQ* 27 (1968), 329-40.

Oswell, Troy. "Above and beyond the Call of Duty." *THQ* 14 (1955), 341-52. Describes Tennessee military heroism in World War II.

Riggs, Joseph H., ed. "A Soldier's Life in the Far-Off Phillipines: Oscar T. Halliburton." *WTHSP* 19 (1965), 121-33.

Skeyhill, Thomas J. *Sergeant York, Last of the Long Hunters.* Philadelphia, Pa.: Winston, 1930. 240 pp.

Sloan, Gene H., comp. *With Second Army, Somewhere in Tennessee.* Kansas City: Yearbook House, 1956. Unpaged. Describes World War II military activity in Tennessee.

Tennessee Laws Relating to Veterans, 1968. Nashville: State of Tennessee, 1968. 45 pp.

Tidwell, Cromwell. "Luke Lea and the American Legion." *THQ* 28 (1969), 70-83.

York, Alvin C. *Sergeant York, His Own Life Story and War Diary,* ed. Thomas J. Skeyhill. New York: Doubleday, 1928. 309 pp.

Economic History

GENERAL HISTORY: 1790-1860

Abernethy, Thomas P. "The Early Development of Commerce and Banking in Tennessee." *MVHR* 14 (1927-28), 311-25.

——. *From Frontier to Plantation in Tennessee.*

Applewhite, Joseph Davis. "Early Trade and Navigation on the Cumberland River." Thesis, Vanderbilt Univ., 1940.

Bailey, Thomas E. "Engine and Iron: A Story of Branchline Railroading in Middle Tennessee." *THQ* 28 (1969), 252-68.

Bancroft, Frederic. *Slave-Trading in the Old South.* Baltimore: J. H. Furst, 1931. Rpt., American Classics Series, introd. Allan Nevins. New York: Ungar, 1959. 415 pp.

Barbee, John D. "Navigation and River Improvement in Middle Tennessee, 1807-1834." Thesis, Vanderbilt Univ., 1934.

Beard, William E. "A Saga of the Western Waters." *THQ* 2 (1943), 316-30.

Belissary, Constantine S. "Industry and Industrial Philosophy in Tennessee, 1850-1860." ETHS*P* 23 (1951), 16-57.

Brooks, Addie Lou. "Beginning of Railroads in West Tennessee, 1830-1861." Thesis, Vanderbilt Univ., 1932.

——. "Early Plans for Railroads in West Tennessee, 1830-1845." *THM* (ser. 2) 3 (1932-37), 20-39.

——. "The Building of the Trunk Line Railroads in West Tennessee, 1852-1861." *THQ* 1 (1942), 99-124; rpt. in *Tennessee Old and New*, II, 188-211.

Broyles, John A., Jr. "A History of Transportation in East Tennessee to 1860." Thesis, George Peabody College, 1929.

Burt, Jesse C. "The Nashville and Chattanooga Railroad, 1854-1872: The Era of Transition." ETHS*P* 23 (1951), 58-76.

Campbell, Claude A. *The Development of Banking in Tennessee.* Diss., Vanderbilt Univ., 1932. Nashville: The Author, 1932. 194 pp.

——. "Banking and Finance in Tennessee during the Depression of 1837." ETHS*P* 9 (1937), 19-30.

——. "Branch Banking in Tennessee prior to the Civil War." ETHS*P* 11 (1939), 34-46.

Campbell, Thomas J. *The Upper Tennessee; Comprehending Desultory Records of River Operations in the Tennessee Valley, Covering a Period of One Hundred Fifty Years, Including Pen and Camera Pictures of the Hardy Craft and the Colorful Characters Who Navigated Them.* . . . Chattanooga: The Author, 1932. 144 pp.

Carroll, Mary Swann. "Tennessee Sectionalism, 1796-1861." Diss., Duke Univ., 1931.

Chamberlain, H. S. "Early Tennessee Iron and Steel Industry." *Manufacturer's Record* 66 (1914), 41-42.

Clark, Blanche Henry. "Agricultural Population of Tennessee, 1840-1860, with Reference to Non-slavery." Diss., Vanderbilt Univ., 1938.

——. *The Tennessee Yeomen, 1840-1860.* Nashville: Vanderbilt Univ. Press, 1942; rpt. New York: Octagon, 1971. 200 pp. The author emphasizes the bearing which land tenure and agriculture had upon social classes in Tennessee of the Old South, particularly upon the small farmer.

Clark, Thomas D. "The Development of Railways in the Southwestern and Adjacent States before 1860." Diss., Duke Univ., 1932.

——. "The Development of the Nashville and Chattanooga Railroad." *THM* (ser. 2) 3 (1932-37), 160-68.

——. *The Beginning of the L & N, the Development of the Louisville and Nashville Railroad and Its Memphis Branches from 1836 to 1860.* Louisville, Ky.: Standard, 1933. 107 pp.

——. *A Pioneer Southern Railroad from New Orleans to Cairo.* Chapel Hill: Univ. of North Carolina Press, 1936. 171 pp.

——. "The Building of the Memphis and Charleston Railroad." ETHS*P* 8 (1936), 9-25.

Clark, Victor S., comp. *History of Manufactures in the United States, 1607-1914.* 2 vols. Washington, D.C.: Carnegie Institution, 1916-1928.

DeBow, J. D. B. "The Southwestern Convention at Memphis." *Hunt's Merchant's Magazine* 15 (1846), 63-67.

Douglas, Byrd. *Steamboatin' on the Cumberland.* Nashville: Tennessee Bk., 1961. 407 pp.

Eubanks, David L. "J. G. M. Ramsey as a Bond Agent: Selections from the Ramsey Papers." ETHSP 36 (1964), 81-99. Ramsey worked for the East Tennessee and Georgia Railroad.

Folmsbee, Stanley J. "State Aid to Internal Improvements in Tennessee, 1836-1861." Diss., Univ. of Pennsylvania, 1932.

——. "The Beginnings of the Railroad Movement in East Tennessee." ETHSP 5 (1933), 81-104.

——. "The Origins of the Nashville and Chattanooga Railroad." ETHSP 6 (1933), 81-95.

——. "The Turnpike Phase of Tennessee's Internal Improvement System of 1836-1838." *JSH* 3 (1937), 453-77.

——. *Sectionalism and Internal Improvements in Tennessee, 1796-1845.* Knoxville: East Tennessee Hist. Soc., 1939. 293 pp. This is a study of the internal improvement mania as it developed in Tennessee. The author considers that unequal distribution of internal improvements in the state accentuated the problems of sectionalism.

Freeman, Thomas H., IV. *An Economic History of Tennessee.* Nashville: State Planning Office, 1965. 59 pp.

Gauding, Harry Hendricks. "A History of Water Transportation in East Tennessee prior to the Civil War." Thesis, Univ. of Tennessee, 1933.

Gifford, James Maurice. "Montgomery Bell, Tennessee Ironmaster." Thesis, Middle Tennessee State Univ., 1970.

Gray, Lewis C., with Esther K. Thompson. *History of Agriculture in the Southern United States to 1860,* Contributions to American Economic History, introd. Henry C. Taylor. 2 vols. Washington, D.C.: Carnegie Institution, 1933; rpt. New York: P. Smith, 1941, 1958; rpt. Clifton, N.J.: Kelley, 1969.

Gray, Warren P. "Development of Banking in Tennessee." Thesis, Rutgers Univ., 1948.

Hall, James. *Statistics of the West at the Close of the Year 1836.* Cincinnati: J. A. James, 1837. 284 pp.

Hillsman, Jack Hines. "The Bank of Tennessee, 1838-1866." Thesis, Univ. of Tennessee, 1937.

Holland, James W. "History of Railroad Enterprise in East Tennessee, 1836-1860." Thesis, Univ. of Tennessee, 1930.

——. "The East Tennessee and Georgia Railroad, 1836-1860." ETHS*P* 3 (1931), 89-107.

——. "The Building of the East Tennessee and Virginia Railroad." ETHS*P* 4 (1932), 83-101.

Holt, Albert C. "The Economic and Social Beginnings of Tennessee." Diss., George Peabody College, 1923.

Hunt, Raymond F., Jr. "The Pactolus Ironworks." *THQ* 25 (1966), 176-96. Relates to Sullivan County, 1789-1830.

"Internal Improvements in Tennessee." *Southern Quarterly Review* 9 (1846), 243 ff.

Jennings, Marjorie. "The Development of Highways in Tennessee to 1840." Thesis, George Peabody College, 1928.

Johnson, Leland R. "Army Engineers on the Cumberland and Tennessee, 1824-1854." *THQ* 31 (1972), 149-69.

Keith, Alice Barnwell. "Commerce on the Mississippi and Its Eastern Tributaries, 1789-1820." Thesis, Univ. of Tennessee, 1928.

Ketchersid, William L. "Campbell Wallace." Thesis, Univ. of Tennessee, 1966. Wallace was president of the East Tennessee and Georgia Railroad.

Lacy, Eric R. "Sectionalism in East Tennessee, 1796-1861." Diss., Univ. of Georgia, 1963.

——. *Vanquished Volunteers: East Tennessee Sectionalism from Statehood to Secession.* Johnson City: East Tennessee State Univ. Press, 1965. 242 pp.

McDonald, Kenneth M. "Milling in Middle Tennessee, 1780-1860." Thesis, Vanderbilt Univ., 1939.

McGrane, Reginald Charles. *The Panic of 1837; Some Financial Problems of the Jacksonian Era.* Chicago: Univ. of Chicago Press, 1924. Rpt. New York: Russell, 1965. 260 pp. This work shows the effect of the panic upon Tennessee.

Mehrling, John C. "The Memphis and Charleston Railroad." WTHS*P* 19 (1965), 21-35.

——. "The Memphis and Ohio Railroad." WTHS*P* 22 (1968), 52-61.

Meyer, Balthasar H., et al. *History of Transportation in the United States before 1860,* Carnegie Institution of Washington Publication no. 215 C. Washington, D.C.: Carnegie Institution, 1917; rpt. New York: P. Smith, 1948. 678 pp.

"Mines and Minerals and Manufacturing in East Tennessee." *De Bow's Commercial Review* 17 (1854), 302-3.

"The Mountain Regions of North Carolina and Tennessee." *De Bow's Commercial Review* 26 (1859), 702-6.

Nichols, George Chester. "Tennessee, Tennesseans and Railroad Conventions, 1845-1852." Thesis, Univ. of Tennessee, 1963.

Owsley, Frank L., and Harriet C. "The Economic Basis of Society in the Late Ante-Bellum South." *JSH* 6 (1940), 24-45.

——. "The Economic Structure of Rural Tennessee, 1850-1860." *JSH* 8 (1942), 161-82,

Phelps, Dawson A., and John T. Willett. "Iron Works on the Natchez Trace." *THQ* 12 (1953), 309-22.

Phillips, Ulrich B. *A History of Transportation in the Eastern Cotton Belt to 1860.* New York: Columbia Univ. Press, 1908; rpt. New York: Octagon, 1968. 405 pp.

Robison, Robert M. "A History of Internal Improvement in Tennessee to 1840: A Study of Legislative Supervision." Thesis, George Peabody College, 1931.

Silver, James W. "Edmund Pendleton Gaines and Frontier Problems, 1801-1849." *JSH* 1 (1935), 320-44.

——. "Edmund Pendleton Gaines: Railroad Propagandist." ETHSP 9 (1937), 3-18.

Sioussat, St. George L. "Memphis as a Gateway to the West." *THM* 3 (1917), 1-27, 77-114.

Stephenson, Wendell Holmes. *Isaac Franklin: Slave Trader and Planter of the Old South: With Plantation Records.* University: Louisiana State Univ. Press, 1938; rpt. New York: P. Smith, 1971. 368 pp. Stephenson, with sometimes only fragmentary official records, attempts to outline the life of one of the South's most important slave-traders, whose primary headquarters were Nashville and Gallatin.

Sutton, Robert M. "The Illinois Central Railroad in Peace and War, 1858-68." Diss., Univ. of Illinois, 1948.

"Tennessee: Her Manufactures and Internal Improvements." *De Bow's Commercial Review* 13 (1852), 156-66.

"Tennessee: Past and Present." *De Bow's Commercial Review* 15 (1853), 65-73.

Wilburn, James R. *The Hazard of the Die: Tolbert Fanning and the Restoration Movement.* Austin, Tex.: Sweet, 1969. 288 pp. Fanning was founder of the Tennessee Agricultural Society.

Wiley, Bell I. "Cotton and Slavery in the History of West Tennessee." Thesis, Univ. of Kentucky, 1929.

——. "Vicissitudes of Early Reconstruction in Farming in the Lower Mississippi Valley." *JSH* 3 (1937), 440-52.

Williams, Samuel C. "The South's First Cotton Factory." *THQ* 5 (1946), 212-21.

——. "Early Iron Works in the Tennessee Country." *THQ* 6 (1947), 39-46.

Wurtele, Lolla. "The Origins of the Louisville and Nashville Railroad." Thesis, Univ. of Louisville, 1939.

GENERAL HISTORY: 1860-1900

Armes, Ethel M. *The Story of Coal and Iron in Alabama.* Birmingham: Chamber of Commerce, 1910. 581 pp. Portions of this work deal with southern Tennessee and the Tennessee Coal and Iron Co.

Bailey, Thomas E. "Engine and Iron: A Story of Branchline Railroading in Middle Tennessee." *THQ* 28 (1969), 252-68.

Ball, Clyde. "The Public Career of Col. A. S. Colyar, 1870-1877." Thesis, Vanderbilt Univ., 1937.

Bejach, Lois D. "The History of Bell County." WTHS*P* 1 (1947), 24-37. Describes implications for railroad development in the southwestern corner of Tennessee.

Belissary, Constantine G. "Tennessee and Immigration, 1865-1880." *THQ* 7 (1948), 229-48.

——. "Rise of the Industrial Spirit in Tennessee, 1865-1885." Diss., Vanderbilt Univ., 1949.

——. "The Rise of Industry and the Industrial Spirit in Tennessee, 1865-1885." *JSH* 19 (1953), 193-215.

Berthoff, Rowland T. "Southern Attitudes toward Immigration, 1865-1914." *JSH* 17 (1951), 328-60.

Biggs, Riley Oakey. "The Development of Railroad Transportation in East Tennessee during the Reconstruction Period." Thesis, Univ. of Tennessee, 1934.

——. "The Cincinnati Southern Railway: A Municipal Enterprise." ETHS*P* 7 (1935), 81-102.

Bokum, Hermann. *The Tennessee Hand-Book and Immigrants Guide: Giving a Description of the State of Tennessee; Its*

Agricultural and Mineralogical Character; Its Waterpower, Timber, Soil, and Climate; Its Various Railroad Lines . . . Its Adaptation for Stock-Raising, Grape Culture, etc., etc., with Special Reference to the Subject of Immigration. Philadelphia: Lippincott, 1868. 164 pp.

Buck, Solon J. *The Agrarian Crusade; a Chronicle of the Farmer in Politics,* The Chronicles of America Series. New Haven: Yale Univ. Press, 1920, 1921. 215 pp. This work follows the farmer from the origin of the Grange through the Populist movement as he worked toward ever greater involvement in political solutions for his problems.

Bull, Jacqueline P. "The General Merchant in the Economic History of the New South." *JSH* 18 (1952), 37-59.

Burt, Jesse C., Jr. "Four Decades of the Nashville, Chattanooga, and St. Louis Railway, 1873-1916." *THQ* 9 (1950), 99-130.

——. "History of N. C. and St. L. Railway, 1873-1916." Diss., Vanderbilt Univ., 1950.

——. "James D. Porter: West Tennessean and Railroad President." WTHSP 5 (1951), 79-89.

——. "The Nashville and Chattanooga Railroad, 1854-1872: Era of Transition." ETHSP 23 (1951), 58-76.

——. "Railroad Promotion of Agriculture in Tennessee." *THQ* 10 (1951), 320-33.

——. "Edmund W. Cole and the Struggle between Nashville and Louisville and Their Railroads, 1879-1880." *FCHQ* 26 (1952), 112-32.

——. "Whitefoord, Russell Cole: A Study in Character." *FCHQ* 28 (1954), 28-54.

Caldwell, Joshua W. *East Tennessee: Its Agricultural and Mineral Resources.* New York: n.p., 1867.

Campbell, Claude A. "Branch Banking in Tennessee since the Civil War." ETHSP 12 (1940), 84-99.

Chamberlain, Morrow. *A Brief History of the Pig Iron Industry of East Tennessee.* Chattanooga: n.p., 1942. 28 pp.

Colton, Henry E. *Coal: Report of Henry E. Colton, Geologist and Inspector of Mines, on the Coal Mines of Tennessee, and Other Minerals, to A. W. Hawkins, Commissioner, Agriculture, Statistics and Mines.* Nashville: A. B. Tavel, 1883. 128 pp.

Curry, Leonard P. *Rail Routes South: Louisville's Fight for the*

Southern Market, 1865-1872. Lexington: Univ. of Kentucky Press, 1969. 150 pp.

De Bow, J. D. B. *Legal History of the Entire System of Nashville, Chattanooga and St. Louis Railway and Possessions, including and Discussing the Charters, Amendments, Rights, Privileges . . . as well as General Powers in Alabama, Georgia, Kentucky and Tennessee.* Nashville: Marshall & Bruce, 1900. 985 pp.

Dodd, James Harvey. "The Development of Manufacturing in Tennessee since the Civil War." Thesis, George Peabody College, 1925.

Donovan, William F. "The Growth of the Industrial Spirit in Tennessee, 1890-1910." Diss., George Peabody College, 1955.

Duggins, Edward Cameron. "The Background for Regulation of the Railroads in Tennessee." Thesis, Univ. of Tennessee, 1939.

Durbin, W. J. "Studies in the Financial History of Tennessee, 1860-1883." Thesis, Univ. of Tennessee, 1925.

Ewing, Robert. "General Robert E. Lee's Inspiration to the Industrial Rehabilitation of the South, Exemplified in the Development of Southern Iron Interests." *THM* 9 (1925), 215-30.

Facts and Figures concerning the Climate, Manufacturing Advantages, and the Agricultural and Mineral Resources of East Tennessee. Knoxville: Knoxville Industrial Assoc., 1869. 26 pp.

Fels, Rendigs. *Wages, Earnings, and Employment, Nashville, Chattanooga & St. Louis Railway, 1866-1896,* Papers of the Institute of Research and Training in the Social Sciences of Vanderbilt Univ., no. 10. Nashville: n.p., 1953. 72 pp.

Fuller, Justin. "History of the Tennessee Coal, Iron, and Railroad Company, 1852-1907." Diss., Univ. of North Carolina, 1966.

Gaston, Paul Morton. *The New South Creed: A Study in Mythmaking.* Diss., Univ. of North Carolina, 1961. New York: Knopf, 1970. 298 pp. Gaston feels that, although it was admirable in vision, the New South creed was manipulated through most of its history by men who served the region poorly and that the myth of the New South obstructed more positive achievements.

Harsh, Alan. "The Development of the Iron Industry in East Tennessee." Thesis, Univ. of Tennessee, 1958.

Hawkins, A. W. and Henry E. Colton. *Hand-Book of Tennessee.* Knoxville: *Whig and Chronicle,* 1882. 168 pp. Rpt. Nashville: McQuiddy, 1903. 292 pp.

Herr, Kincaid A. *The Louisville & Nashville Railroad, 1850-1942.* Louisville, Ky.: *L & N Magazine,* 1943. 221 pp. Rev. 3rd ed., 1959. 234 pp. Rev. 5th ed., 1964. 402 pp.

Howell, Sarah M. "The Editorials of Arthur S. Colyar, Nashville Prophet of the New South." *THQ* 27 (1968), 262-76.

Keith, Jean E. "The Role of the Louisville and Nashville Railroad in the Development of Coal and Iron in Alabama, Tennessee and Kentucky." Thesis, Johns Hopkins Univ., 1959.

Killebrew, Joseph B., et al. *Introduction to the Resources of Tennessee.*

——. *Tobacco: Its Culture in Tennessee, with Statistics of Its Commercial Importance.* Nashville: Tavel, Eastman & Howell, 1876; rpt. Washington, D.C.: GPO, 1884. 286 pp.

——. *Report of the Bureau of Agriculture, Statistics and Mines for 1876.* Nashville: Tavel, Eastman & Howell, 1877. 435 pp.

——. *Tennessee: Its Agricultural and Mineral Wealth, with an Appendix, Showing the Extent, Value and Accessibility of Its Ores, with Analyses of the Same.* Nashville: Tavel, Eastman & Howell, 1877. 196 pp.

——. *Middle Tennessee as an Iron Centre.* Nashville: Tavel, Eastman & Howell, 1879. 15 pp.

——. *Tennessee: The Home for Intelligent Immigrants.* Nashville: *American,* 1879. 58 pp.

——. *West Tennessee: Its Resources and Advantages. Cheap Homes for Immigrants.* Nashville: Tavel, Eastman & Howell, 1879. 93 pp.

——. *Knoxville as an Iron Centre.* Nashville: Tavel, Eastman & Howell, 1880. 15 pp.

——. *Sheep Husbandry. A Work Prepared for the Farmers of Tennessee.* Nashville: Tavel, Eastman & Howell, 1880. 301 pp.

——. *Iron and Coal of Tennessee.* Nashville: Tavel & Howell, 1881. 220 pp.

——. *Information for Immigrants concerning Middle Tennessee and the Counties in That Division. . . .* Nashville: Marshall, 1898. 148 pp.

McWhirter, A. J. *Revised Handbook of Tennessee.* Nashville: Tavel, 1885. 200 pp.

Park, Leah M. "Edwin Mims and the Advancing South." Thesis, Vanderbilt Univ., 1964.

Prince, Richard E. *The Nashville, Chattanooga and St. Louis Railway: History and Steam Locomotives.* Green River, Wyo.: The Author, 1967. 196 pp.

Ralph, J. "Industrial Region of Northern Alabama, Tennessee and Georgia." *Harper's Monthly Magazine,* Mar. 1895, pp. 607-26.

Safford, James M. *Geology of Tennessee.* Nashville: S. C. Mercer, 1869. 550 pp.

Saloutos, Theodore. *Farmer Movements in the South, 1865-1933,* University of California Publications in History, vol. 64. Berkeley: Univ. of California Press, 1960. 354 pp. Rpt., Bison Book, Lincoln: Univ. of Nebraska Press, 1964. The author notes that farmer movements across the land have always foundered upon the rocks of sectionalism. He also contends that constructive agricultural thought came from the South as well as from the Middle West.

Smith, Samuel Boyd. "Joseph Buckner Killebrew and the New South Movement in Tennessee." Diss., Vanderbilt Univ., 1962.

——. "Joseph Buckner Killebrew and the New South Movement in Tennessee." ETHS*P* 37 (1965), 5-22.

Smith, Sarah Frances. "Post Civil War Agriculture in West Tennessee." Thesis, Vanderbilt Univ., 1945.

Stover, John F. *The Railroads of the South, 1865-1900: A Study in Finance and Control.* Chapel Hill: Univ. of North Carolina Press, 1955. 310 pp.

Tachau, Mary K. "Milton Hannibal Smith and the Louisville and Nashville Railroad." Thesis, Univ. of Louisville, 1958.

——. "The Making of a Railroad President: Milton Hannibal Smith and the L & N." *FCHQ* 43 (1969), 125-50.

Vanderford, Charles F. *The Soils of Tennessee.* Knoxville: Bean, Warters & Gaut, 1897. 139 pp.

Ward, Francis Ehl. "A Historical Study of the East Tennessee and Western North Carolina Narrow-Gauge Railroad." Thesis, Appalachian State Univ., 1958.

Weaver, Dempsey. *An Account of the Principal Difficulties and Embarrassments Encountered by the Planter's Bank of Tennessee, from 1860 to the Present Time.* Nashville: *Union and American,* 1872. 37 pp.

Williams, Frank B. "The Pan-Electric Telephone Controversy." *THQ* 2 (1943), 144-62. Discusses an attempt to establish telephone service in Tennessee in the 1880s.

Wilson, Charles W., Jr., John W. Jewell, and Edward T. Luther. *Pennsylvanian Geology of the Cumberland Plateau.* Nashville: Tennessee Dept. of Conservation, Div. of Geology, 1966. 21 pp.

Woodward, Comer Vann. *Origins of the New South, 1877-1913,* A History of the South, vol. 9. Baton Rouge: Louisiana State Univ. Press, 1951, 1966. 542 pp.

GENERAL HISTORY: 1900-1972

Agricultural Economics and Rural Sociology. Rural Research Series, Monographs no. 1-275. Knoxville: Dept. of Agricultural Economics and Rural Sociology, Univ. of Tennessee, 1935-57.

Agricultural Trends in Tennessee 1866-1958. Federal-State Cooperative Crop Reporting Service. Nashville: Tennessee Crop Reporting Service, 1958. 176 pp.

Allred, Charles E. and Samuel W. Atkins. *Human and Physical Resources of Tennessee.* Knoxville: College of Agriculture, Univ. of Tennessee, 1939. 555 pp.

American Forest Products Industries. *Government Land Acquisition; a Summary of Land Acquisition by Federal, State and Local Governments up to 1964. Tennessee Edition.* Washington, D.C.: American Forest Products Industries, 1965. 31 pp.

Anderson, George C. "Tennessee's Railroad and Public Utilities Commission." *TLR* 16 (1941), 974-78.

Appalachian Regional Development Act of 1965: A Rationale and Model for Its Application in Tennessee. Nashville: Tennessee State Planning Office, 1965. 107 pp.

Ashley, G. H. "State Report on Oil and Gas Development in Tennessee." *Scientific American,* Feb. 18, 1911, p. 112.

Barnett, Paul. *Industrial Development in Tennessee: Present Status and Suggested Program,* Bureau of Research, School of Business Administration, Study no. 11. Knoxville: Univ. of Tennessee, Div. of Univ. Extension, 1941. 122 pp.

———. *An Analysis of State Industrial Development Programs in the Thirteen Southern States,* Bureau of Research, School of Business Administration, Study no. 13. Knoxville: Div. of Univ. Extension, Univ. of Tennessee, 1944. 60 pp.

Baughman, James P. *Charles Morgan and the Development of Southern Transportation.* Nashville: Vanderbilt Univ. Press, 1968. 302 pp.

Bird, Elsie Taylor. "Tobacco in East Tennessee." Thesis, Univ. of Tennessee, 1948.

Boyd, Willis Baxter, ed. *Tennessee: A Treatise of Facts about Agricultural Resources and Activities in Tennessee Including a Brief Summary of Related Industries, Institutions, and Sources of Wealth, Conducive to Favorable Living Conditions within the State.* Nashville: Tennessee Dept. of Agriculture, 1934. 111 pp.

Brier, Henry C. "Rise and Decline of Transportation on the Upper Cumberland River." Thesis, George Peabody College, 1928.

Britt, Thomas. "The Marketing of Forest Products in Tennessee." Thesis, Univ. of Tennessee, 1957.

Brown, Louie A. *Measurements of Poverty in East Tennessee,* Institute of Regional Studies, East Tennessee State University, Monograph no. 1. Johnson City: Institute of Regional Studies, East Tennessee State Univ., 1965. 61 pp.

Bruce, Harry James. "Tennessee Spacial Relations and Economic Interaction." Thesis, Univ. of Tennessee, 1959.

Burnett, Edmund C. "Big Creek's Response to the Coming of the Railroad: 'Old Buncombe' Promotes the Better Life in a Rural Community." *Agricultural History* 21 (1947), 129-48.

Campbell, Claude A. "The Diary Industry in Tennessee." Thesis, George Peabody College, 1928.

Campbell, Margaret. "A History of the Tennessee Central Railway." Thesis, George Peabody College, 1927.

Carrier, Ronald E., and William R. Schriver. *Problems Faced by Manufacturers in Tennessee.* Memphis: Memphis State Univ., 1966.

Case, Earl Clark. *The Valley of East Tennessee: The Adjustment of Industry to Natural Environment.* Diss., Univ. of Chicago, 1925. Tennessee Dept. of Education, Div. of Geology, Bulletin 36. Nashville: Tennessee Dept. of Education, 1925. 116 pp.

Changtrakul, Sasithorn. "Patterns of Industrial Growth in the Tennessee Valley States, 1939-1960." Thesis, Univ. of Tennessee, 1964.

Chappell, Vernon Glenn. "The Identification and Evaluation of Factors Affecting Economic Growth in the Tennessee Valley Region, 1950-1960." Diss., Univ. of Tennessee, 1970.

Cockrill, Elizabeth. *Bibliography of Tennessee Geology, Soils, Drainage, Forestry, etc., with Subject Index,* Extract B from State of Tennessee Geological Survey Bulletin no. 1, *Geological*

Work in Tennessee. Nashville: Folk-Keelin, 1911. 119 pp.

Copeland, Lewis C., I. James Pikl, and John M. Peterson. *Estimating Tennessee's Tourist Business,* Univ. of Tennessee, Bureau of Business Research Study no. 26. Knoxville: Bureau of Business Research, Univ. of Tennessee, 1955. 119 pp.

Corry, Ormond C. *Personal Income Trends in Tennessee, 1929-1967.* Knoxville: Center for Business and Economic Research, Univ. of Tennessee, 1969. 141 pp.

Crangle, Charles L., and Norma J. Boardman. *State Public Works in Tennessee,* Tennessee State Planning Commission Publication no. 200. Nashville: State Planning Comm., 1949. 34 pp.

Crawford, Neely. "Ethical Control of Tennessee Utilities." B.D. thesis, Vanderbilt Univ., 1929.

Currence, Mary G., ed. *Tennessee Statistical Abstract, 1971.* Knoxville: Center for Business and Economic Research, Univ. of Tennessee, 1971. 712 pp. Information on all areas of economy and government.

Dahir, James. *Region Building; Community Development Lessons from the Tennessee Valley.* New York: Harper, 1955. 208 pp.

Dale, James. "Historical Survey of Tennessee Agriculture." Thesis, Vanderbilt Univ., 1929.

Davis, Claude J. "Local Governmental Services and Industrial Development." Thesis, Univ. of Tennessee, 1951.

Depriest, William Henry. "Banks Known as the Bank of the State of Tennessee." Thesis, George Peabody College, 1930.

Dickerhoof, H. "Factors Influencing Industrial Plant Location in East Tennessee, 1959 to 1962." Thesis, Univ. of Tennessee, 1965.

Doran, William A. "The Development of the Industrial Spirit in Tennessee, 1910-1920." Diss., George Peabody College, 1965.

Douglas, Richard. "Logging in the Big Hatchie Bottoms." *THQ* 25 (1966), 32-49. Treats the period of the early 1900s.

Duggins, Edward Cameron. "The Background for Regulation of the Railroads in Tennessee." Thesis, Univ. of Tennessee, 1939.

Eberling, Ernest J. *Population and Labor Force Changes during the 1960s: The United States and Tennessee.* Nashville: Tennessee Dept. of Employment Security, 1960. 12 leaves.

Epperson, Terry Elmer, Jr. "Geographic Factors Influencing the Manufacturing Industries of Upper East Tennessee." Diss., Univ. of Tennessee, 1960.

Foust, James Brady. "The Eastern Dark Fired Tobacco Region of Kentucky and Tennessee." Thesis, Univ. of Tennessee, 1966.

Freeman, Thomas H., IV. *An Economic History of Tennessee.* Nashville: Tennessee State Planning Comm., 1965. 59 leaves.

Gaillard, Frye. "Progress Comes to Fall Creek Falls." *Saturday Review,* August 5, 1972, pp. 15ff. Fall Creek Falls is a state park.

Glass, James Jarrett. "Tennessee Development Districts: An Examination of the Relationship between Regional Planning and Politics." Diss., Univ. of Tennessee, 1972.

Glenn, Leonidas C. *Underground Waters of Tennessee and Kentucky West of Tennessee River and of an Adjacent Area in Illinois.* House Doc. 748, 59th Cong., 1st sess. Washington, D.C.: GPO, 1906. 173 pp.

——. *The Northern Tennessee Coal Field Included in Anderson, Campbell, Claiborne, Fentress, Morgan, Overton, Pickett, Roane, and Scott Counties,* Tennessee Geological Survey Bulletin, 33-B. Nashville: Williams, 1925. 478 pp.

Goodlettsville Lamb and Wool Club, the Oldest Cooperative Livestock Marketing Association in the United States, Organized 1877. Nashville: Tennessee Dept. of Agriculture, 1950. 67 pp.

Gore, James L. "The Development of State Banking in Tennessee 1914-1933." Thesis, George Peabody College, 1934.

Gregg, Robert. *Origin and Development of the Tennessee Coal, Iron and Railroad Company.* New York: Newcomen Soc., 1948. 40 pp.

Gresham, Mary Richardson. "The History of the Textile Industry in Tennessee." Thesis, George Peabody College, 1930.

Guide for Organizing Economic Development Districts under Tennessee Enabling Legislation for Participation in the Appalachian Regional Development Act, Economic Development Act, Regional Planning, Housing Act of 1965. Nashville: Tennessee State Planning Off., 1965. 36 leaves.

Harris, W. B. "Splendid Retreat of Alcoa." *Fortune,* Oct. 1955, 114-22.

Hawkins, A. W., and Henry E. Colton. *Hand-Book of Tennessee.*

Herr, Kincaid A. *The Louisville and Nashville Railroad.*

Holly, J. Fred. "The Co-operative Town Company of Tennessee: A Case Study of Planned Economic Development." ETHS*P* 36 (1964), 56-69.

Hoover, Calvin B., and B. U. Ratchford. *Economic Resources and Policies of the South.* New York: Macmillan, 1951. 464 pp.

Howard, Edith Foster. *Riverfront: The Protection of Municipal Waterfronts in Tennessee.* Knoxville: Bureau of Public Administration, Univ. of Tennessee, 1949.

Hurst, Thomas E. "Tennessee Coal Mining and Marketing Trends." Thesis, East Tennessee State Univ., 1951.

Hutchison, Robert S., dir. of study. *Migration and Industrial Development in Tennessee: A Report to the Industrial Development and Migration Subcommittee of the Tennessee Legislative Council.* Nashville: Tennessee State Legislative Council, 1958. 292 pp.

Icenogle, David William. "Rural Non-Farm Population and Settlement in Upper East Tennessee." Diss., Louisiana State Univ., 1970.

Jenkins, Albert Sidney. "An Inventory of Some Economic Agencies and Problems in Tennessee." Thesis, Univ. of Tennessee, 1932.

Johnson, John A. "The Geography of Freight Transportation on the Tennessee River." Thesis, Univ. of Tennessee, 1953.

Johnson, Karen S., and Watkins Thayer. *Delineation of Development Districts in Non-Appalachian Tennessee.* Memphis: Bureau of Business and Economic Research, Memphis State Univ., 1969. 119 pp.

Johnson, R. W. "Land Utilization in Tennessee." *JTAS* 12 (1937), 362-76.

Kelly, Thomas A. "Occupational Trends in Tennessee." Thesis, Vanderbilt Univ., 1940.

Lambert, Robert S. "Logging on Little River, 1890-1940." ETHS*P* 33 (1961), 32-42.

Larsen, William F. *New Homes for Old: Publicly Owned Housing in Tennessee.* Knoxville: Bureau of Public Administration, Univ. of Tennessee, 1948.

Lehman, John W. *Changing Sawmill Industry: A Status Report on 58 Circular Sawmills in the Tennessee Valley, 1950-1960.* Norris: TVA, 1961. 23 pp.

The Lower Cumberland Region: A Study of Its Population, Economic Base and Potential. Memphis: Bureau of Business and Economic Research, Memphis State Univ., 1967. 103 pp.

Lowry, Paul R., et al. *Economic Effects of the Control of Highway Signs in Tennessee.* Memphis: Memphis State Univ., 1967. 157 pp.

McAlpin, Robert. "The Effect of Industrial Development on Rural Welfare in Tennessee." Thesis, Univ. of Tennessee, 1928.

McFerrin, John Berry. *Caldwell and Company: A Southern Financial Empire.* Chapel Hill: Univ. of North Carolina Press, 1939; rev. ed., Nashville: Vanderbilt Univ. Press, 1969. 284 pp.

Magargel, Sue J. *Industrial Atlas of Tennessee.* Memphis: Memphis State Univ., 1967. 46 pp.

Marion Dorset, A Tennessean Whose Genius in Research Enabled Him to Discover the True Serum for Hog Cholera, to Develop Tuberculin for Bovine Tuberculosis, and to Perfect Control Methods for Poultry Pullorum. Nashville: Tennessee Dept. of Agriculture, 1949. 80 pp.

Milton, George F. "Ruhr of America; Huge, Unharnessed Resources in the Tennessee River." *Independent,* June 6, 1925, pp. 631-33.

——. "New Tennessee." *Independent,* Nov. 20, 1926, pp. 577-79.

Outen, Dewey LeRoy. "An Inventory of the Climatic and Mineral Resources of Tennessee." Thesis, Univ. of Tennessee, 1932.

Overman, Edward S. *Taxation of Public Utilities in Tennessee.* Knoxville: Bureau of Public Administration, Univ. of Tennessee, 1962.

Parkison, Samuel Lane. "A Summary of the Records on the Pure-bred Jersey Dairy Herd at the West Tennessee Experiment Station from 1928-1952." Thesis, Univ. of Tennessee, 1960.

Payne, Eddie Wilson. "Economic Growth in the Elk River Region." Thesis, Middle Tennessee State Univ., 1967.

Prince, Richard E. *The Nashville, Chattanooga and St. Louis Railway.*

Quillen, Dennis E. "A Geographic Study of the Tennessee Central Railway: An East-West Transport Route across the Cumberland Plateau of Tennessee." Thesis, Univ. of Tennessee, 1969.

Ray, William Walter. "Glass Manufacture in Tennessee: A Study in Industrial Location." Thesis, Univ. of Tennessee, 1966.

Riggs, Fletcher E. "An Analysis of Southern Economic Development with Particular Reference to Agriculture: Upper Tennessee Valley, 1900-40." Diss., Vanderbilt Univ., 1957.

Robbins, Floy. "Geography of West Tennessee." Diss., George Peabody College, 1930.

Robinson, Nelson M., and John R. Petty. *Public Utility Services in Tennessee.* Knoxville: Bureau of Public Administration, Univ. of

Tennessee, 1966. A study made for the Tennessee Legislative Council Committee.

Robinson, Stephen Bernard. "The Vegetable Canning Industry of East Tennessee." Thesis, Univ. of Tennessee, 1969.

Robock, S. H. "Negro in the Industrial Development of the South." *Phylon* 14 (1953), 319-25.

Rogers, William Robert. "A History of the Smoky Mountain Railroad." Thesis, Univ. of Tennessee, 1969.

Rollins, Leonard Hobson. "The Tennessee River as a Trade Route and Its Relation to the Economic Development of East Tennessee." Thesis, Univ. of Tennessee, 1928.

Schriver, William R. *Factors Affecting the Attraction and Expansion of Industry in Tennessee: The Industrialists' Viewpoint.* Memphis: Memphis State Univ., 1968. 33 leaves.

Schriver, William R., and Joseph D. Thoreson. *Major Sources of Social and Economic Data in Tennessee.* Knoxville: Occupational Research and Development Coordinating Unit, Univ. of Tennessee, 1968. 163 pp.

Sebor, Milos, and Richard Bodamer. *The Economic Geography of Tennessee.* Nashville: Tennessee State Planning Comm., 1966. 65 pp.

Sirison, Sachee. "Economic Growth in Tennessee." Thesis, Univ. of Tennessee, 1964.

Smith, R. W., and G. I. Whitlatch. *The Phosphate Resources of Tennessee,* Division of Geology, Bulletin no. 48. Nashville: Tennessee Dept. of Conservation, 1940. 444 pp.

Spoone, Janice Harrison. "The Textile Industry of Tennessee." Thesis, Univ. of Tennessee, 1964.

Stevenson, William W. "Shift Patterns in Tennessee Valley Region Manufacturing Employment: 1950-1975." Diss., Vanderbilt Univ., 1969.

Stewart, William H. *The Tennessee-Tombigbee Waterway: A Case Study in the Politics of Water Transportation.* University: Univ. of Alabama Press, 1971. 191 pp.

Sulzer, Elmer G. "The Three 'Tennessee Centrals' of Tennessee." *THQ* 39 (1971), 210-14.

"Tennessee." *Manufacturer's Record,* Jan. 1945, pp. 70-101.

"Tennessee Coal and Iron Company Deal and the Panic of 1907." *Nation,* June 15, 1911, p. 594.

Tennessee Dept. of Employment Security. *Population and Labor Force Characteristics of Tennessee Counties.* Nashville: State of Tennessee, 1963. 96 pp.

——. *Tennessee Annual Average Work Force Estimates by Area.* Nashville: State of Tennessee, 1970. 35 leaves.

Tennessee Dept. of Finance and Administration. *Tennessee, Its Resources and Economy.* Nashville: State of Tennessee, 1965. 41 pp.

Tennessee Federal Development Programs Office. *Appalachian Development Plan, 1967-1968.* Nashville: State of Tennessee, 1967. 43 pp.

"Tennessee: New Industrial Empire." *World's Work,* Aug. 1926, pp. 373-88.

Tennessee Office of Urban and Federal Affairs. *Tennessee Appalachian Development Plan, 1969-1970.* Nashville: State of Tennessee, 1969. 279 pp.

Tennessee State Planning Commission. *An Analysis of Aviation in Tennessee and Recommendations for Needed Improvements.* Nashville: State of Tennessee, 1936. 23 pp.

——. *Resource Inventory and Analysis of Tennessee Appalachia.* Nashville: State of Tennessee, 1967. 504 pp.

——. *Tennessee and National Economic Growth.* Nashville: State of Tennessee, 1967. 89 pp.

——. *Tennessee Population, Labor Force, and Employment Projections and Interpretations.* Nashville: State of Tennessee, 1967. 119 pp.

"Tennessee Tourism Booms As Experts Take a New Tack." *Business Week,* Nov. 13, 1954, p. 182.

Thorogood, James E. *A Financial History of Tennessee since 1870.* Sewanee: n.p., 1949. 245 pp.

Tindall, George Brown. *The Emergence of the New South, 1913-1945,* A History of the South, vol. 10. Baton Rouge: Louisiana State Univ. Press, 1967. 807 pp. The author depicts the South as ever moving toward a more diversified, pluralistic society as a result of a rapidly improving industrial and agricultural economy and substantial cultural development.

Tucker, Dorothy. *1970 and 1980 Population Projections for Tennessee and Its Counties by Five Year Age Groups.* Nashville: State Dept. of Finance and Administration, 1965. 96 pp.

U.S. Dept. of Commerce. *Study of the Utilization of Scientific,*

Technical and Professional Resources in the Economic Development of East Tennessee. Washington, D.C.: GPO, 1968.

Wallace, Louis D., ed. *A Century of Tennessee Agriculture.* Nashville: Tennessee Dept. of Agriculture, 1954. 396 pp.

Ward, F. B. "Industrial Development of Tennessee." *Annals* 153 (1931), 141-47.

Whitaker, J. Russell. "Tennessee-Earth Factors in Settlement and Land Use." *THQ* 5 (1946), 195-211.

Whitlatch, George I. "Mileposts in Tennessee's Clay Industry." *JTAS* 11 (1936), 153-63.

——. *The Clays of West Tennessee,* Tennessee Dept. of Conservation, Div. of Geology, Bulletin 49. Nashville: Tennessee Dept. of Conservation, 1940. 368 pp.

——. "Mineral Resources, the Keystone of Tennessee Industry." *Tennessee Planner* 3 (1942), 40-55.

——., comp. *Industrial Resources in Tennessee.* Nashville: State Planning Comm., 1945. 210 pp.

Williams, Frank Jefferson. "Tax Barriers to Industrial Development in Tennessee." Thesis, Univ. of Tennessee, 1943.

Williams, Jerry J., and Leo T. Surla, Jr. *The Incidence of Poverty: Social and Economic Conditions in Tennessee.* Nashville: State Planning Commission, 1965. 36 pp.

Wilson, Charles MacArthur. "An Inter-Industry Analysis of Tennessee with Emphasis on Agriculture." Diss., Univ. of Tennessee, 1968.

Winter, Arthur B. *The Tennessee Utility District: A Problem of Urbanization.* Knoxville: Univ. of Tennessee Press, 1958. 108 pp. A study from the Bureau of Public Administration and Municipal Technical Advisory Service, Univ. of Tennessee.

Night Riders of Middle Tennessee in the Early Century

Grantham, Dewey W., Jr. "Black Patch War: The Story of the Kentucky and Tennessee Night Riders, 1905-1909." *South Atlantic Quarterly* 59 (1960), 215-25.

Miller, John G. *The Black Patch War.* Chapel Hill: Univ. of North Carolina Press, 1936. 87 pp. The series of incidents just after the turn of the 20th century in which tobacco growers in north-central Tennessee and south-central Kentucky used extraordinary tactics to attempt to raise the price paid the farmer for tobacco.

Nall, James O. *The Tobacco Night Riders of Kentucky and Tennessee, 1905-1909.* Louisville, Ky.: Standard, 1939. 221 pp.

Taylor, Marie. "Night Riders in the Black Patch War." Thesis, Univ. of Kentucky, 1934.

——. "Night Riders in the Black Patch." *Register of the Kentucky Historical Society* 61 (1963), 279-99; 62 (1964), 24-40.

Warren, Robert Penn. *Night Rider.* Boston: Houghton, 1939. 460 pp. Rpt. New York: Random, 1948; rpt. London: Eyre & Spottiswoode, 1955. 454 pp. A novel set during the Kentucky-Tennessee conflict at the turn of the century. Warren, born in this area, had firsthand knowledge of the conflict.

THE NEW DEAL

Grubbs, Donald H. "The Southern Tenant Farmers' Union and the New Deal." Diss., Univ. of Florida, 1963. Includes a portion on Tennessee.

——. *Cry from the Cotton: The Southern Tenant Farmers' Union and the New Deal.* Chapel Hill: Univ. of North Carolina, 1971. 218 pp.

McCarthy, James Remington. "The New Deal in Tennessee." *Sewanee Review* 42 (1934), 408-14.

Minton, John D. "The New Deal in Tennessee, 1932-1938." Diss., Vanderbilt Univ., 1959.

National Youth Administration . . . 1935, 1936 . . . in Tennessee. Nashville: National Youth Adm., 1936. 80 pp.

O'Dell, Samuel Robert. "The First 100 Days of the New Deal in Upper East Tennessee." Thesis, East Tennessee State Univ., 1966.

Peterson, Carl I. "The Forestry Work of the Civilian Conservation Corps in Tennessee." *JTAS* 10 (1935), 160-66.

Simpson, Walter L. *Review of Civil Works Administration Activities in Tennessee.* Nashville: CWA, 1935. 82 pp.

TENNESSEE VALLEY AUTHORITY

Bibliography of TVA

Bauer, Harry C., comp. *An Indexed Bibliography of the Tennessee*

Valley Authority. Knoxville: TVA Information Div., 1933-40. Various editions covering the period from 1933 to 1940.

Bauer, Harry C., and Bernard L. Foy, comps. *An Indexed Bibliography of the Tennessee Valley Authority.* Knoxville: TVA Information Div., 1941-42. Various editions covering the period from 1941 to 1942.

Foy, Bernard L., comp. *The TVA Program: A Bibliography.* Knoxville: TVA Information Div., 1943-1968. Various editions covering the period from 1943 to 1968.

Genesis and Development through 1939

Alldredge, J. Haden, et al. *A History of Navigation on the Tennessee River System: An Interpretation of the Economic Influence of This River System on the Tennessee Valley,* House Doc. 254, 75th Cong., 1st sess. Washington, D.C.: GPO, 1937. 192 pp.

Ball, Carleton R. *A Study of the Work of the Land-Grant Colleges in the Tennessee Valley Area in Cooperation with the Tennessee Valley Authority.* Knoxville: U.S. Dept. of Agriculture and TVA, 1939. 76 pp.

Barde, Robert E. "Arthur E. Morgan, First Chairman of TVA." *THQ* 30 (1971), 299-314.

Bennett, James D., II. "Roosevelt, Willkie, and the TVA." *THQ* 28 (1969), 388-96.

——. "Struggle for Power: The Relations between the Tennessee Valley Authority and the Private Power Industry, 1933-1939." Diss., Vanderbilt Univ., 1969.

Bishop, E. L. "TVA's New Deal in Health." *American Journal of Public Health,* Oct. 1934, pp. 1023-27.

Brown, E. F. "Men of TVA." *Commonweal,* Aug. 31, 1934, pp. 419-20.

Brown, Ralph Geron. "Family Removal in the Tennessee Valley." Thesis, Univ. of Tennessee, 1951.

Campbell, Thomas Jefferson. *The Upper Tennessee.*

Chase, Stuart. *Rich Land, Poor Land; A Study of Waste in the Natural Resources of America.* New York: McGraw-Hill, 1936; rpt. New York: AMS, 1969. 361 pp.

Daniel, A. G. "Navigational Development of Muscle Shoals, 1807-1880." *Alabama Review* 14 (1961), 251-58.

Davis, K. C. "Agricultural and Sociological Aspects of the Tennessee Valley Development Project." *JTAS* 9 (1934), 177-79.

Doran, William A. "Early Hydroelectric Power in Tennessee." *THQ* 27 (1968), 72-82.

Draper, E. S. "New TVA Town of Norris, Tennessee." *American City,* Dec. 1933, pp. 67-68.

Droze, Wilmon H. "Tennessee River Navigation: Government and Private Enterprise since 1932." Diss., Vanderbilt Univ., 1960.

———. *High Dams and Slack Waters: TVA Rebuilds a River.* Baton Rouge: Louisiana State Univ. Press, 1965. 174 pp. Droze examines TVA development of navigation on its river and the economic impact of this new commercial artery upon the life of the valley. He concludes that the opening of this waterway to commercial traffic contributes substantially to industrial development and agricultural diversification.

Felsenthal, Edward. "Kenneth Douglas McKellar: The Rich Uncle of the TVA." WTHSP 29 (1966), 108-22.

"From TVA to MVA." *New Republic,* April. 22, 1936, pp. 301-2.

Gorr, Robert Lathrop. "An Analysis of the Tennessee Valley Authority." Thesis, Univ. of Iowa, 1936.

Greene, Lee S. "Personnel Administration in the Tennessee Valley Authority." *Journal of Politics* 1 (1939), 171-94.

Hart, Joseph Kinmont. *Education for an Age of Power; the TVA Poses a Problem.* New York: Harper, 1935. 245 pp.

Harts, William W. "Report upon Improvements of Tennessee River and Its Tributaries." U.S. Engineering Dept. *Report.* Part I, pp. 525-36; part II, pp. 1621-52. Washington, D.C.: GPO, 1907.

"Hatfields and McCoys in the TVA." *New Republic,* Mar. 23, 1938, pp. 192 ff.

Hobson, Leo Guy. "The Agricultural, Cooperative and Rural Electrification Activities of the Tennessee Valley Authority, and the Work of the Farm Credit Administration in the Tennessee River Basin." Diss., Cornell Univ., 1936.

Hodge, Clarence L. *The Tennessee Valley Authority: A National Experiment in Regionalism.* Washington, D.C.: American Univ. Press, 1938; rpt. New York: Russell, 1968. 272 pp.

Horton, Clyde Gibson. "Tennessee Valley Authority Legislation." Thesis, George Peabody College, 1938.

Howard, T. Levron. *The TVA and Economic Security in the South,* Southern Policy Papers, no. 7. Chapel Hill: Univ. of North Carolina Press, 1936. 11 pp.

Hubbard, Preston J. "Story of Muscle Shoals." *Current History,* May 1958, pp. 265-69.

——. "The Muscle Shoals Controversy, 1920-1932." *THQ* 18 (1959), 195-212.

——. *Origins of the TVA; the Muscle Shoals Controversy, 1920-1932.* Diss., Vanderbilt Univ., 1955. Nashville: Vanderbilt Univ. Press, 1961; rpt. New York: Norton, 1968. 340 pp. This work presents the political and economic origins of the TVA through examining the struggle for control of the Tennessee River system from 1920 to 1932. The focal point of this struggle was at Muscle Shoals. Hubbard concludes that TVA owes its existence to a small number of Progressives in the Congress led by Sen. George Norris.

Johnson, D. W. "Tertiary History of the Tennessee River." *Journal of Geology* 13 (1905), 194-231.

Keun, Odette. *A Foreigner Looks at the TVA.* New York: Longmans, Green, 1937. 89 pp.

King, Judson. *Legislative History of Muscle Shoals.* 5 vols. Knoxville: TVA, 1936.

——. *The Conservation Fight, from Theodore Roosevelt to the Tennessee Valley Authority,* introd. Clyde Ellis; foreword Benton J. Stong. Washington, D.C.: Public Affairs Press, 1959. 316 pp.

Lewis, Fred J. "An Engineer Looks at the Tennessee Valley Project." *JTAS* 9 (1934), 167-76.

Lilienthal, David E. "Business and Government in the Tennessee Valley." *Annals,* March 1934, pp. 45-49.

——. *The Journals of David E. Lilienthal,* introd. Henry Steele Commager. 5 vols. New York: Harper, 1964-71. The journal of the man who led in the pioneering development of the Tennessee Valley Authority, widely regarded as the most enduring accomplishment of the New Deal.

McGraw, Thomas K. *Morgan vs. Lilienthal: The Feud within the TVA.* Chicago: Loyola Univ. Press, 1970. 153 pp. Internecine strife during the early days of TVA which resulted in Mr. Arthur E. Morgan's resignation from a TVA directorship.

——. *TVA and the Power Fight, 1933-1939.* Diss., Univ. of Wisconsin, 1970. Critical Periods of History Series. Philadelphia: Lippincott, 1971. 201 pp.

Mackey, Lila Thrasher. "The Social and Educational Aspects of the Tennessee Valley Authority." Thesis, George Peabody College, 1937.

Mank, Russell W., Jr. "Senator Kenneth D. McKellar and the

Tennessee Valley Authority, 1933-1944." Thesis, Univ. of Maryland, 1964.

Milton, George F. "Dawn for the Tennessee Valley." *Review of Reviews,* June 1933, pp. 32-34.

———. "Consumer's View of TVA." *Atlantic Monthly,* Nov. 1937, pp. 653-58.

Moley, Raymond. "Who Owns TVA?" *Newsweek,* Apr. 11, 1938, p. 40.

Morgan, Arthur E. "Planning in the Tennessee Valley." *Current History,* Sept. 1933, pp. 663-68.

———. "Development of the Tennessee Valley." *Literary Digest,* Nov. 18, 1933, pp. 15 ff.

———. "Bench-Marks in the Tennessee Valley." *Survey Graphic,* Jan.-Nov. 1934, pp. 4-10, 105-110, 233-37, 548-52; *Survey Graphic,* Mar. 1935, pp. 112-16.

———. *Log of the TVA.* New York: Survey Associates, 1936. 43 pp.

Morgan, Lucy G. *Finding His World: The Story of Arthur E. Morgan.* Yellow Springs, O.: Kahoe, 1927. 108 pp.

"Dr. Morgan Should Resign." *New Republic,* Mar. 23, 1938, pp. 181 ff.

Moutoux, J. T. "Setback for the Power Trust." *New Republic,* Dec. 27, 1933, pp. 193-95.

"No Quarter for TVA; Private Power Companies Prepare for Finish Fight." *Business Week,* Aug. 29, 1936, p. 18.

Parkins, A. E. "The Tennessee Valley Project—Facts and Fancies." *JTAS* 8 (1933), 345-57.

Poe, J. C. "Morgan-Lilienthal Feud." *Nation,* Oct. 3, 1936. pp. 385-86.

Pope, Adelynne Hiller, "Prelude to TVA: The Wadsworth-Kahn Bill, 1919-1921." Thesis, Trinity Univ., 1966.

Pritchett, C. Herman. "The Development of the Tennessee Valley Authority Act." *TLR* 15 (1938), 128-41.

Rankin, J. E. "TVA Rates as a Yardstick." *Current History,* May 1935, pp. 121-25.

"Reforestation by the Tennessee Valley Authority." *Science,* Dec. 1, 1933, pp. 500- .

Report to the Congress on the Unified Development of the Tennessee River System. Knoxville: TVA, 1936. 105 pp.

Robey, R. "Positive News at Last; Agreement between the TVA and Commonwealth and Southern. *Newsweek,* Feb. 20, 1939, pp. 50- .

Robinson, C. W. "Tennessee River Improvements." *Harper's Weekly,* Apr. 27, 1895, p. 398.

Smallwood, Johnny B., Jr. "George W. Norris and the Concept of a Planned Region." Diss., Univ. of North Carolina, 1963.

Stuart, J. "Tennessee Mountain Poorhouse." *New Republic,* Nov. 21, 1934, pp. 42-43.

Talbert, Roy, Jr., ed. "Arthur E. Morgan's Ethical Code for the Tennessee Valley Authority." ETHSP 40 (1968), 119-27.

———. "Arthur E. Morgan's Social Philosophy and the Tennessee Valley Authority." ETHSP 41 (1969), 86-99.

Taylor, A. W. "TVA Triumphs in Tennessee." *Christian Century,* Aug. 30, 1939, pp. 1054- .

Tennessee Valley Authority. *Tennessee Valley Authority.* Washington, D.C.: GPO, 1934. 8 pp.

———. *Fifty Inches of Rain. A Story of Land and Water Conservation.* Washington, D.C.: GPO, 1939. 111 pp.

———. *Norris Dam.* Washington, D.C.: GPO, 1936. 39 pp.

———. *Tennessee Valley Authority, 1933-1937.* Washington, D.C.: GPO, 1937. 83 pp.

———. *The Scenic Resources of the Tennessee Valley. A Descriptive and Pictorial Inventory.* Washington, D.C.: GPO, 1938. 222 pp.

———. *TVA.* Washington, D.C.: GPO, 1940- . Annual reports, with varying titles, of TVA to Congress.

"TVA Inquiry: Willkie Accuses the New Deal of Trying to Wreck Utilities." *Newsweek,* Dec. 5, 1938, p. 12.

"War on TVA." *Business Week,* Dec. 1, 1934, p. 7.

Wengert, Norman. "Antecedents of TVA: The Legislative History of Muscle Shoals." *Agricultural History* 26 (1952), 141-47,

Whitman, Willson. *God's Valley; People and Power along the Tennessee River.* New York: Viking, 1939. 320 pp.

Willkie, Wendell L. "Political Power." *Atlantic Monthly,* Aug. 1937, pp. 210-18.

"Will Government Operation of Power Utilities Benefit the Public? Opposing Arguments by the National Coal Association." *Congressional Digest,* Oct. 1934, pp. 239- .

Winger, Sarah Elizabeth B. "The Genesis of TVA." Diss., Univ. of Wisconsin, 1959.

1940-49

Blee, C. E. "Miltiple Purpose Reservoir Operation of Tennessee River System." *Civil Engineering,* May 1945, pp. 219-22; June 1945, pp. 263-66.

Ciokolo, Mary. "TVA—a Critique of a Regional Plan." Thesis, Univ. of Rochester, 1948.

Clapp, Gordon. "TVA: A Democratic Method for the Development of a Region's Resources." *Vanderbilt Law Review* 1 (1948), 183-93.

Collins, Frederick Lewis. *Uncle Sam's Billion-Dollar Baby, a Taxpayer Looks at the TVA.* New York: Putnam's, 1945. 174 pp.

Coyle, David Cushman. *Land of Hope: The Way of Life in the Tennessee Valley.* Evanston, Ill.: Row, Peterson, 1941. 64 pp. A short treatment of TVA's impact upon the region.

Davidson, Donald. "Political Regionalism and Administrative Regionalism." *Annals,* Jan. 1940, pp. 138-43.

Duffus, Robert L. "Giant Goes to War; TVA Supplies the Electric Power for National Defense." *New York Times Magazine,* July 27, 1941, pp. 8-9.

———. *The Valley and Its People, a Portrait of TVA.* New York: Knopf, 1944. 167 pp.

Durisch, Lawrence. "The TVA Program and the War Effort." *Journal of Politics* 8 (1946), 531-37.

"Feud: McKellar Loves TVA, Hates Lilienthal." *Time,* May 25, 1942, p. 13.

Finer, Herman. *The T.V.A.; Lessons for International Application,* International Labour Office Studies and Reports, Series B, no. 37. Montreal: International Labor Off., 1944. 289 pp. Rpt., FDR and the Era of the New Deal Series. New York: Da Capo, 1972.

"For Sale: TVA Will Auction Off the Southern Villages." *Business Week,* Mar. 13, 1948, pp. 56-57.

Fox, Portland P., and Thomas M. West. "Geologic Profiles of the Lower Tennessee River." *JTAS* 19 (1944), 150-59.

Gable, William Russell. "The Tennessee Valley Authority and Its Relation to Private Enterprise." Thesis, Louisiana State Univ., 1949.

Green, Clarence Jasper. *An Analysis of the Real Cost of TVA Power, Original and Supplemental Reports.* Washington, D.C.: U.S. Chamber of Commerce, 1948. 91 pp.

Greene, Lee S., Virginia Holmes Brown, and Evan A. Iverson. *Rescued Earth: A Study of the Public Administration of Natural Resources in Tennessee.* Knoxville: Univ. of Tennessee Press, 1948. 204 pp.

Halik, Constance. "The Tennessee Valley Authority: An Examination of Its Historical Background and of Some of the Major Controversies in Which It Has Been Involved." Thesis, Univ. of Rochester, 1947.

Houston, Sam M. "TVA, a Study in Policy Formation." Diss., Univ. of Iowa, 1942.

Howard, T. Levron. "Federal Payments in Lieu of Taxation with Emphasis on the Program of the Tennessee Valley Authority." Diss., Univ. of Wisconsin, 1943.

Howard, Waldorf Vivian. *Authority in TVA Land.* Kansas City: Glenn, 1948. 186 pp.

Huxley, Julian Sorell. *TVA, Adventure in Planning.* Cheam, Surrey, England: Architectural Press, 1943; London: Reader's Union, 1945. 142 pp.

Kirschten, E. "TVA, the First Fifteen Years." *Nation,* June 12, 1948, pp. 656-58.

Kull, Donald C. *Budget Administration in the Tennessee Valley Authority.* Thesis, Univ. of Minnesota. Knoxville: Univ. of Tennessee Record, May 1948. A study sponsored by the Bureau of Research of the College of Business Administration and the Bureau of Public Administration, Univ. of Tennessee.

Lee, Chi Yuen. "The Impact of TVA on Agriculture." Thesis, Univ. of Tennessee, 1949.

Lefferts, Walter. *The Taming of the Tennessee: Continued Study Units in Geographic Backgrounds.* Philadelphia: Davis, 1941. 65 pp.

Lilienthal, David E. "Senator Norris and the TVA." *Nation,* Sept. 23, 1944, pp. 343-44.

———. *TVA: Democracy on the March.* New York: Harper, 1944; rpt. Penguin, 1944. 208 pp. Rev. ed., New York: Harper, 1953. 294 pp.

———. "Shall We Have More TVA's?" *New York Times Magazine,* Jan. 7, 1945, pp. 10- .

Livingood, James W. "The Tennessee Valley in American History." ETHSP 21 (1949), 19-32.

McCarthy, C. J. "Land Acquisition Policies and Proceedings in TVA—a Study of the Role of Land Acquisition in a Regional Agency." *Ohio State Law Journal* 10 (1949), 46-63.

Nielsen, Ralph Leighton. "Socio-Economic Readjustment of Farm Families Displaced by the TVA Land Purchase in the Norris Area." Thesis, Univ. of Tennessee, 1940.

"Norris To Be Sold by TVA." *American City*, Aug. 1947, pp. 101-

Pritchett, C. Herman. *The Tennessee Valley Authority, a Study in Public Administration.* Chapel Hill: Univ. of North Carolina, 1943; rpt. New York: Russell, 1971. 333 pp.

Ransmeier, Joseph Sirera. *The Tennessee Valley Authority: A Case Study in the Economics of Multiple Purpose Stream Planning.* Diss., Columbia Univ., 1942. Nashville: Vanderbilt Univ. Press, 1942. 487 pp.

Ray, Joseph M. "The Influence of the Tennessee Valley Authority on Government in the South." *American Political Science Review* 43 (1949), 922-32.

Russell, Dean. *The TVA Idea.* Irvington-on-Hudson, N.Y.: Foundation for Economic Education, 1949. 108 pp.

Satterfield, M. H. "TVA-State-Local Relationships." *American Political Science Review* 40 (1946), 935-49.

——. "Intergovernmental Cooperation in the Tennessee Valley." *Journal of Politics* 9 (1947), 31-58.

Seigworth, Kenneth J. "Reforestation in the Tennessee Valley." *Public Administration Review* 8 (1948), 280-85.

Selznick, Philip. *TVA and the Grass Roots: A Study in the Sociology of Formal Organization,* University of California Publications in Culture and Society, vol. 3. Berkeley: Univ. of California Press, 1949. 274 pp.; rpt. Torchbooks, New York: Harper, 1966.

Simpich, Frederick. "Around the 'Great Lakes of the South.'" *National Geographic Magazine,* Apr. 1948, pp. 463-91.

"Sold for $2,107,500." *American City,* July 1948, pp. 7 ff. Report of the shift of Norris, Tennessee, from TVA to private ownership.

Strack, Charles Miller. "Agricultural Changes in the TVA Area, 1930-1945." Diss., Univ. of Iowa, 1950.

Taylor, A. W. "TVA Leads in the New South." *Christian Century,* Nov. 27, 1940, pp. 1494-95.

Tennessee State Department of Conservation. *Tennessee Fishing Waters, Featuring TVA Lakes.* Nashville: State of Tennessee, 1948.

Tennessee State Planning Commission. *Towers of Power Back Industrial Opportunities in Tennessee, First Public Power State.* Nashville: State of Tennessee, 1944. 20 pp.

Tennessee Valley Authority. *The Norris Project. A Comprehensive Report on the Planning, Design, Construction, and Initial Operations of the Tennessee Valley Authority's First Water Control Project.* Washington, D.C.: GPO, 1940. 840 pp.

———. *Recreational Development of the Tennessee River System,* House Doc. 565, 76th Cong., 3rd sess. Washington, D.C.: GPO, 1940. 99 pp.

———. *Tennessee Valley Resources; Their Development and Use.* Knoxville: TVA, 1947. 145 pp.

Thiel, Robert Ellis. "Kenneth D. McKellar and the Politics of the Tennessee Valley Authority, 1941-1946." Thesis, Univ. of Virginia, 1967.

"TVA's Riverway." *Business Week,* Dec. 6, 1941, pp. 38- .

"TVA's Ten Years." *Business Week,* May 8, 1943, pp. 19-20.

Whitman, Willson. *David Lilienthal; Public Servant in a Power Age.* New York: Holt, 1948. 245 pp.

"Wilkie and the TVA." *New Republic,* Sept. 2, 1940, pp. 321-24.

Woodhouse, Betty Frost. "Legislative Control of the Tennessee Valley Authority." Thesis, Louisiana State Univ., 1945.

1950-59

Avery, Robert S. *Experiment in Management: Personnel Decentralization in the Tennessee Valley Authority.* Knoxville: Univ. of Tennessee Press, 1954. 224 pp. An analysis of practices in personnel administration.

———. "The TVA and Labor Relations: A Review." *The Journal of Politics,* Aug. 1954.

Blackmore, John. "A Watershed Development Program for the TVA." Diss., Harvard Univ., 1954.

Brown, Ralph Geron. "Family Removal in the Tennessee Valley." Thesis, Univ. of Tennessee, 1951.

Clapp, Gordon R. "National Dividends from the Tennessee Valley." *South Atlantic Quarterly* 49 (1950), 1-7.

——. "TVA after Two Decades." *New Republic,* Sept. 22, 1952, pp. 22-24.

——. *The TVA: An Approach to the Development of a Region.* Chicago: Univ. of Chicago Press, 1955; rpt. New York: Russell, 1971. 206 pp.

Clement, Frank G. "Don't Let TVA Be Wrecked, Mr. President." *Reporter,* Dec. 8, 1953, pp. 28-32.

"Containing the TVA." *Nation,* July 31, 1954, p. 84.

Douglas, William O. "Tennessee across the World." *TLR* 21 (1951), 707-802.

Duffus, Robert L. "TVA's Challenge—after Twenty-Five Years." *New York Times Magazine,* May 18, 1958, p. 27.

Fox, A. J., Jr. "TVA Dam Builders Turn to Steam." *Engineering News-Record,* Feb. 25, 1954, pp. 30-34.

Frank, Bernard and Anthony Netboy. "TVA's Unfinished Business." *Yale Review* 40 (1950), 43-58.

"General Chosen to Administer TVA." *Christian Century,* Aug. 18, 1954, pp. 963- .

Hazlitt, Henry. "The Seamy Side of TVA." *Newsweek,* Aug. 1, 1955, p. 67.

Hill, Lister. "TVA: Democracy in Action." *Progressive,* May 1958, pp. 10-14.

"Isn't TVA Big Enough?" *Fortune,* May 1955, p. 91.

Kyle, John H. *The Building of TVA: An Illustrated History.* Baton Rouge: Louisiana State Univ. Press, 1958. 162 pp.

Lafky, John Delmar. "Tennessee Valley Authority 1933 to 1960: An Investigation of Progress." Thesis, Univ. of Texas, 1960.

Lepawsky, Albert. "Why Public Power Is Here to Stay." *Reporter,* Oct. 6, 1955, pp. 33-37.

Leuchtenburg, William E. "Roosevelt, Norris and the Seven Little TVA's." *Journal of Politics* 14 (1952), 418-41.

McKinley, Charles. "The Valley Authority and Its Alternatives." *American Political Science Review* 44 (1950), 607-49.

Martin, Roscoe C., ed. *TVA: The First Twenty Years.* University: Univ. of Alabama Press, and Knoxville: Univ. of Tennessee Press, 1956. 282 pp. An authoritative review of TVA's many activities.

Meeks, Carl Garnett. "Resources for Physical Recreation in the Tennessee Valley Authority Region." Ed.D. diss., Teachers College, Columbia Univ., 1953.

Moley, Raymond. *Valley Authorities,* National Economic Problems, no. 438. New York: American Enterprise Assoc., 1950. 78 pp.

——. "TVA after Twenty-Five Years." *Newsweek,* May 26, 1958, p. 104.

"Mr. TVA." *New Republic,* Aug. 10, 1953, pp. 4-5.

Peterson, Elmer Theodore. *Big Dam Foolishness; the Problem of Modern Flood Control and Water Storage,* introd. Paul B. Sears. New York: Devin-Adair, 1954. 224 pp.

Roberts, Elliott Phirman. *One River—Seven States; TVA—State Relations in the Development of the Tennessee River.* Diss., Univ. of Wisconsin, 1953. Knoxville: Bureau of Public Administration, Univ. of Tennessee, 1955. 114 pp.

Ruttan, V. W. "Impact of Urban-Industrial Development on Agriculture in the Tennessee Valley and the Southeast." *Journal of Farm Economics,* Feb. 1955, pp. 38-56.

Seneker, Stanley Archibald. "An Economic Analysis of Competition between the Tennessee Valley Authority and Private Power." Thesis, Univ. of Pennsylvania, 1957.

Shah, Robin Chandulal. "What Lessons India Can Learn from the Tennessee Valley Authority." Thesis, Univ. of Pennsylvania, 1958.

Tennessee State Planning Commission. *Reservoir Shore Line Development in Tennessee; a Study of Problems and Opportunities.* Nashville: State of Tennessee, 1958. 77 pp.

"TVA Warns of Power Shortage in Drive for New Steam Plants." *Business Week,* Jan. 7, 1956, p. 84.

Vibhatakarasa, Jin. "The Tennessee Valley Authority: Administrative Development of the Last Two Decades, 1940-1960." Thesis, Duke Univ., 1961.

Wengert, Norman I. "TVA—Symbol and Reality." *Journal of Politics* 13 (1951), 369-92.

——. *Valley of Tomorrow: The TVA and Agriculture.* Diss., Univ. of Wisconsin, 1947. Knoxville: Bureau of Public Administration, Univ. of Tennessee, 1952. 168 pp. An analysis of TVA's policies and program administration in the field of agriculture.

Williams, James Earl. "The Industrial Development Policy of the Tennessee Valley Authority for the Period 1933-1950." Thesis, Univ. of Tennessee, 1950.

"Yardstick That Works." *Reporter,* Mar. 19, 1959, p. 4. "In Reply," *Reporter,* Apr. 30, 1959, pp. 8-9.

THE DIXON-YATES CONTROVERSY

"ABC's of Dixon-Yates." *U.S. News and World Report,* Nov. 19, 1954, pp. 27-29.

Cater, Douglass. "ABC of Dixon-Yates, or, How to Get Less for More." *Reporter,* Oct. 21, 1954, pp. 13-16.

Clapp, Gordon R. "Dixon-Yates Deal."*Nation,* Oct. 2, 1954, pp. 286-87.

"Crisscrossing the Power Lines: Dixon-Yates Power Controversy." *Fortune,* Dec. 1954, p. 92.

"Dixon-Yates Controversy, Background Material, and Pro and Con Discussion." *Congressional Digest,* Jan, 1955, 1-32.

Goodman, Walter, et al. "About Face on Dixon Yates." *New Republic,* July 18, 1955, pp. 6-10.

Kefauver, Estes. "What's Wrong with Dixon-Yates." *Atlantic Monthly,* Jan. 1955, pp. 66-69.

Kenworthy, E. W. "Dixon-Yates: The Riddle of a Self-Inflicted Wound." *Reporter,* Jan. 26, 1956, pp. 19-25. Lister Hill. "In Reply." *Reporter,* Mar. 8, 1956, pp. 7-9.

1960-72

Baker, Willis M. "Reminiscing about the TVA." *American Forests,* May 1969, pp. 31 ff.

Buckley, William F., Jr. "Sell the TVA?" *National Review,* Dec. 3, 1963, pp. 472 ff.

Egerton, John. "TVA: The Halo Slips: The Land Between the Lakes Dispute." *Nation,* July 3, 1967, pp. 11-15.

Gilletta, R. "Crow Creek: Case History of an Ecological Disaster." *Science,* May 26, 1972, pp. 891 ff.

Gray, A. J., and Victor Roterus. *The Tennessee River Valley; A Case Study.* Washington, D.C.: Housing Div., International Cooperation Adm., 1960. 15 pp.

Hechler, K. "TVA Ravages the Land." *National Parks and Conservation Magazine,* July 1971, pp. 15-16.

Hobday, Victor Carr. *Sparks at the Grassroots; Municipal Distribution of TVA Electricity in Tennessee.* Diss., Syracuse Univ., 1966. Knoxville: Univ. of Tennessee Press, 1969. 272 pp.

Hodge, Clarence Lewis. *The Tennessee Valley Authority; a National Experiment in Regionalism.* Washington, D.C.: American Univ. Press, 1938; rpt. New York: Russell, 1968. 272 pp.

Jenkins, Clifford T. *Floods in Tennessee; Magnitude and Frequency.* Nashville: Tennessee Dept. of Highways, 1960.

Kretsch, Jack Louis. "Influence of Reservoir Projects on Land Values." Diss., Harvard Univ., 1963.

Laycock, George. "Land Between the Lakes." *Field and Stream,* Mar. 1965, pp. 130-33.

May, William. "A Case against the Expansion of the Tennessee Valley Authority Electric Generating Facilities." Thesis, Fairleigh Dickinson Univ., 1965.

Moore, John R., ed. *The Economic Impact of TVA.* Knoxville: Univ. of Tennessee Press, 1967. 163 pp. Eight Specialists assess TVA's first 30 years.

Munzer, Martha E. *Valley of Vision: The TVA Years,* Living History Library. New York: Knopf, 1969. 199 pp. Juvenile.

Oberdorfer, Don. "CAP and TVA: Barry's Fine Distinction." *Reporter,* Sept. 10, 1964, pp. 36-38.

Outdoor Recreation for a Growing Nation: TVA's Experience with Man-Made Reservoirs. Knoxville: TVA, 1961. 116 pp.

Palo, G. P., and D. B. Weaver. "TVA's First Nuclear Plant." *Power Engineering,* Apr. 1967, pp. 38-42.

Pearce, John E. "The Creeping Conservatism of TVA." *Reporter,* Jan. 4, 1962, pp. 31-35.

Polite, Douglas William. "Trend Analysis: A Method of Predicting Tennessee River Traffic." Thesis, Univ. of Tennessee, 1969.

Segerberg, J. "Power Corrupts; the TVA and Coal Operators Ruin the Kentucky Hillsides." *Esquire,* March 1972, pp. 138-42.

Smith, Frank E. *The Politics of Conservation.* New York: Pantheon, 1966. 338 pp.; rev. ed., New York: Harper, 1971.

Sweeten, Charles Hugh. "Tennessee Municipalities and TVA Power." Thesis, Univ. of Tennessee, 1966.

Tennessee State Planning Commission. *The Tennessee River Gorge, Its Scenic Preservation; a Report to the 1961 General Assembly,* State Planning Office Publication no. 311. Nashville: n.p., 1961. 104 pp.

Tennessee Valley Authority. *Basic Data on TVA and Its Revenue Bond Financing.* Knoxville: TVA, 1960. 59 pp.

——. Government Relations and Economics Staff. *Manufacturing Employment in the Tennessee Valley Region.* Knoxville: TVA, 1961. 51 pp.

——. *An Appraisal of Coal Strip Mining.* Knoxville: TVA, 1963. 13 pp.

——. *A Short History of the Tennessee Valley Authority.* Knoxville: TVA, 1963. 12 pp.

——. Division of Navigation Development. *The Tennessee River Navigation System: History, Development, and Operation.* Knoxville: TVA, 1964. 423 pp.

——. *TVA—the Valley of Light, 1933-1963.* Washington, D.C.: GPO, 1964. 81 pp.

——. *The Tellico Project of the TVA.* Knoxville: TVA, 1965, 1966. 13 pp.

——. Office of Power. *Comparison of Coal-Fired and Nuclear Power Plants for the TVA System.* Chattanooga: TVA, 1966. 36 pp.

——. Division of Forestry Development. *Forest Resources and Industries in the Tennessee Valley.* Norris: TVA, 1966. 21 pp.

——. *Navigation and Economic Growth—Tennessee River Experience.* Knoxville: TVA, 1966. 64 pp.

"TVA: Coal Gets Cheaper or Else." *Business Week,* Nov. 21, 1970, p. 52.

"TVA Chooses Atom Power." *Business Week,* June 25, 1966, pp. 150ff.

"TVA Is Washington's Watchdog on Industry's Pricing." *Business Week,* Apr. 1, 1961, pp. 62-64.

Walsh, J. "Strip Mining: TVA in Middle in Reclamation Controversy." *Science,* Oct. 8, 1965, pp. 194-98.

Williams, York Wayland. "An Economic Evaluation of the Power Program of the Tennessee Valley Authority." Thesis, Univ. of Colorado, 1961.

Oak Ridge and Atomic Energy

Bissell, A. K. "A Reminiscence of Oak Ridge." ETHSP 39 (1967), 71-86.

Bryan, G. E., Jr. "Youth at Oak Ridge." *Christian Century,* Dec. 26, 1956, pp. 1515-16.

Case, Dale Edward. "Oak Ridge, Tennessee: A Geographic Study." Diss., Univ. of Tennessee, 1955.

"City That Atoms Built." *Business Week,* Oct. 27, 1945, pp. 21-22.

DeVore, R. "Man Who Made Manhattan." *Colliers,* Oct. 13, 1945, pp. 12-13.

Dwyer, Lynn E. "The Social Backgrounds of Scientists and Engineers in Oak Ridge, Tennessee, and Huntsville, Alabama." Thesis, Univ. of Tennessee, 1972.

Falstein, Louis. "Oak Ridge: Secret City." *New Republic,* Nov. 12, 1945, pp. 635-37.

———. "The Men Who Made the A-Bomb." *New Republic,* Nov. 26, 1945, pp. 707-9.

Groueff, Stéphane. *Manhattan Project; the Untold Story of the Making of the Atomic Bomb.* Boston: Little, 1967. 372 pp. An attempt to write a comprehensive story of the manufacture of the atomic bomb. Unfortunately, the author has made use of only a very small bibliography.

Groves, Leslie R. *Now It Can Be Told: The Story of the Manhattan Project.* New York: Harper, 1962; rpt. London: Deutsch, 1963. 464 pp.

Lang, D. "Atomic City." *New Yorker,* Sept. 29, 1945, pp. 48 ff.

———. "Reporter at Large; a Deacon at Oak Ridge." *New Yorker,* Feb. 6, 1954, pp. 37-38.

"Main Street Comes to Oak Ridge." *Business Week,* Sept. 24, 1955, p. 192.

Ogden, Warner. "The A-Bomb's Home." *New York Times Magazine,* Apr. 14, 1946, pp. 16 ff.

Owen, Russell. "Tennessee: From Monkey Trial to Atomic Age." *New York Times Magazine,* July 21, 1946, pp. 17 ff.

Robinson, George O. *The Oak Ridge Story: The Saga of a People Who Share in History.* Kingsport: Southern, 1950. 181 pp.

Skidmore, Owings, & Merrill Co. *Report to the Atomic Energy Commission on the Master Plan, Oak Ridge, Tennessee.* Oak Ridge: The Company, 1948. 102 pp.

Sutton, Horace. "Booked for Travel; Gone Fission." *Saturday Review,* June 12, 1954, pp. 34-35.

Walsh, J. "Oak Ridge: Twenty Years After, Diversification Is the Goal." *Science,* Nov. 12, 1965, pp. 863-65.

White, C. W. "We Visited the Atomic City." *Better Homes and Gardens,* May 1955, pp. 230 ff.

LABOR HISTORY

Belissary, Constantine G. "Behavior Patterns and Aspirations of the Urban Working Classes of Tennessee in the Immediate Post-Civil War Era." *THQ* 14 (1955), 24-42.

Born, Kate. "Organized Labor in Memphis, Tennessee, 1826-1901." WTHS*P* 21 (1967), 60-79.

Brown, Virginia Holmes. *The Development of Labor Legislation in Tennessee.* Thesis, Univ. of Tennessee, 1945. Knoxville: Bureau of Public Administration, Univ. of Tennessee, 1945.

Clouse, R. Wilburn. "The Impact on Workers of an Industrial Plant Shutdown: A Case Study of Du Pont's Rayon Plant Shutdown at Old Hickory, Tennessee." Thesis, Middle Tennessee State Univ., 1968.

Crabtree, Font F. "The Wilder Coal Strike of 1932-33." Thesis, George Peabody College, 1937.

Crooke, Jonas Boyd. "The Labor Characteristics of Low-Wage Manufacturing Industries in East Tennessee: The Berkline Corporation." Thesis, Univ. of Tennessee, 1967.

Davis, Franklin R. "Public Reaction and the Bituminous Coal Strike." Thesis, East Tennessee State Univ., 1968.

Eberling, E. J. "The Employment Security Program (with Special Reference to Tennessee Unemployment Insurance)." *Vanderbilt Law Review* 1 (1947-48), 376-95.

Green, Archie. *Only a Miner: Studies in Recorded Coal-Mining Songs,* Music in American Life Series. Urbana: Univ. of Illinois Press, 1972. 504 pp. This work has one chapter devoted to songs which emanated from the Coal Creek Miners' Insurrection of 1891-92.

Hodges, James A. "The Tennessee Federation of Labor, 1919-1939." Thesis, Vanderbilt Univ., 1959.

——. "Challenge to the New South: The Great Textile Strike in Elizabethton, Tennessee, 1929." *THQ* 23 (1964), 343-57.

Holly, J. Fred, and Bevars D. Mabry. *Protective Labor Legislation and Its Administration in Tennessee.* Knoxville: Univ. of Tennessee Press, 1955. 216 pp.

Horton, Miles. "Witch-Hunt in Tennessee: Highlander Folk School." *New Republic,* Mar. 9, 1959, p. 23.

Hutson, Andrew Carter, Jr. "The Coal Miner's Insurrection 1891-1892." Thesis, Univ. of Tennessee, 1933.

——. "The Coal Miners' Insurrection of 1891 in Anderson County, Tennessee." ETHSP 7 (1935), 103-21.

——. "The Overthrow of the Convict Lease System in Tennessee." ETHSP 8 (1936), 82-103.

Kovach, Bill. "Air-Conditioned Sweatshop; Criticism of Public Financing Programs." *Reporter,* Oct. 7, 1965, pp. 29-31.

Marshall, F. Ray. *Labor in the South,* Wertheim Publications in Industrial Relations Series. Cambridge: Mass.: Harvard Univ. Press, 1967. 406 pp.

Petrie, J. C. "Memphis Makes War on CIO." *Christian Century,* Oct. 13, 1937, pp. 1273- .

Pinkston, Sammy E. "History of Local 309, United Steelworkers of America, Alcoa, Tennessee." Thesis, Univ. of Tennessee, 1970.

Report of Joint Committee on Highlander Folk School 81st Session of the General Assembly of the State of Tennessee. Nashville: State of Tennessee, 1959. 17 pp.

Special Report of the Commissioner of Labor and Inspector of Mines. Nashville: Marshall & Bruce, 1891.

Thomas, Hulan Glyn. "The Highlander Folk School: The Depression Years." *THQ* 23 (1964), 358-71.

——. "History of the Highlander Folk School, 1932-1941." Thesis, Vanderbilt Univ., 1964.

White, Charles P. "Early Experiments with Prison Labor in Tennessee." ETHSP 12 (1940), 45-69.

Wilson, B. M. "Tennessee Workmen's Compensation Law." Thesis, East Tennessee State Univ., 1952.

Political History

GENERAL HISTORY: 1770-1800

Abernethy, Thomas P. "Social Relations and Political Control in the Old Southwest." *MVHR* 16 (1929-30), 529-37.

Black, Roy W., Sr. "The Genesis of County Organization in the Western District of North Carolina and in the State of Tennessee." WTHS*P* 2 (1948), 95-118.

Calhoun, Daniel H. *Professional Lives in America: Structure and Aspiration, 1750-1850,* Center for the Study of the History of Liberty in America Series. Cambridge, Mass.: Harvard Univ. Press, 1965. 231 pp. This work contains a section on the law in frontier Tennessee.

Chambers, William Trout. "Attempts to Adjust Political Life to Pioneer Environment in Tennessee." Thesis, Univ. of Chicago, 1924.

Fink, Miriam L. "Judicial Activities in Early East Tennessee." ETHS*P* 7 (1935), 38-49.

McMurry, Dorothy. "Independent Government of Tennessee and Kentucky, 1771-1790." Thesis, Vanderbilt Univ., 1923.

Waite, Mariella. "Political Institutions in the Trans-Appalachian West, 1770-1800." Diss., Univ. of Florida, 1961.

Wilson, Samuel M. "Washington's Relations to Tennessee and Kentucky." ETHS*P* 5 (1933), 3-21.

GENERAL HISTORY: 1800-64

Alexander, Thomas B. "The Presidential Campaign of 1840 in Tennessee." *THQ* 1 (1942), 21-43.

Bellamy, James W. "The Political Career of Landon Carter Haynes." Thesis, Univ. of Tennessee, 1952.

——. "The Political Career of Landon Carter Haynes." ETHS*P* 28 (1956), 102-26.

Bergeron, Paul H. "Political Struggles in Tennessee, 1839-1843." Thesis, Vanderbilt Univ., 1962.

———., ed. "A Tennessean Blasts Calhoun and Nullification." *THQ* 26 (1967), 383-86. John Wyly of Greeneville was Calhoun's detractor.

Bloomer, Faye Trolson. "The Legislative Career of John Blair." Thesis, East Tennessee State Univ., 1956. Blair was a Jacksonian legislator of the 1820s and 1830s.

Burt, Jesse C., ed. "Tennessee Democrats Employ Editor E. G. Eastman, 1846-1849." ETHS*P* 38 (1966), 83-96.

Brown, Aaron V. *Speeches, Congressional and Political, and Other Writings, of Ex-Governor Aaron V. Brown, of Tennessee. Collected and Arranged by the Editors of the "Union and American."* Nashville: J. L. Marling, 1854-55. 706 pp.

Clark, Patricia P. "A. O. P. Nicholson of Tennessee: Editor, Statesman, and Jurist." Thesis, Univ. of Tennessee, 1965.

Clifton, Frances. "The Life and Activities of John Overton." Thesis, Vanderbilt Univ., 1948.

"Diaries of S. H. Laughlin of Tennessee, 1840-1843: With Introduction and Notes by St. George L. Sioussat." *THM* 2 (1916), 43-85.

Eriksson, Erik McKinley. "Official Newspaper Organs and the Campaign of 1828." *THM* 8 (1924), 231-47.

———. "Official Newspaper Organs and the Campaign of 1832." *THM* 9 (1925), 37-58.

———. "Official Newspaper Organs and the Campaign of 1836." *THM* 9 (1925), 115-30.

Garrett, William R., and John M. Bass, eds. "Origin of the Democratic National Convention." *AHM* 7 (1902), 267-73.

Gass, Edmund C. "The Constitutional Opinions of Justice John Catron." ETHS*P* 8 (1936), 54-73.

Gentry, Amos Leo. "The Public Career of Leonidas Campbell Houk." Thesis, Univ. of Tennessee, 1939.

Goodrich, William. "William Cocke—Born 1748, Died 1828." *AHM* 1 (1896), 224-29.

Harlan, Louis R. "The Public Career of William Berkeley Lewis." Thesis, Vanderbilt Univ., 1947.

———. "Public Career of William Berkeley Lewis." *THQ* 7 (1948), 3-37, 118-51.

Henry, Milton. "Summary of Tennessee Representation in Congress from 1845 to 1861." *THQ* 10 (1951), 140-48.

Hooper, Ernest Walter. "The Presidential Election of 1836 in Tennessee." Thesis, Univ. of North Carolina, 1949.

Horn, Stanley F. "Isham G. Harris in the Pre-War Years." *THQ* 19 (1960), 195-207.

Jordan, Robert D. "Some Phases of the Private Life and Public Career of John Rhea." Thesis, East Tennessee State Univ., 1952. Rhea was a United States congressman from Blountville in the early 1800s.

Kershaw, William Karl. "The Presidential Campaign of 1844 in Tennessee." Thesis, George Peabody College, 1927.

Lacy, Eric Russell. "First District Congressmen and Slavery Issues, 1820-1861." Thesis, East Tennessee State Univ., 1960.

———. "Crossroads in the Highlands: First District Congressmen and the Age of Jackson." ETHS*P* 37 (1965), 23-30.

Lambert, Robert S. "The Democratic National Convention of 1844." *THQ* 14 (1955), 3-23.

Lowe, Gabriel, Jr. "The Early Public Career of John Henry Eaton." Thesis, Vanderbilt Univ., 1951.

———. "John H. Eaton, Jackson's Campaign Manager." *THQ* 11 (1952), 99-147.

Marshall, Kendrick. "Horace Maynard: A Tennessee Statesman." Thesis, Tennessee State A&I Univ., 1960.

Mitchell, Enoch L. "Robert White, Agrarian, Lawyer, Jurist." *THQ* 10 (1951), 3-24.

Mooney, Chase C. "The Political Career of Adam Huntsman." *THQ* 10 (1951), 99-126. Huntsman was a Jacksonian politician from West Tennessee.

Morgan, William G. "The Decline of the Congressional Nominating Caucus." *THQ* 24 (1965), 245-55.

Parks, Joseph H., ed. "Letters from Aaron V. Brown to Alfred O. P. Nicholson, 1844-1850." *THQ* 3 (1944), 170-79.

Partin, Robert Love. "The Administration of Isham G. Harris." Thesis, George Peabody College, 1928.

Rippa, Sol Alexander. "The Development of Constitutional Democracy in Tennessee, 1790-1835." Thesis, Vanderbilt Univ., 1950.

Satterfield, Robert Beeler. "The Early Public Career of Andrew Jackson Donelson." Thesis, Vanderbilt Univ., 1948.

Sioussat, St. George L. "Some Phases of Tennessee Politics in the Jackson Period." *AHR* 14 (1908-9), 51-69.

——. "Tennessee and National Political Parties, 1850-1860." *Annual Report of the American Historical Association for the Year 1914,* 1 (1914), 243-58.

——. "Tennessee, the Compromise of 1850, and the Nashville Convention." *MVHR* 2 (1915), 313-47.

——. "Tennessee, the Compromise of 1850, and the Nashville Convention." *THM* 4 (1918), 215-47.

Sketch of the Life and Public Services of General Wm. B. Campbell of Tennessee. Nashville: *True Whig* and *Republican Banner,* 1851. 16 pp.

Threatte, Bernard Barton. "The Public Life of Robert Hatton, 1855-1862." Thesis, Vanderbilt Univ., 1931.

Tricamo, John E. "Tennessee Politics, 1845-1861." Diss., Columbia Univ., 1965.

Turner, Ruth Osborne. "The Public Career of William Montgomery Churchwell." Thesis, Univ. of Tennessee, 1954. Churchwell was the last Democratic congressman from the 2nd Cong. District in the 1850s.

Walker, Arda S. "John Henry Eaton, Apostate." ETHS*P* 24 (1952), 26-43.

Walton, Brian G. "A Triumph of Political Stability: The Elections of 1847 in Tennessee." ETHS*P* 40 (1968), 3-27.

——. "The Second Party System in Tennessee." ETHS*P* 43 (1971), 18-33.

——. "A Matter of Timing: Elections to the United States Senate in Tennessee before the Civil War." *THQ* 31 (1972), 129-48.

Washburn, Clara Bracken. "Some Aspects of the 1844 Presidential Campaign in Tennessee." *THQ* 4 (1945), 58-74.

Watson, Elbert L. "James Walker of Columbia, Polk's Critic and Compatriot." *THQ* 23 (1964), 24-37.

White, Robert H. "Tennessee's Four Capitals." ETHS*P* 6 (1934), 29-43.

Williams, Frank B., Jr. "Samuel Harvey Laughlin, Polk's Political Handyman." *THQ* 24 (1965), 356-92.

Williams, Gladys Inez. "The Life of Horace Maynard." Thesis, Univ. of Tennessee, 1931.

Williams, Samuel C. "Colonel David Henley." ETHS*P* 18 (1946), 3-24.

Wood, William Henry. "The Administration of Governor Aaron V. Brown of Tennessee." Thesis, George Peabody College, 1928.

MAJOR POLITICAL PERSONALITIES TO 1864

John Bell

Bell, John. *The Life, Speeches and Public Services of John Bell.* New York: Rudd & Carleton, 1860. 118 pp. Includes a sketch of the life of Edward Everett. Bell and Everett were Union candidates for the offices of President and Vice-President of the United States.

Burkett, Benjamin Scott. "The Life of John Bell of Tennessee." Thesis, George Peabody College, 1927.

Caldwell, Joshua W. "John Bell of Tennessee: A Chapter of Political History." *AHR* 4 (1898-99), 652-64.

Goodpasture, Albert V. "John Bell's Political Revolt, and His Vauxhall Garden Speech." *THM* 2 (1916), 254-63; rpt. in *Tennessee Old and New*, I, 371-80.

Grim, Mark Sillers. "The Political Career of John Bell." Thesis, Univ. of Tennessee, 1930.

Parks, Joseph H. "John Bell and the Compromise of 1850." *JSH* 9 (1943), 328-56.

——. "John Bell and Secession." ETHS*P* 16 (1944), 30-47.

——. *John Bell of Tennessee,* Southern Biography Series. Baton Rouge: Louisiana State Univ. Press, 1950. 435 pp.

Parks, Norman L. "The Career of John Bell of Tennessee in the United States House of Representatives." Diss., Vanderbilt Univ., 1942.

——. "The Career of John Bell as Congressman from Tennessee, 1827-1841." *THQ* 1 (1942), 229-49.

Scott, Jesse W. "John Bell: A Tennessee Statesman in National Politics from 1840 to 1860." Thesis, Tennessee State A&I Univ., 1950.

Sioussat, St. George L., ed. "Correspondence of John Bell and Willie Mangum, 1835." *THM* 3 (1917), 196-200.

——., ed. "Letters of John Bell to William B. Campbell, 1839-1857." *THM* 3 (1917), 201-27.

Thomas Hart Benton

Chambers, William N. "Thomas Hart Benton in Tennessee, 1801-1812." *THQ* 8 (1949), 291-331.

——. "Thwarted Warrior: The Last Years of Thomas Hart Benton in Tennessee, 1812-1815." ETHS*P* 22 (1950), 19-44.

——. *Old Bullion Benton, Senator from the New West: Thomas Hart Benton, 1782-1858.* Boston: Little, 1956; rpt. New York: Russell, 1970. 517 pp. Chambers attempts to reconstruct Benton's entire life. He views his subject as one of the representative men of the democratic age in which he lived. Chaps. 2 and 3 cover the period from 1800 to 1815, when Benton lived in Williamson County, Tennessee.

Smith, Elbert B. *Magnificent Missourian; the Life of Thomas Hart Benton.* Philadelphia: Lippincott, 1958. 351 pp.

——. "Thomas Hart Benton: Southern Realist." *AHR* 58 (1953), 795-807.

Willie Blount

Peeler, Elizabeth H. "The Policies of Willie Blount as Governor of Tennessee, 1809-1815." Thesis, Vanderbilt Univ., 1936.

——. "The Policies of Willie Blount as Governor of Tennessee, 1809-1815." *THQ* 1 (1942), 309-27.

George Washington Campbell

Jordan, Weymouth T. "The Public Career of George Washington Campbell." ETHS*P* 10 (1938), 3-18.

——. "The Private Interests and Activities of George Washington Campbell." ETHS*P* 13 (1941), 47-65.

——. *George Washington Campbell of Tennessee: Western Statesman,* Florida State University Studies No. 17. Tallahassee: Florida State Univ., 1955. 214 pp. This work rescues Campbell from obscurity and places him in the front rank of Tennessee statesmen from 1800 to 1848. Friend of every president of this period except Adams, Campbell was one of the first Westerners to achieve a position of national importance.

Newton Cannon

Cassell, Robert B. "The Public Career of Newton Cannon." Thesis, Vanderbilt Univ., 1938.

——. "Newton Cannon and the Constitutional Convention of 1834." *THQ* 15 (1956), 224-42.

——. "Newton Cannon and State Politics, 1835-1839." *THQ* 15 (1956), 306-21.

William Carroll

Golden, Gabriel Hawkins. "William Carroll and His Administration: Tennessee's Business Governor." *THM* 9 (1925), 9-30.

Kegley, Isabelle Green. "The Work of William Carroll as Governor of Tennessee." Thesis, Vanderbilt Univ., 1933.

Rogers, Wallace Rolland. "A History of the Administration of William Carroll, Governor of Tennessee, 1821-1827, 1829-1836." Thesis, Univ. of Tennessee, 1925.

Tucker, Emma Carroll. "Governor William Carroll." *AHM* 7 (1902), 388-96.

Walker, Margaret Leonard. "The Life of William Carroll." Thesis, Univ. of Tennessee, 1929.

William C. C. Claiborne

Hatfield, Joseph T. "The Public Career of William C. C. Claiborne." Diss., Emory Univ., 1962.

——. "William C. C. Claiborne, Congress and Republicanism, 1797-1804." *THQ* 24 (1965), 156-80.

Holmes, Jack D. L., ed. "William C. C. Claiborne Predicts the Future of Tennessee." *THQ* 24 (1965), 181-84.

Volstorff, Vivian V. "William Charles Cole Claiborne: A Study in Frontier Administration." Diss., Niagara Univ., 1932.

Felix Grundy

Baylor, Orval W. "The Career of Felix Grundy, 1777-1840." *FCHQ* 16 (1942), 88-110.

Biddle, Charles. *Senator Grundy's Political Conduct Reviewed.* Nashville: *Republican* and *Gazette* Office, 1832. 25 pp.

Ewing, Frances H. "The Senatorial Career of Felix Grundy, 1829-1840." Thesis, Vanderbilt Univ., 1931.

——. "The Senatorial Career of the Honorable Felix Grundy." *THM* (ser. 2) 2 (1931-32), 3-27, 111-35, 220-24, 270-91.

Howell, R. B. C. "Felix Grundy." *TLR* 16 (1941), 828-42.

Parks, Joseph H. "Felix Grundy and the Depression of 1819 in Tennessee." ETHSP 10 (1938), 19-43.

——. *Felix Grundy, Champion of Democracy,* Southern Biography Series. University: Louisiana State Univ. Press, 1940, 1949. 368 pp. This is the story of one of the great "War Hawks" of the West, statesman, friend of Jackson, and criminal lawyer who died in 1840.

Cave Johnson

Grant, Clement L. "Congressional Years of Cave Johnson of Tennessee, 1829-1845." Thesis, Vanderbilt Univ., 1948.

——. "The Public Career of Cave Johnson." Diss., Vanderbilt Univ., 1951.

——. "The Public Career of Cave Johnson." *THQ* 10 (1951), 195-223.

——. "Cave Johnson and the Presidential Campaign of 1844." ETHSP 25 (1953), 54-73.

——. "Cave Johnson, Postmaster General." *THQ* 20 (1961), 323-49.

James C. Jones

Crittenden, John Ray. "The Public Life of James C. Jones." Thesis, Univ. of Tennessee, 1927.

Osborne, Ray Gregg. "Political Career of James Chamberlain Jones, 1840-1857." *THQ* 7 (1947), 195-228, 322-34.

——. "Study of the Political Career of J. C. Jones, 1840-1857." Thesis, Vanderbilt Univ., 1948.

Woods, Raymond Payne. "The Political Life of James Chamberlain Jones." Thesis, George Peabody College, 1928.

Joseph McMinn

Beard, William E. "Joseph McMinn, Tennessee's Fourth Governor." *THQ* 4 (1945), 154-66.

Garrett, William R., ed. "Letters and Papers of Governor Joseph McMinn." *AHM* 4 (1899), 319-35; 5 (1900), 48-66.

Murphey, Edwin M., Jr. "Joseph McMinn; Governor of Tennessee, 1815-1821: The Man and His Times." *THM* (ser. 2) 1 (1930-31), 3-16.

Slone, Cynthia McCarlie. "The Administration of Governor Joseph McMinn of Tennessee, 1815-1821." Thesis, George Peabody College, 1940.

Thomas A. R. Nelson

Alexander, Thomas B. "Strange Bedfellows: The Interlocking Careers of T. A. R. Nelson, Andrew Johnson, and W. G. (Parson) Brownlow." ETHSP 24 (1952), 68-91.

——. *Thomas A. R. Nelson of East Tennessee.* Nashville: Tennessee Hist. Comm., 1956. 186 pp. Nelson was a Whig political leader who was, from the 1840s to 1873, a key political force in East Tennessee politics.

——. "Thomas A. R. Nelson as an Example of Whig Conservatism in Tennessee." *THQ* 15 (1956), 17-29.

Fraser, Walter Brown. "The Political Career of Thomas A. R. Nelson." Thesis, Univ. of Tennessee, 1930.

John Rhea

Bolden, John. "John Rhea, His Views and Voting Record in Congress, 1803-1815 and 1817-1823." Thesis, Tennessee State A&I Univ., 1958.

Hamer, Marguerite B. "John Rhea of Tennessee." ETHSP 4 (1932), 35-44.

Padgett, James A., ed. "Letters from John Rhea to Thomas Jefferson and James Madison." ETHSP 10 (1938), 114-27.

Daniel Smith

Bryant, Gladys Eugenia. "Daniel Smith, Citizen of the Tennessee Frontier." Thesis, Vanderbilt Univ., 1961.

Garrett, William R., and John M. Bass, eds. "Papers of General Daniel Smith." *AHM* 6 (1901), 213-35.

Sioussat, St. George L., ed. "The Journal of General Daniel Smith, One of the Commissioners to Extend the Boundary Line between the Commonwealth of Virginia and North Carolina, August, 1779, to July, 1780." *THM* 1 (1915), 40-65.

William Trousdale

Allen, B. F. "Governor William Trousdale." *AHM* 7 (1902), 311-14.

Burke, William J. "Career of William Trousdale in Tennessee Politics." Thesis, Vanderbilt Univ., 1967.

Tallant, James Glenn. "The Administration of Governor William Trousdale of Tennessee." Thesis, George Peabody College, 1928.

Tresch, Donna Sue. "The Military and Diplomatic Careers of William Trousdale." Thesis, Middle Tennessee State Univ., 1971.

Trousdale, J. A. "A History of the Life of General William Trousdale." *THM* 2 (1916), 119-36.

Hugh Lawson White

Amburn, F. H. "The Political Career of Hugh Lawson White." Thesis, Univ. of Tennessee, 1933.

Gresham, L. Paul. "The Public Career of Hugh Lawson White." *THQ* 3 (1944), 291-318.

———. "The Public Career of Hugh Lawson White." Diss., Vanderbilt Univ., 1945.

———. "Hugh Lawson White as a Tennessee Politician and Banker, 1807-1827." ETHS*P* 18 (1946), 25-46.

———. "Hugh Lawson White, Frontiersman, Lawyer, and Judge." ETHS*P* 19 (1947), 3-24.

Maybrey, Aileen Smith. "Hugh Lawson White, a Tennessean in State and National Politics from 1817 to 1840." Thesis, Tennessee State A&I Univ., 1955.

Rogers, Daniel Thomas. "Biography of Hugh Lawson White." Thesis, George Peabody College, 1924.

Scott, Nancy N., ed. *A Memoir of Hugh Lawson White, Judge of the Supreme Court of Tennessee, Member of the Senate of the United States, etc., etc. With Selections from His Speeches and Correspondence.* Philadelphia: Lippincott, 1856. 455 pp.

James Winchester

DeWitt, John H. "General James Winchester, 1752-1826." *THM* 1 (1915), 79-105, 183-205.

Griffin, Harry. "The Military Career of Brigadier General James Winchester." Thesis, Tennessee Technological Univ., 1967.

Harrell, David Edwin. "James Winchester: Patriot." *THQ* 17 (1958), 301-17.

Felix K. Zollicoffer

Myers, Raymond E. *The Zollie Tree,* foreword Robert E. McDowell. Louisville, Ky.: Filson Club Press, 1964. 200 pp. A biography of Zollicoffer.

Parks, Edd Winfield. "Zollicoffer: Southern Whig." *THQ* 11 (1952), 346-55.

Stamper, James C. "Felix K. Zollicoffer: Tennessee Editor, Politician, and Soldier." Thesis, Univ. of Tennessee, 1967.

——. "Felix K. Zollicoffer: Tennessee Editor and Politician." *THQ* 28 (1969), 356-76.

WHIG PARTY

Abernethy, Thomas P. "The Origin of the Whig Party in Tennessee." *MVHR* 12 (1926), 504-22.

Bergeron, Paul H. "The Election of 1843: A Whig Triumph in Tennessee." *THQ* 22 (1963), 123-36.

Carroll, E. Malcolm. *Origins of the Whig Party.* Diss., Univ. of Michigan, 1922. Durham: Duke Univ. Press, 1925; rpt. Gloucester, Mass.: P. Smith, 1964. 260 pp.

Cole, Arthur C. *The Whig Party in the South.* Diss., Univ. of Pennsylvania, 1912. Prize Essays of the American Historical Association, 1912. Washington, D.C.: American Hist. Assoc., 1913; rpt. Gloucester, Mass.: P. Smith, 1959, 1962. 392 pp. A very good early analysis of the rise of this political party in opposition to Jackson.

Horton, J. T., Jr. "Evolution of a Whig Editor in Tennessee: Allen A. Hall." Thesis, Vanderbilt Univ., 1966.

Miles, Edwin A. "The Whig Party and the Menace of Caesar." *THQ* 27 (1968), 361-79.

Moore, Powell A. "The Establishment of the Whig Party in Tennessee." Diss., Univ. of Indiana, 1932.

Murphy, James E. "Jackson and the Tennessee Opposition." *THQ* 30 (1971), 50-69.

Parks, Joseph H. "The Tennessee Whigs and the Kansas-Nebraska Bill." *JSH* 10 (1944), 308-30.

Poage, George R. *Henry Clay and the Whig Party.* Chapel Hill: Univ. of North Carolina Press, 1936; rpt. Gloucester, Mass.: P. Smith, 1965. 295 pp.

Riley, Susan B. "Albert Pike in Tennessee." *THQ* 9 (1950), 291-305. Pike was a Whig politician.

Zimmerman, Peter W. "The Whig Party in Tennessee, 1834-1841." Thesis, San Jose State College, 1966.

POLITICAL NATIVISM AND THE KNOW-NOTHING PARTY

Alexander, Thomas B. "Prelude to KuKluxism in Tennessee." Thesis, Vanderbilt Univ., 1940.

Billington, Ray Allen. *The Protestant Crusade, 1800-1860: A Study in the Origins of American Nativism.* New York: Macmillan, 1938; rpt. New York: Rinehart, 1952; rpt. Gloucester, Mass.: P. Smith, 1963. 514 pp.

Gohmann, Sister Mary D. *Political Nativism in Tennessee to 1860.* Diss., Catholic Univ., 1938. Washington, D.C.: Catholic Univ., 1938. 192 pp. This work focuses upon Tennessee's experience with nativism in the 1850s. The author contends that nativism was early to be found in America and appeared in every decade of its history. Her view is that religious fanatics and unprincipled demagogues little representing Tennessee or Americans were the major thrust of nativism.

Hargis, Robert L. "The Know-Nothing Party in Tennessee." Thesis, Vanderbilt Univ., 1931.

Measamer, Murry Bryant. "A History of the Know-Nothing Party in Tennessee." Thesis, Univ. of Tennessee, 1931.

Overdyke, William Darrell. *The Know-Nothing Party in the South.* Baton Rouge: Louisiana State Univ. Press, 1950; rpt. Gloucester, Mass.: P. Smith, 1968. 322 pp.

GENERAL HISTORY: 1865-1900

Abshire, David M. *The South Rejects a Prophet: The Life of Senator D. M. Key, 1824-1900,* foreword by Ralph McGill. New York: Praeger, 1967. 250 pp. David M. Key, postmaster general under Hayes, sought to help lead the South to genuine reunion with the nation.

Alexander, Thomas B. "Persistent Whiggery in the Confederate South, 1860-1877." *JSH* 27 (1961), 305-29.

Archer, Claude A. "The Life of John Chiles Houk." Thesis, Univ. of Tennessee, 1941.

Armstrong, Zella. *Taylor of Tennessee,* Notable Southern Families. Chattanooga: Lookout, 1933. 36 pp.

Atchley, Lucy Elizabeth. "The Attitude of the Tennessee Members of Congress on the Tariff Question, 1865-1894." Thesis, Univ. of Tennessee, 1937.

Ball, Clyde L. "The Public Career of Colonel A. S. Colyar, 1870-1877." *THQ* 12 (1953), 23-47, 106-28, 213-38.

Beagle, Daniel Soyer. "The Farmers' Alliance and the Populist Party in West Tennessee, 1887-1892." Thesis, Univ. of Wisconsin, 1966.

Beeson, Helen Still. "Walter P. Brownlow, Republican." Thesis, East Tennessee State Univ., 1967.

Butler, Margaret. "The Life of John C. Brown." Thesis, Univ. of Tennessee, 1936.

Chesney, William N. "The Public Career of William B. Bate." Thesis, Univ. of Tennessee, 1951.

Folmsbee, Stanley J., and Marguerite B. Hamer. "The Presidential Election of 1896 As Reflected in the Correspondence of Charles McClung McGhee." ETHSP 22 (1950), 158-68.

Foster, J. Price. "The Public Career of John K. Shields." Thesis, Univ. of Tennessee, 1965.

Fox, Elbert Leonard. "A History of Populism in Tennessee." Thesis, George Peabody College, 1930.

Gaither, Gerald. "The Negro in the Ideaology of Southern Populism." Thesis, Univ. of Tennessee, 1967.

Gentry, Amos Leo. "The Public Career of Leonidas Campbell Houk." Thesis, Univ. of Tennessee, 1939.

Hart, Roger Louis. "Bourbonism and Populism in Tennessee, 1875-1896." Diss., Princeton Univ., 1970.

Henry, J. Milton. "What Became of the Tennessee Whigs?" *THQ* 11 (1952), 57-62.

Hicks, John D. *The Populist Revolt; a History of the Farmers' Alliance and the People's Party.* Minneapolis: Univ. of Minnesota Press, 1931. Rpt., Bison Book. Lincoln: Univ. of Nebraska Press, 1959, 1961. 473 pp.

Holloway, Margaret Endsley. "The Reaction in Tennessee to the Federal Elections Bill of 1890." Thesis, Univ. of Tennessee, 1970.

Hutson, Andrew C. "Coal Miners' Insurrections in Tennessee, 1891-1892." Thesis, Univ. of Tennessee, 1933.

Isaac, Paul E. "The Problems of a Republican Governor in a Southern State: Ben Hooper of Tennessee, 1910-1914." *THQ* 27 (1968), 229-48.

Jones, J. S., comp. *Biographical Album of Tennessee Governors.*

Jones, Robert Brinkley III. "The State Debt Controversy in Tennessee, 1865-1883." Diss., Vanderbilt Univ., 1972.

Lewis, J. Eugene. "The Tennessee Gubernatorial Campaign and Election of 1894." *THQ* 13 (1954), 99-126, 224-43, 301-28.

Looney, John Thomas. "Isham G. Harris of Tennessee: Bourbon Senator, 1877-1897." Thesis, Univ. of Tennessee, 1970.

Lynn, Alice. "Tennessee's Public Debt as an Issue in Politics, 1870-1883." Thesis, Univ. of Tennessee, 1934.

McLeary, Ila. "The Life of Isham G. Harris." Thesis, Univ. of Tennessee, 1930.

Marshall, Park. *A Life of William B. Bate, Citizen, Soldier and Statesman; with Memorial Addresses by Edward W. Carmack, Charles H. Grosvenor and A. O. Stanley, and Orations by William B. Bate at Elmwood Confederate Cemetery, and Chickamauga and Chattanooga National Park.* Nashville: Cumberland, 1908. 363 pp.

Miller, Charles A. *The Official and Political Manual of the State of Tennessee.* Nashville: Marshall & Bruce, 1890. 359 pp.

Owsley, Harriet C. "Peace and the Presidential Election of 1864." *THQ* 18 (1959), 3-19.

Queener, Verton M. "The Republican Party in East Tennessee, 1865-1900." Diss., Univ. of Indiana, 1940.

——. "The Origin of the Republican Party in East Tennessee." ETHS*P* 13 (1941), 66-90.

——. "A Decade of East Tennessee Republicanism, 1867-1876." ETHS*P* 14 (1942), 59-85.

——. "The East Tennessee Republicans as a Minority Party, 1870-1896." ETHS*P* 15 (1943), 49-73.

——. "The East Tennessee Republicans in State and Nation, 1870-1900." *THQ* 2 (1943), 99-128.

Robison, Dan M. "Tennessee Politics and the Agrarian Movement, 1886-1896." *MVHR* 20 (1934), 365-80.

Rochester, Anna. *The Populist Movement in the United States.* New York: International, 1944. 128 pp.

Saloutos, Theodore. "The Grange in the South, 1870-1877." *JSH* 19 (1953), 473-87.

——. *Farmer Movements in the South, 1865-1933.*

Seehorn, John B. "The Life and Public Career of Henry Clay Evans." Thesis, Univ. of Tennessee, 1970.

Sharp, Joseph A. "The Farmers' Alliance and Tennessee Politics, 1890-1892." Thesis, Univ. of Tennessee, 1931.

——. "The Entrance of the Farmers' Alliance into Tennessee Politics." ETHS*P* 9 (1937), 77-92.

——. "The Farmers' Alliance and the People's Party in Tennessee." ETHS*P* 10 (1938), 91-113.

Stanbery, George W., II. "The Tennessee Constitutional Convention of 1870." Thesis, Univ. of Tennessee, 1940.

Stanton, William A. "The State Debt in Tennessee Politics." Thesis, Vanderbilt Univ., 1940.

Weems, Martha. "The Grange in Tennessee, 1870-1908, and 1933-1966." Thesis, East Tennessee State Univ., 1969.

Westphal, Corinne. "The Farmers' Alliance in Tennessee." Thesis, Vanderbilt Univ., 1929.

White, Robert H., ed. *Messages of the Governors of Tennessee.*

Williams, Frank B., Jr. "The Poll Tax as a Suffrage Requirement in the South, 1870-1901." *JSH* 18 (1952), 469-96.

Bob and Alf Taylor and the "War of the Roses"

Augsburg, Paul Deresco. *Bob and Alf Taylor; Their Lives and Lectures; the Story of Senator Robert Love Taylor and Governor Alfred Alexander Taylor . . . Followed by the Most Famous of Their Lectures and Speeches, Including the Fiddle and the Bow and Yankee Doodle and Dixie.* Morristown: Morristown Bk., 1925. 334 pp.

Boutwell, Lane L. "The Oratory of Robert Love Taylor." *THQ* 9 (1950), 10-45.

Robison, Dan M. "Robert L. Taylor and the Revolt against Bourbonism." Thesis, Vanderbilt Univ., 1930.

——. "Governor Robert L. Taylor and the Blair Educational Bill in Tennessee." *THM* (ser. 2) 2 (1931-32), 28-49.

——. "Robert L. Taylor and Tennessee Politics, 1886-1896." Diss., Vanderbilt Univ., 1932.

——. "The Political Background of Tennessee's War of the Roses." *ETHSP* 5 (1933), 125-41; rpt. in *Tennessee Old and New,* II, 370-85.

——. "Tennessee Politics and the Agrarian Revolt, 1886-1896." *MVHR* 20 (1933-34), 365-80.

——. *Bob Taylor and the Agrarian Revolt in Tennessee.* Chapel Hill: Univ. of North Carolina Press, 1935. 238 pp. The author considers that during the period of Tennessee's transition from an agricultural to an industrial state Taylor was an important force for political conciliation.

Taylor, James P., Alf A., and Hugh L. *Life and Career of Senator Robert Love Taylor, (Our Bob) by His Three Surviving Brothers, James P. Taylor, Alf A. Taylor, Hugh L. Taylor; Illustrated with Many Interesting Pictures of the Great Orator, from the Age of Fifteen to the Age of Sixty Years, Also with Views of "Happy Valley," Made Famous by His Lectures and Speeches.* Nashville: Bob Taylor Pub., 1913. 370 pp.

Taylor, Robert L. *Gov. Bob Taylor's Tales. "The Fiddle and the Bow," "The Paradise of Fools," "Visions and Dreams" . . . .* Nashville: De Long, Rice, 1896. 204 pp.

——. *Echoes: Centennial and Other Notable Speeches, Lectures and Stories.* Nashville: S. B. Williamson, 1899. 192 pp.

——. *Life Pictures . . . ; Being a Collection of Senator Taylor's Lectures and Public Addresses; Also, His Editorials in "Bob Taylor's Magazine" and "Taylor-Trotwood Magazine."* Nashville: Taylor-Trotwood, 1907. 384 pp.

Taylor, Robert L., Jr. "An Inquiry into the Background and Personalities of Governors Alf and Bob Taylor, 1848-1886." Thesis, Univ. of Tennessee, 1965.

——. "Apprenticeship in the First District: Bob and Alf Taylor's Early Congressional Races." *THQ* 28 (1969), 24-41.

——. "Mainstreams of Mountain Thought: Attitudes of Selected Figures in the Heart of Appalachian South, 1877-1902." Diss., Univ. of Tennessee, 1971. Includes the views of Robert L. Taylor.

Vance, Rupert B. "Tennessee's War of the Roses." *Virginia Quarterly Review* 16 (1940), 413-24.

GENERAL HISTORY: 1900-1960

Archer, Claude Jackson. "The Life of John Chiles Houk." Thesis, Univ. of Tennessee, 1941.

Bagby, Wesley M. "William Gibbs McAdoo and the 1920 Democratic Presidential Nomination." ETHSP 31 (1959), 43-58. McAdoo was an East Tennessean.

Cleghorn, R. "High Noon for Tex Ritter." *New York Times Magazine*, July 12, 1970, pp. 10-11.

Coode, Thomas H. "The Editorial Policy of the Urban Press of Tennessee in the Presidential Elections of 1940, 1948, and 1952." Thesis, Middle Tennessee State Univ., 1961.

———. "The Presidential Election of 1940 As Reflected in the Tennessee Metropolitan Press." ETHSP 40 (1968), 83-100.

Crump, E. H. *See* Shelby County: Political History and Public Administration.

David, Paul T., Malcolm Moos, and Ralph M. Goldman. *Presidential Nominating Politics in 1952*. 5 vols. Baltimore: Johns Hopkins Univ. Press, 1954. Contains a section on Tennessee.

Evans, Edith Snyder. "The Progressive Party in Tennessee in 1912." Thesis, Univ. of Tennessee, 1933.

Foster, Austin P., and Albert H. Roberts. *Tennessee Democracy: A History of the Party and Its Representative Members—Past and Present*. 4 vols. Nashville: Democratic Hist. Assoc., 1940. A primarily political history of the state, concentrating upon personal items and issues, and written from a strongly partisan point of view.

Foster, James Price. "The Public Career of John K. Shields." Thesis, Univ. of Tennessee, 1965. Shields was a United States senator.

Foster, William Thomas. "Legislative Impeachments in Tennessee." Thesis, George Peabody College, 1931.

Goodman, William. *Inherited Domain; Political Parties in Tennessee.* Knoxville: Bureau of Public Administration, Univ. of Tennessee, 1954. 106 pp. A very good account of the background and dynamics of the political structure of Tennessee as it existed at the time this work was prepared.

Gower, Leslie. "Election of 1928 in Tennessee." Thesis, Vanderbilt Univ., 1959.

Grant, Philip A., Jr. "Tennesseans in the 63rd Congress, 1913-1915." THQ 29 (1970), 278-86.

Grantham, Dewey W. "The Southern Senators and the League of Nations, 1918-1920." NCHR 26 (1949), 187-205.

———. *The Democratic South*. Athens: Univ. of Georgia Press, 1963. Rpt., Norton Library. New York: Norton, 1965. 109 pp. Deals with the history of the Democratic party, politics, and government in the southern states.

——. ed. *The South and the Sectional Image: The Sectional Theme since Reconstruction,* Interpretations of American History. New York: Harper, 1967. 191 pp. An interpretive history of the southern states after 1865.

Hansell, J. E. *Hill-Billy Bill, a Biography of Hon. J. Will Taylor of Tennessee.* LaFollette: LaFollette Press, 1932. 128 pp. Taylor was a United States congressman in the 20th century.

Hassler, Shirley. *Fifty Years of Tennessee Elections, 1916-1966.* Nashville: State of Tennessee, Off. of the Sec. of State, 1968. 129 pp.

Havard, William C., ed. *The Changing Politics of the South.* Baton Rouge: Louisiana State Univ. Press, 1972. 755 pp. The essay on Tennessee in this volume is entitled "Tennessee: A Politics of Peaceful Change" and is written by Lee S. Greene and Jack E. Holmes.

Heard, Alexander. *A Two-Party South?* Chapel Hill: Univ. of North Carolina Press, 1952. 334 pp.

Hooper, Ben W. *The Unwanted Boy: The Autobiography of Governor Ben W. Hooper,* ed. Everett Robert Boyce. Knoxville: Univ. of Tennessee Press, 1968. 292 pp. Treats Tennessee history and politics in the early 1900s while describing the career of a man who rose from waif to governor. Hooper later became a national figure in labor-management arbitration.

Key, V. O., Jr., with Alexander Heard. "Tennessee. The Civil War and Mr. Crump." *Southern Politics in State and Nation,* 58-81. New York: Knopf, 1949. Rpt., Vintage Books. New York: Random, 1962. 675 pp. An analysis of Tennessee voting patterns and the matrix for minority rule through the domination of Shelby County and Mr. Crump.

Kilgo, John Wesley. *Campaigning in Dixie, with Some Reflections on Two-Party Government,* foreword B. Carroll Reece. New York: Hobson, 1945. 223 pp. Kilgo was a Greeneville Republican who ran for governor in 1944.

Link, Arthur S. "Democratic Politics and the Presidential Campaign of 1912 in Tennessee." *ETHSP* 18 (1946), 107-30.

——. "The Progressive Movement in the South, 1870-1914." *NCHR* 23 (1946), 172-95. Contains a segment relating to Tennessee.

Majors, William R. "The Political Scene in Twentieth-Century Tennessee: A Bibliography and Evaluation." *WTHSP* 24 (1970), 97-105.

Merritt, D. "Worst Political Mess." *Outlook,* Aug. 15, 1928, pp. 614- .

Mostert, M. "Tennessee's Verdict." *Nation,* Aug. 23, 1952, p. 140.

Perry, Jennings. *Democracy Begins at Home: The Tennessee Fight on the Poll Tax.* New York: Lippincott, 1944. 280 pp.

———. "How Tennessee Killed the Poll Tax." *New Republic,* Feb. 22, 1943, pp. 255-56.

Qualls, J. Winfield. "Fusion Victory and the Tennessee Senatorship, 1910-1911." WTHS*P* 15 (1961), 79-92.

Queener, Verton M. "The East Tennessee Republican Party, 1900-1914." ETHS*P* 22 (1950), 94-127.

Reichard, Gary W. "The Aberration of 1920: An Analysis of Harding's Victory in Tennessee." *JSH* 36 (1970), 33-49.

Sargent, Lawrence Russell. "Protestant Clergymen and the Presidential Campaign of 1928 in Tennessee." Thesis, East Tennessee State Univ., 1966.

Shannon, Jasper Berry. *Toward A New Politics in the South.* Knoxville: Univ. of Tennessee Press, 1949. 108 pp. Fine essays on regional politics.

Spence, Joe Edd. "The Public Career of Andrew Jackson Graves." Thesis, Univ. of Tennessee, 1967.

———. "The Public Career of Andrew Jackson Graves." ETHS*P* 40 (1968), 62-82.

"Tennessee: End of the Road for Pat Sutton." *New Republic,* Aug. 16, 1954, p. 4.

Tennessee State Library and Archives. *Presidential Elections, 1789-1964: Results in Tennessee.* Nashville: State of Tennessee, 1968. 9 leaves.

Terral, Rufus. *Newell Sanders; a Biography.* Kingsport: Privately printed, 1935. 310 pp. This eminent Chattanooga businessman and Republican political leader died in the 1930s.

Tindall, George Brown. *The Disruption of the Solid South.* Athens: Univ. of Georgia Press, 1972. Rpt., Norton Library. New York: Norton, 1972. 98 pp.

"Votes for Mary." *American Magazine,* July 1949, pp. 110ff.

Ward, Keith J. *Metropolitan Cooperation and Coordination: Tennessee Councils of Government.* Knoxville: Bureau of Public Administration, Univ. of Tennessee, 1972.

Wingfield, Marshall. "Legislators Sign Racial Manifesto." *Christian Century,* Jan. 30, 1957, pp. 142-43.

Worden, H. "Pretty Good Politician." *Collier's,* Jan. 14, 1950, pp. 18-19.

Prohibition

Bass, Frank Embrick. "The Work of Edward Ward Carmack in Congress." Thesis, George Peabody College, 1930.

Beard, Mattie Duncan. *The W.C.T.U. in the Volunteer State.* Kingsport: Kingsport Press, 1962. 150 pp.

Crutcher, Robert Franklin. "The Career of Edward Ward Carmack and the Cooper-Sharp Trial." Thesis, Western Kentucky Univ., 1932.

Harris, Mrs. L. H. "Willipus-Wallipus in Tennessee Politics." *Independent,* Mar. 25, 1909, pp. 622-26.

Hooper, Ben W. *The Unwanted Boy.*

Isaac, Paul E. *Prohibition and Politics: Turbulent Decades in Tennessee, 1885-1920.* Knoxville: Univ. of Tennessee Press, 1965. 314 pp. The best account of the evolution and progress of Prohibition sentiment and laws in Tennessee that we have. It also has a good description of the Carmack-Patterson difficulty.

Johns, Charles D. *Tennessee's Pond of Liquor and Pool of Blood: A Complete and Detailed Account of Our Shameless Condition in Tennessee; the Cause and the Remedy.* Nashville: C. D. Johns, 1912. 291 pp.

Lacy, Eric Russell. "Tennessee Teetotalism: Social Forces and the Politics of Progressivism." *THQ* 24 (1965), 219-40.

Leab, Grace. "Temperance Movement in Tennessee, 1860-1907." Thesis, Univ. of Tennessee, 1938.

——. "Tennessee Temperance Activities, 1870-1899." ETHS*P* 21 (1949), 52-68.

Leab, Grace, and Charles Z. Roettger, eds. "A Good Templar's 'Journal.'" ETHS*P* 31 (1959), 83-94.

Martin, Lorena May. "The Development of Prohibition in Tennessee." Thesis, George Peabody College, 1930.

Neville, Lucille. "Edward Ward Carmack in the Fight for Prohibition in Tennessee." Thesis, George Peabody College, 1929.

Piper, David H. "The Administration of Governor Ben W. Hooper of Tennessee." Thesis, George Peabody College, 1929.

"Political Hysteria in Tennessee." *Independent,* Sept. 22, 1910, pp. 663-64.

Priest, Carmen Hamilton. "The History of Temperance in Tennessee, 1910-1918." Thesis, Univ. of Tennessee, 1937.

Pritchard, R. E. "Revolution in Tennessee." *Harper's Weekly,* Nov. 26, 1910, pp. 9- .

Roblyer, Leslie F. "The Road to State-wide Prohibition in Tennessee, 1899-1909." Thesis, Univ. of Tennessee, 1949.

——. "The Fight for Local Prohibition in Knoxville, Tennessee, 1907." ETHS*P* 26 (1954), 27-37.

Smith, Will Dunn. "The Carmack-Patterson Campaign and Its Aftermath in Tennessee Politics." Thesis, Vanderbilt Univ., 1939.

Stockard, Russell L. "Ben W. Hooper, Governor of Tennessee. His Nomination, Campaign, Election and Achievements." Thesis, Tennessee State A & I Univ., 1951.

——. "The Election and First Administration of Ben W. Hooper as Governor of Tennessee." ETHS*P* 26 (1954), 38-59.

——. "The Election and Second Administration of Governor Ben W. Hooper of Tennessee As Reflected in the State Press." ETHS*P* 32 (1960), 51-71.

Women's Suffrage

Burn, Harry T. "A Letter to the Editor." WTHS*P* 19 (1965), 134-35. Treats women's suffrage.

Hoyt, Elizabeth Stone. "Some Phases of the History of the Women's Movement in Tennessee." Thesis, Univ. of Tennessee, 1931.

Louis, James P. "Sue Shelton White and the Woman Suffrage Movement in Tennessee, 1913-1920." *THQ* 22 (1963), 170-90.

Scott, Anne F. "After Suffrage: Southern Women in the Twenties." *JSH* 30 (1964), 298-318.

Taylor, Antoinette Elizabeth. "A Short History of the Woman Suffrage Movement in Tennessee." *THQ* 2 (1943), 195-215; rpt. in *Tennessee Old and New,* II, 386-405.

——. *The Woman Suffrage Movement in Tennessee.* Diss., Vanderbilt Univ., 1943. New York: Bookman, 1957. 150 pp. The author traces the origin of sentiment for woman's suffrage from 19th-century roots through the development of organizational structure at the state and local level to final achievement of state and national enfranchisement.

Tennessee State Federation of Women's Clubs. *Woman's Work in Tennessee.* Memphis: Jones-Briggs Co., 1916. 315 pp.

GENERAL HISTORY: 1960-72

Alexander, Ruth. "Congressional Redistricting in Tennessee from 1796-1936." Thesis, Duke Univ., 1937.

Berenson, William M., Robert D. Bond, and J. Leiper Freeman. "The Wallace Vote and Political Change in Tennessee." *Journal of Politics* 33 (1971), 515-20.

Bird, Agnes Thornton. "Resources Used in Tennessee Senatorial Primary Campaigns, 1948-1964." Diss., Univ. of Tennessee, 1967.

Brown, Philip G. "An Examination of Pressure Politics in Tennessee with Emphasis on the Activities of Six Interest Groups during the Eighty-fifth General Assembly." Thesis, Univ. of Tennessee, 1970.

Buchanan, William, and Agnes Bird. *Money As a Campaign Resource: Tennessee Democratic Senatorial Primaries, 1948-1964,* Citizens' Research Foundation Study No. 10. Princeton, N.J.: The Foundation [1966].

Cleghorn, R. "High Noon for Tex Ritter." *New York Times Magazine,* July 12, 1970, pp. 10-11.

Coomer, James Chester. "The Growth and Development of the Republican Party in Tennessee: 1948-1966." Thesis, Georgia State College, 1968.

Cortner, Richard C. *The Apportionment Cases.* Knoxville: Univ. of Tennessee Press, 1971. 296 pp. A clear, thorough treatment of the reapportionment struggle.

Diamond, Michael Jerome. "The Negro and Organized Labor as Voting Blocs in Tennessee, 1960-1964." Thesis, Univ. of Tennessee, 1965.

Halberstam, David. "Silent Ones Speak Up in Tennessee." *Reporter,* Sept. 1, 1960, pp. 28-30.

Hill, Howard L. *The Herbert Walters Story.* Kingsport: Kingsport Press, 1963; rpt. Morristown: Morristown Print., 1963. 117 pp. Enl. ed., 1966. 232 pp.

King, Roger Earl. "The Tennessee Legislative Council Committee: Reflection of Political Realities." Thesis, Middle Tennessee State Univ., 1968.

Klimasewski, Theodore J. "Political Party Regions in Tennessee; a Study in Electoral Geography." Ed.S. diss., George Peabody College, 1970.

Kovach, Bill, "Racism Wasn't the Issue in Tennessee."*Reporter,* Sept. 24, 1964, pp. 37-38.

Lewis, V. E., and H. Chambers. "New, New Guard of the GOP." *Nation,* Sept. 7, 1964, pp. 85-88.

Locke, Jerry Ross. "The Politics of Legislative Reapportionment in Tennessee: 1962." Thesis, Univ. of Tennessee, 1963.

"Machine v. Style: Democratic Gubernatorial Primary." *Time,* Aug. 12, 1966, pp. 12 ff.

Mahoney, John Hasue. "Apportionments and Gerrymandering in Tennessee since 1870." Thesis, George Peabody College, 1930.

Parks, Norman L. "Tennessee Politics since Kefauver and Reece: A Generalist View." *Journal of Politics* 28 (1966), 144-68.

Terry, Warren W. "The Effects of Reapportionment on the Tennessee Legislature." Thesis, Middle Tennessee State Univ., 1969.

MAJOR POLITICAL PERSONALITIES: 1900-72

Gordon Browning

Bronaugh, Mae M. "The Crump-Browning Political Feud—1937-1938." Thesis, Memphis State Univ., 1959.

Majors, William R. "Gordon Browning and Tennessee Politics." Diss., Univ. of Georgia, 1967.

——. "Gordon Browning and Tennessee Politics, 1937-39." *THQ* 28 (1969), 57-69.

——. "Gordon Browning and Tennessee Politics, 1949-1953." *THQ* 28 (1969), 166-81.

Miller, William D. "The Browning-Crump Battle: The Crump Side." ETHSP 37 (1965), 77-88.

Priest, Marshall F., Jr. "Politics in Tennessee—the 1948 Democratic Gubernatorial Primary." Thesis, Memphis State Univ., 1963.

Joseph W. Byrns

Galloway, Jewell Morrell. "The Public Life of Joseph W. Byrns." Thesis, Univ. of Tennessee, 1962.

———. "Speaker Joseph W. Byrns: Party Leader in the New Deal."
THQ 25 (1966), 63-76.

Frank G. Clement

Boyd, Stephen D. "The Campaign Speaking of Frank Clement in
the 1954 Democratic Primary; Field Study and Rhetorical
Analysis." Diss., Univ. of Illinois, 1972.

Clement, Frank Goad. *Where We Stand; a Report to the 81st General
Assembly of Tennessee.* Nashville: State of Tennessee, 1959.
35 pp.

Davis, William L. "Corruption vs. Morality. A Rhetorical Analysis
of the Campaign of Frank Goad Clement for Governor of
Tennessee, 1952." Thesis, Wake Forest Univ., 1972.

"Ole Frank." *Time,* Aug. 10, 1962, p. 13.

Parmentel, N. E. "Tennessee Spellbinder." *Nation,* Aug. 11, 1956,
pp. 113-17.

Schreiber, F. "Frank Clement: Tennessee's Political Evangelist."
Coronet, July 1956, pp. 97-101.

Albert Gore

Baker, Russell. "Gore Also Runs—but for V.P." *New York Times
Magazine,* Apr. 10, 1960, pp. 15 ff.

Gore, Albert. "Underground Tests Only." *Foreign Policy Bulletin,*
Jan. 15, 1959, pp. 70-71.

———. *The Eye of the Storm: A People's Politics for the Seventies.*
New York: Herder & Herder, 1970. 212 pp.

———. *Let the Glory Out: My South and Its Politics.* New York:
Viking, 1972. 307 pp. The last 20 years of national politics as
viewed by a progressive-minded Tennessean in the United States
Senate, including a vivid account of Gore's bruising loss of his
Senate seat in 1970.

"Gore Stands Pat." *New Republic,* Aug. 18, 1958, pp. 4 ff.

Halberstam, David. "Air-Conditioned Crusade against Albert Gore."
Reporter, Sept. 4, 1958, pp. 24-26.

———. "End of a Populist; Albert Gore." *Harper's Magazine,* Jan.
1971, pp. 35-45.

Harris, Richard E. "Annals of Politics: How the People Feel." *New
Yorker,* July 10, 1971, pp. 34-54. Albert Gore versus William
E. Brock, an analysis of their senatorial contest.

"He Licked the Old Man of the Senate." *Saturday Evening Post,*

Oct. 11, 1952, pp. 38-39. Describes Gore's victory over Sen. Kenneth D. McKellar.

Leiter, K. "Tennessee: Gore vs. the White House." *Nation,* Oct. 26, 1970, pp. 396-99.

"Who Really Won in Tennessee." *U.S. News and World Report,* Aug. 22, 1958, pp. 49ff.

Wieck, P. R. "Blood and Gore." *New Republic,* Oct. 24, 1970, pp. 11-12.

Cordell Hull

Bowers, Robert E. "Hull, Russian Subversion in Cuba, and Recognition of the USSR." *JAH* 53 (1966-67), 542-54.

Burns, Richard Dean. "Cordell Hull: A Study in Diplomacy, 1933-1941." Diss., Univ. of Illinois, 1960.

Chu, Power Y. "A History of the Hull Trade Program, 1934-1939." Diss., Columbia Univ., 1957.

Dougherty, Edward C. "Cordell Hull's Policy toward Japan from 1933 to 1941." Thesis, Univ. of Tennessee, 1949.

Evins, Joe L. "The Cordell Hull Birthplace and Memorial." *THQ* 31 (1972), 111-28.

Grollman, Catherine Anne. "Cordell Hull and His Concept of a World Organization." Diss., Univ. of North Carolina, 1965.

Hinton, Harold B. *Cordell Hull, a Biography,* foreword Sumner Welles. New York: Hurst & Blackett, 1942; rpt. Garden City, N.Y.: Doubleday, 1942. 377 pp. This sympathetic biography depicts Hull as a man of inner sureness, sound judgment, and practical idealism. Hinton considers Hull closely associated with the development of the "Good Neighbor" policy and the ideals of international organization.

Hull, Cordell, with Andrew H. T. Berding. *The Memoirs of Cordell Hull.* 2 vols. New York: Macmillan, 1948. These volumes are Hull's interpretation of events witnessed by him during his 12 years as secretary of state, 1933-44.

Jablon, Howard. "Cordell Hull, the State Department, and the Foreign Policy of the First Roosevelt Administration, 1933-1936." Diss., Rutgers Univ., 1967.

Johnson, Joseph Leland. "Congressional Career of Cordell Hull." Thesis, Univ. of Tennessee, 1965.

Milner, Cooper. "The Public Life of Cordell Hull, 1907-1924." Diss., Vanderbilt Univ., 1960.

Pratt, Julius W. *Cordell Hull, 1933-44,* American Secretaries of

State and Their Diplomacy, vols. 12, 13. 2 vols. New York: Cooper Sq., 1964. Pratt describes Hull's career as secretary of state quite favorably in these volumes.

Schatz, Arthur W. "Cordell Hull and the Struggle for the Reciprocal Trade Agreements Program." Diss., Univ. of Oregon, 1965.

——. "The Anglo-American Trade Agreement and Cordell Hull's Search for Peace, 1936-1938." *JAH* 57 (1970), 85-103.

Estes Kefauver

Anderson, Jack, and Fred Blumenthal. *The Kefauver Story.* New York: Dial, 1956. 240 pp. An account of the Tennessee senator's life from early childhood until his decision to enter the 1956 presidential campaign. Primarily a political tract, the work stresses Kefauver's complexity.

Bender, Frances Kelso. "Crump Falls Victim of Cow Fever: Kefauver's 1948 Victory." Thesis, Wake Forest Univ., 1971.

David, Paul T., Malcolm Moos, and Ralph M. Goldman. *Presidential Nominating Politics in 1952.* Contains a chapter on Tennessee and Kefauver.

Edmundson, C. "How Kefauver Beat Crump." *Harper's Magazine,* Jan. 1949, pp. 78-84.

"Estes Kefauver in Tennessee." *New Republic,* Oct. 11, 1948, pp. 9ff.

"Estes' Strong Right Arm." *New Republic,* Nov. 9, 1953, p. 4.

Everett, Robert B. "The 1948 Senatorial Primary in Tennessee: A History and an Analysis." Thesis, Memphis State Univ., 1962.

Fried, Richard M., ed. "Fighting Words Never Delivered: Proposed Draft of Senator Kefauver's Acceptance Speech." *THQ* 29 (1970), 176-83.

Gorman, Joseph Bruce. "Senator Estes Kefauver and the 1952 New Hampshire Democratic Presidential Primary." Thesis, Univ. of Tennessee, 1964.

——. "The Early Career of Estes Kefauver." *ETHSP* 42 (1970), 57-84.

——. "Estes Kefauver: A Partial Biography 1903-1952." Diss., Harvard Univ., 1970.

——. *Kefauver: A Political Biography.* New York: Oxford Univ. Press, 1971. 434 pp. The first full and detailed biography of Kefauver, it focuses upon his congressional career, particularlay his years in the United States Senate.

Kefauver, Estes. "The Need for Better Executive-Legislative Teamwork in the National Government." *American Political Science Review* 38 (1944), p. 317.

——. "Congressional Reorganization." *Journal of Politics* 9 (1947), 96-107.

——. "How Boss Crump Was Licked." *Collier's,* Oct. 16, 1948, pp. 24-25.

——. *Crime in America,* ed. and introd. Sidney Shalett. Garden City, N.Y.: Doubleday, 1951. 333 pp. Rpt. London: Gollanez, 1952. 254 pp. Rpt., trans. Julio L. Alonso. Barcelona: Carlat, 1960. 302 pp. Rpt. Westport, Conn.: Greenwood, 1968.

——. Crime in the United States." *Saturday Evening Post,* Apr. 7, 1951, pp. 19-21; Apr. 14, 1951, pp. 24-25; Apr. 21, 1951, pp. 26-27; Apr. 28, 1951, pp. 30- .

——. "Executive-Congressional Liaison." *Annals,* Sept. 1953, pp. 108-13.

"Kefauver's Victory." *New Republic,* Aug. 15, 1960, pp. 5- .

Jones, R. "Kefauver's Secret Weapon." *Ladies Home Journal,* Nov. 1954, pp. 64-65.

Kitchens, Allen H. "Political Upheaval in Tennessee: Boss Crump and the Senatorial Election of 1948." WTHSP 16 (1962), 104-26.

Martin, Ralph G., and Ed Plaut. *Front Runner, Dark Horse.* Garden City, N.Y.: Doubleday, 1960. 473 pp.

Parks, Norman. "Coonskin Candidate." *New Republic* 125 (1951), 15 ff.

"Trouble for Estes." *Time,* July 12, 1954, p. 22.

Kenneth D. McKellar

"Farewell to McKellar." *Time,* Aug. 18, 1952, pp. 17 ff.

Graham, Jeanne. "Kenneth D. McKellar's 1934 Campaign: Issues and Events." WTHSP 18 (1964), 107-29.

McKellar, Kenneth D. *Tennessee Senators As Seen by One of Their Successors.* Kingsport: Southern, 1942, 1944. 625 pp.

"McKellar Passes." *New Republic,* Aug. 18, 1952, pp. 7 ff.

Pope, Dean. "The Senator from Tennessee." WTHSP 22 (1968), 102-22.

Riggs, Joseph H. *A Calendar of Political and Occasional Speeches by Senator Kenneth D. McKellar, 1928-1940. With Summaries and Subject Index.* Memphis: Memphis Pub. Libr., 1962. 66 pp.

John R. Neal

Fisher, Gilbert Michael III. "John Randolph Neal, Esq., the Great Objector." Thesis, Tennessee State A&I Univ., 1960.

Hicks, Bobby E. "The Great Objector: The Public Career of Dr. John R. Neal." Thesis, Univ. of Tennessee, 1968.

——. "The Great Objector: The Life and Public Career of Dr. John R. Neal." ETHS*P* 41 (1969), 33-66.

Moutoux, John. "Liberal in Tennessee." *Nation* 112 (1926), 696.

Austin Peay

Macpherson, Joseph T., Jr. "Democratic Progressivism in Tennessee: The Administrations of Governor Austin Peay, 1923-1927." ETHS*P* 40 (1968), 50-61.

——. "Democratic Progressivism in Tennessee: The Administration of Governor Austin Peay, 1923-1927." Diss., Vanderbilt Univ., 1969.

Peay, Austin. *Austin Peay, Governor of Tennessee, 1923-1925, 1925-1927, 1927-1929; a Collection of State Papers and Public Addresses, with a Biography by Truman H. Alexander,* comp. Mrs. Sallie H. Peay. Kingsport: Southern, 1929. 451 pp.

Rouse, Franklin O. "The Historical Background of Tennessee's Administrative Reorganization Act of 1923." ETHS*P* 8 (1936), 104-20.

Rush, F. "Republicans for Revenue Only; Unmasking a Tennessee Patronage Scandal." *Independent,* Dec. 4, 1926, pp. 635-39.

B. Carroll Reece

Hicks, John H. "Congressional Career of B. Carroll Reece, 1920-1948." Thesis, East Tennessee State Univ., 1968.

Alf Taylor

Hale, Lois. "Alf Taylor in Tennessee Politics." Thesis, Duke Univ., 1940.

Martin, Harold B. "The Tennessee Gubernatorial Campaign of 1920." Thesis, Memphis State Univ., 1964.

Reichard, Gary W. "Republican Victory of 1920 in Tennessee." Thesis, Vanderbilt Univ., 1966.

——. "The Aberration of 1920: An Analysis of Harding's Victory in Tennessee." *JSH* 36 (1970), 33-49.

——. "The Defeat of Governor Roberts." *THQ* 30 (1971), 94-109.

TENNESSEE'S GOVERNMENT AND ADMINISTRATIVE AGENCIES OF THE TWENTIETH CENTURY

Bibliography

Cheney, Frances N. "Historical and Bibliographical Study of the Administrative Departments of the State of Tennessee." Thesis, Columbia Univ., c. 1940.

General Issues in State Government

Buck, Arthur E. "Administrative Reorganization in Tennessee." *National Municipal Review* 12 (1923), 592-600.

Butler, Hilton. *The Tennessean and His Government.* Nashville: Rich, 1940. 191 pp. Rpt. New York: Silver Burdett, 1941, 1946. 308 pp.

——. *Government and You! A New Look at Tennessee.* Nashville: n.p., 1955. 235 pp.

Caldwell, Joshua W. *The Government of Tennessee.* New York: Scribners, 1904. 50 pp.

Cole, William Earle, and Ruby S. Johnson. *The Tennessee Citizen.* Oklahoma City: Harlow, 1958. 435 pp. Rpt. Norman: Harlow, 1964. 416 pp.

Combs, William H., and William E. Cole. *Tennessee, A Political Study.* Knoxville: Univ. of Tennessee Press, 1940. 353 pp.

Greene, Lee S., and Robert S. Avery. *Government in Tennessee.* Knoxville: Univ. of Tennessee Press, 1962. 368 pp. 2nd ed., 1966. 384 pp. A descriptive survey history of state government.

Harriss, Julian. "The First Twenty Years of Tennessee's Reorganized State Administration, 1923-1943." Thesis, Univ. of Tennessee, 1946.

Kelly, Harry Freeman, and Charles E. Patterson. *The Tennessee Bureaucrat; A Survey of State Administrators.* Knoxville: Bureau of Public Administration, Univ. of Tennessee, 1970. 94 leaves.

McBain, Howard Lee, and Seymour A. Mynders. *How We Are Governed in Tennessee and the Nation.* Knoxville: Southern School Supply, 1909. 256 pp.; rpt. New York: The Author, 1915.

McClure, Wallace. "Governmental Reorganization, a Constitutional Need in Tennessee." *THM* 2 (1916), 89-97.

McCoy, William J. "The Tennessee Political System: The Relationship of the Socioeconomic Environment to Political Processes and Policy Outputs." Diss., Univ. of Tennessee, 1970.

Miller, Charles A. *The Official and Political Manual of the State of Tennessee.* Nashville: Marshall & Bruce, 1890. 359 pp.

Mize, Ruby Inez. "The Tennessee Parole System: Structure and Administration." Thesis, Univ. of Tennessee, 1955.

Rouse, Franklin Owen. "The Reorganization of the Administrative Machinery of Tennessee." Thesis, Univ. of Tennessee, 1934.

Smith, Daniel. *A Short Description of the Tennassee Government.*

Tennessee Secretary of State. *Tennessee Blue Book and Official Directory.* Nashville: State of Tennessee, 1890- . Issued under various titles.

Tennessee State Planning Commission. *State Government in Tennessee.* 13 vols. Nashville: State of Tennessee, 1938.

White, R. L. C. "The Great Seal of the State of Tennessee. An Inquiry into the True History of Its Origin, with an Investigation of the Trustworthiness of the Statements Made in Col. Wm. A. Henderson's Pamphlet on the Subject." *AHM* 6 (1901), 193-212.

Williams, Samuel Cole. "The Tennessee State Flag." *THQ* 2 (1943), 232-35. Design accepted in 1905.

Agencies of State Government

DEPARTMENT OF CONSERVATION

Coleman, Bevley R. "A History of State Parks in Tennessee." Diss., George Peabody College, 1963.

Greene, Lee S., Virginia H. Brown, and Evan A. Iverson. *Rescued Earth: A Study of the Public Administration of Natural Resources in Tennessee.* Knoxville: Univ. of Tennessee Press, 1948. 214 pp.

Lambert, Walter N. "The Effect of Federal Grants-in-aid on Natural Resource Administration in Tennessee." Thesis, Univ. of Tennessee, 1967.

Tennessee State Planning Commission. *State Parks; a Proposed Program for Tennessee,* State Planning Commission Publication no. 243. Nashville: State of Tennessee, 1952. 23 pp.

——. *A Public Recreation Plan and Program for Tennessee,* State

Planning Commission Publications no. 320, 322-23. 3 vols. Nashville: State of Tennessee, 1962.

Wester, Clyde M. "A Study of a State Wildlife Agency: The Tennessee Game and Fish Commission." Thesis, Univ. of Tennessee, 1968.

DEPARTMENT OF CORRECTIONS

Adams, John C. "Usage of Prisoners' Spare Time at the Tennessee State Prison." Thesis, Vanderbilt Univ., 1937.

Crowe, Jesse C. "Agitation for Penal Reform in Tennessee, 1870-1900." Diss., Vanderbilt Univ., 1954.

———. "The Origin and Development of Tennessee's Prison Problem, 1831-1871." *THQ* 15 (1956), 111-35.

Gibney, Laurence V. "A Descriptive Study of the Guard Force at Brushy Mountain Penitentiary, Petros, Tennessee." Thesis, Univ. of Tennessee, 1970.

"History of the Tennessee Penal Institutions, 1813-1940." Nashville: Unpublished typescript, 1940. 23 pp.

Niceley, Verdel. "History of the Tennessee Penitentiary, 1865-1890." Thesis, Univ. of Tennessee, 1938.

Rankin, Helen K. "Penal Legislation in Tennessee." Thesis, George Peabody College, 1929.

Tennessee Commission on Youth Guidance. *Juvenile Court Statistics for Tennessee, 1962.* Nashville: State of Tennessee, 1964. Unpaged.

Tennessee State Law Enforcement Planning Commission. *The Five-Year Comprehensive Plan for the Improvement of Law Enforcement in the State of Tennessee.* Nashville: State of Tennessee, 1970. 418 pp.

Thompson, E. Bruce. "Reforms in the Penal System of Tennessee, 1820-1850." *THQ* 1 (1942), 291-308.

Winton, Ruth Nellie. "A History of Brushy Mountain Penitentiary." Thesis, Univ. of Tennessee, 1937.

Zimmerman, Jane. "The Penal Reform Movement in the South during the Progressive Era, 1890-1917." *JSH* 17 (1951), 462-92.

DEPARTMENT OF EMPLOYMENT SECURITY

Eberling, E. J. "The Employment Security Program (With Special References to Tennessee Unemployment Insurance)." *VLR* 1 (1947-48), 376-95.

DEPARTMENT OF HIGHWAYS

Tennessee State Highway Planning Survey Division. *History of the Tennessee Highway Department.* Nashville: State of Tennessee, 1959. 126 pp.

DEPARTMENT OF MENTAL HEALTH

Bennett, Billy Nelse, Judith Ann Davenport, and John Ashley McLeod. "A Study of Staff Attitudes toward Philosophy of Treatment at Central State Psychiatric Hospital." Thesis, Univ. of Tennessee, 1970.

Breeding, W. J. "History of the Tennessee State Health Organization." *Centennial History of the Tennessee State Medical Association, 1830-1930,* ed. Philip M. Hamer, 409-47. Nashville: Tennessee State Medical Assoc., 1930. 580 pp.

Craig, Allen R. "A Proposed Vocational Rehabilitation Program for Eastern State Hospital, Knoxville, Tennessee." Thesis, Univ. of Tennessee, 1961.

Elkins, David Eugene, James E. Rhea, and Robert Keck Wyrick. "The Relationship of Home Environment, Sex, Race, and Level of Retardation among Recent Admissions at Tennessee Clover Bottom Hospital and School." Thesis, Univ. of Tennessee, 1964.

Lynch, Jean Puryear. "A Descriptive Study of Children Committed to Central State Hospital in Nashville, Tennessee, from July 1, 1954, through June 30, 1964." Thesis, Univ. of Tennessee, 1965.

Tennessee General Assembly Joint Committee on the Lunatic Asylum. *Report of the Joint Committee on the Lunatic Asylum, submitted to the General Assembly, of the State of Tennessee, on the 9th of December, 1845.* Nashville: B. R. M'Kennie, 1845. 13 pp.

Thompson, E. Bruce. "Reforms in the Care of the Insane in Tennessee, 1830-1850." *THQ* 3 (1944), 319-34.

Wright, Howard Hyder. "A Short History of the Mental Hospitals in Tennessee." Thesis, Univ. of Tennessee, 1956.

DEPARTMENT OF PERSONNEL

McKinney, Ellie Allene. "Personnel Administration in the State Government of Tennessee." Thesis, Univ. of Tennessee, 1945.

DEPARTMENT OF PUBLIC HEALTH

Boren, Gertrude S. "The First State Board of Health in Tennessee." Thesis, Univ. of Tennessee, 1935.

Coles, Harry L., Jr. "The Federal Food Administration of Tennessee and Its Records in the National Archives, 1917-1919." *THQ* 4 (1945), 23-57.

Tennessee Department of Public Health. "Tennessee's Major Identified Health Problems; an Overview." Nashville: Unpublished typescript, 1968. 45 pp.

White, Robert H. "Beginnings of Health and Medical Legislation in Tennessee." *THQ* 2 (1943), 43-51.

Wolfe, Margaret Ripley. "Lucius Polk Brown: Tennessee's First Pure Food and Drug Inspector." Thesis, East Tennessee State Univ., 1969.

——. "Lucius Polk Brown: Tennessee Pure Food and Drug Inspector, 1908-1915." *THQ* 29 (1970), 62-78.

DEPARTMENT OF PUBLIC WELFARE

Ashcraft, Virginia. *Public Care: A History of Public Welfare Legislation in Tennessee.* Thesis, Univ. of Tennessee, 1947. Univ. of Tennessee *Record* 50, no. 6, Knoxville: Univ. of Tennessee, 1947. 91 pp. Publication sponsored by the Bureau of Public Administration of the University.

Cole, William Earle. *Almshouse Policies and Almshouse Care of the Indigent in Tennessee.* Univ. of Tennessee School of Business Administration, Bureau of Research Study no. 3. Knoxville: Research Council of the Univ. of Tennessee, 1938. 76 pp.

Dynes, Russell Rowe. "Almshouse Care in Tennessee." Thesis, Univ. of Tennessee, 1950.

Lisenby, William Foy. "An Administrative History of Public Programs for Dependent Children in North Carolina, Virginia, Tennessee and Kentucky, 1900-1942." Diss., Vanderbilt Univ., 1962.

Spencer, Sue W., ed. *Social Work: Promise and Pressures.* Nashville: School of Social Work, Univ. of Tennessee, 1968. 65 pp.

PUBLIC UTILITIES COMMISSION

Anderson, George C. "Tennessee's Railroad and Public Utilities Commission." *TLR* 16 (1941), 974-78.

Crawford, Neely. "Ethical Control of Tennessee Utilities." B. D. thesis, Vanderbilt Univ., 1929.

Duggins, Edward Cameron. "The Background for Regulation of the Railroads in Tennessee." Thesis, Univ. of Tennessee, 1939.

STATE PLANNING COMMISSION

Becker, Richard Carl. "State Planning Operations in Kansas As

Related to Tennessee—an Evaluation and Comparison." Thesis, Kansas State Univ., 1967.

Garriott, William C., Jr. "The Effects of Environment on Public Planning: The Case of Appalachian Planning in Tennessee." Thesis, Vanderbilt Univ., 1969.

Guess, Eleanor Louise Keeble. *The First Fifteen Years: A History of the Tennessee Planning Commission.* Thesis, Univ. of Tennessee, 1948. Knoxville: Div. of Univ. Extension, Univ. of Tennessee, 1949. 102 pp.

Constitutional, Judicial, Legal, and Legislative History

BIBLIOGRAPHIES AND CHECKLISTS

Preliminary Check-List of Tennessee Legislative Documents. Part I, Check List of Tennessee Session Laws; Part II, Check List of Tennessee Legislative Journals; Part III, Check List of Tennessee Collected Public Documents; Part IV, Check List of Tennessee Statutes. Nashville: State Library and Archives, 1954. Unpaged.

BIOGRAPHIES

Beaumont, Henry Francis. "Biography of Thomas Emmerson." *AHM* 9 (1904), 141-44. Emmerson was a state supreme court justice.

Blake, Morgan, and Stuart Towe. *Lawmakers and Public Men of Tennessee.* Nashville: Eagle, 1915. 197 pp.

Caldwell, Joshua W. *Sketches of the Bench and Bar of Tennessee.*

——. *A Memorial Volume Containing His Biography, Writings and Addresses; Prepared and Edited by a Committee of the Irving Club of Knoxville, Tennessee.* Nashville: Brandon, 1909. 335 pp.

Gass, Edmund C. "The Constitutional Opinions of Justice John Catron." ETHSP 8 (1936), 54-73.

Green, John W. "Five Judges of Our Supreme Court 1894-1910." *TLR* 17 (1942), 355-67.

——. "Six Judges of the United States District Court for Tennessee (1797-1808)." *TLR* 17 (1943), 889-98.

——. Attorneys-General of Tennessee, 1865-1913." *TLR* 19 (1946), 385-91.

——. *Lives of the Judges of the Supreme Court of Tennessee, 1796-1947.* Knoxville: Archer & Smith, 1947. 337 pp.

——. *Law and Lawyers: Sketches of the Federal Judges of Tennessee, Sketches of the Attorneys General of Tennessee, Legal Miscellany, Reminiscences.* Jackson: McCowat-Mercer, 1950. 257 pp.

223

Gresham, L. Paul. "Hugh Lawson White: Frontiersman, Lawyer, and Judge." *ETHSP* 19 (1947), 3-24.

Hollingsworth, Harold M. "George Andrews—Carpetbagger." *THQ* 28 (1969), 310-23. Andrews was a state supreme court justice.

Marshall, Park. "Judge Thomas Stuart." *THM* 8 (1924), 91-101.

Phillips, Harry. "Our Supreme Court Justices." *TLR* 17 (1942), 466-70.

Ragan, Allen E. "Mr. Justice Sanford." *ETHSP* 15 (1943), 74-88. Edward T. Sanford was a Knoxville native and an associate justice, U.S. Supreme Court, during the 1920s.

Wells, Frank L. "Bench and Bar of Tennessee." *East Tennessee Historical and Biographical*, 123-32.

GENERAL CONSTITUTIONAL DEVELOPMENT

Anderson, Douglas. *Tennessee Constitutional Law Compiled from the Opinions of the Supreme Court of Tennessee.* Nashville: Brandon, 1896. 628 pp.

Caldwell, Joshua William. *Studies in the Constitutional History of Tennessee.* Cincinnati: Robert Clarke, 1895. 183 pp.; rev. & enl., 1907. 412 pp.

Garrett, William R., ed. "The Provisional Constitution of Frankland." *AHM* 1 (1896), 48-63.

Haynes, Robert R. "The Origins and Development of the Constitutions of Tennessee." Thesis, George Peabody College, 1927.

Loveless, Walter Alton. "A History of the Constitutional Conventions of Tennessee." Thesis, George Peabody College, 1930.

McClure, Wallace M. "The Development of the Tennessee Constitution." *THM* 1 (1915), 292-314. This article concerns the constitution prior to 1870.

———. *State Constitution-Making, with Especial Reference to Tennessee. A Review of the More Important Provisions of the State Constitutions and of Current Thought upon Constitutional Questions. An Outline of Constitutional Development and Problems in Tennessee.* Nashville: Marshall & Bruce, 1916. 472 pp.

Milton, George Fort. *Constitution of Tennessee Considered with Reference to the Constitutions of Other States. Important Matters That Would Come before a Constitutional Convention.* Knoxville: The Author, 1897. 35 pp.

Rippa, Sol Alexander. "Development of Constitutional Democracy in Tennessee, 1790-1835." Thesis, Vanderbilt Univ., 1949.

Tennessee State General Assembly. *Constitution of the State of Tennessee.* Nashville: State of Tennessee, 1956. 48 pp.

Constitution of 1796

Barnhart, John D. "The Tennessee Constitution of 1796: A Product of the Old West." *JSH* 9 (1943), 532-48.

——. *Valley of Democracy: The Frontier versus the Plantation in the Ohio Valley, 1775-1818,* Indiana University Social Science Series, no. 11. Bloomington: Indiana Univ. Press, 1953. 338 pp.; rpt. Millwood, N.Y.: Kraus, 1953.

Blount, Willie. *A Catechetical Exposition of the Constitution of the State of Tennessee: Intended Principally for the Use of Schools.* Knoxville: G. Roulstone, 1803. 24 pp.

Constitution of the State of Tennessee. Unanimously Established in Convention at Knoxville, on the Sixth Day of February, One Thousand Seven Hundred and Ninety Six. Philadelphia: Thomas Condie, 1796. 33 pp.

Higginbotham, Sanford Wilson. "Frontier Democracy in the Early Constitutions of Tennessee and Kentucky, 1772-1799." Thesis, Louisiana State Univ., 1941.

Journal of the Proceedings of the Tennessee Constitutional Convention, Begun and Held at Knoxville, Jan. 11, 1796. Knoxville: G. Roulstone, 1796. 39 pp. Rpt. Nashville: McKennie & Brown, 1852. 32 pp. The latter edition contains also the proceedings of meetings begun March 28, 1796, and July 30, 1796.

Sanford, Edward Terry. *The Constitutional Convention of Tennessee of 1796.* Nashville: Marshall & Bruce, 1896. 44 pp.

Williams, Samuel C. "The Admission of Tennessee into the Union." *THQ* 4 (1945), 291-319.

Constitution of 1834

Constitutional Convention, 1834. Journal of the Convention. Nashville: W. H. Hunt, 1834. 415 pp.

Constitution of 1870

Butler, Margaret. "The Life of John C. Brown." Thesis, Univ. of Tennessee, 1936. Brown was chairman of the Constitutional Convention of 1870.

Combs, William H. "An Unamended State Constitution: The Tennessee Constitution of 1870." *American Political Science Review* 32 (1938), 514-24.

Journal of the Proceedings of the Convention of Delegates Elected by the People of Tennessee, to Amend, Revise or Form and Make a New Constitution for the State. Assembled in the City of Nashville, January 10, 1870. Nashville: Jones, Purvis, 1870. 467 pp.

The New Constitution of the State of Tennessee, As Revised by the Convention of Delegates, Assembled at Nashville, Jan. 10, 1870. Submitted to the People for Their Ratification or Rejection. Election, March 26th, 1870. Nashville: Jones, Purvis, 1870. 32 pp.

Stanbery, George W. II. "The Tennessee Constitutional Convention of 1870." Thesis, Univ. of Tennessee, 1940.

Limited Constitutional Conventions of the Twentieth Century

Denney, Raymond W. "The Tennessee Constitutional Convention 1953." *TLR* 23 (1953), 15-23.

Journal and Debates. Nashville: State of Tennessee, 1954. 1235 pp. Proceedings of the Limited Constitutional Convention, 1953.

Journal and Debates. Nashville: State of Tennessee, 1959. 416 pp. Proceedings of the Constitutional Convention, 1959.

Journal and Debates. Nashville: State of Tennessee, 1966. 1071 pp. Proceedings of the Constitutional Convention, 1965. (Proceedings of the Constitutional Convention 1971 is still under preparation.)

Sims, Cecil. "The Limited Constitutional Convention in Tennessee." *TLR* 21 (1949), 1-8.

GENERAL BASIC WORKS ON TENNESSEE GOVERNMENT

Alden, George Henry. *New Governments West of the Alleghanies before 1780 (Introductory to a Study of the Organization and Admission of New States).* Diss., Univ. of Wisconsin, 1896. Univ. of Wisconsin Historical Series, vol. 2, no. 1. Madison: Univ. of Wisconsin, 1897; rpt. First American Frontier Series. New York: Arno, 1971. 74 pp.

Brister, John Willard. *The Government of Tennessee; a Supplement to Hughes' Elementary Community Civics.* Boston: Allyn, 1925. 140 pp.

Butler, Hilton. *The Tennessean and His Government.*

Combs, William H., and William E. Cole. *Tennessee: A Political Study.*

Greene, Lee S., and Robert S. Avery. *Government in Tennessee.*

Johnson, Stanley P. *Tennessee Citizenship.* Richmond, Va.: Johnson, 1939. 371 pp.

Karns, Thomas C. *The Government of the People of the State of Tennessee.* Philadelphia: Eldredge, 1896, 1897. 140 pp.

McBain, Howard Lee, and Seymour A. Mynders. *How We Are Governed in Tennessee and the Nation.*

Smith, Daniel. *A Short Description of the Tennassee Government.*

Tennessee's Judicial System: Its History and Development

Bejach, Lois D. "The Chancery Court." *TLR* 20 (1948), 245-54.

Boone, George S. "An Examination of the Tennessee Law of Administrative Procedure." *VLR* 1 (1947-48), 339-75.

Burch, Charles N. "Important Events in the Judicial History of Tennessee." *TLR* 15 (1938), 220-29.

Cason, Palmer Preston. "History of Tennessee's Court System from Its Beginning to 1834." Thesis, George Peabody College, 1930.

Chandler, Walter. "The Judicial System of Tennessee: Its Beginning and Now." *TLR* 16 (1940), 519-28.

Crownover, Arthur. "The Tennessee Court of Appeals." *TLR* 15 (1938), 144-47.

Ewing, Albert, Jr. "Justice of the Peace—Bedrock of Democracy." *TLR* 21 (1950), 484-97.

Greene, Lee S. "The Southern State Judiciary." *The Southern Political Scene, 1938-1948,* rpt. from *The Journal of Politics* X, nos. 2, 3 (May, Aug. 1948), 441-63.

Haywood, John. *The Duty and Office of Justices of Peace, and of Sheriffs, Coroners, Constables, etc., According to the Laws of the State of North Carolina. To Which Is Added an Appendix, Containing the Act Directing the Mode of Recovering Debts of Twenty Pounds and Under; the Declaration of Rights and Constitution of This State; the Constitution of the United States, with the Amendments Thereto; and an Abstract from the Act of Congress, Laying Duties on Stamped Vellum, Parchment and Paper. Together with a Collection of the Most Useful Precedents.*

Halifax, N.C.: Abraham Hodge, 1800. 400 pp. Rpt. Raleigh: William Boylan, 1808. 414 pp.

Keebler, Robert S. "Our Justice of the Peace Courts: A Problem in Justice." *TLR* 9 (1930), 1-21.

Marks, A. D. "Supreme Court of Tennessee." *The Green Bag* 5 (1893), 120-275.

Overton, Elvin E. "The Judicial System in Tennessee and Potentialities for Reorganization." *TLR* 22 (1964-65), 501-72.

Prewitt, Alan M. "The Judicial Structure in Tennessee." *TLR* 29 (1961-62), 1-18.

Sheridan, Richard George. *Urban Justice: Municipal Courts in Tennessee.* Knoxville: Bureau of Public Administration, Univ. of Tennessee, 1964. 101 pp.

Summerford, William A. "The Selection and Removal of Judges in Tennessee and Alternative Techniques." Thesis, Middle Tennessee State Univ., 1969.

Swaney, W. B. "History of the Bar Association of Tennessee from 1924 to June, 1931." *TLR* 10 (1932), 114-19. Swaney was chairman of the Association.

Tennessee Law Revision Commission. *The Judicial System of Tennessee: A Background Survey.* Nashville: State of Tennessee, 1966.

Tennessee Rules of Court, 1970. St. Paul, Minn.: West Pub., 1970. 289 pp.

Williams, Samuel Cole. *History of the Courts of Chancery of Tennessee.* Knoxville: Knoxville Litho., 1923. 19 pp.

——. "The Genesis of the Tennessee Supreme Court." *TLR* 6 (1928), 75-85.

——. *Phases of the History of the Supreme Court of Tennessee.* Johnson City: Watauga, 1944. 5 pp.

——. "Phases of Tennessee Supreme Court History." *TLR* 18 (1944), 323-39.

DEVELOPMENT OF THE TENNESSEE CODE

Caruthers, R. L., and A. O. P. Nicholson. *A Compilation of the Statutes of Tennessee, of a General and Permanent Nature, from the Commencement of the Government to the Present Time. With References to Judicial Decisions, in Notes, to Which Is*

Appended a New Collection of Forms. Nashville: James Smith, 1836. 808 pp.

Gilreath, Sam B., consult. ed. *Tennessee Code Annotated.* Indianapolis: Bobbs-Merrill, 1955. 17 vols., with supplement.

Goodpasture, A. M. "An Account of the Compilations of the Statute Laws of Tennessee." *AHM* 7 (1902), 69-79.

Grayson, D. L. *The Annotated Constitution and Code of the State of Tennessee.* Chattanooga: Chattanooga *Times,* 1895. 1596 pp.

Haywood, John, rev. *A Revisal of All the Public Acts of the State of North Carolina and of the State of Tennessee Now in Force in the State of Tennessee.* Nashville: Thomas G. Bradford, 1809. 474 pp. Rev. & enl., 1810. 560 pp. 3rd ed., 1815. 690 pp.

Meigs, Return, and William F. Cooper, eds. *The Code of Tennessee. Enacted by the General Assembly of 1857-'8,* revs. Joseph B. Heiskell, Micajah Bullock, and Samuel T. Bicknell. Nashville: Eastman, 1858. 1150 pp.

Roulstone, George, ed. *Laws of the State of Tennessee.* Knoxville: Roulstone, 1803. 143 pp. Roulstone's code.

Scott, Edward. *Laws of the State of Tennessee, Including Those of North Carolina Now in Force in This State. From the Year 1715 to the Year 1820, Inclusive.* 2 vols. Knoxville: Heiskell & Brown, 1821. Scott's revisal.

Shannon, R. T., comp., ed., and annot. *Public and Permanent Statutes of a General Nature, Being an Annotated Code of Tennessee, the Annotations Showing the Construction of the Statutes and Constitution of the State by the Supreme Court, and also Its Decisions upon Kindred Subjects . . . and the Chancery Rules.* 2 vols. Nashville: Marshall & Bruce, 1896; 1 vol. rpt., 1896. 1952 pp.

Tennessee Code Commission. *Tennessee Insurance Code and Related Laws.* Nashville: State of Tennessee, 1966. 473 pp.

Tennessee Courts, Rules of Civil Procedure Annotated. Indianapolis: Bobbs-Merrill, 1971. 90 pp.

Thompson, Frank M., et al., revs., eds., and annots. *Thompson's "Shannon's Code of Tennessee," 1917, Containing the Public and Permanent Statutes of a General Nature, with Annotations Showing the Construction of the Statutes and Constitution of the State by the Courts, and Also the Decisions upon Kindred Subjects. Being a Revision of "Shannon's Code" of 1896.* Louisville, Ky.: Baldwin Law Bk., 1917. 3080 pp. Rev. ed., 1918. 3109 pp.

Trabue, Charles C. "The New Tennessee Code." *TLR* 10 (1932), 155-64.

Williams, Samuel Cole, Robert T. Shannon, and George Harsh. *The Code of Tennessee, 1932; Enacted by the General Assembly of 1931, Prepared by the Code Commission.* Kingsport: Southern, 1931. 2829 pp.

——. *History of Codification in Tennessee.* Johnson City: Watauga, 1932. 51 pp.

——, comp. and annot. *Annotated Code of Tennessee, 1934; Containing All Acts of a General and Public Nature in Force January 1, 1934, Including Also the State and Federal Constitutions and Rules of Appellate Courts.* 8 vols. Indianapolis: Bobbs-Merrill, 1934-35.

LEGAL EDUCATION IN TENNESSEE

Blackard, W. Raymond. "Law Schools in Tennessee." *TLR* 14 (1936), 267-72.

Street, Clyde Conley. "A History of Legal Education in Tennessee." Thesis, Univ. of Tennessee, 1941.

Wicker, William, and John W. Wade. "Legal Education in Tennessee." *TLR* 29 (1962), 325-62.

THE GENERAL ASSEMBLY

Alderson, William T. "Legislative Recording by the Tennessee Archives." *American Archivist* 19 (1956), 11-17.

Brown, Philip G. "An Examination of Pressure Politics in Tennessee with Emphasis on the Activities of Six Interest Groups during the Eighty-fifth General Assembly." Thesis, Univ. of Tennessee, 1970.

Fink, Paul M. "The Great Seal of the State of Tennessee, an Inquiry into its Makers." *THQ* 20 (1961), 381-83.

Jewell, Malcolm Edwin, and Lee S. Greene. *The Kentucky and Tennessee Legislatures.* Lexington, Ky.: Dept. of Political Science, Univ. of Kentucky, 1967.

Keen, Herbert F. "Certain Phases of Tennessee Legislation." Thesis, George Peabody College, 1926.

Kelley, Harry F., Jr. *Dimensions of Voting in the Tennessee House of Representatives in 1967.* Thesis, Univ. of Tennessee, 1968. Knoxville: Bureau of Public Administration, Univ. of Tennessee, 1970. 146 pp.

Longley, Lawrence Douglas. "Interest Group Effectiveness and Interaction in the Tennessee General Assembly." Thesis, Vanderbilt Univ., 1964.

———. "The Effectiveness of Interest Groups in a State Legislature." *THQ* 26 (1967), 279-94.

McBride, Robert M. "Tennessee's First State Flag." *THQ* 26 (1967), 354-56.

Robison, Dan M. "Little Men and Big Events: A Passing Look at Some Tennessee Legislators." ETHS*P* 41 (1969), 3-16.

LEGISLATIVE REAPPORTIONMENT

Bickel, A. M. "Great Apportionment Case, with Editorial Comment." *New Republic,* Apr. 9, 1962, pp. 13-14.

Burnham, W. D. "One Man, One Vote? Baker vs. Carr." *Commonweal,* May 4, 1962, pp. 145-58.

Cortner, Richard C. *The Apportionment Cases.*

Edwards, Charles P. "Theoretical and Comparative Aspects of Reapportionment and Redistricting: With Reference to Baker v. Carr." *VLR* 15 (1961-62), 1265-91.

Graham, Gene S. *One Man, One Vote. Baker v. Carr and the American Levellers.* New York: Little, 1972. 328 pp.

Hames, William G. "Baker v. Carr—Mal-apportionment in State Governments Becomes a Federal Constitutional Issue." *VLR* 15 (1961-62), 985-1004.

Katzenbach, Nicholas deB. "Some Reflections on Baker v. Carr." *VLR* 15 (1961-62), 829-36.

Kovach, Bill. "Some Lessons of Reapportionment." *Reporter,* Sept. 21, 1967, p. 26.

Lancaster, Robert. "What's Wrong with Baker v. Carr?" *VLR* 15 (1961-62), 1247-64.

Laughlin, Charles V. "Proportional Representation: It Can Cure Our Apportionment Ills." *American Bar Association Journal* 49 (1963), 1065-69.

Locke, Jerry Ross. "The Politics of Legislative Reapportionment in Tennessee: 1962." Thesis, Univ. of Tennessee, 1963.

Moore, Allen Harris. "Decision Making in Legislative Apportionment: The Tennessee Case, 1965." Thesis, Vanderbilt Univ., 1967.

Williams, Henry N. "Congressional Apportionment in Tennessee, 1796-1941." *Journal of Politics* 4 (1942), 507-21.

MISCELLANEOUS ISSUES

Allenberg, Ann. "A Study of the Ashcroft Case." Thesis, Memphis State Univ., 1955.

Baugh, John C. "Enforcement of Judgments in Tennessee." *TLR* 22 (1953), 873-90.

Coffield, James M. *The Tennessee Justice's Manual and Civil Officer's Guide.* Nashville: A. A. Hall, 1834. 534 pp.

Davidson, Betty Jean. "Tennessee's Proposed Amendments to the Federal Constitution, 1796-1861." Thesis, Univ. of Tennessee, 1959.

DeLozier, Mary Jean. "The Tennessee Supreme Court on Religious Liberty." Thesis, Tennessee Technological Univ., 1966.

Dickinson, J. M. "Tennessee Supreme Court; How It Cleared Its Docket." *American Law Review* 24 (1890), 283-91.

Ewing, Cortez A. M. "Early Tennessee Impeachments." *THQ* 16 (1957), 291-334.

Forms of Precedents for the Use of Justices of the Peace, Sheriffs, Coroners and Constables in the State of Tennessee. Nashville: T. G. Bradford, 1818. 153 pp.

Harrison, Joseph W. "The Bible, the Constitution and Public Education: A Case Study of Religious Instruction in the Public Schools of Knoxville and Knox County, Tennessee." Thesis, Univ. of Tennessee, 1961. Portions of this thesis appeared in his article of the same title published in *Tennessee Law Review* 29 (Spring 1962), 363-418. It was subsequently cited in a decision of the U.S. Supreme Court.

Higgins, Joseph C., and Arthur Crownover, Jr. *Tennessee Procedure in Law Cases; a Treatise Setting Forth the Principles, Pleadings, Practice and Procedure in Lawsuits.* Charlottesville, Va.: Michie, 1937. 1265 pp. Includes revised rules of the supreme court of Tennessee and rules of the court of appeals of Tennessee.

Layman, Edith Belle. "Tennessee's Action on the Proposed Amendments to the Constitution of the United States." Thesis, Univ. of Tennessee, 1934.

McGuire, G. G. W. *McGuire's Tennessee Justice: or, Magistrate's Guide.* Nashville: J. O. Griffith, 1860. 384 pp.

Rodgers, E. C. "Tennessee Courts and the Freedom of the Press." *Public,* Aug. 16, 1919, pp. 877-78.

Smith, L. D. "Land Titles in Tennessee." *Tennessee Bar Association Proceedings* (1911), 49-79.

Whitney, Henry D. *The Land Laws of Tennessee.*

Williams, Samuel Cole. *History of the Courts of Chancery of Tennessee.*

County Government

Bell, Roy. "History of County Government in Tennessee 1834-1860, and Its Failure in the 20th Century." Thesis, Univ. of Tennessee, 1938.

Brock, Robert M. *Knox County Government: A Citizen's Handbook.* Knoxville: Bureau of Public Administration, Univ. of Tennessee, and Knox County Library Board, 1959.

Cameron, Addie Jane. "County Consolidation in Tennessee." Thesis, Univ. of Tennessee, 1940.

Curran, Richard J., Jr. *State of Tennessee County Profile.* Nashville: State of Tennessee, 1969. 45 pp.

Grant, Daniel R. "Metropolitan Problems and Local Government Structure: An Examination of Old and New Issues." *VLR* 22 (1968-69), 757-73.

Greene, Lee S., and Evan A. Iverson. "Tennessee." *County Government Across the Nation,* ed. Paul W. Wager. Chapel Hill: Univ. of North Carolina Press, 1950.

Greene, Lee S., and Victor C. Hobday. "A Short Inquiry into Tennessee County Court Apportionment by the Federal Judiciary." *TLR* 37 (Spring 1970), 528-37.

Grubbs, David H. "Legal Aspects of City-County Consolidation in Tennessee." *TLR* 30 (1962-63), 499-516.

Hinton, Harold B. "County Government in Tennessee." Thesis, Vanderbilt Univ., 1920.

Hobgood, James Lee. "The County Court System of Tennessee." Thesis, George Peabody College, 1929.

Holmes, Jack E., Walter N. Lambert, and Nelson M. Robinson. *The Structure of County Government in Tennessee.* Knoxville: Bureau of Public Administration, Univ. of Tennessee, 1966. 189 pp.

Manning, John W. "County Consolidation in Tennessee." *American Political Science Review* 22 (1928), 733-35.

——. "Tennessee Studies County Consolidation to Reduce Government Costs." *American City,* Fall 1929, p. 98.

Marshall, Jim B. *Fiscal Administration of County Roads.* Knoxville: Bureau of Public Administration, Univ. of Tennessee, 1960.

McBride, Robert M. "Lost Counties of Tennessee." ETHS*P* 38 (1966), 3-15.

Siffin, Catherine Fox. *Shadow over the City.* Thesis, Univ. of Tennessee, 1948. Knoxville: Bureau of Public Administration, Univ. of Tennessee, 1951. A study of local legislation in the General Assembly.

Sims, Carlton C. *County Government in Tennessee.* Diss., Univ. of Chicago, 1930. Ann Arbor: Edwards Bros., 1932. 194 pp.

Tennessee Valley Authority, Department of Regional Planning Studies. *County Government and Administration in the Tennessee Valley States.* Washington, D.C.: GPO, 1940. 144 pp.

Taxation

Anderson, George C. "The Constitutional Basis of Taxation in Tennessee." *TLR* 15 (1938), 280-87.

Brannen, Claude O. "History of Taxation in Tennessee." Thesis, George Peabody College, 1919.

Johnson, Harry L., ed. *State and Local Tax Problems.* Knoxville: Univ. of Tennessee Press, 1969, 1970. 208 pp.

Johnson, Joseph E. *Assessment Administration in Knox County and Knoxville.* Knoxville: Bureau of Public Administration, Univ. of Tennessee, 1959.

——. *Current and Delinquent Tax Collection of Knox County.* Knoxville: Bureau of Public Administration, Univ. of Tennessee, 1960.

McCorkle, C. H. "Taxation in Tennessee." Thesis, Vanderbilt Univ., 1936.

Parker, Eugene L., Jr. "Tax Problems Presented by the Tennessee Constitution." *VLR* 4 (1950-51), 116-44.

White, Charles P. "Some Aspects of Taxation in Tennessee." *TLR* 8 (1930), 170-83.

——. "Problems of Taxation in Tennessee." *Annals* 153 (1931), 238-45.

——. "Recent Developments in Taxation in Tennessee." ETHS*P* 3 (1931), 78-88.

Social and Cultural History

GENERAL HISTORY TO 1860

Allen, Jack. "The Diary of Randal William McGavock, 1852-1862: An Interpretation of a Period." Diss., George Peabody College, 1941.

Arnow, Harriette Simpson. "The Pioneer Farmer and His Crops in the Cumberland Region." *THQ* 19 (1960), 291-327.

——. *Seedtime on the Cumberland.*

——. *Flowering of the Cumberland.*

Atherton, Lewis E. *The Southern Country Store, 1800-1860.* Baton Rouge: Louisiana State Univ. Press, 1949; rpt. Westport, Conn.: Greenwood, 1949. 227 pp.

Babcock, Rufus, ed. *Forty Years of Pioneer Life: Memoir of John Mason Peck.* Philadelphia: American Baptist Pub. Soc., 1864; rpt., Perspectives in Sociology Series, introd. Paul M. Harrison; foreword Herman R. Lanz. Carbondale: Southern Illinois Univ., 1965. 360 pp.

Becker, Carl M. "A Buckeye in Tennessee: Sojourn of Alienation." *THQ* 22 (1963), 335-46. Becker wrote of an Ohioan who spent two years in Tennessee during the 1850s.

Bentley, Blanche. "Tennessee Scotch Irish Ancestry." *THM* 5 (1919), 201-11.

Bond, Octavia Z. *Old Tales Retold; or, Perils and Adventures of Tennessee Pioneers.* Nashville: Smith & Lamar, 1900, 1906; rpt. Nashville: Methodist Church So., 1914; rpt. Vanderbilt Univ. Press, 1941. 262 pp.

Bradford, Thomas G. *Bradford's Tennessee Almanac.* Nashville: Bradford, 1801.

Breazeale, J. W. M. *Life As It Is.*

Burke, Pauline Wilcox. *Emily Donelson of Tennessee.* 2 vols. Richmond, Va.: Garrett & Massie, 1941.

Clark, Isaac. *Clark's Miscellany, in Prose and Verse.* Nashville: T. G. Bradford, 1812. 120 pp.

Clark, Thomas D. *The Rampaging Frontier; Manners and Humors of Pioneer Days in the South and the Middle West.* New York: Bobbs-Merrill, 1939. Rpt., Midland Book Series. Bloomington: Indiana Univ. Press, 1964. 350 pp.

——. *Pills, Petticoats, and Plows: The Southern Country Store.* Indianapolis: Bobbs-Merrill, 1944. 359 pp. Rpt. Norman: Univ. of Oklahoma Press, 1964. 306 pp.

Congleton, Betty Carolyn. "The Southern Poor Whites, 1800-1860, with Particular Reference to Kentucky and Tennessee." Thesis, Univ. of Kentucky, 1948.

Cooper, A. F. "Pioneer Physicians of West Tennessee." *Centennial History of the Tennessee State Medical Association, 1830-1930,* ed. Philip M. Hamer, 244-47. This article covers the period from 1780 to 1820.

Crabb, Alfred L. "Some Early Connections between Kentucky and Tennessee." *FCHQ* 13 (1939), 147-56. Crabb describes the period from 1780 to 1820.

Davenport, F. Garvin. *Cultural Life in Nashville on the Eve of the Civil War.* Diss., Vanderbilt Univ., 1936. Chapel Hill: Univ. of North Carolina Press, 1941. 232 pp.

——. "Culture versus Frontier in Tennessee, 1825-1850." *JSH* 5 (1939), 18-33.

Davis, Richard E. "Views of Early West Tennessee As Seen through the Files of Ancient Newspapers." WTHSP 6 (1952), 64-76. Covers the period between 1830 and 1850.

Denson, Jesse. *A Compendium of Useful Information.* Nashville: The Author, 1813. 234 pp.

Des Champs, Margaret. "Pioneer Life in the Cumberland Country." Thesis, Vanderbilt Univ., 1946.

Douglas, Byrd. *Steamboatin' on the Cumberland.*

Dykeman, Wilma. *The French Broad,* Rivers of America Series. New York: Rinehart, 1955. 371 pp. Rpt. Knoxville: Univ. of Tennessee Press, 1965, 1966. 382 pp. An impressionistic view of the region, its mores, folkways, and institutions, to the late 1800s.

Essary, John Thurman. *Tennessee Mountaineers in Type; a Collection of Stories by J. T. Essary.* New York: Cochrane, 1910. 110 pp.

Fields, William, Jr., comp. *The Literary and Miscellaneous Scrap*

Book. Knoxville: The Author, 1837. 600 pp. Rev. ed., Philadelphia: Lippincott, 1851. 544 pp.

Fisher, John E. "Life on the Common Level: Inheritance, Conflict and Instruction." *THQ* 26 (1967), 304-22. Concerns Middle Tennessee community life between 1844 and the early 1900s.

Frank, John G. "Tennessee in European Literature 1800-1860." *THQ* 7 (1948), 105-17.

Garrett, William R., ed. "Narrative of Capt. Handly, His Defeat and Capture near Crab Orchard, in 1793." *AHM* 2 (1897), 86-90.

———. "Pioneer Documents: A Protest." *AHM* 2 (1897), 336-53.

———. "Pioneer Letters." *AHM* 2 (1897), 90-94.

Garrett, William R., and John M. Bass, eds. "Recollections of Memucan Hunt Howard." *AHM* 7 (1902), 55-68. Howard's reminiscences concern West Tennessee in the early 1800s.

Gaut, John M. "Freedom's Namesake; or The Origin and Historic Import of the Name Cumberland." *AHM* 6 (1901), 99-117.

Gower, Herschel, and Jack Allen, eds. *Pen and Sword; the Life and Journals of Randal W. McGavock.* Nashville: Tennessee Hist. Comm., 1959. 695 pp. Rpt. 1960. 706 pp. One of the most informative diaries of the antebellum South at its zenith.

Gray, John W. *The Life of Joseph Bishop, the Celebrated Old Pioneer in the First Settlements of Middle Tennessee, Embracing His Wonderful Adventures and Narrow Escapes with the Indians, His Animating and Remarkable Hunting Excursions. Interspersed with Racy Anecdotes of Those Early Times.* Nashville: The Author, 1858; rpt., n.p., privately printed, 1962. 236 pp.

Guild, Josephus Conn. *Old Times in Tennessee, with Historical, Personal, and Political Scraps and Sketches.* Nashville: Tavel, Eastman & Howell, 1878; rpt. Knoxville: Tenase, 1971. 503 pp. The recollections of events that occurred during the author's lifetime to 1878.

Gunn, John C. *Gunn's Domestic Medicine, or Poor Man's Friend, in the Hours of Affliction, Pain, and Sickness.* Knoxville: Privately printed, 1830; 12th ed., Louisville, Ky.: C. Pool, 1838; rev. ed., New York: C. M. Saxton, 1853; Philadelphia: T. Cowperthwaite & Co., 1853; New York: C. M. Saxton, 1854; Philadelphia: T. Cowperthwaite, 1854. 893 pp. A work of importance today for its early teaching that good physical health and good mental health go together. Known diseases of the time and suggested remedies are listed.

Hall, James. *Statistics of the West.*

Hamer, Philip M., ed. *Centennial History of the Tennessee State Medical Association, 1830-1930.*

Hesseltine, William B. "Lyman Draper and the South." *JSH* 19 (1953), 20-31.

——. *Pioneer's Mission; the Story of Lyman Copeland Draper.* Madison: State Hist. Soc. of Wisconsin, 1954, 1964; rpt. Westport, Conn.: Greenwood, 1954. 384 pp. The biography of one of the great collectors of historical documents in the nation's history. Draper is important to Tennessee for his visit here in the 1840s; on leaving, he took numerous public and private papers to Wisconsin, thus preserving them for posterity.

Holt, Albert C. "The Economic and Social Beginnings of Tennessee." *THM* 7 (1921), 194-230, 252-313; 8 (1924), 24-86.

Humble, Sallie Lacy. "Life of Frontier Women." Thesis, George Peabody College, 1933.

Ingraham, Joseph Holt, ed. *The Sunny South; or, The Southerner at Home, Embracing Five Years' Experience of a Northern Governess in the Land of the Sugar and the Cotton.* Philadelphia: G. G. Evans, 1860; rpt. New York: Negro Univ. Press, 1968. 526 pp. Describes Tennessee social life and customs.

Kaser, David. "Nashville's Women of Pleasure in 1860." *THQ* 23 (1964), 379-82.

Lacy, Virginia Jayne, and David Edwin Harrell, Jr. "Plantation Home Remedies: Medicinal Recipes from the Diaries of John Pope." *THQ* 22 (1963), 259-65. Covers the period from 1840 to 1865.

Leyburn, James G. *The Scotch-Irish: A Social History.* Chapel Hill: Univ. of North Carolina Press, 1962. 377 pp.

McClary, Ben Harris. "Fun, Fact and Philosophy: The Diary of John Coffee Williamson, 1858-1861." Thesis, Univ. of Tennessee, 1957.

——., ed. "The Education of a Southern Mind: Extracts from the Diary of John Coffee Williamson 1860-1861." *ETHSP* 32 (1960), 94-105.

McDowell, Lucien L. *Songs of the Old Camp Ground. Genuine Religious Folk Songs of the Tennessee Hill Country.* Ann Arbor: Mich.: Edwards, 1937. 85 pp.

McMurry, Donald L. "The Indian Policy of the Federal Government and the Economic Development of the Southwest." *THM* 1 (1915), 21-39.

McMurtrie, Douglas Crawford. *Early Printing in Tennessee, with a Bibliography of the Issues of the Tennessee Press, 1793-1830.* Chicago: Chicago Club of Printing House Craftsmen, 1933. 141 pp.

——. *An Early Tennessee Paper Mill.* Chicago: Privately printed, 1933. 5 pp.

M'Elwee, W. E. "'The Old Road,' from Washington and Hamilton Districts to the Cumberland Settlement." *AHM* 8 (1903), 347-54.

Marshall, Park. "John A. Murrell and Daniel Crenshaw." *THM* 6 (1920), 3-9.

Mathews, Maxine. "Old Inns of East Tennessee." ETHS*P* 2 (1930), 22-33.

Montgomery, James R. "The Nomenclature of the Upper East Tennessee River." ETHS*P* 28 (1956), 46-57.

Morgan, Sarah Sprott. "Thomas Jefferson Eaton, 'The Travelling Surgeon.'" *THQ* 29 (1970), 160-65. Describes the period c. 1856.

Newcomer, Lee Nathaniel, ed. "Two New England Teachers in Nashville, 1818." *THQ* 19 (1960), 74-79.

Owsley, Frank L. *Plain Folk of the Old South.* Baton Rouge: Louisiana State Univ. Press, 1949; rpt. New York: Quadrangle, 1965; rpt. Gloucester, Mass.: P. Smith, 1971. 235 pp.

Pamplin, Lily May. *The Scamps of Bucksnort; Memories of a Nineteenth Century Childhood in Rural Tennessee.* New York: Exposition, 1962. 118 pp.

Penrod, James. "The Folk Mind in Early Southwestern Humor." *TFSB* 18 (1952), 49-54.

Posey, Walter B. "Ecclesiastical Hankerings." *THQ* 23 (1964), 136-44.

Procter, Ben H. "The Early Life of John H. Reagan—from an Unpublished Memoir." ETHS*P* 34 (1962), 106-17. Covers the 1830s.

Radford, P. M. "Block Houses." *AHM* 1 (1896), 247-52. Refers to the period of the 1780s.

Robertson, James I., Jr. "Frolics, Fights and Firewater in Frontier Tennessee." *THQ* 17 (1958), 97-111.

Rogers, Elzia G. *Early Folk Medical Practices in Tennessee.* Murfreesboro: Mid-South, 1941. 68 pp.

Rogers, Tommy W. "Migration from Tennessee during the Nineteenth Century; I. Origin and Destination of Tennessee's Migrants, 1850-1860." *THQ* 27 (1968), 118-22.

Rogers, William Flinn. "Life on the Kentucky-Tennessee Frontier near the End of the 18th Century." Thesis, Univ. of Tennessee, 1925.

——. "Life in East Tennessee near the End of the Eighteenth Century." ETHS*P* 1 (1929), 27-42.

Roper, James E. "Isaac Rawlings, Frontier Merchant." *THQ* 20 (1961), 262-81.

Rose, Kenneth. "Jenny Lind, Diva." *THQ* 8 (1949), 34-48. The singer's visit to Tennessee was in 1851.

Rowland, Maurice L. "The Militia Laws of Tennessee to the Year 1860." Thesis, George Peabody College, 1927.

Royall, Anne. *Sketches of History, Life, and Manners of the United States.* New Haven: The Author, 1826. 392 pp.

Scott, Thomas A. "Migration from Tennessee during the Nineteenth Century; II. The Impact of Tennessee's Migrating Sons." *THQ* 27 (1968), 123-41.

Sioussat, St. George L., ed. "Selected Letters, 1846-1856, from the Donelson Papers." *THM* 3 (1917), 257-91.

Smith, J. Gray. *A Brief Historical, Statistical, and Descriptive Review of East Tennessee, United States of America: Developing Its Immense Agricultural, Mining, and Manufacturing Advantages. With Remarks to Emigrants. Accompanied with a Map & Lithographed Sketch of a Tennessee Farm, Mansion House, and Buildings.* London: J. Leath, 1842, 1843. 71 pp. American Culture Series, 59:5. Ann Arbor: Univ. Microfilms, 1956.

Swint, Henry Lee, ed. "Letters of a College Student to His Sister, 1841-1844." *THQ* 5 (1946), 249-75.

Thompson, Edwin Bruce. "Humanitarian Reforms in Tennessee, 1820-1850." Thesis, Vanderbilt Univ., 1935.

Trollope, Frances. *Domestic Manners of the Americans,* 2 vols. London: Whittaker and Treacher, 1832.

Truett, Randle Bond. *Trade and Travel around the Southern Appalachians before 1830.* Chapel Hill: Univ. of North Carolina Press, 1935. 192 pp.

Utley, Buford C., ed. "The Shadrach Rice Diary." WTHSP 15 (1961), 105-16. First edited by Ralph E. Rice.

Walton, Augustus Q. *A History of the Detection and Trial of John A. Murel, the Great Western Land Pirate; Together with a Biographical Sketch of Mr. Virgil A. Stewart.* Athens: n.p., 1836. 60 pp. At least five editions of this popular work were published, under varying titles and with varying pagings between 1836 and the 1850s.

Watkins, Violet J. "Pioneer Medicine in the Tennessee-Kentucky Frontier Region." Thesis, Vanderbilt Univ., 1941.

White, Robert H. "Tennessee's Four Capitals." ETHSP 6 (1934), 29-43; rpt. in *Tennessee Old and New*, I, 319-32.

Wiley, Edwin. "Eighteenth Century Presses in Tennessee." *Bibliographical Society of America Proceedings* 2 (1908), 70-83.

Williams, Joseph S. *Old Times in West Tennessee. Reminiscences— Semihistoric—of Pioneer Life and the Early Emigrant Settlers in the Big Hatchie Country. By a Descendant of One of the First Settlers.* Memphis: W. G. Cheeney, 1873. 295 pp.

Williams, Samuel Cole, ed. "Journal of Events (1825-1873) of David Anderson Deaderick." ETHSP 8 (1936), 121-37; 9 (1937), 93-110.

——. "The Tennessee State Flag." *THQ* 2 (1943), 232-35; rpt. in *Tennessee Old and New*, II, 406-9.

Wingfield, Marshall, and Earle F. Whittington, eds. "Joshua C. Fleetwood's Diary Made during a Journey on Horseback from North Carolina to Fayette County, Tennessee in 1850." WTHSP 10 (1955), 5-19.

Artists, Artifacts, Crafts and Craftsmen, Musicians

Beasley, Ellen. "Tennessee Cabinetmakers and Chairmakers through 1840." *Antiques,* Oct. 1971, pp. 612-21.

——. "Tennessee Furniture and Its Makers." *Antiques,* Sept. 1971, pp. 425-31.

Bishop, Budd H. "Art in Tennessee: The Early 19th Century." *THQ* 29 (1970), 379-89.

——. "Three Tennessee Painters: Samuel Shaver, Washington B. Cooper, and James Cameron." *Antiques,* Sept. 1971, pp. 432-37.

Caldwell, Benjamin H., Jr. "Tennessee Silversmiths." *Antiques,* Sept. 1971, pp. 382-85.

——. "Tennessee Silversmiths prior to 1860: A Checklist." *Antiques,* Dec. 1971, pp. 906-13.

Cochran, Gifford A., with F. Burrall Hoffman. *Grandeur in Tennessee; Classical Revival Architecture in a Pioneer State.* New York: Augustin, 1946. 132 pp.

Gilchrist, Agnes Addison. *William Strickland, Architect and Engineer, 1788-1854.* Philadelphia: Univ. of Pennsylvania Press, 1950. 145 pp. Enl. ed., Architecture and Decorative Art Series. New York: Da Capo, 1969. Various pagings. A biography of the great 19th century architect from Philadelphia whose Nashville monuments are the State Capitol and St. Mary's Church.

Harper, Herbert L. "The Antebellum Courthouses of Tennessee." *THQ* 30 (1971), 3-25.

Hulan, Richard H. "Music in Tennessee." *Antiques,* Sept. 1971, pp. 418-19.

——. "Tennessee Textiles." *Antiques,* Sept. 1971, pp. 386-89.

Hutchison, Albert W., Jr. "Domestic Architecture in Middle Tennessee." *Antiques,* Sept. 1971, pp. 402-7.

Morrissey, Eleanor Fleming, comp. *Portraits in Tennessee Painted before 1866, Preliminary Checklist.* Nashville: National Soc. of the Colonial Dames of America in Tennessee, 1964. 147 pp.

MacBeth, Jerome R. "Portraits by Ralph E. W. Earl." *Antiques,* Sept. 1971, pp. 390-93.

McNabb, William Ross. "Another Look at William Strickland." Thesis, Vanderbilt Univ., 1971.

Mahoney, Nell Savage. "William Strickland and the Building of Tennessee's Capitol." *THQ* 4 (1945), 99-153.

Parrent, H. Clinton, Jr. "Adolphus Heiman and the Building Methods of Two Centuries." *THQ* 12 (1953), 204-12. Covers the mid-19th-century.

Price, Prentiss. "Samuel Shaver: Portrait Painter." ETHS*P* 24 (1952), 92-105. Mid-19th-century artist.

Tennesseans Abroad

Baylen, Joseph O. "A Tennessee Politician in Imperial Russia, 1850-1853." *THQ* 14 (1955), 227-52. The Tennessean was Neill S. Brown.

——., ed. "Neill S. Brown and Russian Reaction to American Sympathy for the Hungarian Exiles, 1851-1852. Some Documents." ETHSP 29 (1957), 161-71.

Crabb, Alfred Leland, ed. "Letters over the Water: The European Tour of Henry Maney, 1851-1852." THQ 16 (1957), 262-72.

Gower, Herschel. "Tennessee Writers Abroad, 1851: Henry Maney and Randal W. McGavock." THQ 26 (1967), 396-403.

Gower, Herschel, and Jack Allen. Pen and Sword: The Life and Journals of Randal W. McGavock.

Jordan, Weymouth Tyree. "The Public Career of George Washington Campbell." Diss., Vanderbilt Univ., 1937.

——. "The Private Interests and Activities of George Washington Campbell." ETHSP 13 (1941), 47-65.

——. "Excerpts from the Diary of a Tennessean at the Court of the Tsar, 1818-1820." ETHSP 15 (1943), 104-9.

——. "George W. Campbell's Journal of the French Spoliations Claims Commission, 1832-1835." ETHSP 19 (1947), 98-109.

——., ed. "Diary of George Washington Campbell, American Minister to Russia, 1818-1820." THQ 7 (1948), 152-70, 259-80.

——. George Washington Campbell of Tennessee, Western Statesman. Tallahassee: Florida State Univ., 1955. 214 pp.

McBride, John. "A Tennessee Lad on Trial in Paris in 1817." THQ 15 (1956), 269-74.

McGavock, Randal W. A Tennessean Abroad; or, Letters from Europe, Africa, and Asia. New York: Redfield, 1854. 398 pp.

Maney, Henry. Memories over the Water, or, Stray Thoughts on a Long Stroll. Nashville: Toon, Nelson, 1854. 351 pp.

Marraro, Howard R. "William H. Polk's Mission to Naples, 1845-1847." THQ 4 (1945), 222-31.

Marsh, Dwight Whitney. The Tennessean in Persia and Koordistan. Being Scenes and Incidents in the Life of Samuel Audley Rhea. New York: A. D. F. Randolph, 1869. 381 pp.

GENERAL HISTORY: 1860-1900

Baker, William. A Concise Description of Middle Tennessee. McMinnville: McMinnville Enterprise, 1867. 10 pp.

Beaver, R. Pierce. "An Ohio Farmer in Middle Tennessee in 1865." THM (ser. 2) 1 (1930-31), 29-39.

Boom, Aaron M., ed. "Letters from a Tennessean Working on the Mexican Central Railway, 1882-1883." *THQ* 12 (1953), 334-48.

Cates, Ben B. "The Medical Profession of East Tennessee." *East Tennessee. Historical and Biographical,* 132-56.

Clark, Thomas D. "The Country Store in Post-Civil War Tennessee." ETHS*P* 17 (1945), 3-21.

——. "The Country Newspaper: A Factor in Southern Opinion, 1865-1930." *JSH* 14 (1948), 3-33.

——. "The Tennessee Country Editor." ETHS*P* 21 (1949), 3-18.

Cooper, Hobart A. "German and Swiss Colonization in Morgan County, Tennessee." Thesis, Univ. of Tennessee, 1925.

Davenport, F. Garvin. "Scientific Interests in Kentucky and Tennessee, 1870-1890." *JSH* 14 (1948), 500-521.

Donley, David E. "The Flood of March, 1867, in the Tennessee River." ETHS*P* 8 (1936), 74-81.

Ensor, Allison. "The 'Tennessee Land' of the Gilded Age: Fiction and Reality." *Tennessee Studies in Literature* 15 (1970), 15-24.

Fink, Paul M. "The Lighter Side of History." ETHS*P* 39 (1967), 26-41.

Gilmore, James R. [pseud. Edmund Kirke]. *Down in Tennessee, and Back by Way of Richmond.* London: Law, 1864; New York: Carleton, 1864. 282 pp. American Culture Series, 137:3. Ann Arbor: Univ. Microfilms, 1960; rpt. Freeport, N.Y.: Books for Libraries, 1971.

Guide to the Summer Resorts and Watering Places of East Tennessee. n.p.: Privately printed, 1879.

Halley, R. A. "Paper Making in Tennessee." *AHM* 9 (1904), 211-17; rpt. in *Tennessee Old and New,* I, 425-30.

Helm, Susan Evelyn. "Cultural Development of Tennessee, 1865-1900." Thesis, George Peabody College, 1937.

Holding, Charles E. "John Wilkes Booth Stars in Nashville." *THQ* 23 (1964), 73-79. Commemorating the actor's appearance on the Nashville stage in 1864.

Holman, Harriet R., ed. "Thomas Nelson Page's Account of Tennessee Hospitality." *THQ* 28 (1969), 269-72. Page visited Tennessee c. 1893.

Kiger, Joseph C. "Social Thought As Expressed in Rural Newspapers of Middle Tennessee, 1878-1898." Diss., Vanderbilt Univ., 1950.

Kirke, Edmund. *See* Gilmore, James R.

Marius, Richard. *The Coming of Rain.* New York: Knopf, 1969. 437 pp. An outstanding novel set firmly in the Reconstruction Era of East Tennessee. Filled with historical truth and symbolism of larger truths, this work marks the author as a ranking American literary figure.

Ochs, George C. "History of Journalism in East Tennessee." *East Tennessee. Historical and Biographical,* 157-69.

Owsley, Harriet C. "The Fergusson Family Papers—A Bibliographic Note." *THQ* 28 (1969), 324-29.

Richardson, James Daniel, comp. *Tennessee Templars. A Registar of Names, with Biographical Sketches, of the Knights Templar of Tennessee, and Brief Histories of the Grand and Subordinate Commanderies.* Nashville: R. H. Howell, 1833. 277 pp.

Riley, Susan B. "The Hazards of Periodical Publishing in the South during the Nineteenth Century." *THQ* 21 (1962), 365-76.

Scott, Thomas Allan. "National Impact of Tennessee through Her Migrating Sons, 1830-1900." Thesis, Univ. of Tennessee, 1966.

Stewart, Guy H. "History and Bibliography of Middle Tennessee Newspapers, 1799-1876." Diss., Univ. of Illinois, 1957.

Swint, Henry Lee, and D. E. Mohler. "Eugene F. Falconnet, Soldier, Engineer, Inventor." *THQ* 21 (1962), 219-34.

Thorne, Charles B. "The Watering Spas of Middle Tennessee." *THQ* 29 (1970), 321-59.

Wells, Rhea. *An American Farm.* Garden City, N.Y.: Doubleday, 1928. 237 pp. Life on an East Tennessee farm in the late 1800s.

Wiley, Mary C. "With Calvin H. Wiley in Tennessee through Unpublished Letters." *NCHR* 36 (1959), 72-95. Wiley was superintendent of the American Bible Society in Tennessee.

Nineteenth-Century Communitarian Settlements

NASHOBA

Elliott, Helen. "Frances Wright's Experiment with Negro Emancipation." *Indiana Magazine of History* 35 (1939), 141-57.

Emerson, O. B. "Frances Wright and Her Nashoba Experiment." *THQ* 6 (1947), 291-314.

Parks, Edd Winfield. "Dreamer's Vision: Frances Wright at Nashoba 1825-1830." *THM* (ser. 2) 2 (1931-32), 75-86; rpt. in *Tennessee Old and New,* I, 299-310.

——. *Nashoba.* New York: Twayne, 1963. 326 pp.

Pease, William H., and Jane H. Pease. "A New View of Nashoba." *THQ* 19 (1960), 99-109.

——. *Black Utopia; Negro Communal Experiments in America.* Madison: State Hist. Soc. of Wisconsin, 1963, 1972. 204 pp. Includes a description of Nashoba.

RUGBY

Alstetter, Mabel F. "Thomas Hughes in America." *Peabody Journal of Education* 15 (1937), 92-100.

Armytage, W. H. G. "New Light on the English Background of Thomas Hughes' Rugby Colony in Tennessee." ETHS*P* 21 (1949), 69-84.

Bertz, Edward. *Das Sabinergut.* Berlin: Alfred Schall, 1896. A German novel about the Rugby Colony by the first librarian of the Hughes Public Library at Rugby.

Brooks, Nelly Lender. "Sketches of Rugby, Tennessee." Unpublished typescript, 1941. 27 leaves.

Hamer, Marguerite B. "Thomas Hughes and His American Rugby." *NCHR* 5 (1928), 390-412.

——. *Cameos of the South: Historical Word Sketches of Tennessee and of the Old South.* Philadelphia: Winston, 1940. 154 pp. Contains a description of Rugby.

——. "The Correspondence of Thomas Hughes concerning His Tennessee Rugby." *NCHR* 21 (1944), 203-14.

Hughes, Thomas. *Rugby, Tennessee; Being Some Account of the Settlement Founded on the Cumberland Plateau by the Board of Aid to Land Ownership, Limited; a Company Incorporated in England and Authorised to Hold and Deal in Land by Act of the Legislature of the State of Tennessee; by Thomas Hughes. . . . With a Report on the Soils of the Plateau, by the Hon. F. W. [J. B.] Killebrew.* New York: Macmillan, 1881. 168 pp. Rpt. Seaside Library, vol. 51. New York: Monro, 1881. 23 pp.

Jones, Audrey. "Rugby in Tennessee." *TFSB* 14 (1948), 23-27.

Mack, Edward C., and W. H. G. Armytage. *Thomas Hughes: The Life of the Author of "Tom Brown's Schooldays."* London: Benn, 1952. 302 pp.

Maloney, John. "Town of Cultured Ghosts." *Holiday,* Oct. 1948, pp. 81-92.

Mathews, John Joseph. *Life and Death of an Oilman: The Career of E. W. Marland.* Norman: Univ. of Oklahoma Press, 1951.

259 pp. Marland spent his boyhood in Rugby and attended private school there.

McClary, Ben Harris, ed. "Not for the Moment Only: Edward Bertz to Mary Percival, Feb. 18, 1886." *THQ* 24 (1965), 54-62.

Miller, Ernest Ivan. "Some Tennessee Utopias." Thesis, Univ. of Tennessee, 1941.

Montgomery, James Elmer. "Two Resettlement Communities on the Cumberland Plateau." Thesis, Vanderbilt Univ., 1941. These communities are Rugby and Cumberland Homesteads.

Owsley, Harriet C. "The Rugby Papers: A Bibliographic Note." *THQ* 27 (1968), 225-28.

Pemberton, Luola Spangler. "Thomas Hughes in Rugby, Tennessee." Thesis, George Peabody College, 1947.

Stagg, Brian L. "Tennessee's Rugby Colony." *THQ* 27 (1968), 209-24; rpt. in *More Landmarks of Tennessee*, 267-82.

Stone, Grace. "Tennessee: Social and Economic Laboratory." *Sewanee Review* 46 (1938), 36-44, 158-66. Discusses Rugby.

Stott, Kathleen B. "Rugby, Tennessee: An Attempted Utopia." Thesis, Univ. of Missouri, 1938.

"Tennessee Colony Named Rugby after Tom Hughes' Old School." *Time,* Dec. 25, 1939, pp. 9ff.

Walton, Sarah L. *Memories of Rugby Colony.* Rugby: Privately printed, 1952. 15 pp.

——. "Rugby in America." *Georgia Review* 10 (1956), 395-403.

Wichman, Patricia Guion. *Christ Church, Episcopal, Rugby, Tennessee: A Short History.* Rugby: Privately printed, 1959. 47 pp.

——. *Rugby: A Great Man's Dream.* Rugby: Hughes Pub. Libr., 1966. 43 pp.

Young, Arthur C., ed. *The Letters of George Gissing to Eduard Bertz, 1887-1903.* London: Constable, 1961; New Brunswick, N.J.: Rugers Univ. Press, 1961. 337 pp. This book contains information on Bertz's years as a Rugby colonist and on his novel about Rugby, *Das Sabinergut.*

RUSKIN

Braam, J. W. "The Ruskin Cooperative Colony in Tennessee." *American Journal of Sociology* 8 (1903), 667-80.

Broome, Isaac. *The Last Days of the Ruskin Co-operative Association.* Chicago: C. H. Kerr, 1902. 183 pp. The demise of Ruskin as told by an eyewitness to the event.

Butler, Francelia. "The Ruskin Commonwealth: A Unique Experiment in Marxian Socialism." *THQ* 23 (1964), 333-42.

Casson, Herbert N. "The Ruskin Co-operative Colony." *Independent* 51 (1899), 192-95.

Davis, W. G. "Failure of the Ruskin Cooperative Colony." *Gunton's Magazine,* Dec. 1901, pp. 530-37.

Hardiman, Charles E. "A Historical Geography of Ruskin Cave, Tennessee." Thesis, Univ. of Tennessee, 1964.

Kegel, Charles H., ed. "Earl Miller's 'Recollections of the Ruskin Cooperative Association.'" *THQ* 17 (1958), 45-69.

Medill, H. C. "Ruskin Colony: Why It Failed." *Gunton's Magazine,* May 1902, pp. 434-43.

Quint, Howard J. "Julius A. Wayland, Pioneer Socialist Propagandist." *MVHR* 35 (1948-49), 585-606. Wayland was the founder of the Ruskin Colony.

"Ruskin Community's Subterranean Industrial Plant." *Scientific American,* Aug. 5, 1899, pp. 89 ff.

Southworth, J. "Cooperative Colony at Ruskin, Tennessee." *Review of Reviews,* Nov. 1897, pp. 606-7.

"Why All Ruskin Colonies Fail." *Gunton's Magazine,* May 1902, pp. 444-51.

WELSH COLONY

Shepperson, Wilbur S. *Samuel Roberts; a Welsh Colonizer in Civil War Tennessee.* Knoxville: Univ. of Tennessee Press, 1961. 190 pp. The 19th-century colony was located in Scott County.

Tennessee Centennial Celebration, 1897

Anderson, Douglas. "The Centennial Idea and the Centennial Dream." *THM* (ser. 2) 3 (1932-37), 107-10.

Centennial Album of Nashville, Tennessee, Containing Exposition Buildings, Officers of the Exposition, Representative Citizens, Public Buildings, Business Houses, and Private Residences. Nashville: J. Prousnitzer, 1896. 196 pp.

Creighton, Wilbur F. *The Parthenon in Nashville; from a Personal Viewpoint.* Nashville: The Author, 1968. 48 pp.

———. *Building of Nashville.* Nashville: The Author, 1969. 205 pp.

Davis, Louise Littleton. "The Parthenon and the Tennessee Cen-

tennial: The Greek Temple That Sparked a Birthday Party."
THQ 26 (1967), 335-53; rpt. in *More Landmarks of Tennessee,*
209-27.

Fry, Mary A. *Tennessee Centennial Poem. A Synopsis of the History
of Tennessee from Its Earliest Settlement on Watauga to the
Present Time, with Short Biographies of Her Most Prominent
Men.* Chattanooga: The Author, 1896. 174 pp.

Gilchrist, Annie Somers. *A Souvenir of the Tennessee Centennial;
Poems by Annie Somers Gilchrist.* Nashville: *Gospel Advocate,*
1897. 132 pp.

Handley, M. W. "Tennessee and Its Centennial." *Century Magazine,*
May 1897, pp. 92-97.

Justi, Herman, ed. *Official History of the Tennessee Centennial
Exposition, Opened May 1, and Closed October 30, 1897.* Nashville: Brandon, 1898. 495 pp. The best and most comprehensive
single history of this celebration.

Moulder, George B. *The Parthenon at Nashville, Tennessee, U.S.A.*
Nashville: Brandon, 1930. 16 pp.

"Opening of the Tennessee Centennial." *Harper's Weekly,* May 15,
1897, p. 486.

Rogers, W. A. "Tennessee Mountaineers at the Fair." *Harper's
Weekly,* May 29, 1897, p. 546.

Smith, F. H. "Some Notes on Tennessee's Centennial." *Scribner's
Magazine,* Sept. 1897, pp. 333-44.

Starr, F. "First Days at Tennessee's Centennial." *Outlook,* May 29,
1897, pp. 251-53.

Stephenson, Nathaniel W. *The Tennessee Centennial Exposition.*
Nashville: Brandon, 1897. 32 pp.

Tennessee Centennial and International Exposition. *Commemoration of the One Hundredth Anniversary of Tennessee's Admission into the American Union.* Nashville: W. S. Rainey, 1896.
59 pp.

——. *Catalogue (Illustrated). Fine Arts Department.* Nashville:
Brandon, 1897. 266 pp.

——. *Official Guide to the Tennessee Centennial and International
Exposition and City of Nashville.* Nashville: Marshall & Bruce,
1897. 183 pp.

——. *Tennessee. Her Illustrious History, Marvelous Resources,
Wonderful Capabilities, Developed by the Tennessee Centennial
Exposition.* Nashville: Foster & Webb, 1897. 192 pp.

——. *The Wayne Hand-Book of Nashville, and the Tennessee Centennial Exposition . . . . A Complete Guide-Book for Tourists.* Fort Wayne, Ind.: Wayne, 1897. 119 pp.

——. *Woman's Department Catalogue, May 1 to October 1, 1897.* Nashville: Burch, Hinton, 1897. 59 pp.

——. *Art Album of the Tennessee Centennial and International Exposition, Held in Nashville, May 1, 1897 to October 31, 1897.* Nashville: Marshall & Bruce, 1898. Unpaged.

"The Tennessee Centennial Exposition." *Harper's Weekly,* May 23, 1896, p. 522.

"Tennessee Centennial Exposition." *Scientific American,* Jan. 16, 1897, pp. 36-37; Apr. 17, 1897, pp. 242 ff.

Thruston, Gates P. "The Department of History at the Tennessee Centennial." *AHM* 3 (1898), 3-21.

White, R. L. C. "A Centennial Dream." *AHM* 2 (1897), 187-93, 280-98.

Wilson, Benjamin Franklin, III. *The Parthenon of Pericles and Its Reproduction in America.* Nashville: Parthenon Press, 1937, 1941. 140 pp.

Yenowine, G. H. "Tennessee Centennial." *Harper's Weekly,* Jan. 2, 1897, pp. 11-12.

General History: 1900-1972

Bailey, Bernadine Freeman. *Picture Book of Tennessee.* Chicago: Whitman, 1952, 1959. Unpaged. Rev. ed., 1966. 32 pp. Juvenile.

Boebel, Clarence W., comp. *Tennessee's Aging: Full Report and Recommendations.* Nashville: State of Tennessee, 1960. 184 pp. Report resulting from the Governor's Planning Committee for the 1961 White House Conference on Aging.

Boswell, George W. "Some Characteristics of Folksongs in Middle Tennessee." *TFSB* 15 (1949), 63-69.

Botkin, B. A., ed. *A Treasury of Southern Folklore: Stories, Ballads, Traditions, and Folkways of the People of the South.* New York: Crown, 1949. 776 pp.

Brigham, Clarence Saunders, comp. *Bibliography of American Newspapers, 1690-1820,* American Antiquarian Soc. Proceedings, vol. 35, pp. 79-160. Worcester, Mass.: American Antiquarian Soc., 1926.

Burt, Jesse. "The Savor of Old Time Railroading. . . ." *Bulletin of the Railway and Locomotive Historical Society.* Fall 1956, pp. 36-45.

Burton, Thomas G., and Ambrose N. Manning. *Collection of Folklore by Undergraduate Students of East Tennessee State University.* Johnson City: East Tennessee State Univ. Press, 1967. 80 pp.

Caton, Joseph L. *Pictorial Handbook of the Tennessee Valley.* Knoxville: The Author, 1935. 29 pp.

Chandler, Walter. *The Challenge of Handicap; How Four Tennesseans Met the Dare and Won!* Nashville: The Author, c. 1964. 95 pp. These persons were Edward E. Barnard, Francis J. Campbell, Marion Dorsett, Matthew Fontaine Maury.

Chatfield, E. Charles. "The Southern Sociological Congress: Organization of Uplift." *THQ* 19 (1960), 328-47.

——. "The Southern Sociological Congress: Rationale of Uplift." *THQ* 20 (1961), 51-64.

Cody, Annie E. *History of the Tennessee Division, United Daughters of the Confederacy.* Nashville: Cullom & Ghertner, 1947. 374 pp.

Combs, Jerry Walker. "Population Migration in the State of Tennessee." Thesis, Univ. of Tennessee, 1948.

Cox, Lawrence Eugene. "The Tennessee Scenic Rivers System." Thesis, Univ. of Tennessee, 1969.

Coyle, David Cushman. *Land of Hope.* A short treatment of TVA's impact upon the region.

Crabb, Alfred Leland. "The Disappearing Smokehouse." *THQ* 25 (1966), 155-68.

DeWitt, John H. "Report of the George Washington Bi-centennial Commission of Tennessee." *THM* (ser. 2) 2 (1931-32), 179-85.

Donabauer, Elton Henry. "Some Annual Tennessee Celebrations." Thesis, George Peabody College, 1951.

Dykeman, Wilma. "Too Much Talent in Tennessee." *Harper's Magazine,* Mar. 1955, pp. 48-53.

Federal Writers' Project. *These Are Our Lives As Told by the People and Written by Members of the Federal Writers' Project of the Works Progress Administration in North Carolina, Tennessee, and Georgia.* Chapel Hill: Univ. of North Carolina Press, 1939. Rpt. New York: Arno, 1969; rpt. Detroit: Gale, 1972.

421 pp. Self-portraits of tenant farmers, farm owners, factory workers, persons in service trades, mining, etc., showing working of society at this level during the 1930s.

Fisher, H. D. "Recreation in Tennessee." *Survey,* Apr. 23, 1921, p. 117.

Fisher, Mary Bell. "Robert Sparks Walker, Naturalist and Writer." Thesis, George Peabody College, 1937.

Flowers, Paul. "Place Names in Tennessee." WTHSP 14 (1960), 113-23.

Freels, Edward Theodore. "A Geographic Study of a Cross Section of the Great Valley of East Tennessee." Diss., Univ. of Tennessee, 1970.

Fuller, Wayne E. "The South and the Rural Free Delivery of Mail." *JSH* 25 (1959), 499-521.

Hamer, Philip M., ed. *The Centennial History of the Tennessee State Medical Association, 1830-1930.*

Harder, Kelsie B. "The Vocabulary of Hog-Killing." *TFSB* 25 (1959), 111-15.

Hart, John Fraser. *Kentucky and Tennessee,* Know Your America Program Series. Garden City, N.Y.: Doubleday, 1965. 64 pp. Prepared with the cooperation of the American Geographical Society.

Hatcher, Mildred. "Superstitions in Middle Tennessee." *Southern Folklore Quarterly* 19 (1955), 150-55.

Hayes, Harold. "Settlement Pattern of Upper East Tennessee." Thesis, East Tennessee State Univ., 1966.

Holden, Alfred H. "The Way It Was When We Rode 'Mike.'" *THQ* 18 (1959), 345-52. Railroading from Collierville to Memphis, 1914.

Howse, Ruth W. "Folk Music of West Tennessee." *TFSB* 13 (1947), 77-88.

Hunter, Kermit. "Some Aspects of Outdoor Historical Drama with Special Reference to 'Unto These Hills.'" ETHSP 26 (1954), 3-6.

Jackson, George P. *The Story of "The Sacred Harp," 1844-1944; a Book of Religious Folk Songs as an American Institution.* Nashville: Vanderbilt Univ. Press, 1944. 46 pp. *The Sacred Harp, a Collection of Psalm and Hymn Tunes, Odes, and Anthems* was published in many editions beginning in 1844.

Johnson, Rayburn W. "Population Trends in Tennessee from 1940-1950." *THQ* 11 (1952), 254-62.

Joiner, James. "A History of Sunday Laws in Tennessee." Thesis, Univ. of Tennessee, 1954.

Jones, Madison. *History of the Tennessee State Dental Association*, comp. Thomas D. Dow. Nashville: Tennessee Dental Assoc., 1958. 300 pp.

Keating, B. "Fresh Look at Tennessee." *Holiday*, Nov. 1962, pp. 94-97.

Kiger, Joseph C. "Social Thought As Voiced in Rural Middle Tennessee Newspapers, 1878-1898." *THQ* 9 (1950), 131-54.

Knox, John Ballenger. *The People of Tennessee; a Study of Population Trends*, introd. William E. Cole. Knoxville: Univ. of Tennessee Press, 1949. 191 pp. A basically demographic study, this work bridges all of the social sciences to describe the people of the state in their political, economic, and social condition.

Kollmorgen, Walter M. "Observations on Cultural Islands in Terms of Tennessee Agriculture." ETHSP 16 (1944), 65-78.

Krueger, Thomas A. *And Promises to Keep: The Southern Conference for Human Welfare, 1938-1948.* Nashville: Vanderbilt Univ. Press, 1967. 218 pp. This is the story of a voluntary organization devoted to propagating the New Deal in the South, 1938-1948. Krueger rejects the charge that the organization was in any way related to the Communist party, but asserts that it was important in preparing the way for desegregation in the South.

McClenahan, F. M. "National Asset in East Tennessee." *Scientific American*, Sept. 29, 1917, pp. 236ff.

McDowell, Lucien L., and Flora L. McDowell, comps. *Folk Dances of Tennessee; Folk Customs and Old Play Party Games of the Caney Fork Valley.* Ann Arbor, Mich.: Edwards, 1938. 78 pp. Rpt. Delaware, O.: Cooperative Research Service, 1953. 64 pp.

Mason, Robert Leslie. "Ten Old English Ballads in Middle Tennessee." *Southern Folklore Quarterly* 11 (1947), 119-37.

Massengill, Samuel Evans. *A Sketch of Medicine and Pharmacy and a View of Its Progress by the Massengill Family from the Fifteenth to the Twentieth Century.* Bristol: Massengill Co., 1942. 445 pp.

May, William Frederick. "Population Fertility in Tennessee." Thesis, Univ. of Tennessee, 1969.

Meredith, Kenneth Ross. "Conversations with Potters in the Mountains of North Carolina and Tennessee." Thesis, East Tennessee State Univ., 1967.

Moneymaker, B. C. "Earthquakes in Tennessee and Nearby Sections of Neighboring States, 1901-1925." *JTAS* 32 (1957), 91-105.

———. "Earthquakes in Tennessee and Nearby Sections of Neighboring States, 1926-1950." *JTAS* 33 (1958), 224-39.

Neville, Bert. *Directory of Tennessee River Steamboats (1821-1928)*. Selma, Ala.: The Author, 1963. 272 pp.

Parr, Jerry S. "Folk Cures of Middle Tennessee." *TFSB* 28 (1962), 8-12.

Rogers, E. G. "Some Experiences at Staging." *TFSB* 12 (1946), 6-13.

———. "Some East Tennessee Figurative Expressions." *TFSB* 19 (1953), 36-39.

———. "More Tall Tales from Tennessee." *Southern Folklore Quarterly* 25 (1961), 178-83.

Roy, L. C. "Tennessee: Highlights of the Volunteer State." *National Geographic Magazine*, May 1939, pp. 553-94.

Sears, Joseph Hamblen. *Tennessee Printers, 1791-1945: A Review of Printing History from Roulstone's First Press to Printers of the Present*. Kingsport: Kingsport Press, 1945. 47 pp.

Sixty Years of Columbianism in Tennessee: A History of the Knights of Columbus in Tennessee. Nashville: Scott, 1962. 118 pp.

Snodgrass, Charles Albert. *The History of Freemasonry in Tennessee, 1789-1943*. Nashville: Ambrose, 1944. 542 pp.

Spellings, William W. "The Spread of Population in Tennessee." Thesis, George Peabody College, 1929.

Tennessee Commission on the Performing Arts. *Report and Recommendations of the Commission on the Performing Arts to the Governor and General Assembly of the State of Tennessee*. Nashville: State of Tennessee, 1967. 20 pp.

Tennessee Governor's Commission on the Status of Women. *Report of the Governor's Commission on the Status of Women in Tennessee*. Nashville: State of Tennessee, 1964. 20 pp.

Tennessee State Planning Division. *Population in Tennessee*. Nashville: State of Tennessee, 1970. 130 pp.

Teuton, Frank L. *Steamboat Days on the Tennessee River: A History of the St. Louis and Tennessee River Packet Company.* Washington, D.C.: South Capitol Press, 1967. 72 pp. A history of captains and craft which plied the waters of the Tennessee until 1942.

Thompson, Lawrence S., ed. "Foreign Books about Tennessee, 1900-1950." *THQ* 11 (1952), 274-81.

United States Department of Agriculture. *Hull-York Lakeland Resource Conservation and Development Association.* Fort Worth: U.S. Dept. of Agriculture, 1966.

White, Robert H. "Historical Background re Capital Punishment in Tennessee." WTHS*P* 19 (1965), 69-93.

Wood, Mayme Parrott. *Hitch Hiking along the Holston River from 1792-1962; a Peep at East Tennessee from King's Meadows (Bristol) to White's Fort (Knoxville) Via McBee's Ferry (Straw-berry Plains). How? Let's See!* Gatlinburg: Brazos, 1964. 237 pp. Local manners and customs.

———. *Drifting down Holston River Way, 1756-1966.* Maryville: The Author, 1966. 240 pp. Local manners and customs.

Appalachia

[*See also* Great Smoky Mountains and Great Smoky Mountains National Park.]

Abbott, Martin, ed. "A Mountain School in Tennessee: Some Reconstruction Letters." *THQ* 17 (1958), 70-73.

Auer, Maria. "The Uncanny in East Tennessee." *TFSB* 29 (1963), 60-63.

Buckley, Samuel B. *Mountains of North Carolina and Tennessee.* New Haven, Conn.: n.p., 1859. 8 pp.

Burleson, Nell P. "The Evolution of Southern Appalachian Culture As Evidenced in Folklore." Thesis, East Tennessee State Univ., 1963.

Cambiaire, Célestin Pierre, comp. *East Tennessee and Western Virginia Mountain Ballads (the Last Stand of American Pioneer Civilization).* London: Mitre, 1934; rpt. New York: Mitre, 1935. 179 pp.

Clark, Joe. *Hill Folk.* Nashville: Vanderbilt Univ. Press, 1972. 96 pp. Photographs and captions by Clark, with an essay by Jesse Stuart.

Eaton, Allen H. *Handicrafts of the Southern Highlands: With an*

Account of the Rural Handicraft Movement in the United States and Suggestions for the Wider Use of Handicrafts in Adult Education and in Recreation. New York: Russell Sage, 1937; rpt. New York: Dover, 1972. 370 pp.

Gannaway, Mary Ann. "The Singing Games of the Cumberland Mountains in Tennessee." Thesis, George Peabody College, 1935.

Gaut, John M. *Cumberland: The Story of a Name.* Nashville: Cumberland Presbyterian Pub. House, 1903. 47 pp.

Hogue, Albert R. *One Hundred Years in the Cumberland Mountains along the Continental Line.* McMinnville: Standard, 1933. 92 pp. This work is a potpourri of information about the Cumberlands, including names of early settlers.

Humes, Thomas William. *The Loyal Mountaineers of Tennessee.* Knoxville: Ogden, 1888. 400 pp.

Jackson, George P. *White Spirituals in the Southern Uplands; the Story of the Fasola Folk, Their Songs, Singings, and "Buckwheat" Notes.* Chapel Hill: Univ. of North Carolina Press, 1933; rpt. New York: Dover, 1965; rpt. Santa Fe: Gannon, 1965. 444 pp.

Jillson, Willard Rouse. *A Bibliography of the Cumberland River Valley in Kentucky and Tennessee; Citations of Printed Manuscript Sources Touching upon Its History, Geology, Cartography, Coal, Iron, Salt, Fluorspar, Phosphate, Clays, Oil and Gas, with Annotations.* Frankfort, Ky.: Perry, 1960. 46 pp.

Lanman, Charles. *Letters from the Alleghany Mountains.* New York: Putnam, 1849. 198 pp. Rpt. in *Adventures in the Wilds of the United States and British American Provinces,* vol. 1. Philadelphia: Moore, 1856. Microfilm, American Culture Series, 189:8. Ann Arbor: Univ. Microfilms, 1962.

McDowell, Lucien L. *Songs of the Old Camp Ground: Genuine Religious Songs of the Tennessee Hill Country.* Ann Arbor, Mich.: Edwards Bros., 1937. 85 pp.

McDowell, Lucien L., and Flora Lassiter McDowell, comps. *Folk Dances of Tennessee.*

———. *Memory Melodies; a Collection of Folk Songs from Middle Tennessee.* Smithville: The Authors, 1947. 128 pp.

McNeer, May Yonge. *The Story of the Southern Highlands.* New York: Harper, 1945. 32 pp.

Matthews, Elmora Messer. *Neighbor and Kin; Life in a Tennessee Ridge Community.* Nashville: Vanderbilt Univ. Press, 1965, 1966. 178 pp. The author, pondering the role of conflict and violence in a Tennessee rural community, concludes that violence occurs when families sharing a culture that is egalitarian attempt to secure for their descendants resources believed to be in excess of those available to others.

Moffat, A. "Mountaineers of Middle Tennessee." *Journal of American Folklore* 4 (1891), 314-20.

Montague, M. P. "Big Draft: The Tennessee Mountains." *North American Review,* July 1922, pp. 111-20.

Montgomery, James E. "Three Appalachian Communities: Cultural Differentials As They Affect Levels of Living and Population Pressure." Diss., Vanderbilt Univ., 1944.

Patton, James Welch. "White Spirituals in the Southern Uplands." *THM* (ser. 2) 3 (1932-37), 121-24.

Pearsall, Marion. "Some Aspects of Culture Change in a Mountain Neighborhood of East Tennessee." Diss., Univ. of California (Berkeley), 1950.

Rhea, Caroline McQueen. "Sketches and Legends of Upper East Tennessee." Thesis, George Peabody College, 1932.

Shapiro, Henry David. "A Strange Land and Peculiar People: The Discovery of Appalachia, 1870-1920." Diss., Rutgers Univ., 1966.

Shearin, Hubert G. "British Ballads in the Cumberland Mountains." *Sewanee Review* 19 (1911), 313-27.

Snyder, Ann E. *On the Watauga and the Cumberland.* Nashville: Methodist Pub. House, 1895, 1903. 33 pp.

Thompson, Samuel Hunter. *The Highlanders of the South.* New York: Eaton & Mains, 1910; rpt. Cincinnati: Jennings & Graham, 1910. 86 pp.

Walker, Robert S., ed. *Outdoors in the Cumberlands.* Chattanooga: The Author, 1933.

Weeks, Stephen B. "Tennessee: A Discussion on the Sources of Its Population and the Lines of Immigration." *THM* 2 (1916), 245-53.

Williams, M. C. "Homespun Age; Pioneer Life in Western Tennessee." *Magazine of American History,* Mar. 1891, pp. 239-43.

Wirt, Alvin Bryan. *The Upper Cumberland of Pioneer Times.* Washington, D.C.: The Author, 1954. 82 pp.

Tennessee Sesquicentennial

Courtenay, Walter Rowe, D.D. "Tennessee Sesquicentennial Sermon." *THQ* 5 (1946), 343-55.

McCord, Gov. Jim Nance. "Tennessee's Sesquicentennial." *THQ* 5 (1945), 99-110, 294-303; rpt. in *Tennessee Old and New,* II, 475-85.

"Other Sesquicentennial Activities Described." *THQ* 5 (1946), 356-404.

Tennessee's Sesquicentennial Exhibition Held at the Library of Congress, Washington, D. C., June 1, 1946-October 21, 1946. Washington, D.C.: GPO, 1946. 71 pp.

Tennessee Walking Horse and Thoroughbred

Anderson, Douglas. *Making the American Thoroughbred, Especially in Tennessee, 1800-1845.* Norwood, Mass.: Plimpton, 1916. 300 pp.

"Big Lick; Tennessee Walking Horse National Celebration." *Newsweek,* Sept. 11, 1972, pp. 62 ff.

Green, Ben A. *Biography of the Tennessee Walking Horse.* Nashville: Parthenon Press, 1960. 236 pp.

McGill, W. J. "The Superior Speed and Breed of Tennessee Walking Horses." *Tennessee Walking Horse* 4 (1948), 11-15. Covers the period from 1789 to 1946.

Wallace, Louis D., ed. *The Horse and Its Heritage in Tennessee.* Nashville: Tennessee Dept. of Agriculture, 1945, 1951. 88 pp.

Warden, Margaret L. "The Fine Horse Industry in Tennessee." *THQ* 6 (1947), 134-47.

——. "A Brief History of Middle Tennessee Horse Shows." *Tennessee Walking Horse* 6 (1950), 15-23.

Webb, Joe. *The Care and Training of the Tennessee Walking Horse.* Searcy, Ark.: The Author, 1962. 120 pp.

Institutions and Personalities Important in the Preservation of Tennessee History

Beard, William E. "Albert Virgil Goodpasture: Gentleman and Scholar." *THQ* 2 (1943), 52-58. Goodpasture was editor of the *American Historical Magazine* from 1902 to 1904.

Chandler, Walter. "A Century of the Tennessee Historical Society and of Tennessee History." *THQ* 9 (1950), 3-9.

Creekmore, Pollyanna, comp. "A Bibliography of the Historical Writings of Samuel Cole Williams." ETHSP 20 (1948), 9-15.

Crouch, Billy Joe. "Judge Samuel Cole Williams, Businessman, Lawyer, Jurist, Dean and Historian." Thesis, East Tennessee State Univ., 1956.

Crownover, Arthur, Jr. "Judge John Hibbert DeWitt: A Biographical Sketch." *THQ* 1 (1942), 44-48. DeWitt established the *Tennessee Historical Magazine* in 1915.

Davidson, Donald. "John H. DeWitt: A Southern Gentle Man." *THQ* 1 (1942), 48-50.

DeWitt, John H. "William A. Provine, 1867-1935." *THM* (ser. 2) 3 (1932-37), 280-82. Provine was one of the editors of the Tennessee Historical Society's publication, the *Tennessee Historical Magazine.*

Easterly, Ambrose. "The Tennessee Library Association's First Fifty Years, 1902-1951." Thesis, George Peabody College, 1954.

Fink, Paul M. "Samuel Cole Williams." ETHSP 20 (1948), 3-8.

Folmsbee, Stanley J., ed. "Samuel Cole Williams: An Evaluation." *THQ* 7 (1948), 101-4.

Foster, Austin P. "Tennessee Department of Library Archives and History." *THM* 6 (1920), 266-78.

Garrett, William, and John M. Bass, eds. "The State Library and Museum." *AHM* 6 (1901), 350-52. Description of some of the collections housed there.

Goodpasture, Albert V. "William Robertson Garrett, A.M., Ph.D.: Founder of the *American Historical Magazine." AHM* 9 (1904), 105-12.

Green, Claud B. *John Trotwood Moore; Tennessee Man of Letters.* Athens: Univ. of Georgia Press, 1957. 189 pp.

Halley, R. A. "The Preservation of Tennessee History." *AHM* 8 (1903), 49-63.

Hesseltine, William B. *Pioneer's Mission.* Lyman Copeland Draper's biography includes his work on the preservation of Tennessee records.

Historical Records Survey, Tennessee. "The Tennessee Historical Records Survey: A Review of Five Years." ETHSP 13 (1941), 91-101.

Horn, Stanley F. "Samuel Cole Williams: In Memoriam." *THQ* 7 (1948), 99-100.

Lea, John M. "History of the Tennessee Historical Society." *AHM* 6 (1901), 353-62.

Leach, Douglas Edward. "Coming of Age: The First Twenty-One Years of the *Tennessee Historical Quarterly.*" *THQ* 22 (1963), 266-79.

Lewis, Charles Lee. "Robert Thomas Quarles and the Archives of Tennessee." *THM* 9 (1925), 3-8.

Lloyd, Ralph W. "Verton Madison Queener: An Appreciation." ETHS*P* 31 (1959), 59-62.

Luttrell, Laura E. "Historical Activities in and Respecting Tennessee, 1923-1929." ETHS*P* 2 (1930), 94-95.

Miles, Guy. "The Tennessee Antiquarian Society and the West." ETHS*P* 18 (1946), 87-106.

Moore, Mrs. John Trotwood. "The First Century of Library History in Tennessee, 1813-1913." ETHS*P* 16 (1944), 3-21.

——. "The Tennessee Historical Society, 1849-1918." *THQ* 3 (1944), 195-225; rpt. in *Tennessee Old and New*, II, 344-69.

——. "The Tennessee State Library in the Capitol." *THQ* 12 (1953), 3-22.

Owsley, Harriet C. "The Tennessee Historical Society: Its Origin, Progress and Present Condition." *THQ* 29 (1970), 227-42.

Rooker, Henry Grady. "Nathaniel Cross, the Father of the Tennessee Historical Society." *THM* (ser. 2) 3 (1932-37), 135-44.

Rothrock, Mary U. "Laura Elizabeth Luttrell." ETHS*P* 29 (1957), 3-9.

——. "Fifty Years of Lawson McGhee Library, 1917-1967." ETHS*P* 39 (1967), 7-12.

Settlemire, Claude L. "The Tennessee State Library, 1854-1923." Thesis, George Peabody College, 1951.

Smith, Michael J. "Historic Preservation in the 1970's." *THQ* 31 (1972), 187-95.

Smith, Samuel Boyd. "Remarks in Honor of Miss Mary Utopia Rothrock and the Fiftieth Anniversary of Lawson McGhee Library." ETHS*P* 39 (1967), 3-6.

Swint, Henry Lee. "The Historical Activities of the State of Tennessee." *THQ* 17 (1958), 291-300.

Williams, Samuel Cole. "The Works of Goodpasture: An Appraisal." *THQ* 2 (1943), 58-60.

JAMES G. M. RAMSEY

Eubanks, David L., ed. "J. G. M. Ramsey as a Bond Agent: Selections from the Ramsey Papers." ETHS*P* 36 (1964), 81-99.

——. "Dr. J. G. M. Ramsey of East Tennessee: A Career of Public Service." Diss., Univ. of Tennessee, 1965.

——. "The Last Years of Dr. J. G. M. Ramsey." ETHS*P* 38 (1966), 48-61.

——. "Ramsey and Draper vs. Bancroft: History for the Common Man." ETHS*P* 33 (1961), 3-16.

Hoskins, M. Margaret. "James Gettys McGready Ramsey, the Man and His Work." Thesis, Univ. of Tennessee, 1929.

Inge, M. Thomas. "G. W. Harris's 'The Doctor's Bill': A Tale about Dr. J. G. M. Ramsey." *THQ* 24 (1965), 185-94.

Garrett, William R., and J. M. Bass, eds. "Letter from Dr. J. G. M. Ramsey." *AHM* 7 (1902), 38-54. This letter was written to Gov. James D. Porter on the expulsion of William Blount from the U.S. Senate.

Ramsey, James G. M. *Annals of Tennessee.*

——. *History of Lebanon Presbyterian Church "In the Fork Five Miles East of Knoxville."* Knoxville: Larew, 1918; rpt. Knoxville: Archer & Smith, 1952. 23 pp.

——. *Autobiography and Letters,* ed. William B. Hesseltine. Nashville: Tennessee Hist. Comm., 1954. 367 pp.

Historic Sites, Preservation and Resources of Tennessee History

Alderson, William T. "Tennessee's Historic Sites Business." *THQ* 21 (1962), 318-25.

——. ed. "A Plea for the Men of the Past."*THQ* 23 (1964), 237-45. An 1852 plea for the Tennessee Historical Society.

——. *Tennessee: A Student's Guide to Localized History,* Localized History Series. New York: Teacher's College Press, 1966. 36 pp.

Alderson, William T., and Robert M. McBride. *Landmarks of Tennessee.* A compendium of cover articles appearing in the *THQ* in the 1960s.

Alderson, William T., and Hulan Glyn Thomas. *Historic Sites in Tennessee.* Nashville: Tennessee Hist. Comm., 1963. Unpaged.

Allen, Richard Sanders. *Covered Bridges of the South.* Brattleboro, Vt.: Stephen Greene, 1970. 56 pp.

Beach, Ursula Smith. "Tennessee's Covered Bridges—Past and Present." *THQ* 28 (1969), 3-23; also in *More Landmarks of Tennessee,* 53-73.

Benedict, Sarah. "Group Action in Preservation." *Antiques,* Mar. 1969, pp. 388-89.

Binkley, William C. "Some Undeveloped Phases of Tennessee History." ETHS*P* 15 (1943), 3-18.

Brown, Campbell H. "History on the Highways." *THQ* 9 (1950), 362-66. A listing of state historical markers.

Carver, Martha Cummins. "Vitalizing Tennessee History in the Junior High School." Thesis, Univ. of Tennessee, 1949.

The Charter and By-Laws of the Tennessee Historical Society, Revised October, 1878. With a List of Members. Nashville: Tennessee Hist. Soc., 1880. 24 pp.

Comstock, Charles. "Lest We Forget." *THM* 9 (1925), 31-36. Argument for need to write state and local history.

Davidson, Donald. "State History." *THM* (ser. 2) 1 (1930-31), 139-41.

Giddings, Frederick. "Early Tennessee Surveys and Maps." *TLR* 4 (1926), 115-24.

Hammond, Thomas Clark. "Planning for Preservation in Tennessee: Methods of Identification, Evaluation and Utilization of Historical and Architectural Resources." Thesis, Univ. of Tennessee, 1969.

Henneman, J. B. "Recent Tennessee History by Tennesseans." *Sewanee Review* 4 (1896), 439-66.

Horn, Stanley F. "Twenty Tennessee Books." *THQ* 17 (1958), 3-18.

——. "Twenty More Tennessee Books." *THQ* 30 (1971), 26-49.

Keeble, Edwin A. "Housing History." *THQ* 1 (1942), 147-51.

Kelley, Norma, and Jane Sparks. *Tennessee History; Resources for Teaching and Learning.* Knoxville: Knoxville City Schools, 1967. 181 pp.

McBride, Robert M., ed. *More Landmarks of Tennessee.* A continuation of the work initiated by the editor in cooperation with William T. Alderson, this is a compendium of more recent cover articles from the *THQ*.

——. "Historic Sites in Tennessee." *Antiques,* Sept. 1971. 394-401.

Moore, Frederick W. "The Recent Revival of Interest in Historical Teaching and Investigation in the South." *AHM* 9 (1904), 201-10.

Munsey, Lee A., Jr. "The Teaching of Tennessee History." Ed.D. diss., George Peabody College, 1960.

Pope, Edith. "The Necessity of Preserving Southern Historical Material." *THM* (ser. 2) 3 (1932-37), 152-59.

Schafer, Joseph. "Cooperation between State Universities and State Historical Societies." *THM* 7 (1921), 69-73.

Scofield, Edna. "The Evolution and Development of Tennessee Houses." *JTAS* 11 (1936), 229-39.

Tennessee Historical Commission. *Tennessee Historical Markers, Erected by Tennessee Historical Commission: Guide.* 5th ed., Nashville: State of Tennessee, 1962. 208 pp. 6th ed., rev. & enl., 1972. 242 pp. First published in 1952, titled *Guide to Tennessee Historical Markers.*

——. *Tennessee Junior Historian.* Nashville: State of Tennessee, 1968- . Several numbers of this publication have been issued since 1968.

Washington County Chapter, Association for the Preservation of Tennessee Antiquities. *Some Historic Landmarks of Upper East Tennessee.* Johnson City: East Tennessee State Univ., 1963. Unpaged.

Whitley, Edythe R. "Preservation and Publication of Historical Records." *DAR Magazine,* Nov. 1967, pp. 808ff.

Wingfield, Marshall, comp. "Notes: The Preservation of History in Tennessee." WTHSP 23 (1969), 129-33.

Education

Arnow, Harriette Simpson. "Education and the Professions in the Cumberland Region." *THQ* 20 (1961), 120-58.

Baughn, Milton L. "An Early Experiment in Adult Education: The Nashville Lyceum, 1830-1832." *THQ* 11 (1952), 235-45.

Beasley, Wallis. "The Life and Educational Contributions of James D. Porter." Diss., George Peabody College, 1950.

Carroll, Rosemary F. "Margaret Clark Griffis, Plantation Teacher." *THQ* 26 (1967), 295-303. Covers the period from 1858 to 1861.

Clough, Dick B. "Teacher Institutes in Tennessee, 1870-1900." *THQ* 31 (1972), 61-73.

Cummings, Charles M. "Richard Owen, Teacher in Tennessee." *THQ* 28 (1969), 273-96. Covers the years from 1840 to 1860.

Dabney, Charles William. *Universal Education in the South.* 2 vols. Chapel Hill: Univ. of North Carolina, 1936; rpt. American Education: Its Men, Institutions and Ideas Series. New York: Arno, 1969. This is an outstanding effort to trace the evolution and development of universal public education in the South from the ideas of Jefferson through the early portion of the 20th century.

Doak, H. M. "The Development of Education in Tennessee." *AHM* 8 (1903), 64-90; rpt. in *Tennessee Old and New,* II, 21-44. Treats educational history in the state before 1880.

Enslow, Ella. *See* Murray, Lena Davis.

Foster, Isabelle. "Washington College and Washington College Academy." *THQ* 30 (1971), 241-58.

Graf, LeRoy P. "Education in East Tennessee, 1867-1869: Selections from the John Eaton, Jr., Papers." *ETHSP* 23 (1951), 97-114.

Higher Education. *See* Higher Education to 1972.

McMillin, Laurence. *The Schoolmaker: Sawney Webb and the Bell Buckle Story.* Chapel Hill: Univ. of North Carolina Press, 1971.

The biography of one of the greatest figures in private school education in the history of the state. A stern disciplinarian, "Old Sawney" stood for classical education and character building.

McMurtry, Horace. "Readings on Tennessee's Rural Educational History prior to 1873." Thesis, George Peabody College, 1923.

Middlebrooks, John Enoch. "A History of the Rise and Fall of the Academies in Tennessee." Thesis, George Peabody College, 1923.

Murray, Lena Davis [pseud. Ella Enslow], with Alvin F. Harlow. *Schoolhouse in the Foothills.* New York: Simon, 1935. 239 pp. Relates to early 19th-century schools.

Nagy, J. Emerick. "Wanted: A Teacher for the Nashville English School." *THQ* 21 (1962), 171-86. Covers the period from 1821 to 1830.

O'Donnell, James H., III. "Taylor Thistle: A Student at the Nashville Institute, 1871-1880." *THQ* 26 (1967), 387-95.

Parks, Edd Winfield. "Sawney Webb: Tennessee's Schoolmaster." *NCHR* 12 (1935), 233-51.

Pridgen, Esther Pritchett. "The Influence of Samuel Doak upon Education in Early East Tennessee." Thesis, East Tennessee State Univ., 1952.

Provine, William A. "Tennessee's Earliest Educational Institutions." *THM* (ser. 2) 2 (1931-32), 165-78.

Purcell, Richard J. "Pioneer Irish Educators in Tennessee." *Catholic Educational Review* 34 (1936), 406-13.

Rogers, Lucille. *Light from Many Candles; a History of Pioneer Women in Education in Tennessee.* Nashville: McQuiddy, 1960. 318 pp.

Schuler, Elizabeth. "History of Education in Tennessee during the Reconstruction Period." Thesis, George Peabody College, 1918.

Todd, Herbert H. "The History of Educational Legislation in Tennessee to 1860." Thesis, George Peabody College, 1927.

Underwood, Betsy Swint. "The Life of a Young Girl in a Female Academy, 1848-1850: The Letters of Rachel Jackson Lawrence." *THQ* 21 (1962), 162-70.

Utley, Buford C. "The Early Academies of West Tennessee." *WTHSP* 8 (1954), 5-38.

Ward, Harold F. "Academy Education in Tennessee prior to 1861." Thesis, George Peabody College, 1926.

Webb, William R., Jr. "Swaney Webb, My Father and His Ideals of Education." *Sewanee Review* 50 (1942), 227-40.

Whitaker, Arthur P. "The Public School System of Tennessee, 1834-1860." *THM* 2 (1916), 1-30.

White, Robert H. *The Development of the Tennessee State Education Organization, 1796-1929.* Diss., George Peabody College, 1929. Kingsport: Southern, 1929. 289 pp.

Williams, Emma Inman, ed. "Some Letters of Elijah Bigelow and His Family." WTHS*P* 1 (1947), 103-16. Bigelow was a pioneer West Tennessee educator of the 1820s.

Williams, Samuel Cole. "Moses Fisk." ETHS*P* 20 (1948), 16-36. Fisk was an early Middle Tennessee educator.

GENERAL HISTORY: 1900-72

Anderson, Louis V. "The Effects of Desegregation on the Achievement and Personality Patterns of Negro Children." Diss., George Peabody College, 1966.

Anderson, Margaret. *The Children of the South,* foreword Ralph McGill. New York: Farrar, 1966. 208 pp. Desegregation at Clinton, 1956.

Batts, William O. *Private Preparatory Schools for Boys in Tennessee since 1867.* Nashville: Parthenon Press, 1957. 86 pp.

Bullock, Henry Allen. *A History of Negro Education in the South: From 1619 to Present.* Cambridge, Mass.: Harvard Univ. Press, 1967; rpt. New York: Praeger, 1970. 339 pp. Bullock treats Negro education as a force for social change and, in fact, the main thrust by which the fight has continued to complete the emancipation of the Negro American.

Carr, Margaret Thompson. "A History of the Tennessee School for the Deaf." Thesis, Univ. of Tennessee, 1941.

Carter, Judson McGilvray. "Development of the Tennessee Education Association." Thesis, Duke Univ., 1938.

Cheshier, Cavit C. "The Teacher Tenure Movement in Tennessee." Thesis, George Peabody College, 1961.

Cohron, Mary N. "A History of State Care of the Blind and Deaf in Tennessee." Thesis, Univ. of Tennessee, 1932.

Cushing, Arthur Leavitt. "A Comparative Analysis of the North Carolina and Tennessee Tax Support of Public Education." Thesis, Middle Tennessee State Univ., 1967.

Egerton, John. "Pebbles." *Southern Education Report*, Sept.-Oct. 1965, pp. 14-18. A residential summer school at Tennessee Technological University for Appalachian youth.

——. "One Teacher Schools Are Still Around." *Southern Education Report*, Oct. 1966, pp. 5-9. There were 160 such schools in Tennessee in 1966.

——. "Pebbles Revisited." *Southern Education Report*, Oct. 1967, pp. 7-11.

England, Lurad R. "The Development of Public Vocational Education in Tennessee." Diss., George Peabody College, 1952.

Gibbs, James E. *Public Education in Tennessee: Grades 1 through 12. Digest of a Report to the Education Survey Subcommittee of the Tennessee Legislative Council. Submitted November 18, 1957, by James E. Gibbs, Director of the Study.* Nashville: State of Tennessee, 1957. 90 pp.

Griffith, Chester Clinton. "Constitutional and Legal Status of Compulsory Education in Tennessee." Thesis, George Peabody College, 1935.

Hale, Anna Beatryce. "A Study of the Negro Department of the Tennessee School for the Deaf." Thesis, Univ. of Tennessee, 1948.

Harlan, Louis R. "The Southern Education Board and the Race Issue in Public Education." *JSH* 23 (1957), 189-202.

Hearn, Edell Midgett. "Public Educational Changes through Legislation in Tennessee." Diss., Univ. of Tennessee, 1959.

Hill, Claude M., Jr. "The Administration of Educational Services of the State of Tennessee State Board of Education." Thesis, George Peabody College, 1954.

Holcomb, Marjoriebell S. "A Recent History and the Present Status of the Tennessee School for the Deaf." Thesis, Univ. of Tennessee, 1957.

Holt, Andrew David. *The Struggle for a State System of Public Schools in Tennessee, 1903-1936.* Diss., Columbia Univ., 1938. New York: Teachers College, Columbia Univ., 1938; rpt. New York: AMS, 1972. 502 pp. An outstanding survey of 20th-century efforts to establish a strong public school system.

Howard, George C., Jr., and Edith Foster Howard. *City-County Educational Relationships in Tennessee.* Knoxville: Bureau of Public Administration, Univ. of Tennessee, 1950. 32 leaves.

Hughes, Owen Rogers. "The Evolution of the Tennessee Public School System." Thesis, George Peabody College, 1920.

Knight, Edgar W. *A Documentary History of Education in the South before 1860.* 5 vols. Chapel Hill: Univ. of North Carolina Press, 1949-1953; 3rd ed., Westport, Conn.: Greenwood, 1951.

Lewis, Charles Lee. *Philander Priestly Claxton: Crusader for Public Education.* Knoxville: Univ. of Tennessee Press, 1948. 380 pp. Claxton was one of the most distinguished educators Tennessee has produced. He was the central figure of the educational revival, 1900-1912, was United States commissioner of education, and was later president of Austin Peay State University.

McKinstry, E. Richard. "The 1953 Tennessee Textbook Investigation." Thesis, Univ. of Tennessee, 1971.

McMillen, Neil R. "Organized Resistance to School Desegregation in Tennessee." *THQ* 30 (1971), 315-28.

Myllymaki, Kathy Kay. "Behind the Fence. A Study of the Tennessee Vocational School at Tullahoma." Thesis, Middle Tennessee State Univ., 1965.

Nants, J. Stanley. "Comparative Study of the Common School Systems of Massachusetts, Tennessee and Washington and the Laws under Which They Are Organized and Operated." Thesis, Teachers College, Columbia Univ., 1910.

Nicholson, William B. "History of the Education of the Blind in Tennessee." Thesis, George Peabody College, 1928.

100th Anniversary of the Tennessee School for the Deaf, 1845-1945. Knoxville: Archer & Smith, 1945. 193 pp.

Parsons, Rhey Boyd. . . . *Teacher Education in Tennessee* . . . . Diss., Univ. of Chicago, 1935. Chicago: Privately printed, 1935. 265 pp.

Pearson, Eugene L. *Tennessee Education, 1780-1962.* Nashville: Tennessee Dept. of Education, 1963. 38 pp.

Simmons, Ira Fred. "The Private Chartered Educational Institutions of Tennessee." Diss., George Peabody College, 1934.

Sinclair, Francis. "Sir Francis Joseph Campbell, Noted Educator of Blind, Was Tennessean." *THM* (ser. 2) 3 (1932-37), 185-88.

Smith, Samuel Boyd. "Tennessee Department of Education." *Education in the States: Historical Development and Outlook,* 1173-98. Washington, D.C.: Nat. Ed. Assoc., 1969. A history of the department's development.

Smith, Will Dunn. "History of the Tennessee Education Association." Diss., George Peabody College, 1952.

Tennessee State Department of Education. *Statistical Report.* Nashville: State of Tennessee, 1870- . The annual reports were included in the general report of the Tennessee State Department of Education before the 1940-41 publication.

———. *Public Education in Tennessee; a Study of Tennessee's Program of Public Education and Suggestions for Continuing Its Development.* Nashville: State of Tennessee, 1946. 407 pp. A report prepared in accordance with chap. 121, *Public Acts of Tennessee, 1945.*

———. "Public Education for Negroes in Tennessee." Nashville: Unpublished typescript, 1950. 60 pp.

Turner, William E. "A Survey of Negro High Schools in Tennessee." Thesis, Univ. of Tennessee, 1933.

Wade, Bailey Meador. "The Development of Secondary Education in Tennessee." Diss., George Peabody College, 1938.

Whitaker, John Ulna, Jr. "Influence of the Governors on Education in Tennessee, 1937-1957." Thesis, Univ. of Tennessee, 1958.

Williams, Frank B., Jr. "The East Tennessee Education Association, 1903-1954." ETHS*P* 27 (1955), 49-76.

Womack, Bob J. "The Enactment of a State School Program in Tennessee." Ed.D. diss., George Peabody College, 1956.

HIGHER EDUCATION TO 1972

Come, Donald R. "The Influence of Princeton on Higher Education in the South before 1825." *William and Mary Quarterly* (ser. 3) 2 (1945), 359-96.

Diekhoff, John Siemon, Ida Long Rogers, and Monnie S. Hatcher. *A Study of Private Higher Education in Tennessee. A Study Sponsored by Tennessee Council of Private Colleges and Tennessee Higher Education Commission.* Nashville: Tennessee Council of Private Colleges and the Tennessee Higher Ed. Comm., 1970. 71 pp.

Egerton, John. *The Black Public Colleges: Integregation and Disintegregation.* Nashville: Race Relations Information Center, 1971. 31 pp.

Horton, Allison Norman. "Origin and Development of the State College Movement in Tennessee." Ed.D. diss., George Peabody College, 1953.

Long, Herman H. "The Status of Desegregated Higher Education in Tennessee." *Journal of Negro Education* 27 (1958), 311-17.

——. "The Negro Public College in Tennessee." *Journal of Negro Education* 31 (1962), 341-48.

Merriam, Lucius S. *Higher Education in Tennessee,* Contributions to American Educational History, no. 16. Washington, D. C.: GPO, 1893. 287 pp.

Mitchell, Enoch L. "College Life in Ante-bellum Tennessee." WTHSP 12 (1958), 5-39.

Rankin, Robert Stanley. "The Oldest College West of the Alleghenies." ETHSP 1 (1929), 19-26. Refers to Greeneville College chartered in 1794.

Rensi, Ray C. "Josephus Hopwood: Christian Educator." Thesis, East Tennessee State Univ., 1964.

Roberts, S. O. "Negro Higher and Professional Education in Tennessee." *Journal of Negro Education* 17 (1948), 361-72.

Swint, Henry Lee. "Higher Education in the Tennessee-Kentucky Region a Century Ago." *THQ* 2 (1943), 129-43.

Tennessee General Assembly, Legislative Council Committee. *General Plan; Survey of Higher Education in Tennessee.* Nashville: State of Tennessee, 1956. 21 leaves.

Tennessee Higher Education Commission. *Biennial Report.* Nashville: State of Tennessee, 1970- . The first report covered the years 1967 to 1969. 36 pp.

Ward, Richard Hiram. "The Development of Baptist Higher Education in Tennessee." Diss., George Peabody College, 1953.

INDIVIDUAL FOUR-YEAR COLLEGE AND UNIVERSITY HISTORIES

Belmont College

Duncan, Ivar Lou M. *A History of Belmont College.* Nashville: n.p., 1967. 15 pp.

Bethel College

Newton, James A. "Early History of Bethel College." WTHSP 9 (1955), 119-37.

Burritt College

West, Francis Marion. "Pioneer of the Cumberlands: A History of

Burritt College, 1848-1938." Thesis, Tennessee Technological Univ., 1969.

Carson-Newman College

Carr, Isaac N. *History of Carson-Newman College, 1851-1959.* Jefferson City: Carson-Newman College, 1959. 421 pp.

Hall, William Franklin. "The History of Carson-Newman College." Thesis, Univ. of Tennessee, 1936.

Cumberland Female College

Nunley, Joe Edwin. "A History of Cumberland Female College, McMinnville, Tennessee." Ed.D. diss., Univ. of Tennessee, 1964.

Cumberland University

Bone, Winstead Paine. *A History of Cumberland University, 1842-1935.* Lebanon: The Author, 1935. 303 pp.

Crabb, Alfred Leland. "James Priestley, Pioneer Schoolmaster." *THQ* 12 (1953), 129-34.

David Lipscomb College

Hooper, Robert Eugene. "The Political and Educational Ideas of David Lipscomb." Diss., George Peabody College, 1965.

Neil, Robert G. "A History of David Lipscomb College." Thesis, George Peabody College, 1938.

West, Earl. *The Life and Times of David Lipscomb.* Henderson: Religious Bk., 1954. 287 pp.

East Tennessee State University

Burleson, David Sinclair. *History of the East Tennessee State College.* Johnson City: n.p., 1947. 102 pp.

Fisk University

Campbell, Robert F. "Negro Colleges Have a Job." *Southern Educational Report,* Nov. 1967, pp. 3-9.

Richardson, Joe M. "Fisk University: The First Critical Years." *THQ* 29 (1970), 24-41.

Taylor, Alrutheus A. "Fisk University and the Nashville Community

1866-1900." *Journal of Negro History* 39 (1954), 111-26.

Tipton, C. Robert. "The Fisk Jubilee Singers." *THQ* 29 (1970), 42-48.

Franklin College

Scobey, James E., ed. *Franklin College and Its Influences.* Nashville: McQuiddy, 1906. 454 pp.

George Peabody College

Bailey, Joseph C. "Seaman A. Knapp, Schoolmaster of American Agriculture." Diss., Columbia Univ., 1944.

Baird, James O. "The Life and Works of Charles Edgar Little." Diss., George Peabody College, 1949. Little was a professor at George Peabody College.

Bass, John M. "Rev. Thomas Craighead." *AHM* 7 (1902), 88-96.

Boom, Aaron M., ed. "A Student at the University of Nashville: Correspondence of John Donelson Coffee, 1830-1833." *THQ* 16 (1957), 141-59. The University of Nashville was a predecessor of George Peabody College.

Connor, R. D. W. "The Peabody Education Fund." *South Atlantic Quarterly* 4 (1905), 169-81.

Crabb, Alfred Leland. *The Genealogy of George Peabody College for Teachers Covering a Period of One Hundred and Fifty Years.* Nashville: n.p., 1935. 56 pp.

——. *The Historical Background of Peabody College, Covering a Period of One Hundred and Fifty-five Years.* Nashville: George Peabody College, 1941. 41 pp.

Cullum, Edward Neely. "George Peabody College for Teachers, 1914-1937." Ed.D. diss., George Peabody College, 1963.

Dillingham, George A., Jr. "Peabody Normal College in Southern Education 1875-1909." Diss., George Peabody College, 1970.

Duncan, Ruth Batterton. "A History of the George Peabody College Library, 1785-1910." Thesis, George Peabody College, 1940.

Garrett, William R. "The Genesis of the Peabody College for Teachers." *AHM* 8 (1903), 14-25.

Garrett, William R., and John M. Bass, eds. "Memorial of the

President and Trustees of the University of Nashville to the Congress of the United States." *AHM* 7 (1902), 80-87.

George Peabody College for Teachers. *The Semicentennial of George Peabody College for Teachers, 1875-1925. The Proceedings of the Semicentennial Celebration February 18, 19, and 20, 1925,* ed. Charles E. Little. Nashville: George Peabody College, 1925. 188 pp.

Halsey, LeRoy Jones. *A Sketch of the Life and Educational Labors of Philip Lindsley, D.D., Late President of the University of Nashville.* Hartford, Conn.: Williams, Wiley & Turner, 1859. 46 pp.

Haunton, Richard H. "Education and Democracy: The Views of Philip Lindsley." *THQ* 21 (1962), 131-39.

Kegley, Tracy M. "Bushrod Rust Johnson: Soldier and Teacher." *THQ* 7 (1948), 249-58.

Kelton, Allen. "The University of Nashville: 1850-1875." Diss., George Peabody College, 1969.

Lindsley, Philip. *The Cause of Education in Tennessee. An Address Delivered to the Young Gentlemen Admitted to the Degree of Bachelor of Arts, at the First Commencement of the University of Nashville, October 4, 1826.* Nashville: Hunt, Tardiff, 1826, 1832, 1833. 39 pp.

———. *The Works of Philip Lindsley, D.D., Formerly Vice-President and President Elect of the College of New Jersey, Princeton; and Late President of the University of Nashville, Tennessee . . . . With Introductory Notices of His Life and Labours,* ed. Le Roy Jones Halsey. 3 vols. Philadelphia: Lippincott, 1866.

Little, Charles E. "John Berrien Lindsley." *AHM* 3 (1898), 32-41.

———, comp. *George Peabody College for Teachers: Its Evolution and Present Status, September 1912.* Nashville: George Peabody College, 1912. 164 pp.

McCann, Bess. "The Faculty of George Peabody College for Teachers, 1914-1936." Thesis, George Peabody College, 1936.

Mason, Julian. "The Wit and Wisdom of Philip Lindsley." Thesis, George Peabody College, 1954.

Morgan, Kenimer Houze. "The University of Nashville, 1825-1850." Diss., George Peabody College, 1960.

Parker, Franklin. *George Peabody, 1796-1869, Founder of Modern Philanthropy.* Nashville: George Peabody College, 1955. 32 pp.

——. "George Peabody, Founder of Modern Philanthropy." 3 vol. Ed.D. diss., George Peabody College, 1956.

——. "George Peabody's Influence on Southern Educational Philanthropy." *THQ* 20 (1961), 65-74.

——. *George Peabody: A Biography.* Nashville: Vanderbilt Univ. Press, 1971. 233 pp. The first great 19th-century philanthropist, founder of Peabody College.

Poret, George Cleveland. "The Contributions of William Harold Payne to Public Education." Diss., George Peabody College, 1930.

Shapiro, Jacob W. "Growth of a Philosophy: Hanor A. Webb." Thesis, George Peabody College, 1963. A 20th-century Peabody professor.

Windrow, John Edwin. *John Berrien Lindsley: Educator, Physician, Social Philosopher.* Diss., George Peabody College, 1937. Chapel Hill: Univ. of North Carolina Press, 1938. 240 pp. A fine biography of this distinguished educator who headed the University of Nashville from 1855 to 1870 and founded its medical school.

Woolverton, John F. "Philip Lindsley and the Cause of Education in the Old Southwest." *THQ* 19 (1960), 3-22.

Johnson Bible College

Brown, Alva Ross. *Standing on the Promises: A Memorial to Two of the Grandest Lives That This World Ever Has Known or Ever Shall Know.* Knoxville: Newman, 1928. 271 pp. Treats Ashley S. and Emma Strawn Johnson, and Johnson Bible College.

Lambuth College

Herron, W. W. "A History of Lambuth College." WTHSP 10 (1956), 20-37.

Hinton, David Edgar. "Origin, Development, and Aims of Lambuth College." Thesis, George Peabody College, 1936.

Lane College

Adair, Thomas Jackson. "Bishop Isaac Lane, a Portrait: 1834-1914." Thesis, Tennessee State A&I Univ., 1956.

Savage, Horace C. *Life and Times of Bishop Isaac Lane.* Nashville: National, 1958. 240 pp.

Le Moyne-Owen College

Qualls, J. Winfield. "The Beginnings and Early History of the Le Moyne School at Memphis—1871-1874." Thesis, Memphis State Univ., 1952.

——. "The Beginnings and Early History of the Le Moyne School at Memphis, 1871-1874." WTHSP 7 (1953), 5-37.

Lincoln Memorial University

Shumate, Mildred B. *Our Story, Lincoln Memorial University.* Harrogate: n.p., 1966.

Madison College

Sandborn, William Cruzan. "The History of Madison College." Ed.D. diss., George Peabody College, 1953.

Martin College

Allen, Paul F. *A History of Martin College: The First 100 Years.* Pulaski: Martin College, 1971. 49 pp.

Maryville College

Lloyd, Ralph Waldo. *Maryville College: A History of 150 Years, 1819-1969.* Maryville: Maryville College Press, 1969. 287 pp.

Robinson, John J. *Memoir of Rev. Isaac Anderson, Late President of Maryville College, and Professor of Theology.* Knoxville: J. Addison Rayl, 1860. 300 pp.

Wilson, Samuel Tyndale. *A Century of Maryville College, 1819-1919, a Story of Altruism.* Maryville: Maryville College, 1916. 265 pp. Rpt. in *Chronicles of Maryville College,* bk. 1. Maryville: Maryville College, 1935. 334 pp.

——. *Isaac Anderson, Founder and First President of Maryville College: A Memorial Sketch.* Maryville: Privately printed, 1932. 168 pp.

——. *Chronicles of Maryville College; a Story of Altruism: A Century of Maryville College and Second Century Beginnings.* 2 vols. in 1.

Meharry Medical School

Flake, Tom. "Meharry Is Convinced It Is Needed." *Southern Education Report,* Nov. 1967, pp. 10-11.

"Medical Discoveries on a Shoe String." *Business Week,* June 15, 1968, pp. 92-94. Concerns Meharry Medical School.

Memphis State University

Chumney, James R., Jr. "West Tennessee College Teacher: Nellie Angel Smith at Memphis State 1927-1952." WTHSP 21 (1967), 80-92.

Ford, Helen Lytle. "An Academic History of the State Teachers College, Memphis." Thesis, George Peabody College, 1937.

Stathis, John C. "The Establishment and Early Development of the West Tennessee State Normal School 1909-1914." Thesis, Memphis State Univ., 1951.

——. "The Establishment of the West Tennessee State Normal School 1909-1914." WTHSP 10 (1956), 78-99.

Wooten, Rebecca Grantham. "A History of Memphis State College." Thesis, Univ. of Texas, 1942.

Middle Tennessee State University

Pittard, Homer P. "Middle Tennessee State College: Its Historical Aspects and Its Relation to Significant Teacher Education Movements." Ed.D. diss., George Peabody College, 1957.

Southwestern at Memphis

Cooper, Waller Raymond. *Southwestern at Memphis, 1848-1948.* Richmond, Va.: John Knox Press, 1949. 172 pp.

Tennessee State Agricultural and Industrial University

Lloyd, Raymond Grann. *Tennessee Agricultural and Industrial State University, 1912-1962; Fifty Years of Leadership through Excellence, 1912-1962.* Nashville: n.p., 1962. 73 pp.

Tennessee Technological University

Smith, Austin Wheeler. *The Story of Tennessee Tech.* Cookeville: n.p., 1957; rpt. Nashville: McQuiddy, 1957. 326 pp.

Tennessee Wesleyan College

Martin, LeRoy Albert. *A History of Tennessee Wesleyan College, 1857-1957.* Athens: Tennessee Wesleyan College, 1957. 296 pp.

Tusculum College

Bailey, Gilbert L. "A History of Tusculum College, 1944-1964." Thesis, East Tennessee State Univ., 1965.

Haynes, Grace. *The Daddy Haynes Story, The Life of Professor Landon Carter Haynes.* Morristown: Morristown Printing, 1968; rpt. Charlotte, N.C.: Carolina Ruling, 1968. 319 pp. Professor of mathematics at Tusculum College for 40 years, Haynes died in 1956.

Ragan, Allen E. *A History of Tusculum College, 1794-1944.* Greeneville: Tusculum Sesquicentennial Comm., 1945. 274 pp.

Union University

Rutledge, Rosa Dyer. "Union University through the Century (1834-1950)." WTHSP 4 (1950), 83-96.

University of the South [Sewanee]

Chitty, Arthur B., Jr. *Reconstruction at Sewanee: The Founding of the University of the South and Its First Administration, 1857-1872.* Sewanee: Univ. of the South Press, 1954; rpt. Memphis: LeMoyne, 1970. 206 pp.

Du Bose, William P. "The Romance and Genius of a University." *Sewanee Review* 13 (1905), 496-502.

Fairbanks, George R. *History of the University of the South at Sewanee, Tennessee, from Its Founding by the Southern Bishops, Clergy and Laity of the Episcopal Church in 1857 to the Year 1905.* Jacksonville, Fla.: H. & W. B. Drew, 1905. 403 pp.

Finney, Raymond A. "History of the Private Educational Institutions of Franklin County, Tennessee." Thesis, Univ. of Tennessee, 1939. Includes the University of the South.

Gailor, Thomas Frank. *Some Memories.* Kingsport: Southern, 1937. 339 pp. The author was vice chancellor at the University of the South from 1908 to 1935.

Gessell, J. M. "Test at Sewanee." *Christian Century,* May 16, 1962, pp. 626-27.

Guerry, Moultrie. *Men Who Made Sewanee, for Makers of Sewanee To-day; Biographical Sketches.* Sewanee: Univ. of the South Press, 1932. 102 pp.

Helvenston, Reginald H. *A Common Heritage; Franklin County, Tennessee, and the University of the South at Sewanee, Tennessee.* Sewanee: Sewanee Univ. Press, 1970.

Keene, Charles Jonas, Jr. "Alexander Guerry: Educator." Diss., George Peabody College, 1952.

McCrady, James Waring, and Bruce Rodarmor. *Under the Sun at Sewanee.* Sewanee: Univ. of the South Press, 1967. 117 pp.

Percy, William Alexander. *Sewanee.* Sewanee: n.p., n.d.

University of Tennessee

Davis, Curtis Carroll. "James Hays Piper, a Sketch." *THQ* 10 (1951), 46-54. Piper was president of East Tennessee College, a predecessor of the University of Tennessee.

De Carlo, Vincent R. "The Net Direct Economic Effect of the University of Tennessee on the City of Knoxville and on Knox County Resulting from the Expansion of the Knoxville Campus since 1962." Thesis, Univ. of Tennessee, 1969.

Dabney, Charles W. "Educational Work in Tennessee." *Annals,* Sept. 1903, pp. 284-86.

Egerton, John. "Suit Unresolved on Dual Colleges." *Race Relations Reporter,* May 3, 1971, pp. 4-6. Involves the University of Tennessee at Nashville, and Tennessee State University.

Folmsbee, Stanley J., ed. "The Laws of East Tennessee College, 1821." *ETHSP* 16 (1944), 97-108.

———. *Blount College and East Tennessee College, 1794-1840: The First Predecessors of the University of Tennessee.* ETHSP 17 (1945), 22-50; rpt. Knoxville: Univ. of Tennessee *Record* 49, no. 1 (Jan. 1946). 50 pp.

———. "East Tennessee University, Pre-war Years, 1840-1861." *ETHSP* 22 (1950), 60-93.

———. *East Tennessee University, 1840-1879, Predecessor of The University of Tennessee.* Knoxville: Univ. of Tennessee *Record* 62, no. 3 (May 1959). 143 pp.

———. *Tennessee Establishes a State University: First Years of The*

University of Tennessee, 1879-1887. Knoxville: Univ. of Tennessee *Record* 64, no. 3 (May 1961). 214 pp.

——. "The Early History of The University of Tennessee: An Address in Commemoration of Its 175th Anniversary." ETHS*P* 42 (1970), 3-19.

Gaither, Gerald H., and James R. Montgomery, eds. "Letters of Samuel Henry Lockett: Professor and Commandant at the University of Tennessee." ETHS*P* 42 (1970), 108-23.

Holt, Andrew David. *The University of Tennessee; Dynamic Spirit of the Volunteer State.* New York: Newcomen Soc., 1966. 28 pp.

Laws of the College of East Tennessee. Knoxville: Ramsey & Craighead, 1838. 22 pp.

Montgomery, James Riley. *The University of Tennessee Builds for the Twentieth Century; a History of The University of Tennessee during the Administration of President Brown Ayres, 1904-1919.* Thesis, Univ. of Tennessee, 1956. Knoxville: Univ. of Tennessee *Record* 60, no. 4 (July 1957). 97 pp.

——., ed. "Benton White's Recollections of the University of Tennessee." ETHS*P* 33 (1961), 78-96.

——. "The Summer School of the South." *THQ* 22 (1963), 361-81.

——. *The Volunteer State Forges Its University: The University of Tennessee, 1887-1919.* Diss., Columbia Univ., 1961. Knoxville: Univ. of Tennessee *Record* 69, no. 6 (Nov. 1966). 231 pp. Montgomery traces the development of the state university from a small school upon a hill in Knoxville to a statewide campus.

——. *Threshold of a New Day: The University of Tennessee, 1919-1946.* Knoxville: Univ. of Tennessee *Record* 74, no. 6 (Nov. 1971). 432 pp.

Oakes, William Oscar. "An Organizational Structure for the University of Tennessee Systems-Level Administration." Ed.D. diss., Univ. of Tennessee, 1970.

Sanford, Edward T. *Blount College and the University of Tennessee. An Historical Address Delivered before the Alumni Association and Members of the University of Tennessee, June 12th, 1894.* Knoxville: Univ. of Tennessee, 1894. 119 pp.

Simpson, Evelyn Shipe. "The Development of Home Economics at the University of Tennessee." Diss., Univ. of Tennessee, 1961.

Sims, Almon James. *A History of Extension Work in Tennessee;*

Twenty-five Years of Service to Rural Life, 1914-1939. Knoxville: Agricultural Extension Service, Univ. of Tennessee, 1939. 44 pp.

"Summer School of the South." *Outlook,* Aug. 2, 1902, pp. 894-96.

Tennessee Agricultural Hall of Fame. *Harcourt Alexander Morgan; Scientist—Teacher—Public Servant, Philosopher Who Inspired Others to Higher Vision, Builder of Soil and Men.* Nashville: State of Tennessee, 1950. Various pagings.

The University of Tennessee Sesqui-centennial, 1794-1944. Knoxville: Univ. of Tennessee Press, 1945. 217 pp.

White, Moses. *Early History of the University of Tennessee. Address Delivered before the Alumni Association. With a Poem by Rev. J. H. Martin. June 17, 1879.* Knoxville: Board of Trustees, Univ. of Tennessee, 1879. 80 pp.

Wills, U. G. "How Nixon Used the Media, Billy Graham and the Good Lord to Rap with Students at the University of Tennessee." *Esquire,* Sept. 1970, pp. 119-22.

ACADEMIC FREEDOM IN THE 1920s

"Dismissal of Professors at the University of Tennessee." *School and Society,* Apr. 26, 1924, pp. 487-88.

"Monkeying." *Nation,* Aug. 1, 1923, pp. 104ff. Relates to difficulties at the University of Tennessee.

"Professorial Fiasco." *New Republic,* May 28, 1924, pp. 6-7.

MILITARY AND SPORTS PROGRAMS

Arwood, Victor B. "The History of Varsity Basketball at the University of Tennessee." Thesis, Univ. of Tennessee, 1968.

Harris, Edward M. *Bob Neyland: 37 Years a Volunteer.* Knoxville: n.p., 1962. Unpaged.

Jarrell, John Eben. "The History and Development of the Air Force Reserve Officers' Training Corps at the University of Tennessee." Thesis, Univ. of Tennessee, 1956.

Siler, Thomas T. *The Volunteers, an Informal History of Tennessee Football, 1890-1950; Glamour and Pathos, Laughter and Tears, Victory and Defeat at the University of Tennessee.* Knoxville: Archer & Smith, 1950. 102 pp.

——. *Tennessee: Football's Greatest Dynasty.* Knoxville: Holston, 1961. 90 pp.

——. *Tennessee's Dazzling Decade, 1960-1970.* Knoxville: Hodge, 1970. 112 pp.

UNIVERSITY OF TENNESSEE AT CHATTANOOGA

Govan, Gilbert E., and James W. Livingood. *The University of Chattanooga: Sixty Years.* Chattanooga: Univ. of Chattanooga, 1947. 271 pp. The evolution of this institution, now a part of The University of Tennessee system, from its beginning in 1886 to 1946.

UNIVERSITY OF TENNESSEE AT MARTIN

Inman, Elmer B. "A History of the Development of the University of Tennessee, Martin Branch." Ed.D. diss., Univ. of Tennessee, 1960.

Vanderbilt University

Binkley, William C. "The Contribution of Walter Lynwood Fleming to Southern Scholarship." *JSH* 5 (1939), 143-54.

Brown, Oswald E., James H. Kirkland, and Edwin Mims. *God and the New Knowledge.* Nashville: Cole Lecture Foundation, Vanderbilt Univ., 1926. 109 pp.

Gross, John O. "The Bishops versus Vanderbilt University." *Methodist History* 2 (1963-64), 23-34; *THQ* 22 (1963), 53-65.

Hardacre, Paul H. "History and Historians at Vanderbilt, 1875-1918." *THQ* 25 (1966), 22-31.

Hargrove, R. K. "The Founders and Organizers of Vanderbilt University." *Vanderbilt University Quarterly* 1 (1901), 99-115.

Kirkland, James H. "Twenty-five Years of University Work." *Vanderbilt University Quarterly* 1 (1901), 86-99.

Lee, John David, Jr. "The Separation of Vanderbilt University from the Methodist Episcopal Church South." B.D. thesis, Duke Univ., 1934.

McGaw, Robert A. "A Brief History of Vanderbilt University." Unpublished typescript, 1964. 16 pp.

"Methodist Church and the University." *Independent,* Jan. 3, 1907, pp. 52-53.

Mims, Edwin. *Chancellor Kirkland of Vanderbilt.* Nashville: Vanderbilt Univ. Press, 1940. 362 pp. The best profile of this distinguished head of Vanderbilt University from 1893 to 1937.

——. *History of Vanderbilt University.* Nashville: Vanderbilt Univ. Press, 1946. 497 pp. The best survey of Vanderbilt's origin and development as an outstanding regional university, covering the period from 1875 to 1945.

Nelson, J. R. "Vanderbilt's Time of Testing." *Christian Century*, Aug. 10, 1960, pp. 921-25.

Snyder, Henry Nelson. *Vanderbilt University in Some of Its Relations to Higher Education in the South.* Nashville: Methodist Pub. House, 1898.

Swint, Henry Lee. "William Campbell Binkley, 1889-1970: Historian, Editor, Teacher." *JSH* 37 (1971), 353-66.

Tigert, John J. *Bishop Holland Nimmons McTyeire: Ecclesiastical and Educational Architect.* Nashville: Vanderbilt Univ. Press, 1955. 279 pp.

Washington College

Calhoun, William Gunn. *Samuel Doak, 1749-1830, His Life, His Children [and] Washington College.* Washington College: Pioneer, 1966. 51 pp.

Carr, Howard Ernest. *Washington College; a Study of an Attempt to Provide Higher Education in Eastern Tennessee.* Thesis, Duke Univ., 1935. Knoxville: Newman, 1935. 282 pp.

Foster, Isabelle. "Washington College and Washington College Academy." *THQ* 30 (1971), 241-58.

Pridgen, Esther P. "The Influence of Doctor Samuel Doak upon Education in Early East Tennessee." Thesis, East Tennessee State College, 1952.

The Negro since the Civil War

GENERAL HISTORY: 1860-1900

Buggs, John Allen. "Racial Legislation in Tennessee: A Contribution to the Natural History of Laws Regarding Race and Social Status." Thesis, Fisk Univ., 1941.

Bullock, Henry A. *A History of Negro Education in the South: From 1619 to the Present.* Cambridge: Harvard Univ. Press, 1967; rpt. New York: Praeger, 1970. 339 pp.

Cartwright, Joseph H. "The Negro in Tennessee Politics, 1880-1891." Thesis, Vanderbilt Univ., 1968.

Corlew, Robert E. "The Negro in Tennessee, 1870-1900." Diss., Univ. of Alabama, 1954.

Folmsbee, Stanley J. "The Origin of the First 'Jim Crow' Law." *JSH* 15 (1949), 235-47.

Gaither, Gerald H. "Blacks and the Populist Revolt: Balance and Bigotry in the New South." Diss., Univ. of Tennessee, 1972.

Johnson, Clifton H. "Some Archival Sources on Negro History in Tennessee." *THQ* 28 (1969), 417-27.

Jordan, Weymouth T. "The Negro in Tennessee during Reconstruction." Thesis, Vanderbilt Univ., 1934.

Kennedy, Elizabeth Carolyn. "The Development of Higher Education in Tennessee for Negroes from 1865-1900." Thesis, Fisk Univ., 1950.

Marsh, J. B. T. *The Story of the Jubilee Singers: With Their Songs.* London: Hodder & Staughton, 1877, 1903. 248 pp. Rpt. Boston: Houghton, 1880; rev. ed., Westport, Conn.: Greenwood, 1881; rpt. New York: Green, 1883; rpt., 1880 ed., New York: AMS, 1971.

——. *The Story of the Jubilee Singers, Including Their Songs. With Supplement, Containing an Account of their Six Years' Tour around the World, and Many New Songs, by F. J. Loudin.* Cleveland, O.: Cleveland Printing, 1892; rpt. London: Hodder & Staughton, 1903. 311 pp.

Pike, Gustavus D. *The Jubilee Singers, and Their Campaign for Twenty Thousand Dollars.* London: Hodder & Staughton, 1873; rpt. Boston: Lee & Shepard, 1873. 219 pp. American Culture Series, 51:8. Ann Arbor: Univ. Microfilms, 1956. Rpt. New York: AMS, 1971.

Quarles, Benjamin. *The Negro in the Civil War.* Boston: Little, 1953, 1969; rpt. New York: Russell, 1968. 379 pp.

Richardson, J. M., ed. "The Negro in Post-Civil War Tennessee: A Report of a Northern Missionary." *Journal of Negro Education* 34 (1966), 419-24.

Scott, Mingo, Jr. *The Negro in Tennessee Politics and Governmental Affairs, 1865-1965: The Hundred Years Story.* Nashville: Rich, 1965. 352 pp. This work seeks to explain the kinds of offices Negroes have held at all levels of government. It also analyzes the importance of Negro voting patterns in the state.

Seward, Theodore F. *The Singing Campaign for 10,000 Pounds; or, The Jubilee Singers in Great Britain.* New York: American Missionary Assoc., 1875. 272 pp.

Sneed, Pauline Lucy. "Education of the Negroes in Tennessee during the Reconstruction Period." Thesis, Fisk Univ., 1935.

Stubblefield, Ruth Louise. "The Education of the Negro in Tennessee during Reconstruction." Thesis, Fisk Univ., 1943.

Taylor, Alrutheus Ambush. *The Negro in Tennessee, 1865-1880.*

Tipton, C. Robert. "The Fisk Jubilee Singers." *THQ* 29 (1970), 42-48.

Walker, Joseph Alexander. "The Negro in Tennessee Politics, 1865-1880." Thesis, Fisk Univ., 1941.

Walker, Joseph E. "The Negro in Tennessee during the Reconstruction Period." Thesis, Univ. of Tennessee, 1933.

Wiley, Bell Irwin. *Southern Negroes, 1861-1865,* Historical Publications Miscellany, 31; foreword C. Vann Woodward. New Haven: Yale Univ. Press, 1965. 366 pp.

Woodward, C. Vann. *The Strange Career of Jim Crow.* New York: Oxford Univ. Press, 1955. 155 pp.; rev. ed., 1957. 2nd rev. ed., 1966. 205 pp. An effort to probe the question of how and why Jim Crow laws arose and how they relate to the rapid change in race relations of the last few years.

———. "The Birth of Jim Crow." *AH* 15 (1964), 52.

GENERAL HISTORY: 1900-72

Anderson, Margaret. *The Children of the South.*

Antone, George Peter, Jr. "Willis Duke Weatherford: An Interpretation of His Work in Race Relations, 1906-1946." Diss., Vanderbilt Univ., 1969.

Ashmore, Harry S. *An Epitaph for Dixie.* New York: Norton, 1958. 189 pp. Ashmore admonishes the South to forget its past of race prejudice and inwardness and join the mainstream of national life. The South can do this, he says, without losing the finer qualities of its life.

Baker, Earlene T. "The Ku Klux Klan of the 1920's." Thesis, Memphis State Univ., 1960.

Bartley, Numan V. *The Rise of Massive Resistance: Race and Politics in the South during the 1950's.* Baton Rouge: Louisiana State Univ. Press, 1969. 390 pp. This work is a study of politics and race relations in the South focusing primarily upon the 11 southern states of the former Confederacy which chose to hamper, or prevent, enforcement of the *Brown* v. *Topeka* decision.

Bledsoe, Thomas. *Or We'll All Hang Separately; The Highlander Idea.* Boston: Beacon, 1969. 266 pp.

Brent, Michael J., and Ellen F. Greene. *Rural Negro Health.* Nashville: Julius Rosenwald Fund, 1937. 85 pp. Report of a 5-year experiment in health education in Tennessee.

Brown, Charles Caswell. "The History of Negro Education in Tennessee." Thesis, Washington Univ., 1929.

Brown, Harold Spencer. "The Distribution of Funds for Salaries between the Racial Groups in Tennessee." Thesis, Fisk Univ., 1933. Treats teachers' salaries.

Cansler, Charles W. *Three Generations; the Story of a Colored Family of Eastern Tennessee.* Kingsport: Privately printed, 1939. 173 pp.

Caudill, R. "Plight of the Negro Intellectuals." *Christian Century,* Aug. 20, 1930, pp. 1012-14.

Cohn, David Lewis. *Where I Was Born and Raised.* Boston: Houghton, 1948; rpt. Notre Dame: Univ. of Notre Dame Press, 1967. 380 pp. Implications of life for a Negro in Tennessee.

Diamond, Michael Jerome. "The Negro and Organized Labor as Voting Blocs in Tennessee, 1960-1964." Thesis, Univ. of Tennessee, 1965.

——. "The Impact of the Negro Vote in Contemporary Tennessee Politics." *TLR* 34 (1966-67), 435-81.

Dykeman, Wilma. *Prophet of Plenty: The First Ninety Years of W. D. Weatherford.* Knoxville: Univ. of Tennessee Press, 1966, 1967. 288 pp. Weatherford was a great humanitarian who gave his life to the cause of human uplift in Appalachia and elsewhere among the blacks and poor whites of the South.

Dykeman, Wilma, and James Stokely. *Neither Black nor White.* New York: Rinehart, 1957. 371 pp. An effort to probe the most profound dilemma of the South—racial prejudice—this work is written with humility, great humanity, and deep insight.

——. *Seeds of Southern Change: The Life of Will Alexander.* Chicago: Univ. of Chicago Press, 1962. 343 pp. A deeply sensitive biography of a man who was leader of the Interracial Commission for a quarter century after World War I, officer of the Rosenwald and Stern funds, and founder of Dillard University.

——. "Hopeful Dialogue of the Races." *New York Times Magazine,* Aug. 10, 1963, pp. 10ff.

Egerton, John. *A Mind to Stay Here; Profiles from the South.* New York: Macmillan, 1970. 190 pp. A series of profiles of southern black civil rights leaders and white liberals who defied and endured personal danger to fight for the cause of human freedom and dignity.

Ford, Jesse Hill. *The Liberation of Lord Byron Jones,* an *Atlantic Monthly* Press Book. Boston: Little, 1965; rpt. New York: NAL, 1967. 364 pp. A novel of life in Somerton, a fictional Tennessee rural community, which shows smoldering racial antagonisms flaring into violence.

Gibson, D. Parke. *The Thirty Billion Dollar Negro.* New York: Macmillan, 1969. 311 pp. A study of the Negro as consumer.

Giovanni, Nikki. *Gemini.* New York: Bobbs-Merrill, 1971. 403 pp. An autobiography picturing life in Knoxville and Nashville.

Graham, Hugh Davis. "Tennessee Editorial Response to Changes in the Bi-racial System, 1954-1960." Diss., Stanford Univ., 1965.

——. *Crisis in Print: Desegregation and the Press in Tennessee.* Nashville: Vanderbilt Univ. Press, 1967. 338 pp. A comprehensive effort to describe the reaction of the Tennessee press to the issue of desegregation in the state from 1954 to 1964. Graham concludes that, with few exceptions, the press fulfilled its responsibility for decency and fair reporting rather well.

Green, Ely. *Ely: Too Black, Too White,* eds. Elizabeth N. Chitty and Arthur Ben Chitty. Amherst: Univ. of Massachusetts Press, 1970. 637 pp. The autobiography of a Sewanee native born of white father and black mother.

Harrell, David Edwin. *White Sects and Black Men in the Recent South.* Nashville: Vanderbilt Univ. Press, 1971. 161 pp.

"If You're Black Stay out of Tennessee." *Trans-Action,* Oct. 1969, pp. 11 ff.

Jackson, Kenneth T. *The Ku Klux Klan in the City, 1915-1930.* New York: Oxford Univ. Press, 1967; rpt., Urban Life in America Series, ed. Richard C. Wade, 1969. 326 pp. Memphis and Knoxville are included here.

Johnson, Charles Spurgeon. *Bibliography.* Nashville: Fisk Univ., 1947. 2 pp.

Johnson, Clifton H. "Some Archival Sources on Negro History in Tennessee." *THQ* 28 (1969), 397-416.

Johnson, Lena B. "An Investigation of News of Negroes in a Select Number of Tennessee Newspapers from September, 1960 through February, 1961." Thesis, Tennessee State A & I Univ., 1961.

Kelly, Clarence L. "Robert A. Church, a Negro Tennessean, in Republican State and National Politics from 1912-1932." Thesis, Tennessee State A & I Univ., 1954.

Koontz, William Edward. "A Follow-up Study of the Negro Students Who Entered Clinton, Tennessee High School, 1956-1965." Thesis, Univ. of Tennessee, 1965.

Lamon, Lester. "Negroes in Tennessee 1900-1930." Diss., Univ. of North Carolina, 1971.

Lincoln, C. E. "Key Man in the South: The Negro Minister." *New York Times Magazine,* July 12, 1964, pp. 20 ff.

Long, Herman H., and Vivian W. Henderson. *Negro Employment in Tennessee State Government; a Report from Nashville Community Conference on Employment Opportunity.* Nashville: Tennessee Council on Human Relations, 1962. 9 pp.

"Martin Luther King, Jr.: Man of 1963." *Negro History Bulletin,* Mar. 1964, pp. 136-37.

"Martin Luther King, Jr.; Nonviolence: The Only Road to Freedom." *Ebony,* Oct. 1966, pp. 27-30.

"Medical Discoveries on a Shoe String." *Business Week,* June

15, 1968, pp. 92-94. Concerns Meharry Medical School.

Morley, F. "What Makes Integration Work?" *Nation's Business,* Dec. 1966, pp. 27-28.

Morrison, Marshall L. "Issues Vital to Negroes in Tennessee." Ed.D. diss., Univ. of Tennessee, 1962.

Morrow, Martha Barrett. "The Reaction in Tennessee to the Supreme Court Desegregation Decision of 1954: From May, 1954 through December, 1957." Thesis, Memphis State Univ., 1964.

Muse, Benjamin. *Ten Years of Prelude: The Story of Integration since the Supreme Court's 1954 Decision.* New York: Viking Press, 1964. 308 pp. A chapter on the Clinton integration difficulty is included.

Nolen, Claude H. *The Negro's Image in the South; the Anatomy of White Supremacy.* Lexington: Univ. of Kentucky Press, 1967. 232 pp.

Peelle, Elizabeth Brown. "An Empirical Test of the Relationship between Church Attendance and Attitudes toward Negroes." Thesis, Univ. of Tennessee, 1964.

Petrie, J. C. "Demand Justice for Negroes." *Christian Century,* July 4, 1934, pp. 910ff.

Powell, Ruth Marie. "The History of Negro Educational Institutions Sponsored by the Baptists of Tennessee from 1864-1934." Thesis, Tennessee State A&I Univ., 1953.

"Race in One State." *Nation's Business,* Aug. 1970, pp. 24-30.

Redd, George N. "Educational Desegregation in Tennessee—One Year Afterward." *Journal of Negro Education* 24 (1955), 333-47.

———. "The Status of Educational Desegregation in Tennessee." *Journal of Negro Education* 25 (1956), 324-33.

"Requiem for Jim Crow." *Nation,* Mar. 12, 1960, pp. 218ff.

Roberts, S. O. "The Education of Negroes in Tennessee." *Journal of Negro Education* 16 (1947), 417-24.

Schuster, Louis H., Edgar G. Epps, and Vivian W. Henderson. *Business Enterprises of Negroes in Tennessee,* Small Business Management Research Study. Nashville: Small Business Administration, 1961. 93 pp.

Scott, Mingo, Jr. *The Negro in Tennessee Politics and Governmental Affairs, 1865-1965.*

Sibley, Elbridge. *Differential Mortality in Tennessee, 1917-1928 . . . a Statistical Study Conducted Jointly by Tennessee State Department of Health and Fisk University.* Diss., Columbia Univ., 1930. Nashville: Fisk Univ. Press, 1930; rpt. Westport, Conn.: Greenwood, 1930. 152 pp.

Sitton, Claude. "Southern Negro Drives for the Vote." *New York Times Magazine,* Sept. 28, 1963, pp. 28-29.

Snead, Edward. "A Study of the Status of Music in the Negro High Schools of Tennessee." Thesis, Fisk Univ., 1953.

"Tender Loving Care; Hubbard Hospital." *Ebony,* Nov. 1961, pp. 48-50.

Tennessee State Department of Education. *The Negro; A Selected List for School Libraries of Books by or about the Negro in Africa and America.* Nashville: State of Tennessee, 1941. 48 pp.

Tennessee State Planning Commission. *Human Relations in Tennessee.* Nashville: State of Tennessee, 1970. 28 leaves.

Tinsley, Lacy Bradley. "A Study of Adult Education for Negroes under Public Auspices in the State of Tennessee." Thesis, Fisk Univ., 1953.

Valien, Preston. "Expansion of Negro Suffrage in Tennessee." *Journal of Negro Education* 26 (1957), 362-68.

Waskow, Arthur. *From Race Riot to Sit-in, 1919 and the 1960s; a Study of the Connections between Conflict and Violence.* Gloucester, Mass.: P. Smith, 1966; rpt. Garden City, N.Y.: Doubleday, 1966. 380 pp.

Wynes, Charles E., ed. *The Negro in the South since 1865; Selected Essays in American Negro History,* Southern Historical Publications no. 10. University: Univ. of Alabama Press, 1965. 253 pp.

Religion

[For local church and religious group histories, see county histories.]

GENERAL HISTORY

Bailey, Kenneth K. *Southern White Protestantism in the Twentieth Century.* New York: Harper, 1964; rpt. Gloucester, Mass.: P. Smith, 1968. 180 pp. Bailey feels that the Southern identity is best delineated in the sphere of religion, primarily Christian, Protestant religion. His effort is to examine its response to the challenge of this century.

Carty, James W. *Nashville As a World Religious Center.* Nashville: Cullom & Ghertner, 1958. 24 pp.

Cleveland, Catherine C. *The Great Revival in the West, 1797-1805.* Diss., Univ. of Chicago, 1914. Chicago: Univ. of Chicago Press, 1916; rpt. Gloucester, Mass.: P. Smith, 1959. 215 pp. The story of the greatest of the frontier revivals, which shook the religious life of the area west of the Appalachians.

Collins, J. B. *Tennessee Snake Handlers.* Chattanooga: Collins, 1945. 36 pp.

A Concise Narrative of the Rise and Progress of the East Tennessee Missionary Society. Knoxville: Heiskell & Brown, 1824. 17 pp.

Griggs, Guy P., Jr. "Environment as a Factor in the Great Revival of 1797-1805 in Frontier Tennessee and Kentucky." Thesis, Univ. of Arkansas, 1963.

Johnson, Charles A. "The Frontier Camp Meeting: Contemporary and Historical Appraisals, 1805-1840." *MVHR* 37 (1950-51), 91-110.

———. *The Frontier Camp Meeting; Religious Harvest Time.* Dallas: Southern Methodist Univ. Press, 1955. 325 pp.

Landing, James E. "The Failure of Amish Settlements in the Southeastern United States: An Appeal for Inquiry." *Mennonite Quarterly Review* 44 (1970), 376-88.

McBride, Robert M. "A Camp Meeting at Goshen Church." *THQ* 22 (1963), 137-42.

Maurer, Beryl B. "The Rural Church and Organized Community:

A Study of Church-Community Relations in Two East Tennessee Communities." Thesis, Univ. of Tennessee, 1953.

Posey, Walter B. "The Earthquake of 1811 and Its Influence on Evangelistic Methods in the Churches of the Old South." *THM* (ser. 2) 1 (1930-31), 107-14.

———. *Religious Strife on the Southern Frontier.* Baton Rouge: Louisiana State Univ. Press, 1965. 112 pp. Posey studies the conflict which developed among Protestant sectarian groups in the 18th and 19th centuries; he concludes that they found strength in exclusiveness, individualism, and, eventually, in divisiveness.

———. *Frontier Mission: A History of Religion West of the Southern Appalachians to 1861.* Lexington: Univ. of Kentucky Press, 1966. 436 pp. A survey history of religion in its many forms and increasingly pluralistic groups.

Preece, Harold, and Celia Kraft. *Dew on Jordan.* New York: Dutton, 1946. 221 pp. Relates to snake handlers in Tennessee.

Rogers, E. E. "Pioneering Accounts of Frontier Religion." *TFSB* 17 (1951), 32-40.

Shurter, Robert L. "The Camp Meeting in the Early Life and Literature of the Mid-West." ETHSP 5 (1933), 142-49.

Sweet, William Warren. *Religion on the American Frontier, 1783-1840.* 4 vols. New York: Holt, 1931-46; rpt. Cooper Sq., 1964. A study of pioneer Baptist, Presbyterian, Congregationalist, and Methodist churches.

"Tennessee Develops a Creative Evangelism: Appalachian Preaching Mission." *Christian Century,* Dec. 19, 1956, pp. 1469-70.

Tennessee State Planning Commission. *Guide to Church Vital Statistics in Tennessee.* Nashville: State of Tennessee, 1942. 510 pp.

White, John Bowman. "The German Christian in Tennessee and Western North Carolina prior to 1800." B.D. thesis, Vanderbilt Univ., 1932.

Wingfield, Marshall. "Tennessee's Mormon Massacre." *THQ* 17 (1958), 19-36.

DENOMINATIONAL HISTORIES

Baptist

Barnes, William W. *The Southern Baptist Convention, 1845-1953.* Nashville: Broadman, 1954. 330 pp.

Bond, John. *History of the Baptist Concord Association of Middle Tennessee and North Alabama.* Nashville: Graves & Mark, 1860. 104 pp.

Borum, Joseph H. *Biographical Sketches of Tennessee Baptist Ministers.* Memphis: Rogers, 1880. 640 pp.

Brooks, Richard Donoho. *One Hundred and Sixty-two Years of Middle Tennessee Baptists, 1796-1958.* Nashville: Cullom & Ghertner, 1958. 140 pp.

Burnett, James J. *Sketches of Tennessee's Pioneer Baptist Preachers, Being, Incidentally, a History of Baptist Beginnings in the Several Associations in the State; Containing, Particularly, Character and Life Sketches of the Standard-Bearers and Leaders of Our People; Commencing with the Oldest Communities of Baptists and Covering, Substantially but Not in Detail, a Period of One Hundred Years (1775-1875) of Baptist Effort and Achievement in Tennessee; with Photo Illustrations and an Appendix of Curious Documents and Bits and Fragments of Church History.* Nashville: Marshall & Bruce, 1919- .

Canaday, Dayton W., ed. "A Check List of Tennessee Baptist Imprints, 1809-1849." *THQ* 12 (1953), 323-33.

Edgar, Lewis M. *A History of the Primitive Baptists in the Western Districts of Tennessee and Kentucky. . . .* Paris: *Intelligencer* Office, 1881. 184 pp.

Edwards, Lawrence. "History of the Baptists of Tennessee with Particular Attention to the Primitive Baptists of East Tennessee." Thesis, Univ. of Tennessee, 1941.

Fuller, T. O. *History of the Negro Baptists of Tennessee.* Memphis: Haskins, 1936. 346 pp.

Graves, James Robinson. *The Watchman's Reply.* Nashville: Graves & Shankland, 1853. 83 pp.

——. *The Great Iron Wheel; or, Republicanism Backwards and Christianity Reversed.* Nashville: The Author, 1856; rpt. Baptist Bk. House, 1885. 570 pp.

Grime, John H. *History of Middle Tennessee Baptists with Special References to Salem, New Salem, Enon, and Wiseman Associations, Containing Sketches of Associations, Churches, Deceased Ministers, and Deacons, with Ministerial Directory: Also Chapters on Separate Baptists, Christian Baptists, Feet Washing.* Nashville: *Baptist and Reflector,* 1902; rpt. Lebanon: J. Hall Grime, 1972. 565 pp.

Hood, John O. *History of the Chilhowee Baptist Association.* Nashville: Curley, 1970. 370 pp.

Jordan, Lewis G. *Negro Baptist History, 1750-1930.* Nashville: Sunday School Pub. Bd., N.B.C., 1930. 394 pp.

Posey, Walter B. "The Frontier Baptist Ministry." ETHSP 14 (1942), 3-10.

——. *The Baptist Church in the Lower Mississippi Valley, 1776-1845.* Lexington: Univ. of Kentucky Press, 1957. 166 pp.

Spain, Rufus B. *At Ease in Zion: A Social History of Southern Baptists, 1865-1900.* Diss., Vanderbilt Univ., 1961. Nashville: Vanderbilt Univ. Press, 1967. 247 pp.

Taylor, Oury W. *Early Tennessee Baptists, 1769-1832.* Nashville: Tennessee Baptist Conv., 1957. 314 pp.

Tindall, S. W. "Buffalo Ridge Church." *The Baptists of Tennessee,* 17-67. Kingsport: Southern, 1930. 67 pp.

Torbet, Robert G. *A History of the Baptists,* foreword Kenneth Scott Latourette. Philadelphia: 1950. 538 pp. Rev. ed., Valley Forge, Pa.: Judson, 1963; rpt. London: Carey Kingsgate, 1963, 1966. 553 pp.

Williams, Samuel Cole. "Tidence Lane, Tennessee's First Pastor." *THM* (ser. 2) 1 (1930-31), 40-48; rpt. in Tindall, *The Baptists of Tennessee,* 5-18.

Wooley, Davis C., and Norman W. Cox, eds. *Encyclopedia of Southern Baptists.* 3 vols. Nashville: Broadman, 1958-1971. Contains an excellent monograph on Tennessee Baptists.

Christian, Church of Christ, Disciples of Christ

Caldwell, Charles Grover III. "Alexander Campbell: Adversary and Advocate of Missionary Organization among Disciples of Christ." Thesis, Tennessee State Univ., 1970.

Chalk, John Allen. "A History of the *Gospel Advocate,* 1866-1868: Its Social and Political Conscience." Thesis, Tennessee Technological Univ., 1967.

Edwards, Arthur B. "Alexander Campbell's Philosophy of Education." Thesis, East Tennessee State Univ., 1957.

Garrison, Winfred E. *Religion Follows the Frontier: A History of the Disciples of Christ.* New York: Harper, 1931. 317 pp.

Garrison, Winfred E., and Alfred T. De Groot. *The Disciples of*

Christ; A History. St. Louis: Christian Board of Pub., 1948; rev. ed., Bethany, 1958. 592 pp.

Grant, J. W. "A Sketch of the Reformation in Tennessee." Unpublished typescript, 1897. 88 leaves. Located in the Tennessee State Library and Archives.

Harrell, David Edwin, Jr. "Disciples of Christ Pacifism in Nineteenth Century Tennessee." *THQ* 21 (1962), 263-74.

——. "The Sectional Origins of the Churches of Christ." *JSH* 30 (1964), 261-77.

——. "The Disciples of Christ and Social Force in Tennessee, 1865-1900." ETHS*P* 38 (1966), 30-47.

——. *Quest for a Christian America: The Disciples of Christ and American Society to 1866*. Nashville: Disciples of Christ Hist. Soc., 1966. 256 pp.

Johnson, T. H. "History of the Restoration Movement in Tennessee." B.D. thesis, Eugene Bible Univ., 1928.

Lipscomb, David. *Life and Sermons of Jesse L. Sewell*. Nashville: *Gospel Advocate*, 1891. 318 pp.

Norton, Herman A. *Tennessee Christians: A History of the Christian Church in Tennessee*. Nashville: Reed, 1971. 309 pp. Norton depicts Tennessee as the pivotal state in the development of the Christian Church in its many forms from its 19th-century origins to 1962.

Roland, Clifford. "History of the Disciples of Christ in Tennessee to 1850." Thesis, Vanderbilt Univ., 1931.

Wagner, Harry C. "History of the Disciples of Christ in Upper East Tennessee." Thesis, Univ. of Tennessee, 1943.

——. "The Beginnings of the Christian Church in East Tennessee." ETHS*P* 20 (1948), 49-58.

Ware, Charles C. *Barton Warren Stone: Pathfinder of Christian Union; a Story of His Life and Times*, introd. Elmer E. Snoddy. St. Louis: Bethany, 1932. 357 pp.

West, William G. *Barton Warren Stone: Early American Advocate of Christian Unity*. Nashville: Disciples of Christ Hist. Soc., 1954. 245 pp.

Wooten, Raleigh Ray. "The Early Career of a Restoration Preacher: Barton Warren Stone." Thesis, Middle Tennessee State Univ., 1962.

Wrather, Eva Jean. "Alexander Campbell in Nashville." *The Scroll* 43 (1946), 289-98.

Congregational

Wingfield, Marshall. "Tennessee's Oldest Congregational Church." WTHSP 8 (1954), 55-94.

Cumberland Presbyterian

Beard, Richard. *Brief Biographical Sketches of Some of the Early Ministers of the Cumberland Presbyterian Church.* Nashville: Cumberland Presbyterian Board of Pub., 1867, 1874. 408 pp.

Blake, Thaddeus C. *The Old Log House: A History and Defense of the Cumberland Presbyterian Church.* Nashville: Cumberland Presbyterian Board of Publ., 1878. 293 pp.

Campbell, Thomas H. *Studies in Cumberland Presbyterian History.* Nashville: Cumberland Presbyterian Board of Education, 1944. 361 pp.

Cossitt, Franceway R. *The Life and Times of Rev. Finis Ewing, One of the Fathers and Founders of the Cumberland Presbyterian Church.* Louisville, Ky.: L. R. Woods, 1853. 501 pp.

Foster, Robert V. *A Sketch of the History of the Cumberland Presbyterian Church.* New York, 1894. 53 pp.

Hubbard, Donald Peyton. "A Historical Study of the Cumberland Presbyterian Church in Tennessee, 1810-1860." Thesis, Univ. of Tennessee, 1966.

McDonnold, B. W. *History of the Cumberland Presbyterian Church.* Nashville: Cumberland Presbyterian Pub. House, 1899. 679 pp.

Miller, A. B. *Doctrines and Genius of the Cumberland Presbyterian Church.* Nashville: Cumberland Presbyterian Pub. House, 1892.

Episcopal

Douglas, Hiram K. "The First Bishop of Tennessee." *American Church Monthly* 20 (1927), 454-62.

Green, William Mercer. *Memoir of Rt. Rev. James Hervey Otey, D.D., L.L.D., the First Bishop of Tennessee.* New York: J. Pott, 1885. 359 pp.

Hendrick, John Thilman. *A Historical Contrast between the Episcopal and Presbyterian Churches.* Clarksville: C. O. Faxon, 1851. 44 pp.

Noll, Arthur H. *History of the Church in the Diocese of Tennessee.* New York: J. Pott, 1900. 229 pp. A survey history up to 1899.

Pennington, Edgar. "The Organization of the Episcopal Church in

Tennessee." *Historical Magazine of the Protestant Episcopal Church* 22 (1953), 13-44.

Polk, William M. *Leonidas Polk, Bishop and General.* 2 vols. New York: Longmans, Green, 1893, 1915.

Posey, Walter B. "The Protestant Episcopal Church: An American Adaptation." *JSH* 25 (1959), 3-30.

Rodgers, Ellen Davies. *The Romance of the Episcopal Church in West Tennessee, 1832-1964.* Brunswick: Plantation, 1964. 232 pp. The development of the church in West Tennessee from the first parishes at La Grange, Jackson, Brownsville, and Memphis to the strong institution it had become throughout the region by 1963.

Sharber, Patricia Farrell. "The Social Attitudes of the Episcopal Church in Tennessee, 1865-1898." Thesis, Vanderbilt Univ., 1970.

Lutheran

Cassell, Charles W., W. J. Finck, and Elon O. Henkel, eds. *History of the Lutheran Church in Virginia and East Tennessee.* Strasburg, Va.: Shenandoah Pub. House, 1930. 401 pp.

Fox, Luther A. "The Genesis of the Tennessee Synod." *Lutheran Quarterly* 52 (1922), 87-107.

Henkel, Socrates. *History of the Evangelical Lutheran Tennessee Synod.* New Market, Va.: Henkel, 1890. 275 pp.

Methodist

Asbury, Francis. *The Journal of the Rev. Francis Asbury, Bishop of the Methodist Episcopal Church, from August 7, 1771, to December 7, 1815.* 3 vols. New York: Bangs & Mason, 1821. Rpt. Elmer E. Clark, J. Manning Potts, and Jacob S. Payton, eds. Nashville: Abingdon, 1958; rpt. London: Epworth, 1958.

Barnes, Annie Maria. *Scenes in Pioneer Methodism.* Nashville: Methodist Pub. House, 1890. 397 pp.

Bucke, Emory S., ed. *The History of American Methodism.* 3 vols. New York: Abingdon, 1964.

Carter, Cullen T. *History of the Tennessee Conference and a Brief Summary of the General Conferences of the Methodist Church from the Frontier in Middle Tennessee to the Present Time.* Nashville: Parthenon Press, 1948. 556 pp. An outline of the consecutive general conferences of the Tennessee Conference from frontier days to 1948.

——. *History of Methodist Churches and Institutions in Middle Tennessee, 1787-1956.* Nashville: Parthenon Press, 1956. 443 pp.

——. *Methodism in the Wilderness, 1786-1836.* Nashville: Parthenon Press, 1960. 123 pp.

——. *Methodist Leaders in the Old Jerusalem Conference, 1812-1962.* Nashville: Parthenon Press, 1961. 222 pp.

——. *History of the Columbia District of the Tennessee Conference of the Methodist Church.* Nashville: Parthenon Press, 1962. 95 pp.

Cartwright, Peter. *Autobiography of Peter Cartwright, the Backwoods Preacher,* ed. W. P. Strickland. New York: Hunt & Eaton, 1856 (525 pp.); rpt., Carlton & Porter, 1857; rpt. Cincinnati: Swormstedt & Poe, 1859; rpt. London: Hall, 1859 (240 pp.). Rpt., introd., bibliog., index Charles L. Wallis, Nashville: Abingdon, 1956 (349 pp.). American Culture Series, 57:1. Ann Arbor: University Microfilms, 1956. Rpt. Cincinnati: Cranston & Curtis, 1956. Rpt., 1st ed., New York: Methodist Bk., 1958; rpt. Louisville, Ky.: Lost Cause, 1958.

Cooper, Freeman Marco. "A Study of Attitudes Regarding Church Financial Support in the African Methodist Episcopal Church, Nashville, Tennessee Area." Thesis, Tennessee State A & I Univ., 1959.

Cullom, Jeremiah W. *Warm Hearts and Saddlebags: Journal of the Reverend Jeremiah W. Cullom (1828-1915),* ed. James R. Cox. Nashville: Tennessee Conference Hist. Soc., n.d. 321 pp.

Duvall, Sylvanus M. *The Methodist Episcopal Church and Education up to 1869.* Diss., Columbia Univ., 1928. Teachers College, Columbia Univ., Contributions to Education no. 284. New York: Columbia Univ. Press, 1928; rpt. AMS, 1972. 127 pp.

Fair, Harold L. "Southern Methodists on Education and Race 1900-1920." Diss., Vanderbilt Univ., 1972.

Fitzgerald, Oscar P. *Dr. Summers: A Life-Study.* Nashville: Methodist Pub. House, 1884, 1886. 352 pp. Biography of Thomas O. Summers.

——. *John B. McFerrin: A Biography.* Nashville: Meth. Pub. House, 1888, 1890, 1901. 448 pp.

Garnett, Bernard E. *Black Protest: Will It Split the United Methodists?* Nashville: Race Relations Report, 1969. 23 pp.

Godbold, Albea. "Bishop William McKendree and His Contribution to Methodism." *Methodist History* 8 (1969-70), 3-12.

Graves, James Robinson. *The New Great Iron Wheel. An Examina-*

tion of the New M. E. Church, South, in a Series of Letters Addressed to Bishop McTyeire. Memphis: Baptist Bk. Store, 1884. 574 pp.

Green, Rev. William M. *Life and Papers of A. L. P. Green, D.D.,* ed. T. O. Summers. Nashville: Methodist Pub. House, 1877. 592 pp. Green was a Methodist minister c. 1845.

Historical Records Survey, Tennessee, Work Projects Administration. *Outline Development of Methodism in Tennessee.* Sponsored by the Tennessee State Planning Commission. Nashville: Hist. Records Survey, 1940. 16 leaves.

History of the Organization of the Methodist Episcopal Church, South: Comprehending All the Official Proceedings of the General Conference; the Southern Annual Conferences, and the General Convention; with Such Other Matters As Are Necessary to a Right Understanding of the Case. Nashville: *Southwestern Christian Advocate,* 1845. 267 pp.

Hoss, Elijah Embree. *David Morton, a Biography.* Nashville: Methodist Pub. House, 1916. 214 pp. Morton was an eminent Methodist minister whose work in south-central Kentucky had wide impact upon Tennessee.

———. *William McKendree, A Biographical Study.* Nashville: Methodist Pub. House, 1914. 206 pp. An early, but good, biography of this outstanding Methodist circuit rider who was a powerful force in the church in Middle Tennessee until his death in 1833.

Kennedy, Rhoda Lee. "The Methodist Church in Tennessee, 1800-1824." Thesis, George Peabody College, 1929.

Ledford, Allen James. "Methodism in Tennessee, 1783-1866." Thesis, Univ. of Tennessee, 1941.

Life and Work of Lucinda B. Helm, Founder of the Woman's Parsonage and Home Missions Society of the Methodist Episcopal Church South. Nashville: Methodist Pub. House, 1898. 117 pp.

Little, Brooks B., ed. *Methodist Union Catalog of History, Biography, Disciplines, and Hymnals.* Prelim. ed., Lake Junaluska, N.C.: Assoc. of Methodist Hist. Socs., 1967. 478 pp.

Lundy, Clyde E. *Holston Horizons.* Bristol, 1947.

McAnally, David R. *Life and Times of Reverend S. Patton, D.D., and Annals of the Holston Conference.* St. Louis: Methodist Bk. Depository, 1859. 343 pp.

McFerrin, John Berry. *History of Methodism in Tennessee.* 3 vols. Nashville: A. H. Redford, 1869-73, 1874, 1875. Covers the period from 1783 to 1840.

Martin, A. E. "Anti-slavery Activities of the Methodist Episcopal Church in Tennessee." *THM* 2 (1916), 98-109.

Martin, Isaac Patton. *Elijah Embree Hoss, Ecumenical Methodist.* Nashville: Parthenon Press, 1942, 1944. 487 pp.

——. *Methodism in Holston.* Knoxville: Methodist Hist. Soc. of Holston Conference, 1945. 459 pp.

——. *A Minister in the Tennessee Valley: Sixty-seven Years.* Nashville: Methodist Hist. Soc. of Holston Conference, 1954. 234 pp.

Methodist Publishing House. *Since 1789; the Story of the Methodist Publishing House.* Nashville: Abingdon, 1964. 61 pp.

Morrow, Ralph E. "Northern Methodism in the South during Reconstruction." *MVHR* 41 (1954-55), 197-218.

Neely, Thomas B. *American Methodism: Its Divisions and Unification.* New York: Revell, 1915. 407 pp.

Paine, Robert. *Life and Times of William McKendree, Bishop of The Methodist Episcopal Church South.* 2 vols. Nashville: Methodist Pub. House, 1869, 1885; 2 vols. in 1, 1880. 500 pp.

Perez, Joseph A. "Some Effects of the Central Jurisdiction upon the Movement to Make the Methodist Church an Inclusive Church." Diss., Boston Univ., 1964.

Phillips, Elmer Harrell. "Methodism in the Jackson Purchase, 1818-1845." Thesis, Memphis State Univ., 1968.

Pilkington, James Penn. *The Methodist Publishing House. A History.* Nashville: Abingdon, 1968- . 563 pp. Vol. 1 of this series, *Beginnings to 1870,* traces the history of this venerable institution, in existence since 1789, from its small, frontier operation to 1870.

Pinson, William Washington. *Walter Russell Lambuth, Prophet and Pioneer.* Nashville: Cokesbury, 1924. 261 pp.

——. *George R. Stuart, Life and Work, 1857-1926.* Nashville: Cokesbury, 1927. 276 pp. Lambuth was an East Tennessee Methodist minister.

Poole, C. H. "Thomas O. Summers: A Biographical Study." Thesis, Vanderbilt Univ., 1957.

Posey, Walter B. *The Development of Methodism in the Old Southwest, 1783-1824.* Diss., Vanderbilt Univ., 1933. Tuscaloosa: Ala.: Weatherford, 1933. 151 pp. Traces the growth of Southern Methodism under the leadership of pioneer preachers and circuit riders who spread the Word and shared the hardships of frontiersmen while ministering to their spiritual needs.

——. "Bishop Asbury Visits Tennessee, 1788-1815; Extracts from His Journal." *THQ* 15 (1956), 253-68.

Price, Richard N. *Holston Methodism. From Its Origin to the Present Time.* 5 vols. Nashville: Methodist Pub. House, 1903-13.

——. "Methodism in East Tennessee: Before, during and since the War." *Methodist Quarterly Review* 57 (1908), 293-303.

Purifoy, Lewis McCarroll. "The Methodist Episcopal Church South and Slavery, 1844-1865." Diss., Univ. of North Carolina, 1965.

Rawls, Margaret B. "Peter Cartwright and His Times." Thesis, Univ. of Tennessee, 1932.

Redford, Albert H. *History of the Organization of the Methodist Episcopal Church, South.* Nashville: The Author, 1871. 660 pp.

Rutledge, Norman E. "A Study of Methodist Child Care Institutions." Thesis, Univ. of Tennessee, 1957.

Strickland, William P. *The Pioneer Bishop: or, The Life and Times of Francis Asbury,* introd. Nathan Bangs. New York: Carlton & Porter, 1858; rpt. Cincinnati: Hitchcock & Wolden, 1858; rpt. New York: Nelson & Phillips, 1858; rpt. Louisville, Ky.: Lost Cause, 1956. 496 pp.

Summers, Thomas O., ed. *Biographical Sketches of Eminent Itinerant Ministers Distinguished, for the Most Part, as Pioneers of Methodism within the Bounds of the Methodist Episcopal Church, South.* Nashville: Stevenson & Owen, 1858; rpt. Nashville: Methodist Pub. House, 1859. 384 pp.

Sweet, William W., ed. *The Rise of Methodism in the West: Being the Journal of the Western Conference, 1800-1811.* Nashville: Smith & Lamar, 1920; rpt. New York: Methodist Bk., 1920. 207 pp.

Thompson, E. Bruce. "Richard Abbey and the Methodist Publishing House." *Journal of Mississippi History* 6 (1944), 145-60.

Townsend, Newton. "His Spirit Was Willing." *THQ* 21 (1962), 275-86. Jesse J. Ellis was a Methodist circuit rider from 1842 to 1851.

Travis, Joseph. *Autobiography of the Rev. Joseph Travis, A.M., a Member of the Memphis Annual Conference. Embracing a Succinct History of the Methodist Episcopal Church, South; Particularly in Part of Western Virginia, the Carolinas, Georgia, Alabama, and Mississippi. With Short Memoirs of Several Local Preachers, and an Address to His Friends,* ed. Thomas O. Summers. Nashville: Stevenson & Evans, 1856. 238 pp.

Whitehead, Paul. *The Odd Hour, or, Recreations of a Presiding Elder.* Nashville: n.p., 1865.

Wright, Absalom B. *Autobiography of Rev. A. B. Wright, of the Holston Conference, Methodist Episcopal Church South,* ed. J. C. Wright. Cincinnati: Cranston & Curtis, 1896. 447 pp.

Presbyterian

Alexander, J. E. *A Brief History of the Synod of Tennessee from 1817-1887.* Knoxville: Ross & Goodheart, 1890. 155 pp.

Alexander, Theron, Jr. "The Covenanters Come to East Tennessee." Thesis, Univ. of Tennessee, 1939.

——. "The Covenanters Come to Tennessee." ETHSP 13 (1941), 36-46.

Posey, Walter B. *The Presbyterian Church in the Old Southwest, 1778-1838.* Richmond, Va.: John Knox, 1952. 192 pp. Posey's theme is that the church was a strong social factor in the development of a new land. He contends that, although other sectarian groups were larger, the Presbyterians had an importance out of proportion to their numbers because of their strong stand for a literate church membership pledged to religion, virtue, and knowledge.

Queener, Verton M. "Gideon Blackburn." ETHSP 6 (1934), 12-28. Blackburn was an early Presbyterian minister, educator, and missionary to the Cherokees.

Thompson, Ernest T. *Presbyterians in the South: 1607-1861,* vol. 1. Richmond, Va.: John Knox, 1963- . 608 pp.

Roman Catholic

Daniel, Victor Francis. *The Faith of the Church in Tennessee; or the Life, Times, and Character of the Right Reverend Richard Pius Miles o.p., the First Bishop of Nashville.* Washington, D.C.: Dominicans, 1926. 607 pp. Miles was the founder of the Catholic church in Tennessee.

Flanigen, George J., ed. *Catholicity in Tennessee: A Sketch of Catholic Activities in the State, 1541-1937.* Nashville: Ambrose, 1937. 176 pp. A fine survey history.

——., ed. "Diocese of Nashville." *New Catholic Encyclopedia,* vol. 10, pp. 215-16. New York: McGraw, 1967.

Fox, Sister Mary Loyola. *A Return of Love: The Story of the*

Sisters of Mercy in Tennessee, 1866-1966. Nashville: Bruce, 1967. 188 pp. The story of the 100 years since the coming of Mother Clare and the five pioneers to war-stricken Nashville in 1866. St. Mary's Hospital in Knoxville is one of the enduring legacies of this group.

Haile, Mrs. Herbert, ed. *Catholic Women of Tennessee, 1937-1956.*

The *Tennessee Register.* Nashville: Diocese of Nashville, 1937- . The *Register* is the official weekly newspaper of the Diocese of Nashville.

EVOLUTION CONTROVERSY AND THE SCOPES TRIAL

Allen, Leslie Henri, ed. and comp. *Bryan and Darrow at Dayton: The Record and Documents of the "Bible-Evolution Trial."* New York: Lee, 1925; rpt. New York: Russell, 1967. 218 pp. The first book to appear shortly after the Scopes trial, this work features court transcripts and testimony.

Allen, Warren. "Background of the Scopes Trial at Dayton, Tennessee." Thesis, Univ. of Tennessee, 1959.

"Anti-evolution Statute of Tennessee." *Scientific American,* Apr. 1927, pp. 269 ff.

Armstrong, O. K. "Bootleg Science in Tennessee." *North American Review* (Fall 1929), 138-42.

Bailey, Kenneth K. "The Enactment of Tennessee's Anti-evolution Law." Thesis, Vanderbilt Univ., 1949.

——. "The Enactment of Tennessee's Anti-evolutionary Law." *JSH* 16 (1950), 472-90.

"Baiting of Judge Raulston." *New Republic,* July 29, 1925, pp. 249-50.

"Battle of Tennessee." *Nation,* May 27, 1925, pp. 589-90.

Darrow, Clarence S. *The Story of My Life.* New York: Scribners, 1932; rpt. Grosset's Universal Library no. 27, Grosset, 1957; rpt. Clifton, N.J.: Kelley, 1971. 465 pp. Rpt. New York: Scribners, 1960. 495 pp.

"Dayton, and After." *Nation,* Aug. 5, 1925, pp. 155-56.

DeCamp, L. Sprague. *The Great Monkey Trial.* Garden City, N.Y.: Doubleday, 1968. 538 pp.

——. "End of the Monkey War." *Scientific American,* Feb. 1969, pp. 15-21.

"Evolution Unproven; Tennessee House Votes 67 to 20 for the Anti-evolution Law." *Literary Digest,* Mar. 2, 1935, pp. 22 ff.

"Foreign Amazement at Tennessee." *Literary Digest,* July 25, 1925, pp. 18-19.

Gatewood, Willard B., Jr., ed. *Controversy in the Twenties: Fundamentalism, Modernism, and Evolution.* Nashville: Vanderbilt Univ. Press, 1969. 459 pp. The basic purpose of this work is to indicate the nature and dimension of the confrontation between modernists and fundamentalists in the 1920s.

Ginger, Ray. *Six Days or Forever? Tennessee v. John Thomas Scopes.* Boston: Beacon, 1958; rpt. New York: Quadrangle, 1969. 258 pp. A highly interpretative account of this court case which symbolized the tension between modernism and religious fundamentalism in the 1920s.

Grebstein, Sheldon Norman, ed. *Monkey Trial: The State of Tennessee vs. John Thomas Scopes,* Houghton Mifflin Research Series no. 4. Boston: Houghton, 1969. 221 pp.

Harrison, Charles Y. *Clarence Darrow.* New York: Cape & Smith, 1931. 380 pp.

Hays, Arthur G. "Strategy of the Scopes Defense." *Nation,* Aug. 5, 1925, pp. 157-58.

Hicks, Bobby E. "The Great Objector: The Public Career of Dr. John R. Neal." Thesis, Univ. of Tennessee, 1968. Dr. Neal was active in the Scopes trial.

"John T. Scopes Redivivus." *Christian Century,* Apr. 5, 1967, pp. 429 ff.

Jordan, R. "Tennessee Goes Fundamentalist." *New Republic,* Apr. 29, 1925, pp. 258-60.

Keebler, Robert Samuel. *The Tennessee Evolution Case.* Memphis: Davis, 1925. 34 pp.

Krutch, Joseph W. "Tennessee: Where Cowards Rule." *Nation,* July 15, 1925, pp. 88-89.

——. "Darrow vs. Bryan." *Nation,* July 29, 1925, pp. 136-37.

——. "Monkey Trial." *Commentary,* May 1967, pp. 83-84.

Levine, Lawrence W. *Defender of the Faith—William Jennings Bryan: The Last Decade, 1915-1925.* Diss., Columbia Univ., 1962; copy, Ann Arbor: Univ. Microfilms, 1962. New York: Oxford Univ. Press, 1965, 1968. 386 pp.

McGeehan, W. O. "Why Pick on Dayton?" *Harper's Monthly Magazine,* Oct. 1925, pp. 623-27.

Mencken, H. L. "In Tennessee." *Nation,* July 1, 1925, pp. 21-22.

Miller, E. E. "Tennessee: Three-Quarters of Bewilderment." *Nation,* Sept. 20, 1922, pp. 273-76.

Milton, George F. "Dayton Postscript." *Outlook,* Aug. 19, 1925, pp. 550-52.

Montgomery, James R., and Gerald Gaither. "Evolution and Education in Tennessee: Decisions and Dilemmas." *THQ* 28 (1969), 141-55.

Montoux, J. T. "Liberal in Tennessee." *Nation,* June 23, 1926, pp. 696-97. Relates to John R. Neal.

Pattie, Frank A., ed. "The Last Speech of William Jennings Bryan." *THQ* 6 (1947), 265-83.

Scopes, John T., and James Presley. *Center of the Storm: Memoirs of John T. Scopes.* New York: Holt, 1967. 277 pp. A memoir written 41 years after the Scopes trial. Scopes concluded that if what he did advanced the cause of freedom an inch, he was satisfied.

"Scopes Retrial." *Life,* May 9, 1955, pp. 119-20.

Shaw, B. "Scopes Reviews the Monkey Trial." *Esquire,* Nov. 1970, pp. 86ff.

Smith, S. D. "Great Monkey Trial." *New York Times Magazine,* July 4, 1965, pp. 8-9.

Szasz, Ferenc M. "The Scopes Trial in Perspective." *THQ* 30 (1971), 288-98.

"Tennessee Sticks to Genesis." *Literary Digest,* July 11, 1931, pp. 21-22.

Tompkins, Jerry R., ed. *D-Days at Dayton: Reflections on the Scopes Trial.* Baton Rouge: Louisiana State Univ. Press, 1965. 173 pp. An excellent short survey of the Scopes trial.

The World's Most Famous Court Trial, Tennessee Evolution Case; Complete Stenographic Report of the Famous Court Test of the Tennessee Anti-evolution Act, at Dayton, July 10 to 21, 1925, Including Speeches and Arguments of Attorneys, Testimony of Noted Scientists, and Bryan's Last Speech. Cincinnati: Nat. Bk., 1925. Rpt., Civil Liberties in American History Series, New York: Da Capo, 1971. 339 pp.

Natural History

BIBLIOGRAPHIES

Cockrill, Elizabeth. *Bibliography of Tennessee Geology, Soils, Drainage, Forestry, etc., with Subject Index.* Extract from Tennessee Geological Survey Bulletin no. 1. Nashville: Folk-Keelin, 1911. 119 pp.

Wilson, Charles W. *Annotated Bibliography of the Geology of Tennessee through December 1950,* Tennessee Dept. of Conservation, Division of Geology Bulletin 59. Nashville: Tennessee Dept. of Conservation, 1953. 308 pp.

GEOGRAPHIES, INCLUDING SCHOOL TEXTS

Amick, Harold C., and L. H. Rollins. *The Geography of Tennessee.* Boston: Ginn, 1937. 48 pp.

Barrett, Albert T. *Tennessee.*

Hewitt, Edwin C. *The Geography of Tennessee, a Supplement to the Eclectic Series of Geographies.* Cincinnati: Van Antwerp, Bragg, 1878. 16 pp.

Law, Harry L. *A Brief Geography of Tennessee.* Clarksville: Queen City Bk., 1949, 1954. 101 pp.

——. *Tennessee Geography.* Oklahoma City: Harlow Pub., 1954. 171 pp.

——. *Tennessee: Its Lands and People.* Ann Arbor, Mich.: n.p., 1962. 306 pp.

Monteith, James W. *Geography of Tennessee: Physical, Political, and Historical.* New York: Barnes, 1877. 8 pp. Special supplement to the Tennessee edition of Monteith's school geographies.

Yoakley, Ina. *Geography of Tennessee,* supplement to Stull and Hatch, *Our World Today* (a textbook in the new geography). New York: Allyn, 1943. 75 pp.

Geologies, Including School Texts

Currey, Richard Owen. *A Sketch of the Geology of Tennessee: Embracing a Description of Its Minerals and Ores, Their Variety and Quality, Modes of Assaying and Value; with a Description of Its Soils and Productiveness, and Palaeontology.* Knoxville: Kinsloe & Rice, 1857. 128 pp.

Glenn, Leonidas Chalmers. "The Growth of Our Knowledge of Tennessee Geology." *Resources of Tennessee,* vol. 2, pp. 167-219. Nashville: Tennessee Dept. of Conservation, Div. of Geology, 1912.

Rooker, Henry Grady. "A Sketch of the Life and Work of Dr. Gerard Troost." *THM* (ser. 2) 3 (1932-37), 3-19. Rpt. in *Tennessee Old and New,* II, 288-303. Dr. Troost was Tennessee's first geologist.

Safford, James Merrill. *A Geological Reconnaissance of Tennessee.* Nashville: State of Tennessee, 1856. 120 pp.

———. *Geology of Tennessee.*

Safford, James Merrill, and Joseph Buckner Killebrew. *The Elements of the Geology of Tennessee. Prepared for the Use of the Schools of Tennessee, and for All Persons Seeking a Knowledge of the Resources of the State.* Nashville: Tavel, Eastman & Howell, 1876 (255 pp.); rpt. Foster & Webb, 1900; rpt. Ambrose & Bostelman, 1904 (264 pp.).

Troost, Gerard. *Geological Reports to the General Assemblies of the State of Tennessee.* Nashville: Nye, 1835-47.

Flora and Fauna

Bailey, James L., comp. *Tennessee Timber Trees.* Nashville: Tennessee Dept. of Conservation and Commerce, 1962. 32 pp.

Barr, Thomas C., Jr. *Caves of Tennessee.* Tennessee Geological Survey Bulletin no. 64. Nashville: Tennessee Dept. of Conservation, 1961. 567 pp.

Craig, John L., et al. *Birds of Tennessee in Verse and Story.* Nashville: Cullom & Ghertner, 1939; rpt. Nashville: Rich, 1944. 76 pp.

Emerson, Frederick B. *Tennessee Valley Wildlife: An Outlook for Year 2000.* Norris: Div. of Forestry Development, TVA, 1968. 26 pp.

Ganier, Albert F. *A Distributional List of the Birds of Tennessee.*

Nashville: Tennessee Dept. of Game and Fish, 1933. 64 pp.

Glenn, Leonidas Chalmers. "Natural Setting for Tennessee Gardens." *History of Homes and Gardens of Tennessee,* 1st ed., 29-32.

——. "Iris in Nashville." *History of Homes and Gardens of Tennessee,* 1st ed., 502-3.

Hazard, James O. "The Work of the Tennessee Forest Service." *JTAS* 6 (1931), 130-39.

Headden, Harmon C., and Damon Headden. *Conservation of Wildlife and Forests in Tennessee.* Kingsport: Southern, 1936; rpt. Nashville: McQuiddy, 1941. 242 pp.

Jennison, Harry Milliken. *A Preliminary Check-list of the Spring Wild Flowers and the Ferns of Tennessee,* Supplement to the *Journal* of the Tennessee Academy of Science, vol. 4, no. 2. Nashville: Williams, 1929. 32 pp.

Killebrew, Joseph B. *The Grasses of Tennessee; Including Cereals, and Forage Plants.* Nashville: *American* Co., 1878. 511 pp.

Kuhne, Eugene R. *A Guide to the Fishes of Tennessee and the Mid-South.* Nashville: Tennessee Dept. of Conservation, Div. of Game & Fish, 1939. 124 pp.

Maddox, Rufus Sherrill, et al. *Common Forest Trees of Tennessee, How to Know Them; a Pocket Manual.* Nashville: Tennessee Dept. of Conservation, 1922. 72 pp. 10th ed., rev., Clarksville: Lloyd's, 1938. 80 pp.

Schultz, Vincent, et al. *Statewide Wildlife Survey of Tennessee, a Study of the Land, Wildlife, Farmer, Hunter and Trapper; Final Report of Work Accomplished with Federal Aid to Wildlife Restoration Funds under Pittman-Robertson Project no. W-16-R.* Nashville: Tennessee Game and Fish Commission, 1954. 506 pp.

Scribner, Frank Lamson. *Grasses of Tennessee.* 2 vols. Knoxville: Agricultural Experiment Station, Univ. of Tennessee, 1892-94.

Shanks, Royal E., and Aaron J. Sharp. *Summer Key to Tennessee Trees.* Knoxville: Univ. of Tennessee Press, 1950, 1963, 1968. 24 pp. All trees of the state, native or naturalized, identified by leaves and other characteristics.

Svenson, Henry. *Tennessee Wildflowers.* Nashville: Division of Information, Tennessee Dept. of Conservation, 1964. 28 pp.

Tennessee Department of Conservation and Commerce, Education Service. "Some Tennessee Trees—a Simple, Illustrated Key." Nashville: Unpublished typescript. 1966. 31 pp.

Tennessee State Game and Fish Commission. *Amphibians and Reptiles of Tennessee.* Nashville: State of Tennessee, 1965. 28 pp.

Wiesehuegel, E. G. "Forest Tree Improvement Progress in Tennessee." *Southern Lumberman,* June 1, 1956, pp. 34-39.

Augustin Gattinger

Gattinger, Augustin. *The Tennessee Flora: With Special Reference to the Flora of Nashville. Phaenogams and Vascular Cryptogams.* Nashville: The Author, 1887. 109 pp.

———. *The Medicinal Plants of Tennessee Exhibiting Their Commercial Value, with an Analytical Key, Descriptions in Aid of Their Recognition, and Notes Relating to Their Distribution, Time and Mode of Collection, and Preparation for the Drug Market,* arr. T. F. P. Allison. Nashville: F. M. Paul, 1894. 128 pp.

———. *The Flora of Tennessee and a Philosophy of Botany, Respectfully Dedicated to the Citizens of Tennessee.* Nashville: *Gospel Advocate,* 1901. 296 pp.

Goodpasture, Albert V., ed. "Dr. Augustin Gattinger." *AHM* 9 (1904), 153-78; rpt. in *Tennessee Old and New,* II, 317-39. Some persons attribute the writing of this article to Robert A. Halley.

Halley, Robert A. *Dr. Augustin Gattinger: The Pioneer Botanist of Tennessee.* Nashville: Cumberland, 1904. 28 pp.

Oakes, Henry N. *A Brief Sketch of the Life and Works of Doctor Augustin Gattinger.* Thesis, George Peabody College, 1932. *JTAS* 7 (1932), 261-412; rpt. Nashville: Cullom & Ghertner, 1932. 152 pp.

GREAT SMOKY MOUNTAINS AND GREAT SMOKY MOUNTAINS NATIONAL PARK

[*See also* Social and Cultural History.]

Bibliographies

McCoy, George William. *A Bibliography for the Great Smoky Mountains.* Asheville, N.C.: n.p., 1932. 31 pp.

Mason, Robert L., and Myron H. Avery. *A Bibliography for the Great Smokies,* rpt. from *Appalachia* 18 (3), 271-77. Boston: n.p., 1931. 7 pp.

General History and Description

Adams, Paul J. *Mt. Le Conte.* Knoxville: Holston, 1966. 63 pp.

Bowman, Elizabeth Skaggs. *Land of High Horizons.* Kingsport: Southern, 1938, 1948. 212 pp.

Callahan, North. *Smoky Mountain Country,* American Folkways Series, ed. Erskine Caldwell. New York: Duell, Sloan & Pearce, 1952. 257 pp.

Campbell, Carlos C. *Birth of a National Park in the Great Smoky Mountains; an Unprecedented Crusade Which Created, as a Gift of the People, the Nation's Most Popular Park.* Knoxville: Univ. of Tennessee Press, 1960 (155 pp.); rev. ed., 1970 (184 pp.). The finest description we have of the enormous effort put forth by many dedicated people during the period from 1920 to 1940 to bring into being the Great Smoky Mountains National Park. Includes 29 photographs, 5 maps.

——. "Flora of the Great Smokies." *History of Homes and Gardens of Tennessee,* 121-22.

Campbell, Carlos C., William F. Hutson, and Aaron J. Sharp. *Great Smoky Mountains Wildflowers.* Knoxville: Univ. of Tennessee Press, 1962 (40 pp.); enl. ed., 1964, 1965, 1966, 1969 (88 pp.); 3rd ed., 1970, 1972 (112 pp.). Superb photographs in natural color of 175 wildflowers.

Connelly, Thomas L. *Discovering the Appalachians. What to Look for from the Past and in the Present along America's Eastern Frontier.* Harrisburg, Pa.: Stackpole Bks., 1968. 223 pp. An account of the great recreation and travel opportunities throughout the Appalachians; although often impressionistic, it maintains one's high interest.

Douglas, William O. "The People of Cades Cove." *National Geographic Magazine,* July 1962, pp. 60-95.

Fink, Paul M. "Early Explorers in the Great Smokies." ETHSP 5 (1933), 55-68; rpt. in *Tennessee Old and New,* II, 304-16.

——. "Smoky Mountains History As Told in Place Names." ETHSP 6 (1934), 3-11.

——. *That's Why They Call It . . . . The Names and Lore of the Great Smokies. Have You Ever Wondered Why the Mountains and Valleys of the Smokies Were So Named? These Are the Romantic Stories behind Them.* Jonesboro: The Author, 1956. 20 pp.

Fink, Paul M., and Myron H. Avery. "The Nomenclature of the Great Smoky Mountains." ETH*SP* 9 (1937), 53-64.

Fitzgerald, Mary Newman. *The Cherokee and His Smoky Mountain Legends.*

Frome, Michael. *Strangers in High Places: The Story of the Great Smoky Mountains.* Garden City, N.Y.: Doubleday, 1966. 394 pp. The story of the Great Smoky Mountains National Park, its social and cultural history, and its opportunities to enjoy and commune with nature in some of its greatest beauty.

Gatewood, Willard B., Jr. "North Carolina's Role in the Establishment of the Great Smoky Mountains National Park." *NCHR* 37 (1960), 165-84.

Gilbert, Vernon Collis. "Vegetation of the Grassy Balds of the Great Smoky Mountains." Thesis, Univ. of Tennessee, 1954.

The Great Smoky Mountains National Park, Tennessee and North Carolina. Knoxville: Great Smoky Mtns. Pub., 1928. 80 pp.

Hall, Joseph Sargent. *The Phonetics of Great Smoky Mountain Speech.* Diss., Columbia Univ., 1941. Rpt., American Speech Reprints and Monographs no. 4. New York: King's Crown, 1942. 110 pp.

———. *Smoky Mountain Folk and Their Lore.* Asheville: N.C.: Great Smoky Mtn. Natural Hist. Assoc., 1960, 1964. 68 pp.

Hart, Val. "Pack Trip through the Smokies." *National Geographic Magazine,* Oct. 1952, pp. 473-502.

Hesler, L. R. *Mushrooms of the Great Smokies; a Field Guide to Some Mushrooms and Their Relatives.* Knoxville: Univ. of Tennessee Press, 1960. 304 pp. Descriptions of 183 species, with over 200 excellent illustrations; useful to mushroom hunters of the eastern states.

Hoyt, Edwin Palmer [pseud. Christopher Martin]. *Your National Parks: Great Smoky Mountains.* New York: Putnam, 1965. 127 pp. Juvenile.

Huheey, James E., and Arthur Stupka. *Amphibians and Reptiles of Great Smoky Mountains National Park.* Knoxville: Univ. of Tennessee Press, 1967, 1972. 112 pp.

Hunnicutt, Samuel J. *Twenty Years of Hunting and Fishing in the Great Smoky Mountains.* Knoxville: Newman, 1926; rpt. Maryville: n.p., 1951. 216 pp.

Hutchens, Ross E. *Hidden Valley of the Smokies.* New York: Dodd, 1971.

Justus, May. *The Complete Peddler's Pack: Games, Songs, Rhymes, and Riddles from Mountain Folklore,* illus. Jean Tamburine. Knoxville: Univ. of Tennessee Press, 1967. 100 pp. A fine treasure for collectors of folklore and cultural heritage of the Great Smoky Mountains.

Keats, J. "To Meet Spring Halfway." *Holiday,* April 1971, pp. 66-69.

Kephart, Horace. *Our Southern Highlanders.* New York: Outing, 1913. 305 pp. Enl. ed., New York: Macmillan, 1922. 469 pp.

King, P. B., and Arthur Stupka. "Great Smoky Mountains; Their Geology and Natural History." *Scientific Monthly,* July 1950, pp. 31-43.

Lambert, Robert S. "Logging the Great Smokies, 1880-1930." *THQ* 20 (1961), 350-63.

Linzey, Alicia W., and Donald W. Linzey. *Mammals of Great Smoky Mountains National Park.* Knoxville: Univ. of Tennessee Press, 1971, 1972. 148 pp. 32 plates of illus. Valuable to amateur naturalists.

Maloney, J. "Time Stood Still in the Smokies." *Saturday Evening Post,* Apr. 27, 1946, pp. 16-17.

Martin, Christopher. *See* Hoyt, Edwin Palmer.

Mason, Robert Lindsay. *The Lure of the Great Smokies.* Boston: Houghton, 1927. 320 pp.

Mathes, C. Hodge. *Tall Tales from Old Smoky.* Kingsport: Southern, 1952. 241 pp.

Peattie, Roderick, ed. *The Great Smokies and the Blue Ridge: The Story of the Southern Appalachians,* American Mountain Series, vol. 1. New York: Vanguard, 1943. 372 pp.

Porter, Eliot. *Appalachian Wilderness: The Great Smoky Mountains.* New York: Dutton, 1970. 123 pp. Natural and human history by Edward Abbey; epilogue, Harry M. Caudill.

Roy, Leonard C. "Rambling around the Roof of Eastern America." *National Geographic Magazine,* Aug. 1936, pp. 242-66.

Schlatter, John. "Great Smokies Trails, the Backpacking Permit System." *National Parks and Conservation Magazine,* Sept. 1972, pp. 13-17.

Seeman, Elizabeth. *In the Arms of the Mountain; an Intimate Journal of the Great Smokies,* illus. Glen H. Rounds. New York: Crown, 1961. 251 pp.

Shields, A. Randolph. "Cades Cove, in the Great Smoky Mountains National Park." *THQ* 24 (1965), 103-20; rpt. in *More Landmarks of Tennessee,* 33-50.

Snyder, Opal. "History of the Great Smoky Mountains National Park." Thesis, George Peabody College, 1935.

Stupka, Arthur. *Notes on the Birds of Great Smoky Mountains National Park.* Knoxville: Univ. of Tennessee Press, 1963, 1968. 256 pp. Observations of more than 200 species, based on 25 years of field work.

———. *Trees, Shrubs, and Woody Vines of Great Smoky Mountains National Park.* Knoxville: Univ. of Tennessee Press, 1964, 1968. 196 pp., 16 pp. illus. The detailed notes are based upon field observations of many years.

Tennessee General Assembly. *Joint Legislative Committee Report on the Great Smoky Mountains and Other Areas for a National or State Park.* Nashville: State of Tennessee, 1925.

Thornburgh, Laura [pseud. Laura Thornborough]. *The Great Smoky Mountains,* drawings Vivian Moir. New York: Thomas Y. Crowell, 1937. 147 pp. Rpt. Knoxville: Univ. of Tennessee Press, 1956; rev. ed., 1962 (180 pp.); 10th rpt., 1971 (224 pp.). Written by one born and reared in sight of the Great Smokies, this work has a special quality which makes it personal and interesting.

Wharton, D. "Our Most Popular National Park." *Saturday Evening Post,* June 5, 1954, pp. 34-35.

Wright, James B. *Great Smoky Mountains National Park. Statement of Jas. B. Wright of Knoxville, Tennessee, Elicited by the Park Investigation Committee Appointed by the Sixty-sixth General Assembly (1929) under House Resolution no. 21, the Senate Concurring.* Knoxville: Rich, 1929. 72 pp.

Young, Gordon. "Great Smokies National Park: Solitude for Millions." *National Geographic Magazine,* Oct. 1968, pp. 522-49.

Literature Relating to Tennessee History

BIBLIOGRAPHY

Rubin, Louis D., and Robert D. Jacobs, eds. *Southern Renascence: The Literature of the Modern South*. Baltimore: Johns Hopkins Univ. Press, 1953. 450 pp.

HISTORICAL AND BIOGRAPHICAL FICTION

Blanton, Margaret Gray. *The White Unicorn*. New York: Globus, 1961. 424 pp. Concerns the Tennessee Centennial.

Chapman, John S. H., and Mary I. Chapman [pseud. Maristan Chapman]. *Rogue's March*. Philadelphia: Lippincott, 1949. 384 pp. Describes Tennesseans in the American Revolution, especially in the battle of Kings Mountain.

——. *Tennessee Hazard*. Philadelphia: Lippincott, 1953. 367 pp. Treats the Spanish Conspiracy in the Tennessee country, with John Sevier and John Tipton as prominent figures.

Churchill, Winston. *The Crossing*. New York: Macmillan, 1904; 1912. 598 pp. Rpt. Green and Blue Library Series, introd. Alice Jordan. New York: Macmillan, 1930. 296 pp. Rpt. Boston: Gregg, 1969. 598 pp.

Crabb, Alfred Leland. *Home to the Hermitage, a Novel of Andrew and Rachel Jackson*. Indianapolis: Bobbs-Merrill, 1948. 318 pp.

——. *Home to Tennessee, a Tale of Soldiers Returning*. Indianapolis: Bobbs-Merrill, 1952. 299 pp. Relates to Tod Carter and the battles of Franklin and Nashville.

——. *Journey to Nashville, a Story of the Founding*. Indianapolis: Bobbs-Merrill, 1957. 291 pp. Describes the Donelson party's journey from Fort Patrick Henry to Fort Nashborough.

Craddock, Charles Egbert. *See* Murfree, Mary N.

Farrar, Rowena Rutherford. *Bend Your Heads All: A Novel*. New York: Holt, 1965. 288 pp. Describes Fort Nashborough and the Donelson party.

——. *A Wondrous Moment Then.* New York: Holt, 1968. 343 pp. Details the women's suffrage movement in Nashville.

Gerson, Noel B. *The Cumberland Rifles.* Garden City, N.Y.: Doubleday, 1952. 314 pp. About the Lost State of Franklin.

——. *The Yankee from Tennessee.* Garden City, N.Y.: Doubleday, 1960. 382 pp. A novel of Andrew Johnson.

——. *Old Hickory.* Garden City, N.Y.: Doubleday, 1964. 372 pp. A novel of Andrew Jackson.

——. *The Slender Reed; a Biographical Novel of James K. Polk, Eleventh President of the United States.* Garden City, N.Y.: Doubleday, 1965. 394 pp.

——. *Sam Houston.* Garden City, N.Y.: Doubleday, 1968. 297 pp. A biographical novel.

——. *Clear for Action!* Garden City, N.Y.: Doubleday, 1970; rpt. New York: Popular Library, 1971. 254 pp. A novel of David Glasgow Farragut.

Gordon, Caroline. *None Shall Look Back.* New York: Scribners, 1937; rpt. New York: Cooper Sq., 1972. 378 pp. Concerns Nathan Bedford Forrest and the battle of Chickamauga in the Civil War.

——. *Green Centuries.* New York: Scribners, 1941; rpt. New York: Cooper Sq., 1972. 469 pp. Relates to East Tennessee in pioneer and Indian days.

Kroll, Harry Harrison. *Rogues' Company.* Indianapolis: Bobbs-Merrill, 1943. 412 pp. A novel of the Tennessee desperado, John Murrell, in the 1820s.

——. *Darker Grows the Valley.* Indianapolis: Bobbs-Merrill, 1947. 400 pp. A description of the Clinch Valley of East Tennessee from 1778 to modern times.

Lytle, Andrew. *The Long Night.* New York: Bobbs-Merrill, 1936. 331 pp. Describes the battle of Shiloh in the Civil War.

——. *At the Moon's Inn.* New York: Bobbs-Merrill, 1941. 400 pp. Describes DeSoto and the Spaniards at Chickasaw Bluffs (Memphis) in 1539.

McSpadden, J. Walker. *Storm Center, a Novel about Andy Johnson.*

Miller, Helen Topping. *Shod with Flame.* Indianapolis: Bobbs-Merrill, 1946. 270 pp. A novel of the Civil War in East Tennessee.

——. *The Sound of Chariots; a Novel of John Sevier and the State of Franklin.* Indianapolis: Bobbs-Merrill, 1947. 288 pp.

Moore, John Trotwood. *Hearts of Hickory; a Story of Andrew Jackson and the War of 1812.* Nashville: Cokesbury, 1926. 450 pp.

Murfree, Mary N. [pseud. Charles Egbert Craddock]. *Where the Battle Was Fought.* Boston: Osgood, 1884; rpt. New York: Houghton, 1884. 423 pp. Treats the battle of Stones River in the Civil War.

——. *The Story of Old Fort Loudoun.* New York: Macmillan, 1899. Rpt. Boston: Gregg, 1970. 409 pp. About a British fort built in 1756-57 in East Tennessee.

Nicholson, Meredith. *The Cavalier of Tennessee.* New York: Bobbs-Merrill, 1928. 402 pp. A novel of Andrew Jackson.

Parks, Edd Winfield. *Nashoba.* Describes Frances Wright's West Tennessee experiment in utopian living.

Rowell, Adelaide. *On Jordan's Stormy Banks. A Novel of Sam Davis, Confederate Scout.*

Stone, Irving. *The President's Lady; a Novel about Rachel and Andrew Jackson.* Garden City, N.Y.: Doubleday, 1951, 1959; rpt. New York: NAL, 1968. 338 pp.

Wellman, Paul I. *Magnificent Destiny; a Novel about the Great Secret Adventure of Andrew Jackson and Sam Houston.* Garden City, N.Y.: Doubleday, 1962. 479 pp.

SOCIAL AND CULTURAL LIFE IN FICTION

Agee, James. *A Death in the Family.* New York: McDowell, Oblensky, 1957; rpt. Avon, 1957. 339 pp. Rpt. in Maurois, *The Titans,* Books Abridged Series, New York: Bks. Abridg., 1958. 448 pp. Rpt. New York: Avon, 1964. An autobiographical account of life in Knoxville in 1915.

Armstrong, Anne W. *This Day and Time.* New York: Knopf, 1930. 269 pp. Depicts life in the East Tennessee mountains.

Boone, Jack. *Dossie Bell is Dead, a Novel.* New York: Stokes, 1939. 291 pp. Depicts life in rural West Tennessee.

De la Motte, Roy [pseud. Gregory Wilson]. *The Valley of Time.* Garden City, N.Y.: Doubleday, 1967. 449 pp. The effect of the TVA on people in East Tennessee.

Dykeman, Wilma. *The Tall Woman.* New York: Holt, 1962. 312 pp. A novel set in the Great Smoky Mountains during the Civil War.

———. *The Far Family.* New York: Holt, 1966; rpt. Avon, 1972. 372 pp. A sequel to *The Tall Woman,* set in an East Tennessee town near the Smokies.

Ford, Jesse Hill. *Mountains of Gilead, a Novel.* Boston: Little, 1961. 342 pp. Life in the fictional West Tennessee town of Somerton.

———. *The Liberation of Lord Byron Jones.* Racial problems in Somerton.

Gordon, Caroline. *The Women on the Porch.* New York: Scribners, 1944; rpt. Cooper Sq., 1972. 316 pp. The story is laid in Montgomery County.

———. *The Strange Children.* New York: Scribners, 1951; rpt. Cooper Sq., 1972. 303 pp. Family life in Middle Tennessee.

Govan, Christine Noble. *Jennifer's House.* Boston: Houghton, 1945. 337 pp. Life on a Middle Tennessee country estate.

Gowen, Emmett. *Mountain Born.* Indianapolis: Bobbs-Merrill, 1932. 307 pp. Rural family life in Middle Tennessee.

———. *Dark Moon of March.* Indianapolis: Bobbs-Merrill, 1933. 335 pp. Life on a Middle Tennessee farm.

Haun, Mildred. *The Hawk's Done Gone.* New York: Bobbs-Merrill, 1940. Rpt., ed. Herschel Gower. Nashville: Vanderbilt Univ. Press, 1968. 290 pp. Rural life in Cocke and Hancock counties.

Huddleston, Edwin G. *The Claybrooks.* New York: Macmillan, 1951. 297 pp. Family life in Nashville in 1910.

Huie, William B. *Mud on the Stars.* New York: Fisher, 1942. 341 pp. The TVA figures prominently in this novel set in Alabama and Tennessee.

Jones, Madison. *The Innocent.* New York: Harcourt, 1957; rpt. Popular Lib., 1971. 370 pp. Middle Tennessee rural life.

———. *Forest of the Night.* New York: Harcourt, 1960. 305 pp. Middle Tennessee frontier life.

———. *A Buried Land, a Novel.* New York: Viking, 1963. 295 pp. The effect of TVA on farm life in Middle Tennessee.

———. *An Exile.* New York: Viking, 1967. 153 pp. Middle Tennessee rural justice.

———. *A Cry of Absence.* New York: Crown, 1971; rpt. PB, 1972. 280 pp. Racial tension in a Middle Tennessee Town.

Kroll, Harry Harrison. *The Mountainy Singer.* New York: Morrow, 1928. 310 pp. Customs and social life of people in the Tennessee mountains.

———. *The Cabin in the Cotton.* New York: Long & Smith, 1931. 288 pp. The life of West Tennessee sharecroppers.

———. *Lost Homecoming.* New York: Coward, 1950. 311 pp. Life in a West Tennessee town.

Lytle, Andrew. *The Velvet Horn.* New York: McDowell, Oblensky, 1957. 373 pp. Middle Tennessee rural life shortly after the Civil War.

McCarthy, Cormac. *The Orchard Keeper.* New York: Random, 1965; rpt. London: Deutsch, 1966. 246 pp. East Tennessee rural life.

———. *Outer Dark.* New York: Random, 1968; rpt. New York: Ballantine, 1971. 242 pp. A Gothic novel of East Tennessee mountain people.

Marius, Richard. *The Coming of Rain.* East Tennessee life in 1885.

Moore, John Trotwood. *The Bishop of Cottontown: A Story of the Southern Cotton Mills.* Philadelphia: Winston, 1906. 644 pp. Life in a Tennessee mill town.

Murfree, Mary N. [pseud. Charles Egbert Craddock]. *In the Tennessee Mountains.* Boston: Houghton, 1884. 322 pp. Rpt. Tennesseanna Editions, introd. Nathalia Wright, Knoxville: Univ. of Tennessee Press, 1970. 356 pp. A superior example of local color fiction, these eight short stories are Miss Murfree's best work.

Parks, Edd Winfield. *Backwater.* New York: Twayne, 1957. 186 pp. Life on a West Tennessee farm beside the Mississippi River.

Ramsey, Robert W. *The Mockingbird.* New York: Dutton, 1951. 223 pp. Family life in Memphis in the 1930s.

Stuart, Jesse. *Daughter of the Legend.* New York: McGraw-Hill, 1965. 249 pp. Melungeon life in Hancock County.

Sullivan, Walter. *Sojourn of a Stranger.* New York: Holt, 1957. 316 pp. Middle Tennessee life after the Civil War.

———. *The Long, Long Love.* New York: Holt, 1959. 255 pp. Life in a Middle Tennessee town.

Taylor, Peter H. *A Woman of Means.* New York: Harcourt, 1950. 160 pp. A novelette set in a West Tennessee town.

———. *The Widows of Thornton.* New York: Harcourt, 1954. 310 pp. A novelette with a West Tennessee town setting.

———. *Happy Families Are All Alike.* New York: McDowell, Oblensky, 1959; rpt. Stamford, Conn.: Astor-Honor, 1959. 305 pp. Short stories laid in Middle and West Tennessee communities.

——. *Miss Leonora When Last See, and Fifteen Other Stories.* New York: Oblensky, 1963; rpt. Stamford, Conn.: Astor-Honor, 1963. 398 pp. More short stories laid in Middle and West Tennessee towns.

Warren, Robert Penn. *Flood, a Romance of Our Time.* New York: Random, 1964. 440 pp.

Wilson, Gregory. *See* De la Motte, Roy.

Winslow, Anne Goodwin. *The Dwelling Place.* New York: Knopf, 1943. 256 pp. Family life in West Tennessee.

——. *A Quiet Neighborhood.* New York: Knopf, 1947. 240 pp. Life in a West Tennessee town.

——. *It Was Like This.* New York: Knopf, 1949. 223 pp. Life in a West Tennessee town.

——. *The Springs.* New York: Knopf, 1949. 227 pp. Social life at Raleigh Springs, a fashionable spa near Memphis.

Nashville Fugitives and Agrarians

Beatty, Richmond Croom. "Fugitive and Agrarian Writers at Vanderbilt." *THQ* 3 (1944), 3-23.

Connelly, Thomas Lawrence. "The Vanderbilt Agrarians: Time and Place in Southern Tradition." *THQ* 22 (1963), 22-37.

Couch, William T., ed. *Culture in the South.* Chapel Hill: Univ. of North Carolina Press, 1934; rpt. Westport, Conn.: Greenwood, 1971. 711 pp. An answer to *I'll Take My Stand* (s.v. Twelve Southerners).

Cowan, Louise. *The Fugitive Group; a Literary History.* Baton Rouge: Louisiana State Univ. Press, 1959, 1968. 277 pp.

Cullen, Charles T. "The Nashville Agrarians; A History of the Southern Protest Movement, 1919-1936." Thesis, Florida State Univ., 1963.

Daniel, Robert. "The Critics of Nashville." *Tennessee Studies in Literature* 1 (1956), 19-26.

Davenport, F. Garvin, Jr. *The Myth of Southern History; Historical Consciousness in Twentieth-Century Southern Literature.* Nashville: Vanderbilt Univ. Press, 1970. 212 pp. Contains a chapter on the Nashville Agrarians.

Davidson, Donald. *Still Rebels, Still Yankees, and Other Essays.* Baton Rouge: Louisiana State Univ. Press, 1957; 2nd ed., Library of Southern Civilization, 1971. 284 pp.

Irish, Marion D. "Proposed Roads to the New South, 1941, Chapel Hill Planners vs. Nashville Agrarians." *Sewanee Review* 49 (1941), 1-27.

Knickerbocker, William S. "The Fugitives of Nashville." *Sewanee Review* 36 (1928), 211-24.

Owsley, Frank L. *The South: Old and New Frontiers; Selected Essays*, ed. Harriet C. Owsley. Athens: Univ. of Georgia Press, 1969. 284 pp. A series of important essays which together point up the impact which Owsley had upon changing the national attitude toward the South, determining that both thinking and writing would be more objective, based upon evidence.

Santmyer, Sue. "The 'Nashville Agrarians' as Critics of American Society." Thesis, Vanderbilt Univ., 1951.

Stewart, John L. *The Burden of Time: The Fugitives and Agrarians; the Nashville Groups of the 1920's and 1930's, and the Writing of John Crowe Ransom, Allen Tate, and Robert Penn Warren.* Princeton: Princeton Univ. Press, 1965. 551 pp. An analysis of the importance of this literary movement upon literature and upon its dominant participants.

Twelve Southerners. *I'll Take My Stand; the South and the Agrarian Tradition.* New York: Harper, 1930, 1962; rpt. P. Smith, 1951. 359 pp. Twelve southern writers argue for a more agrarian society, as opposed to the industrial, which they consider a materialistic, dehumanizing technology representing a decaying culture.

Weaver, Richard M. "Agrarianism in Exile." *Sewanee Review* 58 (1950), 586-606.

Wilson, Edmund. "Tennessee Agrarians." *New Republic*, July 29, 1931, pp. 279-81.

Young, Thomas D., and M. Thomas Inge. *Donald Davidson: An Essay and a Bibliography*. Nashville: Vanderbilt Univ. Press, 1965. 118 pp. Rpt. New York: Twayne, 1971. 173 pp.

County Histories

BIBLIOGRAPHIES AND GENERAL WORKS

Foster, Austin P. *Counties of Tennessee.* Nashville: State of Tennessee, 1923. 124 pp.

Goodspeed Publishing Company. *History of Tennessee.*

Killebrew, Joseph Buckner. *Introduction to the Resources of Tennessee.* This work contains detailed information on most of the counties of the state.

Luttrell, Laura E., and Pollyanna Creekmore, comps. *Writings on Tennessee Counties.* Nashville: Tennessee Hist. Comm., 1944. 50 pp. Rpt. from *THQ* 2 (1943), 257-79, 336-61; 3 (1944), 81-83.

Paine, Thomas H. *Short Sketches of the Counties of Tennessee.* Nashville: Tennessee Dept. of Agriculture, 1901.

Tennessee State Library and Archives. *Writings on Tennessee Counties Available on Interlibrary Loan from the Tennessee State Library and Archives.* Nashville: State of Tennessee, 1971. 47 pp.

Wagner, Paul W., ed. *County Government Across the Nation.*

ANDERSON COUNTY
Historian: Mrs. G. D. Hoskins, Box 86, Clinton 37716.

"Anderson County." *History of Tennessee,* East Tennessee Edition, ed. Weston A. Goodspeed et al., pp. 837-40, 1104-23. Nashville: Goodspeed Pub., 1887.

Bradley, Frank H. *Geological Report: Coal Creek Mining and Manufacturing Company of Tennessee.* New York: David H. Gildersleeve, 1872. 16 pp.

Harris, Luther Calvin. "An Educational Survey of Coal Creek Community, Anderson County, Tennessee." Thesis, Univ. of Tennessee, 1932.

Historical Records Survey, Tennessee. *Inventory of the County*

Archives of Tennessee: Anderson County. Nashville: The Survey, WPA, 1941. 89 leaves.

History of Andersonville Baptist Church and Andersonville Institute. Knoxville: Coleman's, 1966. 84 pp.

McMillan, Fay E. "A Biographical Sketch of Joseph Anderson (1757-1937)." ETHSP 2 (1930), 81-93. Anderson County is named for this man.

Oak Ridge. *See* Economic History: Oak Ridge.

Seeber, Raymond Clifford. "A History of Anderson County, Tennessee." Thesis, Univ. of Tennessee, 1928.

Stevenson, C. "Contrast in Perfect Towns: Norris and Kingsport, Tennessee; Federal Showcase and Industry's Yardstick Town." *Nation's Business,* Dec. 1937, pp. 18-20.

Tennessee Valley Authority, Industry Division. *Agricultural-Industrial Survey of Anderson County, Tennessee.* Knoxville: TVA, 1934. 174 pp.

Weaver, Mary. *One Hundred Years: A Story of the First Baptist Church, Clinton, Tennessee.* Clinton: Clinton *Courier-News,* 1940. 35 pp.

School Desegregation Problems of the 1950s

Anderson, Margaret. "Clinton, Tennessee: Children in a Crucible." *New York Times Magazine,* Nov. 2, 1958, pp. 12ff.

———. *The Children of the South.* The story of a courageous teacher who experienced the throes of desegregation in her community, Clinton. Bombings, threats, violence, compassion are all interwoven in this narrative.

Barrett, George. "Study in Desegregation: The Clinton Story." *New York Times Magazine,* Sept. 16, 1956, pp. 11ff.

Dykeman, Wilma, and James Stokely. "Courage in Action in Clinton, Tennessee." *Nation,* Dec. 22, 1956, pp. 531-33.

———. "Clinton, Tennessee: A Town on Trial." *New York Times Magazine,* Oct. 26, 1958, pp. 9ff.

———. "'The South' in the North." *New York Times Magazine,* Apr. 17, 1960, pp. 8ff. Concerns Clinton.

Halberstam, David. "Town That Became Everybody's Test Tube." *Reporter,* Jan. 10, 1957, pp. 32-36. Relates to Clinton.

———. "Patching the Roof at Clinton High." *Reporter,* Sept. 17, 1959, pp. 39-40.

Morrell, Ken. "The Equation at Oak Ridge." *Southern Education Report,* Mar. 1968, pp. 15-18. A story of successful integration.

"Now: Dynamite in School Unrest." *U.S. News and World Report,* Sept. 20, 1957, pp. 74-76.

Phillips, Wayne. "Integration: The Pattern Emerges." *New York Times Magazine,* Sept. 29, 1957, pp. 19 ff.

Rorty, James. "Hate Monger with Literary Trimmings." *Commentary,* Dec. 1956, pp. 533-42.

——. "In Contempt of the Law." *New Republic,* Dec. 17, 1956, pp. 7-8.

BEDFORD COUNTY
Historian: Richard Poplin, 112 Lee Lane, Shelbyville 37160.

"Bedford County." *History of Tennessee,* ed. Weston A. Goodspeed et al., 861-84, 1126-89. Nashville: Goodspeed Pub., 1886.

Bedford County Historical Society. *Doors of the Past, Homes of Shelbyville and Bedford County.* Shelbyville: Shelbyville *Times-Gazette,* 1969. 88 pp.

Biographical Directory: Bedford County Members of the Tennessee General Assembly, 1796- . Nashville: State Library and Archives, 1968- . 58 pp.

Centennial Celebration, Fourth of July, 1876, at Shelbyville, Bedford County, Tennessee. Chattanooga: W. I. Crandall, 1877. 31 pp.

Cogswell, Robert E. *The History of the First Presbyterian Church, Shelbyville, Tennessee, 1815-1865.* Nashville: Parthenon Press, c. 1965. 279 pp.

Davidson, H. Lewis. *History of Bedford County.* Chattanooga: W. I. Crandall, 1877. 31 pp.

Green, Ben A. *Biography of the Tennessee Walking Horse.*

Gunter, Charles Raymond. "Bedford County during the Civil War." Thesis, Univ. of Tennessee, 1963.

Historical Records Survey, Tennessee. *Inventory of the County Archives of Tennessee: Bedford County.* Nashville: The Survey, WPA, 1940.

History of Fairfield, Tennessee, from 1796 to 1963. Eagleville: n.p., c. 1963. 21 pp.

Hutson, J. L. *Old Times in Bedford County, Tennessee.* Shelbyville: n.d. 20 pp.

Ingram, Joe Mason. "The Educational History of Shelbyville, Tennessee, 1870-1954." Thesis, George Peabody College, 1954.

Jacobs, Lucile Frizzell. *Duck River Valley in Tennessee and Its Pioneers.* n.p., 1968. 124 pp.

Owsley, Harriet C., ed. "William Eakins's Memoirs." *THQ* 23 (1964), 269-78. Eakin was a Bedford County resident c. 1840.

Poplin, Richard H. "The Letters of W. Thomas Osborne." *THQ* 22 (1963), 152-69. Osborne was a Spanish-American War soldier from Bedford County.

——. *Silhouettes from Walking Horse Country.* Shelbyville: Central Pub. Co., 1969. 67 pp.

Shelbyville "Times-Gazette." Sesqui-centennial Historical Edition 1819-1969. Shelbyville: Shelbyville *Times-Gazette,* 1969. 262 pp.

Stewart, Rose Tate. *Pioneer Schools of Bedford County and Their Masters.* n.p., n.d.

Tennessee State Department of Education. *Bedford County and Shelbyville City Educational Survey.* Nashville: State of Tennessee, 1967. Various pagings.

Tennessee State Library and Archives. "Inventory of Bedford County Records." Nashville: State Library and Archives, 1964- . Unpublished typescript.

Tennessee Valley Authority, Industry Division. *Agricultural-Industrial Survey of Bedford County.* 2 vols. Knoxville: TVA, 1934.

BENTON COUNTY
Historian: J. D. Melton, Route 2, Camden 38320.

"Benton County." *History of Tennessee,* ed. Weston A. Goodspeed et al., 832-46, 935-54. Nashville: Goodspeed Pub., 1887.

Biographical Directory: Benton County Members of the Tennessee General Assembly, 1796- . 36 pp. This volume also includes Decatur County.

Burchard, Ernest F. "Benton and Humphreys Counties." *Tennessee State Geological Survey Bulletin* no. 39, pp. 51-53. Nashville, 1934.

Little, Arthur D., Inc. *The Opportunity for Industrial Development in Benton, Houston, and Humphreys Counties, Tennessee; Report to the Area Redevelopment Administration, C-65063.* Cambridge, Mass.: The Company, 1964. 135 pp.

Smith, Jonathan Kennon. *A History of Benton County, Tennessee, to 1900.* Memphis: J. Edge Co., 1970. 151 pp.

Tennessee State Library and Archives. "Inventory of Benton County Records." Nashville: State Library and Archives, 1964- . Unpublished typescript.

BLEDSOE COUNTY
Historian: Elizabeth Robnett, Route 1, Pikeville 37367.

Biographical Directory: Bledsoe County Members of the Tennessee General Assembly, 1796- . 51 pp. This volume also includes Marion and Sequatchie counties.

"Bledsoe County." In *History of Tennessee,* East Tennessee Edition, ed. Weston A. Goodspeed et al., 1071.

Brown, Dalton Milford. "An Educational and Economic Survey of Bledsoe County, Tennessee." Thesis, Univ. of Tennessee, 1926.

——. *Educational, Economic and Community Survey, Bledsoe County.* Knoxville: School of Education, Univ. of Tennessee, 1927. 39 pp.

Guild, Josephus Conn. *A Report on Coal Lands Lying in Bledsoe County.* Nashville, 1887.

Hiatt, Ellen O. M. *Sequatchie Valley, a Historical Sketch,* photographs Marguerite Hiatt. Nashville: Methodist Pub. House, 1916. 32 pp.

Robnett, Elizabeth Parham. "A History of Bledsoe County, Tennessee: 1807-1957." Ed.S. diss., George Peabody College, 1957.

Scott, John H., Jr. "Pikeville, Market Center of the Upper Sequatchie Valley." Thesis, Univ. of Tennessee, 1951.

Tennessee State Library and Archives. "Inventory of Bledsoe County Records." Nashville: State Library and Archives, 1964- . Unpublished typescript.

Tennessee Valley Authority, Industry Division. *Agricultural-Industrial Survey of Bledsoe County.* Knoxville: TVA, 1934. 124 pp.

BLOUNT COUNTY
Historian: Inez Burns, 1308 Brannon Drive, Maryville 37801.

Bartlett, Alex. *The History of New Providence Church, Maryville, Tennessee.* Maryville: College Printing, 1876. 10 pp.

Battaglia, Joseph Charles. "The Social and Economic History of Maryville since 1890." Thesis, Univ. of Tennessee, 1936.

Best, Edwin J. "New Providence Presbyterian Church." ETHSP 30 (1958), 75-95.

Biographical Directory: Blount County Members of the Tennessee General Assembly, 1796- . 47 pp.

"Blount County." History of Tennessee, East Tennessee Edition, ed. Weston A. Goodspeed et al., 828-33, 1088-96.

Burns, Inez E. "Settlement and Early History of the Coves of Blount County, Tennessee." ETHSP 24 (1952), 44-67.

———. History of Blount County, Tennessee, from War Trail to Landing Strip, 1795-1955. Nashville: Tennessee Hist. Comm., 1957. 375 pp.

Eusebia Presbyterian Church, Blount County, Tennessee: Eusebia Church History. Maryville: n.p., 1924.

Historical Records Survey, Tennessee. Inventory of the County Archives of Tennessee: Blount County. Nashville: The Survey, WPA, 1941.

Hood, John O. History of the Chilhowee Baptist Association. This association is located in Blount County.

Houts, Paul G. "An Educational, Economic, and Community Survey of Blount County, Tennessee." Thesis, Univ. of Tennessee, 1928.

Howard, George Craft. "The Louisville Area Development Association." Thesis, Univ. of Tennessee, 1948.

Hutchison, Robert S., and David C. Hodge. An Economic Survey of Blount County, Tennessee, a Study of Resources and Industrial Potentials. Knoxville: Bureau of Business Research, Univ. of Tennessee, 1957. 92 pp.

McTeer, William A. History of New Providence Presbyterian Church, Maryville, Tennessee, 1786-1921. Maryville: New Providence Church, 1921. 111 pp.

Maryville College Students. "Social Survey of Blount County, Tennessee." Maryville: Unpublished typescript, 1930. 43 leaves.

Parham, W. E. "Old Blount County Papers." THM 7 (1921), 92-95.

Rittgers, Fred Henry. "A Geographical Survey of Blount County, Tennessee." Thesis, Univ. of Tennessee, 1941.

Tennessee State Library and Archives. "Inventory of Blount County Records." Nashville: State Library and Archives, 1964- . Unpublished typescript.

Wright, Nathalia. "Montvale Springs under the Proprietorship of Sterling Lanier, 1857-1863." ETHS*P* 19 (1947), 48-63.

BRADLEY COUNTY
Historian: James F. Corn, Box 67, Cleveland 37311.

Biographical Directory: Bradley County Members of the Tennessee General Assembly, 1796- . 37 pp. This volume also contains Polk County.

"Bradley County." *History of Tennessee,* East Tennessee Edition, ed. Weston A. Goodspeed et al., 798-804, 962-87.

Burkhead, Homer. *Guest's Guide; Points of Interest in Cleveland.* Cleveland: n.p., n.d. 13 pp.

Cleveland Chamber of Commerce. *Bradley County, Tennessee.* 2 vols. Cleveland: Historical & Pictorial Advertising, 1929.

Cleveland Chamber of Commerce. *City and County with a Future! Cleveland, Bradley County, Tennessee.* Cleveland: Historical & Pictorial Advertising, 1929. 64 pp.

Corn, James Franklin. *Red Clay and Rattlesnake Springs.*

Edwards, R. M. "Bradley County and the Town of Cleveland." *East Tennessee. Historical and Biographical,* 355-78.

Hardy, Lucina Elizabeth. *An Album of Historical Memories. Chatata-Tasso, Bradley County, Tennessee, 1830-1961.* N.p., 1962. 84 pp.

Historical Records Survey, Tennessee. *Inventory of the County Archives of Tennessee: Bradley County.* Nashville: The Survey, WPA, 1941. 137 leaves.

Hurlburt, J. S. *History of the Rebellion in Bradley County, East Tennessee.* Indianapolis: Downey & Brause, 1866. 280 pp.

Long, Grady M. "Folk Medicine in McMinn, Polk, Bradley and Meigs Counties, Tennessee, 1910-1927." *TFSB* 28 (1962), 1-8.

McClary, Ben H., and LeRoy P. Graf, eds. " 'Vineland' in Tennessee, 1852: The Journal of Rosine Parmentier." ETHS*P* 31 (1959), 95-111.

McGhee, Lucy Kate, comp. *Cherokee and Creek Indians. Returns of Property Left in Tennessee and Georgia, 1838,* vol. 64. Includes Bradley County property.

Pieper, Mary Gladys Brown. "Church Organization in Bradley County, Tennessee, in 1950." Thesis, Univ. of Tennessee, 1952.

Ross, Ernest Lafayette. "An Educational Study of Bradley County, Tennessee." Thesis, Univ. of Tennessee, 1940.

Slay, James Linwood. "A History of Bradley County, Tennessee, to 1861." Thesis, Univ. of Tennessee, 1967.

Tennessee State Department of Education. *Bradley County Schools Survey Report.* Nashville: State of Tennessee, 1966. Various pagings.

Trewhitt, Frank G. "Ghost Tales from Bradley County." *TFSB* 29 (1963), 10-12.

Wooten, John Morgan. *A History of Bradley County.* Cleveland: Bradley Co. Post 81, American Legion, in cooperation with Tennessee Hist. Comm., 1949. 323 pp.

——. *Centennial of the First Presbyterian Church, United States, in Cleveland, Tennessee, 1837-1937.* Cleveland: The Author, 1937. 33 pp.

——. *Red Clay in History.*

——. *Red Clay Council Ground.*

CAMPBELL COUNTY
Historian: T. H. Miller, 314 East Prospect Street, LaFollette 37766.

"Campbell County." *History of Tennessee,* East Tennessee Edition, ed. Weston A. Goodspeed et al., 844-46, 1125-35.

Hassell, Bluford Leslie. "An Administrative and Educational Survey of the Schools of Campbell County, Tennessee." Thesis, Univ. of Tennessee, 1933.

Ridenour, George L. *The Land of the Lake: A History of Campbell County, Tennessee.* LaFollette: LaFollette Pub., 1941. 104 pp.

Siler, James Hayden. *A History of Jellico, Tennessee, Containing Information on Campbell County, Tennessee, and Whitley County, Kentucky.* Jellico, 1938. 44 pp. First published in the summer and autumn of 1938 as a series of sketches in the Jellico *Advance-Sentinel.*

Smith, G. Hobart. "An Economic, Social and Educational Survey of Campbell County, Tennessee." Thesis, Univ. of Tennessee, 1934.

Tennessee State Department of Education. *Campbell County School Survey.* Nashville: State of Tennessee, 1962. Various pagings.

Tennessee State Library and Archives. *A Study of the Community of LaFollette, Tennessee.* Nashville: State of Tennessee, 1957. 55 pp.

Tennessee Valley Authority, Industry Division. *Agricultural-Industrial Survey of Campbell County.* Knoxville: TVA, 1934. 79 pp.

CANNON COUNTY
Historian: No appointment made.

Biographical Directory: Cannon County Members of the Tennessee General Assembly, 1796- . 46 pp. This volume also contains De Kalb County.

Brown, Sterling Spurlock. *History of Woodbury and Cannon County, Tennessee.* Manchester: Doak, 1936. 235 pp.

"Cannon County." *History of Tennessee,* ed. Weston A. Goodspeed et al., 854-60, 987-92.

Mason, Robert L. "Folk Songs and Folk Tales of Cannon County, Tennessee." Thesis, George Peabody College, 1939.

——. "The Life of the People of Cannon County, Tennessee." Diss., George Peabody College, 1946.

Northcutt, Dixon L. "A Geographic Survey of Cannon County, Tennessee." Thesis, Univ. of Tennessee, 1954.

CARROLL COUNTY
Historian: Lucy Williams Brown, Box 87, Huntingdon 38344.

Biographical Directory: Carroll County Members of the Tennessee General Assembly, 1796- . 48 pp.

"Carroll County." *History of Tennessee,* ed. Weston A. Goodspeed et al., 797-813, 847-88.

De Vault, Mary Ruth. *Carroll County Sesquicentennial Booklet.* McKenzie: McKenzie *Banner,* 1972. 192 pp.

McKenzie's Past, 1869-1969. McKenzie, Tennessee, Hub of the Tri-Counties, Carroll, Henry and Weakley. McKenzie: Centennial Corp., 1969. 156 pp.

Rothrock, Mary U., ed. "Family Letters: Home Life in Madison and Carroll Counties, Tennessee, 1864-1867." WTHSP 23 (1969), 110-28; 24 (1970), 106-29.

——, ed. "Family Letters: Home Life in Carroll and Gibson

Counties, Tennessee, 1868." WTHSP 25 (1971), 107-34.

Smith, W. A., ed. "The Autobiographical Sketch of Thomas Hamilton." WTHSP 16 (1962), 127-32. Hamilton was a member of the first Carroll County Court, 1822.

Wingfield, Marshall, ed. "The Diary of Williamson Younger, 1817-1876." WTHSP 13 (1959), 55-77.

CARTER COUNTY
Historian: Ben Allen, Route 3, Elizabethton 37643.

Allen, Ben, and Dennis T. Lawson. "The Wataugans and the Dangerous Example." THQ 26 (1967), 137-47.

Biographical Directory: Carter County Members of the Tennessee General Assembly, 1796- . 61 pp. This volume also contains Johnson and Unicoi counties.

Bohn, Frank. "Tennessee's New Silkworm; Industrial Germany Comes to America." *Review of Reviews,* Oct. 1928, pp. 367-72.

"Carter County." *History of Tennessee,* East Tennessee Edition, ed. Weston A. Goodspeed et al., 906-12, 1289-99.

Goff, John S. "Col. James P. T. Carter of Carter County." THQ 26 (1967), 372-82.

Holly, J. Fred. "The Social and Economic Effects Produced upon Small Towns by Rapid Industrialization." Thesis, Univ. of Tennessee, 1938. Elizabethton is described in this study.

Hyder, N. E. "Watauga Old Fields." AHM 8 (1903), 253-55.

Merritt, Frank. *Early History of Carter County, 1760-1861.* Thesis, Univ. of Tennessee, 1950. Knoxville: East Tennessee Hist. Soc., 1950. 213 pp.

Morgan, Charles McKinley. "An Educational Survey of Carter County, Tennessee. Thesis, Univ. of Tennessee, 1936.

Nave, Robert Tipton. "History of the Iron Industry in Carter County to 1860." Thesis, East Tennessee State Univ., 1953.

Nelson, Selden. "The Tipton Family of Tennessee." ETHSP 1 (1929), 67-76.

Perry, Henry Wacaster. "A Sampling of the Folklore of Carter County, Tennessee." Thesis, George Peabody College, 1938.

Scott, Samuel W., and Samuel P. Angel. *History of the Thirteenth Regiment, Tennessee Voluntary Cavalry, U.S.A.* Treats Carter County.

Sharp, Karl Wayne. "A Study of Debt History in Carter County, Tennessee, 1892-1952." Thesis, Univ. of Tennessee, 1952.

Tennessee State Library and Archives. "Inventory of Carter County Records." Nashville: State Library and Archives, 1964- . Unpublished typescript.

Tennessee Valley Authority, Industry Division. *Agricultural-Industrial Survey of Carter County.* Knoxville: TVA, 1934. 137 pp.

CHEATHAM COUNTY
Historian: James B. Hallums, 106 Smith Street, Ashland City 37015.

Biographical Directory: Cheatham County Members of the Tennessee General Assembly, 1796- . 47 pp. This volume also contains Dickson County.

"Cheatham County." *History of Tennessee,* ed. Weston A. Goodspeed et al., 947-74, 1358-88.

Historical Records Survey, Tennessee. *Inventory of the County Archives of Tennessee: Cheatham County.* Nashville: The Survey, WPA, 1941.

Tennessee State Library and Archives. "Inventory of Cheatham County Records." Nashville: State Library and Archives, 1964- . Unpublished typescript.

CHESTER COUNTY
Historian: Corley Orick, North Avenue, Henderson 38340.

Biographical Directory: Chester County Members of the Tennessee General Assembly, 1796- . 43 pp. This volume also contains McNairy County.

"Chester County." *History of Tennessee,* ed. Weston A. Goodspeed et al., 806-13, 862-69.

Henderson Area Centennial. *Henderson Centennial Celebration Commemorating 100 Years of Progress. "From Indians to Industry."* Jackson: Laycock, 1960. 64 pp.

Reid, Mrs. S. E. *A Brief History of Chester County, Tennessee, Then and Now. An Historical Comparison, Facts of the Past and Present Which the Future Will Want to Remember.* Jackson: McCowat-Mercer Press, 1924, 1967. 24 pp.

Tennessee Valley Authority, Industry Division. *Agricultural-Industrial Survey of Chester County.* Knoxville: TVA, 1936.

CLAIBORNE COUNTY
Historian: Edgar A. Holt, Route 1, Tazewell 37879.

Alvarez, Eugene. "Impressions of Cumberland Gap." *Virginia Cavalcade* 14 (1964), 11-19.

Borah, Leo A. "Home Folk around Historic Cumberland Gap." *National Geographic Magazine,* Dec. 1943, pp. 741-68.

"Claiborne County." *History of Tennessee,* East Tennessee Edition, ed. Weston A. Goodspeed et al., 847-50, 1136-45.

Cumberland Gap; Its Geographical and Commercial Features and Importance as a Railroad Centre. New York: Fleming, Brewster, n.d. 54 pp.

Edwards, Lawrence, ed. *Minutes of Davis Creek Church, 1897-1907.* Montevallo, Ala.: *Times* Printing, 1968. 244 pp. This is a Baptist church.

Fetterman, John. "The People of Cumberland Gap." *National Geographic Magazine,* Nov. 1971, pp. 591-621.

Hamilton, Alice M. *A Doctor's Pilgrimage.* Harrogate: Cumberland Gap Hotel and Park, 1892. 44 pp.

Kincaid, Robert L. "Cumberland Gap, Gateway of Empire." *FCHQ* 15 (1941), 25-40.

——. *The Wilderness Road.*

Luckett, William W. "Cumberland Gap National Historical Park." *THQ* 23 (1964), 303-20; rpt. in *Landmarks of Tennessee,* 179-96.

McFarland, Robert W. *The Surrender of Cumberland Gap.* Columbus, O.: Smythe, 1898.

Polhemus, Richard R., and James H. Polhemus. "The McCullough Bend Site." *Tennessee Archaeologist* 22 (1966), 13-24.

Vaughn, Lawrence M. *Just the Little Story of Cumberland Gap.* Middlesboro, Ky.: Middlesboro Chamber of Commerce, 1927. 16 pp.

CLAY COUNTY
Historian: Mrs. W. B. Upton, Celina 38551.

Gaskill, Gordon. "Backyard Bonanza." *American Magazine* 129 (1940), 36-37, 124-26. Oil wells in Clay County.

Powell, James Curtis. "Farm Taxation and County Government in

Overton, Clay and Pickett Counties, Tennessee." Thesis, Univ. of Tennessee, 1930.

Stone, William Curtis. "Historical Sketches of Clay County, Tennessee." Nashville: Unpublished typescript, 1962. 15 leaves.

COCKE COUNTY
Historian: Mary R. Ruble, 1210 East Broadway, Newport 37821.

"Cocke County." *History of Tennessee,* East Tennessee Edition, ed. Weston A. Goodspeed et al., 864-67, 1194-99.

Godshalk, Rolfe F., ed. *Newport.* Newport: Cliftan Club, 1970. 261 pp.

Haun, Mildred. "Cocke County Ballads and Songs." Thesis, Vanderbilt Univ., 1937.

——. "The Traditions of Cocke County." *TFSB* 33 (1967), 72-79.

O'Dell, Ruth Webb. *Over the Misty Blue Hills: The Story of Cocke County, Tennessee.* Newport [?], 1951. 369 pp.

"Sketches of Pioneer Medical Doctors of Cocke County." Unpublished typescript, 1968.

Rakestraw, Isaac Knox. "Negro Education in Cocke County." Thesis, Univ. of Tennessee, 1956.

Tennessee Valley Authority, Industry Division. *Agricultural-Industrial Survey of Cocke County.* Knoxville: TVA, 1934.

COFFEE COUNTY
Historian: David L. Jacobs, Beech Grove 37018.

Biographical Directory: Coffee County Members of the Tennessee General Assembly, 1796- . 42 pp. This volume also contains Grundy County.

"Coffee County." *History of Tennessee,* ed. Weston A. Goodspeed et al., 827-45, 921-51.

Ewell, Leighton. *History of Coffee County, Tennessee.* Manchester: Doak, 1936. 85 pp.

Hoyer, Raymond A. "The Soldier Town." *Journal of Educational Sociology* 15 (1942), 487-97. Relates to Tullahoma during World War II.

Jernigan, V. H. "Fort Nash—Outpost of the 1790's." *THQ* 29 (1970), 130-38.

Martinez, Corinne. *Coffee County from Arrowheads to Rockets; A History of Coffee County, Tennessee.* Tullahoma: Coffe Co. Conservation Bd., 1969. 360 pp.

Old Stone Fort. *See* Early Period: Prehistory and Archaeology, Middle Tennessee.

Tennessee State Library and Archives. "Inventory of Coffee County Records." Nashville: State Library and Archives, 1964- . Unpublished typescript.

Tennessee Valley Authority, Industry Division. *Agricultural-Industrial Survey of Coffee County.* Knoxville: TVA, 1934.

CROCKETT COUNTY
Historian: No appointment made.

Armentrout, W. W. *Educational, Economic and Community Survey, Crockett County.* Knoxville: School of Education, Univ. of Tennessee, 1924. 31 pp.

"Crockett County." *History of Tennessee,* ed. Weston A. Goodspeed et al., 830-42, 947-71.

Historical Records Survey, Tennessee. *Inventory of the County Archives of Tennessee: Crockett County.* Nashville: The Survey, WPA, 1936. 115 leaves.

Whatley, Thomas J. *Significant Trends in Agriculture in Crockett County, Tennessee, 1879-1945.* Knoxville: Agricultural Experiment Station, Univ. of Tennessee, 1947. 37 leaves.

CUMBERLAND COUNTY
Historian: Laverne M. Tabor, Crossville 38555.

Allred, Charles Ernest. *Significant Changes in Agriculture of Cumberland County, Tennessee.* Knoxville: Agricultural Experiment Station, Univ. of Tennessee, 1942. 38 leaves.

Bonser, H. J., et al. *Neighborhoods and Communities of Cumberland County, Tennessee.* Knoxville: Agricultural Experiment Station, Univ. of Tennessee, 1941. 20 leaves.

——, et al. *Local Leadership in Rural Communities of Cumberland County, Tennessee.* Knoxville: Agricultural Experiment Station, Univ. of Tennessee, 1942. 79 leaves.

Brookhart, Mary Bishop. *A Brief History of the First Congregational Church, Crossville, Tennessee, 1887-1962.* Crossville: *Chronicle,* Pub., 1962. 40 pp.

Cooper, Herston. *Crossville.* Miami, Fla. [?]: Adams Press, 1965. 155 pp. A description of the World War II interment camp.

Dodge, Emma Florence. *History of Pleasant Hill; a History of Pleasant Hill Academy and Who's Who of Alumni.* Kingsport: Kingsport Press, 1938. 192 pp.

Fleming, Arklie Lee. "Economic Set-up of the Cumberland Homesteads, Crossville, Tennessee." Thesis, George Peabody College, 1941.

Gray, John W. *The Life of Joseph Bishop, the Celebrated Old Pioneer in the First Settlements of Middle Tennessee, Embracing His Wonderful Adventures and Narrow Escapes with the Indians, His Animating and Remarkable Hunting Excursions. Interspersed with Racy Anecdotes of Those Early Times.* Nashville: The Author, 1858; rpt. Wayne [?], Ill.: Fleming, 1962. 236 pp. Bishop was one of the early settlers of Cumberland County.

Harvey, Stella Mowbray. *Tales of the Civil War Era.* Crossville: *Chronicle* Pub., 1963. 51 pp. Publication of this volume was sponsored by the Cumberland County Civil War Centennial Committee.

Krechniak, Helen B., and Joseph M. Krechniak. *Cumberland County's First Hundred Years.* Crossville: Crossville Centennial Comm., 1956. 377 pp.

Loomis, Charles P. *Social Relationships and Institutions in Seven Rural Communities,* United States Farm Security Administration Social Research Report no. 18. Washington, D.C.: 1940. 82 pp. Reproduced from typewritten copy. Includes Cumberland County.

——, and Dwight M. Davidson. *Standards of Living of the Residents of Seven Rural Resettlement Communities,* United States Farm Security Administration Social Research Report no. 11. Washington, D.C.: 1938. 93 pp. Reproduced from typewritten copy. Includes Cumberland County.

Cole, M. "Mob Rule in Crossville." *Nation,* June 9, 1951, pp. 539-41.

Montgomery, James Elmer. "Two Resettlement Communities on the Cumberland Plateau." Thesis, Vanderbilt Univ., 1941. Includes Cumberland Homesteads.

Moore, James C. "An Analysis of the New Deal Subsistence Homesteads Program in Cumberland County, Tennessee." Thesis, Tennessee Technological Univ., 1967.

Stratton, Cora S. *And This Is Grassy Cove.* Crossville: *Chronicle* Pub., 1938. 54 pp.

Tennessee State Library and Archives. "Inventory of Cumberland County Records." Nashville: State Library and Archives, 1964- . Unpublished typescript.

Tennessee Valley Authority, Industry Division. *Agricultural-Industrial Survey of Cumberland County.* Knoxville: TVA, 1935. 206 pp.

Webb, George Willis. "The Resources of the Cumberland Plateau As Exemplified by Cumberland County, Tennessee: A Geographic Analysis." Thesis, Univ. of Tennessee, 1956.

Wharton, May Cravath. *Doctor Woman of the Cumberlands; the Autobiography of May Cravath Wharton, M.D.* Pleasant Hill: Uplands, 1953. 208 pp.

DAVIDSON COUNTY
Historian: Hugh Walker, Nashville *Tennessean,* 1100 Broadway, Nashville 37203.

Bibliographies

Cundiff, Ruby Ethel, comp. *Nashville, Past and Present, Portrayed in Books: A Bibliography.* Nashville: American Assoc. of Univ. Women, Nashville, 1936. 20 leaves.

Hyde, Grace V. "A Bibliographical Checklist of Nashville Imprints, 1867-1876, with an Introductory Essay on Nashville Literature and Publishers of the Era." Thesis, Univ. of Tennessee, 1953.

Geology and Topography

Marshall, Park. "The Topographical Beginnings of Nashville." *THM* 2 (1916), 31-39.

Wilson, Charles William. *The Geology of Nashville, Tennessee,* Tennessee Dept. of Conservation, Division of Geology Bulletin 53. Nashville: State of Tennessee, 1948. 172 pp.

General History and Early Settlement

Aiken, Leona Taylor. *Donelson, Tennessee: Its History and Landmarks.* Nashville: n.p., 1968. 366 pp.

Anderson, James Douglas. *The Historic Blue Grass Line: A Review of the History of Davidson and Sumner Counties, Together with Sketches of Places, and Events along the Route of the Nashville-*

Gallatin Interurban Railway. Nashville: Nashville-Gallatin Inter-urban Railway, c. 1913. 93 pp.

Andrews, J. D., and Son. *Atlas of the Suburbs of Greater Nashville, Tennessee. Compiled from the Plan Books and Other Official Records in the Register's Office of Davidson County, Showing Recent Additions and Subdivisions.* Nashville: The Authors, 1906. 11 maps.

Arnow, Harriette Simpson. *Seedtime on the Cumberland.* Empha-sizes the pioneer's ability to conquer his environment in the valley of the Cumberland from 1780 to 1803.

———. *Flowering of the Cumberland.* Emphasizes the social and political organizations formed by the early settlers along the valley of the Cumberland from 1780 to 1803.

Beard, William E., comp. *It Happened in Nashville, Tennessee; a Collection of Historical Incidents Which Occurred in Nashville, Are Commemorated There, or in Which Nashville People Were Actors.* Nashville: Davie, 1912. 65 pp.

———. *Red Letter Days in Nashville; Written for the Semi-centennial Edition of the "Nashville Banner," April 5, 1925.* Nashville: Nashville *Banner,* 1925. 22 pp.

———. *Nashville, the Home of History Makers.* Nashville: Civitan Club, 1929. 93 pp.

Boylin, Gerald, comp. *Nashville Illustrated in Colors.* Nashville: Benson, 1937. 36 pp.

Bright, John M. *Donelson and the Pioneers of Middle Tennessee.* Washington, D.C.: Globe, 1880. 35 pp.

Burt, Jesse C. *Nashville, Its Life and Times,* foreword Robert T. Quarles, Jr. Nashville: Tennessee Bk., 1959. 182 pp.

Bushnell, E., ed. *An Early Description of Middle Tennessee.* Chicago: Sleepeck-Helman, 1939. 8 pp.

Cate, Wirt Armistead. "Timothy Demonbreun." *THQ* 16 (1957), 214-27.

Centennial Album of Nashville, Tennessee.

Clarke, Ida Clyde. *All about Nashville: A Complete Historical Guide Book to the City.* Nashville: Marshall & Bruce, 1912. 231 pp.

Clayton, W. Woodford. *History of Davidson County, Tennessee, with Illustrations and Biographical Sketches of Its Prominent Men and Pioneers.* Philadelphia, Pa.: J. W. Lewis, 1880; rpt. Nashville: Charles Elder, 1971. 499 pp. A combination of brief narrative historical, biographical, and institutional sketches, together with general information, it is fragmented, but contains useful information.

Crabb, Alfred Leland. *Journey to Nashville*. Fiction with a strong and accurate regional flavor, it describes the Donelson party's journey from Fort Patrick Henry to Fort Nashborough.

——. *Nashville: Personality of a City*. Indianapolis: Bobbs-Merrill, 1960. 288 pp.

——. *Andrew Jackson's Nashville*. [Nashville]: n.p., 1966. 20 pp.

Creighton, Wilbur Foster. *Building of Nashville*. Nashville: Privately printed, 1969. 205 pp.

Des Champs, Margaret Burr. "Early Days in the Cumberland Country." *THQ* 6 (1947), 195-229.

Elliott, Lizzie P. *Early History of Nashville*. Nashville: Nashville Bd. of Ed., 1911; rpt. Nashville: Nashville Pub. Lib., 1963. 286 pp. Originally published as a textbook.

Federal Writers' Project. "Nashville." *Tennessee*, 179-205.

Garrett, William R. and John M. Bass, eds. "Records of the Cumberland Association." *AHM* 7 (1902), 114-35, 254-66.

Henderson, Archibald. *The Founding of Nashville, Second of the Transylvania Towns: Boonesboro, Kentucky, Nashville, Tennessee, Henderson, Kentucky*. Henderson, Ky.: Transylvanians, 1932. 15 pp.

——. *Richard Henderson: The Authorship of the Cumberland Compact and the Founding of Nashville*. Nashville: n.p., 1916. 20 pp. Rpt. from *THM* 2 (1916), 155-74.

Jones, Ira P. *City of Nashville Illustrated*. Nashville: n.p., 1890. 101 pp.

Kress, S. H., and Co. *Nashville, the Gateway of the South*. Portland, Me.: L. H. Nelson, 1907; rpt. Nashville: Curley, 1970. 32 pp.

Lewis, Eugene C. "James Robertson, Nashville's Founder." *AHM* 8 (1903), 285-94.

McNeilly, J. H., comp. *Memorial: Colonel John Overton and Mrs. Harriet Maxwell Overton*. Nashville: n.p., 1899. 122 pp.

McRaven, William Henry. *Life and Times of Edward Swanson, One of the Original Pioneers Who with General James Robertson Founded Nashville, Tennessee, 1779; First Recorded Settler of Williamson County, Tennessee, March, 1780*. Nashville: The Author, 1937. 240 pp.

——. *Nashville: Athens of the South*. Chapel Hill, N.C.: Scheer & Jervis, 1949. 303 pp. A description of Nashville as a community where quality of educational opportunity and appreciation of the fine arts have been reflected in its history.

May, Charles. *The Pioneers of Nashville and of Tennessee! Who They Were! Where They Came From! How They Got Here! What They Achieved! One Hundred Years Ago! "Honor to Whom Honor Is Due." A Historical Novel of Narrative, about the First Settlers of This Commonwealth in 1780. To Which Is Added: An Historical Sketch about Robertson's and Donaldson's Exploits and Adventures in the Foundation on the Cumberland. A Contribution to the Celebration of Our Centennial in 1880*. Nashville: Nashville *American*, 1880. 157 pp.

Morrison, Andrew. *The City of Nashville*. [Nashville: George W. Engelhardt, 1891?]. 159 pp.

Nashville and Davidson County Metropolitan Government Planning Commission. *History and Physical Setting, Nashville and Davidson County, Tennessee*, Fact Book Series, vol. 1. Nashville: The Comm., 1965. 10 leaves.

Nashville City and Business Directory for 1860-61, vol. 5. Nashville: L. P. Williams, 1860. 303 pp. One of a series begun in 1853, this early city directory contains a good historical sketch and map of the city.

Nashville First American National Bank. *Firsts in Nashville, a Pictorial History*. Nashville: First American Nat. Bank, 1951. 21 pp.; rev. ed., 1966. 31 pp.

Nashville Chamber of Commerce. *Nashville in the 20th Century. Pictorial Edition*. Nashville: Foster & Webb, 1900. 44 pp.

Nelson, Anson. "Brief Annals of Nashville." *Nashville Board of Health Second Report . . . July 4, 1877*, pp. 185-216. Nashville: Tavel, Eastman & Howell, 1877. 230 pp.

Pen and Sunlight Sketches of Nashville, the Most Progressive Metropolis of the South. Nashville: American Illustrating, [1911]. 168 pp.

Pope, Charles M. "John Donelson: Pioneer." Thesis, Univ. of Tennessee, 1969.

Profitt, Waldo. "A Study of Social Conditions in Davidson County, Tennessee." Thesis, Vanderbilt Univ., 1926.

Provine, W. A. "Lardner Clark, Nashville's First Merchant and Foremost Citizen." *THM* 3 (1917), 28-50, 115-33.

Ranson, James Morris. "The Life and Career of James Robertson." Thesis, Univ. of Tennessee, 1966.

Robertson, Laura Lea. *A Country Home in Town*. [Nashville]: n.p., 1937. 15 pp. A brochure to interest buyers in homesites.

Rogers, Linell Chenault. "Francis Nash, Soldier and Patriot." *THM* (ser. 2) 3 (1932-37), 269-79. Nash was the Revolutionary War soldier for whom Nashville is named.

Stealey, John Edmund III. "French Lick and the Cumberland Compact." *THQ* 22 (1963), 323-34.

Taylor, Alfred W., comp. *Index to the Private Acts of the General Assembly which Apply to Davidson County from Creation of County 1783-1937 Inclusive, and the City of Nashville from Adoption of New Charter 1923-37 Inclusive*. Nashville: McDaniel, 1937. 24 pp.

Tennessee State Library and Archives, Manuscript Division. *Index to Interments in the Nashville City Cemetery, 1846-1962*. Nashville: State of Tennessee, 1964. 89 pp.

Thomas, Jane Henry. *Old Days in Nashville, Tennessee. Reminiscences*. Nashville: Methodist Pub. House, 1897. 135 pp. Rpt. Nashville: Charles Elder, 1969. 190 pp.

Thruston, Gates P. "Nashville, the Advance Guard of Western Civilization." *Historic Towns of the Southern States,* American Historic Towns Series, ed. Lyman P. Powell, 477-501. New York: Putnam's, 1900. 604 pp.

Tootle, Margaret Marie. "A History of Old Hickory, Tennessee." Thesis, George Peabody College, 1953.

Waller, William, ed. *Nashville in the 1890's*. Nashville: Vanderbilt Univ. Press, 1970. 342 pp. A history of Nashville's "decisive decade." A fine sequel to Wooldridge's *History of Nashville* (Nashville, 1890), it concentrates upon business, politics, and social life.

——, ed. *Nashville, 1900-1910*. Nashville: Vanderbilt Univ. Press, 1972. 390 pp.

Weidner, Maude. *Nashville Then and Now, 1780-1930*. Nashville: Hermitage Pub., 1930. 85 pp.

Whitley, Edythe J. R. "Revolutionary Soldiers of Davidson County, Tennessee." *William and Mary Quarterly* 11 (1931), 13-19.

——. *Tennessee Genealogical Records: Davidson County Pioneers; Revolutionary and War of 1812 Soldiers*. Nashville: The Author, 1965. 84 leaves.

Williams, Samuel C. "Ann Robertson: An Unsung Tennessee Heroine." *THQ* 3 (1944), 150-55.

——. "Generals Francis Nash and William Lee Davidson." *THQ* 1

(1942), 250-68. The two North Carolinian generals of the American Revolution for whom Nashville and Davidson County were named.

——. "Nashville As Seen by Travellers, 1801-1821." *THM* (ser. 2) 1 (1930-31), 182-206.

Woods, Fayla. *History of Davidson County.* Nashville [?]: 1946 [?]. 32 pp.

Wooldridge, John. *History of Nashville, Tennessee, with Full Outline of the Natural Advantages, Accounts of the Mound Builder, Indian Tribes, Early Settlement, Organization of the Mero District, and General and Particular History of the City Down to the Present Time.* Nashville: Methodist Pub. House, 1890; rpt. Nashville: Charles Elder, 1970. 656 pp.

Nashville during the Civil War and Reconstruction

Armistead, George H., Jr. "'He Is a Great Rascal': A Sketch of Byrd Douglas." *THQ* 27 (1968), 37-39. Douglas was a Civil War cotton broker of Nashville.

Battle of Nashville. *See* Civil War.

Caldwell, May Winston. *A Chapter from the Life of a Little Girl of the Confederacy.* Nashville: Parthenon Press, 1936. 25 pp.

Crabb, Alfred Leland. "The Twilight of the Nashville Gods." *THQ* 15 (1956), 291-305.

Horn, Stanley F. "Nashville during the Civil War." *THQ* 4 (1945), 3-22; rpt. in *Tennessee Old and New,* II, 223-41.

——. "Dr. John Rolfe Hudson and the Confederate Underground in Nashville." *THQ* 22 (1963), 38-52.

Houk, Eliza P. T. *A Tribute to General Gates Phillips Thruston.* Dayton, O.: United Brethren Pub. House, 1914. 129 pp.

Kornell, Gary L. "Reconstruction in Nashville, 1867-1869." *THQ* 30 (1971), 277-87.

Plaisance, Aloysius F., and Leo F. Schelver III. "Federal Military Hospitals in Nashville, May and June, 1863." *THQ* 29 (1970), 166-75.

Watson, McMillan S. "Nashville during the Civil War." Thesis, Vanderbilt Univ., 1926.

Economic History

Alexander, Attie B. "The Development of Motor Bus Transportation in Nashville, Tennessee." Thesis, George Peabody College, 1927.

Bacon, Hollis Phillip II. "The Historical Geography of Ante-bellum Nashville." Ed.D. diss., George Peabody College, 1955.

———. "Nashville's Trade at the Beginning of the Nineteenth Century." *THQ* 15 (1956), 30-36.

———. "Some Problems of Adjustment to Nashville's Site and Situation, 1780-1860." *THQ* 15 (1956), 322-29.

Beaumont, Henry Francis. *West Nashville, Manufacturing Metropolis of the South.* Nashville: The Author, 1908. 52 pp.

Campbell, John P., comp. *The Nashville, State of Tennessee, and General Commercial Directory.* 5 vols. Nashville: n.p., 1853-60.

Cornelius, Edward Gordon. "A Study of Economic Conditions in Davidson County." Thesis, Vanderbilt Univ., 1926.

Cummings, James Barnett. "The Clay Products Industries of Nashville." Thesis, George Peabody College, 1928.

Dawson, Clarence Colton. "History of the Flour Milling Industry of Nashville, Tennessee." Thesis, George Peabody College, 1931.

Halley, Robert A. *The City of Nashville: Advantages Possessed by Tennessee's Capital as a Home and as a Place of Business.* Nashville: Foster & Webb, 1903. 32 pp.

Haynes, M. A. "Nashville, Tennessee." *De Bow's Commercial Review* 1 (1846), 503-8.

Kennamer, Lorrin Garfield. "The Woodworking Industries of Nashville. A Study in Economic Geography and Conservation." Thesis, George Peabody College, 1922.

Killebrew, Joseph B. *Life and Character of James Cartwright Warner. A Memorial Volume.* Nashville: Methodist Pub. House, 1897. 150 pp. Warner was an iron-making entrepreneur of the late 19th century.

Larkin, Lee Roy. "An Economic Study of the Nashville Fluid Milk Market." Thesis, Univ. of Tennessee, 1952.

Miller, Laura Kate. "Geographical Influences in the Growth of Nashville." Thesis, George Peabody College, 1923.

"Nashville's Flashiest Merchant Fights to Save Store; Harvey Co. and Cain-Sloan Co." *Business Week,* Mar. 27, 1954, pp. 124-26.

"Nashville: A Story of Progress." *Forbes,* May 15, 1968, pp. 51-52.

Nashville Third National Bank. *Nashville, 1927-1952; Twenty-five Years of Progress.* Nashville: Third Nat. Bank, 1952. 48 pp.

"Nativity Display." *Business Week,* Dec. 26, 1953, p. 82.

Owsley, Harriet C., ed. "William Eakin's Memoirs." *THQ* 23 (1964), 269-78. Eakin was a Nashville merchant of the 1840s.

Pierce, John E. *Structure of the Nashville Economy; an Input-Output Analysis in Terms of Moneyflows.* Knoxville: Center for Business and Economic Research, Univ. of Tennessee, 1969. 268 pp.

Roberts, Charles E. *Nashville and Her Trade for 1870.* Nashville: Roberts & Purvis, 1870. 480 pp.

Taylor, A. W. "TVA Power Is a Boon to Nashville." *Christian Century,* Sept. 27, 1944, p. 1110.

Thursby, Vincent V. "The Nashville TVA Contract as an Instrument of Public Policy." Thesis, Vanderbilt Univ., 1947.

Political History and Public Administration

Boddie, Rufus Foster. "Murder Prosecutions in Davidson County, Tennessee (1907-1916) vs. (1919-1928)." Thesis, George Peabody College, 1929.

Bradford, Thomas Gamaliel. *By-laws of the Town of Nashville.* Nashville: The Author, 1814. 36 pp.

"City in the Hands of a Receiver." *Outlook,* Sept. 1, 1915, pp. 11 ff. Refers to Nashville.

Clark, Mary Katherine. "Activities of the Davidson County Court." Thesis, George Peabody College, 1931.

Community Services Commission for Davidson County and the City of Nashville. *A Future for Nashville: A Report.* Nashville: Community Services Comm., 1952. 201 pp.

Creswell, Richard, et al. "Nashville Model Cities: A Case Study." *VLR* 25 (1972), 727-844.

Crittenden, Marvin C. "A History of the Welfare Commission of Davidson County, Tennessee." Thesis, Univ. of Tennessee, c. 1956.

Garrett, William R., and John M. Bass, eds. "Davidson County Land Warrants." *AHM* 6 (1901), 236-42.

———. "The Earliest Records of Davidson County." *AHM* 7 (1902), 315-21.

Halberstam, David. "Good Jelly's Last Stand." *Reporter,* Jan. 19, 1961, pp. 40-41. Description of a colorful black politician.

Head, J. M. "Nashville, Tennessee, Municipal Government." *Arena,* Apr. 1903, pp. 345-51.

Jenkins, Sandra Laureen. "Evolution of Local Government Services by Nashville and Bangkok Residents: A Comparative Study." Thesis, Vanderbilt Univ., 1966.

Nashville Housing Authority. *Capitol Hill Redevelopment Project.* Nashville: The Authority, 1952. 46 pp.

Provine, William A. "A Davidson Political Circular, 1843." *THM* 5 (1919), 195-96.

Rains, James E., comp. *A Compilation of the General Laws of the City of Nashville: Together with the Charters of the City, Granted by the States of North Carolina and Tennessee, and a List of the Chief Officers of the Municipal Government of Nashville . . . from 1806 to 1860.* Nashville: J. O. Griffith, 1860. 280 pp.

Taylor, Alfred W., comp. *Index to the Private Acts of the General Assembly of Tennessee Which Apply to Davidson County, from Creation of the County, 1783 to 1937 Inclusive, and the City of Nashville from . . . 1923 to 1937. . . .* Nashville: McDaniel Print. Co., 1937. 24 pp.

Thompson, Linda D. (Wynn). "The Political Career of Robert Emmitt Lillard; A Black Politician of Nashville, Tennessee, 1951-1962." Thesis, Tennessee State Univ., 1971.

Todd, Henry F. *The Colemere Handbook of City and County Government.* Nashville: n.p., 1949.

Tennessee State Library and Archives. "Inventory of Davidson County Records." Nashville: State Library and Archives, 1964- . Unpublished typescript.

METROPOLITAN GOVERNMENT

Bolin, Imogene Wright. "Planning in Metropolitan Nashville and Davidson County before and after Consolidation." Thesis, Univ. of Tennessee, 1968.

Grant, Daniel R. "Metropolitics and Professional Political Leadership: The Case of Nashville." *Annals,* May 1964, pp. 72-83.

———. "Urban and Suburban Nashville: A Case Study in Metropolitanism." *Journal of Politics* 17 (1955), 82-99.

Hawkins, Brett W. "Sources of Opposition and Support for Metropolitan Reorganization: The Nashville Experience." Diss., Vanderbilt Univ., 1964. This study traces developments in Nashville and Davidson County government from 1957 to the June 1962 referendum which consolidated the city and county governments. The author gives the late Mayor Ben West's policies much credit for the electorate's acceptance of consolidation.

——. *Nashville Metro: The Politics of City-County Consolidation.* Nashville: Vanderbilt Univ. Press, 1966. 162 pp.

——. "Public Opinion and Metropolitan Reorganization in Nashville." *Journal of Politics* 28 (1966), 408-18.

League of Women Voters of Nashville. *Your Metropolitan Government, a Handbook about Nashville and Davidson County, Tennessee.* Nashville: Rich, 1968. 48 pp.

McArthur, Robert E. "The Impact of Metropolitan Government on the Rural-Urban Fringe: The Nashville-Davidson County Experience." Diss., Vanderbilt Univ., 1967.

Metropolitan Charter Commission. *Charter of the Metropolitan Government of Nashville and Davidson County, Tennessee.* Charlottesville, Va.: Michie, 1967. 279 pp.

"Metropolitan Government." *American City,* Aug. 1962, pp. 7 ff.

Mikesell, Phillip Dean. "The Impact of Nashville's Metropolitan Consolidation on Administrative Departments: A Study of Change and Non-change." Thesis, Vanderbilt Univ., 1968.

"Nashville Thrives on a City-County Merger." *Business Week,* Sept. 25, 1971, pp. 133-58.

Race Relations Information Center. *Nashville Model Cities Program.* Nashville: The Center, 1971. 34 pp.

Zuzak, Charles A., Kenneth E. McNeil, and Frederic Bergerson. *Beyond the Ballot: Citizen Participation in Metropolitan Nashville.* Nashville: Urban Observatory of Metropolitan Nashville and Bureau of Public Administration of Univ. of Tennessee, 1971. 308 pp.

Social and Cultural History

TO 1900

Adallis, Dio. *Fiftieth Anniversary, "The Athens of the South": Historical Sketch, Nashville, Tennessee, Greek Community, 1884-1934.* Nashville: Nashville Greek Community, 1934. 16 pp.

Bell, Lilly Cartwright. *History of the Dickinson Road.* Nashville: Robert Cartwright Chap., D. A. R., 1936. 40 pp.

Bowling, William K. *An Account of the Cholera, As It Appeared at Nashville in the Year 1873.* Nashville: *Union & American,* 1873. 63 pp.

Burt, Jesse C., Jr. "Anna Russell Cole, a Study of a Grand Dame." *THQ* 13 (1954), 127-55.

Chavis, Douglas Carr. "The Underworld of Nashville: Its Character and Function As Based on Records of Personal Experience of Prisoners in the Tennessee State Prison." Thesis, Fisk Univ., 1945.

Christie, Amos. "Early History of Medical Education in Nashville." *Journal of the Tennessee Medical Association* 42 (1969), 819-29.

Colleges and Universities. *See* Education and Individual Colleges and Universities Histories.

Crabb, Alfred Leland. "Wilkins Tannehill, Business and Cultural Leader." *THQ* 7 (1947), 314-31.

Crabb, Alfred Leland, Jr. "The Nashville Literary Societies, 1825-1860." Thesis, George Peabody College, 1941.

Creighton, Wilbur F., Jr. "Wilbur Fisk Foster, Soldier and Engineer." *THQ* 31 (1972), 261-75.

Crutchfield, James A. *The Harpeth River: A Biography.* Nashville: Blue & Gray Press, 1972. 120 pp.

Davenport, Francis Garvin. *Cultural Life in Nashville on the Eve of the Civil War.* Diss., Vanderbilt Univ., 1936. Chapel Hill: Univ. of North Carolina Press, 1941. 232 pp.

———. "Cultural Life in Nashville on the Eve of the Civil War." *JSH* 3 (1937), 326-47.

Dreyfus, Frederick Jonas. "Life and Works of George Michael Wharton, M.D. (Pseudonym 'Stahl'), 1825-1853." *THQ* 6 (1947), 315-36. Wharton was a literary figure and a medical scholar.

Eastman, Roger. *Old and New Names of Cross-Town Streets.* Nashville: Brandon, c. 1905. 3 pp.

Flanagan, James J. "The Irish Element in Nashville, 1810-1890." Thesis, Vanderbilt Univ., 1951.

Flint, M. "Trips from Nashville to Red River." *Knickerbocker Magazine* 3 (1834 or 1835), 112ff.

Frank, John G. "Adolphus Heiman: Architect and Soldier." *THQ* 5 (1946), 35-57.

Gay, William H. "Lincoln's Assassination: How Nashville Received the News." *THM* 5 (1919), 38-39.

Gilmore, Rose Long. *Davidson County Women in the World War, 1914-1919.* Nashville: Foster & Parkes, 1923. 509 pp.

Goodpasture, Albert V. "Dr. James White, Pioneer, Politician, Lawyer." *THM* 1 (1915), 282-91.

Gower, Herschel, and Jack Allen, eds. *Pen and Sword.* Randal W.

McGavock was a Harvard law student, diarist, European traveler, mayor of Nashville, and Confederate soldier killed in battle.

Grise, George C. "Samuel Watkins." *THQ* 6 (1947), 251-64. Watkins, a successful businessman and philanthropist interested in adult education, founded Watkins Institute.

Halley, R. A. "Dr. J. P. Dake—a Memoir." *AHM* 8 (1903), 297-346. Nashville physician from 1870 to 1890.

——. "John McCormick Lea—the Ideal Citizen." *AHM* 9 (1904), 1-30. Lea (1818-1903) was an attorney, mayor, and president of the Tennessee Historical Society.

——. "Paul Fitzsimmons Eve, A.M., M.D., LL.D." *AHM* 9 (1904), 281-342. Eve was a prominent Nashville physician.

Hallum, John. *The Diary of an Old Lawyer: or, Scenes behind the Curtain.* Nashville: Southwestern, 1895. 458 pp.

Hicks, Edward D. "Origin of the Name Harpeth." *AHM* 5 (1900), 128-31.

History of Woman's Mission Home and Annual Reports for the Year 1893. Nashville: Marshall & Bruce, 1894. 16 pp. Home for unwed mothers.

Houk, Eliza P. *A Tribute to General Gates Phillips Thruston.*

Howell, Morton B. "First Streets of Nashville." *AHM* 7 (1902), 179-89.

——. *Memoirs [of] Morton Boyte Howell.* Nashville: Reproduced from typewritten copy, 1945. 100 leaves.

Howell, R. B. C. "Early Corporate Limits of Nashville." *THM* 2 (1916), 110-18.

Hunt, Douglas L. *The Nashville Theatre, 1830-1840,* Birmingham-Southern College Bulletin, vol. 39, no. 1. Birmingham: Birmingham-Southern College, 1935. 89 pp.

Johnson, Mary Elizabeth. "Stories and Legends of Donelson, Tennessee." Thesis, George Peabody College, 1938.

Kaser, David. "Nashville's Women of Pleasure in 1860." *THQ* 23 (1964), 379-82.

Knox, Jack. *Riverman.* Nashville: Abingdon, 1971. 159 pp. Juvenile.

Lloyd, A. Dennis. "The Legend of Granny White." *THQ* 27 (1968), 257-61.

Macpherson, Joseph T., Jr. "Nashville's German Element." Thesis, Vanderbilt Univ., 1957.

Maiden, Lewis Smith. "A Chronicle of the Theatre in Nashville, Tennessee, 1876-1900." Diss., Vanderbilt Univ., 1955.

Mayfield, George R., ed. and trans. "The Diary of a German Immigrant." *THQ* 10 (1951), 249-81.

Miles, Guy S. "Literary Beginnings in Nashville, 1815-1825." Diss., Vanderbilt Univ., 1941.

Milner, James W. "Memorial to Robert Dyas, 1861 to 1928." *THM* (ser. 2) 1 (1930-31), 146-48. Dyas was a prominent member of the Tennessee Historical Society.

Nashville Senior Citizens. *Leadership in Nashville: A Listing of 116 of the Most Prominent Citizens in Nashville Leadership, with Brief Accompanying Sketches.* Nashville: The Authors, 1961. 41 leaves.

Nunn, Roscoe. "William Ferrell." *THM* 3 (1917), 192-95. Ferrell was a teacher and meteorologist of the 1850s.

Owsley, Harriet C. "The Morton B. Howell Papers." *THQ* 25 (1966), 287-309.

Provine, William A., ed. "An Early Temperance Society at Nashville in 1829." *THM* 5 (1919), 142-44.

——. ed. "Centennial Anniversary of the Birth of George Washington As Observed in Nashville, Feb. 22, 1832." *THM* (ser. 2) 2 (1931-32), 195-97.

Rose, Kenneth. "A Nashville Musical Decade, 1830-1840." *THQ* 2 (1943), 216-31.

Rose, Stanley Frazer. "Nashville and Its Leadership Elite, 1861-1869." Thesis, Univ. of Virginia, 1965.

Smith, Earl. "The Free, Foreign-born Population of Nashville in the 1850's." Thesis, Vanderbilt Univ., 1968.

Stevens, Eva. "History of the Theatre in Nashville, 1871-1875." Thesis, Vanderbilt Univ., 1934.

Tennessee Centennial. *See* Social and Cultural History: Tennessee Centennial Celebration, 1897.

Thruston, Gates P. "The Nashville Inn." *AHM* 7 (1902), 174-77. This inn burned in 1856.

Whitley, Edythe J. R. "Reminiscence of Granny White Pike and Its Neighbors." Unpublished typescript, 1934. 58 leaves.

Williams, Samuel Cole. "Nashville As Seen by Travelers, 1801-1821." *THM* (ser. 2) 1 (1930-31), 182-206.

1900 TO 1972

Coleman, Daniel M. *A History of the Nashville Workshop for the Blind, 1918-1945.* Nashville: Tennessee Dept. of Public Welfare, 1946. 80 pp.

DeWitt, John H., Jr. "Early Radio Broadcasting in Middle Tennessee." *THQ* 31 (1972), 80-94.

Galloway, J. M. "The Public Life of Norman L. Davis." *THQ* 27 (1968), 142-56.

Hargrove, Margery Hollister. "A History of the Community Theatre Movement in Nashville, Tennessee, 1926-1951." Thesis, Tennessee Technological Univ., 1965.

Henderson, Jerry. "Nashville's Ryman Auditorium." *THQ* 27 (1968), 305-28; rpt. in *More Landmarks of Tennessee,* 285-308.

Morrow, Sara Sprott. "A Brief History of Theatre in Nashville, 1807-1970." *THQ* 30 (1971), 178-89.

Profitt, Waldo. "A Study of Social Conditions in Davidson County." Thesis, Vanderbilt Univ., 1926.

Provine, William A., ed. "Peter Ross Calvert." *THM* (ser. 2) 1 (1930-31), 386-88. Calvert was a prominent local photographer.

Reynolds, Morgan B. *Seventy Years of Belle Meade Country Club.* Nashville: McQuiddy, 1971. Unpaged.

Stokes, Walter, Jr. "Hillsboro Pike and Something Personal." *THQ* 24 (1965), 70-84.

Weaver, Blanche Henry Clark. "Shifting Residential Patterns of Nashville." *THQ* 8 (1959), 20-34.

EDUCATION

Baughn, Milton L. "An Early Experiment in Adult Education: The Nashville Lyceum, 1830-1832." *THQ* 11 (1952), 235-45.

Benkovitz, Miriam Jeanette. "History of Women's Educational Institutions in Nashville, Tennessee." Thesis, George Peabody College, 1942.

Clark, Stewart Sandy. "A Study of Negro Education in Davidson County, Tennessee." Thesis, George Peabody College, 1919.

Harris, Kenneth LeRoy. "A History of the Tennessee Industrial School." Thesis, Middle Tennessee State Univ., 1953.

Hogan, Walter Edwin. "Changing Conceptions of the Aim of Negro Education As Seen in the History of Colored Schools in Nashville, Tennessee." Thesis, George Peabody College, 1917.

Howell, Isabel. "Montgomery Bell Academy: A Chapter in the History of the University of Nashville." Thesis, George Peabody College, 1940.

Hubbard, G. W., comp. *A History of the Colored Schools of Nashville, Tennessee.* Nashville: Wheeler, Marshall & Bruce, 1874. 34 pp.

Hume, Leland. *Early History of the Nashville Public Schools.* Nashville [?]: n.p., 1921. 36 pp.

Rule, James C. *History of Montgomery Bell Academy.* Nashville: n.p., 1954. 78 pp. A brief history of this private boys' school from its inception in 1785 as Davidson Academy to 1954.

Stinson, Harold N. "The Nashville Education Improvement Project." *Southern Education Report,* July-Aug. 1965, pp. 11-15.

Windrow, John E. "Collins D. Elliott and the Nashville Female Academy." *THM* (ser. 2) 3 (1932-37), 74-106.

Work, Helen E. "An Historical Study of the Colored Public Schools of Nashville, Tennessee." Thesis, Fisk Univ., 1933.

Wyatt, Charles T. *History of the Development of Watkins Institute.* Nashville: State of Tennessee, 1935. 31 pp.

RELIGIOUS GROUPS

Baptist

Burroughs, Prince Emanuel. *The Spiritual Conquest of the Second Frontier: The Biography of an Achieving Church, 1820-1942.* Nashville: Broadman, 1942. 222 pp. Describes the Nashville First Baptist Church.

Both Sides: A Full Investigation of the Charges Preferred against Elder J. R. Graves by R. B. C. Howell and Others, September 8 and October 12, 1858, by a Council Composed of Delegates from Twenty Churches, of Concord Association, Held in Odd Fellow's Hall, March 1-3, 1859. Together with the Report of the Council and the Action of the Church. Nashville: Spring St. Baptist Church, 1859. 238 pp.

"Epistle to the First Baptist Churches in Nashville: Invitation for Negro and White Baptists to Unite." *Christian Century,* Jan. 26, 1966, p. 102.

May, Lynn E., Jr. *The First Baptist Church of Nashville, Tennessee, 1820-1970.* Nashville: First Baptist Church, 1970. 331 pp.

Spain, Rufus B. "R. B. C. Howell, Tennessee Baptist, 1801-1868." Thesis, Vanderbilt Univ., 1948.

——. "R. B. C. Howell: Virginia Baptist Tradition Comes to the Old Southwest." *THQ* 14 (1955), 99-119.

——. "R. B. C. Howell: Progressive Baptist Minister in the Old Southwest." *THQ* 14 (1955), 195-226.

——. "R. B. C. Howell: Nashville Baptist Leader in the Civil War Period." *THQ* 14 (1955), 323-40.

Trial of Rev. J. R. Graves before the First Baptist Church of Nashville. Nashville: First Baptist Church, 1858. 126 pp.

Disciples of Christ

Cochran, Bess W. *The Wonder of Woodmont: A More or Less Light-Hearted Look at the History of Woodmont Christian Church, Nashville, Tennessee, on the Occasion of Its Twenty-fifth Birthday, July 18, 1968*. Nashville: Woodmont Christian Church, 1968. 57 pp.

Norton, Herman. "Fall of Vine Street." Thesis, Vanderbilt Univ., 1951.

Walker, William P. "History of the Nashville Disciples of Christ, 1820-1895." Thesis, Vanderbilt Univ., 1931.

Episcopal

Rankin, Anne P., ed. *Christ Church, Nashville, 1829-1929*. Nashville: Marshall & Bruce, 1929. 297 pp.

St. George's Episcopal Church. *St. George's Church: The First Ten Years, 1949-1959*. Nashville: The Church, 1959. 28 pp.

Jewish

Frank, Fedora Small. *Five Families and Eight Young Men (Nashville and her Jewry, 1850-1861)*. Nashville: Tennessee Bk., 1962. 184 pp.

Nashville Y.M.H.A. *The Nashville Jewish Community*. Nashville: Cullom & Ghertner, 1933. 91 pp.

Methodist

Clark Memorial Methodist Church. *A Century of Witness for Christ; 1867-1967*. Nashville: Hemphill, 1967. 42 pp.

The History of McKendree Methodist Church. Nashville: Parthenon Press, 1962. 36 pp.

Kirby, James E. "The McKendree Chapel Affair." *THQ* 25 (1966), 360-70.

Presbyterian

Avery, Mrs. Roy C., ed. "The Second Presbyterian Church of Nashville during the Civil War." *THQ* 11 (1952), 356-75.

Gant, Norwood J. *A History of Trinity Presbyterian Church, Nashville, Tennessee, 1942-1958.* Nashville: n.p., 1958. 38 pp.

Hollins, Mrs. Eugene T., and Mrs. J. L. Weakley. *Sixty-five Years of Story and History [of] Moore Memorial Presbyterian Church, Nashville, Tennessee, 1873-1938.* Nashville: The Church, 1938. 16 leaves.

Jacobs, William S. *Presbyterianism in Nashville: A Compilation of Historic Data.* Nashville: Ministers' Alliance of the Presbyterian Church, 1904. 118 pp.

Taylor, A. W. "Deny Freedom to Nashville Pastor, Dr. T. C. Barr of the First Presbyterian Church." *Christian Century,* Oct. 21, 1942, p. 1293.

Wills, Jesse E. *The Towers See One Hundred Years. The Story of the First Presbyterian Church Building.* Nashville: First Presbyterian Church, 1951. 12 pp.

——. "An Echo from Egypt: A History of the Building Occupied by the First Presbyterian Church, Nashville, Tennessee." *THQ* 11 (1952), 63-77.

Roman Catholic

Barr, Daniel F. *Souvenir of St. Mary's Cathedral, Including the Century's Annals of the Roman Catholic Church in Nashville, 1897.* Nashville: Burton & Fick, 1897. 64 pp.

Flanigen, George J. *One Hundredth Anniversary of the Church of the Assumption, Nashville, Tennessee: An Historical Sketch from 1859-1959.* Nashville: Assumption Parish, 1959. 78 pp.

——. "Diocese of Nashville." *New Catholic Encyclopedia,* vol. 10, pp. 215-16.

O'Daniel, V. F. *The Father of the Church in Tennessee; or, The Life, Times, and Character of the Right Reverend Richard Pius Miles, O.P., The First Bishop of Nashville.* Washington, D.C.: Dominicana, 1926. 607 pp.

Old St. Mary's; An Historical Sketch of St. Mary's Church, Nashville, Tennessee, 1847-1947. Nashville: n.p., 1947. 52 pp.

General

Bearden, Lillie. "The Religious Situation in the Fensterwald

Settlement Area of Nashville, Tennessee." Thesis, Vanderbilt Univ., 1929.

Carty, James W., Jr. *Nashville as a World Religious Center.* Nashville: Cullom & Ghertner, 1958. 24 pp.

Claiborne, Thomas. *History and True Position of the Church of Christ in Nashville: With an Examination of the Speculative Theology Recently Introduced from Neologists, Universalists, etc.* Nashville: Cameron & Fall, 1854. About 60 pp.

Historical Records Survey, Tennessee. *Directory of Churches, Missions, and Religious Institutions of Tennessee,* no. 19. *Davidson County.* Nashville: The Survey, WPA, 1940- . 79 pp.

Kester, Howard. "A Study of Negro Ministers in Nashville." B.D. thesis, Vanderbilt Univ., 1931.

Seven Early Churches of Nashville, foreword Alfred Leland Crabb. Nashville: Elder, 1972. 124 pp.

COUNTRY MUSIC

Bart, Teddy. *Inside Music City, U.S.A.* Nashville: Aurora, 1970. 164 pp.

Becker, Paula. *Let the Song Go On: The Speer Family Biography.* Nashville: Benson, 1971. 175 pp.

Burt, Jesse. "Chester Burton Atkins." *Tennessee Valley Historical Review,* 1 (1971), 12-19.

Burt, Jesse, and Duane Allen. *The History of Gospel Music.* Nashville: K & S Press, 1971. 205 pp.

Burt, Jesse, and Bob Ferguson. *So You Want to Be in Music!,* foreword Chet Atkins. Nashville: Abingdon, 1970. 175 pp.

"Country Music Gets Soul; L. Martell at the Grand Ole Opry." *Ebony,* Mar. 1970, pp. 66-68.

"Country Music Snaps Its Regional Bounds." *Business Week,* Mar. 19, 1966, pp. 96-98.

Dunkleburger, A. C. *King of Country Music: The Life and Story of Roy Acuff.* Madison: n.p., 1971. 137 pp.

Fox, W. P., Jr. "Night at the Opry." *Holiday,* May 1967, pp. 99-100.

Hemphill, Paul. *The Nashville Sound: Bright Lights and Country Music.* New York: Simon, 1970; rpt. New York: PB, 1971. 289 pp.

Henderson, Jerry. "Nashville's Ryman Auditorium." *THQ* 27 (1968), 305-28; rpt. in *More Landmarks of Tennessee,* 285-308.

King, Larry L. "Grand Ole Opry." *Harper's Magazine,* July 1968, pp. 43-50.

Malone, Bill C. *Country Music USA: A Fifty-Year History,* Memoir Series, vol. 54. Austin: Univ. of Texas Press, 1968. 422 pp.

"Nashville Sound; Country Music Festival." *Time,* Nov. 27, 1964, p. 76.

Polk, Linda Sue. "An Analysis of Country-Western Music as a Communicative Art Form." Thesis, Murray State Univ., 1970.

Portis, C. "That New Sound from Nashville." *Saturday Evening Post,* Feb. 12, 1966, pp. 30-34.

Scruggs, Louise. "History of the 5-String Banjo." *TFSB* 27 (1961), 1-5.

Shelton, Robert. *The Country Music Story; a Picture History of Country and Western Music,* photographs Burt Goldblatt. Indianapolis: Bobbs-Merrill, 1966; rpt. New Rochelle, N.Y.: Arlington House, 1971. 256 pp.

Simcoe, George. "Critical-Historical Analysis of Rock Music as a Medium of Communication." Thesis, Murray State Univ., 1970. Relates to the Nashville music industry.

HISTORIC STRUCTURES AND PLACES

Art Work of Nashville. Chicago: Gravure Illus., 1901. 18 leaves.

Beard, Mrs. William E., comp. *The Story of the Tennessee Capitol.* Nashville: Brandon, n.d. 21 pp. Compiled for the Tennessee Capitol Association.

Brumbaugh, Thomas B. "The Architecture of Nashville's Union Station." *THQ* 27 (1968), 3-12; rpt. in *More Landmarks of Tennessee,* 371-80.

Carter, H. "Master of Belle Meade." *Outlook,* July 27, 1912, pp. 725-30.

Caldwell, Mrs. James E., comp. *Historical and Beautiful Country Homes near Nashville, Tennessee.* Nashville: Brandon, 1911. 165 pp.

Dardis, George. *Description of the State Capitol of Tennessee.* Nashville: B. R. McKennie, 1854; G. C. Torbett, 1855; Cameron, 1859; Tennessee Capitol Assoc., 1925. 8 pp.

Dekle, Clayton B. "The Tennessee State Capitol." *THQ* 25 (1966), 213-38; rpt. in *More Landmarks of Tennessee,* 5-30.

Denis, J. W. "The Nashville City Cemetery." *THQ* 2 (1943), 30-42.

Denis, Virginia H. "The Old City Cemetery, Nashville, Tennessee." *DAR Magazine,* Jan. 1969, pp. 7 ff.

Dickinson, Margaret S. *Travelers Rest.* Boston: Christopher, 1944. 148 pp.

Estes, P. M., A. P. Foster, and John Trotwood Moore, comps. *Historic Places in Davidson, Williamson, Maury and Giles Counties.* Nashville: Nashville Automobile Club, 1928. 29 pp.

Frank, John G. "Adolphus Heiman: Architect and Soldier." *THQ* 5 (1946), 35-57.

Gower, Herschel. "Belle Meade: Queen of Tennessee Plantations." *THQ* 22 (1963), 203-22; rpt. in *Landmarks of Tennessee,* 25-44.

Henderson, Jerry. "Nashville's Ryman Auditorium." *THQ* 27 (1968), 305-28; rpt. in *More Landmarks of Tennessee,* 285-308.

June, Orrin Wickersham. "Living with Antiques: The Nashville Home of Dr. and Mrs. Benjamin H. Caldwell, Jr." *Antiques,* Sept. 1971, pp. 438-41.

"Living with Antiques: Harpeth House, the Nashville Home of Mr. and Mrs. Roupen M. Gulbenk." *Antiques,* Oct. 1971, pp. 602-5.

McBride, Robert M. "The Historical Enrichment of the Governor's Residence." *THQ* 30 (1971), 215-19.

Macdonald-Millar, Donald. "The Grundy-Polk Houses, Nashville." *THQ* 25 (1966), 281-86.

Mahoney, Nell Savage. "The Building of the Tennessee State House, 1845-1854." Thesis, Vanderbilt Univ., 1939.

———. "William Strickland and the Building of Tennessee's Capitol, 1845-1854." *THQ* 4 (1945), 99-153.

———. "William Strickland's Introduction to Nashville, 1845." *THQ* 9 (1950), 46-63.

Milton, Alice Warner. "A Saga of Belle Meade Mansion—Queen of Tennessee Plantations." *DAR Magazine,* Feb. 1971, pp. 115 ff.

Orr, Mary T. "John Overton and Traveller's Rest." *THQ* 15 (1956), 216-23.

Rudy, Jeanette C. *Historic Two Rivers: The Story of a Historic Tennessee Home in Text and Illustration.* Nashville: Blue & Gray, 1972. 127 pp.

Senkevitch, Anatole, Jr. "Nineteenth-Century Public Buildings in Nashville." *Antiques,* Aug. 1971, pp. 222-27.

Swint, Henry Lee. "Traveler's Rest: Home of Judge John Overton." *THQ* 26 (1967), 119-36; rpt. in *More Landmarks of Tennessee,* 329-46.

Tennessee State Library and Archives. *Index to Interments in the Nashville City Cemetery, 1846-1962.* Nashville: State of Tennessee, 1964. 89 pp.

West, Edward William. "A Visitor to Bellemeade in 1874." *THM* (ser. 2) 1 (1930-31), 62-63.

White, Robert H. "The Governors' Mansions of Tennessee." *THQ* 25 (1966), 327-39; rpt. in *More Landmarks of Tennessee,* 155-67.

The Hermitage

Arnold, James. "The Hermitage Church." *THQ* 28 (1969), 113-25.

Caldwell, Mary French. *Andrew Jackson's Hermitage; the Story of a Home in the Tennessee Blue-Grass Region, Which, from Pioneer Log Cabin to Ante-Bellum Mansion, Furnished the Background of "Old Hickory's" Dramatic and Colorful Career.* Nashville: Ladies' Hermitage Assoc., 1933. 106 pp.

——. "Another Breakfast at the Hermitage. Part II, 1934." *THQ* 26 (1967), 249-54.

Dorris, Mary C. *Preservation of the Hermitage, 1889-1915: Annals, History, and Stories. The Acquisition, Restoration, and Care of the Home of General Andrew Jackson by the Ladies' Hermitage Association for over a Quarter of a Century.* Nashville: Smith & Lamar, 1915. 221 pp.

Frazer, Mrs. James S., and Mrs. Reau E. Folk. *The Hermitage.* 2d rev. ed., Nashville: n.p., 1927. 52 pp.

Goodpasture, Virginia P. "Another Breakfast at the Hermitage. Part III, 1967." *THQ* 26 (1967), 255-62.

Helton, Ginger, and Susan Van Riper, eds. *Hermitage Hospitality from the Hermitage Library.* Nashville: Aurora, 1970. 268 pp. Cookbook.

Horn, Stanley F. *The Hermitage, Home of Old Hickory.* Richmond, Va.: Garrett & Massie, 1938. 225 pp. Rpt. New York: Greenberg, 1950; rpt. Nashville: Ladies' Hermitage Assoc., 1960. 226 pp. The best description of the Hermitage and of Jackson's personal life at home.

——. "The Hermitage; Home of Andrew Jackson." *THQ* 20 (1961), 3-19; rpt. in *Landmarks of Tennessee,* 5-21.

——. "The Hermitage, Home of Andrew Jackson." *Antiques,* Sept. 1971, pp. 413-17.

Ladies' Hermitage Association. *The Historic Hermitage Properties.* Hermitage: Ladies' Hermitage Assoc., 1972. 57 pp.

Lawrence, Stephen S. "Tulip Grove: Neighbor to the Hermitage." *THQ* 26 (1967), 3-22; rpt. in *More Landmarks of Tennessee,* 349-68.

Strand, Wilson E. "Jackson's Hermitage Today." *DAR Magazine,* Nov. 1969, pp. 757-60.

White, Robert H. "Another Breakfast at the Hermitage. Part I, 1907." *THQ* 26 (1967), 241-48.

JOURNALISM

Beard, William E. "Henry Watterson—Last of the Oracles." *THM* (ser. 2) 1 (1930-31), 233-52. Watterson was editor of the Nashville *Republican Banner,* 1865-68.

Burt, Jesse. "Harvey Watterson Discharges a Nashville Editor." *FCHQ* 41 (1967), 263-78. E. G. Eastman was the man discharged.

Donnald, Morrill. "Study on Nashville Newspapers, 1850-1875." Thesis, Vanderbilt Univ., 1957.

Elder, Robert. "Partisan Press: Nashville Tennessean's Campaign for Poll Tax Repeal, 1936-1943." Thesis, Vanderbilt Univ., 1967.

Howell, Sarah H. "Editorial Career of A. S. Colyar, 1882-1888." Thesis, Vanderbilt Univ., 1967. Colyar was a Nashville journalist, editor of the *Union and American.*

Millspaugh, Kathryn. "Notes on Early Nashville Newspapers, 1797-1850." Thesis, Vanderbilt Univ., 1936.

Sutherland, Sallie Bralliar. "Newspapers of Nashville, Tennessee, before 1868." Thesis, George Peabody College, 1933.

THE NEGRO

Booze, Dorothe Mae. "Consumer Habits of Negroes in Nashville, Tennessee." Thesis, Fisk Univ., 1951.

England, James Merton. "The Free Negro in Davidson County, Tennessee, 1780-1860." Thesis, Vanderbilt Univ., 1937.

Giovanni, Nikki. *Gemini.* An autobiography picturing life in Knoxville and Nashville.

Mooney, Chase C. "Slavery in Davidson County, Tennessee." Thesis, Vanderbilt Univ., 1936.

"Sociological Studies upon the Negro in Nashville, Tennessee." *Vanderbilt University Quarterly* 4 (1904), 79-113. Covers religion, crime, economics.

Weatherford, Willis D. *A Survey of the Negro Boy in Nashville, Tennessee.* New York: YMCA Press, 1932. 157 pp. A study by the YMCA of the condition and needs of the Negro boy in Nashville. Careful physical and medical examinations were given 340 boys in junior high schools, and studies were made of their economic, educational, home, and family life.

Williams, Cordell Hull. "The Life of James Carroll Napier from 1845 to 1940." Thesis, Tennessee State A&I Univ., 1955.

Desegregation: 1955-

"Already Underway: '67 Racial Flare-ups." *U.S. News and World Report,* Apr. 24, 1967, pp. 10 ff.

Egerton, John. "De Facto Segregation: A Tale of Three Cities." *Southern Education Report,* Sept. 1967, pp. 10-16. Includes Nashville.

Geier, Woodrow A. "Nashville Schools Face Integration." *Christian Century,* Sept. 4, 1957, pp. 1051 ff.

——. "Nashville Halts School Violence." *Christian Century,* Oct. 9, 1957, pp. 1206-8.

——. "Sit-ins Prod a Community." *Christian Century,* Mar. 30, 1960, pp. 379-82.

——. "Nashville Sit-ins." *Christian Century,* Apr. 27, 1960, pp. 525-26.

"Go for the Honkies: Aftermath of Stokely Carmichael Visit." *Newsweek,* Apr. 24, 1967, p. 28.

Graham, Hugh D. "Desegregation in Nashville: The Dynamics of Compliance." *THQ* 25 (1966), 135-54.

Halberstam, David. "A Good City Gone Ugly." *Reporter,* Mar. 31, 1960, pp. 17-19.

Harris, Edwin Hale. "Desegregation: Metropolitan Nashville-Davidson County Public Schools, 1955-1971." Ed.S. diss., George Peabody College, 1971.

"It Happened in Nashville." *Reporter,* May 26, 1960, pp. 2 ff. Description of sit-ins.

Jackson, L. "Tennessee Rebels; Nashville Liberation School." *New Republic,* Sept. 9, 1967, pp. 9-10.

"Nashville Creates Bi-racial Committee." *Christian Century,* May 29, 1963, pp. 700 ff.

"Nashville Lesson; Integrated without Fanfare or Violence." *Time,* May 26, 1961, pp. 17 ff.

"Nashville's Method." *Commonweal,* May 27, 1960, pp. 220 ff. Description of sit-ins.

Street, Sorena Roberta Lee. "Partial Desegregation of Nashville

City Public Schools, 1954-1957: The Beginning." Thesis, Tennessee State A & I Univ., 1962.

Toby, J. "Bombing in Nashville: A Jewish Center and the Desegregation Struggle." *Commentary*, May 1958, pp. 385-89. *See also* "Reply with Rejoinder," by L. H. Silberman, *Commentary*, July 1958, pp. 79-80.

"Trouble at Nashville." *Commonweal*, Apr. 4, 1958, p. 4.

"Why Riots Erupted in a 'Show Case' City." *U.S. News and World Report*, May 11, 1964, pp. 6ff.

DECATUR COUNTY

Historian: Mrs. Lillye Younger, 212 N. Georgia Avenue, Parsons 38363.

Biographical Directory: Decatur County Members of the Tennessee General Assembly, 1796- . 36 pp. This volume also contains Benton County.

"Decatur County." *History of Tennessee,* ed. Weston A. Goodspeed et al., 814-19, 880-94.

Younger, Lillye. *People of Action.* Jackson: Brewer, 1969. 68 pp.

DEKALB COUNTY

Historian: Thomas G. Webb, Route 1, Box 5, Smithville 37166.

Biographical Directory: DeKalb County Members of the Tennessee General Assembly, 1796- . 46 pp. This volume also contains Cannon County.

"DeKalb County." *History of Tennessee,* ed. Weston A. Goodspeed et al., 845-53, 951-87.

Hale, William Thomas. *History of DeKalb County, Tennessee.* Nashville: P. Hunter, 1915; rpt. McMinnville: Ben Lomond, 1969. 254 pp.

Love, Jolee. *Love's Valley.* Nashville: Ambrose, 1954. 556 pp.

Marler, Mike, comp. "Name Index to [Hale's] History of DeKalb County, Tennessee." Nashville: Unpublished typescript, 1971.

Tennessee State Library and Archives. "Inventory of DeKalb County Records." Nashville: State Library and Archives, 1964- . Unpublished typescript.

Webb, Thomas G. "The Pottery Industry of DeKalb, White and Putnam Counties." *THQ* 30 (1971), 110-12.

DICKSON COUNTY
Historian: Clifton Goodlett, Dickson 37055

Biographical Directory: Dickson County Members of the Tennessee General Assembly, 1796- . 47 pp. This volume also contains Cheatham County.

Burchard, Ernest F. *The Brown Iron Ores of the Western Highland Rim, Tennessee,* Tennessee Dept. of Education, Division of Geology Bulletin 39. Nashville: State of Tennessee, 1934. 227 pp. This report covers Dickson County.

Corlew, Robert E. "Some Aspects of Slavery in Dickson County, Tennessee." Thesis, Vanderbilt Univ., 1949.

——. "Some Aspects of Slavery in Dickson County." *THQ* 10 (1951), 224-48, 344-65.

——. *A History of Dickson County, Tennessee.* Nashville: Tennessee Hist. Comm., 1956. 243 pp.

"Dickson County." *History of Tennessee,* ed. Weston A. Goodspeed et al., 920-47, 1329-57.

Ruskin Commonwealth. *See* Social and Cultural History: Nineteenth-Century Communitarian Settlements in Tennessee.

Teachers of Dickson County, comps. *A History of Dickson County.* Dickson: n.p., 1945.

Tennessee State Library and Archives. "Inventory of Dickson County Records." Nashville: State Library and Archives, 1964- . Unpublished typescript.

DYER COUNTY
Historian: Elmer Gardner, Dyersburg 38024.

Donaldson, R. C. "Key Corner, Dyer County, Tennessee." WTHSP 17 (1963), 126-27.

"Dyer County." *History of Tennessee,* ed. Weston A. Goodspeed et al., 842-52, 1024-73.

First Presbyterian Church. *One Hundredth Anniversary, 1854-1954. First Presbyterian Church, Dyersburg, Tennessee.* Dyersburg: The Church, 1954. 16 pp.

Tennessee Valley Authority, Industry Division. *Agricultural-Industrial Survey of Dyer County.* Knoxville: TVA, 1935.

Tennessee State Library and Archives. "Inventory of Dyer County Records." Nashville: State Library and Archives, 1964- . Unpublished typescript.

FAYETTE COUNTY
Historian: Mrs. J. R. Morton, Moscow 38057.

Barraclough, S. "No Plumbing for Negroes; Ames Plantation." *Atlantic,* Sept. 1965, pp. 105-9.

DeBerry, John H. "LaGrange-La Belle Village." *THQ* 30 (1971), 133-53.

Denenberg, R. V. "Students Get the Vote Out; Fayette County, Tennessee." *Nation,* Aug. 10, 1964, pp. 45-49.

Egerton, John. *Racial Protest in the South—1969 Style.* Nashville: Race Relations Information Center, 1969. 33 pp. This is a case study of Forrest City, Ark. and Somerville, Tenn.

Ewing, John Arthur. "Planning the Ames Plantation Project." Diss., Harvard Univ., 1956.

"Fayette County." *History of Tennessee,* ed. Weston A. Goodspeed et al., 797-817, 840-87.

Mitchell, Francis H. "Tent City, Tennessee." *Ebony,* Mar. 1961, pp. 61-67.

Parsons, Mildred. "Negro Folklore from Fayette County." *TFSB* 19 (1953), 67-70.

Tennessee Valley Authority, Industry Division. *Agricultural-Industrial Survey of Fayette County.* Knoxville: TVA, 1935.

Walls, Dwayne E. *Fayette County, Tennessee: Tragedy and Confrontation.* Atlanta: Southern Regional Council, 1969. 36 pp.

FENTRESS COUNTY
Historian: Ruble Upchurch, Pall Mall 38577.

Biographical Directory: Fentress County Members of the Tennessee General Assembly, 1796- . 49 pp. This volume also contains Overton and Pickett counties.

Clarke, James N., and Annetta Gernt. "History of Allardt." *THM* 9 (1925-26), 185-89.

Ensor, Allison. "The Birthplace of Samuel Clemens: A New Mark Twain Letter." *Tennessee Studies in Literature* 14 (1969), 31-34.

Fentress, Willie Blount. "James Fentress." *AHM* 7 (1902), 178.

Goodpasture, Albert V. "Mark Twain, Southerner." *THM* (ser. 2) 1 (1931), 253-60; rpt. in *Tennessee Old and New,* II, 280-87.

Hale, William Thomas. *True Stories of Jamestown and Its Environs.* Nashville: Methodist Pub. House, 1907. 156 pp.

Hogue, Albert R. *History of Fentress County, Tennessee, the Old Home of Mark Twain's Ancestors.* Nashville: Williams, 1916, 1920. 165 pp.

——. *One Hundred Years in the Cumberland Mountains along the Continental Line.*

——. *Mark Twain's Obedstown and Knobs of Tennessee; a History of Jamestown and Fentress County, Tennessee.* Jamestown: Cumberland, 1951. 91 pp.

——. *Davy Crockett and Others in Fentress County Who Have Given the County a Prominent Place in History.*

Tennessee Valley Authority, Industry Division. *Agricultural-Industrial Survey of Fentress County.* Knoxville: TVA, 1934. 99 pp.

Wright, Absalom B. "Jamestown Circuit." *Autobiography of Rev. A. B. Wright of the Holston Conference, Methodist Episcopal Church South,* 63-78, 94-173.

FRANKLIN COUNTY
Historian: Howard M. Hannah, Estill Springs 37330.

Biographical Directory: Franklin County Members of the Tennessee General Assembly, 1796- . 44 pp. This volume also contains Moore County.

Chitty, Arthur B., Jr. *Reconstruction at Sewanee.*

Finney, Raymond Alfred. "History of the Private Educational Institutions of Franklin County, Tennessee." Thesis, Univ. of Tennessee, 1939.

"Franklin County." *History of Tennessee,* ed. Weston A. Goodspeed et al., 785-804, 820-46.

Hall, Howard, "Franklin County in the Secession Crisis." *THQ* 17 (1958), 37-44.

Hannah, Howard M. *Confederate Action in Franklin County, Tennessee.* Sewanee: Franklin Co. Civil War Centennial Comm., 1963. 69 pp.

Henderson, Mrs. Jesse Arn. "Unmarked Historic Spots of Franklin County." *THM* (ser. 2) 3 (1932-37), 111-20.

Hill, James Otto. "Sewanee, a Unique Community." Thesis, Middle Tennessee State Univ., 1952.

Hunter, Catherine H. "A History of Higher Education in Franklin County, Tennessee." Thesis, Univ. of Tennessee, 1940.

Kennedy, Harold. "A History of St. Andrew's School." Thesis, Middle Tennessee State Univ., 1952.

Kollmorgen, Walter Martin. *The German-Swiss in Franklin County, Tennessee; a Study of the Significance of Cultural Considerations in Farming Enterprises.* Diss., Columbia Univ., 1940. Washington, D.C.: U.S. Dept. of Agriculture, 1940. 113 leaves.

McKellar, William H. "Churvallic's Chronicle of Franklin County, Tennessee." Unpublished typescript. 150 pp.

Mary Sharp College Club of Nashville, Tennessee. *Dr. Z. C. Graves and the Mary Sharp College, 1850-1896.* Nashville: Baptist Bd. of Pub., 1926. 150 pp.

Pennington, Egar Legare. "The Battle at Sewanee."*THQ* 9 (1950), 217-90.

Ray, A. Herman. "An Economic, Educational and Social Survey of Franklin County, Tennessee." Thesis, Univ. of Tennessee, 1937.

Rhoton, Thomas Foster. "A Brief History of Franklin County, Tennessee." Thesis, Univ. of Tennessee, 1941.

Rogers, Evelyn. *Focus on Franklin County.* Winchester: n.p., 1966. 151 pp.

Tennessee State Library and Archives. "Inventory of Franklin County Records." Nashville: State Library and Archives, 1964- . Unpublished typescript.

Tennessee Valley Authority, Industry Division. *Agricultural-Industrial Survey of Franklin County, Tennessee.* Knoxville: TVA, 1934. 144 pp.

GIBSON COUNTY
Historian: Fred Culp, Route 1, Trenton 38382.

Bright, R. E. "The History of Secondary Education in Gibson County, Tennessee." Thesis, Univ. of Tennessee, 1931.

Culp, Frederick M., and Mrs. Robert E. Ross. *Gibson County, Past and Present; the First General History of One of West Tennessee's Pivotal Counties.* Trenton: Gibson Co. Hist. Soc., 1961. 583 pp.

"Gibson County." *History of Tennessee,* ed. Weston A. Goodspeed et al., 797-816, 857-931.

Greene, W. P., ed. *Gibson County, Tennessee: A Series of Pen and Picture Sketches; Comprising a Passing Glance at the History, Progress, and Present State of Industrial and Social Development in Gibson County. Historical, Descriptive, and Biographical.* Nashville: *Gospel Advocate,* 1901. 144 pp.

Hargrove, Mrs. Gordon Brame. *The Honor Roll. Gibson County, Tennessee, U.S.A., 1917-1918-1919.* Eaton: The Author, 1920. 200 pp.

Johnson, R. W. "Truck Farming in the Northern Part of the Cotton Belt—Gibson County, Tennessee." *JTAS* 16 (1941), 266-89.

Presbyterian Church in the U.S.A. *A Rural Survey in Tennessee, Made by the Department of Church and Country Life of the Board of Home Missions of the Presbyterian Church in the U.S.A.* New York: Redfield, 1912. 48 pp. This report relates to Gibson County.

Rauchle, Bob C. "The Germantown near Milan, Tennessee." WTHSP 20 (1966), 61-76.

Rooks, C. W. *Humboldt—Past, Present and Future.* Humboldt: Humboldt Chamber of Commerce, 1925. 16 pp.

Rothrock, Mary U., ed. "Family Letters: Home Life in Carroll and Gibson Counties, Tennessee, 1868." WTHSP 25 (1971), 107-34.

——, ed. "Family Letters: Home Life in Gibson County, Tennessee, January-June, 1869." WTHSP 26 (1972), 94-130.

Smith, Conrad Frederick. *The Gibson County Story. A Historical Drama of Gibson County, Tennessee, from Indian Times through Eventful, Tragic and Romantic Years of War and Peace to the Present.* Trenton: *Herald-Register,* 1960. 121 pp.

Tennessee Valley Authority, Industry Division. *Agricultural-Industrial Survey of Gibson County, Tennessee.* Knoxville: TVA, 1935. 164 pp.

Williamson, Harry. "A History of Laneview College of Gibson County, Tennessee," ed. Ernest Thompson, Jr. WTHSP 18 (1964), 130-35.

GILES COUNTY

Historian: No appointment made.

Biographical Directory: Giles County Members of the Tennessee General Assembly, 1796- . 53 pp.

Cohen, Nelle Roller. *Pulaski History, 1809-1950; the Beginning, the Building, the Development, the Institutions, and the People of the Town of Pulaski, Tennessee.* Pulaski: M. Cohen, 1951. Unpaged.

Estes, P. M., A. P. Foster, and John Trotwood Moore, comps. *Historic Places in Davidson, Williamson, Maury and Giles Counties.*

"Giles County." *History of Tennessee,* ed. Weston A. Goodspeed et al., 749-66, 846-76.

Giles County Sesqui-centennial Assoc. *Official Souvenir Program [of] Giles County, Tennessee, Sesqui-centennial, 1809-1959. July 11-18, 1959.* Pulaski: n.p., 1959. 128 pp.

Killebrew, Joseph B. *Resources of Giles County: Resources of Lincoln County.* Nashville: *Union & American,* 1871. 14 pp.

Knox, Robert Doyle. "A History of Public Education in Giles County, Tennessee." Thesis, Tennessee Technological Univ., 1965.

Lightfoot, Marise P., and Evelyn B. Shackelford. *Maury County Neighbors: Records of Giles, Lewis, and Marshall Counties, Tennessee.* Mt. Pleasant: The Authors, 1967. 288 pp.

McCallum, James. "Brief Sketch of the Settlement and Early History of Giles County." *AHM* 2 (1897), 303-23.

——. *A Brief Sketch of the Settlement and Early History of Giles County, Tennessee, 1876.* Pulaski: Pulaski *Citizen,* 1928. 125 pp.

Parker, Elizabeth C. "History of Giles County, Tennessee." Thesis, Middle Tennessee State Univ., 1953.

Richardson, William Thomas. *Historic Pulaski, Birthplace of the Ku Klux Klan, Scene of the Execution of Sam Davis.* Nashville: Methodist Pub. House, 1913. 108 pp.

Tennessee Industrial and Agricultural Development Commission. "Pulaski and Giles County Industrial Data." Pulaski: Unpublished typescript, 1958. 20 leaves.

Tennessee Valley Authority, Industry Division. *Agricultural-Industrial Survey of Giles County, Tennessee.* 2 vols. Knoxville: TVA, 1934.

Thomas, W. O. "Giles County and Pulaski." *Trotwood's Monthly* 3 (1906), 249-57.

GRAINGER COUNTY
Historian: Mrs. Jerry Jarnagan, New Corinth Road, Blaine 37709.

Caruthers, Amelia Leer. "Bean Station." *National Historical Magazine* 77 (1943), 31-35.

"Grainger County." *History of Tennessee,* East Tennessee Edition, ed. Weston A. Goodspeed et al., 853-56, 1152-60.

Official Booklet of Grainger County, Tennessee. Rutledge: Progressive Club: 1926. 16 pp.

Polhemus, Richard R., and James H. Polhemus. "The McCullough Bend Site." *Tennessee Archaeologist* 22 (1966), 13-24.

Tennessee State Department of Education. *Grainger County Schools Survey Report.* Nashville: State of Tennessee, 1965. 144 pp.

Tennessee Valley Authority, Industry Division. *Agricultural-Industrial Survey of Grainger County.* Knoxville: TVA, 1934. 163 pp.

GREENE COUNTY

Historian: T. Elmer Cox, Sevier Heights, Greeneville 37743.

Allen, Charles W. *Historic Greeneville, Tennessee. A City among the Mountains.* New York: Moss, 1899. 48 pp.

Burgner, Goldene F., Marian K. Crosby, and A. C. Duggins, comps. *Kirchen Buch (Church Book) Register, 1815-1828, St. James Lutheran Church, Greene County, Tennessee.* Greeneville: The Authors, 1964. 74 leaves.

Connally, Ernest Allen. "The Andrew Johnson Homestead at Greeneville, Tennessee." ETHSP 29 (1957), 118-40.

Duggins, A. C. *Lest We Forget: First Baptist Church, Greeneville, Tennessee, 1871-1960.* Kingsport: Kingsport Press, 1960. 372 pp.

Graf, LeRoy P. "The Greeneville Legal Association (1858): A Document." ETHSP 24 (1952), 155-60.

"Greene County." *History of Tennessee,* East Tennessee Edition, ed. Weston A. Goodspeed et al., 881-90, 1239-61.

Hayes, Carl N. *Neighbor against Neighbor, Brother against Brother; Greene County in the Civil War.* Greeneville: The Author, c. 1966. 31 pp.

Holly, J. Fred. *The Economy of Greeneville, Tennessee; a Study of the Information and Data Related to the Greeneville, Tennessee, Economic Community,* Bureau of Research, College of Business Administration Study no. 21. Knoxville: Univ. of Tennessee, 1950. 62 pp.

Lawing, Hugh A. "Andrew Johnson National Monument." *THQ* 20 (1961), 103-19; rpt. in *Landmarks of Tennessee,* 199-215.

Pageant of East Tennessee Commemorating the Sesquicentennial of Greene County at Greeneville, August 18, 1933. Greeneville: n.p., 1933. 16 pp.

Tennessee Valley Authority, Industry Division. *Agricultural-Industrial Survey of Greene County, Tennessee.* Knoxville: TVA, 1934. 67 pp.

University of Tennessee. Bureau of Public Administration. *Greeneville's Government; a Study of the Organization and Administration of the Government of Greeneville, Tennessee.* Knoxville: Univ. of Tennessee, 1950. 160 leaves.

GRUNDY COUNTY
Historian: Lewis F. Fults, Altamont 37301.

Allred, Charles E., et al. *How the Swiss Farmers Operate on the Cumberland Plateau.* Knoxville: Agricultural Experiment Station, Univ. of Tennessee, 1937. 30 leaves.

American Public Welfare Association. "Public Welfare and Related Problems in Grundy County, Tennessee." Chicago: Unpublished typescript, 1940. 178 pp.

Bentley, Blanche S. *Sketch of Beersheba Springs: and: Chickamauga Trace.* Chattanooga: Lookout, c. 1928. 34 pp.

Biographical Directory: Grundy County Members of the Tennessee General Assembly, 1796- . 42 pp. This volume also contains Coffee County.

Highlander Folk School. *See* Economic History: Labor History; Education; and The Negro since the Civil War.

Howell, Isabel. "John Armfield of Beersheba Springs." *THQ* 3 (1944), 46-64, 156-67.

Jackson, Frances Helen. "The German-Swiss Settlement at Gruetli, Tennessee." Thesis, Vanderbilt Univ., 1933.

McCampbell, Vera Cleo. "An Educational Survey of the Elementary Schools of Grundy County, Tennessee." Thesis, Univ. of Tennessee, 1935.

McCormick, Allen. "Development of the Coal Industry of Grundy County, Tennessee." Thesis, George Peabody College, 1934.

Neskaug, Selmer Reinhart. "Agricultural and Social Aspects of the Swiss Settlement in Grundy County, Tennessee." Thesis, Univ. of Tennessee, 1936.

Porter, Curt. "Chautauqua and Tennessee: Monteagle and the Independent Assemblies." *THQ* 22 (1963), 347-60.

Stone, Grave. "Tennessee: Social and Economic Laboratory." *Sewanee Review* 46 (1938), 36-44, 158-66, 312-36. Swiss colonists in Grundy County.

Stevens, A. "Monteagle, Tennessee: Small-Town America." *Nation,* June 29, 1946, pp. 784 ff.

Tennessee State Library and Archives. "Inventory of Grundy County Records." Nashville: State Library and Archives, 1964-. Unpublished typescript.

Hamblen County

Historian: Mrs. Burwin Haun, Green Hills, Russellville 37860.

Brooks, Cora Davis. *History of Morristown, 1787-1936.* Nashville: The Survey, WPA, 1940.

Caldwell, Kate Livingston. *Diary of Kate Livingston, 1859-1868.* Nashville: WPA, 1938.

Davy Crockett Tavern and Pioneer Museum.

"Hamblen County." *History of Tennessee,* East Tennessee Edition, ed. Weston A. Goodspeed et al., 868-71, 1200-16.

Hill, Howard L. *The Herbert Walters Story.* 2 vols. Morristown: Morristown Printing, 1963-66.

Howard, James Edward. "Migration Patterns of Residents in a High In-Migration County, Hamblen County, Tennessee." Thesis, Univ. of Tennessee, 1969.

Morristown Centennial Corporation. *Morristown Centennial, 1855-1955.* Morristown: The Authors, c. 1955. Unpaged.

Paye, Burrall. "A Political History of Morristown and Hamblen County, Tennessee." Thesis, Univ. of Tennessee, 1965.

Rudicil, Rowland K., Mrs. Feamster Taylor, and Mrs. W. H. Inman. *Historic Hamblen, 1870-1970.* Morristown: Morristown Print. Co., 1970. 104 pp.

Tennessee Valley Authority, Industry Division. *Agricultural-Industrial Survey of Hamblen County, Tennessee.* Knoxville: TVA, 1935.

Hamilton County

Historian: Creed F. Bates, "The Cabins," Signal Mountain 37377.

General History and Early Settlement

Allen, Penelope Johnson, comp. *Guide Book of Chattanooga*

and Vicinity. Chattanooga: USD of 1812, 1935. 27 pp.

Armstrong, Zella. *The History of Hamilton County and Chattanooga, Tennessee.* 2 vols. Chattanooga: Lookout, 1931-40. A detailed presentation of persons and developments from prehistoric times until the coming of TVA.

Brown, John P. *Pioneers of Old Frontiers,* with supplements: Penelope J. Allen, *Pioneer Settlers of the Chattanooga Area,* and *The Story of Another Pioneer: A Brief History of Pioneer Bank.* Chattanooga: Pioneer Bank, 1962. 54 pp.

Federal Writers' Project. "Chattanooga." *Tennessee,* 251-69.

Govan, Gilbert E. "Some Sidelights on the History of Chattanooga." *THQ* 6 (1947), 148-60.

Govan, Gilbert E., and James W. Livingood. *The Chattanooga Country, 1540-1951: From Tomahawks to TVA.* New York: Dutton, 1952. 509 pp. Rev. ed., Chapel Hill: Univ. of North Carolina Press, 1963. 526 pp. The story of this Tennessee city and the surrounding region is traced from exploration by DeSoto until the early 1960s. An excellent area history.

"Hamilton County." *History of Tennessee,* East Tennessee Edition, ed. Weston A. Goodspeed et al., 932-38.

"James County." *History of Tennessee,* East Tennessee Edition, ed. Weston A. Goodspeed et al., 797-98, 955-62. James County is now a part of Hamilton County.

Lynde, Francis. "Historic and Picturesque Chattanooga." *Southern Magazine* 5 (1895), 517-35.

MacGowan, J. E. "Chattanooga, Tennessee." *East Tennessee Historical and Biographical,* 173-353.

McBride, Robert M. "The Search for Jesse James." *THQ* 24 (1965), 241-44.

McGuffey, Charles D., ed. *Standard History of Chattanooga, Tennessee, with Full Outline of the Early Settlement, Pioneer Life, Indian History and General and Particular History of the City to the Close of the Year 1910.* Knoxville: Crew & Dorey, 1911. 503 pp.

McMurry, Charles A. *Chattanooga, Its History and Geography.* Morristown: Globe, 1923. 309 pp. School text.

Meeker, Mrs. A. M. *Eliza Ross; or, Illustrated Guide of Lookout Mountain.* Atlanta: Franklin, 1870. 36 pp.

Oakes, George W. Ochs-. *Chattanooga and Hamilton County, Tennessee.* Chattanooga: Tennessee Centennial Exposition

Comm., Chattanooga and Hamilton Co., Tenn., 1897. 64 pp.

Parham, Louis L. *Chattanooga, Tennessee; Hamilton County, and Lookout Mountain. An Epitome of Chattanooga from Her Early Days Down to the Present; Hamilton County, Its Soil, Climate, Area, Population, Wealth, etc. Lookout Mountain, Its Battlefields, Beauties, Climate, and Other Attractions.* Chattanooga: The Author, 1876. 116 pp.

Patten, Cartter. *Signal Mountain and Walden's Ridge.* Chattanooga: The Author, 1961. 76 pp. A good history of this area, very personal in its approach.

Patten, Elizabeth Bryan. *History of Summertown, Walden's Ridge, Tennessee.* Chattanooga: The Author, 1959. 20 leaves.

Walker, Robert S. *Chattanooga, Its History and Growth.* Chattanooga: Chattanooga Community Assoc., c. 1930. 35 pp.

——. *Lookout, the Story of a Mountain.* Kingsport: Southern, 1941; rpt. Chattanooga: George C. Hudson, 1952. 282 pp.

——. *The Chickamauga Dam and Its Environs.* Chattanooga: Andrews, 1949. 32 pp.

——. *This Is Chattanooga.* Chattanooga: Andrews, c. 1949. 45 pp.

Webster, Susie McCarver. *Historic City, Chattanooga; Containing Views and Descriptive Matter of Historic Points of Interest, Scenery, Pictures of Old and New Buildings, Leading Men, etc., all Artistically and Pleasingly Intermingled.* Chattanooga: McGowan-Cooke, 1915. 230 pp.

Hamilton County during the Civil War and Reconstruction

[*See also* Civil War; Reconstruction.]

Armstrong, Zella. *Hamilton County Confederate Soldiers.* Chattanooga: Lookout, n.d. 33 pp.

"Chattanooga Choo-Choo; Mayor Hijacks the General." *Newsweek,* Sept. 25, 1967, p. 33.

Downey, Fairfax Davis. *Storming of the Gateway; Chattanooga, 1863.*

Govan, Gilbert E., and James W. Livingood. "Chattanooga under Military Occupation, 1863-1865." *JSH* 17 (1951), 23-47.

Henry, Robert S. "Chattanooga and the War." *THQ* 19 (1960), 222-30.

Livingood, James W. "The Chattanooga Country in 1860." *THQ* 20 (1961), 159-66.

Lynde, Francis. *Chickamauga and Chattanooga National Military Park. With Narratives of the Battles of Chickamauga, Lookout Mountain, and Missionary Ridge.*

——. *Battles of Chattanooga and Vicinity* . . . . Chattanooga: Chattanooga Community Assoc., 1930[?]. 36 pp.

Newberry, Elizabeth. "Civil War Anecdotes and Legends of Chattanooga." Thesis, George Peabody College, 1928.

Norwood, Charles W., comp. *The Chickamauga and Chattanooga Campaign and Battle-fields. A Chronological Historic Guide, August 16-November 25, 1863* . . . . Chattanooga: Connelly, c. 1898. 84 pp.

Patten, Z. C., and Cartter Patten. *So Firm a Foundation.* Chattanooga: The Authors, 1968. 159 pp. Hamilton County during the Civil War.

Rogers, Jesse Littleton. *Civil War Battles of Chickamauga and Chattanooga.*

Economic History

Buchanan, Cecil. "Municipal Ownership of Public Utilities in Chattanooga, Tennessee." Thesis, Louisiana State Univ., 1941.

Chattanooga Chamber of Commerce. *Chattanooga, Industrial Center of the South.* Chattanooga: Chattanooga Community Advertising Assoc., 1929. 50 pp.

Doster, James F. "The Chattanooga Rolling Mill: An Industrial By-product of the Civil War." *ETHSP* 36 (1964), 45-55.

Lee, Mary Law. "The Influence of Geography on the Growth of Chattanooga Industries." Thesis, Vanderbilt Univ., 1931.

Livingood, James W. "Chattanooga, Tennessee: Its Economic History in the Years Immediately following Appomatox." *ETHSP* 15 (1943), 35-48.

——. "Chattanooga: A Rail Junction of the Old South." *THQ* 6 (1947), 230-50.

The Past, Present, and Future of Chattanooga, Tennessee, the Industrial Center of the South. Chattanooga: *Times*, 1885. 71 pp.

Stein, John G. *Hamilton County, Economic and Social: A Laboratory Study in the Department of Agricultural Economics Under the Direction of Professor C. E. Allred.* Knoxville: Dept. of Agricultural Economics, Univ. of Tennessee, 1925. 36 pp.

Political History and Public Administration

Biographical Directory: Hamilton County Members of the Tennessee General Assembly, 1796- . 84 pp.

Historical Records Survey, Tennessee. *Inventory of the County Archives of Tennessee: Hamilton County, Tennessee.* Nashville: The Survey, WPA, 1937.

Social and Cultural History

Beene, William Virgil. *In Retrospect: Reminiscencies [sic] and Observations of a Hamilton County, Tennessee, Retired Teacher.* Chattanooga: Target, 1958. 158 pp.

"Competition Makes a Comeback: Merger Ended: *Times* and the *News-Free Press.*" *Time,* Sept. 9, 1966, pp. 70 ff.

Coulter, Roy D. "The Negroes of Chattanooga, Tennessee." B.D. thesis, Vanderbilt Univ., 1934.

Davis, Virgil H. "Coordination of Anti-poverty Programs in Chattanooga." Thesis, Middle Tennessee State Univ., 1971.

Govan, Gilbert E., and James W. Livingood. "Adolph S. Ochs: The Boy Publisher." ETHS*P* 17 (1945), 84-104. Ochs published the Chattanooga *Times.*

Johnson, Gerald W. *An Honorable Titan: A Biographical Study of Adolph S. Ochs.* New York: Harper, 1946. 313 pp. Ochs (1858-1935) was an outstanding Chattanooga journalist who came to control the *New York Times.* This work covers his entire life.

Jones, Frank Anderson. "The Incidence of Social Diseases among Negroes in Chattanooga, Tennessee, and the Educational Implications." Thesis, Fisk Univ., 1944.

Partin, Robert. "T. H. Roddy: A Nineteenth Century Physician of Old James County, Tennessee." *THQ* 11 (1952), 195-211.

Walker, Robert Sparks. *As the Indians Left It: The Story of the Chattanooga Audubon Society and Its Elise Chapin Wildlife Sanctuary.* Chattanooga: G. C. Hudson, 1955. 239 pp.

RELIGIOUS GROUPS

Armstrong, Zella. *History of the First Presbyterian Church of Chattanooga.* Chattanooga: Lookout, 1945. 161 pp.

Centenary . . . the Story of a Church. Chattanooga: n.p., 1962. 100 pp. This is a Methodist church.

Flanigen, George J. *The Centenary of St. Peter and St. Paul's*

Parish, Chattanooga, Tennessee. The Story of the First 100 Years of the Catholic Church in Hamilton County. Chattanooga: St. Peter and St. Paul's Parish, 1952. 69 pp.

Historical Records Survey, Tennessee. *Directory of Churches, Missions, and Religious Institutions of Tennessee, no. 33. Hamilton County.* Nashville: The Survey, WPA, 1940. 75 pp.

Peacock, Mary Thomas. *The Circuit Rider and Those Who Followed; Sketches of Methodist Churches Organized before 1860 in the Chattanooga Area with Special Reference to Centenary.* Chattanooga: Hudson, 1957. 465 pp.

HISTORIC STRUCTURES AND PLACES

Art Works in Hamilton County. Chattanooga: W. H. Parrish, 1895. 12 pp.

Baker, Clarence W. *Guide Book to Lookout Mountain and a Brief Account of Battles Fought near Chattanooga, Tennessee.* Chattanooga: C. W. Baker, 1876. 36 pp.

Bate, William B. *The Dedication of the Chickamauga and Chattanooga National Park. Address by Gen. Wm. B. Bate, One of the Speakers Appointed by the Secretary of War for the Above Occasion, Delivered on September 20, 1895.* Nashville: Brandon, 1895. 38 pp.

Boynton, Henry V. *The National Military Park, Chickamauga-Chattanooga. An Historical Guide.* Cincinnati: Clarke, 1895. 307 pp. Rosters of both armies at Chickamauga, pp. 60-87, and at Chattanooga, pp. 140-166, compiled by J. W. Kirkley.

Ferger, Edward. *Guide to Chattanooga, Lookout Mountain and Chickamauga National Military Park.* Chattanooga: Ferger & Taylor, 1895. 54 pp.

Govan, Gilbert E. "The Chattanooga Union Station." *THQ* 29 (1970), 372-78.

Lewis, J. Eugene. "Cravens House: Landmark of Lookout Mountain." *THQ* 20 (1961), 203-21; rpt. in *Landmarks of Tennessee,* 157-75.

Livingood, James W. "Chickamauga and Chattanooga National Military Park." *THQ* 23 (1964), 3-23; rpt. in *Landmarks of Tennessee,* 91-111.

McGuffey, Charles D., ed. *Chattanooga and Her Battlefields.* Chattanooga: MacGowan-Cooke, 1912. 64 pp.

HANCOCK COUNTY
Historian: Chris D. Livesay, Eidson 37731.

Barr, Phyllis Cox. "The Melungeons of Newman's Ridge." Thesis, East Tennessee State Univ., 1965.

"Hancock County." *History of Tennessee,* East Tennessee Edition, ed. Weston A. Goodspeed et al., 871-72, 1216-25.

Price, Prentiss, ed. "Two Petitions to Virginia of the North of Holston Men, 1776, 1777." ETHS*P* 21 (1949), 95-110. Area includes Hancock County.

Stuart, Jesse. *Daughter of the Legend.* Historical fiction of Melungeon people of Hancock County.

HARDEMAN COUNTY
Historian: Fay Tennyson Davidson, 234 Central Street, Bolivar 38008.

Alexander, Herbert L. R. "The Armstrong Raid Including the Battles of Bolivar, Medon Station and Britton Lane." *THQ* 21 (1962), 31-46.

Armour, Quinnie. "The Development of Secondary Education in Hardeman County, Tennessee." Thesis, George Peabody College, 1937,

Barraclough, S. "No Plumbing for Negroes: Ames Plantation." *Atlantic,* Sept. 1965, pp. 105-9.

Black, Roy W., comp. "Hardeman County, Tennessee, Cemetery Records." Bolivar: Unpublished typescript, 1965. Unpaged.

Clifft, Warner Wardell. "Early History of Hardeman County, Tennessee." Thesis, George Peabody College, 1930.

Deming, Raymond McCoy. "Hardeman County: Its Origin and Economic Development." Ed.D. diss., George Peabody College, 1958.

Ewing, John Arthur. "Planning the Ames Plantation Project." Diss., Harvard Univ., 1956.

"Hardeman County." *History of Tennessee,* ed. Weston A. Goodspeed et al., 818-40, 887-963.

Haywood, Marshall D. *Calvin Jones, Physician, Soldier and Freemason, 1755-1846, Being an Account of His Career in North Carolina and Tennessee.* Oxford, N.C.: Press of Oxford Orphanage, 1919. 31 pp.

Kirksey, Howard G. "History and Comparative Growth of Public Schools in Hardeman County, 1867-1936." Thesis, George Peabody College, 1937.

Owsley, Harriet C. "Westward to Tennessee." *THQ* 24 (1965), 31-38. This article describes Calvin Jones, who settled near Bolivar c. 1832.

Pirtle, James Riley. "The Military History of the Hatchie River Valley in Hardeman County, Tennessee." Thesis, George Peabody College, 1957.

Rivers, Ernest Lynwood. "The History of Allen White High School, Whiteville, Hardeman County, Tennessee from 1930-1948." Thesis, Tennessee State A & I Univ., 1954.

HARDIN COUNTY
Historian: Grace Patterson, Box 304, Savannah 38372.

Bingham, James M. "Northwest Hardin County: A Study in Industrial Development." Thesis, Memphis State Univ., 1965.

Biographical Directory: Hardin County Members of the Tennessee General Assembly, 1796- . 61 pp. This volume also contains Lawrence County.

Brazelton, B. G. *A History of Hardin County, Tennessee.* Nashville: Cumberland Presbyterian Pub. House, 1885. 135 pp. Rpt. Savannah: Savannah Pub., 1965. 109 pp.

Burchard, Ernest F. *The Brown Iron Ores of the Western Highland Rim, Tennessee.*

Campbell, Bernard T. "Shiloh National Military Park." *THQ* 21 (1962), 3-18; rpt. in *Landmarks of Tennessee,* 301-16.

Durbin, Lear Pearl. "Economic and Social Development of Hardin County, Tennessee since 1965." Thesis, George Peabody College, 1930.

Harbert, P. M. "Early History of Hardin County." WTHSP 1 (1947), 38-67.

"Hardin County." *History of Tennessee,* ed. Weston A. Goodspeed et al., 829-41, 894-908.

Jewell, W. B. *Geology and Mineral Resources of Hardin County, Tennessee,* Tennessee Dept. of Education, Division of Geology Bulletin 37. Nashville: Tennessee Dept. of Education, 1931. 117 pp.

Swanson, James M. "An Educational Survey of Hardin County, Tennessee." Thesis, Univ. of Tennessee, 1933.

Swanson, Lois. "A Way of Living: Study of a Hundred Homes in the Morris Chapel Community in Hardin County, Tennessee." Thesis, Univ. of Tennessee, 1933.

Tennessee Valley Authority, Industry Division. *Agricultural-Industrial Survey of Hardin County, Tennessee.* Knoxville: TVA, 1934. 171 pp.

HAWKINS COUNTY
Historian: Blanche Grigsby, Huffmaster Street, Rogersville 37857.

Anderson, Isaac. *A Sermon, Delivered on September 8th, 1813 . . . .* Rogersville: The Author, 1814. 20 pp.

Davis, James H. "A Study of Seven School Communities of Hawkins County, Tennessee." Thesis, Univ. of Tennessee, 1937.

First Baptist Church, Rogersville, Tennessee. Diamond Anniversary, 1890-1965. Rogersville: n.p., 1965.

"Hawkins County." *History of Tennessee,* East Tennessee Edition, ed. Weston A. Goodspeed et al., 873-80, 1225-39.

Long, Alton Blanton. "An Economic and Educational Survey of Rogersville Community." Thesis, Univ. of Tennessee, 1940.

Park, James. *The Fiftieth Anniversary of the Rogersville Synodical College.* McMinnville: Standard, 1899. 17 pp.

Price, Prentiss, ed. "Two Petitions to Virginia of North of Holston Men, 1776, 1777." ETHSP 21 (1949), 95-110. Area includes much of Hawkins County.

Vance, Carl Taylor. "A Study of High Schools in Hawkins County, Tennessee." Thesis, George Peabody College, 1922.

Williams, Samuel Cole. "Hawkins County." *Phases of Southwest Territory History,* 18-20.

With the Colors from Hawkins County: 1917-1918-1919. Pressmen's Home: Dunwoody & Reed, 1920. 92 pp.

HAYWOOD COUNTY
Historian: Morton Felsenthal, 513 Key Corner, Brownsville 38012.

Hamner, Virginia. "Biography of John Alexander Taylor As

Revealed by His Journals, 1842-1881." Thesis, Trinity Univ., 1959. Taylor was a small planter near Brownsville.

"Haywood County." *History of Tennessee,* ed. Weston A. Goodspeed et al., 818-29, 921-47.

Historical Records Survey, Tennessee. *Inventory of the County Archives of Tennessee: Haywood County.* Nashville: The Survey, WPA, 1939.

Provine, William A., ed. "In Memoriam—Col. George C. Porter." *THM* 5 (1919), 137-41.

Taylor Kinsfolk Association at Tabernacle Church. *The Taylors of Tabernacle; the History of a Family, Including the Genealogy of Its Descendants with Biographical Sketches and Family Journals with Daily Accounts of Life in Haywood County, Tennessee, for Over a Century.* Brownsville: Tabernacle Hist. Comm., 1957. 628 pp.

Tennessee Valley Authority, Industry Division. *Agricultural-Industrial Survey of Haywood County, Tennessee.* Knoxville: TVA, 1935. 168 pp.

HENDERSON COUNTY
Historian: G. Tillman Stewart, Superintendent, Henderson County Board of Education, Lexington 38351.

Biographical Directory: Henderson County Members of the Tennessee General Assembly, 1796- . 30 pp.

Bolen, H. J. *Henderson County's History.* Murfreesboro: *Home Journal,* 1922. 14 pp.

"Henderson County." *History of Tennessee,* ed. Weston A. Goodspeed et al., 797-806, 841-62.

Powers, Auburn. *History of Henderson County, Comprising an Account of the Facts Connected with the Early Settlement of the County; the Origin and the Development of the County; Slavery, the Civil War, and the Reconstruction Days; the World War and Present Conditions.* N. p.: n.p., 1930. 169 pp.

Tennessee Valley Authority, Industry Division. *Agricultural-Industrial Survey of Henderson County, Tennessee.* Knoxville: TVA, 1935. 103 pp.

HENRY COUNTY
Historian: W. O. Inman, 602 Jackson Street, Paris 38242.

Bearss, Edwin C. "The Fall of Forth Henry, Tennessee." WTHSP 17 (1963), 85-107. A Civil War engagement.

Biographical Directory: Henry County Members of the Tennessee General Assembly, 1796- . 58 pp.

Field, Maurice Houston. "A History of E. W. Grove High School, Henry County, Tennessee." Thesis, Univ. of Tennessee (Martin), 1960.

Fox, Susan E., and Margaret L. Morris. *Paris, the City Beautiful.* Paris: n.p., 1934. 23 pp.

Greene, W. P. *The City of Paris and Henry County, Tennessee, Historical, Descriptive, and Biographical.* Paris: Paris Pub., 1900. 96 pp.

"Henry County." *History of Tennessee,* ed. Weston A. Goodspeed et al., 813-32, 888-935.

Howard, John R. *An Anniversary Address on Female Education, Delivered in Paris, Tennessee, at the First Annual Examination of the Pupils of Henry Academy, under the Management of Mr. Thos. Johnson, on 30th June.* Paris: Gates & McCowat, 1837. 15 pp.

Hurdle, Virginia Jo. "Folklore of a Negro Couple in Henry County." *TFSB* 19 (1953), 71-78.

Johnson, E. McLeod. "A History of Henry County, Tennessee." Vol. 1. Paris: Unpublished typescript, 1958. 284 pp.

Provine, William A. "A Diary of the Travels of William G. Randle, Daguerreotypist, of Henry County, Tennessee, 1852." *THM* 9 (1925), 195-208.

Rennolds, Edwin H. *A History of the Henry County Commands Which Served in the Confederate States Army, Including Rosters of the Various Companies Enlisted in Henry County, Tennessee.* Jacksonville, Fla.: Sun Pub., 1904; rpt. Kennesaw, Ga.: Continental, 1961. 301 pp.

Tennessee State Library and Archives. "Inventory of Henry County Records." Nashville: State Library and Archives, 1964- . Unpublished typescript.

Tennessee Valley Authority, Industry Division. *Agricultural-Industrial Survey of Henry County, Tennessee.* Knoxville: TVA, 1934. 74 pp.

Van Dyke, Roger Raymond. "A History of Henry County, Tennessee, through 1865." Thesis, Univ. of Tennessee, 1966.

HICKMAN COUNTY

Historian: Edward Dotson, County Court Clerk, Centerville 37033.

Biographical Directory: Hickman County Members of the Tennessee

General Assembly 1796- . 100 pp. This volume also contains Maury County.

Hickman County Sesquicentennial Commemorating 150 Years of Progress: A Presentation to the People of Hickman County, Tennessee, Sponsored by the Hickman County Sesquicentennial Corporation and Business and Professional Men with the Cooperation of Our Civil, Service and Social Organizations . . . . Columbia: Columbia Printing, 1957. 76 pp.

"Hickman County." *History of Tennessee,* ed. Weston A. Goodspeed et al., 788-801, 910-23.

McDonaugh, James L. "Forgotten Empire: Sam Graham's Pinewood." *THQ* 27 (1968), 40-49.

Spence, W. Jerome D., and David L. Spence. *A History of Hickman County, Tennessee.* Nashville: *Gospel Advocate,* 1900; rpt. Lawrenceburg: Norval Gilbert, 1955. 509 pp.

Tennessee Valley Authority, Industry Division. *Agricultural-Industrial Survey of Hickman County, Tennessee.* Knoxville: TVA, 1934. 103 pp.

HOUSTON COUNTY
Historian: No appointment made.

"Houston County." *History of Tennessee,* ed. Weston A. Goodspeed et al., 974-98, 1388-1402.

Irwin, David. "Land Utilization in Houston County, Tennessee." Thesis, Univ. of Tennessee, 1949.

Little, Arthur D., Inc. *The Opportunity for Industrial Development in Benton, Houston and Humphreys Counties, Tennessee.*

McClain, Iris Hopkins. "A History of Houston County." Columbia: Unpublished typescript, 1966. 241 pp.

Tennessee State Library and Archives. "Inventory of Houston County Records." Nashville: State Library and Archives, 1964- . Unpublished typescript.

HUMPHREYS COUNTY
Historian: Mrs. Bill Anderson, Waverly 37185.

Garrett, Jill K. "A History of Humphreys County, Tennessee." Columbia: Unpublished typescript, 1963. 376 pp.

"Humphreys County." *History of Tennessee,* ed. Weston A. Goodspeed et al., 868-94, 1205-88.

Little, Arthur D., Inc. *The Opportunity for Industrial Development in Benton, Houston, and Humphreys Counties, Tennessee.*

Waverly Regional Planning Commission. *Humphreys County School Survey.* Nashville: School Survey, 1958. 40 pp.

JACKSON COUNTY
Historian: Mrs. H. M. Haile, Jr., Gainesboro 38562.

Draper, R. C. "Early History of Jackson County, Tennessee." Gainesboro: *Jackson County Sentinel,* 1928-29. Published as a series of newspaper articles.

Haille, Ann Byrne. "History of the Development of Education prior to 1900 in Jackson County, Tennessee." Thesis, Tennessee Technological Univ., 1961.

Overton, Walter Bruce. "An Educational Economic, and Community Survey of Jackson County, Tennessee." Thesis, Univ. of Tennessee, 1927.

Smith, Ed M. "History of Educational Development in Jackson County, Tennessee, 1800 to 1950." Thesis, Tennessee Technological Univ., 1967.

JEFFERSON COUNTY
Historian: J. C. Thornton, Route 4, Dandridge 37725.

Beaumont, Henry Francis. "Dandridge: The Namesake of Martha Washington." *AHM* 7 (1902), 274-80, 296-305.

Cockrum, James Earl. "A Study of the Development of Organized Religion in Jefferson County, Tennessee (1785-1950)." Thesis, Univ. of Tennessee, 1951.

Couch, Robert Clarence. "The Zinc Industry of Jefferson County, Tennessee." Thesis, Univ. of Tennessee, 1953.

"Jefferson County." *History of Tennessee,* East Tennessee Edition, ed. Weston A. Goodspeed et al., 856-64, 1160-93.

McGhee, Lucy Kate, comp. *Historical Records of East Tennessee. Jefferson County, Dandridge Edition.* 2 vols. Washington, D.C.: n.p., 1954.

Tennessee State Department of Education. *Jefferson County Survey*

Report. Nashville: State of Tennessee, 1965. 128 pp. Relates to the schools of the county.

Toomery, Glen A. *The Romance of a Sesquicentennial. The Dumplin Creek Baptist Church of Christ, Jefferson County, Tennessee, Organized 1797.* N.p.: n.p., 1947. 93 pp.

Wood, Mayme Parrott. *Shunem Church and Cemetery Speak: A Living Memorial to Those Who Sleep Here, 1824-1965.* Gatlinburg: Brazos, 1965. 56 pp.

JOHNSON COUNTY
Historian: Mrs. L. F. Kent, Route 1, Mountain City 37683.

Biographical Directory: Johnson County Members of the Tennessee General Assembly, 1796- . 61 pp. This volume also contains Carter and Unicoi Counties.

Jennings, George. "The History of Watauga Academy of Butler, Tennessee." Thesis, Appalachian State Univ., 1950.

"Johnson County." *History of Tennessee,* East Tennessee Edition, ed, Weston A. Goodspeed et al., 922-25, 1312-17.

Lawrence, Robert A. "A New Manganese Mine in Johnson County, Tennessee." *JTAS* 15 (1940), 396-401.

Scott, Samuel W., and Samuel P. Angel. *History of the Thirteenth Regiment, Tennessee Voluntary Cavalry, U.S.A.* Includes Johnson County history.

Tennessee Valley Authority, Industry Division. *Agricultural-Industrial Survey of Johnson County, Tennessee.* Knoxville: TVA, 1934. 51 pp.

KNOX COUNTY
Historian: Mrs. Park Niceley, 1216 Weisgarber Road, Knoxville 37919.

Bibliography

Ballentine, Nelle. "A Bibliographical Checklist of Knoxville and Memphis Imprints, 1867-1876, with an Introductory Essay on the Knoxville and Memphis Press." Thesis, Univ. of Tennessee, 1957.

General History and Early Settlement

Branson, H. M. *Annual Handbook of Knoxville, Tennessee, for the*

Year 1892. A Concise Statement of the Financial, Commercial and Manufacturing Interests of This City; Its Climate, and the Magnificent Scenery of Its Surroundings; Its Mineral, Marble and Timber Interests, as well as a Complete Memoranda of the Laws of Tennessee, and Other Matters of Interest to Homeseekers and Capitalists. Knoxville: *Tribune,* 1892. 104 pp.

Caldwell, Joshua William. "History of Knoxville, Tennessee." *East Tennessee. Historical and Biographical,* 455-87.

———. "Knoxville, the Metropolis of Eastern Tennessee." *Historic Towns of the Southern States,* ed. Lyman P. Powell, 449-75.

Creekmore, Betsy Beeler. *Knoxville.* Knoxville: Univ. of Tennessee Press, 1958, 1959; 2nd ed., 1967. 324 pp. Developments in the Knoxville area from Indian times until the late 1960s.

Creswell, J. B. *Brief Historical Sketch of the Village of Bearden.* Knoxville: Newman, 1899. 19 pp.

Federal Writers' Project. "Knoxville," Tennessee, 232-50.

Folmsbee, Stanley J., and Lucile Deaderick. "The Founding of Knoxville." ETHSP 13 (1941), 3-20.

Hicks, Nannie Lee. *Community Historical Sketches in Knox County, Tennessee: Corryton—Harbison's Cross Roads—Smithwood,* Community Historical Sketches, no. 1. Knoxville: Knox Co. Lib., 1958. 25 pp.

———. *Historic Treasure Spots of Knox County, Tennessee.* Knoxville: DAR, 1964. 82 pp.

———. *The John Adair Section of Knox County, Tennessee.* Knoxville: n.p., 1968. 98 pp.

Historical, Pictorial, Fraternal Souvenir of Knoxville, Tennessee. Knoxville: n.p., 1903. 100 pp.

History and Illustrations of Knoxville, Tennessee. Knoxville: n.p., 1896, 1900.

Humes, Thomas William. *An Address . . . before the Citizens of Knoxville, on the 10th Day of February, 1842, the Semi-centennial Anniversary of the Settlement of the Town.* Knoxville: Eastman, 1842; rpt. Knoxville *Register,* 1852. 26 pp. Rpt. in *Tennessee Old and New,* I, 452-79.

Kirke, E. "Knoxville, Tennessee in the Olden Time." *Harper's New Monthly Magazine* 71 (1885), 68-77.

"Knox County." *History of Tennessee,* East Tennessee Edition, ed. Weston A. Goodspeed et al., 925-31.

"Knox County and Knoxville." *History of Tennessee,* Knox

County and Knoxville Edition, ed. Weston A. Goodspeed et al., 797-1072. Knoxville: Goodspeed Pub., 1887.

Knoxville, Tennessee, the Queen City of the Mountains. Knoxville: Knoxville Board of Trade, 1909. 24 pp.

Luttrell, Laura E., comp. "Some Founders of Campbell's Station, Tennessee: A Geneaology of Alexander, David, and James Campbell." ETHS*P* 25 (1953), 89-110; 26 (1954), 107-31.

Pilcher, Margaret Campbell. "Sketch of Captain David Campbell." *AHM* 8 (1903), 154-59.

Pentecost, Percy M. "A Corporate History of Knoxville, Tennessee, before 1860." Thesis, Vanderbilt Univ., 1946.

Progressive Knoxville: A Pictorial Review of the City, 1903-1904. 2 vols. Knoxville: Russell Harrison, 1904.

Reilly, J. S. *Knoxville, Past, Present and Future.* n.p.: The Author, 1884. 156 pp.

Rothrock, Mary U., ed. *The French Broad-Holston Country: A History of Knox County, Tennessee.* Knoxville: East Tennessee Hist. Soc., 1946, 1972. 573 pp.

Rule, William, George F. Mellen, and J. Wooldridge, eds. *Standard History of Knoxville, Tennessee, with Full Outline of the Natural Advantages, Early Settlement, Territorial Government, Indian Troubles and General and Particular History of the City Down to the Present Time.* Chicago: Lewis, 1900. 590 pp.

Williams, Samuel Cole. "George Farragut." ETHS*P* 1 (1929), 77-94. Father of Admiral David Farragut.

——, "George Roulstone: Father of the Tennessee Press." ETHS*P* 17 (1945), 51-60.

——. "Colonel David Henley." ETHS*P* 18 (1946), 3-24.

Knoxville during the Civil War and Reconstruction

Boeger, Palmer H. "General Burnside's Knoxville Packing Project." ETHS*P* 35 (1963), 76-84.

Brearley, William H. *Recollections of the East Tennessee Campaign, Battle of Campbell Station, 16th Nov., 1863; Siege of Knoxville, 17th Nov.-5th Dec., 1863.* Detroit: *Tribune,* 1871. 48 pp.

Davidson, James F. "Michigan and the Defense of Knoxville, Tennessee, 1863." ETHS*P* 35 (1963), 21-53.

Going, Allen J. "A Shooting Affray in Knoxville with Interstate Repercussions: The Killing of James H. Clanton by David M. Nelson, 1871." ETHS*P* 27 (1955), 39-48.

Kennerly, Wesley Travis. *The Battle of Fort Sanders. An Address Delivered November 28th, 1814 . . . at the Unveiling and Dedication of the Monument Erected by the Knoxville Chapter, United Daughters of the Confederacy, to the Memory of the Confederate Soldiers Who Lost Their Lives during the Siege of Knoxville, Tennessee, November 29, 1863.* Knoxville: Breen, 1914. 14 pp.

Klein, Maury. "The Knoxville Campaign." *Civil War Times Illustrated*, Oct. 1971, pp. 4 ff.

Poe, Orlando M. *Personal Recollections of the Occupation of East Tennessee and the Defense of Knoxville.*

Seymour, Digby Gordon. *Divided Loyalties.*

Williams, Samuel Cole. "John Mitchell, the Irish Patriot, Resident of Tennessee." ETHSP 10 (1938), 44-56. Mitchell was a pro-Confederate activist during the Civil War.

Economic History

Chang, Po Shin. "History of the Hamilton National Bank of Knoxville." Thesis, Univ. of Tennessee, 1962.

Clark, Joseph Harold. "History of the Knoxville Iron Company." Thesis, Univ. of Tennessee, 1948.

De Carlo, Vincent R. "The Net Direct Economic Effect of the University of Tennessee on the City of Knoxville and on Knox County Resulting from the Expansion of the Knoxville Campus since 1962." Thesis, Univ. of Tennessee, 1969.

Dodge, Richard L. "Factors Influencing the Development of the Broadway Shopping Center at Knoxville, Tennessee." Thesis, Univ. of Tennessee, 1958.

Dorman, Coy. "Manufacturing in the West Central Knoxville Area." Thesis, Univ. of Tennessee, 1959.

Goodman, William, ed. *Souvenir History of Knoxville, the Marble City and Great Jobbing Market. Its Importance as a Manufacturing Center . . . .* Knoxville: Knoxville Engr., 1907. Unpaged.

Grady, James T., ed. and comp. *The City of Knoxville, Tennessee and Vicinity and Their Resources.* Knoxville: Knoxville Bd. of Trade, 1906. Unpaged.

Greater Knoxville Illustrated. A Glance at Her History, a Review of Her Commerce . . . . Nashville: n.p., 1910.

Hammer and Company Associates. *The Economy of Metropolitan Knoxville. A Study Focused on the Economic Base and Potentials of Knoxville and Knox County.* Washington, D.C.: Metro. Planning Comm. of Knoxville and Knox County, 1962. 181 pp.

Hind, James Fox. "The History of Transportation Advertising, 1850-1956, and a Study of Its Importance in Knoxville, Tennessee." Thesis, Univ. of Tennessee, 1958.

Hoss, Hugh F. *Knoxville: Commercial and Industrial Survey of Knoxville, Tennessee.* Knoxville: n.p., 1939.

Hyde, Victor A. "A Geographical Survey of Knoxville, Tennessee." Thesis, Univ. of Tennessee, 1939.

Killebrew, Joseph B. *Knoxville as an Iron Center.* Nashville: Eastman & Howell, 1880. 15 pp.

"Knoxville Plans to Be First Big Federal Power User." *Newsweek,* July 28, 1934, p. 32.

Manufacturing and Mercantile Resources of Knoxville, Tennessee. Knoxville: n.p., 1882. 409 pp.

Pentecost, Percy M. "A Corporate History of Knoxville, Tennessee before 1860." Thesis, Univ. of Tennessee, 1946.

The Prospector's Guide: Showing the Resources and Advantages of East Tennessee, and of Her Central and Largest City, Knoxville, Tennessee. Knoxville: W. T. Ragsdale, 1888 [?]. 24 pp.

Rush, John DeWitt. "Relation of Land Base Quality to the Agricultural Economy of Knox County, Tennessee." Thesis, Univ. of Tennessee, 1940.

Smith, James Clenton. "The Economic Impact of the University of Tennessee upon Metropolitan Knoxville." Thesis, Univ. of Tennessee, 1964.

Teng, Hai Chuan. "Marble Deposits and Marble Industry of the Knoxville Area." Thesis, Univ. of Tennessee, 1948.

Walters, Joe Parks. "The Marble Industry of the Knoxville Area." Thesis, Univ. of Tennessee, 1958.

Wayland, Mrs. Charles F. "An Old Book of Stock Marks and Brands of Knox County, Tennessee." ETHSP 22 (1950), 148-57.

Political History and Public Administration

Baker, Todd. "The Office of Knox County Sheriff: An Administrative Study." Thesis, Univ. of Tennessee, 1959.

——. "Politics of Innovation." Diss., Univ. of Tennessee, 1968. A study of 20 demands made in Knoxville and Knox County between 1955-63.

Beaumont, Henry Francis. "Thomas Emmerson—the First Mayor of Knoxville." *AHM* 8 (1903), 183-88.

Bell, Robert Monroe. "The Cost of Administering Criminal Justice in Memphis and Knoxville, Tennessee." Thesis, Univ. of Tennessee, 1931.

Biographical Directory: Knox County Members of the Tennessee General Assembly, 1796- . 124 pp.

Brock, Robert M. *Knox County Government.*

Green, John Webb. *Bench and Bar of Knox County, Tennessee.* Knoxville: Archer & Smith, c. 1947. 267 pp.

Historical Records Survey, Tennessee. *Inventory of the County Archives of Tennessee: Knox County.* Nashville: The Survey, WPA, 1941.

Lambert, Walter N. *Governments in Knox County.* Knoxville: Bureau of Public Administration, Univ. of Tennessee, 1965. 145 pp.

Lord, Gerald D. "Federal Centralization versus Local Values: A Case Study of Federal-Local Relations in the Knoxville-Knox County Community Action Committee." Thesis, Univ. of Tennessee, 1969.

Holmes, Jack E., Nelson Robinson, and Walter Lambert. *Structure of County Government in Tennessee.*

McComb, Thomas, and Martha Donaldson. *Knoxville-Knox County Consolidation and the County and City School Systems.* Knoxville: Bureau of Public Administration, Univ. of Tennessee, 1958.

Metropolitan Government Charter Commission. *Proposed Metropolitan Government Charter for Knoxville and Knox County, Tennessee.* Knoxville: The Commission, Jan. 1959. 72 pp.

Philips, Claude S. "The Influence of the Baptist Church on Knoxville Government." Thesis, Univ. of Tennessee, 1950.

Richardson, Charles H. "A History of Municipal Government in Knoxville since 1911." Thesis, Univ. of Tennessee, 1945.

Spence, Joe Edd. "The Public Career of Andrew Jackson Graves." Thesis, Univ. of Tennessee, 1967. Graves was a Democratic political leader of Knox County in the 1920s.

——. "The Public Career of Andrew Jackson Graves." ETHSP 40 (1968), 62-82.

Social and Cultural History

Baker, Joe L., and Stuart Towe. *Men of Affairs in Knoxville.* Knoxville: Knoxville Litho., 1917. 202 pp.

Catalogue of the Fine Arts Section of the Appalachian Exposition. Knoxville: Newman, 1910. 78 pp.

Clark, John B., Jr. "Fire Protection in Old Knoxville." ETHS*P* 31 (1959), 32-42.

Crews, E. Katherine. "Early Musical Activities in Knoxville, Tennessee, 1791-1861." ETHS*P* 32 (1960), 3-17.

——. "Musical Activities in Knoxville, Tennessee, 1861-1891." ETHS*P* 34 (1962), 58-85.

——. "The Golden Age of Music in Knoxville, Tennessee, 1891-1910." ETHS*P* 37 (1965), 49-76.

Curry, Kenneth. "The Knoxville of James Agee's *A Death in The Family.*" *Tennessee Studies in Literature* 14 (1969), 1-14.

Fowler, James Alexander. *Memoirs.* 6 vols. Knoxville: Unpublished typescript, n.d.

Gilbert, Dorothy Lloyd. "Quaker Migration to the Western Waters." ETHS*P* 18 (1946), 47-58. The group paused in Knox County before moving on.

Goodman, William M., ed. *The First Exposition of Conservation and Its Builders; an Official History of the National Conservation Exposition, Held at Knoxville, Tenn., in 1913 and of Its Forerunners, the Appalachian Expositions of 1910-11, Embracing a Review of the Conservation Movement in the United States from Its Inception to the Present Time.* Knoxville: Knoxville Litho., 1914. 411 pp.

Hanlon, Russell W. *Men of Affairs in Knoxville.* Knoxville: *Journal & Tribune,* 1921. 137 pp.

Knox County in the World War: 1917-1918-1919. Knoxville: Knoxville Litho., c. 1919. 448 pp.

Lauritzen, Mrs. J. R. *Some Sketches from My Life, Written for My 80th Birthday, May 1, 1910.* Knoxville: n.p., 1910. 24 pp.

Lawson McGhee Library. *Calvin M. McClung Historical Collection.*

Luttrell, Laura E., and Mary U. Rothrock, comps. *Calvin Morgan McClung Historical Collection.*

Mellen, George F. "Calvin Morgan McClung." *THM* 7 (1921), 3-28.

Official Souvenir and History, Sesquicentennial Celebration, Knoxville, August 28 through September 1, 1941. Knoxville: n.p., 1941. 50 pp.

Palmer, Susan Tate. *Thomas Hope of Tennessee, 1757-1820, House Carpenter and Joiner.* Knoxville: Privately printed, 1972. 175 pp.

Rothrock, Mary U. "Mrs. Calvin M. McClung." ETHS*P* 30 (1958), 3-6.

Temple, Mary Boyce. *Sketch of Margaret Fuller Ossoli.* Knoxville: Ossoli Soc., 1886. 48 pp.

White, Kate. "The Diary of a '49-er'—Jacob Stuart." *THM* (ser. 2) 1 (1930-31), 279-85. A Knoxville citizen in search of California gold.

Williams, W. D. *Whittle Springs Hotel and Golf and Country Club.* Knoxville: n.p., c. 1911. Unpaged.

EDUCATION

History of the Knoxville Public Schools. Knoxville: Dept. of Secondary Educ., 1953. 90 pp.

Lothrop, Laura Egerton. "A History of the Webb School of Knoxville. Knoxville, Tennessee." Thesis, Univ. of Tennessee, 1972.

Luttrell, Laura E. "One Hundred Years of a Female Academy: The Knoxville Female Academy, 1811-1846; the East Tennessee Female Institute, 1846-1911." ETHS*P* 17 (1945), 71-83.

McComb, Thomas, and Martha Donaldson. *Knoxville-Knox County Consolidation and the County and City School Systems.*

Morgan, Le Berta H., ed. *Staub School. A Brief History of Its First Fifty Years' Service to the Community.* Knoxville: Staub PTA, 1947. 74 pp.

Pratt, C. W. "The History and Development of Education in Knox County, Tennessee." Thesis, Univ. of Tennessee, 1959.

White, Kate. "Knoxville's Old Educational Institutions." *THM* 8 (1924), 4-6.

RELIGIOUS GROUPS

Baptist

Egerton, Cecil Baker. "A History of the First Baptist Church of Knoxville, Tennessee." Thesis, Univ. of Tennessee, 1960.

Hamby, Robert P. *History of Meridian Baptist Church, Old Sevierville Pike, Knoxville, Tennessee: Church Directory and Church Roll in Celebration of the Seventy-sixth Anniversary.* Knoxville: n.p., 1950. 54 pp.

Shipley, Gertrude G., comp. *Centennial Celebration of Island Home Baptist Church, Knoxville, Tennessee, October 2, 1960-December 11, 1960.* Knoxville: Coleman, 1960. 52 pp.

Episcopal

Humes, Thomas William. *Historical Discourse of St. John's Church, Knoxville, Tennessee.* Knoxville: n.p., 1886. 16 pp.

St. James Church, Knoxville, Tennessee. Knoxville: n.p., 1929.

Seymour, Charles M., comp. *A History of One Hundred Years of St. John's Episcopal Church in Knoxville, Tenn., 1846-1946.* Knoxville: St. John's Parish, [1947]. 295 pp.

Methodist and Evangelical United Brethren

Bennecker, Ruth. *He That Serveth; Twenty-five Years' Adventures in Christian Ministry; George Creswell and Second Church.* Knoxville: Second Methodist Church, 1945. 345 pp.

McDaniel, Harold W. *History of Forestdale Evangelical United Brethren Church.* Knoxville: The Church, 1956. 138 pp.

Martin, Isaac Patton. *Church Street Methodists, Children of Francis Asbury: A History of Church Street Methodist Church. Knoxville, Tennessee, 1816-1947.* Knoxville: Methodist Hist. Soc. of Holston Conference, 1947. 212 pp.

Presbyterian

Bachman, J. W., and J. H. McNeilly. *Memorial of the Rev. James Park.* Nashville: Smith & Lamar, 1912. 38 pp. Park was pastor of the First Presbyterian Church at Knoxville.

Briscoe, W. Russell, and Katherine Boies Buehler. *Her Walls before Thee Stand: History of the Second Presbyterian Church, 1818-1968.* Knoxville: n.p., 1969. 53 pp.

Centennial Anniversary of the First Presbyterian Church of Knoxville, Tennessee, and the Semi-centennial Anniversary of the Ministry of Rev. James Park, D.D., Knoxville, Tennessee, Oct. 11, 1896. Knoxville: Bean, Warters & Gaut, 1897. 55 pp.

Hassall, Harry Sharp. *A History of Concord Presbyterian Church, Concord, Tennessee.* Knoxville: Letter Shop, 1963. 96 leaves.

Homecoming, First Presbyterian Church, Knoxville, Tennessee, 1796-1925. Knoxville: n.p., 1925.

McMullen, Robert B. *History of the First Presbyterian Church in Knoxville, Tennessee.* Knoxville: John B. G. Kinsloe, 1855. 28 pp.

Old First Church, Synod of Appalachia, Presbytery of Knoxville. Knoxville: n.p., 1942.

Orr, Horace E. "One Hundred Years of New Prospect Presbyterian Church, Knox County, Tennessee, 1834-1934." ETHSP 7 (1935), 50-63.

Park, James. *History of the First Presbyterian Church in Knoxville, Tennessee.* Knoxville: Ramage, 1876. 29 pp.

Ramsey, James G. McGready. *History of Lebanon Presbyterian Church, 'In the Fork,' Five Miles East of Knoxville.* Knoxville: Archer & Smith, 1918; 1952. 23 pp.

Shannondale Presbyterian Church Historical Committee. *Seventy-Five Years: Shannondale Presbyterian Church, Knoxville, Tennessee, 1886-1961.* Knoxville: n.p., 1962. 103 pp.

General

Edington, John F., comp. *A Church Census of the 134 Churches in the City of Knoxville, Tennessee as of Date January 31, 1925.* Knoxville: Southside, 1925. 15 pp.

Historical Records Survey, Tennessee. *Directory of Churches, Missions, and Religious Institutions of Tennessee,* no. 47. *Knox County.* Nashville: The Survey, WPA, 1941. 99 pp.

Humphreys, Flynn G. "The Status and Problems of the Ministry in Knox County." Thesis, Univ. of Tennessee, 1936.

HISTORIC STRUCTURES AND PLACES

Art Work of Knoxville, with sketch of Knoxville by Moses White. Chicago: W. H. Parish, 1895. About 16 leaves.

The Blount Mansion Association. *The Blount Mansion, Built 1792.* Knoxville: Knoxville Engr., 1930. 13 pp.

Bowman, Elizabeth Skaggs. "Swan Pond: Francis Alexander Ramsey's Stone House." ETHS*P* 27 (1955), 9-18.

Bowman, Elizabeth Skaggs, and Stanley J. Folmsbee. "The Ramsey House: Home of Francis Alexander Ramsey." *THQ* 24 (1965), 203-318; rpt. in *More Landmarks of Tennessee,* 231-46.

Cates, Alice Smith. "Blount Mansion—'The Cradle of Tennessee.'" *DAR Magazine* 69 (1935), 344-49.

Dempster, G. R. "History in Houses; Craighead-Jackson House." *Antiques,* July 1970, pp. 110-14.

Folmsbee, Stanley J., and Susan Hill Dillon. "The Blount Mansion, Tennessee's Territorial Capitol." *THQ* 22 (1963), 103-22; rpt. in *Landmarks of Tennessee,* 47-66.

McNabb, W. R. "The Knoxville City Hall." *THQ* 31 (1972), 256-60.

Porter, Matilda A. "Historic Homes and Gardens of Tennessee—'Swan Pond,' The Ramsey Home." *THM* (ser. 2) 3 (1932-37), 283-86.

Rose, Norvell Sevier. "John Sevier and Marble Springs." *THQ* 29 (1970), 205-26.

Ryan, Arthur Frank, and Mrs. Floyd Hancock, eds. *Historical Forts and Houses in Knoxville and Nearby Vicinity.* Knoxville: Knox Co. Libr., 1962. 24 pp.

JOURNALISM

Haley, Nancy Marlene. "Cry Aloud and Spare Not; the Formative Years of Brownlow's *Whig,* 1839-1841." Thesis, Univ. of Tennessee, 1966.

McClary, Ben H., ed. "The Sale of Brownlow's Knoxville Whig." ETHS*P* 35 (1963), 96-99.

McGill, J. T. "George Wilson." *THM* 4 (1918), 157-60. The Knoxville journalist who succeeded Roulstone.

Masterson, Clara Estelle. "A History of Knoxville Journalism." Thesis, George Peabody College, 1933.

Taylor, Jerome Gregg. "The Public Career of Joseph Alexander Mabry." Thesis, Univ. of Tennessee, 1968. Mabry was editor of the Knoxville *Whig.*

Vincent, Bert. *Bert Vincent's Strolling, Being Sort of a Side-Glance at the Little Odds and Ends of Life in These Parts.* Knoxville: W. L. Warters, 1940. 42 pp. Vincent was a feature writer for the Knoxville *News-Sentinel.*

——. *The Best Stories of Bert Vincent,* ed. Willard Yarbrough. Maryville: Brazos, 1968. 208 pp.

——. *More of the Best Stories of Bert Vincent.* Maryville: Brazos, 1970. 208 pp.

Welsh, John R. "George F. Mellen: A Versatile Tennessean." *THQ* 8 (1949), 220-47. Mellen, a professor at the Univ. of Tennessee, was associate editor of the Knoxville *News-Sentinel.*

THE NEGRO

Davis, J. H. *A Social Study of the Colored Population of Knoxville, Tennessee.* Knoxville: n.p., 1926.

Dunn, Larry W. "Knoxville Negro Voting and the Roosevelt Revolution, 1928-1936." ETHS*P* 43 (1971), 71-93.

Giovanni, Nikki. *Gemini.* An autobiography picturing life in Knoxville and Nashville.

Lamon, Lester C. "Tennessee Race Relations and the Knoxville Riot of 1919." ETHS*P* 41 (1969), 67-85.

Proudfoot, Merrill. *Diary of a Sit-in.* Chapel Hill: Univ. of North Carolina, 1962; rpt. New Haven, Conn.: College & Univ. Press, 1962. 204 pp.

Wilson, Barto G., comp. *Knoxville Negro.* Knoxville: n.p., 1929. 92 pp.

LAKE COUNTY
Historian: Emmett Lewis, 321 Walnut Street, Tiptonville 38257.

Burt, Jesse. "Reelfoot Lake—Child of Violence." *Natural History,* Feb. 1955, pp. 95-114.

Callis, Ruby. *Ridgley Panorama.* N.p.: n.p., 1967. 113 pp.

Carter, John Ray. "Life and Lore of Reelfoot Lake." Ed.S. diss., George Peabody College, 1958.

Donaldson, R. C. *By Gone Days.* N.p., n.d.

Eagle, R. E. Lee. *Reelfoot Lake, Fishing and Duck Shooting. History of Reelfoot Lake.* Nashville: McQuiddy, 1915.

Franco, Alfred. *Early Inhabitants of This Region.* N.p., n.d.

Humphreys, Cecil C. "The History of the Reelfoot Lake Region." Thesis, Univ. of Tennessee, 1938.

——. "The Formation of Reelfoot Lake and Consequent Land and Social Problems." WTHSP 14 (1960), 32-73.

"Lake County." *History of Tennessee,* ed. Weston A. Goodspeed et al., 852-57, 1073-87.

Lowe, Walter Edgar. "History of Reelfoot Lake." Thesis, George Peabody College, 1930.

McGill, J. T., and W. W. Craig. "The Ownership of Reelfoot Lake." *JTAS* 8 (1933), 13-21.

Nelson, Wilbur A. "Reelfoot—an Earthquake Lake." *National Geographic Magazine,* Jan. 1924, pp. 95-114.

Purcell, Martha Graham. *Birth of Reelfoot Lake and the Legend of Kalopin.* Paducah, Ky.: Paducah Printing, 1929. 19 pp.

Taylor, Hillsman. "The Night Riders of West Tennessee." WTHSP 6 (1952), 77-86.

Vanderwood, Paul J. "Night Riders of Reelfoot Lake." *THQ* 28 (1969), 126-40.

——. *Night Riders of Reelfoot Lake.* Memphis: Memphis State Univ. Press, 1969. 159 pp. Vanderwood views the Night Rider episode of the early 20th century as a classic example of the continuing struggle of the American pioneer to pursue his ways against a changing society.

Van Dresser, C. "Reelfoot, a Dying Lake." *Nature Magazine,* Feb. 1955, pp. 90-93.

Walker, Paul E. *Illustrated History of Reelfoot Lake.* Ridgely: The Author, 1929. 30 pp.

White, Lonnie J. "Federal Operations at New Madrid and Island Number Ten." WTHSP 17 (1963), 47-67.

LAUDERDALE COUNTY

Historian: Mrs. Jennie Forsburg, Asbury Road, Ripley 38063.

Gerslaecker, Fredrich. *The Wanderings and Fortunes of Some German Emigrants.* New York: n.p., 1848. Account of effort to establish a communitarian settlement near the mouth of Big Hatchie River.

"Lauderdale County." *History of Tennessee,* ed. Weston A. Goodspeed et al., 797-807, 842-85.

McKinney, Colin P. "History of Lauderdale County." N.p.: Unpublished typescript, n.d. 157 pp. Microfilm copy at Tennessee State Library and Archives.

Peters, Kate Johnston, ed. *Lauderdale County from Earliest Times; an Intimate and Informal Account of the Towns and Communities, Its Families and Famous Individuals, Written by Descendants of Its Pioneer Citizens.* Ripley: Lauderdale Co. Libr., 1957. 377 pp.

Williams, Joseph S. *Old Times in West Tennessee.*

LAWRENCE COUNTY

Historian: Mrs. Edward M. Lindsley, Box 431, Lawrenceburg 38464.

Alexander, William F., Jr., and John F. Morrison, Jr., comps. *Early Sales and Ownership of Lots in Lawrenceburg, Tennessee.* Lawrenceburg: Lawrence Co. Hist. Soc., 1970. 97 leaves.

Annals of Lawrence County, Tennessee. July 1970- . Quarterly publication of Lawrence County Historical Society.

Biographical Directory: Lawrence County Members of the Tennessee General Assembly, 1796- . 61 pp. This volume also contains Hardin County.

"Lawrence County." *History of Tennessee,* ed. Weston A. Goodspeed et al., 749-63, 807-49.

Moore, Lewis E., ed. *Glimpses of Lawrence County History; a Class Anthology for American History 2121L, Columbia State Community College.* Columbia: Columbia State Community College, 1970. 74 leaves.

Morrison, John, and Bob Hamsley. *The Real David Crockett.*

Morrison, John F., Jr. *Life of David Crockett in Lawrence County.* Nashville: *Democratic-Union,* 1967.

———. "A Brief History of Early Lawrence County, Tennessee." Lawrenceburg: Unpublished typescript, 1968. 50 leaves.

Reeves, Charles E. "Loretto in the Happy Long Ago, 1800 to 1954." Lawrenceburg: Unpublished typescript, 1954. 15 leaves.

Rowles, W. P. *Life and Character of Capt. Wm. B. Allen, of Lawrence County, Tenn., Who Fell at the Storming of Monterey, on the 21st of September, 1846. With an Appendix, Containing a Number of His Essays and Speeches.* Columbia: J. J. McDaniel, 1853. 228 pp. Published posthumously; completed by A. O. P. Nicholson.

Tennessee Valley Authority, Industry Division. *Agricultural-Industrial Survey of Lawrence County, Tennessee.* Knoxville: TVA, 1934. 141 pp.

Wilson, Charles M. "The Impact of Industrial Development on Lawrence County, Tennessee." Thesis, Univ. of Tennessee, 1965.

LEWIS COUNTY

Historian: No appointment made.

Biographical Directory: Lewis County Members of the Tennessee General Assembly, 1796- . 43 pp. This volume also contains Perry and Wayne counties.

"Lewis County." *History of Tennessee,* ed. Weston A. Goodspeed et al., 801-7, 923-24.

Nicholson, John. *The Tennessee Massacre and Its Causes; or, The Utah Conspiracy, a Lecture by John Nicholson, Delivered in the Salt Lake Theatre, on Monday, September 22, 1884. Steonographically Reported by John Irvine.* Salt Lake City: Juvenile Instructor Off., 1884. 48 pp.

Tennessee Valley Authority, Industry Division. *Agricultural-Industrial Survey of Lewis County.* Knoxville: TVA, 1934. 119 pp.

Wingfield, Marshall. "Tennessee's Mormon Massacre." *THQ* 17 (1958), 19-36.

LINCOLN COUNTY
Historian: Battle Bagley, Sr., Box 470, Fayetteville 37334.

Biographical Directory: Lincoln County Members of the Tennessee General Assembly, 1796- . 53 pp.

Foster, Austin P. "Camp Blount." *THM* (ser. 2) 1 (1930-31), 270-73. Relates to the War of 1812.

Killebrew, Joseph B. *Resources of Giles County: Resources of Lincoln County.*

"Lincoln County." *History of Tennessee,* ed. Weston A. Goodspeed et al., 767-84, 876-924.

Tennessee Valley Authority, Industry Division. *Agricultural-Industrial Survey of Lincoln County, Tennessee.* 2 vols. Knoxville: TVA, 1934.

LOUDON COUNTY
Historian: Edmund McQueen II, Route 4, Mason Place, Loudon 37774.

Biographical Directory: Loudon County Members of the Tennessee General Assembly, 1796- . 44 pp. This volume also contains Monroe County.

Daughters of the American Revolution, Tennessee. *Beloved Landmarks of Loudon County, Tennessee.* Loudon: Hiwassee Chap., DAR, 1962. 66 pp.

Hawn, Ashley T. "The Lenoir City Company, an Attempt in Community Development." Thesis, Univ. of Tennessee, 1940.

Historical Records Survey, Tennessee. *Inventory of the County Archives of Tennessee: Loudon County.* Nashville: The Survey, WPA, 1941.

"Loudon County." *History of Tennessee,* East Tennessee Edition, ed. Weston A. Goodspeed et al., 825-28, 1081-88.

Marfield, Samuel. "Lenoir City, Tennessee." *East Tennessee. Historical and Biographical,* 421-33.

Martel Methodist Church, 1795-1962. N.p., n.d.

Tennessee State Library and Archives. "Inventory of Loudon
County Records." Nashville: State Library and Archives, 1964- .
Unpublished typescript.

Tennessee Valley Authority, Industry Division. *Agricultural-
Industrial Survey of Loudon County, Tennessee.* Knoxville:
TVA, 1935. 244 pp.

McMinn County
Historian: James Burn, Edgewood Farms, Niota 37826.

*Athens "Press" Presents the Story of Niota, Tennessee; Its History,
Products and Services in Words and Pictures.* Niota: Athens
Press, 1961. 12 pp.

*Biographical Directory: McMinn County Members of the Tennessee
General Assembly, 1796- .* 37 pp.

*Early History of McMinn County from the Time It Was Organized
to the Year 1887.* Athens: *Herald,* n.d. 13 pp.

Johnson, George Q. "Weena and Connestoga: A Legend Which
Centers around Two Trees in the Heart of Athens." *THM* 8
(1924), 153-66.

Long, Grady M. "Folk Medicine in McMinn, Polk, Bradley, and
Meigs Counties, Tennessee, 1910-1927." *TFSB* 28 (1962), 1-8.

"McMinn County." *History of Tennessee,* East Tennessee Edition,
ed. Weston A. Goodspeed et al., 811-15, 1012-32.

Nankivel, J. R. *History and Times of Mars Hill Presbyterian Church,
1823-1923.* Athens: Session Bd., n.d. 26 pp.

Russell, Thomas R. "History of McMinn County, Tennessee." *East
Tennessee. Historical and Biographical,* 387-405.

Sharp, John McClure. *Recollections of Hearsays of Athens, Fifty
Years and Beyond.* Athens: The Author, 1933. 78 pp.

Tennessee State Library and Archives. "Inventory of McMinn County
Records." Nashville: State Library and Archives, 1964- . Unpublished typescript.

Tennessee Valley Authority, Industry Division. *Agricultural-
Industrial Survey of McMinn County, Tennessee.* Knoxville: TVA,
1934. 70 pp.

Political Difficulties in Athens: 1946-47

"Athens Now." *Newsweek,* Sept. 9, 1946, p. 38.

"G.I. Revolution." *Commonweal,* Aug. 16, 1946, p. 419.

Perry, J. "Rebellion in Tennessee." *Nation,* Aug. 10, 1946, p. 147.

"Veterans Rule by Fist." *Newsweek,* Jan. 27, 1947, p. 25.

White, T. H. "The Battle of Athens, Tennessee." *Harper's Magazine,* Jan. 1947, pp. 54-61.

McNAIRY COUNTY
Historian: C. L. Majors, Ramer 38367.

Adams, J. Louis. *Old Purdy, The History of the First County Seat of McNairy County, Tennessee.* Jackson: McCowat-Mercer, 1952. 31 pp. Rpt. in WTHSP 6 (1952), 5-33.

Alexander, Frank D. "Owners and Tenants of Small Farms in the Life of a Selected Community: A Cultural Analysis." Diss., Vanderbilt Univ., 1938. Relates to McNairy County.

Biographical Directory: McNairy County Members of the Tennessee General Assembly, 1796- . 43 pp. This volume also contains Chester County.

"McNairy County." *History of Tennessee,* ed. Weston A. Goodspeed et al., 819-28, 870-80.

Morris, W. R. *The Twelfth of August; the Story of Buford Pusser.* Nashville: Aurora, 1971. 240 pp. Pusser is a contemporary crime-busting sheriff.

Tennessee Valley Authority, Industry Division. *Agricultural-Industrial Survey of McNairy County, Tennessee.* Knoxville: TVA, 1934. 171 pp.

Wright, Marcus J. *Reminiscences of the Early Settlement and Early Settlers of McNairy County, Tennessee.* Washington, D.C.: Commercial, 1882; rpt. Ramer: C. L. Majors, 1968. 96 pp.

MACON COUNTY
Historian: Harold Blankenship, Lafayette 37083.

Bandy, Lewis David. "Folklore of Macon County, Tennessee." Thesis, George Peabody College, 1940.

Biographical Directory: Macon County Members of the Tennessee General Assembly, 1796- . 100 pp. This volume also contains Sumner and Trousdale counties.

"Macon County." *History of Tennessee,* ed. Weston A. Goodspeed et al., 834-41, 971-88.

MADISON COUNTY
Historian: Judge Andrew T. Taylor, Courthouse, Jackson 38301.

Cisco, Jay G. "Madison County." *AHM* 7 (1902-3), 328-48; 8 (1902-3), 26-48.

Drake, Robert Y., Jr. "Casey Jones: The Man and the Son." *TFSB* 19 (1953), 95-101.

Hawkins, Hermon. "The Story of George Frederick Burgoyne Howard: The Holy Cheat." WTHS*P* 16 (1962), 56-69. Howard was pastor of the First Baptist Church, Jackson, in 1883.

Irby, Henry Clay. *History of the First Baptist Church, Jackson, Tennessee, 1837-1912.* Jackson: McCowat-Mercer, c. 1912. 96 pp.

Jackson-Madison County Chamber of Commerce. *Jackson-Madison County Industrial Survey.* Jackson: n.p., 1958. 50 leaves.

Jackson *Sun. The Jackson "Sun" of Jackson "The Hub City of West Tennessee" in the Geographical Center of a Three Hundred Eighty Million Dollar Annual Market.* Jackson: McCowat-Mercer, 1960. 23 pp.

James, Lena Graham. *Historic St. Luke's Episcopal Church, Jackson: Glimpses Past and Present.* Jackson: The Author, 1962. 67 pp.

Kuhlman, Augustus F. *Social Survey of the City of Jackson and Madison County, Tennessee.* Jackson: Jackson-McClaran Chap., Am. Red Cross, 1920. 139 pp.

"Madison County." *History of Tennessee,* ed. Weston A. Goodspeed et al., 797-917.

Mercer, Mrs. Frank A. "A Survey of Family Living Conditions in Madison County, Tennessee." Thesis, Univ. of Tennessee, 1935.

Moody, James W., Jr. "Casey Jones Railroad Museum." *THQ* 25 (1966), 3-21; rpt. in *More Landmarks of Tennessee,* 187-205.

Phillips, Elizabeth C. "John Tomlin: The 'Literary Postmaster' of Jackson, Tennessee." WTHS*P* 8 (1954), 39-54. Tomlin was a correspondent of Edgar Allen Poe and other literary figures.

Price, A. Lacy. *The History of Jackson Lodge No. 45, Free and Accepted Masons of Tennessee; with the Story of Masonry Through the Ages.* Jackson: Jackson Lodge, 1965. 343 pp.

Rothrock, Mary U., ed. "Family Letters: Home Life in Madison and Carroll Counties, Tennessee, 1864-1867." WTHS*P* 23 (1969), 110-28; 24 (1970), 106-29.

Tennessee State Library and Archives. "Inventory of Madison County Records." Nashville: State Library and Archives, 1964-. Unpublished typescript.

Wiley, J. W. *St. Mary's Church, Jackson, Tennessee. The Story of Catholicity in Jackson, Tennessee, from Earliest Times.* Jackson: McCowat-Mercer, 1951. 71 pp.

Williams, Emma Inman. "Jackson and Madison County; an Inland Cotton Center of the Growing West, 1821-1850." *THQ* 3 (1944), 24-45.

——. *Historic Madison: The Story of Jackson and Madison County, Tennessee, from the Prehistoric Moundbuilders to 1917.* Jackson: Madison Co. Hist. Soc., 1946; rpt. Jackson: Jackson Service Leagues, 1972. 553 pp. A contribution to the sesquicentennial celebration of Tennessee statehood, 1946.

MARION COUNTY
Historian: J. Leonard Raulston, South Pittsburg 37380.

Biographical Directory: Marion County Members of the Tennessee General Assembly, 1796- . 51 pp. This volume also contains Bledsoe and Sequatchie counties.

Cameron, Walter M. *Memoirs of Marion County, Tennessee, 1893-1946.* Jasper: Jasper *Journal,* 1946. 48 pp.

Garner, Isaac Leonard. "A Study of Certain Phases of the Educational and Economic Conditions of Marion County, Tennessee." Thesis, Univ. of Tennessee, 1930.

Hiatt, Ellen O. M. *Sequatchie Valley, a Historical Sketch,* photographs Marguerite Hiatt.

Link, Gertrude Bible. "A History of Marion County." Thesis, Middle Tennessee State Univ., 1953.

South Pittsburg on the Tennessee River, Marion County, Tennessee. N.p.: Privately printed, 1887. 29 pp.

Tennessee State Library and Archives. "Inventory of Marion County Records." Nashville: State Library and Archives, 1964- . Unpublished typescript.

Tennessee Valley Authority, Industry Division. *Agricultural-Industrial Survey of Marion County, Tennessee.* 2 vols. Knoxville: TVA, 1934.

MARSHALL COUNTY

Historian: Ralph D. Whitesell, 612 Woodlawn Avenue, Lewisburg 37091.

Biographical Directory: Marshall County Members of the Tennessee General Assembly, 1796- . 38 pp.

Fisher, John E. "Life on the Common Level: Inheritance, Conflict, and Instruction." *THQ* 26 (1967), 304-22.

Gamble, Barnett J. "The History of Secondary Education in Petersburg, Tennessee." Thesis, George Peabody College, 1956.

"Marshall County." *History of Tennessee,* ed. Weston A. Goodspeed et al., 884-903, 1190-1232.

Rogers, Eliza Guy. "Stories and Legends of Marshall County, North of Duck River." Thesis, George Peabody College, 1936.

Tennessee Valley Authority, Industry Division. *Agricultural-Industrial Survey of Marshall County, Tennessee.* 2 vols. Knoxville: TVA, 1934.

Veterans of Foreign Wars of the United States, Tennessee, Bill Lowe Wheatley Post no. 5109, Lewisburg. *Service Record, World War I and II, Marshall County, Tennessee.* Marceline, Mo.: Walsworth, c. 1948. 161 pp.

Wright, Mitchel. *A History of Marshall County, Tennessee.* Franklin: The Author, 1963. 144 leaves. Reproduced from typewritten copy.

MAURY COUNTY

Historian: Mrs. T. T. Garrett, Jr., 610 Terrace Place, Columbia 38401.

Alexander, Charles C., and Virginia W. Alexander. "Historic Ebenezer (Reese's Chapel), Presbyterian Church and Cemetery, Maury County, Columbia, Tennessee." Columbia: Unpublished typescript, 1968. 94 pp.

Baxter, Nathaniel. "Reminiscences." *AHM* 8 (1903), 262-70. Baxter was a young attorney in Columbia in the 1830s.

Bergeron, Paul H. "My Brother's Keeper: William H. Polk Goes to School." *NCHR* 44 (1967), 188-294.

Biographical Directory: Maury County Members of the Tennessee General Assembly, 1796- . 100 pp. This volume also contains Hickman County.

Campbell, Andrew Jackson. *Civil War Diary,* ed. Jill K. Garrett.

Century Review, 1805-1905, Maury County, Tennessee. A Condensation of the Most Important Events of the Past One Hundred Years, and Descriptive Sketches of the Cities and Villages. Columbia and Mt. Pleasant in Detail. Directory of the Cities and Mail Lists for Thirty-seven Rural Routes of Maury County. Columbia: Bd. of Mayor and Aldermen, 1905; rev. ed., Columbia: Maury Co. Hist. Soc., 1970. 336 pp.

Circular of the Tennessee and Alabama Railroad Co. to the Inhabitants of Maury County. Nashville: J. F. Morgan, 1855. 11 pp.

Compilation of the General Laws of the City of Columbia: Together with the Charters of the City, Granted by the State of Tennessee. Columbia: Columbia *Herald* Book and Job Print. Co., 1866. 81 pp. Nashville: Marshall & Bruce, 1885. 170 pp.

Enfield, Gertrude Dixon, ed. "Early Settlement in Maury County: The Letters of Christopher Houston." *THQ* 18 (1959), 54-68.

Enterprise Publishing Company. *Columbia, Maury County, Tennessee. Her Progress and Importance. Manufacturing Advantages, Business and Transportation Facilities, with Sketches of Representative Merchants, Manufacturers and Professional Men. September 1885.* Nashville: A. B. Tavel, 1885. 58 pp.

Estes, P. M., A. P. Foster, and John Trotwood Moore, comps. *Historic Places in Davidson, Williamson, Maury and Giles Counties.*

Evins, S. C. *Memoir of the Late Elder Elijah Hanks of Maury County, Tennessee; Together with a Synopsis of His Views on the Atonement of Christ, and Other Subjects.* Nashville: *Union & American*, 1872. 55 pp.

Fleming, William S. *A Historical Sketch of Maury County, Read at the Centennial Celebration in Columbia, Tennessee, July 4, 1876.* Columbia: Excelsior, 1876; rpt. Columbia: Maury Co. Hist. Soc., 1967. 65 pp.

Fox, Wilburn M. *History and Pictures of the Fifty Churches of Christ in Maury County, Tennessee.* Columbia: The Author, 1962.

Fowler, William Ewing. "Stories and Legends of Maury County, Tennessee." Thesis, George Peabody College, 1937.

Galloway, Donnel M. "An Economic, Social and Educational Survey of Maury County, Tennessee." Thesis, Univ. of Tennessee, 1930.

Garrett, Jill K. "Maury County, Tennessee Newspapers." 2 vols. Columbia: Unpublished typescript, 1965. Vol. 1 covers the period from 1810 to 1844; vol. 2, from 1846 to 1850.

——. "Maury County, Tennessee Historical Sketches." Columbia: Unpublished typescript, 1967. 282 pp.

——. "St. John's Church, Ashwood." *THQ* 29 (1970), 3-23.

Garrett, Jill K., and Virginia Alexander. *A Guide to Points of Interest in Maury County, Tennessee.* Columbia: Assoc. for the Preservation of Tennessee Antiquities, Maury Co. Chap., 1969. 32 pp.

Garrett, Jill K., Virginia W. Alexander, and Evelyn B. McAnally, eds. *Confederate Soldiers and Patriots of Maury County, Tennessee.* Columbia: UDC, Capt. James Madison Sparkman Chap., 1970. 381 pp.

Garrett, Jill K., and Marise P. Lightfoot. "The Civil War in Maury County, Tennessee." Columbia: Unpublished typescript, 1966. 265 pp.

——, comps. "Maury County, Tennessee, Wills and Settlements, 1807-1824 and 1820 Census." Columbia: Unpublished typescript, 1964. 220 pp.

Gracy, Mary Irene. "Economic Structure of Maury County from 1840-1860." Thesis, George Peabody College, 1938.

Greenlaw, R. Douglass. "Outline History of Maury County." *THM* (ser. 2) 3 (1935), 145-51.

Highsaw, Mary Wagner. "A History of Zion Community in Maury County, 1806-1860." *THQ* 5 (1946), 3-34, 111-40, 222-33.

Historic Maury. 1965- . Ed. Jill K. Garrett, 1965-67; Virginia Wood Alexander, Evelyn B. Shacklford, 1968- . Annual publication of the Maury County Hist. Soc.

Jackson, Blanche Scott. *Reese's Church and Its Founders.* Columbia, 1940.

Jones, Nathaniel Willis. *A History of Mount Pleasant, Especially, and the Western Part of Maury County Generally, As He Remembers It.* Nashville: McQuiddy, 1903; rpt. Columbia: Maury Co. Hist. Soc., 1965. 78 pp.

King, Alice Siviter. "Intra-County Shift in Negro Population in Maury County, Tennessee, 1860-1870." Thesis, George Peabody College, 1968.

Kunstling, Frances Williams. "The Cooper Family Papers—a Bibliographic Note." *THQ* 28 (1969), 197-205.

Leach, Douglas Edward. "John Gordon of Gordon's Ferry." *THQ* 18 (1959), 322-44. Gordon was an early citizen of Maury County.

Lightfoot, Marise P., ed. *Historic Maury County in Pictures.* Columbia: Maury Co. Hist. Soc., 1966. Unpaged pamphlet.

Little, D. D. *History of the Presbytery of Columbia, Tennessee.* Columbia: Maury *Democrat,* 1928.

"Maury County." *History of Tennessee,* ed. Weston A. Goodspeed et al., 749-87, 904-65.

Maury County, the Blue-Grass Region of Tennessee. Its Agricultural and Mineralogical Resources, Including a View of the County Seat, the City of Columbia. Her Commerce and Industries, Schools and Churches, Past Development and Future Possibilities. Facts for Practical Minds. Columbia: *Herald,* 1884. 24 pp.

Polk, George W. "St. John's Church, Maury County, Tennessee." *THM* 7 (1921), 147-53.

Quillen, Eva Pearl. "A Study of the Life of Franklin Gillette Smith." Thesis, Tennessee Technological Univ., 1960. Smith was the rector and principal of the Columbia Female Institute from 1837 to 1852.

Rivers, Flournoy. "The Beginnings of Maury County." *AHM* 3 (1898), 139-50.

"Riverside Methodist Church, History." Columbia: Unpublished typescript, 1965. 16 pp.

Ryan, Thornton A. *St. Peter's Episcopal Church, Columbia, Tennessee, the First 125 Years of the Parish, 1829-1954.* Columbia: n.p. 1954.

Smith, Frank H. *Frank H. Smith's History of Maury County, Tennessee.* Columbia: Maury Co. Hist. Soc., 1969. 391 pp.

Tennessee State Library and Archives. "Inventory of Maury County Records." Nashville: State Library and Archives, 1964- . Unpublished typescript.

Tennessee Valley Authority, Industry Division. *Agricultural-Industrial Survey of Maury County, Tennessee.* 2 vols. Knoxville: 1934.

Turner, William Bruce. *History of Maury County, Tennessee.* Nashville: Parthenon Press, 1955. 404 pp.

Wagner, Mary Church. "Settlement of Zion Community in Maury County." Thesis, Vanderbilt Univ., 1945.

Waller, Charlot Clay. "Maury County, Tennessee, and the Civil War." Thesis, Vanderbilt Univ., 1951.

Weaver, Herbert, and William G. Eidson. "The James K. Polk Home."

THQ 24 (1965), 3-19; rpt. in *Landmarks of Tennessee,* 281-97.

Williams, Samuel C. "Major-General Richard Winn: South Carolinian and Tennessean." *THQ* 1 (1942), 8-20. Winn, a Revolutionary War veteran, settled in Maury County in 1812.

Yeatman, Trezevant P., Jr. "St. John's—a Plantation Church of the Old South." *THQ* 10 (1951), 334-43.

MEIGS COUNTY
Historian: Mrs. James F. Gallaher, Decatur 37322.

Allen, Valentine C. *Rhea and Meigs Counties in the Confederate War.* N.p.: The Author, 1908. 126 pp.

Biographical Directory: Meigs County Members of the Tennessee General Assembly, 1796- . 37 pp. This volume also contains Rhea County.

Long, Grady M. "Folk Medicine in McMinn, Polk, Bradley and Meigs Counties, Tennessee, 1910-1927." *TFSB* 28 (1962), 1-8.

"Meigs County." *History of Tennessee,* East Tennessee Edition, ed. Weston A. Goodspeed et al., 815-17, 1032-46.

Tennessee State Library and Archives. "Inventory of Meigs County Records." Nashville: State Library and Archives, 1964- . Unpublished typescript.

Tennessee Valley Authority, Industry Division. *Agricultural-Industrial Survey of Meigs County, Tennessee.* Knoxville: TVA, 1934. 131 pp.

MONROE COUNTY
Historian: No appointment made.

Biographical Directory: Monroe County Members of the Tennessee General Assembly, 1796- . 44 pp. This volume also contains Loudon County.

Boyer, Reba B. *Monroe County Records, 1820-1870.* 2 vols. Athens: The Author, 1969, 1970.

Fort Loudoun. *See* Early Period: Early Settlement; Fort Loudoun.

Lenoir, William B. "Monroe County and the Town of Sweetwater." *East Tennessee. Historical and Biographical,* pp. 407-17.

——. *History of Sweetwater Valley.* Sweetwater: The Author, 1916. 414 pp.

"Monroe County." *History of Tennessee,* East Tennessee Edition, ed. Weston A. Goodspeed et al., 807-11, 994-1012.

Patten, Z. Cartter. "A History of the Mansion on the Tellico River." *THQ* 10 (1951), 366-69.

Ray, Worth S. "Early Days in Monroe County, Tennessee." Austin, Tex.: Unpublished typescript, 1943. 26 pp.

Stanley, Isaac Newton. "An Educational and Economic Survey of Monroe County, Tennessee." Thesis, Univ. of Tennessee, 1926.

Tennessee Valley Authority, Division of Forestry. *Forest Conditions in Monroe County, Tennessee.* Knoxville: TVA, 1935.

Tennessee Valley Authority, Industry Division. *Agricultural-Industrial Survey of Monroe County, Tennessee.* Knoxville: TVA, 1934. 198 pp.

Van Benthuysen, Robert N., Jr. "The Sequent Occupance of Tellico Plains, Tennessee." Thesis, Univ. of Tennessee, 1951.

Young, D. C., ed. *History of the First Presbyterian Church, Sweetwater, Tennessee, 1860-1960.* Knoxville: n.p., n.d.

MONTGOMERY COUNTY
Historian: Mrs. Oscar Beach, 512 Madison Street, Clarksville 37040.

Beach, Ursula Smith. *Along the Warioto; or, A History of Montgomery County, Tennessee.* Nashville: Kiwanis Club of Clarksville and Tennessee Hist. Comm., 1964, 1965. 390 pp. One of the better county histories that we have, particularly strong through the Civil War and Reconstruction Era.

———. *A Commemorative History of the First Christian Church, Clarksville, Tennessee, 1842-1972.* Clarksville: Christoph, 1972. 65 pp.

Beach, Ursula S., and Anne E. Alley. *1798 Property Tax List and 1820 Census of Montgomery County, Tennessee.* Clarksville: The Authors, 1969. 83 pp.

Biographical Directory: Montgomery County Members of the Tennessee General Assembly, 1796- . 62 pp.

Daniel, Mrs. William M., Mrs. J. Moore Dickson, and Mrs. E. H. Harrison, comps. *History of Madison Street Methodist Church.* Clarksville: n.p., c. 1960. 79 pp.

Goodpasture, Albert V. "William Little Brown." *AHM* 7 (1902), 97-111. Brown was a Tennessee Supreme Court judge of the early 19th century.

——. "Beginnings of Montgomery County." *AHM* 8 (1903), 193-215.

——. "Colonel John Montgomery." *THM* 5 (1919), 145-50.

Henry, Gustavus A. *Reminiscences of the Clarksville Bar.* Nashville: n.p., 1877.

Hyatt, Lewis Paul. "The Clarksville *Leaf-Chronicle,* 1808-1956—a History." Diss., George Peabody College, 1957.

Killebrew, Joseph B. *Montgomery County: Its Agricultural and Mineral Wealth; Its Topography and Geology; Its Healthfulness and Desirableness. Also a Description of Clarksville, Together with an Address Delivered before the Montgomery County Farmers' Club.* Clarksville: Ingram & Doak, 1870. 61 pp.

Life and Times of Elder Reuben Ross by his son with Introduction and Notes by J. M. Pendleton. Philadelphia, Pa.: Grant, Faires & Rogers, 1882. 427 pp.

McCord, Franklyn. "J. E. Bailey: A Gentleman of Clarksville." *THQ* 23 (1964), 246-68.

"Montgomery County." *History of Tennessee,* ed. Weston A. Goodspeed et al., 749-827, 999-1124.

Morris, Wentworth S. "The Davie Home and the Register of the Federal Military Prison at Clarksville." *THQ* 8 (1949), 248-51.

Morrow, G. Juneau. *Historical Notes, Clarksville, Tennessee, 1784-1865.* Clarksville: Clarksville *Leaf-Chronicle,* 1934. 30 pp.

Smith, Samuel Boyd. "Joseph Buckner Killebrew and the New South Movement in Tennessee." Diss., Vanderbilt Univ., 1962.

Smith, Ursula Lee. "A Literary History of Montgomery County, Tennessee." Thesis, Austin Peay State College, 1954.

Tennessee State Library and Archives. "Inventory of Montgomery County Records." Nashville: State Library and Archives, 1964- . Unpublished typescript.

Titus, William P. *Picturesque Clarksville, Past and Present. A History of the City of the Hills. Its Institutions, Tobacco Interests, Mercantile Pursuits and Manufactories, together with Biographical Sketches of Its Early and Present Citizens.* Clarksville: The Author, 1887. 522 pp.

U.S. Congress. *Report on Survey of Red River, Tennessee.* House Exec. Doc. no. 57, 46th Congress, 3rd Sess. Vol. XVIII, Jan. 25, 1881. Washington, D.C.: n.p., 1881. 18 pp.

Whittle, Arthur E. *The First Hundred Years. A History of Trinity Church, Clarksville, Tennessee.* Nashville: Baird-Ward, 1932. 99 pp.

——. *Through the Mist of the Years, Presented at the Sesqui-centennial of Clarksville, Tennessee, June 10-13, 1934.* Clarksville: The Author, 1934. 60 pp. A historical drama.

Williams' Clarksville Directory, City Guide and Business Mirror, 1859-1860, vol. 1. Clarksville: n.p., 1859. 72 pp.

Williams, Nannie H. *History of the Clarksville Female Academy.* Clarksville: W. P. Titus, 1899. 32 pp.

Williams, Samuel C. "The Clarksville Compact of 1785." *THQ* 3 (1944), 237-47.

Winters, Ralph L. *Historical Sketches of Adams, Robertson County, Tennessee, and Port Royal, Montgomery County, Tennessee, from 1779-1968.* Clarksville: The Author, 1968. 280 pp. A fine local history by a competent layman. Although primarily family history, it includes a generous treatment of economic and social history as well.

MOORE COUNTY
Historian: Mrs. Elizabeth Cobble, Lynchburg 37352.

Bigger, Jeanne Ridgway. "Jack Daniel Distillery and Lynchburg: A Visit to Moore County, Tennessee." *THQ* 31 (1972), 3-21.

Biographical Directory: Moore County Members of the Tennessee General Assembly, 1796- . 44 pp. This volume also contains Franklin County.

"Moore County." *History of Tennessee,* ed. Weston A. Goodspeed et al., 804-19, 924-34.

Tennessee State Library and Archives. "Inventory of Moore County Records." Nashville: State Library and Archives, 1964- . Unpublished typescript.

MORGAN COUNTY
Historian: Mrs. Glena K. Ott, Wartburg 37887.

Bradley, Frank H. "Geological Report of F. H. Bradley." *Wilcox Mining Company of Tennessee, Annual Report,* 11-39. New York: E. Wells Sackett, 1871. 39 pp. Relates to Morgan and neighboring counties.

Cooper, Hobart S. "German and Swiss Colonization in Morgan County, Tennessee." Thesis, Univ. of Tennessee, 1925.

Freytag, Ethel, and Glena Kreis Ott. *A History of Morgan County, Tennessee.* Wartburg: Specialty, 1971. 379 pp.

Jones, Reece A. "A Geographical Survey of Morgan County, Tennessee." Thesis, Univ. of Tennessee, 1940.

"Morgan County." *History of Tennessee,* East Tennessee Edition, ed. Weston A. Goodspeed et al., 841-43, 1123-25.

Rugby Colony. *See* Social and Cultural History: Nineteenth-Century Communitarian Settlements.

Stagg, Brian L. *Deer Lodge, Tennessee, Its Little-Known History.* Oak Ridge: The Author, 1964. 28 pp.

Tennessee Valley Authority, Industry Division. *Agricultural-Industrial Survey of Morgan County, Tennessee.* Knoxville: TVA, 1935. 59 pp.

Wilson, Ross Harlen. "A Study of Secondary Schools of Morgan County." Thesis, Univ. of Tennessee, 1941.

Wright, Absalom B. "Morgan County." *Autobiography of Rev. A. B. Wright of the Holston Conference, Methodist Episcopal Church South,* 78-93, 158-73, 208-27.

Wust, Klaus. *Wartburg: Dream and Reality of the New Germany in Tennessee,* 31st Report, Society for the History of the Germans in Maryland. Baltimore: J. H. Furst, 1963. 25 pp.

OBION COUNTY
Historian: Rebel C. Forrester, Route 1, Union City 38261.

Allen, Alberta K. *Once upon a Time in Rives. A History of Rives, Obion County, Tennessee.* Union City: H. A. Lanzer, 1969. 124 pp.

Carter, John Ray. "Life and Lore of Reelfoot Lake." Ed.S. diss., George Peabody College, 1958.

Cavanaugh, John. *Historical Sketch of Obion Avalanche, Company H, Ninth Tennessee Infantry, Confederate States of America.* Union City: Commercial, 1922. 52 pp.

Centennial Committee. *"A Century on Parade." Centennial Diadem of Dixie: Union City, 1854-1954, Celebration June 20 to 30, 1954.* Union City: n.p., 1954. 92 pp.

Eagle, R. E. Lee. *Reelfoot Lake, Fishing and Duck Shooting.*

Forrester, Rebel C. *Glory and Tears: Obion County, Tennessee,*

1860-1870. Union City: H. A. Lanzer, 1966, 1970. 222 pp.

Humphreys, Cecil C. "History of the Reelfoot Lake Region." Thesis, Univ. of Tennessee, 1938.

———. "The Formation of Reelfoot Lake and Consequent Land and Social Problems." WTHSP 14 (1960), 32-73.

Lowe, Walter Edgar. "History of Reelfoot Lake." Thesis, George Peabody College, 1930.

McGill, J. T., and W. W. Craig. "The Ownership of Reelfoot Lake." *JTAS* 8 (1933), 13-21.

Marshall, Edwin H., ed. *History of Obion County; Towns and Communities, Churches, Schools, Farming, Factories, Social and Political.* Union City: *Daily Messenger,* 1941; rpt. Union City: Lanzer, 1970. 272 pp.

Nelson, Wilbur A. "Reelfoot—an Earthquake Lake." *National Geographic Magazine,* Jan. 1924, pp. 95-114.

"Obion County." *History of Tennessee,* ed. Weston A. Goodspeed et al., 816-31, 932-84.

Purcell, Martha Graham. *Birth of Reelfoot Lake and the Legend of Kalopin.*

Taylor, Hillsman. "The Night Riders of West Tennessee." WTHSP 6 (1952), 77-86.

Tennessee Valley Authority, Industry Division. *Agricultural-Industrial Survey of Obion County, Tennessee.* Knoxville: TVA, 1934. 208 pp.

Vanderwood, Paul J. "Night Riders of Reelfoot Lake." *THQ* 28 (1969), 126-40.

———. *The Night Riders of Reelfoot Lake.*

Van Dresser, C. "Reelfoot, a Dying Lake." *Nature Magazine,* Feb. 1955, pp. 90-93.

Walker, Paul E. *Illustrated History of Reelfoot Lake.*

Overton County
Historian: Robert L. Eldridge, Livingston 38570.

Allred, Charles E., and Samuel W. Atkins. *An Economic Analysis of Farming in Overton County, Tennessee.* Knoxville: Dept. of Agricultural Education, Univ. of Tennessee, 1927. 127 pp.

Atkins, Samuel W. "An Economic Analysis of Farming in Overton County, Tennessee." Thesis, Univ. of Tennessee, 1927.

Biographical Directory: Overton County Members of the Tennessee General Assembly, 1796- . 49 pp. This volume also contains Fentress and Pickett counties.

Crabtree, Lillian Gladys. "Songs and Ballads Sung in Overton County, Tennessee—a Collection." Thesis, George Peabody College, 1936.

Eldridge, Robert L., and Mrs. Robert L. Eldridge. *A History of the First Methodist Church in Livingston, Tennessee, Established 1836.* Livingston: *Enterprise,* 1962. 56 pp.

Goodpasture, Albert V. *Overton County Address of Albert V. Goodpasture Delivered at Livingston, Tennessee, July 4, 1876.* Nashville: Cumberland Presbyterian Pub. House, 1877; rpt. Nashville: B. C. Goodpasture, 1954. 27 pp.

Goodpasture, Albert V., and William H. Goodpasture. *Life of Jefferson Dillard Goodpasture; to Which Is Appended a Genealogy of the Family of James Goodpasture.* Nashville: Cumberland Presbyterian Pub. House, 1897. 308 pp.

Hatfield, Gilbert Harris. "A Study of Rural Cooperative Organizations in Overton County, Tennessee." Thesis, Univ. of Tennessee, 1929.

Livingston Academy, Class of 1951. *Echoes from the Foothills.* Livingston: n.p., 1951.

Mitchell, R. L., Jr. "Fifty Years Ago, a History of Overton County, Tennessee, around the Year 1850." A scrapbook of articles printed in the Livingston *Enterprise,* 1931-32.

Whitaker, Sarah G. "A History of Livingston Academy from 1909 through 1947." Thesis, Tennessee Technological Univ., 1964.

Whitley, Edythe J. R. *Tennessee Genealogical Records: Overton County.* Nashville: The Author, 1966. 97 pp.

Wirt, Alvin B. *The Upper Cumberland of Pioneer Times.* Washington, D.C.: The Author, 1954. 82 leaves.

PERRY COUNTY

Historian: Gus A. Steele, Box 105, Linden 37096.

Biographical Directory: Perry County Members of the Tennessee General Assembly, 1796- . 43 pp. This volume also contains Wayne and Lewis counties.

Harder, Kelsie B. "Weather Expressions and Beliefs in Perry County, Tennessee." *TFSB* 23 (1957), 832-86.

———. "Hay-Making Terms in Perry County." *TFSB* 33 (1967), 41-48.

"Perry County." *History of Tennessee,* ed. Weston A. Goodspeed et al., 777-88, 889-909.

Tennessee Valley Authority, Industry Division. *Agricultural-Industrial Division of Perry County, Tennessee.* Knoxville: TVA, 1935.

PICKETT COUNTY
Historian: Tim Huddleston, Box 66, Ooltewah 37363.

Biographical Directory: Pickett County Members of the Tennessee General Assembly, 1796- . 49 pp. This volume also contains Fentress and Overton counties.

Evins, Joe L. "The Cordell Hull Birthplace and Memorial." *THQ* 31 (1972), 111-28.

Holt, C. L. *Seventy Years in the Cumberlands.* N.p., 1970.

Huddleston, Tim. *Pioneer Families of Pickett County, Tennessee.* Collegedale: College Press, 1968. 180 pp.

Sanders, Charles H. "An Educational and Economic Survey of Pickett County, Tennessee." Thesis, Univ. of Tennessee, 1924.

Smith, Charles G. "A Social and Economic Survey of Pickett County." Thesis, Vanderbilt Univ., 1928.

Wright, Absalom B. *Autobiography of Reverend A. B. Wright of the Holston Conference.*

POLK COUNTY
Historian: Roy G. Lillard, Benton 37307.

Barclay, R. E. *Ducktown Back in Raht's Time.* Barclay presents developments in the southeast Tennessee Copper Basin from the 1830s to the 1890s, centering his work around the life of Julius Eckhardt Raht, whom he considers the area's most significant personality during these decades.

Biographical Directory: Polk County Members of the Tennessee General Assembly, 1796- . Nashville: State Library and Archives, 1968- . 37 pp. This volume also contains Bradley County.

Blair, Reuben Moore. "The Development of Education in Polk County, Tennessee." Thesis, Univ. of Tennessee, 1941.

Clemmer, James D. "J. D. Clemmer's Scrapbooks, 1884-1934." Unpublished typescript. Microfilm copy (5 reels) at Tennessee State Library and Archives. A history of Polk County in possession of the Clemmer family.

Coulter, E. Merton. "The Georgia-Tennessee Boundary Line." *Georgia Historical Quarterly* 35 (1951), 269-306.

Goff, John H. "Retracing the Old Federal Road." *Emory University Quarterly* 6 (1950), 159-71.

Lillard, Roy G. "A Brief History of the First Baptist Church (Ocoee Baptist Church), Benton, Tennessee, 1836-1959." Benton: Unpublished typescript, 1964. About 50 pp. In possession of author.

——. "Some Aspects of Polk County Politics." Benton: Unpublished typescript, 1962. About 50 pp. In possession of author.

——. "The Ocoee Lodge no. 212, F. & A.M., Benton, Tennessee." Benton: Unpublished typescript, 1963. About 10 pp. In possession of author.

Long, Grady M. "Folk Medicine in McMinn, Polk, Bradley, and Meigs Counties, Tennessee, 1910-1927." *TFSB* 28 (1962), 1-8.

Patton, Sadie S. *Sketches in Polk County History.* Hendersonville, N.C.: n.p., 1950. 161 pp.

"Polk County." *History of Tennessee,* East Tennessee Edition, ed. Weston A. Goodspeed et al., 804-7, 987-94.

Polk County Historical Society. *Studies in Polk County History,* no. 1, 1965. Benton: Polk Co. Hist. Soc., 1965. 24 pp.

Teale, E. W. "Murder of a Landscape; Ducktown Desert." *Natural History,* Oct. 1951, pp. 352-56.

Tennessee State Library and Archives. "Inventory of Polk County Records." Nashville: State Library and Archives, 1964- . Unpublished typescript.

Tennessee Valley Authority, Industry Division. *Agricultural-Industrial Survey of Polk County, Tennessee.* Knoxville: TVA, 1935. 152 pp.

Williams, A. J. *A Confederate History of Polk County, Tennessee, 1860-1866.* Nashville: McQuiddy, 1923. 31 pp.

Williamson, W. H. "A History of Polk County." Unpublished typescript, n.d.

Wooten, John M., comp. *Scrapbook History of Polk County, Tennessee.* N.p.: n.p., 1927-39. Microfilm copy at Tennessee State Library and Archives.

Polk County Politics, Post-World War II

"Dog-Day Elections." *Newsweek,* Aug. 20, 1951, pp. 23 ff.

Lemond, Thomas Addison. "The Good Government League and Polk County Politics, 1946-1965." Thesis, Vanderbilt Univ., 1970.

"Pistol-Packing Polkers." *Newsweek,* Apr. 2, 1951, p. 25.

"Polk County Draws Its Guns." *Life,* Apr. 9, 1951, pp. 47-48.

"Shotgun Politics in Polk." *Newsweek,* Mar. 24, 1958, p. 38.

PUTNAM COUNTY

Historian: James P. Buck, Tennessee Technological University Library, Cookeville 38501.

Grime, John Harvey. *Recollections of a Long Life.* Lebanon: n.p., 1930. 26 pp.

Hatfield, James Monroe. "A History and Educational Survey of Putnam County, Tennessee." Thesis, Univ. of Tennessee, 1937.

McClain, Walter S. *A History of Putnam County, Tennessee,* chap. 8 by Quimby Dyer. Cookeville: Q. Dyer, 1925. 152 pp. A short history emphasizing geography, demography, institutions, and personalities.

Webb, Thomas G. "The Pottery Industry of DeKalb, White, and Putnam Counties." *THQ* 30 (1971), 110-12.

Whitney, Gertrude. *Cookeville in Retrospect.* Dallas: n.p., 1943. 47 pp.

RHEA COUNTY

Historian: Dr. Theodore C. Mercer, Bryan College, Dayton 37321.

Allen, Valentine Collins. *Rhea and Meigs Counties in the Confederate War.*

Biographical Directory: Rhea County Members of the Tennessee General Assembly, 1796- . 37 pp. This volume also contains Meigs County.

Campbell, Thomas Jefferson. *Records of Rhea; a Condensed County History.* Dayton: Rhea Pub., 1940. 204 pp.

Cash, James I. *Autobiography and Sermons.* Spring City: n.p., 1934. 252 pp.

Grandview Student Body Association. *Old Grandview: Grandview Normal Institute, Grandview, Tennessee, 1884-1919: A History.* Grandview: The Assoc., 1966. 168 pp.

Johnson, G. W. "The Growing Town of Dayton, Tennessee."*East Tennessee. Historical and Biographical,* 435-39.

"Rhea County." *History of Tennessee,* East Tennessee Edition, ed. Weston A. Goodspeed et al., 817-21, 1046-71.

Spring City High School Alumni Association. *Spring City High School, 1912-1962, Golden Anniversary Celebration, May 12, 1962.* Collegedale: College Press, 1962. 32 pp.

Tennessee State Library and Archives. "Inventory of Rhea County Records." Nashville: State Library and Archives, 1964- . Unpublished typescript.

Tennessee Valley Authority, Industry Division. *Agricultural-Industrial Survey of Rhea County.* Knoxville: TVA, 1934. 159 pp.

ROANE COUNTY
Historian: Mrs. L. G. McCluen, Box 209, Rockwood 37854.

Banker, Katherine Thomas. *A Church Called Bethel.* Kingston: n.p., 1968. 58 pp. A Presbyterian church.

Banker, Luke H. "Fort Southwest Point, Tennessee: The Development of a Frontier Post, 1792-1807." Thesis, Univ. of Tennessee, 1972.

Biographical Directory: Roane County Members of the Tennessee General Assembly, 1796- . 43 pp.

Bradley, Frank Howe. "Geological Report of F. H. Bradley." *Wilcox Mining Company of Tennessee, Annual Report,* 11-39. Relates to Roane and neighboring counties.

Burkett, Elsie May Staples, ed. *Historical Review, Rockwood's Centennial Year, 1868-1968.* Rockwood: Rockwood *Times,* 1968. Unpaged.

Donovan, William F., Jr. "Real Estate Speculation in Cardiff and Harriman, 1890-1893." *THQ* 14 (1955), 253-56.

Fowler, William Joseph. "History of Roane County, Tennessee, 1860-1870." Thesis, Univ. of Tennessee, 1964.

Hayward, James. "History of Harriman, Tennessee." *East Tennessee. Historical and Biographical,* 491-541.

Kingston Iron Company. *Prospectus Showing the Advantages of*

Kingston for the Development of Iron. New York: J. J. Canlon, 1874.

McCluen, Marilyn N. *Roane County, Tennessee: Abstracts of Estate Book "A" 1801-1824.* Rockwood: n.p., 1965. 96 pp.

Moore, William H. "Rockwood: A Prototype of the New South." Thesis, Univ. of Tennessee, 1965.

——. "Preoccupied Paternalism: The Roane Iron Company in Her Company Town—Rockwood, Tennessee." ETHS*P* 39 (1967), 56-70.

Pickel, Eugene. "A History of Roane County to 1860." Thesis, Univ. of Tennessee, 1971.

"Roane County." *History of Tennessee,* East Tennessee Edition, ed. Weston A. Goodspeed et al., 821-25, 1072-81.

Seward, Harry M. *Scenes and Information about Rockwood, Tennessee, in the Heart of the Great Tennessee Valley Development.* Rockwood: Rockwood *Times,* c. 1935. 61 pp.

Stith, Lee Street. "Rural Leadership in Roane County, Tennessee." Thesis, Univ. of Tennessee, 1942.

Tennessee State Library and Archives. "Inventory of Roane County Records." Nashville: State Library and Archives, 1964- . Unpublished typescript.

Thornton, Mable Harvey. *Pioneers of Roane County, Tennessee, 1801-1830; (Tax Lists, Muster Rolls, Election Lists, Petitions, etc.).* Rockwood: n.p., 1965. 185 pp.

Two Years of Harriman, Tennessee. Established by the East Tennessee Land Company, February 26, 1890. New York. South, 1892. 104 pp.

Wells, Emma H. M. *The History of Roane County, Tennessee, 1801-1870.* Chattanooga: Lookout Pub., 1927- . 308 pp.

——. "The History of Roane County, Tennessee, 1801-1870." Chattanooga: Unpublished typescript, n.d. 71 pp. Copy in Roane County library.

ROBERTSON COUNTY
Historian: Mrs. Charles Durrett, 403 North Pawnee Drive, Springfield 37172.

Biographical Directory: Robertson County Members of the Tennessee General Assembly, 1796- . 47 pp.

Conn, Hardin H. *Robercrest in the Snow.* Springfield: n.p., 1940. 26 pp.

DeWitt, John H., Jr. "Early Radio Broadcasting in Middle Tennessee." *THQ* 31 (1972), 80-94. Describes the early years of WSIX at Springfield.

Dorsey, A. L. "Miscellaneous Collection of Pamphlets and Materials Relating to Robertson County and Springfield, 1908-1940." Unpublished typescript. Microfilm copy at Tennessee State Library and Archives.

Garrett, William R., ed. "Sketches of Sevier and Robertson Counties." *AHM* 5 (1900), 310-25.

Gunn, Lovie Mai. *Childhood Memories of Oak Lawn.* Springfield: n.p., 1967. 10 leaves.

——. *The House with Open Doors.* Springfield: n.p., 1967. 7 pp.

Holman, Catherine, and Jean Durrett. *Historic Robertson County, Places and Personalities.* Springfield: n.p., 1970. 40 pp.

Love, Charles H. *The Springfield I Have Known.* Springfield: *Robertson County Times,* 1943. 92 pp.

Miller, Harriet Parks. *Pioneer Colored Christians.* Clarksville: W. P. Titus, 1911. Rpt. Black Heritage Library Collection, Freeport, N.Y.: Bks. for Libraries, 1972. 103 pp. Relates to Robertson County.

Morton, Jacob C., and Virdner D. Moore, Jr. *Robertson County Negro Yearbook.* Springfield: n.p., 1938. Unpaged pamphlet.

Mulloy, James S. *Reminiscences of Robertson County.* Springfield: n.p., n.d. 23 leaves.

"Robertson County." *History of Tennessee,* ed. Weston A. Goodspeed et al., 827-67, 1124-1205.

Tennessee State Library and Archives. "Inventory of Robertson County Records." Nashville: State Library and Archives, 1964-. Unpublished typescript.

Thomas, Mrs. Archie, comp. *Chronicles of Robertson County, As Appears in Springfield "Record," August, 1902.* Springfield: n.p., 1922. 56 leaves.

U.S. Army Corps of Engineers. *Flood Plain Information, Sulphur Fork, Springfield, Tennessee, Prepared for the City of Springfield by the Dept. of the Army, Nashville District, Corps of Engineers, Nashville, August, 1972.* Nashville: Army Corps of Engineers, 1972. 29 pp.

Willett, Charles. *Bygone Days in Tennessee.* Springfield: The Author, 1961. 7 pp. Reproduced from articles in the Robertson County *Times,* Feb.-Mar. 1961.

Winters, Ralph L. *Historical Sketches of Adams, Robertson County, Tennessee, and Port Royal, Montgomery County, Tennessee, from 1779-1968.* A fine local history by a competent layman. Although primarily family history, it includes a generous treatment of economic and social history as well.

———. *Hospitality Homes and Historic Sites in Western Robertson County, Tennessee.* Clarksville: The Author, 1971. 128 pp.

Folklore of the Bell Witch

Barr, Gladys H. *The Bell Witch at Adams.* Nashville: D. Hutchinson, 1969. 107 pp.

Bell, Charles Bailey. *The Bell Witch: A Mysterious Spirit.* Nashville: Lark, 1934; rpt. Nashville: Charles Elder, 1972. 228 pp.

Ingram, Martin Van Buren. *An Authenticated History of the Famous Bell Witch. The Wonder of the 19th Century, and Unexplained Phenomenon of the Christian Era. The Mysterious Talking Goblin That Terrorized the West End of Robertson County, Tennessee, Tormenting John Bell to His Death. The Story of Betsy Bell, Her Lover and the Haunting Sphinx.* Clarksville: W. P. Titus, 1894; rpt. Nashville: Rare Bk. Rpts., 1961. 316 pp.

Miller, Harriet Parks. *The Bell Witch of Middle Tennessee.* Clarksville: *Leaf-Chronicle,* 1930; rpt. Nashville: Charles Elder, 1972. 72 pp.

RUTHERFORD COUNTY

Historian: Dr. Homer Pittard, Middle Tennessee State University, Murfreesboro 37130.

Baumstark, Michael P. "Recreational Demand Study for Rutherford County." Thesis, Middle Tennessee State Univ., 1971.

Biographical Directory: Rutherford County Members of the Tennessee General Assembly, 1796- . 63 pp.

Galloway, Jesse J. *Geology and Natural Resources of Rutherford County, Tennessee,* Tennessee Dept. of Education, Division of Geology Bulletin 22. Nashville: Williams, 1919. 81 pp.

Glass, P. T. "Sketch of Henry Rutherford." *AHM* 5 (1900), 225-29. The man for whom Rutherford County was named.

Greene, Samuel Goldsby. "Availability of Education to Negroes in Rutherford County, Tennessee." Thesis, Fisk Univ., 1940.

Handbook of Murfreesboro and Rutherford County, Tennessee. Murfreesboro: Mutual Realty & Loan, 1923. 128 pp.

Henderson, C. C. *The Story of Murfreesboro.* Murfreesboro: *News-Banner,* 1929. 145 pp.

Historical Records Survey, Tennessee. *Inventory of the County Archives of Tennessee: Rutherford County.* Nashville: The Survey, WPA, 1938.

Hoover, Walter King. *A History of the Town of Smyrna, Tennessee.* Nashville: McQuiddy, 1968. 559 pp.

Hughes, Mary B. *Hearthstones. The Story of Historic Rutherford County Homes.* Murfreesboro: Mid-South, 1942. 68 pp.

Lanier, Doris, ed. "Mary Noailles Murfree: An Interview." *THQ* 31 (1972), 276-78.

Lokey, James L. "History of Dairying in Rutherford County, Tennessee." Thesis, George Peabody College, 1937.

McBride, Robert M. "Oaklands: A Venerable Host: A Renewed Welcome." *THQ* 22 (1963), 303-22; rpt. in *Landmarks of Tennessee,* 259-78.

Meredith, Owen Nichols. "The Sam Davis Home." *THQ* 24 (1965), 303-20; rpt. in *More Landmarks of Tennessee,* 101-18.

Middle Tennessee State College. *History of Rutherford County.* Murfreesboro: Middle Tennessee State College, 1939. 52 leaves.

Miller, Julia C. "The Status of Women in Industry in Rutherford County." Thesis, Middle Tennessee State Univ., 1969.

Pittard, Homer P. "Legends and Stories of Civil War Rutherford County." Thesis, George Peabody College, 1940.

———. *The First Fifty Years,* illus. Nora Smith Hinton; photographs Bealer Smotherman. Murfreesboro: Courier, 1961. 273 pp.

———. *Pillar and Ground.* Murfreesboro: Courier, 1968. 166 pp. History of the First Baptist Church of Murfreesboro.

"Rutherford County." *History of Tennessee,* ed. Weston A. Goodspeed et al., 810-40, 1019-76.

Sims, Carlton C., ed. *A History of Rutherford County.* Murfreesboro: The Editor, 1947. 236 pp.

Tennessee State Library and Archives. "Inventory of Rutherford County Records." Nashville: State Library and Archives, 1964- . Unpublished typescript.

Walker, Watson Frank. *Ten Years of Rural Health Work, Rutherford*

County, Tennessee, 1924-1933. New York: Commonwealth Fund, 1935. 82 pp.

Walker, Watson Frank, and Carolina R. Randolph. *Influence of a Public Health Program on a Rural Community: Fifteen Years in Rutherford County, Tennessee, 1924-1938.* New York: Commonwealth Fund, 1940. 106 pp.

Willett, Ann Wilson. "A History of the Stones River National Military Park." Thesis, Middle Tennessee State Univ., 1958.

Womack, Bob. "Stone's River National Military Park." *THQ* 21 (1962), 303-17; rpt. in *More Landmarks of Tennessee,* 311-25.

Scott County
Historian: John Roy Thompson, Box B, Oneida 37841.

Burke, Carmel E. "Geographic Factors Influencing the Development of Scott County, Tennessee." Thesis, Univ. of Tennessee, 1959.

"Luck of Roaring Oneida; Oil Boom in Scott County." *Time,* Nov. 30, 1970, pp. 74- .

Pemberton, Olson. "Educational, Economic and Community Survey of Scott County, Tennessee." Thesis, Univ. of Tennessee, 1934.

Sanderson, Esther Sharp. *County Scott and Its Mountain Folk.* Huntsville: n.p., 1958. 254 pp.

Shepperson, Wilbur S. "A Welsh Settlement in Scott County, Tennessee." *THQ* 18 (1959), 162-68.

——. *Samuel Roberts: A Welsh Colonizer in Civil War Tennessee.* 190 pp. The 19th-century colony was located in Scott County.

U.S. Army Corps of Engineers. "Big South Fork, Cumberland River (Kentucky-Tennessee), Interagency Field Task Group Report." Unpublished typescript, 1969. 451 pp.

Sequatchie County
Historian: Mrs. Ora Lane, Box 563, Dunlap 37327.

Biographical Directory: Sequatchie County Members of the Tennessee General Assembly, 1796-. 51 pp. This volume also contains Bledsoe and Marion counties.

Bowron, William M. *Hand-Book to the Sequatchie Valley.* Nashville: Foster & Webb, 1888. 26 pp.

Hiatt, Ellen O. M. *Sequatchie Valley, A Historical Sketch,* photographs Marguerite Hiatt.

Layne, Ora. *Sequatchie County: History and Development.* Dunlap: The Author, 1969. 57 pp.

Martin, Robert Lewis. "The Sequatchie Valley, Tennessee, a Study in Land Utilization." Diss., George Peabody College, 1941.

Tennessee State Library and Archives. "Inventory of Sequatchie County Records." Nashville: State Library and Archives, 1964- . Unpublished typescript.

Torrey, B. "Week on Walden's Ridge." *Atlantic Monthly,* May-June 1895, pp. 605-13, 776-84.

SEVIER COUNTY
Historian: Mrs. Beulah D. Linn, 204 Country Club Road, Pigeon Forge 37863.

Crozier, Ethelred W. *The White-Caps: A History of the Organization in Sevier County.* Knoxville: The Author, 1899. 217 pp. Rev. ed., Knoxville: n.p., 1937. Rpt., 1899 ed., Sevierville: Brazos, 1963. Lawless factionalism in Sevier County of the 1890s.

Duggan, W. L. "Sketches of Sevier and Robertson Counties." *AHM* 5 (1900), 310-25.

——. *Facts about Sevier County.* Sevierville: n.p., 1910.

Edwards, Rapha O. Jones, and Ina Wear Roberts. *Descendants of East Tennessee Pioneers.* Gatlinburg: n.p., 1963. 315 pp.

Foscue, Edwin Jay. *Gatlinburg, Gateway to the Great Smokies,* American Resort Series no. 1. Dallas: Southern Methodist Univ. Press, 1946. 19 pp. A brief history of the community.

Greve, Jeanette S. *The Story of Gatlinburg (White Oak Flats).* Strasburg, Va.: Shenandoah, 1931; rpt. Gatlinburg: n.p., 1964. 136 pp.

——. "Traditions of Gatlinburg." ETHSP 3 (1931), 62-77.

Hodges, Sidney Cecil. "Handicrafts in Sevier County, Tennessee." Thesis, Univ. of Tennessee, 1951.

Matthews, Fred D. *History of Sevier County.* Knoxville: Master, c. 1950. 56 pp. Rev. ed., Knoxville: n.p., 1960. 55 pp.

Maupin, Juanita. "A Study of Living Conditions in the Pittman Center Community, 1934-1935." Thesis, Univ. of Tennessee, 1936.

Pyle, Ernest T. (Ernie). *Gatlinburg and the Great Smokies.* Gatlinburg: Mountain Press, 1951. 27 pp.

"Sevier County." *History of Tennessee,* East Tennessee Edition, ed. Weston A. Goodspeed et al., 834-37, 1096-1104.

Tennessee State Planning Commission. *A Proposed Plan for Development: Sevier County, Tennessee.* Nashville: n.p., 1964. 28 pp.

Tennessee Valley Authority, Industry Division. *Agricultural-Industrial Survey of Sevier County.* Knoxville: TVA, 1934.

SHELBY COUNTY

Historian: Mrs. Hillman P. Rodgers, Davies Plantation, Memphis 38128.

Bibliography

Ballentine, Nelle. "A Bibliographical Checklist of Knoxville and Memphis Imprints, 1867-1876, with an Introductory Essay on the Knoxville and Memphis Press." Thesis, Univ. of Tennessee, 1957.

General History and Early Settlement

Bejach, Lois D. "The Seven Cities Absorbed by Memphis." WTHSP 8 (1954), 95-103.

Bridges, George C. *Memphis in Pictures.* Memphis: S. C. Toof, 1940. Unpaged.

Burrow, Rachael Herring Kennon. *Arlington: A Short Historical Writing of the Town.* Memphis: E. H. Clarke, 1962. 124 pp.

Capers, Gerald M., Jr. "Where South Met West: Memphis, Tennessee, 1819-1900." Diss., Yale Univ., 1936.

——. *The Biography of a River Town; Memphis: Its Heroic Age.* Chapel Hill: Univ. of North Carolina Press, 1939. 292 pp. Rpt. New Orleans, 1966. 316 pp. Memphis from the 16th century to 1890; the author contends that an understanding of this city's past is invaluable for understanding the entire Lower West.

Chandler, Walter. "Personal Recollections of Memphis." WTHSP 22 (1968), 86-92.

Coppock, Paul R. "Pigeon Roost Road: A Chickasaw Trail." WTHSP 18 (1964), 59-69.

Davis, James D. *History of Memphis. The History of the City of Memphis, Being a Compilation of the Most Important Documents and Historical Events Connected with the Purchase of Its Territory, Laying Off of the City and Early Settlement. Also, the "Old Times Papers," Being a Series of Reminiscences and*

Local Stories Written by the Author, and Published in the "Daily Appeal" over the Signature of "Old Times." Memphis: Hite, Crumpton & Killy, 1873; rpt. West Tennessee Hist. Soc., 1972. 320 pp.

Gambill, Louise. *Municipal Progress in Memphis. From Frontier Post to Modern City.* Memphis: Municipal Reference Library, 1937. 16 pp.

Hamilton, Green P. *The Bright Side of Memphis; a Compendium of Information concerning the Colored People of Memphis, Tennessee, Showing Their Achievements in Business, Industrial and Professional Life and Including Articles of General Interest on the Race.* Memphis: N.p., 1908. 294 pp.

Historical Facts and Incidents Pertaining to Shelby County, Tennessee, vol. 1. Memphis, 1874.

Holmes, Jack D. L. "Three Early Memphis Commandants: Beauregard, Deville Degoutin, and Folch." WTHSP 18 (1964), 5-38.

House, Boyce. "Memphis Memories of Fifty Years Ago." WTHSP 14 (1960), 103-12.

Hutchins, Fred L. *What Happened in Memphis.* Kingsport: n.p., 1965. 134 pp.

Keating, John M. *History of the City of Memphis and Shelby County, Tennessee, with Illustrations and Biographical Sketches of Some of Its Prominent Citizens.* 2 vols. in 1. Syracuse, N.Y.: D. Mason, 1888; 2 vol. ed., Syracuse, N.Y.: Mason, 1889. Vol. 2 of each edition by O. F. Vedder.

Larson, Melvin G. *Skidrow Stopgap; the Memphis Story.* Wheaton, Ill.: Van Kampen, 1950. 112 pp.

Lindsay, Bertha B. "The Early Development of Memphis, Tennessee." Thesis, Univ. of Wisconsin, 1928.

McIlwaine, Shields. *Memphis Down in Dixie,* Society in America Series no. 3. New York: Dutton, 1948. 400 pp. Concentrating on the four generations between the 1820s and the 1940s, the author tells the story of his hometown. Noting that the ancient Egyptian placename Memphis meant "good abode," he feels that the Tennessee city has been, and remains, true to its name.

Mallory, Loula G. "The Three Lives of Raleigh." WTHSP 13 (1959), 78-94.

Memphis and Shelby County Centennial Commission. *Memphis Centennial Celebration May 19-24, 1919: Blossoming of the Century Plant . . . 1819-1919.* Memphis: Hood, 1919. 64 pp.

Meriwether, Lee. "Recollections of Memphis." WTHSP 3 (1949), 90-109.

Miller, William D. *Memphis during the Progressive Era, 1900-1917.* Diss., Univ. of North Carolina, 1954. Memphis: Memphis State Univ. Press, 1957. 242 pp. A superior example of the writing of urban history in Tennessee.

——. *Mr. Crump of Memphis,* Southern Biography Series. Baton Rouge: Louisiana State Univ. Press, 1964. 373 pp. The best biography of one of Tennessee's most colorful political figures. Crump was the state's first, and perhaps last, political boss.

Morrison, Andrew. *Memphis, Tennessee, the Bluff City, Mistress of the Lower River.* St. Louis: George L. Englehart, 1892. 168 pp.

Nickolds, Mary Costillo. "Reminiscences of My Childhood and Youth." WTHSP 12 (1958), 80-108. Mrs. Nickolds recalls late-19th-century Memphis.

Robinson, James Troy. "Fort Assumption: The First Recorded History of White Man's Activity on the Present Site of Memphis." WTHSP 5 (1951), 62-78.

Roper, James E. "Marcus Winchester and the Earliest Years of Memphis." *THQ* 21 (1962), 326-51.

——. "The Founding of Memphis, August, 1818 through December 1820." WTHSP 23 (1969), 5-29.

——. *The Founding of Memphis, 1818-1820.* Memphis: Memphis Sesquicentennial, Inc., 1970. 100 pp.

——. "Fort Adams and Fort Pickering." WTHSP 24 (1970), 5-29.

"Shelby County." *History of Tennessee,* ed. Weston A. Goodspeed et al., 797-1063.

Young, John Preston, ed. *Standard History of Memphis, Tennessee, from a Study of the Original Sources,* asst. writer and comp. Miss A. R. James. Knoxville: H. W. Crew, 1912. 606 pp.

——. "Happenings in the White Haven Community, Shelby County, Tennessee, Fifty or More Years Ago." *THM* 7 (1921), 96-103.

——. "Centennial History of Memphis." *THM* 8 (1924), 277-98; rpt. in *Tennessee Old and New,* II, 413-30.

Memphis during the Civil War and Reconstruction

Burns, Vincent L. "The Memphis Race Riot of 1866." Thesis, Memphis State Univ., 1972.

Ellis, John H. "Henry Morton Woodson—Confederate Veteran; Historian; Memphian." WTHSP 14 (1960), 74-90.

Holmes, Jack D. L. "Forrest's 1864 Raid on Memphis." *THQ* 18 (1959), 295-321.

——, ed. "Documents: Joseph A. Gronauer and the Civil War in Memphis." WTHS*P* 13 (1959), 148-58.

Hooper, Ernest W. "Memphis, Tennessee: Federal Occupation and Reconstruction, 1862-1870." Diss., Univ. of North Carolina, 1957.

Meriwether, Elizabeth Avery. *Recollections of 92 Years, 1824-1916.*

Newcomer, Lee N. "The Battle of Memphis, 1862." WTHS*P* 12 (1958), 40-57.

Parks, Joseph H. "A Confederate Trade Center under Federal Occupation: Memphis, 1862 to 1865." *JSH* 7 (1941), 289-314.

——. "Memphis under Military Rule, 1862 to 1865." ETHS*P* 14 (1942), 31-58.

Rayner, Juan. "An Eye-Witness Account of Forrest's Raid on Memphis." WTHS*P* 12 (1958), 134-37.

United States Congress. *Memphis Riots and Massacres. House Report* 101, 39th Cong., 1st sess.; Elihu B. Washburne, comp. Washington, D.C.: GPO, 1866. 394 pp. More commonly known as the "Washburne Report."

Economic History

Arrington, Raymond O'Neal. "Memphis, Tennessee, as a Wholesale Trade Center: Analysis of Its Development and Present Position." Thesis, Univ. of Tennessee, 1966.

Chandler, Walter. "The Memphis Navy Yard: An Adventure in Internal Improvement." WTHS*P* 1 (1947), 68-72.

Commercial and Statistical Review of the City of Memphis, Tennessee, Showing Her Manufacturing, Mercantile and General Business Interests . . . with Historical Sketches of the Growth . . . of the "Bluff City." Memphis: Reilly & Thomas, 1883. 181 pp.

Cooper, W. Raymond. "Four Fateful Years—Memphis, 1858-1861." WTHS*P* 11 (1957), 36-75.

Coppock, Paul R. "Huntington's Pacific to Atlantic Rails through Memphis." WTHS*P* 9 (1955), 5-28.

Cotterill, Robert S. "Memphis Railroad Convention, 1849." *THM* 4 (1918), 83-94.

Frigg, Martelle Daisy. "An Analysis of Illegitimacy by Natural Areas in Memphis, Tennessee." Thesis, Fisk Univ., 1954.

Gambill, Louise. *Memphis in the Heart of the Mid-South. A Story of Progress Made Possible by Taxes.* Memphis: n.p., 1930. 40 pp.

Hammer, Greene, Siler Associates. *The Economy of Metropolitan Memphis.* Memphis: Memphis and Shelby Co. Planning Comm., 1965. 228 pp.

Hensley, Andrew A. *Memphis: An Illustrated Review of Its Commercial Progress and Importance.* Memphis: Enterprise, 1886. 152 pp.

"An Island of Mud That Threatens Memphis Harbor." *Scientific American,* April 29, 1916, pp. 447 ff.

Johnson, R. W. "Geographic Influence in the Location and Growth of the City of Memphis." *Journal of Geography* 27 (1928), 85-97.

Kirkpatrick, C. C. "Second Awakening of Memphis." *Collier's,* Oct. 2, 1915, pp. 36 ff.

Lax, Forrest Orren. "The Memphis Cotton Exchange from Beginning to Decline." Thesis, Memphis State Univ., 1970.

Lindsay, Bertha B. "The Early Development of Memphis, Tennessee." Thesis, Univ. of Wisconsin, 1928.

Long, George Baker. "An Analysis of the Development of Manufacturers and Wholesalers in the Memphis, Tennessee Area, Their Land Use Requirements, and Effects upon Industrial Land Values 1950-1960." Thesis, Memphis State Univ., 1962.

MacDonald, W. "As Memphis Sees the Future." *Nation,* Mar. 8, 1919, pp. 348-49.

"The Memphis Convention." *De Bow's Commercial Review* 1 (1846), 7-21; 8 (1850), 217-32.

"Memphis, Tennessee, and Its Manufacturing Advantages." *De Bow's Commercial Review* 10 (1851), 525-29.

Miller, William D. "The Progressive Movement in Memphis." *THQ* 15 (1956), 3-16.

Morrison, Andrew. *Memphis, Tennessee, the Bluff City, Mistress of the Lower River.*

Ozment, Thomas Daniel. "Transportation and the Growth of Memphis." Thesis, George Peabody College, 1926.

Plaisance, Aloysius, O.S.B. "The Chickasaw Bluffs Factory and Its Removal to the Arkansas River, 1818-1822." *THQ* 11 (1952), 41-56.

Rust, John. "The Origin and Development of the Cotton Picker." *WTHSP* 7 (1953), 38-56. The author, inventor of the cotton picker, lived in Memphis for a short while.

Sioussat, St. George L. "Memphis as a Gateway to the West: A Study in the Beginnings of Railway Transportation in the Old Southwest." *THM* 3 (1917), 1-27, 77-114.

Tennessee Valley Authority, Industry Division. *Agricultural-Industrial Survey of Shelby County, Tennessee.* Knoxville: TVA, 1934.

Twyman, R. B. J. *Twyman's Memphis Directory and General Business Advertiser for 1850; with a Brief History of Memphis Annexed.* Memphis: The Author, 1849. 112 pp.

Waschka, Ronald W. "Transportation at Memphis before the Civil War." Thesis, Memphis State Univ., 1970.

Williams, Bobby Joe. "Let There Be Light: History of the Development of Public Ownership of Electric Utilities in Memphis, 1933-1940." Thesis, Memphis State Univ., 1972.

Williams, Edward F. *Early Memphis and Its River Rivals.* Memphis: Hist. Hiking Trails, c. 1968. 35 pp.

——. "Memphis' Early Triumph over Its River Rivals." WTHSP 22 (1968), 5-27.

Williams, Joseph R. *The Builders of the Pyramid: The Story of Shelby County: Its Resources and Developments.* Memphis: De Garis, 1897. 96 pp.

Political History and Public Administration

Bejach, Lois D. "The Taxing District of Shelby County." WTHSP 4 (1950), 5-27.

Bell, Robert M. "The Cost of Administering Criminal Justice in Memphis and Knoxville, Tennessee." Thesis, Univ. of Tennessee, 1931.

Brandon, Elvis Denby. "The Background and Operation of the Commission System in Memphis, Tennessee." Thesis, Duke Univ., 1952.

Capers, Gerald M. "Memphis, Satrapy of a Benevolent Despot." *Our Fair City,* ed. Robert S. Allen, 211-34. New York: Vanguard, 1947. 424 pp.

"Crimp in Crump." *Time,* Nov. 1, 1937, p. 22.

Daniels, Jonathan. "He Suits Memphis." *Saturday Evening Post,* June 10, 1939, pp. 22-23. Remarks on Mr. Crump.

Davis, Henry Clifton. "Some Aspects of the Formation, Operation and Termination of the Taxing District of Shelby County, Tennessee." Thesis, Memphis State Univ., 1964.

"Dixie's Mother Confessor: Judge Camille Kelley of the Juvenile Court." *American Magazine,* July 1938, pp. 51 ff.

Flowers, Paul. "In Memoriam: Walter Chandler, October 5, 1887-October 1, 1967." WTHS*P* 22 (1968), 93-94.

Gambill, Louise. *Memphis in the Heart of the Mid-South.*

——. *Municipal Progress in Memphis.*

Hinton, H. B. "Crump of Tennessee: Portrait of a Boss." *New York Times Magazine,* Sept. 29, 1946, pp. 15 ff.

Historical Records Survey, Tennessee. *Inventory of the County Archives of Tennessee: Shelby County.* Nashville: The Survey, WPA, 1939.

——. *History and Organization of the Shelby County Judiciary.* Nashville: The Survey, WPA, 1939. 14 pp.

Holmes, Jack D. L., ed. "The First Laws of Memphis: Instructions for the Commandant of San Fernando De Las Barrancas, 1795." WTHS*P* 15 (1961), 93-104.

Kelley, Camille. *A Friend in Court.* New York: Dodd, 1942. 266 pp. Mrs. Kelley was judge of the juvenile court in Memphis during the Crump years.

Kitchens, Allen H. "Ouster of Mayor Edward H. Crump, 1915-1916." WTHS*P* 19 (1965), 105-20.

——. "The Browning-Crump Battle: The Crump Side." ETHS*P* 37 (1965), 77-88.

Miller, William D. "J. J. Williams and the Greater Memphis Movement." WTHS*P* 5 (1951), 14-30.

——. "E. H. Crump: Family Background and Early Life." *THQ* 20 (1961), 364-80.

Phillips, Virginia. "Rowlett Paine's First Term as Mayor of Memphis, 1920-1924." Thesis, Memphis State Univ., 1958.

——. "Rowlett Paine, Mayor of Memphis, 1920-1924." WTHS*P* 13 (1959), 95-116.

Rauchle, Robert C. "The Political Life of the Germans in Memphis, 1848-1880." *THQ* 27 (1968), 165-75.

Roper, James E. "Marcus B. Winchester, First Mayor of Memphis: His Later Years." WTHS*P* 13 (1959), 5-37.

Scott, M. L. "Edward Crump and Commission Government in Memphis, 1909-1911." Thesis, Vanderbilt Univ., 1949.

Shelby County Codes Commission. *A Compilation of Acts of the General Assembly of the State of Tennessee Relating to Shelby*

County, Containing Certain Acts, Private Acts and Public Acts for the Years 1819 through 1955. Memphis: S. C. Toof, 1960. 376 pp.

Sorrels, William Wright. "Memphis' Greatest Debate: A Study of the Development of Its Public Water System." Thesis, Memphis State Univ., 1969.

Street, J. "Mista Crump Keeps Rollin' Along." *Collier's,* Apr. 9, 1938, p. 16.

Tucker, David M. "Black Politics in Memphis, 1865-75." WTHS*P* 26 (1972), 13-19.

Wax, Jonathan I. "Program of Progress: The Recent Change in the Form of Government of Memphis." WTHS*P* 23 (1969), 81-109; 24 (1970), 74-96.

Social and Cultural History

Bobbitt, Charles A. "The North Memphis Driving Park, 1901-1905: The Passing of an Era." WTHS*P* 26 (1972), 40-55.

Boom, Aaron M. "Early Fairs in Shelby County." WTHS*P* 10 (1956), 38-52.

Bristow, Eugene K. "Variety Theatre in Memphis, 1859-1862." WTHS*P* 13 (1959), 117-27.

——. "From Temple to Barn: The Greenlaw Opera House in Memphis, 1860-1880." WTHS*P* 21 (1967), 5-23.

Brooks, B. F. C. *Memphis; Her Great Men, Their Sayings, Writings and Doings as Secession Leaders . . . .* Memphis: n.p., 1864.

Bruesch, S. R. "Early Medical History of Memphis (1819-1861)." WTHS*P* 2 (1948), 33-94.

Chisman, Margaret Sue. "Literature and the Drama in Memphis, Tennessee, to 1860. . . . ." Thesis, Duke Univ., 1942.

Cohn, D. L. "Sing No Blues for Memphis." *New York Times Magazine,* Sept. 4, 1955, p. 14.

Coppock, Paul R. "History in Memphis Street Names." WTHS*P* 11 (1957), 93-111.

——. "W. W. Busby's Memories." WTHS*P* 22 (1968), 95-101.

Creekmore, H. "That's Memphis." *Holiday,* May 1954, pp. 106-13.

Edson, Andrew S. "How Nineteenth Century Travellers Viewed Memphis before the Civil War." WTHS*P* 24 (1970), 30-40.

Edwall, Harry R. "Some Famous Musicians on the Memphis Concert Stage prior to 1860." WTHS*P* 5 (1951), 90-105.

——. "The Golden Era of Minstrelsy in Memphis—a Reconstruction." WTHS*P* 9 (1955), 29-47.

Fakes, Turner J., Jr. "Memphis and the Mexican War." WTHS*P* 2 (1948), 119-44.

Falsone, Anne Marie M. "The Memphis Howard Association: A Study in the Growth of Social Awareness." Thesis, Memphis State Univ., 1968.

Fox, Jesse W. "Beale Street and the Blues." WTHS*P* 13 (1959), 128-47.

"The Great Bridge at Memphis." *Harper's Weekly,* May 14, 1892, pp. 473 ff.

Greene, Maude. "Folklore of Shelby County, Tennessee." Thesis, George Peabody College, 1940.

——. "The Background of the Beale Street Blues." *TFSB* 7 (1941), 1-10.

Haile, A. Arthur. "History of the Memphis Cotton Carnival." WTHS*P* 6 (1952), 34-63.

Halliburton, Richard. *Richard Halliburton, His Story of His Life's Adventure, As Told in Letters to His Mother and Father.* Indianapolis: Bobbs-Merrill, 1940; rpt. Garden City, N.Y.: Garden City Pub., 1942. 433 pp. Halliburton, a Memphis native, was a world traveler, journalist, and adventurer.

Handy, William Christopher. *Father of the Blues; an Autobiography,* ed. Arna Bontemps; foreword Abbe Niles. New York: Macmillan, 1941; rpt. London: Sidgwick & Jackson, 1957; rpt. New York, Macmillan, 1970. 317 pp.

Hill, Raymond S. "Memphis Theatre—1836-1846." WTHS*P* 9 (1955), 48-58.

Hutchings, Fred L. "Beale Street As It Was." WTHS*P* 26 (1972), 56-63.

Jackson, S. M. "Memphis Street Lighting Now 100 Per Cent Electric." *American City,* July 1931, pp. 162-63.

Jones, Otis H. "Reminiscences of Shiloh Park." WTHS*P* 23 (1969), 45-64.

Kahlin, Berkley. "Isaac L. Myers: A Man Who Brought the Best in the Arts to Memphis." WTHS*P* 26 (1972), 74-93.

Lanier, Robert A., Jr. "Memphis Greets War with Spain." WTHS*P* 18 (1964), 39-58.

Lasch, R. "You Can't Blow Your Horn in Memphis." *Popular Science,* Jan. 1954, pp. 151-54.

Lee, George Washington. *Beale Street, Where the Blues Began,* foreword W. C. Handy. New York: Ballou, 1934; rpt. Washington, D.C.: McGrath, 1969. 296 pp. Here is an annecdotal history to the 1930s of what the author considers "the Main Street of Negro America." Concentrating on a few of many events and sometimes using fictitious names, Lee seeks to preserve the memory of this famous street.

——. "Poetic Memories of Beale Street." WTHSP 26 (1972), 64-73.

McIntyre, Florence M. "The History of Art in Memphis." WTHSP 7 (1953), 79-92.

Matthews, James S. "Sequent Occupance in Memphis, Tennessee: 1819-1860." WTHSP 11 (1957), 112-34.

Miller, William D. "Rural Ideals in Memphis Life at the Turn of the Century." WTHSP 4 (1950), 41-49.

——. "Rural Values and Urban Progress: Memphis, 1900-1917." *Mississippi Quarterly* 21 (1968), 263-74.

Mitchell, Enoch L. "A Dentist Looks at Memphis, 1897." WTHSP 14 (1960), 91-102.

Pittman, Carolyn. "Memphis in the Mid-1840's." WTHSP 23 (1969), 30-44.

Prescott, Grace Elizabeth. "The Woman Suffrage Movement in Memphis—Its Place in the State, Sectional, and National Movements." Thesis, Memphis State Univ., 1953.

——. "The Woman Suffrage Movement in Memphis: Its Place in the State, Sectional, and National Movements." WTHSP 18 (1964), 87-106.

Rauchle, Robert C. "Social and Cultural Contributions of the German Population in Memphis, Tennessee, 1848-1880." Thesis, Univ. of Tennessee, 1964.

——. "Biographical Sketches of Prominent Germans in Memphis, Tennessee in the Nineteenth Century." WTHSP 22 (1968), 73-85.

——. "The Reactions of the Germans in Memphis to the Franco-Prussian War, 1870-1871." THQ 30 (1971), 205-9.

Ritter, Charles C. "'The Drama in Our Midst'—The Early History of the Theater in Memphis." WTHSP 11 (1957), 5-35.

Roark, Eldon. *Memphis Bragabouts. Characters I have Met,* illus. Frank L. Miller. New York: McGraw, 1945. 224 pp.

Root, Jonathan. *Halliburton, the Magnificent Myth: A Biography.* New York: Coward-McCann, 1965. 288 pp. The story of a

Memphis native who dazzled the world in the 1920s and '30s with his world travels and exploits in exotic places. He lost his life attempting to sail from Hong Kong to San Francisco in a Chinese junk.

Sawrie, Paul J. "The Porter-Leath Home, Memphis." WTHS*P* 17 (1963), 118-25. Porter-Leath is a home for widows and orphans.

Shankman, Samuel. *The Peres Family.* Kingsport: Southern, 1938. 241 pp. An important Jewish family in 19th-century Memphis.

Sorrels, William. *Memphis' Greatest Debate: A Question of Water.* Memphis: Memphis State Univ. Press, 1970. 139 pp.

Stanton, William M. "The Irish of Memphis." WTHS*P* 6 (1952), 87-118.

Taylor, Hillsman. "The History of the Memphis Open Air Theater." WTHS*P* 7 (1953), 93-100.

Tilly, Bette B. "Memphis and the Mississippi Valley Flood of 1927." WTHS*P* 24 (1970), 41-56.

Tracy, Sterling. "The Immigrant Population of Memphis." WTHS*P* 4 (1950), 72-82.

Watson, Samuel. *A Memphian's Trip to Europe with Cook's Educational Party: To Which Is Added Letters from Revs. T. W. Hooper, A. B. Whipple, and C. W. Cushing; Also, Letters from Several Ladies and Gentlemen of the Party.* Nashville: Methodist Pub. House, 1874. 352 pp.

Whittington, Earle Ligon. "A History of the Young Men's Christian Association of Memphis and Shelby County." WTHS*P* 12 (1958), 109-20.

Wingfield, Marie Gregson. "Memphis As Seen through *Meriwether's Weekly.*" WTHS*P* 5 (1951), 31-61.

Wingfield, Marshall. *Literary Memphis, a Survey of Its Writers and Writings.* Memphis: West Tennessee Hist. Soc., 1942. 223 pp.

——. "The Life and Letters of Dr. William J. Armstrong." WTHS*P* 4 (1950), 97-114.

EDUCATION

Bailey, Ralph P. "The Establishment and Development of Memphis Junior Academy." Thesis, Memphis State University, 1954.

Durham, Louise. "The Old Market Street School 1872-1920." Thesis, Memphis State University, 1953.

——. "The Old Market Street School, 1872-1920." WTHS*P* 7 (1953), 57-71.

Hamilton, Sister Margaret. *History of Saint Agnes Academy, Memphis, Tennessee, 1851-1926.* Memphis: John Gasser, 1926. 119 pp.

Hilliard, David Moss. *The Development of Public Education in Memphis, Tennessee, 1848-1945.* Diss., Univ. of Chicago, 1945. Chicago: n.p., 1946. 191 pp.

Holmes, Jack D. L. "On the Practicability and Advantages of a First-Class University in Memphis: A Letter from Dr. Ashbel Smith in 1849." *THQ* 19 (1960), 64-73.

Pool, Charles, Sam Shankman, and Annie Mayhew Fitzpatrick. "Three Views of Old Higbee School." WTHSP 20 (1966), 46-60.

RELIGIOUS GROUPS

Baptist

Coleman, Leslie H. "The Baptists in Shelby County to 1900." WTHSP 15 (1961), 8-39.

———. "The Baptists in Shelby County, 1903-1950." WTHSP 16 (1962), 70-103.

Episcopal

Davies-Rodgers, Ellen. *The Holy Innocents: The Story of a Historic Church and Country Parish (Haysville, Wythe Depot), Arlington, Shelby County, Tennessee, Including the Unpublished Diaries of Capt. Kenneth Garrett, Churchman and Civil War Soldier,* photographs Nadia Price. Brunswick: Plantation, 1965. 460 pp.

Davis, John H. *St. Mary's Cathedral, 1858-1958; a History of Saint Mary's Episcopal Church, Memphis, Which Became the Cathedral of the Diocese of Tennessee in 1871.* Memphis: Memphis Chap. of St. Mary's Cathedral (Gailor Memorial), 1958. 264 pp.

Greek Orthodox

Frey, Sara. "A History of the Annunciation Greek Orthodox Community in Memphis." WTHSP 18 (1964), 70-86.

Jewish

Shankman, Samuel. *Baron Hirsch Congregation; from Ur to Memphis.* Memphis: n.p., 1957. 153 pp.

Wax, Rabbi James A. "The Jews of Memphis: 1860-1865." WTHSP 3 (1949), 39-89.

Methodist

Perkins, J. E. "Highlights in the Life of the First Methodist Church of Memphis, Tennessee, 1826-1963." WTHS*P* 18 (1964), 136-46.

Whittington, Earle L. *St. John's Methodist Church: Centennial History, 1859-1959.* Memphis: McCowat-Mercer, 1960. 95 pp.

Presbyterian

Curry, Albert Bruce. *History of the Second Presbyterian Church of Memphis, Tennessee.* Memphis: Adams, 1937. 128 pp.

McCaslin, Robert H. *Presbyterianism in Memphis, Tennessee.* Memphis: Adams, c. 1945. 141 pp.

Mitchell, Enoch L. "Nicholas M. Long, Liberal Theologian." WTHS*P* 3 (1949), 110-25. Long was both a Presbyterian and Congregational minister.

General

Davis, John H. "Marshall Wingfield: In Memory." WTHS*P* 15 (1961), 5-7.

Fuller, Thomas O. *The Story of the Church Life among Negroes in Memphis, Tennessee, for Students and Workers, 1900-1938.* Memphis: n.p., 1938. 52 pp.

Historical Records Survey, Tennessee. *Directory of Churches, Missions, and Religious Institutions of Tennessee, no. 79. Shelby County.* Nashville: The Survey, WPA, 1941. 114 pp.

Meyers, Lawrence Charles. "Evolution of the Jewish Service Agency in Memphis, Tennessee: 1847-1963." Thesis, Memphis State Univ., 1965.

Wingfield, Marie Gregson. "The Memphis Council of Churches." WTHS*P* 17 (1963), 5-19.

———. "The Memphis Round Table of the National Conference of Christians and Jews." WTHS*P* 23 (1969), 65-80.

Wingfield, Marshall. *Strangers—First; a History of the Congregational Church in Memphis, Tennessee, Which Bore the Name Union, 1862-1867; the Name First, 1867-1881; the Name Strangers, 1881-1910; and the Name First since 1910.* Memphis: First Congregational Church, 1958. 71 pp.

Wooten, Fred Thomas, Jr. "Religious Activities in Civil War Memphis." Thesis, Univ. of Texas, 1942.

———. "Religious Activities in Civil War Memphis." *THQ* 3 (1944), 131-49, 248-72.

HISTORIC STRUCTURES AND PLACES

Art Work of Memphis. Chicago: Gravure Illus., 1912. 11 leaves.

Chandler, Walter. "The Court Houses of Shelby County." WTHSP 7 (1953), 72-78.

Coppock, Paul R. "Parks of Memphis." WTHSP 12 (1958), 120-33.

——. "The Memphis and Charleston Depot." WTHSP 21 (1967), 48-59.

Crawford, Charles W., and Robert M. McBride. "The Magevney House, Memphis." THQ 28 (1969), 345-55.

"Expressway to Bisect Memphis' Overton Park." *Parks and Recreation,* Sept. 1968, pp. 62- .

Gambill, Louise. *De Soto Park, Its Romance and History.* Written for Hernando De Soto Expedition Quadricentennial, 1541-1941. Memphis: City of Memphis, 1941. 23 pp.

Hughes, Eleanor. "The Fontaine House of the James Lee Memorial." THQ 27 (1968), 107-17; rpt. in *More Landmarks of Tennessee,* 141-51.

Morton, Terry B. "Victorian Mansions in Memphis." *Antiques,* Sept. 1971, pp. 409-13.

Nash, Charles H., and Rodney Gates, Jr. "Chucalissa Indian Town." THQ 21 (1962), 103-21; rpt. in *Landmarks of Tennessee,* 115-33.

Roper, James. "Memphis Historical Markers: Some Corrections and New Locations." WTHSP 22 (1968), 62-72.

"Showdown in the Park; Conservationists' Action over Building U.S. Highway through Overton Park." *Time,* Mar. 15, 1971. p. 44.

Thomas, William A. "The Road to Overton Park: Parklands Statutes in Federal Highway Legislation." *TLR* 39 (1972), 433-58.

JOURNALISM

Baker, Thomas Harrison III. "The Memphis *Appeal,* 1841-1865." Thesis, Univ. of Texas, 1962.

——. *The Memphis "Commercial Appeal": The History of a Southern Newspaper.* Baton Rouge: Louisiana State Univ. Press, 1972. 323 pp.

——. "The Early Newspapers of Memphis, Tennessee, 1827-1860." WTHSP 17 (1963), 20-46.

——. "Refugee Newspaper: The Memphis *Daily Appeal,* 1862-1865." *JSH* 29 (1963), 326-44.

——. "The Memphis *Commercial Appeal,* 1865-1941." Diss., Univ. of Texas, 1965.

Bridges, Lamar Whitlow. "Editor Mooney versus Boss Crump." WTHS*P* 20 (1966), 77-107.

——. "The Memphis *Daily Appeal*'s 'Dixie': Civil War Capital Correspondent." *THQ* 28 (1969), 377-87.

Fraser, Walter J., Jr. "Lucien Bonaparte Eaton: Politics and the Memphis *Post,* 1867-1869." WTHS*P* 20 (1966), 20-45.

Halley, R. A. "A Rebel Newspaper's War Story: Being a Narrative of the War History of the Memphis *Appeal.*" *AHM* 8 (1903), 124-53; rpt. in *Tennessee Old and New* II, 247-72.

House, Boyce. *Cub Reporter, Being Mainly about Mr. Mooney and the "Commercial Appeal."* Dallas: Hightower, 1947. 175 pp.

Silver, J. W. "C. P. J. Mooney of the Memphis *Commercial Appeal,* Crusader for Diversification." *Agricultural History* 17 (1943), 81-89.

Sisler, George. "The Arrest of a Memphis *Daily Appeal* War Correspondent on Charges of Treason." WTHS*P* 11 (1957), 76-92.

Stanton, Mary Imelda. "Life and Editorial Style of C. P. J. Mooney." Thesis, George Peabody College, 1930.

Talley, Robert. *One Hundred Years of the "Commercial Appeal." The Story of the Greatest Romance in American Journalism, 1840 to 1940.* Memphis: *Commercial Appeal,* 1940. 71 pp.

Taylor, Heber, and Forrest Martin. "The Sunday *Times:* A Memphis Paper That Failed." WTHS*P* 24 (1970), 57-73.

Tollison, Grady. "Andrew J. Kellar, Memphis Republican." WTHS*P* 16 (1962), 29-55. Kellar was editor of the Memphis *Avalanche* in the post-Civil War era.

THE NEGRO

The Race Riot of 1866

Holmes, Jack D. L. "The Effects of the Memphis Race Riot of 1866." WTHS*P* 12 (1958), 58-79.

——. "The Underlying Causes of the Memphis Race Riot of 1866." *THQ* 17 (1958), 195-221.

"The Moral of the Riots at Memphis, 1866." *Nation* 2 (1866), 616- .

Richardson, Joe M., ed. "The Memphis Race Riot and Its Aftermath." *THQ* 24 (1965), 63-69.

Strong, John E. "Memphis Environs 1816-1860, with Some Considerations on the Establishment of Beale Street." Thesis, Tennessee State A&I Univ., 1962.

United States Congress. *Memphis Riots and Massacres,* Elihu B. Washburne, comp.

Turn-of-the-Century Race Relations

Fuller, Thomas O. *Twenty Years in Public Life, 1890-1910, North Carolina-Tennessee.* Nashville: Nat. Bapt. Pub., 1910. 279 pp. Fuller was a prominent Memphis Negro leader.

Roitman, Joel M. "Race Relations in Memphis, Tennessee, 1880-1905." Thesis, Memphis State Univ., 1964.

Race Relations of the 1950s

Slavick, W. H. "Trouble Comes to Memphis." *Commonweal,* July 24, 1953, pp. 392-94.

Wingfield, Marshall. "Memphians Plan for Integration." *Christian Century,* Aug. 8, 1956, pp. 928-29.

——. "Memphis Stirred by Racial Debate." *Christian Century,* Dec. 12, 1956, pp. 1461-62.

——. "Memphis Studies Housing Pattern; Church Projects Build Racial Good Will." *Christian Century,* Mar. 27, 1957, p. 402.

Race Relations: 1960-72

"Bloody Memphis and More to Come?" *U.S. News and World Report,* Apr. 8, 1968, pp. 8ff.

Leifermann, H. P. "A Year Later in Memphis." *Nation,* Mar. 31, 1969, pp. 401-3.

"Memphis Blues; Demonstrations and School Boycotts for Desegregation of School Administration." *Newsweek,* Nov. 24, 1969, pp. 38-39.

"Memphis: How Assassination Changed a City in Three Years." *U.S. News and World Report,* Apr. 5, 1971, pp. 66-68.

"Memphis Is Also America." *Nation,* Apr. 22, 1968, pp. 529-31.

"Memphis Moves toward Racial Justice." *Christian Century,* Sept. 9, 1964, pp. 1102-3.

Muse, Benjamin. *Memphis.* Atlanta: Southern Regional Council, 1964. 49 pp.

Osborne, J. "King's Men Return to Memphis." *New Republic,* Aug. 24, 1968, pp. 12-14.

Stanfield, J. E. "Memphis: More Than a Garbage Strike; Excerpts from Report of Southern Regional Council." *Current,* May 1968, pp. 10-18.

"What Union Won in Garbage Strike." *U.S. News and World Report*, Apr. 29, 1968, pp. 82- .

Willis, G. "Martin Luther King Is Still on the Case." *Esquire*, Aug. 1968, pp. 98-104.

Wingfield, Marie Gregson. "The Memphis Interracial Commission." WTHSP 21 (1967), 93-107.

YELLOW FEVER

Capers, Gerald M. "Yellow Fever in Memphis in the 1870's." *MVHR* 24 (1937-38), 483-502.

Carroll, Ann Barron. "The Life of General Luke E. Wright." Thesis, Univ. of Tennessee, 1942. Wright, a community leader during the yellow fever epidemic, was also a military and diplomatic leader.

Davis, John Henry. "Two Martyrs of the Yellow Fever Epidemic of 1878." WTHSP 26 (1972), 20-39.

Dromgoole, John P., et al. *Dr. Dromgoole's Yellow Fever Heroes, Honors, and Horrors of 1878. A List of Over Ten Thousand Victims, Martyr Death-Roll of Volunteer Physicians, Nurses, etc.* Louisville, Ky.: J. P. Morton, 1879. 176 pp.

Ellis, John H. "Yellow Fever and the Origins of Modern Public Health in Memphis, Tennessee." Diss., Tulane Univ., 1962.

——. "Memphis' Sanitary Revolution, 1880-1890." *THQ* 23 (1964), 59-72.

——. "Business Leadership in Memphis Public Health Reform, 1880-1900." WTHSP 19 (1965), 94-104.

Hicks, Mildred, ed. *Yellow Fever and the Board of Health, Memphis, 1878.* Memphis: Memphis and Shelby Co. Health Dept., 1964. 41 pp.

Hurt, Mary Elizabeth. "The Yellow Fever Epidemic of 1878 in Memphis." Thesis, George Peabody College, 1938.

Keating, John M. *A History of the Yellow Fever. The Yellow Fever Epidemic of 1878, in Memphis, Tenn., Embracing a Complete List of the Dead, the Names of the Doctors and Nurses Employed, Names of All Who Contributed Money or Means, and the Names and History of the Howards, together with Other Data, and Lists of the Dead Elsewhere.* Memphis: Howard Assoc., 1879. 454 pp.

Merrill, Ayres P. *Yellow Fever, As It Appeared in Memphis, Tennessee, in 1855.* Memphis: *Morning Bulletin* Steam Job Off., 1855. 38 pp.

Quinn, Denis A. *Heroes and Heroines of Memphis; or, Reminiscences of the Yellow Fever Epidemics That Afflicted the City of Memphis during the Autumn Months of 1873, 1878 and 1879, to Which Is Added: A Graphic Description of Missionary Life in Eastern Arkansas.* Providence, R. I.: Freeman, 1887. 306 pp.

SMITH COUNTY

Historian: The Reverend R. D. Brooks, Carthage 37030.

Biographical Directory: Smith County Members of the Tennessee General Assembly, 1796- . 112 pp. This volume also contains Wilson County.

Bowen, John W. *Smith County History.* N.p.: n.d. 67 leaves. Available at the Tennessee State Library and Archives.

Gold, W. D. *The County of Smith.* Carthage: Carthage *Post,* 1903; rpt. Livingston: n.p., 1968. 48 pp. Newspaper articles made into a scrapbook.

Handbook of Smith County. Ed. E. H. Burk. Supplement to the Carthage *Post.* Carthage: Carthage *Post,* 1903. 48 pp.

"Smith County." *History of Tennessee,* ed. Weston A. Goodspeed et al., 821-34, 929-71.

Tennessee State Library and Archives. "Inventory of Smith County Records." Nashville: State Library and Archives, 1964- . Unpublished typescript.

Young, S. M. "Major Tilman Dixon." *THM* (ser. 2) 2 (1931-32), 207-15.

STEWART COUNTY

Historian: No appointment made.

Battle of Fort Donelson. *See* Civil War.

Brandon, Helen Gould. "A History of Stewart County, Tennessee." Thesis, Univ. of Tennessee, 1944.

Cooling, B. Franklin. "Fort Donelson National Military Park." *THQ* 23 (1964), 203-20; rpt. in *More Landmarks of Tennessee,* 121-38.

Guerin, Wayne. "Some Folkways of a Stewart County Community." *TFSB* 19 (1953), 49-58.

McClain, Iris Hopkins. *A History of Stewart County, Tennessee.* Columbia: Unpublished typescript, 1965. 152 pp.

Mark, L. *The New Bamberg Colony in the State of Tennessee in North America.* Bamberg, Germany: n.p., 1846. The site of the colony was Stewart County.

Mooney, Chase C., ed. "Some Letters from Dover, Tennessee, 1814-1855." *THQ* 8 (1949), 154-84, 252-83, 345-65; 9 (1950), 64-83, 155-70. Written by William Williams.

Stewart County." *History of Tennessee,* ed. Weston A. Goodspeed et al., 894-920, 1289-1329.

Tennessee State Library and Archives. "Inventory of Stewart County Records." Nashville: State Library and Archives, 1964- . Unpublished typescript.

Voight, Robert Charles. "Defender of the Common Law: Aaron Goodrich, Chief Justice of Minnesota Territory." Diss., Univ. of Minnesota, 1962. Before going to Minnesota, Goodrich was a Stewart County attorney and state legislator in the 1840s.

SULLIVAN COUNTY
Historian: No appointment made.

Ahern, L. R., Jr., and R. F. Hunt, Jr., eds. "The Boatyard Store, 1814-1825." *THQ* 14 (1955), 257-77.

Allred, Charles E., and J. C. Fitch. *Effects of Industrial Development on Rural Life in Sullivan County, Tennessee.* Univ. of Tennessee *Record,* vol. 5, no. 3. Knoxville: Division of Univ. Extension, Univ. of Tennessee, 1928. 45 pp.

Anderson, Paul Fain. "The History of Educational Development in Sullivan County, Tennessee." Thesis, Univ. of Tennessee, 1936.

Chase, Lewis. "Changes in Social and Economic Status of the People in Sullivan County for a Thirty Year Period." Thesis, Univ. of Tennessee, 1936.

Clark, Joe. *Back Home. Kingsport, Tennessee.* Kingsport: Kingsport Press, 1965. Unpaged.

Counce, Paul A. "Social and Economic History of Kingsport before 1908." Thesis, Univ. of Tennessee, 1939.

DeFriece, Pauline M., and Frank B. Williams, Jr. "Rocky Mount: The Cobb-Massengill Home, First Capitol of the Territory of the United States South of the River Ohio." *THQ* 25 (1966), 119-34; rpt. in *More Landmarks of Tennessee,* 249-64.

Fuller, Hugh Eckel. "Joseph Ketron and His Kingsley Seminary, Sullivan County, Tennessee." Thesis, East Tennessee State Univ., 1953.

Haden, Ben. *Kingsport, Tennessee—A Modern American City—Developed through Industry.* Kingsport: Kingsport Rotary Club, 1963. Unpaged.

Hamer, Marguerite B. "John Rhea of Tennessee." ETHS*P* 4 (1932), 35-44.

Historical Records Survey, Tennessee. *Summary of Special Legislation Relating to the Government of Sullivan County.* Nashville: The Survey, WPA, 1940. 19 leaves.

——. *Inventory of the County Archives of Tennessee: Sullivan County.* Nashville: The Survey, WPA, 1942.

Holland, Carl W. "Educational Facilities and Economic Development of Bristol, 1930-1950." Thesis, East Tennessee State Univ., 1956.

Holly, John Fred. "The Social and Economic Effects Produced upon Small Towns by Rapid Industrialization." Thesis, Univ. of Tennessee, 1938. Includes Kingsport.

Hunt, Raymond F., Jr. "The Pactolus Ironworks." *THQ* 25 (1966), 176-96.

Isaacs, I. J., comp. *The City of Bristol, Virginia-Tennessee, Its Interests and Industries; Compiled under the Auspices of the Board of Trade. Also a Series of Comprehensive Sketches of Representative Business Enterprises.* Bristol: King, 1915. 88 pp.

Long, Howard. *Kingsport: A Romance of Industry.* Kingsport: Sevier, 1928. 304 pp.

Loving, Robert S. *Double Destiny: The Story of Bristol, Tennessee-Virginia.* Bristol: n.p., 1955, 1956. 232 pp.

New Bethel Presbyterian Church. *The New Bethel Sesquicentennial 1782-1932.* Bristol: King, 1932. 110 pp.

Nicks, Roy S. "City-County Separation in Tennessee. A Case Study of Kingsport and Sullivan County." Thesis, Univ. of Tennessee, 1957.

Petro, Sylvester. *The Kingsport Strike.* New Rochelle, N.Y.: Arlington House, 1967. 238 pp. Refers to labor difficulty at the Kingsport Press.

Piquet, John A., ed. *Kingsport, City of Industries, Schools, Churches and Homes.* Kingsport: Kingsport Rotary Club, 1937. 234 pp.

——. *Kingsport, the Planned Industrial City.* Kingsport: Kingsport Rotary Club, 1946. 349 pp.

Pitts, John Abram. *Personal and Professional Reminiscences of an Old Lawyer.* Kingsport: Southern, 1930. 381 pp. Except for the last chapter, first published as weekly articles in the Nashville *Citizen Appeal,* beginning in June, 1929.

Preston, Thomas W. *The Story of Bristol.* N.p., n.d.

——. *Historical Sketches of the Holston Valleys,* Holston Historical Library no. 1. Kingsport: Kingsport Press, 1926. 186 pp.

——. "The Netherland Inn at Old Kingsport." ETHS*P* 4 (1932), 32-34.

Price, Prentice, ed. "Two Petitions to Virginia of the North of Holston Men, 1776, 1777." ETHS*P* 21 (1949), 95-110. The area includes Sullivan County.

Ross, Charles C., ed. *Story of Rotherwood, from the Autobiography of Rev. Frederick A. Ross.* Knoxville: Bean, Warters, 1923. 35 pp.

Smith, Homer H. *Memoirs.* Blountville: King, 1948. 121 pp.

Spoden, Muriel Clark. *Kingsport, Tennessee: Historical Map of Long Island of the Holston.* Kingsport: n.p., 1969.

Stevenson, C. "Contrast in Perfect Towns: Norris and Kingsport, Tennessee, Federal Show Case and Industry Yardstick Town." *Nation's Business,* Dec. 1937, pp. 18-20.

"Sullivan County." *History of Tennessee,* East Tennessee Edition, ed. Weston A. Goodspeed et al., 912-21, 1300-1312.

Taylor, Oliver. *Historic Sullivan: A History of Sullivan County, Tennessee, with Brief Biographies of the Makers of History.* Bristol: King, 1909; rpt. Nashville: Charles Elder, 1971. 330 pp. A good county history prepared under difficult circumstances, since the written records of the county were burned during the battle of Blountville, 1863.

Tennessee Valley Authority, Industry Division. *Agricultural-Industrial Survey of Sullivan County.* Knoxville: TVA, 1934. 124 pp.

"Test Tube Love Seat, Kingsport, Tennessee." *Time,* Feb. 26, 1940, p. 74.

Van Cleve, Dorothy. "History of the First Presbyterian Church, Bristol." Thesis, East Tennessee State Univ., 1959.

Whitman, W. "Three Southern Towns: Kingsport: They Planned It." *Nation,* Jan. 21, 1939, pp. 88-90.

——. "Slum Clearance in Kingsport." *Nation,* June 3, 1939, p. 656.

Williams, Samuel Cole. "Fort Robinson on the Holston." ETHS*P* 4 (1932), 22-31.

——. "Shelby's Fort." ETHS*P* 7 (1935), 28-37.

Wilson, Mary Allison. "The Symphony Orchestra of Kingsport." Thesis, East Tennessee State Univ., 1965.

SUMNER COUNTY

Historian: E. L. Ferguson, Route 3, Portland 37148.

Allen, Ward. "Cragfont: Grandeur on the Tennessee Frontier." *THQ* 23 (1964), 103-20; rpt. in *Landmarks of Tennessee,* 137-54.

Anderson, James Douglas. *The Historic Blue Grass Line: A Review of the History of Davidson and Sumner Counties.*

Barnes, Dovie, Mrs. Owen Donoho, and Mrs. Homer Bradley. *A Brief History of Cairo Community.* Gallatin: Cairo Community Club, 1964. 12 pp.

Biographical Directory: Sumner County Members of the Tennessee General Assembly, 1796- . 100 pp. This volume also contains Macon and Trousdale counties.

Carr, John. *Early Times in Middle Tennessee.* An important account of early days in the area by an eyewitness to the events.

Cisco, Jay Guy. *Historic Sumner County, Tennessee, with Genealogies of the Bledsoe, Cage, and Douglas Families, and Genealogical Notes of Other Sumner County Families.* Nashville: Folk-Keelin, 1909; rpt. Nashville: Charles Elder, 1971. 319 pp. After a short narrative history of the county, the author concentrates upon county genealogy and specific family histories to around 1820.

Clark, Isaac. *Clark's Miscellany.*

Connor, Thomas K. "Living with Antiques: Fairvue, the Tennessee home of Mr. and Mrs. William Wemyss." *Antiques,* Oct. 1971, pp. 606-10.

Delaney, Joseph D. *A Historical Study of Rock Castle.* Nashville: Tennessee Hist. Comm., 1969. 47 pp.

Dickson, D. Bruce. *Excavations at Rock Castle, Sumner County, Tennessee. August, 1972.* Nashville: Tennessee Hist. Comm., 1972. 9 pp. Report of work done for the Tennessee Historical Commission.

Durham, Anna T. "Tyree Springs." *THQ* 28 (1969), 156-65.

Durham, Walter T. *The Great Leap Westward: A History of Sumner County, Tennessee, from Its Beginning to 1805.* Gallatin: Sumner Co. Pub. Lib. Bd., 1969. 225 pp. Durham emphasizes the lure which cheap and abundant land had for the people of colonial

America and concludes that the "leap" to the Cumberland settlements was a phenomenon in that it took settlers well beyond firmly held Indian boundaries to points that could be reached from the eastern colonies only through the Indian country.

———. *Old Sumner: A History of Sumner County, Tennessee.* Gallatin: Sumner Co. Pub. Lib. Bd., 1972. 530 pp.

Garrett, W. R., ed. "Rock Castle." *AHM* 5 (1900), 291-94.

Guild, George B. "Reconstruction Times in Sumner County." *AHM* 8 (1903), 355-68.

Hall, William. *Early History of the South West by General William Hall: Pioneer, Indian Fighter, Governor of Tennessee, United States Congressman,* ed. Robert H. Horsley. Nashville: Parthenon Press, 1968. 45 pp.

Hendrickson, Mrs. T. J. *A Short History of Sumner County, 1786-1957.* Gallatin: Sumner Co. Pub. Libr. Bd., 1958. 46 pp.

Jenkins, William T. "History of Sumner County, Tennessee." Thesis, Vanderbilt Univ., 1949.

Law, Harry L. "The Strawberry Industry in Sumner County, Tennessee." Thesis, George Peabody College, 1930.

Matlock, J. W. L. *History of the Methodist Church at Hendersonville, Tennessee.* Hendersonville: First Methodist Church, 1960. 90 pp.

"Sumner County." *History of Tennessee,* ed. Weston A. Goodspeed et al., 797-821, 848-929.

Tennessee State Library and Archives. "Inventory of Sumner County Records." Nashville: State Library and Archives, 1964- . Unpublished typescript.

Todd, Pauline M. *Sumner County Sesquicentennial, 1787-1937.* Nashville: Marshall & Bruce, 1937. 64 pp.

TIPTON COUNTY
Historian: Dr. J. S. Ruffin, Jr., Covington 38019.

Historical Records Survey, Tennessee. *Inventory of the County Archives of Tennessee: Tipton County.* Nashville: The Survey, WPA, 1941.

"Tipton County." *History of Tennessee,* ed. Weston A. Goodspeed et al., 808-18, 885-921.

Wingfield, Marshall. "Tipton County, Tennessee." *WTHSP* 3 (1949), 5-26.

UNION COUNTY / 443

TROUSDALE COUNTY
Historian: Mrs. Henry Haynie, Hartsville 37074.

Biographical Directory: Trousdale County Members of the Tennessee General Assembly, 1796- . 100 pp. This volume also contains Macon and Sumner counties.

McMurtry, J. C. *History of Trousdale County.* Hartsville: Vidette, 1970. 332 pp.

Tennessee Valley Authority, Industry Division. *Agricultural-Industrial Survey of Trousdale County.* Knoxville: TVA, 1934.

"Trousdale County." *History of Tennessee,* ed. Weston A. Goodspeed et al., 841-48, 988-91.

Young, S. M. "The Old Rock House." *THM* (ser. 2) 3 (1932-37), 59-64; rpt. in *Tennessee Old and New,* II, 9-14.

UNICOI COUNTY
Historian: Pat Alderman, Box 699, Erwin 37650.

Alderman, Pat. *The Wonders of the Unakas in Unicoi County.* Erwin: Erwin Business and Professional Women's Club, 1964. 44 pp. A promotional pamphlet primarily for tourists.

Barnes, Florence. "An Educational History of Unicoi County, Tennessee." Thesis, George Peabody College, 1935.

Biographical Directory: Unicoi County Members of the Tennessee General Assembly, 1796- . 61 pp. This volume also contains Carter and Johnson counties.

Pratt, Audree W. "Unicoi County Court: 1876-1918." Thesis, East Tennessee State Univ., 1960.

Tennessee Valley Authority, Industry Division. *Agricultural-Industrial Survey of Unicoi County.* Knoxville: TVA, 1934. 62 pp.

Thrasher, James Arvin. "An Educational Survey of Unicoi County, Tennessee." Thesis, Univ. of Tennessee, 1932.

"Unicoi County." *History of Tennessee,* East Tennessee Edition, ed. Weston A. Goodspeed et al., 904-6, 1287-89.

UNION COUNTY
Historian: No appointment made.

Duggan, Benjamin O., M. L. Hardin, and W. H. Thomas. *Educational*

Survey, Union County. University of Tennessee *Record* Extension Series, Vol. 1, no. 2. Knoxville: Div. of University Extension, Univ. of Tennessee, 1924. 48 pp.

"Union County." *History of Tennessee,* East Tennessee Edition, ed. Weston A. Goodspeed et al., 850-52, 1146-52.

VAN BUREN COUNTY

Historian: Creed B. Shockley, Box 65, Spencer 38585.

Biographical Directory: Van Buren County Members of the Tennessee General Assembly, 1796- . 92 pp. This volume also contains Warren and White counties.

Tennessee State Library and Archives. "Inventory of Van Buren County Records." Nashville: State Library and Archives, 1964- . Unpublished typescript.

WARREN COUNTY

Historian: Walter Womack, 114 College Street, McMinnville 37110.

Biographical Directory: Warren County Members of the Tennessee General Assembly, 1796- . 92 pp. This volume also contains White and Van Buren counties.

Clark, Carroll H. *My Grandfather's Diary of the War.* McMinnville: n.p., 1963. Relates to the Civil War.

Grizzell, Mary Frances. "A Historical Survey of Education in Warren County, Tennessee." Thesis, Tennessee Technological Univ., 1964.

Grove, J. G. *This Is My Story.* Commerce, Tex.: n.p., 1966. 167 pp.

Hale, William T. *Early History of Warren County,* ed. J. W. Womack, Jr. McMinnville: Standard, 1930. 59 pp. First published in a special edition of the *Southern Standard,* Oct. 4, 1902.

Hill, Louise Biles. *History of Mt. Zion Methodist Episcopal Church, South of Mount Zion, Warren County, Tenn., 1809-1930.* McMinnville: Standard, 1930. 107 pp.

Killebrew, Joseph B. *Warren County, Its Organization, Scenery, Resources and Representative Men.* Nashville: *Union & American,* 1871. 36 pp.

Population Schedule of the United States Census of 1850 (Seventh Census) for Warren County, Tennessee. McMinnville: Womack, 1958. 173 pp.

Savage, John H. *Life of John H. Savage, Citizen, Soldier, Lawyer, Congressman. Written by Himself.* Nashville: The Author, c. 1903. 200 pp. Savage served in the Mexican War, and was colonel of the 16th Tennessee regiment, 1861-63.

Tennessee State Library and Archives. "Inventory of Warren County Records." Nashville: State Library and Archives, 1964- . Unpublished typescript.

"Warren County." *History of Tennessee,* ed. Weston A. Goodspeed et al., 812-27, 884-921.

Womack, James J. *The Civil War Diary of Capt. J. J. Womack.*

Womack, Walter. *McMinnville at a Milestone, 1810-1960: A Memento of the Sesquicentennial Year of McMinnville, Tennessee, 1960, and Warren County, Tennessee, 1958.* McMinnville: Standard, 1960. 327 pp.

Woodward, J. Fletch. *Fletch Woodward, His Fights with Those Bad, Bad Town Boys.* McMinnville: n.p., 1878.

WASHINGTON COUNTY
Historian: Paul M. Fink, Box 82, Jonesboro 37659.

Archer, Cordelia Pearl. "History of the Schools of Johnson City, Tennessee, 1868-1950." Thesis, East Tennessee State Univ., 1953.

Baratte, John J. "The Tipton-Haynes Place II. The Later Years." *THQ* 29 (1970), 125-29.

Bradshaw, Grace Beatrice. "Some Phases of the Social and Economic History of Washington County, Tennessee, 1865-1917." Thesis, Univ. of Tennessee, 1942.

Browning, Howard Miller. "Washington County Court: The Government of a Tennessee Frontier Community." Thesis, Vanderbilt Univ., 1938.

——. "The Washington County Court, 1778-1789: A Study in Frontier Administration." *THQ* 1 (1942), 328-43.

Brumit, Robert F. "History of Boone's Creek School, 1851-1958." Thesis, East Tennessee State Univ., 1958.

Centennial of Holston Presbytery Celebrated in the Jonesboro Presbyterian Church, Jonesboro, Tennessee, October 18-19, 1926. Greeneville: John R. Self, 1927. 43 pp.

Crutcher, Charlotte. "Asiatic Cholera in Jonesboro, 1873." *THQ* 31 (1972), 74-79.

Daniels, Ophelia Cope. "Formative Years of Johnson City, Tennessee; 1885-1890." Thesis, Tennessee State A&I Univ., 1948.

Eberling, May Dean. "History in Towns: Jonesboro, Tennessee's Oldest Town." *Antiques,* Sept. 1971, pp. 420-24.

Finchum, George A. "Washington County Court, 1796-1836." Thesis, East Tennessee State Univ., 1959.

Fink, Miriam L. "Some Phases of the Social and Economic History of Jonesboro, Tennessee, prior to the Civil War." Thesis, Univ. of Tennessee, 1934.

——. "Judicial Activities in Early East Tennessee." ETHS*P* 7 (1935), 38-49.

Fink, Paul M. "The Early Press of Jonesboro." ETHS*P* 10 (1938), 57-70.

——. "The Bumpass Cove Mines and Embreeville." ETHS*P* 16 (1944), 48-64.

——. "Fifty Years of Freemasonry, 1823-1872; Rhea Lodge no. 47, Jonesboro, Tennessee." ETHS*P* 19 (1947), 25-47.

——. "Methodism in Jonesboro, Tennessee." ETHS*P* 22 (1950), 45-59.

——. "Jonesboro's Chester Inn." ETHS*P* 27 (1955), 19-38.

——. "Some Phases of the History of the State of Franklin." *THQ* 16 (1957), 195-213.

——. "Russell Bean, Tennessee's First Native Son." ETHS*P* 37 (1965), 31-48.

——. "The Rebirth of Jonesboro." *THQ* 31 (1972), 223-39.

First Presbyterian Church, Johnson City, 100th Anniversary: History and Directory, 1869-1969. St. Louis: Pictorial Church Directories of America, 1970. Unpaged.

Garrett, William R., ed. "The Records of Washington County." *AHM* 5 (1900), 326-84; 6 (1901), 51-93, 191-92, 283-88.

——. "Controverted Points in Tennessee History." *AHM* 6 (1901), 140-47. Washington County boundary dispute.

Hamlett, James Clifton. "Long-Lots in Washington County with Reference to Past and Present Landholding Shapes." Thesis, East Tennessee State Univ., 1962.

Harris, Nathaniel E. *Autobiography: The Story of an Old Man's Life, with Reminiscences of Seventy-five Years.* Macon, Ga.: J. W. Burke, 1925. 550 pp.

Hash, Judith Hawes. "History of the First Presbyterian Church,

Jonesboro, Tennessee." Thesis, East Tennessee State Univ., 1965.

Hill (Eric) Associates. *Johnson City, Tennessee, Population and Economic Base Study.* 2 vols. in 1. Atlanta: Johnson City Regional Planning Comm., 1964-65. 89 pp.

Historical Records Survey, Tennessee. *Directory of Churches, Missions, and Religious Institutions of Tennessee,* no. 90. *Washington County.* Nashville: The Survey, WPA, 1942. 47 pp.

Lawson, Dennis T. "The Tipton-Haynes Place I. A Landmark of East Tennessee." *THQ* 29 (1970), 105-24.

McBride, Robert M., ed. "A Note on Washington County." *THQ* 31 (1972), 279.

McCown, Mary H. *Brief Chronological History of Johnson City, Tennessee and Three Suggested Historical Tours of the Johnson City Area.* Johnson City: Chamber of Commerce, 1963. 22 leaves.

——. *100th Anniversary History and Directory, 1871-1971, First Christian Church, Johnson City, Tennessee.* Johnson City: n.p., 1971. 160 pp.

——, ed. *Washington County, Tennessee, Records, Transcribed by Mary Hardin McCown.* Vol. 1, *Washington County Lists of Taxables, 1778-1801,* ed. Nancy E. Jones Stickley and Inez Burns. Johnson City: Privately printed, 1964- . 257 pp.

Maher, James A. "Johnson City, Tennessee." *East Tennessee. Historical and Biographical,* 441-51.

Robinson, Blackwell Pierce. "Willie Jones of Halifax." *NCHR* 18 (1941), 1-26, 133-70. Jones was the North Carolina statesman for whom Jonesboro is named.

Rodgers, John. *Geology and Mineral Deposits of Bumpass Cove, Unicoi and Washington Counties, Tennessee,* Tennessee Dept. of Conservation, Division of Geology Bulletin 54. Nashville: State of Tennessee, 1948. 82 pp.

Smith, Ross. *Reminiscences of an Old-Timer.* N.p.: Privately printed, 1930. 86 pp.

Tennessee State Library and Archives. "Inventory of Washington County Records." Nashville: State Library and Archives, 1964- . Unpublished typescript.

Tennessee Valley Authority, Industry Division. *Agricultural-Industrial Survey of Washington County, Tennessee.* Knoxville: TVA, 1934.

Thomas, James F. "The History of the First Baptist Church of

Jonesboro, Tennessee." Thesis, East Tennessee State Univ., 1955.

"Washington County." *History of Tennessee,* East Tennessee Edition, ed. Weston A. Goodspeed et al., 891-904, 1262-86.

Weaver, Clarence E. *Illustrated Johnson City, Tennessee.* Johnson City: Chamber of Commerce, 1915. 23 pp.

Williams, Samuel Cole. "Washington County Bar—the First Bar West of the Alleghanies." *Tennessee Bar Association Proceedings* 16 (1897), 95-111.

——. "The Founder of Tennessee's First Town: Major Jesse Walton." ETHS*P* 2 (1930), 70-80.

——. "The First Territorial Division Named for Washington." *THM* (ser. 2) 2 (1931-32), 153-64.

——. *History of Johnson City and Its Environs.* Johnson City: Watauga, 1940. 31 pp.

——, ed. "Journal of Events (1825-1873) of David A. Deaderick." ETHS*P* 8 (1936), 121-37; 9 (1937), 93-110.

WAYNE COUNTY
Historian: Charles D. Gallaher, Box 451, Waynesboro 38485.

Biographical Directory: Wayne County Members of the Tennessee General Assembly, 1796- . 43 pp. This volume also contains Lewis and Perry counties.

Tennessee State Library and Archives. "Inventory of Wayne County Records." Nashville: State Library and Archives, 1964- . Unpublished typescript.

Tennessee Valley Authority, Industry Division. *Agricultural-Industrial Survey of Wayne County.* Knoxville: TVA, 1934. 216 pp.

"Wayne County." *History of Tennessee,* ed. Weston A. Goodspeed et al., 763-77, 849-89.

WEAKLEY COUNTY
Historian: Mrs. Wilbur Vaughn, Martin 38237.

Coppock, Paul R. "The Killgore Killing." WTHS*P* 15 (1961), 40-54. Civil War in Weakley County.

Gardner, John A. "Early Times in Weakley County: *An Address Delivered by Col. John A. Gardner."* WTHS*P* 17 (1963), 68-84.

Prins, Dixie Eldridge. *The Life and Times of Greenfield, Tennessee, with Sketches of Weakley County,* introd. Blake Clark. Greenfield: Greenfield Hist. Soc., 1965. 220 pp.

Tennessee Valley Authority, Industry Division. *Agricultural-Industrial Survey of Weakley County, Tennessee.* Knoxville: TVA, 1935.

"Weakley County." *History of Tennessee,* ed. Weston A. Goodspeed et al., 831-42, 985-1024.

White County

Historian: Mrs. B. K. Mitchell, Sparta 38583.

Biographical Directory: White County Members of the Tennessee General Assembly, 1796- . 92 pp. This volume also contains Van Buren and Warren counties.

Comstock, Charles. *Freemasonry in Pioneer Times, White County.* Sparta: n.p., 1929.

Doran, Edwina Bean. "Folklore in White County, Tennessee." Diss., George Peabody College, 1969.

Fowler, Walter. "An Educational, Economic and Community Survey of White County, Tennessee." Thesis, Univ. of Tennessee, 1932.

Prater, Otto. "Economic History of White County, Tennessee." Thesis, George Peabody College, 1932.

Seals, Monroe. *History of White County.* N.p., 1935. 152 pp.

Souvenir Supplement. Sparta Exposition, January, 1902. Sparta: n.p., 1902. 56 pp.

Tennessee State Library and Archives. "Inventory of White County Records." Nashville: State Library and Archives, 1964- . Unpublished typescript.

Tennessee Valley Authority, Industry Division. *Agricultural-Industrial Survey of White County.* Knoxville: TVA, 1934. 127 pp.

Webb, Thomas G. "The Pottery Industry of DeKalb, White, and Putnam Counties." *THQ* 30 (1971), 110-12.

"White County." *History of Tennessee,* ed. Weston A. Goodspeed et al., 797-812, 860-84.

Williams, Coral. "Legends and Stories of White County, Tennessee." Thesis, George Peabody College, 1930.

WILLIAMSON COUNTY

Historian: Mrs. Joe Bowman, Lewisburg Pike, Franklin 37064.

Biographical Directory: Williamson County Members of the Tennessee General Assembly, 1796- . 52 pp.

Battle of Franklin. *See* Civil War.

Bowman, Virginia. *Historic Williamson County: Old Homes and Sites.* Nashville: Blue & Gray, 1971. 194 pp. Reprint of an earlier, undated edition.

Crutchfield, James A. *The Harpeth River.*

Estes, P. M., A. P. Foster, and John Trotwood Moore, comps. *Historical Places in Davidson, Williamson, Maury and Giles Counties.*

Field, Henry Martyn. *Bright Skies and Dark Shadows.* New York: Scribners, 1890. Rpt., Select Bibliographies Reprint Series, Freeport, N.Y.: Bks. for Libraries, 1972. 316 pp. Field traveled through the South, including much of Tennessee, late in the 19th century. His "dark shadows" are the problems of race, to which he hoped "common sense" might be applied.

Greer, Nancy Amelia. "Legends of Franklin, Tennessee." Thesis, George Peabody College, 1930.

Kinard, Frances M. "Frontier Development of Williamson County, Tennessee." Thesis, Vanderbilt Univ., 1948. Covers the period from the earliest settlement until 1812.

———. "Frontier Development of Williamson County." *THQ* 8 (1949), 3-33, 127-53.

McGann, Will Spencer. "The Old Carter House at Franklin, Tennessee." *THM* (ser. 2) 3 (1932-37), 40-44.

McRaven, William H. *Life and Times of Edward Swanson, One of the Original Pioneers Who with General James Robertson Founded Nashville, Tennessee, 1779; First Recorded Settler of Williamson County, Tennessee, March, 1780.* Nashville: n.p., 1937. 240 pp.

Morgan, Marshall. *Tennessee Town: Franklin, Tennessee.* Franklin: James D. Dustin, 1936. 116 pp.

Powell, John K. *History of St. Paul's Church, with an Account of the Introduction of the Episcopal Church into Tennessee.* Chattanooga: Morgan, 1925. 106 pp.

Robison, Dan M. "The Carter House, Focus of the Battle of Franklin." *THQ* 22 (1963), 3-21; rpt. in *Landmarks of Tennessee,* 69-87.

Tennessee State Library and Archives. "Inventory of Williamson County Records." Nashville: State Library and Archives, 1964- . Unpublished typescript.

Williamson County Historical Society. *Williamson County Historical Society Publication,* no. 1. Franklin: The Society, Fall 1970. 137 pp.

"Williamson County." *History of Tennessee,* ed. Weston A. Goodspeed et al., 787-810, 965-1019.

WILSON COUNTY
Historian: R. D. Lawlor, 112 Hatten Avenue, Lebanon 37087.

Anderson, T. C. *Life of Rev. George Donnell, First Pastor of the Church in Lebanon; with a Sketch of the Scotch-Irish Race.* Nashville: The Author, 1858. 334 pp.

Biographical Directory: Wilson County Members of the Tennessee General Assembly, 1796- . 112 pp. This volume also contains Smith County.

Chambers, W. R. "Some Reminiscences of an Old Lawyer." *THM* (ser. 2) 2 (1931), 67-70.

Drake, James V. *A Historical Sketch of Wilson County, Tennessee, from Its First Settlement to the Present Time.* Nashville: Tavel, Eastman & Howell, 1879. 33 pp.

Historical Records Survey, Tennessee. *Inventory of the County Archives of Tennessee: Wilson County.* Nashville: The Survey, WPA, 1938.

History Associates of Wilson County. *The History of Wilson County: Its Land and Its Life,* ed. and senior contributor Dixon Merritt. Nashville: Benson, 1961. 453 pp.

Lawlor, Virginia. "Historical Background of Cultural Forces in Wilson County, Tennessee." Thesis, Vanderbilt Univ., 1961.

——, ed. "I, Mary Morriss Smith, Do Recollect . . . ." *THQ* 29 (1970), 79-87. Relates to early-19th-century Wilson County history.

Macon, Drake, Alice Chastain, and Hershell Ligon. *A History of Green Hill.* N.p., 1946. 20 pp.

Tennessee State Library and Archives. "Inventory of Wilson County Records." Nashville: State Library and Archives, 1964- . Unpublished typescript.

Walton, Julie Hasselkus. "Consensus and Pluralism in a Small

Town (Watertown, Tennessee)." Thesis, Vanderbilt Univ., 1967.

"Wilson County." *History of Tennessee,* ed. Weston A. Goodspeed et al., 840-61, 1077-1125.

Author Index

Subject Index

WITHDRAWAL